SERBO~CROATIAN–ENGLISH
ENGLISH–SERBO~CROATIAN
DICTIONARY

Моја једина Оксанкице,

Можда сам ову посвету требао написати на пољском или енглеском, али је потпуно свеједно; јер ни један језик не може изразити оно што осјећам према Теби...

Дакле, само за Тебе...

Твој
Ванка

20. јануар 2001.

HIPPOCRENE PRACTICAL DICTIONARY

SERBO-CROATIAN–ENGLISH
ENGLISH–SERBO-CROATIAN
DICTIONARY

by

NICHOLAS AWDE

HIPPOCRENE BOOKS

New York

For information, address:
HIPPOCRENE BOOKS, INC.
171 Madison Avenue
New York, NY 10016

Library of Congress Cataloging-in-Publication Data

Awde, Nicholas.
    Serbo-Croatian-English, English-Serbo-Croatian
  Dictionary / by Nicholas Awde.
          p.   cm. — (Hippocrene practical dictionary)
    ISBN 0-7818-0445-0 (pbk.)
    1. Serbo-Croatian language—Dictionaries—English.
  2. English language—Dictionaries—Serbo-Croatian.
  I. Title. II. Series
  PG1376.A95   1996
  491.8′2321—dc20   96-26010
                                             CIP

Typesetting and font design by Nicholas Awde / Desert Hearts

Printed in the United States of America.

CONTENTS

Acknowledgements

I would like to thank Jadran Jolivić and Nenad Klarić for their invaluable editorial contributions at, respectively, the initial and final stages of compiling this dictionary.

I would also like to thank Silvana Perovich, Damian Manestar, DeeDee Edwards and Dr Isabelle Miller for their inspiration.

Special thanks go to Fred Hill and Emma Hill, Michael Wylde, Emanuela Losi (who helped typeset), Evie Arup, Will Harvey, Peter Davies, Laurence Chabert, Kevin Smith, Andrew Honey, Ian Carnochan, John Wright, Imad Al-Assir, Hugh Mulcahey, Jan Barrington, Richard Brow, Saidi el-Gheithy, Farouque Abdillah, Bruce Ingham, Ippolita Vigo, Anne Raufaste, and most of all George Blagowidow, Jennifer Pigeon and all at Hippocrene.

NICHOLAS AWDE
London

Abbreviations

acad.	academic / *akademski*
adj	adjective / *pridev*
adv	adverb / *prilog*
conj	conjunction / *veznik*
Chr.	Christian / *hrišćanski; kršćanski*
ec.	economics / *ekonomika*
ed.	education / *obrazovanje*
f	feminine / *ženski*
fin.	finance / *finansije; financije*
Isl.	Islamic / *islamski*
leg.	legal / *sudski*
m	masculine / *muški*
mar.	maritime / *pomorski*
med.	medicine / *medicina*
mil.	military / *vojni*
mus.	music / *muzika*
n	[English:] noun / *imenica*
	[Serbo-Croatian:] neuter / *srednji*
Orth.	Orthodox / *pravoslavan*
pl	plural / *plural*
pol.	politics / *politika*
prep	preposition / *predlog*
rel.	religion / *religija*
sl.	slang / *sleng*
spor.	sports / *sport*
tel.	telecommunications / *telekomunikacije*
UK	British English / *britanski engleski*
US	American English / *američki engleski*
v	verb / *glagol*

Notes on use

1. Brackets following an English verb contain its past tense and past participle.

2. Brackets following an English noun contain its plural.

3. In the Serbo-Croatian–English section, British–American variants are separated by a semi-colon, e.g. **metre; meter**, **lift; elevator**.

4. In the English–Serbo-Croatian section, ekavian–jekavian and Eastern–Western variants are separated by a semi-colon, e.g. **reka; rijeka, voz; vlak**.

THE ENGLISH ALPHABET

a	[ei]	**n**	[en]
b	[biː]	**o**	[əu]
c	[siː]	**p**	[piː]
d	[diː]	**q**	[kjuː]
e	[iː]	**r**	[aː]
f	[ef]	**s**	[es]
g	[dʒiː]	**t**	[tiː]
h	[eitʃ]	**u**	[juː]
i	[aːi]	**v**	[viː]
j	[jei]	**w**	[dʌbljuː]
k	[kei]	**x**	[eks]
l	[el]	**y**	[wai]
m	[em]	**z**	[zed; ziː]

THE SERBO-CROATIAN ALPHABET: ROMAN

Serbo-Croatian letter	Serbo-Croatian name of letter	Approximate English equivalent
A a	[a]	fat
B b	[be]	box
C c	[ce]	bits
Č č	[čə]	church
Ć ć	[ćə]	church
D d	[de]	dog
DŽ dž	[džə]	jet
Đ đ	[də]	jet
E e	[e]	set
F f	[ef]	fat
G g	[ge]	get
H h	[ha]	hot / loch – *as in Scottish English*
I i	[i]	sit
J j	[jə]	yes
K k	[ka]	kick
L l	[el]	let
LJ lj	[ljə]	million
M m	[em]	mat
N n	[en]	net
NJ nj	[njə]	onion
O o	[o]	cot
P p	[pe]	pet
R r	[er]	rat – *but 'rolled'*
S s	[es]	sit
Š š	[šə]	shut
T t	[te]	ten
U u	[u]	put
V v	[ve]	van
Z z	[ze]	zebra
Ž ž	[žə]	erasure

THE SERBO-CROATIAN ALPHABET: CYRILLIC

Serbo-Croatian letter	Roman equivalent
А а	a
Б б	b
В в	v
Г г	g
Д д	d
Ђ ђ	đ
Е е	e
Ж ж	ž
З з	z
И и	i
Ј ј	j
К к	k
Л л	l
Љ љ	lj
М м	m
Н н	n
Њ њ	nj
О о	o
П п	p
Р р	r
С с	s
Т т	t
Ћ ћ	ć
У у	u
Ф ф	f
Х х	h
Ц ц	c
Ч ч	č
Џ џ	dž
Ш ш	š

SERBO~CROATIAN
– ENGLISH

A

a *conj* and
abeceda *f* alphabet
ablendovati *v* to dip headlights
abnormalan *adj* abnormal
abolicija *f* abolition
abolitirati *v* to abolish
abortirati *v* to abort
abortus *m* abortion
ada *f* islet
adaptacija *f* adaptation
adaptirati *v* to adapt
adekvatan *adj* adequate
administracija *f* administration
administrativan *adj* administrative
admiral *m* admiral
adresa *f* address
adresar *m* directory
adresirati, adresovati *v* to address
adut *m* trump
advokat *m* lawyer; attorney
adutant *m* adjutant
aerodinamičan, aerodinamički
  adj streamlined
aerodrom *m* airport
aeromiting *m* air show
afektirati *v* to be affected
afera *f* 1. affair 2. scandal
afinitet *m* affinity
afirmacija *f* affirmation
afirmisati *v* to affirm
afrički *adj* African
Afrika *f* Africa
Afrikanac *m*, **Afrikanka** *f* African
agencija *f* 1. agency 2. novinarska
  agencija news agency 3.
  turistička agencija travel
  agency

agent *m* 1. agent 2. tajni agent
  secret agent
agitacija *f* agitation
agitator *m* agitator
agitirati *v* to agitate
agonija *f* agony
agrarni *adj* agrarian
agresija *f* aggression
agresivan *adj* aggressive
agresor *m* aggressor
agronom *m* agronomist
agronomija *f* agronomy
ah! oh!
ajde! come on!
ajkula *f* shark
akademija *f* academy
akademik *m* 1. academic 2.
  academician
akademski *adj* academic
akcelerator *m* accelerator
akcenat *m* accent
akcenovati *v* to accent
akcija *f* 1. action 2. (fin) share
akcionar *m* (fin) shareholder,
  stockholder
aklimatizovati se *v* to acclimatize
ako *conj* if
akontacija *f* payment in advance
akord *m* 1. accord 2. piecework
akreditiv *adj* credentials
akreditovati *v* to accredit
akrobacija *f* 1. acrobatics 2. stunt
akrobat *m* acrobat
akrobatski *adj* acrobatic
akt *m* 1. act 2. file
aktentašna *f* briefcase
aktiva *f* assets

aktivan *adj* active
aktivirati *v* to activate
aktivnost *f* activity
aktuelan *adj* current
aktuelozivati *v* to up-date
akumulator *m* battery
akušer *m* obstetrician
akustika *f* acoustics
akutan *adj* acute
akuzativ *m* accusative
akvarel *m* watercolour
akvarij *m* aquarium
akviziter *m* collector
alarm *m* alarm
alarmantan *adj* alarming
alarmirati *v* to alarm
alat *m* tools
alat za lemljenje *m* soldering iron
album *m* album
alegorija *f* allegory
alergičan *adj* allergic
alergija *f* allergy
alfabet *m* alphabet
alfabetizam *m* illiteracy
alga *f* seaweed
algebra *f* algebra
ali *conj* but
alibi *m* alibi
alimentacija *f* 1. sustenance 2. alimony
aljkav *adj* careless
alkohol *m* alcohol
alkoholan *adj* alcoholic
alkoholičar *m* alcoholic
alkoholizam *m* alcoholism
Alpe *fpl* the Alps
alt *m* (mus) alto
alternativa *f*, **alternativan** *adj* alternative
aludirati *v* to allude
aluminij *m* aluminium; aluminum
aluzija *f* allusion

ama *conj* but
amandman *m* amendment
amanet *m* will (and testament)
amater *m* amateur
ambalaža *f* 1. container 2. packing
ambasada *f* embassy
ambasador *m* ambassador
ambicija *f* ambition
ambiciozan *adj* ambitious
ambijent *m* ambience
ambulanta *f* (med) out-patient department
amemija *f* anaemia
američki *adj* American
Amerika *f* America
Amerikanac *m* American
amnestija *f* amnesty
amo here
amo tamo to and fro
amonijak *m* ammonia
amorfan *adj* amorphous
amortizacija *f* amortization
amortizer *m* shock absorber
amortizovati *v* to amortize
amputacija *f* amputation
amputirati *v* to amputate
analfabet *m* illiterate person
analfabetski *adj* illiterate
analitički *adj* analytical
analiza *f* analysis
analizator *m* analyst
analizirati *v* to analyse
analogija *f* analogy
ananas *m* pineapple
anarhički *adj* anarchistic
anarhija *f* anarchy
anarhist *m* anarchist
anatomija *f* anatomy
anatomski *adj* anatomic
anđeo *m* angel
anegdota *f* anecdote
aneksija *f* annexation

anemičan *adj* anaemic
anestetičar *m* anaesthetist
anestezija *f* anaesthetic
angažirati *v* to engage
angažman *m* engagement
angažovati *v* to engage
angina *f* 1. angina 2. tonsilitis
anketa *f* 1. poll 2. survey 3. questionnaire
anketirati *v* to poll
anketni listić *m* questionnaire
anlaser *m* starter
anoniman *adj* anonymous
anorganski *adj* inorganic
ansambl *m* ensemble
antena *f* aerial
antenatalni *adj* prenatal
antibiotik *m* antibiotic
antifriz *m* anti-freeze
antika *f* antiquity
antikoncipijens *m* contraceptive
antikvarijat *m* 1. antique dealer 2. second-hand bookshop
antikvarnica *f* antique shop
antilop *m* suede
antipatičan *adj* unpleasant
antipatija *f* antipathy
antiseptik *m* antiseptic
antitelo, antitijelo *n* antibody
antologija *f* anthology
anuitet *m* annuity
aparat *m* 1. apparatus 2. appliance 3. machine
aparat za brijanje *m* razor
aparat za fotokopiranje *m* photocopier
apartman *m* apartment; suite
apatičan *adj* apathetic
apel *m* appeal
aperitiv *m* aperitif
apetit *m* appetite
aplauz *m* applause

apoen *m* denomination
apostol *m* apostle
apoteka *f* chemist's; pharmacy
apotekar *m* chemist; pharmacist
april *m* April
apsolutan *adj* 1. absolute 2. mitigated
apsolutno *adv* absolutely
apsorbovati *v* to absorb
apsurdan *adj* absurd
aranžirati *v* to arrange
aranžman *adj* arrangement
Arapin *m* Arab
arbitraža *f* arbitration
argument *m* argument
arhaičan *adj* archaic
arheolog *m* archaeologist
arheologija *f* archaeology
arheopiskop *m* archbishop
arhipelag *m* archipelago
arhitekt(a) *m* architect
arhitektura *f* architecture
arhiv *m* archives
arija *f* 1. aria 2. tune
aristokrat *m* aristocrat
aristokratija *f* aristocracy
aritmetika *f* arithmetic
armija *f* army
armirani beton *m* reinforced concrete
arogantan *adj* arrogant
aromatičan *adj* aromatic
arterija *f* artery
artiljerija *f* artillery
artiljerijsko gađanje *n* (mil.) shelling
asfalt *m* asphalt
asistent *m* 1. assistant 2. (acad.) teaching fellow
asistirati *v* to assist
asocijacija *f* association
asocijalan *adj* asocial

asocirati *v* to associate
asortiman *m* assortment
ašov *m* spade
astma *f* asthma
astrofizika *f* astrophysics
astronaut *m* astronaut
astronomija *f* astronomy
ataše *m* attaché
ateist(a) *m* atheist
ateizam *m* atheism
atelje *m* studio
atentat *m* assassination attempt
atentator *m* (would-be) assassin
aterirati *v* to land
atlas *m* atlas
atlet(a) *m/f* athlete
atletičar *m* athlete
atletika *f* athletics
atletski *adj* athletic
atmosfera *f* atmosphere
atom *m* atom
atomista *f* nuclear
atomistika *f* nuclear physics
atomski *adj* atomic
audicija *f* audition
audijencija *f* audience
august *m* August
Australija *f* Australia
Austrija *f* Austria
austrijaski *adj* Austrian
autentičan *adj* authentic
auto *m* car; automobile
autobiografija *f* autobiography
autobus *m* bus
autogram *m* autograph
automat *m* 1. submachine gun 2. vending machine

automatski *adj* automatic
automehaničar *m* mechanic
automobil *m* car
automobilist *m* motorist
autonoman *adj* autonomous
autonomija *f* autonomy
autoput *m* motorway; superhighway
autor *m* author
autoritet *m* authority
autorsko pravo *n* copyright
autoservis *m* garage; auto service shop
autostop *m* 1. hitchhiking 2. **putovat autostopom** to hitchhike
autostrada *f* motorway; superhighway
autsajder *m* outsider
avangarda *f* 1. advance guard 2. avant-garde
avans *m* (fin) advance
avantura *f* adventure
avenija *f* avenue
avet *f* ghost
avgust *m* August
avijacija *f* 1. aviation 2. air force
avijatičar *m* pilot
avion *m* 1. airplane 2. **borbeni avion** warplane
avionom by air
azbest *m* asbestos
Azija *f* Asia
azil *m* 1. asylum 2. **pravo azila** right of asylum
azot *m* nitrogen
aždaja *f* dragon
ažuriranje *n* update
ažurirati *v* to update

B

baba *f* grandmother
babica *f* midwife
babura *f* green pepper
bacati u zrak *v* to blow up
bacati, baciti *v* to throw
bacil *m* bacillus
baciti *v* to throw
bačva *f* 1. barrel 2. oil drum
badava *f* free (of charge)
badem *m* almond
bademantil *m* bathrobe
Badnjak, Badnji Dan *m* Christmas Eve
bager *m* excavator
bagrem *m* acacia
bahat *adj* arrogant
bajka *f* fairy tale
baka *f* grandmother
bakalar *m* cod
bakalin *m* grocer
bakalnica *f* grocery
bakar *m* copper
baklja *f* torch
bakropis, bakrorez *m* etching
bakšiš *m* tip
bakteriologija *f* bacteriology
bal *m* ball
bala *f* bale
balast *m* ballast
balerina *f* ballerina
balet *m* ballet
baletan *m* ballet dancer
balkon *m* balcony
balon *m* balloon
balon mantil *m* raincoat
Baltičko more *n* the Baltic Sea
balvan *m* beam

balzamirati *v* to embalm
bambus *m* bamboo
banalan *adj* banal
banana *f* banana
bančiti *v* to have a good time
banda *f* 1. band 2. gang
bandera *f* pole
banja *f* spa
banka *f* bank
bankar *m* banker
bankarstvo *n* banking
bankina *f* road verge; road shoulder
banknota *f* banknote; bill
bankovni činovnik *m* bank clerk
bankrot *m* bankruptcy
bankrotirati *v* to go bankrupt
bar *m* 1. bar 2. nightclub
bar, barem *adv* at least
bara *f* 1. puddle 2. pond
baraka *f* shed
barikada *f* barricade
barikada na putu *f* roadblock
barka *f* boat
barokan *adj* baroque
barometar *m* barometer
baršun *m* velvet
barun *m* baron
barut *m* gunpowder
bas *m* bass
basen *m* 1. basin 2. swimming pool
basna *f* fable
baš 1. just 2. quite 3. *adj* senior
bašta *f* garden
baština *f* 1. inheritance 2. heritage
baštinik *m* heir
baštiniti *v* to inherit
baštovan *m* gardener

batak *m* leg
baterija *f* battery
batina *f* stick
batine *fpl* beating
baviti se *v* to be occupied with
baza *f* 1. base 2. basis
bazen *m* 1. basin 2. swimming pool
baždariti *v* to gauge
bdeti, bdjeti *v* to watch over
beba *f* baby
beda *f* misery
bedak *m* fool
bedan *adj* wretched
bedast *adj* foolish
bedastoća *f* foolishness
bedem *m* wall
bedinerka *f* cleaner
bedro *n* thigh
begstvo *n* escape
bek *m* (spor.) back
belančevina *f* egg-white
beleška *f* notice
beletristika *f* fiction
beležiti *v* to note
beležnica *f* notebook
Belgija *f* Belgium
beli luk *m* garlic
benzin *m* petrol; gasoline
benzin bez dodatka olova *m* unleaded petrol
benzinska stanica *f* petrol station; filling station
benzinski rezervoar *m* petrol tank; gas tank
beo *adj* white
berba, berba grožđa *f* vintage
berberin *m* barber
berbernica *f* barbershop
berza *f* stock exchange
bes *m* 1. fury 2. tantrum
besanica *f* insomnia
bescarinska zona *f* duty-free zone

bescarinski *adj* duty-free
besciljan *adj* aimless
beskamatan, beskamatni *adj* interest-free
beskaslan, besklasni *adj* classless
beskičmenjak *m* invertebrate
beskompromisan *adj* uncompromising
beskonačan *adj* limitless
beskorisnost *f* uselessness
beskoristan *adj* useless
beskraj *m* infinity
beskrajan *adj* infinite
beskrajnost *f* infinity
beskrupulozan *adj* unscrupulous
beskućnik *m* homeless person
besmisao *f* nonsense
besmislen *adj* absurd
besmrtan *adj* immortal
besmrtnost *f* immortality
besnilo *n* fury
besperspektivan *adj* unpromising
besplatan *adj*, **besplatno** *adv* free of charge
bespomoćan *adj* helpless
besposlen *adj* idle
besposličiti *v* to idle about
bespravan *adj* without rights
besprijekoran *adj* impeccable
besprimjeran *adj* unprecedented
besprincipijelan *adj* unprincipled
besraman *adj* shameless
bešika *f* bladder
bešuman *adj* noiseless
bešćutan *adj* callous
bestežinski *adj* weightless
beton *m* concrete
bez *prep* 1. without 2. -less
bezakonje *n* lawlessness
bezalkoholan *adj* non-alcoholic
bezalkoholno piće *n* soft drink
bezazlen *adj* harmless

bezbedan *adj* safe
bezbojan *adj* colourless
bezbolan *adj* painless
bezbožan *adj* godless
bezbrižan *adj* carefree
bezbroj *m* multitude
bezbrojan *adj* countless
bezdan *m/f* abyss
bezdušan *adj* heartless
bezdušnost *f* heartlessness
bezglav *adj* confused
bezgraničan *adj* infinite
bezgraničan *adj* unlimited
bezimen *adj* 1. nameless 2. unknown
bezizlazan *adj* hopeless
bezizražajan *adj* expressionless
bezličan *adj* impersonal
beznačajan *adj* insignificant
beznadan, beznadežan *adj* hopeless
bezobrazan *adj* impudent
bezobrazan *adj* rude
bezobziran *adj* 1. inconsiderate 2. reckless 3. ruthless
bezobzira na *adj* irrespective of
bezopasan *adj* harmless
bezosećajan *adj* insensitive
bezukusan *adj* tasteless
bezuslovan *adj* unconditional
bezuslovna predaja *f* unconditional surrender
bezuvjetan *adj* unconditional
bezuvjetna predaja *f* unconditional surrender
bezvazdušan *adj* airless
bezvodan *adj* waterless
bezvoljan *adj* apathetic
bezvredan, bezvrijedan *adj* worthless

bežati *v* to run away
bežični *adj* wireless
beživotan *adj* lifeless
biber *m* pepper
biblija *f* the Bible
biblioteka *f* library
bibliotekar *m* librarian
bič *m* whip
bičevati *v* to whip
bicikl *m* bicycle
biciklist *m* cyclist
biće *n* 1. being 2. creature
bide *m* bidet
bife *m* 1. buffet 2. bar
biftek *m* steak
bijeda *f* misery
bijedan *adj* wretched
bijeg *m* escape
bijel *adj* white
bijeliti *v* to whitewash
bijes *m* 1. fury 2. tantrum
bijesan *adj* furious
bik *m* bull
bikini *m* bikini
bilanca, bilans *f* (fin) balance
bilijar *m* billiards
bilijun *m* billion; milliard
biljar *m* billiards
bilje *n* plants
biljeg *m* duty stamp
bilješka *f* note
biljeter *m* ticket collector
bilježiti *v* to note
bilježnica *f* notebook
bilježnik *m* town clerk
biljka *f* plant
biljni *adj* vegetable
bilo 1. -ever, any 2. *n* pulse
bilo kad *conj* no matter when
bilten *m* 1. fact sheet 2. bulletin
biografija *f* biography
biologija *f* biology

bioskop *m* cinema
birač *m* voter
biračko pravo *n* right to vote
birati *v* 1. to choose 2. to vote
biro *m* office
birokracija, birokratija *f* bureaucracy
birokratizam *m* bureaucratism
birokratski *adj* bureaucratic
bis! encore!
biser *m* pearl
biskup *m* bishop
biskupija *f* diocese
biskvit *m* biscuit; cookie
bistar *adj* clear
bistrina *f* clarity
bistriti (se) *v* 1. to clear up 2. to clarify
bit *f* essence
bitan *adj* essential
bitanga *m/f* good-for-nothing
biti *v* 1. to be 2. to exist 3. to live
biti dosta *f* to suffice
bitka *f* battle
bitno *adv* essentially
bivo, bivol *m* buffalo
bivši *adj* former
biznis *m* business
bižuterija *f* costume jewellery
bjegunac *m* 1. fugitive 2. **vojni bjegunac** (mil.) deserter
bjelance, bjelančevina *f* egg-white
bjelilo *n* bleach
bjelina *f* white
bjelokost *f* ivory
bjesnjeti *v* to rage
bjesnoća *f* rabies
bježati *v* to escape
blag *adj* gentle
blagajna *f* 1. pay-point 2. ticket office
blagajnica *f*, **blagajnik** *m* cashier

blagdan *m* holiday
blage naravi *adj* good-tempered
blago 1. *adv* gently 2. **blago vama!** lucky you! 3. *n* treasure 4. wealth
blagodareći *prep* thanks to
blagodat *f* advantage
blagonaklon *adj* benevolent
blagoslov *m* blessing
blagosloviti *v* to bless
blagost *f* gentleness
blagostanje *n* 1. prosperity 2. welfare
blagotvoran *adj* beneficial
blagovaonica *f* dining room
blagovremeno *adv* in time
blajhan *adj* bleached
blamaža *f* disgrace
blamažirati se *v* to be disgraced
blanja *f* plane
blanjati *v* to plane
blanket *m* form
blanko *adj* blank
blatan *adj* muddy
blato *n* mud
blatobran *m* mudguard; fender
blaziran *adj* blasé
blaženstvo *n* bliss
blebetati *v* to babble
bled *adj* pale
blef *m* bluff
blefirati *v* to bluff
blenuti *v* to gape
blesak *m* flash
blesa *m/f*, **blesan** *m* stupid person
blesav *adj* stupid
blezgarija *f* nonsense
blic *m* flashgun
blijed *adj* pale
blijesak *m* dazzle
blijeskati *v* to dazzle
Bliski istok *m* Middle East
bliskost *f* nearness

blistati *v* to sparkle
blistav *adj* dazzling
blizak *adj* near
blizak korisniku *adj* user-friendly
blizanac *m* twin
blizina *f* nearness
blizu *adv/prep* near
bliži *adj* nearer
bližnji fellow man
bljedilo *n*, **bljedoća** *f* pallor
bljutav *adj* tasteless
bljuvati *v* to vomit
bljuzgavica *f* slush
blok *m* 1. block 2. (pol) bloc
blokada *f* blockade
blokirati puteve *v* to set up a
  roadblock
blud *m* promiscuity
bludnica *f* prostitute
bluza *f* blouse
bob *m* broad bean
bobica *f* berry
boca *f* bottle
bočni *adj* lateral
bod *m* stitch
bodar *adj* brisk
bodež *m* dagger
bodlja, bodljika *f* thorn
bodljikav *adj* thorny
bodljikava žica *f* barbed wire
bodovanje *n* score
bodrenje *n* pep-talk
bodriti *v* to encourage
bog *m* god
bogalj *m* 1. invalid 2. cripple
bogat *adj* rich
bogat industrijalac *m* tycoon
bogataž *m* wealthy person
bogatstvo *n* wealth
boginja *f* goddess
boginje *n* smallpox
bogomoljka *f* praying mantis

bogosluženje *n* (rel) 1. mass 2.
  service
boj *m* battle
boja *f* 1. colour 2. paint 3. **uljena
  boja** oil paint
bojadisati *v* to paint
bojati se *v* to fear
bojazan *f* fear
bojažljiv *adj* timid
bojeva glava *f* warhead
bojište *n* battlefield
bojkot *m* boycott
bojkotirati *v* to boycott
bojler *m* boiler
bojni brod *m* battleship
bojni otrov *m* poison gas
bok *m* 1. side 2. **bok uz bok** side
  by side
bokal *m* pitcher
boks *m* boxing
boks meč *m* boxing match
boksač *m* boxer
boksati *v* to box
bol *m/f* 1. pain 2. **porođajni bolovi**
  labour pains
bolan *adj* painful
bolesnik *m* patient
bolest *f* 1. illness 2. disease
bolestan *adj* sick
bolje *adj* better
boljeti *v* to hurt
bolji *adj* better
bolnica *f* hospital
bolničar *m* 1. nurse 2. orderly
bolničarka *f* nurse
bolnička kola *f* ambulance
bolovati *v* to suffer from
bomba *f* 1. bomb 2. **ručna bomba**
  hand grenade
bombarder *m* bomber
bombardirati, bombardovati *v* to
  bombard

bombardovanje *n* (mil.)
bombardment
bombon *m*, **bombona** *f* sweet;
candy
bon *m* 1. ticket 2. token
bor *m* pine
bora *f* wrinkle
borac *m* fighter
boranija *f* string beans
boravak *m*, **boravište** *n* 1. stay 2.
residence
boraviti *v* 1. to stay 2. to dwell
borba *f* 1. struggle 2. combat 3.
grupa borba infighting
borbena tehnika *f* (mil.) ordnance
borbeni avion *m* warplane
boriti se *v* to struggle
borna kola *f* armoured car
borovnica *f* blueberry
bos *adj* barefoot
bostan *m* melon patch
bosti *v* to prick
botanički *adj* botanical
botanika *f* botany
božanski *adj* divine
božica *f* goddess
Božić *m* Christmas
božji *adj* divine
bračni *adj* 1. matrimonial 2. married
bračno putovanje *n* honeymoon
braća *m* brethren
brada *f* beard
bradat *adj* bearded
bradavica *f* wart
bradavica sise *f* nipple
bradva *f* axe
brak *m* marriage
brana *f* dam
branič *m* (spor) back
branik *m* bumper; fender
branilac *m* 1. defender 2. (leg)
defence lawyer

braniti *v* to defend oneself
braon *adj* brown
brašno *n* flour
brat *m* brother
bratanac *m* nephew
bratanica *f* niece
brati *v* to gather
bratić *m* cousin
bratoub(oji)ica *f* fratricide
bratski *adj* fraternal
bratstvo *n* fraternity
brav *m* 1. head of cattle 2. wether
brava *f* lock
bravar *m* locksmith
brazda *f* 1. furrow 2. (mar.) wake
brazgotina *f* scar
brbljarija *f* chatter
brbljati *v* to chatter
brbljav *adj* chatty
brčići *mpl* moustache
brdo *n* 1. hill 2. mountain
brdovit *adj* 1. hilly 2. mountainous
brdski *adj* 1. hill 2. mountain
breme *n* burden
breskva *f* peach
brest *m* elm
breza *f* birch
brežuljak *m* hill
brid *m/f* edge
bridak *adj* sharp
briga *f* worry
brigada *f* brigade
brijač *m* barber
brijačnica *f* barber's
brijanje *n* shaving
brijati se *v* to shave oneself
brijati *v* to shave (someone)
brijeg *m* mountain
brilijant, briljant, briljantan *adj*
brilliant
brinuti se *v* 1. to worry 2. to take
care of

bris *m* smear test
brisač *m* wiper
brisač stakla *f* windscreen wiper
brisati *v* to wipe
britva *f* razor
brizantni eksploziv *m* high explosive
brizgalica *f* syringe
brižljiv *adj* careful
brižljivo *adv* carefully
brižljivost *f* carefulness
brk *m* moustache
brkati *v* to confuse
brklja *f* barrier
brnjica *f* muzzle
brod *m* 1. ship 2. **na brodu** aboard 3. **ratni brod** warship
brodogradiliš, brodogradiliše *n* 1. shipyard 2. dockyard
brodogradnja *f* shipbuilding
brodolom *m* shipwreck
brodovlasnik *m* shipowner
brodska agencija *f* shipping agency
brodski tovar *m* cargo
broj *m* 1. number 2. **poštanski broj** postal code; zip code
brojan *adj* numerous
brojati *v* to count
brojčanik *m* dial
brojilo *n* meter
brojiti *v* to count
brojka *f* digit
bronca *f* bronze
bronhitis *m* bronchitis
bronza *f* bronze
broš *m* brooch
brošura *f* brochure
bršljan *m* ivy
brstiti *v* to browse
brujati *v* to hum
brundati *v* to grumble

brus *m* grindstone
brusiti *v* to grind
brusnica *f* cranberry
bruto-težina *f* gross weight
brvnara *f* log cabin
brvno *n* footbridge
brz *adj* rapid
brzaci *mpl* rapids
brzina *f* 1. speed 2. **najvećom brzinom** at top speed
brzinomjer *m* speedometer
brzo *adv* rapidly
brzojav *m* telegram
brzojaviti *v* to send a telegram
brzoplet *adj* hasty
brzovozna roba *f* express goods
brže 1. faster 2. hurry up!
buba *f* insect; bug
bubamara *f* ladybird
bubanj *m* drum
bubnjar *m* drummer
bubnjati *v* to drum
bubnjić *m* eardrum
bubreg *m* kidney
bubrežni *adj* renal
bubrežnjak *m* loin
bubuljica *f* pimple
buča *f* marrow
bučan *adj* noisy
bučiti *v* to make a noise
bucmast *adj* plump
budala *m/f* fool
budalaština *f* foolishness
budalast *adj* foolish
budan *adj* 1. awake 2. alert
budilica *f*, **budilnik** *m* alarm clock
buditi se *v* to wake up
budnost *f* vigilance
budući da *conj* since
budući *adj* future
budućnost *f* future
budžet *m* budget

budžetska godina *f* financial year; fiscal year
budžetski *adj* fiscal
Bugarin *m* Bulgarian
Bugarska *f* Bulgaria
bugarski *adj* Bulgarian
buha *f* flea
bujan *adj* dense
bujati *v* to swell
bujica *f* torrent
buka *f* noise
buket *m* bouquet
buknuti *v* to break out
buktinja *f* torch
bukva *f* beech
bukvalan *adj* literal
bukvar *m* (ed) primer
buldog *m* bulldog
buldožer *m* bulldozer
bulevar *m* boulevard
buljiti *v* to stare
bum *m* (fin.) boom
bumbar *m* bumblebee
buna *f* revolt
bunar *m* well
buncati *v* to be delirious
bunda *f* sheepskin coat
bundeva *f* pumpkin

bungalov *m* bungalow
bunilo *n* delirium
buniti se *v* to rebel
buniti *v* to stir up
bunker *m* (mil) bunker
bunovan *adj* sleepy
buntovan, buntovnički *adj* rebellious
buntovnik *m* 1. rebel 2. rioter
bura *f* storm
burag *m* tripe
buran *adj* stormy
bure *n* barrel
burza *f* 1. stock exchange 2. **crna burza** blackmarket
burza rada *f* labour exchange
buržoazija *f* bourgeoisie
buržujski *adj* bourgeois
busen *m* turf
busola *f* compass
bušilica *f* drill
bušiti *v* to drill
bušotina *f* hole
but *m* 1. leg 2. thigh
butan *m* butane
buva *f* flea
buvara *f* (sl.) prison
buvlja pijaca *f* flea market

C

car *m* emperor
carevina *f* empire
carica *f* empress
carina *f* 1. customs 2. tariff
carinarnica *f* customs house
carinik *m* customs officer
carski *adj* imperial
carski rez *m* (med) Caesarean section
carstvo *n* empire
cedar *m* cedar
cediti *v* to drain
cedulja *f* note
ceh *m* guild
celer *m* celery
celina *f* entirety
celishodan *adj* suitable
celofan *m* cellophane
celokupan *adj* entire
celuloid *m* celluloid
celuloza *f* cellulose
cement *m* cement
cementirati *v* to cement
cena *f* 1. value 2. price
cena vožnje *n* fare
cenjen *adj* valued
cenovik *m* price list
centar *m* 1. centre 2. **smučarski centar** ski resort
centarfor *m* (spor) centre forward
centarhalf *m* (spor) centre half
centimetar *m* centimetre
centrala *f* 1. headquarters 2. central station 3. power station
centralan *adj* central
centralizirati *v* to centralize
centralno grijanje *n* central heating

centrifuga *f* spin-dryer
centrifugalan *adj* centrifugal
cenzura *f* censorship
cenzurirati *v* to censor
ceo *adj* whole
cepelin *m* airship
cepidlački *adj* fussy
cerada *f* tarpaulin
ceriti se *v* to grimace
cermonija *f* ceremony
cesta *f* road
cestarina *f* toll
cev *m* tube
cevanica *f* shin
cičati *v* to squeak
ciferšlus *m* zip
cifra *f* cipher
Ciganin *m* Gypsy
ciganski *adj* Gypsy
cigara *f* cigar
cigareta *f* cigarette
cigla *f* brick
cijediti se *v* to trickle
cijediti *v* to filter
cijeli 1. entire 2. **7 cijela 25** seven point two five
cijena *f* price
cijena vožnje *n* fare
cijeniti *v* to appreciate
cijepati *v* to split
cijepiti *v* 1. to vaccinate 2. to graft
cijepljenje *n* vaccination
cijev *m* 1. tube 2. hose
cik-cak *m* zig-zag
cikcak *adj* zigzag
cikla *f* beetroot
ciklon *m* cyclone

ciklus *m* 1. cycle 2. series
cilindar *m* cylinder
cilj *m* aim
ciljati *v* to aim
cimet *m* cinnamon
ciničan *adj* cynical
cinik *m* cynic
cinizam *m* cynicism
cink *m* zinc
cipela *f* shoe
cirkulacija *f* circulation
cirkulirati *v* to circulate
cirkus *m* circus
ciroza *f* cirrhosis
cista *f* cyst
cisterna *f* 1. cistern 2. tank
cistitis *m* cystitis
citat *m* quotation
citirati *v* to quote
citra *f* zither
civil *m* civilian
civilan *adj* civil
civilizacija *f* civilization
cjedilo *n* strainer
cjelina *f* 1. whole 2. **u cjelini** as a whole
cjelokupan *adj* total
cjelovit *adj* entire
cjenik *m* price-list
cjenkati se *v* to bargain
cjepanica *f* log
cjepidlački *adj* fussy
cjepivo *n* vaccine
cmizdriti *v* to whine
col *m* inch
crep *m* tile
crevo *n* intestine
crijep *m* tile
crijevni *adj* intestinal
crijevo *n* intestine
crknuti *v* to die
crkva *f* church

crkven *adj* ecclesiastical
crkvica *f* chapel
crkvnjak *m* verger
crn *adj* 1. black 2. dark
crna burza *f* blackmarket
Crna Gora *f* Montenegro
crnka *f* brunette
Crnogorac *m* Montenegrin
crnogorica *f* pine forest
crnogorski *adj* Montenegrin
crnomanjast *adj* dark
crpka *f* pump
crpsti *v* 1. to pump 2. to draw
crta *f* line
crtač *m* draughtsman
crtanje *n* drawing
crtani film *m* cartoon film
crtati *v* 1. to draw 2. to design
crtež *m* drawing
crv *m* worm
crven *adj* red
crvendać *m* robin
Crveni krst/križ *m* Red Cross
crvenilo *n* red
crvenjeti *v* to redden
crvenkast *adj* reddish
curenje informacija *n* information leak
curica *f* girl
curiti *v* to flow
cvasti *v* to bloom
cvat *m* bloom
cvećar *m* florist
cveće, cvijeće *n* flowers
cvet, cvijet *m* flower
cviljeti *v* to whine
cvjetača *f* cauliflower
cvjećar *m* florist
cvjećarna *f* florist's
cvrčak *m* cicada
cvrčati *v* to chirp
cvrkutati *v* to twitter

Č

čabar *m* bucket
čačkalica *f* toothpick
čađa *f* soot
čađav *adj* sooty
čahura *f* 1. cocoon 2. (mil) cartridge
čaj *m* tea
čajnik *m* teapot
čak *adv* even
čamac *m* boat
čamac za spasavanje *m* life-boat
čangrizav *adj* morose
čaplja *f* heron
čar *m* 1. charm 2. fascination
čarapa *f* 1. sock 2. stocking
čarape *fpl* 1. socks 2. stockings 3. tights
čarati *v* to cast a spell
čaroban *adj* magical
čarobnjak *m* magician
čarolija *f* magic
čaršav *adj* table cloth
čas *m* 1. hour 2. moment 3. policijski čas curfew
časni *adj* honorable
časno *adv* honourably
časopis *m* 1. periodical 2. magazine
časovnik *m* 1. watch 2. clock
čaša *f* glass
čast *f* honour
častan *adj* honourable
častiti *v* to honour
častohlepan *adj* ambitious
čavao *adj* nail
čavka *f* jackdaw
čavrljati *v* to chatter
čedan *adj* modest

čednost *f* modesty
čega what
čegrtati *v* to rattle
Čeh *m* Czech
ček *m* cheque; check
čekanje *n* 1. waiting 2. expectation 3. lista čekanja waiting list
čekaonica *f* waiting-room
čekati *v* to wait (**na** for)
čekinja *f* bristle
čekić *m* hammer
čekovna knjižica *f* cheque book
čekrk *m* winch
čeličan *adj* steel
čeličana *f* steel works
čelik *m* 1. steel 2. **valoviti čelik** corrugated iron
čelikolji ne rđa *f* stainless steel
čeljust *f* jaw
čelni *adj* frontal
čelo *n* 1. forehead 2. front 3. cello
čempres *m* cypress
čemu 1. why? 2. what?
čep *m* 1. cork 2. plug 3. tampon
čepić *m* suppository
čeprkati *v* to scratch
čerupati *v* to pluck
česma *f* 1. well 2. fountain
češalj *m* comb
češati *v* to scratch
Češka *f* Bohemia
češki *adj* Czech
češljaonica *f* hairdresser's
češljati *v* to comb
češnjak *m* garlic
češće *adv* fairly often
čest *adj* frequent

čestica *f* 1. particle 2. fraction
čestit *adj* honest
čestitanje *n* congratulation
čestitati *v* to congratulate
čestitka *f* 1. congratulations 2. greetings card
čestitost *f* honesty
često *adj* frequently
četa *f* (mil) company
četinar *m* conifer
četiri four
četka *f* brush
četka za kosu *f* hairbrush
četkati *v* to brush
četkica za zube *f* toothbrush
četrdeset forty
četrnaest fourteen
četvero *n* foursome
četverokut *m* quadrangle
četveronožac *m* quadruped
četvorica four
četvorici, četvorke *n* quadruplets
četvorni *adj* square
četvorougao *adj* quadrangle
četvrt *f* 1. quarter 2. district
četvrtak *m* Thursday
četvrtgodišnji *adj* quarterly
četvrti *adj* fourth
četvrtina *f* quarter
čeznuti *v* to yearn
čeznuti za domovinom *v* to be homesick
čežnja *f* yearning
čičak *m* burr
čigra *f* top
čiji? whose?
čik *m* stub
čil *adj* healthy
čim *conj* 1. as soon as 2. since
čime what with?
čimpanza *m* chimpanzee
čin *m* 1. act. 2. action 3. rank

činija *f* bowl
činilac *m* factor
činiti *v* 1. to do 2. to make 3. to work
činiti se *v* to seem
činjenica *f* fact
činovnik *m* 1. official 2. office worker 3. employee
čioda *f* pin
čipka *f* lace
čips-krompir/krumpir *m* potato chips
čir *m* 1. ulcer 2. boil
čist *adj* 1. clean 2. pure 3. refined 4. (fin.) net
čista srijeda *f* Ash Wednesday
čista zarada *f* net profit
čistač *m*, **čistačica** *f* cleaner
čistilište *n* Purgatory
čistina *f* open space
čistiti *v* 1. to clean 2. to purify
čistka *f* purge
čistokrvan *adj* thoroughbred
čistoća *f* 1. cleanness 2. purity
čitač *m* scanner
čitak *adj* legible
čitalac *m*, **čitanka** *f* textbook
čitanje *n* reading
čitanje s usana *n* lip-reading
čitaonica *f* reading room
čitati s usana *f* to lip-read
čitati *v* to read
čitav *adj* 1. whole 2. intact
čizma *f* boot
član *m* member
članak *m* 1. article 2. **uvodni članak** leading article
članstvo *n* membership
čmar *m* anus
čoban, čobanin *m* shepherd
čokolada *f* chocolate
čopor *m* flock, herd, pack

čorba *f* soup
čovečan, čovječan *adj* humane
čovečanstvo, čovječanstvo *n* mankind
čovečnost, čovječnost *f* humanity
čovek, čovjek *m* 1. person 2. human being
čovekova prava *f* human rights
črčkati *v* to scribble
čučati *v* to squat
čudak *m* eccentric
čudan *adj* strange
čuđenje *n* surprise
čudesan *adj* marvellous
čuditi se *v* to marvel
čudo *n* marvel
čudotvoran *adj* miraculous
čudovište *n* monster
čujan *adj* audible
čulan *adj* sensual

čulnost *f* sensuality
čulo *n* sense
čun *m* canoe
čupati *v* to pull
čupav *adj* unkempt
čuti *v* to hear
čuvanje *n* protection
čuvar *m* 1. keeper 2. guard 3. guardian
čuvati *v* 1. to keep 2. to guard 3. to protect
čuven *adj* famous
čuvenje *n* reputation
čuvstvo *n* feeling
čvor *m* 1. knot 2. junction
čvorak *m* starling
čvorište *n* junction
čvoruga *f* bump
čvrst *adj* hardy
čvrstina, čvrstoća *f* hardiness

Ć

ćaknut *adj* crazy
ćar *m* profit
ćasa *f* dish
ćaskanje *n* chat
ćaskati *v* to chatter
ćebe *n* blanket
ćelav *adj* bald
ćelija *f* cell
ćelim *m* **1.** rug **2.** carpet
ćevapčić *m* kebab
ćilibar *m* amber
ćilim *m* **1.** rug **2.** carpet
ćirilica *f* Cyrillic script/alphabet
ćopav *adj* lame

ćorac, ćorak *m* blank (cartridge)
ćorav *adj* **1.** one-eyed **2.** blind
ćorsokak *m* dead-end
ćosav *adj* beardless
ćošak *m* corner
ćud *f* **1.** mood **2.** temper
ćudljiv *adj* moody
ćuk *m* owl
ćup *m* clay pot
ćuran *m* turkey
ćuška *f* slap
ćušnuti *v* to slap
ćutanje *n* silence
ćutati *v* to keep silent

D

da 1. yes **2.** *conj* that **3.** if **4. da ne bi** lest

dabar *m* beaver

dabome of course

dadilja *f* nanny

dah *m* breath

dahtati *v* to gasp

dakako of course

dakavac *m* yes-man

dakle 1. well **2.** therefore

daktilograf *m*, **daktilografkinja** *f* typist

dalek *adj* far

daleko *adv* far away

dalekosežan *adj* far-reaching

dalekovidan *adj* long-sighted; far-sighted

dalekovod *m* power line

dalekozor *m* binoculars

dalje *adj* farther, further

daljina *f* distance

daljnji *adj* **1.** far **2.** next

Dalmacija *f* Dalmatia

Dalmatinac *m* Dalmatian

dalmatinski *adj* Dalmatian

dama *f* lady

dan *m* day

dan-danas *adv* nowadays

dan isplate *m* payday

dan izbora *m* election day

dan za danom *adv* day after day

Danac *m* Dane

danak *m* tax

danas *adv* today

danas navečer *adv* tonight

današnji *adj* present-day

dangubiti *v* to waste time

Danska *f* Denmark

danski *adj* Danish

danju *adv* by day

dapače *adv* even

dar *m* gift

darežljiv *adj* generous

darežljivost, darost *f* generosity

darovati *v* to present

darovit *adj* talented

darovitost *f* talent

daska *f* board

daska-koturaljka *f* skateboard

daščara *f* shed

dati *v* to give

dati ostavku *v* to resign

datirati *v* to date

dativ *m* dative

datoteka *f* computer file

datula, datulja *f* date (fruit)

datum *m* date (time)

davalac *m* **1.** giver **2.** donor

davalac krvi *m* blood donor

daviti *v* to choke

davni *adj* ancient

davno *adv* long ago

daze 1. *n* omama **2.** *v* omamiti

dažbina *f* tax

de-luks *adj* deluxe

debata *f* debate

debatirati *v* to debate

debeljuškast *adj* plump

debeo *adj* fat

debi *m* debut

debil *m* idiot

debilan *adj* idiotic

debl *m* (spor) doubles

debljati se *v* to get fat

debljina *f* fat
deblo *n* tree trunk
dečak *m* 1. boy 2. youth
decembar *m* December
decenij *m*, **decenija** *f* decade
decentralizacija *f* decentralization
decentralizirati *v* to decentralize
decilitar *m* decilitre
decimal *m* decimal
decimalni zarez *m* decimal point
dečko *m* boyfriend
deda *m* grandfather
defekt *m* defect
defektan *adj* defective
defektolog *m* teacher of the disabled
defetist(a) *m* defeatist
deficit *m* deficit
defile *n* (mil) parade
defilovati *v* to parade
definicija *f* definition
definirati, definisati *v* to define
definitivan *adj* definitive
deflacija *f* (ec.) deflation
deformacija *f* deformity
deformiran *adj* deformed
deformirati *v* to deform
deformirati se *v* to be deformed
degeneracija *f* degeneration
degeneriran *adj* degenerate
degradirati *v* 1. to degrade 2. to demote
dejstvo *n* effect
deka *f* blanket
deklamovati *v* to recite
deklaracija *f* declaration
deklarirati *v* to declare
dekompresija *f* decompression
dekor *m* decor
dekoracija *f* decoration
dekoracije *n* scenery
dekorater *m* decorator

dekorativan *adj* decorative
dekret *m* decree
dekubitus *m* (med) bed sore
dekuražirati *v* to discourage
delati *v* to act
delatnost *f* activity
delegacija *f* delegation
delegat *m* delegate
delegirati *v* to delegate
delfin *m* dolphin
delikatan *adj* delicate
delikates *m*, **delikatesa** *f* delicacy
delikatesna radnja *f* delicatessen
delikatna situacija *f* delicate situation
delikatnost *f* delicacy
delilac *m* distributor
delimičan *adj* partial
delirij *m* delirium
deliti *v* 1. to divide 2. to distribute
delo *n* action
delom *adv* partially
demagog *m* demagogue
demant, demanti *m* denial
demantirati *v* to deny
demantirati se *v* to contradict oneself
demarkaciona linija *f* demarcation line
demaskirati *v* to unmask
demilitarizovana zona *f* demilitarized zone
demobilizacija *f* demobilization
demobilizirati *v* to demobilize
demografska eksplozija *f* population explosion
demokracija, demokratija *f* democracy
demokrat(a) *m* democrat
demokratizacija *f* democratization
demokratizovati *v* democratize
demolirati *v* to demolish

demon *m* demon
demonstracija *f* demonstration
demonstrant *m* demonstrator
demonstrirati *v* to demonstrate
demontirati *v* to dismantle
denacionalizacija *f* denationalization
denacionalizovati *v* denationalize
denuncijant *m* 1. denouncer 2. informer
denuncirati *v* to denounce
deo *m* part
deoba *f* division
deodorant *m* deodorant
deonica *f* share
depeša *f* telegram
depilator *m* hair-remover
deplasiran *adj* inappropriate
deponirati, deponovati *v* to deposit
deportirac *m* deportee
deportacija *f* deportation
deportirati, deportovati *v* to deport
depozit *m* deposit
depresija *f* depression
deprimiran *adj* depressed
deprimirati *v* to depress
derati se *v* 1. to be torn 2. to yell
derati *v* to tear
derivat *m* derivative
dernjava *f* yelling
desant *m* landing
desantni tenkonosac *m* tank lander
desen *m* design
desert *m* dessert
deset ten
desetar *m* (mil) corporal
deseti *adj* tenth
desetina *f* a tenth
desetkovati *v* to decimate
desiti se *v* to happen

desni 1. *adj* right 2. *fpl* gums
desnica *f* right
desničar *m* right-winger
desničarski *adj* right-wing
desno *adv* to the right
despot *m* despot
dešifrovati *v* to decode
destilacija *f* distillation
destilerija *f* distillery
destilirati *v* distill
destilovana voda *f* distilled water
destimulirati *v* to discourage
destruktivan *adj* destructive
detalj *m* detail
detaljan *adj* detailed
detaljno *adv* in detail
detant *m* détante
dete *n* child/children
detektiv *adj* detective
detektor *m* detector
detektor laži *m* lie dectector
detektor mina *m* mine dectector
deterdžent *m* detergent
detinjstvo *n* childhood
deva *f* camel
devalvacija *f* devaluation
devedeset ninety
devedeseti *adj* ninetieth
dever *m* brother-in-law
devet nine
deveti *adj* ninth
devetnaest nineteen
devetnaesti *adj* nineteenth
devica *f* virgin
deviza *f* motto
devize *fpl* currency
devojka *f* young lady
dezaktiviranje mina *f* mine disposal
dezavuirati *v* to disown
dezen *m* design
dezerter *m* deserter
dezertirati *v* to desert

dezinfekcija *f* disinfection
dezinfekciono sredstvo *n* disinfectant
dezinficirati *v* to disinfect
dezodorans, dezodorant *m* deodorant
dezorganizacija *f* disorganization
dezorganizirati se *v* to be disorganised
dežuran *adj* on duty
dežurstvo *n* duty
dići *v* to raise
diferencijal *m* differential
difterija *f* diphtheria
diftong *m* diphthong
dignuti *v* to raise
dignuti se *v* to rise
dihovitost *f* wit
dijabetes *m* diabetes
dijabetičar *m* diabetic
dijabetičan, dijabetski *adj* diabetic
dijafragma *f* diaphragm
dijagnoza *f* diagnosis
dijagonalan *adj* diagonal
dijagram *m* diagram
dijalekt *m* dialect
dijalektičan *adj* dialectical
dijalog *m* dialogue
dijamant *m* diamond
dijapozitiv *m* (film) slide
dijela *f see* dio
dijeliti *v* 1. to separate 2. to share
dijeljenje *n* division
dijeta *f* diet
dijete *n* child
diktat *m* 1. dictation 2. order
diktator *m* dictator
diktirati *v* to dictate
dilema *f* dilemma
dim *m* smoke
dimenzija *f* dimension
dimnjak *m* chimney

dina *f* sand dune
dinamičan *adj* dynamic
dinamičnost *f* dynamism
dinamit *m* dynamite
dinamo *n* dynamo
dinar *m* dinar
dinastija *f* dynasty
dinja *f* melon
dinosaur *m* dinosaur
dio *m* part
dionica *f* share
dioničar *m* shareholder
dionička glavnica *f* share capital
diploma *f* 1. diploma 2. certificate 3. degree
diplomat(a) *m* diplomat
diplomatska pošta *f* diplomatic pouch
diplomatski *adj* diplomatic
diplomirati *v* to graduate
dirati *v* to touch
direkcija *f* 1. headquarters 2. head office
direktan *adj* direct
direktan pogodak *m* direct hit
direktan prenos *m* live broadcast
direktno *adv* directly
direktor *m* 1. director 2. manager 3. headmaster; principal
direktorijum *m* board of directors
dirigent *m* conductor
dirigirati *v* to conduct
dirljiv *adj* touching
dirnuti *v* to touch
disanje *n* breathing
disati *v* to breath
disciplina *f* discipline
discipliniran *adj* disciplined
disciplinirati *v* discipline
discriminacija *f* discrimination
disidencija *f* dissent
disident *m* dissident

disidentstvo *n* dissidence
disketa *f* diskette
disko, disko-club *m* disco
diskont *m* discount
diskoteka *f* disco
diskrecija *f* discretion
diskretan *adj* discreet
diskusija *f* discussion
diskutirati *v* to discuss
diskvalificirati *v* to disqualify
dispanzer *m* clinic
dišni *adj* respiratory
distributer *m* distributor
div *m* giant
divan *adj* wonderful
diverzant *m* 1. commando 2. saboteur
diverzija *f* 1. diversion 2. sabotage
dividenda *f* dividend
diviti se *v* to admire
divljač *m* (hunting) game
divljak *m* barbarian
divlje bekstvo/bjekstvo *n* stampede
divljenje *n* admiration
divlji *adj* wild
divljina *f* wilderness
divota *f* splendour
dizač tegova/utega *m* weightlifter
dizajn *m* design
dizajner *m* designer
dizalica *f* 1. crane 2. lift; elevator
dizalo *n* lift; elevator
dizanje tegova/utega *f* weightlifting
dizel *m* diesel engine
dizel-gorivo *n* diesel fuel
dizgini vlasti *mpl* reins of power
djeca *f* children
dječak *m* boy
djed *m* grandfather
djelatnost *f* activity

djeljiv *adj* divisible
djelo *n* work
djelokrug *m* area
djelomice *adv* partly
djelotvoran *adj* effective
djelovanje *n* activity
djelovati *v* 1. to work 2. to take effect
djetinjarija *f* childishness
djetinjast *adj* childish
djetinjstvo *n* childhood
djevica *f* virgin
djevojka *f* 1. girl 2. girlfriend
dlaka *f* hair
dlakav *adj* hairy
dlan *m* palm
dlijeto *n* chisel
dnevni *adj* daily
dnevnica *f* 1. wages 2. expenses
dnevnik *m* diary
dno *n* bottom
do *prep* 1. to 2. up to 3. beside
do viđenja!, doviđenja! goodbye!
dob *f*, **doba** *n* 1. time 2. period
dobaciti *v* to throw
dobar *adj* good
dobavljač *m* supplier
dobavljanje *n* supply
dobavljati *v* 1. to get 2. to provide 3. to supply
dobit *f*, **dobitak** *m* 1. profit 2. gain
dobitak i gubitak profit and loss
dobiti *v* 1. to get 2. to gain
dobiti gorivo *v* to refuel
dobitnik *m* winner
dobitnik medalje *m* medalist
doboš *m* drum
dobošar *m* drummer
dobra volja *f* goodwill
dobro 1. *adv* well 2. okay! 3. *n* farm 4. property 5. *see* dobar
dobrobit *f* 1. benefit 2. welfare

dobročinitelj *m* benefactor
dobroćudan *adj* good-natured
dobrodošao *adj* welcome
dobrodošlica *f* welcome
dobrohotan *adj* benevolent
dobronamjeran *adj* well-meaning
dobrota *f* 1. good 2. kindness
dobrotvor *m* benefactor
dobrotvoran *adj* charitable
dobrotvorna priredba *f* charity
dobrovoljac *m* volunteer
dobrovoljan *adj* voluntary
dobrovoljan radnik *m* voluntary
   worker
docent *m* assistant lecturer
dockan *adj* late
docniti *v* to be late
doček *m* reception
dočekati *v* to meet
dočepati se *v* to seize
dočuti *v* to hear
doći *v* 1. to come 2. to arrive
dodatak *m* addition
dodatak za jelo *m* food additive
dodatan *adj* additional
dodati *v* 1. to add 2. to pass
dodijati *v* to be fed up with
dodijavati *v* to bother
dodijeliti *v* to assign
dodir *m* touch
dodirnuti *v* to touch
dodjela *f* assignment
doduše 1. *adv* indeed 2. *conj*
   although
doga *m/f* mastiff
događaj *m* event
dogled *m* binoculars
dogledan *adj* near
dogmatičan *adj* dogmatic
dogoditi se *v* to happen
dogorijevati *v* to die down
dogovati *v* to owe

dogovor *m* 1. arrangement 2.
   agreement
dogovoriti se *v* to arrange
dogradnja *f* annex
dohodak *m* 1. income 2. yield
dohodak po stanovniku *m* per
   capita income
dohvat *m* reach
dohvatiti *v* to reach
doista *adv* indeed
dojaditi *v* to be fed up with
dojam *m* impression
dojiti *v* to breast-feed
dojka *f* breast
dojmiti se *v* to be impressed
dok 1. *conj* until 2. *m* dock
dokaz *m* proof
dokazati *v* to prove
dokazni materijal *m* evidence
dokle *conj* 1. until 2. how long?
dokle god *conj* as long as
dokolica *f* leisure time
dokopati se *v* to come by
dokrajčiti *v* to end
doktor *m* doctor
doktorat *m* doctorate
doktrina *f* doctrine
dokument *m* document
dokumentirati *v* to document
dolar *m* dollar
dolazak *m* arrival
dole *adv* down
dolikovati *v* to be suitable
dolina *f* valley
doliti *v* 1. to add 2. to fill
dolje *adv* down
dom *m* 1. home 2. centre 3. hall 4.
   (pol) **Donji Dom** Lower House
   5. **Gornji Dom** Upper House
doma *f* reach
domašaj *m* range
domaći *adj* domestic

domaćica *f* 1. housewife 2. hostess
domaćin *m* 1. householder 2. host 3. (spor.) home team
domaćinstvo *n* household
domen *m* domain
domet *m* range
dominacija *f* 1. domination 2. muška dominicija sexism
dominantan *adj* dominant
dominirati *v* to dominate
domišljat *adj* ingenious
domoradac *m* native
domovina *f* homeland
domoći se *v* to get hold of
donde *adv* so far
donedavni *adj* recent
donedavna *adv* until recently
donekle *adv* to a certain extent
doneti, donijeti *v* to bring
donji *adj* lower
donji dom *m* (pol) lower house
donositi zakone *v* to legislate
dopadljiv *adj* attractive
dopasti se *v* to attract/like
dopirati *v* to reach
dopis *m* report
dopisivanje *n* correspondence
dopisivati se *v* to correspond
dopisnica *f* postcard
dopisnik *m* 1. correspondent 2. ratni dopisnik war correspondent
doplatak *m* (fin) allowance
dopodne *n* in the morning
dopratiti *v* to escort
doprema *f* 1. supply 2. delivery
dopremiti *v* 1. to supply 2. to deliver
doprijeti *v* to reach
doprinijeti *v* to contribute
doprinos *m* contribution
dopuna *f* supplement
dopuniti *v* to supplement

dopunski *adj* supplementary
dopuštenje *n* permission
dopust *m* leave
dopustiti *v* to allow
dopustiv *adj* permissible
doputovati *v* to arrive
doraditi *v* to finish
dorastao *adj* equal to
doručak *m* breakfast
doručkovati *v* to have breakfast
dosad *adv* so far
dosada 1. *adv* so far 2. *f* boredom
dosadan *adj* boring
dosadašnji *adj* 1. last 2. past
dosaditi *v* to be bored
dosađivati se *v* to be bored
dosađivati *v* to bother
doseg *m* reach
doseliti se *v* 1. to settle 2. to immigrate
doseljenik *m* 1. settler 2. immigrant
dosetka *f* joke
dosije *n* file
dosjetiti se *v* to understand
doskočiti *v* to solve
doskora *adv* 1. recently 2. soon
doskorašnji *adj* recent
dosljedan *adj* consistent
dosljedno *adv* consistently
dosljednost *f* consistency
doslovan *adj* verbatim
doslovce *adv* literally
doslovno *adv* verbatim
dospeti, dospjeti *v* 1. to arrive 2. to mature 3. to expire
dospjeće *n* 1. maturity 2. expiry
došapnuti *v* to whisper to
došljak *m* newcomer
dosta *adv* enough
dostava *f* delivery
dostaviti *v* to deliver
dostignuće *n* achievement

dostići *v* to catch up with
dostojan *adj* worthy
dostojanstven *adj* dignified
dostojanstvo *n* dignity
dostupan *adj* accessible
dostupnost *f* accessibility
dosuditi *v* to award
dotacija *f* 1. grant 2. subsidy
dotad *adv* till then
dotaknuti, dotaći *v* to touch
doticaj *m* touch
dotičan *adj* referred to
dotirati *v* to subsidise
dotjeran *adj* tidy
dotjerati *v* 1. to tidy 2. to drive to
dotle *adv* 1. till then 2. at that time
dotrajao *adj* used
dotrčati *v* to run up
dotući *v* to finish
doušnik *m* informer
dovdje *adv* this far
dovesti *v* 1. to bring 2. to lead
dovesti se *v* to come over
doviknuti *v* to summon
dovinuti se *v* to reach
dovitljiv *adj* inventive
dovle *adv* so far
dovoljan *adj* sufficient
dovoljno *adv* enough
dovoz *m* 1. supply 2. transport
dovratnik *m* doorpost
dovršenje *n* completion
dovršiti *v* to complete
dovući *v* to drag
doza *f* 1. dose 2. prevelika doza overdose
dozirnaje *n* dosage
dozivati *v* to call
doznačiti *v* to remit
doznaka *f* 1. voucher 2. token 3. money order 4. assignment
doznati *v* to find out

dozreti *v* to ripen
dozvati *v* to call back
dozvola *f* 1. permission 2. permit
dozvola za pretres *f* search warrant
dozvoliti *v* to permit
doživjeti *v* to experience
doživljaj *m* experience
doživotan zatvor *m* (leg) life sentence
drač *m* brambles
drag *adj* 1. dear 2. nice
draga *adj/f* girlfriend
dragi *adj/m* boyfriend
drago 1. -ever, any 2. *adj* glad
dragocen, dragocjen *adj* precious
dragocenost, dragocjenost *f* value
dragocenosti, dragocjenosti *fpl* valuables
dragulj *m* jewel
draguljar *m* jeweller
drama *f* drama
dramatičan *adj* dramatic
dramatizirati *v* to dramatise
dramski *adj* dramatic
drap *adj* beige
draperije *n* drapery
drapirati *v* to drape
draškati *v* to caress
drastičan *adj* drastic
draž *f* charm
dražba *f* auction
dražbovaonica *f* auction house
dražest *f* charm
dražestan *adj* charming
dražiti *v* to provoke
drečati *v* to scream
dreka *f* screaming
dremljiv *adj* sleepy
dremuckanje *n* nap
dremuckanjeti *v* to nap

dreser *m* trainer
dresirati *v* to train
dresura *f* training
drevan *adj* ancient
drhtati *v* 1. to tremble 2. to shiver
drhtav *adj* trembling
driblati *v* (spor) to dribble
drijemanje *n* nap
drmati *v* to shake
drndati *v* to strum
drobiti *v* to crush
droga *f* 1. drug/drugs 2. **uzimati droge** to take drugs 3. **uzimaje droga** drug addiction
drogerija *f* chemist's; pharmacy
drolja *f* prostitute
dronjak *m* **u dronjcima** in tatters
dronjci *mpl* rags
drozak *m* thrush
drskost *f* insolence
drška *f* handle
drug *m*, **drugarica** *f* 1. friend 2. companion 3. comrade
drugarstvo *n* 1. companionship 2. camaraderie
drugde, drugdje elsewhere
drugi *adj* 1. second 2. next 3. another
drugo *adv* 1. else 2. secondly
drugorazredan *adj* second-class
drukčije *adv* differently
drukčiji *adj* different
drum *m* road
drumarina *f* toll
društven *adj* sociable
društvene nauke *fpl* social sciences
društveni *adj* social
društveno-ekonomski *adj* socioeconomic
društveno-politički *adj* sociopolitical
društvenost *f* sociability

društvo *n* 1. society 2. association 3. company
družina *f* group
družiti se *v* to associate
drvarnica *f* 1. woodshed 2. coal cellar
drven *adj* wooden
drvenarija *f* woodwork
drveće *n* trees
drvo *n* 1. tree 2. wood
drvodjelac *m* carpenter
drvored *m* avenue
drvorez *m* carving
drvosječa *m* lumberjack
drzak *m* insolent
držak *m* handle
držanje *n* attitude
držati *v* 1. to hold 2. to keep 3. **ne držati** to renege
držati u frižideru *v* to refrigerate
država *f* 1. state 2. **nacionalna država** nation state
državljanin *m* citizen, national
državljanstvo *n* citizenship
državni *adj* 1. state 2. public
državni sektor *m* public sector
državnik *m* statesman
dubin *m* dolphin
dubina *f* depth
dublirati *v* to dub
dubok *m* deep
dubokouman *adj* profound
dućan, dućan *m* shop; store
dud *m* mulberry
duda *f* dummy
duet *m* duet
dug *adj* long
dug *m* debt
duga *f* rainbow
dugirični *adj* long-term
dugme *n* button
dugo *adv* for a long time

dugogodišnji *adj* long-term
dugotrajan *adj* long lasting
dugovanje *n* debt
duh *m* 1. spirit 2. mind
duhan *adj* tobacco
duhandžija *f* tobacconist
duhovit *adj* witty
duhovita primedba/primjedba *f* wisecrack
duhovni *adj* 1. spiritual 2. intellectual
duhovnik *m* priest
duljina vala *f* wavelength
Dunav the Danube
dunja *f* quince
duo *m* duet
dupli *adj* double
duplikat *m* 1. duplicate 2. copy
duplja *f*, **duplje** *n* 1. hole 2. cave
dupsti *v* to hollow out
duriti se *v* to sulk
duša *f* soul
dušek *m* mattress
duševni *adj* spiritual
dušik *m* nitrogen
dušman, dušmanin *m* enemy
dušmanski *adj* violent
dušnik *m* larynx
duvan *m* tobacco
duvandžija *f* tobacconist
duvati *v* to blow
duž 1. *f* straight line 2. *prep* along
dužan *adj* 1. obliged 2. in debt
dužica *f* iris
dužina *f* length
dužina vala *f* wavelength
dužnik *m* debtor
dužnost *f* 1. duty 2. position
dva two
dvadeset twenty
dvadeseti *adj* twentieth
dvanaesnik *m* colon

dvanaest twelve
dvanaesti *adj* twelfth
dvaput *adv* twice
dvije two
dvije tačke *fpl* colon
dvjesta *f* two hundred
dvoboj *m* duel
dvojba *f* doubt
dvojben *adj* doubtful
dvojci *mpl* twins
dvoje *n* couple
dvojezičan *adj* bilingual
dvojica *f* couple
dvojka *f* twosome
dvojni *adj* 1. double 2. bipartite
dvojnik *m* double
dvokrevetna soba *f* twin-bed room
dvoličan *adj* hypocritical
dvoličnost *f* hypocrisy
dvomotorac *m* twin-engine plane
dvopartijski *adj* two-party
dvopartijski sistem *m* two-party system
dvopek *m* biscuit
dvor *m* 1. palace 2. court
dvorac *m* manor
dvorana *f* 1. hall 2. auditorium
dvorana velikana *f* hall of fame
dvorište *n* courtyard
dvoriti *v* to serve
dvorkinja *f* cleaner
dvosjed *m* two-seater
dvosjekli *adj* two-edged
dvosmerni, dvosmjerni *adj* two-way
dvosmislen *adj* ambiguous
dvosmislenost *f* ambiguity
dvostran *adj* bilateral
dvostruk *m* double
dvotočka *f* colon
dvoumiti se *v* to hesitate
dvoženstvo *n* bigamy

DŽ

džabe *adv* free of charge
džak *m* sack
džamija *f* mosque
džbun *m* bush
džem *m* jam
džemper *m* sweater
dženaza *m* (Isl.) funeral
džentlmen *adj* gentleman
džep *m* pocket
džepar *m* pickpocket
džeparac *m* pocket money

džeparoš *m* pickpocket
džepna lampa *f* torch; flashlight
džez *m* jazz
džigerica *f* liver
džin *m* giant
džip *m* jeep
džokej *m* jockey
džoker *m* joker
džumbus *m* chaos
džungla *f* jungle
džus *m* juice

đak *m* pupil
đavo, đavao *m* devil
đon *m* sole
đubre *n* **1.** manure **2.** rubbish; garbage
đubretar *m* dustman

đubrište *n* rubbish heap
đubrivo *n* fertiliser
đulad *f* (mil.) shells
đumbir *m* ginger
đus *m* juice
đuture *adv* **u đuture** all together

E

ebanovina *f* ebony
edicija *f* edition
efekt, efekat *m* effect
efektan *adj* effective
efektivan, efikasan *adj* 1. effective 2. efficient
efikasnost *f* 1. effectiveness 2. efficiency
egiosta *f* egoist
egzaktan *adj* exact
egzaltiran *adj* sensitive
egzemplar *m* 1. example 2. model
egzistencija *f* 1. existence 2. survival
egzistirati *v* to exist
egzotičan *adj* exotic
eho *m* echo
ej! hey!
ejakulacija *f* ejaculation
ejakulirati *v* to ejaculate
ekcem *m* eczema
ekipa *f* team
ekipa za spasavanje *f* rescue team
eklatantan *adj* obvious
ekonom *m* 1. economist 2. manager
ekonomičan *adj* economical
ekonomija *f* 1. economy 2. economics
ekonomika *f* economy
ekonomist, ekonomista *f* economist
ekonomizirati *v* to economize
ekonomska kriza *f* economic crisis
ekonomska politika *f* economic policy

ekonomske nauke *fpl* economics
ekonomski *adj* economic
ekran *m* screen
ekscentričan *adj* eccentric
eksces *m* excess
ekselencija *f* excellency
ekser *m* nail
ekshibicija *f* exhibition
ekskurzija *f* 1. trip 2. tour
eksluzivan *adj* exclusive
ekspansivan *adj* expansive
ekspanzionist(a) *m* expansionist
ekspanzionistički *adj* expansionist
ekspanzionizam *m* expansionism
ekspedicija *f* expedition
ekspeditivan *adj* prompt
ekspeditivnost *f* promptness
eksperiment *m* experiment
eksperimentalan *adj* experimental
ekspert *m* expert
eksploatacija *f* exploitation
eksploatator *m* exploiter
eksploatirati, eksploatisati *v* to exploit
eksplodirati *v* to explode
eksplozija *f* explosion
eksploziv *adj* explosive
eksponat *m* 1. display 2. exhibit
eksponaža *f* exposure
eksponirati *v* to expose
ekspoze *m* 1. exposé 2. report
ekspozitura *f* branch
ekspres, ekspresni *adj* express
ekspres-restoran *m* fast-food restaurant
ekstaza *f* ecstasy
ekstra *adj/adv* extra

ekstradicija *f* extradition
ekstradirati *v* to extradite
ekstrakt *m* extract
ekstravagantan *adj* extravagant
ekstravagantnost *f* extravagance
ekstrem *m* extreme
ekstreman *adj* extreme
ekstremist(a) *m* extremist
ekstremistički *adj* 1. extremist 2. (pol.) ultra
ekstremizam *m* extremism
ekvator *m* equator
ekvivalent *m* equivalent
elaborat *m* 1. plan 2. proposal 3. survey
elan *m* enthusiasm
elastičan *adj* 1. elastic 2. flexible
elastičnost *f* flexibility
elegancija *f* elegance
električar *m* electrician
elektrana *f* power station
elektricitet *m* electricity
električna bušilica *f* power drill
električni vodovi *mpl* wiring
elektrika *f* electricity
elektron *m* electron
elektronika *f* electronics
elektronski *adj* eletronic
elektrotehničar *m* electrician
elektrotehnika *f* electrical engineering
element *m* element
elementaran *adj* 1. basic 2. fundamental
eliminisati *v* to eliminate
elipsa *f* ellipse
elita, elitan *adj* elite
elitne trupe *fpl* crack troops
emajl *m* enamel
embrio, embrion *m* embryo
emigracija *f* emigration
emigrant *m* emigrant

emigrirati *v* to emigrate
emisija *f* 1. transmission 2. broadcast 3. programme
emisija vesti/vijesti *f* newscast
emitirati *v* 1. to transmit 2. to broadcast
emocija *f* emotion
emocionalan *adj* emotional
enciklopedija *f* encyclopaedia
energija *f* 1. energy 2. power
Engleska *f* 1. England 2. United Kingdom
engleski *adj* English
Engleskinja *f* Englishwoman
Englez *m* Englishman
eno *adv* there
enterijer *m* interior
entuzijazam *m* enthusiasm
epidemija *f* epidemic
epileptički *adj* epileptic
epilog *m* epilogue
episkop *m* bishop
epitaf *m* epitaph
epizoda *f* episode
epoha *f* epoch
epruveta *f* test tube
epski *adj* epic
era *f* era
ergela *f* stud farm
erkondišn *m* airconditioner, airconditioning
erotičan, erotički, erotski *adj* erotic
erupcija *f* eruption
esej *m* essay
eskadra *f* squadron
eskalacija *f* escalation
eskalator *m* escalator
estetika *f* aesthetics
estetski *adj* aesthetic
etapa *f* 1. stage 2. phase 3. (spor) lap

etar, eter *m* 1. air 2. atmosphere
etažni *adj* storey
etičan *adj* ethical
etika *f* ethics
etiketa *f* 1. etiquette 2. label
etnički *adj* ethnic
eto *adv* there
eukaliptus *m* eucalyptus
evakuacija *f* evacuation
evakuisati *v* to evacuate
evanđelje *n* gospel
evazija *f* evasion
eventualan *adj* possible
eventualno *adv* possibly
evidencija *f* records

evidentirati *v* to keep a record
evo! here!
evolucija *f* evolution
evro- euro-
evrokomunizam *m* eurocommunism
Evropa *f* Europe
Evropljanin *m* European
Evropska zajednica *f* European Community
evropski *adj* European
Evropski savet/savje *m* Council of Europe
Evropsko vijeće *n* Council of Europe

F

fabrika *f* factory
fabrika municije *f* munition factory
fabrikant *m* manufacturer
fabrikat *m* 1. manufacture 2. product
fabula *f* story
fah *m* 1. profession 2. field
fakt, fakat *m* fact
fakin *m* rogue
faks, faksimil *m* fax
faktičan *adj* actual
faktura *f* invoice
fakturisati *v* to invoice
fakultativan *adj* optional
fakultet *m* 1. faculty 2. college
faliti *v* to lack
falsifikat *m* forgery
fanatičan *adj* fanatical
fantastičan *adj* fantastic
fantazija *f* 1. fantasy 2. imagination
fantom *m* phantom
far *m* headlight
farbati *v* to paint
farma *f* farm
farmaceut *m* chemist; pharmacist
farmaceutski *adj* pharmaceutical
farmacija *f* chemist's; pharmacy
farmakolog pharmacologist
farmakologija *f* pharmacology
farmerice *fpl* jeans
farovi *mpl* headlights
fasada *f* facade
fasciki *adj* folder
fascinirati *v* to fascinate
fasung *m* socket

fašist(a) *m*, **fasistički** *adj* fascist
fašizam *m* fascism
fatalan *adj* fatal
faul *m* foul
favele *fpl* slums
favorit *m* (spor.) favourite
faza *f* phase
fazan *adj* pheasant
februar *m* February
feder *m* (metal) spring
federacija *f* federation
federalna rezervna banka *f* federal reserve bank
federalna vlada *f* federal government
federalni *adj* federal
federativan *adj* federative
federativni *adj* federal
federovanje *n* (car) suspension
feljton *m* sketch
feministkinja *f* feminist
feminizam *m* feminism
fen *m* hair-dryer
fenjer *m* lamp
fenomen *m* phenomenon
fer *adj/adv* fair
feribot *m* ferry
ferije *fpl* holidays
festival *m* festival
fetiš *m* fetish
fetus *m* fetus
figura *f* figure
figurativan *adj* figurative
fijasko *m* fiasco
fijuk *m* whistle
fijukati *v* to whistle
fikcija *f* fiction

fiksan *adj* fixed
fiktivan *adj* fictitious
filc *m* felt
filharmonija *f* philharmonic
filijala *f* branch
film *m* film
filmska industrija *f* film industry
filmska zvezda/zvijezda *f* film star
filologija *f* philology
filozofija *f* philosophy
filozofski *adj* philosophical
filter *m* filter
filtrirati *v* to filter
fin *m* fine
finalan *adj* final
finale *m* (spor) 1. final(s) 2. **polu-finale** semi-final(s)
finalista *f* finalist
financije *n* finance
financirati *v* to finance
finansije *fpl* finance(s)
finansirati *v* to finance
finiš *m* finish
fino *adj/adv* 1. fine 2. finely
finoća *f* refinement
fioka *f* drawer
fioka za novac *f* cash till
firma *f* 1. firm 2. company
firnajz *m* 1. varnish 2. premazati firnajzom to varnish
fiskultura *f* 1. physical training 2. body-building
fišek *m* 1. bag 2. cartridge
fitilj *m* fuse
fizičar *m* physicist
fizički *adj* physical
fizika *f* physics
fiziologija *f* physiology
fizioterapija *f* physiotherapy
flanel *m* flannel
flaša *f* flask

flaster *m* plaster
flauta *f* flute
flegma *f* phlegm
fleka *f* fleck
fleksibilan *adj* flexible
fleksibilni disk *m* floppy disc
flert *m* flirting
flertovati *v* to flirt (s with)
fleš *m* 1. flash 2. torch; flashlight
flota *f* 1. navy 2. fleet
fluorescentna svetiljka/svjetiljka *f* fluorescent light tube
foaje *m* foyer
fobija *f* phobia
foka *f* seal
folija *f* foil
folklor *m* folklore
fond *m* fund
fondacija *f* foundation
fonetika *f* phonetics
fontana *f* fountain
forma *f* form
formacija *f* formation
formalan *adj* formal
formalnost *f* formality
format *m* 1. format 2. size
formirati *v* to form
formula *f* formula
formular *m* form
formulisanje *n* wording
forsirati *v* to force
forum *m* forum
fosfat *m* phosphate
fosfor *m* phosphorus
fosil *m* fossil
fotelja *f* armchair
foto-aparat *m* camera
fotograf *m* photographer
fotografija *f* 1. photograph 2. photography
fotografski *adj* photographic
fotokopija *f* photocopy

fotokopiranje *n* aparat za fotokopiranje photocopier
fotokopirati *v* to photocopy
foto-teka *f* photo library
fozgen *m* phosgene
fragment *m* fragment
frakcija *f* 1. fraction 2. (pol.) faction 3. splinter group
fraktura *f* fracture
franak *m* franc
Francuska *f* France
francuski *adj* French
francuski ključ *m* spanner; wrench
Francuz *m* Frenchman
franko *adj* 1. post-paid 2. free on board (FOB)
franko-kanadski *adj* French-Canadian
frapantan *adj* amazing
frapirati *v* to amaze
fratar *m* monk
fraza *f* phrase
fregata *f* frigate
frekvencija *f* frequency
freska *f*, **fresko** *m* fresco
fri-šop *m* duty-free shop
frigati *v* to fry

frigidan *adj* frigid
frizer *m* 1. freezer 2. hairdresser
frizerski salon *m* hairdresser's
frizura *f* hair-do
frižider *m* refrigerator
front *m* (mil.) front
frontalan *adj* frontal
frontalan napad *m* frontal attack
frotir *m* bath towel
frotirati *v* to rub
fudbal *m* football
fudbaler *m* footballer
fuj! shame!
fundamentalan *adj* fundamental
fundamentalist(a) *f* fundamentalist
funkcija *f* function
funkcijska tipka *f* function key
funkcionalan *adj* functional
funkcionar, funkcioner *m* official
funta *f* pound
furija *f* fury
furnir *m* veneer
fusnota *f* footnote
futrola *f* 1. case 2. cover
fuzija *f* 1. fusion 2. (fin) merger
fuzionirati *v* 1. to fuse 2. (fin) to merge

G

gaće *fpl* underpants; shorts
gaćice *fpl* knickers; panties
gadan *adj* disgusting
gađanje *n* artilerijsko gađanje (mil.) shelling
gađati *v* to aim
gađenje *n* disgust
gajde *fpl* bagpipes
gajenje *n* 1. cultivation 2. upbringing
gajgerov brojač *m* Geiger counter
gajiti *v* to bring up
gajtan *m* braid
gakati *v* to quack
gala predstava *f* gala
galaksija *f* galaxy
galama *f* noise
galamiti *v* to make a noise
galantan *adj* gallant
galanterija *f* haberdashery
galanterista *f* haberdasher's
galeb *m* seagull
galerija *f* gallery
galon *m* gallon
galopirati *v* to gallop
gamad *f* vermin
gangrena *f* gangrene
gangster *m* gangster
ganut *adj* 1. moved 2. emotional
ganuti *v* to touch an emotion
ganutljiv *adj* moving
ganuće *n* emotion
garancija *f* guarantee
garantirati *v* to guarantee
gar *m/f* soot
garav *adj* sooty
garaža *f* garage

garda *f* guard(s)
garderoba *f* 1. wardrobe 2. cloak-room; checkroom 3. left-luggage
garnitura *f* set
garnizon *m* garrison
gas *m* gas
gasiti *v* 1. to put out 2. to switch off
gasmaska *f* gas-mask
gasna komora *f* gas cylinder
gasovod *m* gas line
gat *m* 1. dam 2. wharf
gatanje *n* fortune-telling
gatara *f* fortune-teller
gatati *v* to tell fortunes
gavran *m* raven
gaz *m* ford
gaza *f* gauze
gazda *m* 1. landlord 2. owner 3. boss
gazdarica *f* 1. landlady 2. housewife
gazdinstvo *n* farm
gazeća površina *f* tyre tread
gaziti *v* to tread
gde, gdje where
gdegde, gdjegdje here and there
gdegod, gdjegod somewhere
gdekoji, gdjekoji some
gegalo *n* toddler
gel *m* gel
gen *m* gene
genealogija *f* genealogy
generacija *f* generation
general *m* general
Generalna skupština *f* General Assembly
general-potpukovnik *m* major-general

generalni sekretar *m* secretary general
generalštab *m* headquarters
generator *m* generator
genetičan, genetski *adj* genetic
genetika *f* genetics
geneza *f* genesis
genijalan *adj* ingenious
genitalije *n* genitals
genitiv *m* genitive
genocid *m* 1. genocide 2. **sprovesti genocid** to commit genocide
geodezija *f* surveying
geofizika *f* geophysics
geografija *f* geography
geologija *f* geology
geometrija *f* geometry
geometrijski *adj* geometrical
gerijatrija *f* geriatrics
gerila *f* guerrilla warfare
gerilac *m* guerrilla
gerilski rat *m* guerrilla warfare
gerund, gerundij *m* gerund
geslo *n* slogan
gestikulirati *v* to gesticulate
geto *m* ghetto
gibak *adj* flexible
gibanje *n* motion
gibanti *v* to move
gimnastičar *m* gymnast
gimnastička dvorana *f* gymnasium
gimnastika *f* gymnastics
gimnazija *f* secondary school
gimnazijalac *m* secondary-school student
ginekolog *m* gynaecologist
ginekologija *f* gynaecology
ginekološka klinika *f* gynaecological clinic
ginekološki *adj* gynaecological
ginuti *v* to get killed
gipkost *f* flexibility

gips *m* 1. plaster 2. cast
git *m* putty
gitara *f* guitar
gitarist(a) *m* guitarist
glačalo *n* iron
glačati *v* 1. to smooth 2. to iron
glad *m/f* 1. hunger 2. famine
gladak *adj* smooth
gladan *adj* hungry
gladiti *v* to smooth
gladovati *v* to starve
glagol *m* verb
glagoljica *f* Glagolitic
glagolski *adj* verbal
glas *m* 1. sound 2. voice 3. vote 4. reputation
glasač *m* voter
glasan *adj* loud
glasanje *n* 1. voting 2. **tajno glasanje** secret vote 3. **jednoglasno glasanje** unanimous vote
glasanje o nepovjerenju/nepovjerenju *n* vote of no-cofidence
glasanje o povjerenju/povjerenju *n* vote of cofidence
glasanje u bloku *n* block voting
glasati *v* to vote (**za** for; **na** on)
glasiti *v* to run
glasnice *fpl* vocal cords
glasnik *m* messenger
glasno *adv* aloud
glasovit *adj* famous
glatko *adv* smoothly
glava *f* 1. head 2. self
glavar *m* chief
glavčina *f* hub
glavica *f* mound
glavna pošta *f* general post office
glavni grad *m* capital
glavni *adj* main

glavnica f capital
glavnokomandujući m commander-in-chief
glavobolja f headache
glazba f music
gle! look!
glečer m glacier
gledalac m spectator
gledalište n 1. audience 2. auditorium
gledanje n watching
gledati v 1. to look at 2. to watch
gledište n standpoint
gležanj m ankle
glib m silt
glikoza f glucose
glina f clay
gliser m motor boat
glista f worm
gljiva f mushroom
globa f penalty
globalan adj global
globiti v to fine
globtroter m globetrotter
globus m globe
glodar m rodent
glodati v to gnaw
glodavac m rodent
glog m hawthorn
glomazan adj 1. bulky 2. clumsy
glosar m glossary
gluh adj deaf
gluhonijem adj deaf-mute
gluhoća f deafness
gluma f acting
glumac m actor
glumica f actress
glumiti v to act
glup adj stupid
glupost f stupidity
gluv adj deaf
gluvonem adj deaf-mute

gluvoća f deafness
gmaz m reptile
gmizati v to crawl
gmizavac m reptile
gnev m fury
gnezdo, gnijezdo n nest
gnilost f rot
gniti v to rot
gnjavator m bore
gnjavaža f boredom
gnjaviti v to bother
gnječiti v to squeeze
gnjev m fury
gnjida f nit
gnjida f pest
gnjil, gnjio adj rotten
gnjurac m diver
gnjuriti v to dive
gnjusan adj loathsome
gnoj m manure
gnušati se v to loathe
go adj naked
godina f 1. year 2. prošle godine last year 3. ove godine this year 4. iduće godine next year 5. prestupna godina leap year 6. budžetska godina financial year; fiscal year 7. poreska godina tax year 8. svetlosna godina; svjetlosna godina light year 9. svake godine yearly
godina vina f vintage
godišinjca f anniversary
godišnjak m almanac
godišnji adj yearly, annual
godište n year
goditi v to please
godpodar m master
gojaznost f obesity
gojiti v to cultivate
gol 1. adj naked 2. m goal
golem adj enormous

golman *m* goalkeeper
goloruk *adj* unarmed
golotinja *f* nakedness
golub *m* pigeon
golubica *f* dove
gomila *f* crowd
gomolj *m* bulb
gonič *m* driver
goniti *v* to chase
gonoreja *f* gonorrhea
gora *f* 1. mountain 2. forest
gorak *adj* bitter
gorčina *f* bitterness
gord *adj* proud
gordost *f* pride
gore *adv* 1. above 2. worse
goreti *v* to blaze
gorila *m* gorilla
gorivo *n* fuel
gorjeti *v* burn
gorljiv *adj* eager
gorljivost *f* eagerness
gornji *adj* upper
gornji dom *m* (pol) upper house
gorostas *m* giant
gorovit *adj* 1. mountainous 2. hilly
gorski lanac *m* mountain chain
gorušica *f* mustard
gorući *adj* burning
gospod *m* lord
gospodar *m* 1. lord 2. boss
gospodariti *v* 1. to rule 2. to manage
gospodarstvo *n* management
gospodin *m* 1. gentleman 2. Mr
gospodstvo *n* power
gospođa *f* 1. lady 2. Mrs
gospođica *f* Miss
gost *m* 1. guest 2. visitor
gostionica *f* 1. pub 2. inn
gostioničar *m* publican
gostiti *v* to entertain

gostoljubivost *f* hospitality
gošća *f* 1. guest 2. visitor
gotov *adj* 1. finished 2. ready
gotovina *f* cash
goveče *n* head of cattle
goveda *f* cattle
govedina *f* beef
govedo *n* head of cattel
govno *n* shit
govor *m* speech
govoriti *v* to speak
govorljiv *adj* talkative
govorna mana *f* speech defect
govornik *m* speaker
govor prstima *f* sign language
gozba *f* feast
graba *f* ditch
grabež *m* looting
grabiti *v* to grab
grablje *n* rake
graciozan *adj* graceful
gracioznost *f* grace
grad *m* 1. place 2. town 3. city
gradilište *n* 1. plot of land 2. site
graditelj *m* builder
graditi *v* to build
gradivo *n* material
gradić *m* town
gradnja *f* construction
gradonačelnik *m* mayor
grad-satelit *m* satellite city
gradska čistoća *f* sanitary department
gradski *adj* 1. municipal 2. urban
građa *f* material
građani *adj* citizens
građanin *m* 1. citizen 2. city dweller
građanski *adj* civic
građanski rat *m* civil war
građanski stalež *m* middle class
građanstvo *n* the public

građen *adj* built
građevina *f* 1. building 2. construction
građevinar *m* 1. civil engineer 2. architect
građevinarstvo *n* 1. civil engineering 2. architecture
građevinski materijal *m* building materials
grafičar *m* graphic artist
grafika *f* 1. graphic art(s) 2. graphics
grafikon *m* 1. graph 2. diagram
grafit *m* graphite
grah *m* bean
graktati *v* to croak
gram *m* gramme
gramatički *adj* grammatical
gramatika *f* grammar
gramofon *m* record player
gramzljiv *adj* greedy
grana *f* branch
granata *f* (mil) 1. grenade 2. shell
granica *f* 1. border 2. boundary
granica dozvoljenih greška *f* margin of error
graničar *m* border guard
grančica *f* twig
graničiti se *v* to border on
granit *m* granite
grašak *m* pea
graver *m* engraver
gravirati *v* to engrave
gravitacija *f* gravity
gravura *f* engraving
grb *m* coat of arms
grba *f* hump
grč *m* 1. cramp 2. **porođajni grčevi** labour contractions
Grčka *f* Greece
grčki *adj* Greek
grditi *v* to scold

grdoba *f* monstrosity
grdoban *adj* ugly
grdosija *f* monster
grebati *v* to scratch
greben *m* 1. cliff 2. reef
greda *f* beam
greh *m* 1. sin 2. offence
grehota *f* shame
grejanje *n* heating
grejpfrut *m* grapefruit
grepsti *v* to scratch
grešiti *v* 1. to make a mistake 2. to be wrong
greška *f* 1. mistake 2. fault
greškom *adv* by mistake
grešnik *m* sinner
grgeč *m* perch
grgljati *v* to gargle
grickati *v* to nibble
grijalica *f* heater
grijanja *f* heating
grijati *v* to heat
grijeh *m* sin
griješiti *v* 1. to sin 2. to make a mistake
grimiz *m* crimson
grip *m*, **gripa** *f* flu
gristi *v* to bite
griva *f* mane
griz *m* semolina
grjaj *m* noise
Grk *m* Greek
grkljan *m* larynx
grliti *v* to embrace
grlo *n* throat
grm *m* bush
grmjeti *v* to thunder
grmljavina *f* thunder
grmlje *n* bushes
grnčarija *f*, **grnčarstvo** *n* pottery
grob *m* grave
groblje *n* graveyard

grobnica *f* tomb
grof *m* count
grofica *f* countess
groktati *v* to grunt
grom *m* thunder
groza *f* horror
grozan *adj* horrible
grozd *m* bunch
groziti se *v* to threaten
groznica *f* fever
grozota *f* horror
grožnja *f* threat, menace
grožde *n* grapes
grub *adj* rude
grubost *f* rudeness
gruda *f* 1. lump 2. ball
grudi *fpl* 1. breasts 2. chest
grudica *f* clot
grudnjak *m* bra
grupa *f* group
grupa borba *f* infighting
grupna ekskurzija *f* field trip
grupno putovanje *n* package tour
grušati se *v* to clot
guba *f* leprosy
gubica *f* nose
gubici *mpl* (mil.) losses
gubilište *n* scaffold
gubitak *m* loss
gubiti *v* to lose
gudalo *n* bow

gudura *f* ravine
gulaš *m* goulash
gulikoža *f* extortioner
guliti *v* 1. to peel 2. to skin
guma *f* 1. rubber 2. gum 3. tyre; tire
gumb *m* button
gumeni pečat *m* rubber stamp
gungula *f* riot
gunj *m* blanket
gunđati *v* to grumble
gurati *v* to push
gusar *m* pirate
gusarstvo *n* piracy
gusenica, gusjenica *f* caterpillar
gusjeničar *m* tracked vehicle
guska *f* goose
guša *f* throat
gušiti *v* to choke
guštara *f* thicket, shrubs
gušter *m* lizard
gušterača *f* pancreas
gust *adj* dense
gustina, gustoća *f* density
gutati *v* to swallow
guverner *m* governor
guzica *f* buttock
gužva *f* crowd
gužvati *v* to crumple
gvozden *adj* iron
gvoždarski radnja *f* hardware store
gvožde *n* iron

H

hadži *m/f/pl*, **hadžija** *m* haji
hadžiluk *m* hajj
hajduk *m* outlaw, 'haiduk'
halabuka *f* uproar
halaliti *v* to bless
half *m* (spor) half
haljina *f* dress
halo! hello!
halucinacija *f* hallucination
halucinantan *adj* hallucinatory
halucinogen *adj* 1. hallucinogenic
   2. **halucinogena sredstva**
   hallucinogens
hambar *m* barn
hapsiti *v* to arrest
hapšenje *n* arrest
harati *v* to devastate
hardver *m* hardware
haringa *f* herring
harmoničan *adj* harmonious
harmonija *f* harmony
harmonika *f* accordion
harmonikaš *m* accordionist
hauba *f* bonnet; hood
hazard *m* gamble
hazarder *m* gambler
hazardirati *v* gambler
heftalica *f* stapler
hej! hey!
helikopter *m* helicoper
heljda *f* buckwheat
hemoragija *f* hemorrhage
hemoroidi *mpl* haemorrhoids
hemung *m* inhibition
hendikep *m* handicap
heretik *m* heretic
hereza *f* heresy

hermetički *adj* 1. hermetic
   2. -proof
heroin *m* heroin
heterogen *adj* heterogeneous
heteroseksualan *adj* heterosexual
hidrauličan *adj* hydraulic
hidrocentrala *f* hydroelectric
   power station
hidroelektričan *adj* hydroelectric
hidroelektrična energija *f*
   hydroelectric power
hidrogen *m* hydrogen
hidrogenska bomba *f* hydrogen
   bomb
higijena *f* hygiene
higijenski *adj* hygienic
hihotati *v* to giggle
hijerarhija *f* hierarchy
hiljada thousand
himna *f* anthem
hiperprodukcija *f* overproduction
hipertenzija *f* hypertension
hipnotizirati *v* to hyponotize
hipodrom *m* racecourse
hipoteka *f* mortgage
hipoteza *f* hypothesis
hir *m* whim
hirovit *adj* capricious
histeričan *adj* hysterical
histerija *f* hysteria
hitac *m* shot
hitan *adj* urgent
hitan sastanak *m* emergency
   session
hlače *fpl* trousers
hlad *m* shade
hladan *adj* cold

hladetina *f* jelly
hladiti *v* to cool
hladnjak *m* radiator
hladnokrvan *adj* cool
hladnokrvnost *f* coolness
hladnoća *f* cold
hlapiti *v* to evaporate
hlapljiv *adj* volatile
hleb, hljeb *m* 1. bread 2. loaf
hobi *m* hobby
hobotnica *f* octopus
hod *m* walk
hodati *v* to walk
hodnik *m* walkway
hodočasnik *m* pilgrim
hodža *m* mullah
hohštapler *m* 1. imposter 2. social climber
hohštaplirati *v* to show off
hokej na ledu *m* ice hockey
hol *m* lobby
Holandija *f* Netherlands
homoseksualac *m*, **homoseksualan** *adj* homosexual
honorar *m* fee
honorarac *m* freelancer
honorarni rad *m* freelance work
horizontalan *adj* horizontal
hormon *m* hormone
hostija *f* (rel) host
hotel *m* hotel
hotelski gost *m* hotel guest
hrabar *m* courageous
hrabrenje *n* encouragement
hrabriti *v* to encourage
hrabrost *f* courage
hram *m* temple
hramati *v* to limp

hrana *f* food
hraniti *v* to feed
hranjenik *m* fosterchild
hranljivost *f* nutrition
hrapav *adj* rough
hrapavost *f* roughness
hrast *m* oak
hrbat *m* back
hridina *f* cliff
hripavac *m* whooping-cough
hrkati *v* to snore
hrom *adj* lame
hrpa *f* pile
Hrvat *m*, **Hrvatica** *f* Croat
Hrvatska *f* Croatia
hrvatski *adj* Croatian
hrvatskosrpski *adj* Serbo-Croatian
htjeti *v* to want
hučiti *v* to roar
huckati *v* to urge
hula *f* blasphemy
hula-hopke *fpl* tights
hulja *m/f* villain
human *adj* humane
humanitarac *m* humanitarian
humanitaran *adj* humanitarian
humanost *f* humaneness
humor *m* humour
hunjavica *f* (med) cold
hunta *f* junta
hura! hooray!
huškač *m* agitator
huškanje *n* agitation
huškati *v* to agitate
hvala thank you
hvalisati se *v* to brag
hvaliti se *v* to boast
hvaliti *v* to praise
hvatati *v* to catch

I

i *conj* 1. and 2. also
i... i *conj* both... and
iako *conj* although
ići *v* 1. to go 2. to walk
ideal *m* ideal
idealist(a) *f* idealist
idealistički *adj* idealistic
idealizam *m* idealism
ideja *f* 1. idea 2. policy 3. principle
identičan *adj* identical
identitet *m* identity
ideolog *m* ideologist
ideologija *f* ideology
ideologiški *adj* ideological
idila *f* idyll
idiličan *adj* idyllic
idiot *m* idiot
idiotizam *m* idiocy
idiotski *adj* idiotic
idući *adj* next
igde, igdje anywhere
igla *f* needle
ignorisati *v* to ignore
igra *f* 1. play 2. game 3. performance 4. acting
igrač *m* player
igračka *f* toy
igralište *n* 1. playground 2. playing field
igralište za golf *n* golf course
igranka *f* dance
igrati nerešeno/neriješeno *v* (spor.) to draw
igrati *v* to play
iguman *m* abbot
igumanija *f* abbotess
ijedan *adj* any, anyone

ikad, ikada *adv* ever
ikakav *adj* any
ikako *adv* at all
iko anybody, anyone, whoever
ikona *f* icon
ikonostas *m* iconostasis
ikra *f* 1. roe 2. caviar
ilegalac *m* 1. illegal resident 2. (pol) member of illegal organization
ilegalan *adj* 1. illegal 2. (pol) underground
ilegalnost *f* 1. illegality 2. (pol) underground
ili *conj* or
ili... ili *conj* either... or
ilovača *f* clay
ilustracija *f* illustration
ilustrariti *v* to illustrate
ilustrator *m* illustrator
iluzija *f* illusion
iluzoran *adj* fictitious
ima li? is/are there?
imaginacija *f* imagination
imaginaran *adj* imaginary
imalo *adv* at all
imam *m* imam
imanje *n* 1. plot of land 2. estate 3. property
imati *v* 1. to have 2. to own
imbecilan *adj* imbecilic
ime *n* name
imendan *m* name-day
imenica *f* noun
imenik *m* directory
imenjak *m* namesake
imenovanje *n* appointment

imenovati v 1. to appoint 2. to nominate
imenski adj normal
imetak m property
imigracija f immigration
imitacija f imitation
imitator m imitator
imitirati v to imitate
imovina f 1. assets 2. belongings 3. property
imperativ adj imperative
imperator m emperor
imperfekt m imperfect
imperija f empire
imperijalist m imperialist
imperijalistički adj imperialstic
imperijalizam m imperialism
imponirati, imponovati v to impress
import m import
impotencija, impotentnost f impotence
impotentan adj impotent
impozantan adj impressive
impregniran adj waterproof
impresija f impression
improvizacija f improvisation
improviziran adj improvised
improvizirati, improvizovati v to improvise
impuls m impulse
impulzivan adj impulsive
imun adj immune
imunitet m 1. immunity 2. diplomatski imuntet diplomatic immunity
imunizacija f immunization
imunizirati, imunizovati v to immunize
imunost f immunity
imućan adj wealthy
inače adv 1. otherwise 2. anyway

inat m spite
inauguracija f inauguration
inaugurirati v to inaugurate
inč m inch
incest m incest
incident m incident
indeks m index
indiferentan adj indifferent
indignirati se v to be indignant
indigo m 1. indigo 2. carbon paper
Indija f India
Indijac m Indian
indikacija f indication
indirektan adj indirect
indirektno adv indirectly
indiskretan adj indiscreet
indisponirati v to indispose
individua f individual
individualizam m individualism
individualnost f individuality
indoktrinacija f indoctrination
indoktrinirati v to indoctrinate
indolencija f indolence
indosirati v to endorse
indukcija f induction
industrija f 1. industry 2. **laka industrija** light industry 3. **teška industrija** heavy industry 4. **filmska industrija** film industry
industrija f 1. industry 2. manufacture
industrijalac m **bogat industrijalac** tycoon
industrijalizacija f industrialization
industrijalizovati (se) v to industrialize
inercija f inertia
infantilan adj infantile
infekcija f infection
inferioran adj inferior
infinitiv m infinitive
inflacija f inflation

informacija *f* information
informativan *adj* informative
informirati *v* to inform
informirati se *v* to find out
infracrven *adj* infrared
infrastruktura *f* infrastructure
infuzija *f* infusion
inhalacija *f* inhalation
inicijal *m* initial
inicijativa *f* initiative
inidividualan *adj* individual
injekcija *f* injection
inkasant *m* collector
inkasirati *v* to collect
inkomodirati *v* to incovenience
inkubacija *f* incubation
inkubator *m* incubator
inkvizicija *f* inquisition
inokosan *adj* 1. solitary 2. alone
inostran *adj* foreign
inostranstvo *n* 1. foreign country 2. abroad
inozemni *adj* foreign
inscenirati *v* to stage
insekt *m* insect
insekticid *m* insecticide
insistirati *v* to insist
inspekcija *f* 1. inspection 2. supervision
inspektor *m* 1. inspector 2. supervisor
inspiracija *f* inspiration
inspirisati *v* to inspire
instalacija *f* installation
instalater *m* 1. fitter 2. plumber 3. electrician
instalirati *v* to instal
instinkt *m* instinct
instinktivno *adv* instinctively
institucija *f* institution
institut *m* institute
instrukcija *f* instruction

instruktor *m* instructor
instrument *m* instrument
integracija *f* integration
intelekt *m* intellect
intelektualac *m* intellectual
inteligencija *f* 1. intelligence 2. intelligentsia
inteligentan *adj* intelligent
intenzitet *m* intensity
interes *m* 1. interest 2. profit
interesantan *adj* interesting
interesirati, interresovati *v* to interest
interesovanje *n* interest
interfejs *m* interface
interkontinentalni *adj* intercontinental
internacija *f* internment
internat *m* boarding school
interni *adj* internal
internice *n* **logor za internice** internment camp
internirac *m* internee
interniranje *n* internment
internirati *v* to intern
interpretacija *f* interpretation
interpretirati *v* to interpret
interpunkcija *f* punctuation
interurban *m* long-distance call
intervencija *f* intervention
intervencija *f* **oružana intervencija** armed intervention
intervju *m* interview
intervjuisati *v* to interview
intervjuist *m* interviewer
intiman *adj* intimate
intimnost *f* intimacy
intonacija *f* intonation
intriga *f* 1. plot 2. intrigue
intriga *f* intrigue
introdukcija *f* introduction
intuicija *f* intuition

intuitivan *adj* intuitive

invalid *m* 1. invalid 2. disabled person

invaliditet *m* 1. being an invalid 2. disability

invalidska kolica *f* wheelchair

invazija *f* invasion

invencija *f* imaginaton

invencija *f* inventiveness

inventar *m* inventory

inventarisati robu *v* to stock-take

inventivan *adj* inventive

inventura *f* stock-take

investicija *f* investment

investicioni fond *m* investment fund

investirati *v* to invest

investitor *m* investor

inženjer, inžinjer *m* engineer

inženjer brodogradnje *m* naval architect

inženjer elektrotehnike *m* electrical engineer

inženjering *m* engineering

iole *adv* at all

ipak *conj* however

Irac *m* Irishman

iracionalan *adj* irrational

Irci *mpl* the Irish

iritirati *v* to irritate

Irkinja *f* Irishwoman

ironičan *adj* ironical

ironički *adj* ironic

ironija *f* irony

Irska *f* Ireland

irski *adj* Irish

irvas *m* reindeer

iscediti *v* to squeeze

iscepan *adj* torn

iscrpan *adj* exhaustive

iscrpljen *adj* exhausted

iscrpljenost *f* exhaustion

iscrpsti *v* to exhaust

iscuriti *v* to leak

iseckati *v* to chop

iseliti *v* 1. to remove 2. to evacuate

iseljavanje *n* emigration

iseljenik *m* emigrant

iseći *v* to cut off

ishlapiti *v* to evaporate

ishod *m* result

ishrana *f* 1. food 2. diet 3. nutrition

isisati *v* 1. to suck out 2. to drain

isitniti *v* to chop up

isjeckati *v* to chop

iskapanje *n* excavation

iskapati *v* to excavate

iskapiti *v* to drain

iskašljati *v* to cough up

iskaz *m* statement

iskazati *v* to state

iskaznica *f* identity card (ID)

iskidati *v* to tear to pieces

iskititi *v* to decorate

isklesati *v* to sculpt

isključenje *n* 1. expulsion 2. exclusion 3. elimination

isključiti *v* 1. to expel 2. to exclude 3. to eliminate 4. to turn off 5. to unplug

isključiv *adj* exclusive

iskočiti *v* 1. to jump off 2. to derail

iskopati, iskopavati *v* to dig (up)

iskopčati *v* to switch off

iskopina *f* excavation

iskoristiti *v* 1. to utilize 2. to exploit

iskra *f* spark

iskrcati se *v* to disembark

iskrcati *v* to unload

iskrcavanje *n* 1. unloading 2. disembarkation

iskrčiti *v* to clear land

iskren *adj* sincere

iskreno *adv* sincerely

iskrenost *f* sincerity

iskrenuti *v* to turn upside down/ inside out

iskričavo vino *n* sparkling wine

iskriviti *v* to twist

iskrojiti *v* to cut out

iskrpiti *v* to mend

iskrsnuti *v* to crop up

iskrvariti *v* to bleed to death

iskusan *adj* 1. experienced 2. practised

iskusiti *v* 1. to experience 2. to practise

iskušati, iskušavati *v* 1. to try out 2. to tempt

iskušenje *n* 1. trial 2. temptation

iskustvo *n* 1. experience 2. practice

iskvaren *adj* 1. ruined 2. corrupt

iskvariti *v* corrupt

islam *m* Islam

islednik *m* investigator

isleđenje *n* investigation

ismijati *v* to ridicule

ismijavanje *n* ridicule

ispad *m* outrage

ispaliti *v* to fire

ispaliti torpedo *v* to launch a torpedo

isparavati se *v* to evaporate

ispasti *v* to come off

ispavati se *v* to sleep well

ispeći *v* to roast

ispijen *adj* haggard

ispirati *v* to rinse

ispis *m* withdrawal

ispisati se *v* to withdraw

ispit *m* 1. examination 2. **usmeni ispit** oral examination 3. **proći na ispitu** to pass an exam 4. **pasti na ispitu** to fail an exam

ispitati, ispitivati *v* to examine

ispiti *v* 1. to drink 2. to waste

ispitivanje javnog mnenja *n* opinion poll

isplahnuti *v* to rinse

isplata *f* payment

isplatiti *v* to pay

isplatiti se *v* to be worthwhile

isplesti *v* to knit

isplivati *v* 1. to come up 2. to swim out

ispljunuti *v* to spit out

isploviti *v* to set sail

ispod *prep* 1. under 2. below

ispoljiti *v* to show

isporučiti *v* to deliver

isporuka *f* delivery

isposlovati *v* to arrange

ispostava *f* 1. branch 2. section

ispostaviti se *v* to turn out

ispoved, ispovijed *f* confession

ispovedati se, ispovijedati se *v* to confess

isprati *v* to wash out

ispratiti *v* to see off

isprava *f* 1. document 2. I.D. 3. passport

ispravak *m* 1. correction 2. (leg/pol) amendment

ispravan *adj* 1. correct 2. exact

ispraviti *v* 1. to correct 2. (leg/pol) to amend

ispravka *f* correction

isprazan *adj* vain

isprazniti *v* to clear out

isprazniti creva/crijeva *v* to defecate

ispraćaj *m* farewell

isprebijati *v* to beat up

ispred *prep* 1. in front of 2. before

isprekidan *adj* interrupted

isprevijati *v* to bandage up

ispričati *v* 1. to tell 2. to excuse

ispričati se *v* 1. to apologize 2. to make an excuse

isprika *f* 1. apology 2. excuse

isprobati *v* 1. to try out 2. to check

ispružiti *v* to stretch

isprva, isprve *adv* at first

ispucan *adj* cracked

ispucati *v* to crack

ispumpati *v* to deflate

ispuniti *v* 1. to fill 2. to fulfil

ispuniti se *v* to be fulfilled

ispunjen *adj* filled

ispupčen *adj* 1. bulging 2. convex 3. prominent

ispupčenje *n* 1. bulge 2. convexity

ispušni *adj* exhaust

ispust *m* outlet

ispustiti *v* 1. to drop 2. to let out 3. to flush

istaknut *adj* prominent

istaknuti *v* to emphasize

istaknuti se *v* to be prominent

istaći *v* to emphasize

istegnuti *v* to stretch

istek *m* expiry

isteći *v* 1. to run out 2. to expire

isti *adj* same

isticanje *n* emphasis

istina *f* truth

istinit *adj* true

istinitost *f* truth

istinski *adj* true

istisnuti *v* to oust

istjerati *v* to expel

isto *adv* in the same way

istočni *adj* eastern

istok *m* east

istoimen *adj* of the same name

istorija *f* history

istosmeran, istosmjeran *adj* direct

istovar *m* unloading

istovariti, istovarivati *v* to unload

istovetan, istovjetan *adj* identical

istovjetnost *f* identity

istovremen *adj* simultaneous

istraga *f* 1. inquiry 2. inquest

istražiti *v* 1. to investigate 2. to explore 3. to research

istraživač *m* 1. investigator 2. explorer 3. researcher

istraživačka vasionska stanica *f* spacelab

istraživački institut *m* research institute

istraživanje *n* 1. investigation 2. exploration 3. research

istraživati *v* 1. to investigate 2. to explore 3. to research

istražna komisija *f* fact-finding committee

istrčati *v* to run out

istrebljenje *n* extermination

istresti *v* 1. to shake out 2. to dump

istrezniti se *v* to sober up

istrgnuti *v* to wrench away

istrijebiti *v* to exterminate

istrljati *v* to rub

istrošiti *v* 1. to wear out 2. to use up

istrugati *v* to scrape away

istrunuti *v* to decay

istup *m* 1. action 2. withdrawal

istupanje *n* appearance

istupiti *v* 1. to take action 2. to withdraw 3. to resign

isturiti *v* to protrude

istuširati se *v* to take a shower

istući *v* to beat

isušiti *v* to dry

isuštiti *v* to drain

išamarati *v* to slap

iščašenje *n* (med) 1. sprain 2. dislocation

iščašiti *v* (med) 1. to sprain 2. to dislocate
iščekivanje *n* anticipation
iščupati *v* to pull out
išijas *m* sciatica
išta, išto anything
Italija *f* Italy
itd. etc.
itko anyone
iver *m* splinter
iverploča *f* plywood
ivica *f* 1. edge 2. **na ivici rata** on the verge of war
ivičnjak *m* curb
iz *prep* 1. from 2. because of
iza *prep* 1. behind 2. after
izabran *adj* chosen
izabrati *v* 1. to choose 2. to elect
izadati se *v* to betray oneself
izaslanik *m* delegate
izaslanstvo *n* delegation
izazivati *v* 1. to challenge 2. to provoke
izazov *m* 1. challenge 2. provocation
izazovan *adj* 1. challenging 2. provocative
izažeti *v* to wring
izaći *v* 1. to exit 2. to appear
izbaciti *v* 1. to omit 2. to eject 3. to fire
izbaviti *v* to relieve
izbavljenje *n* deliverance
izbegavanje *n* avoidance
izbeglica *m/f* 1. refugee 2. fugitive
izbeglištvo *n* 1. exile 2. refuge
izbezumiti *v* to perturb
izbezumljen *adj* perturbed
izbijati, izbiti *v* 1. to knock out 2. to break out
izbirljiv *adj* fussy
izbirljivost *f* fussiness

izbistriti *v* to clear up
izbiti *v* 1. to beat 2. to knock out 3. to break out
izbivati *v* 1. to be absent 2. to leave
izbjeglica *m/f* refugee
izbjeći, izbjegavati *v* to avoid
izbliza *f* closely
izbočen *adj* protruding
izbor *m* choice
izbori *mpl* 1. elections 2. **opšti izbori** general elections 3. **slobodni izbori** free elections
izborna jedinica *f* electorate
izborni *adj* electoral
izborni glas *m* suffrage
izbrbljati *v* to blurt
izbrijati *v* to shave
izbrisati *v* 1. to wipe 2. to wipe out
izbrojati *v* to count
izbušiti *v* to drill
izdahnuti *v* 1. to exhale 2. to die
izdaja *f* 1. treason 2. betrayal
izdajica *m* traitor
izdaleka *adv* from a distance
izdanje *n* 1. edition 2. publication
izdašan *adj* abundant
izdatak *m* expense
izdati *v* 1. to publish 2. to betray 3. to desert
izdati viza *f* to issue a visa
izdavač *m* publisher
izdavački *adj* publishing
izdavanje *n* distribution
izdavati *v* 1. to distribute 2. to issue
izderati *v* to wear out
izdiktirati *v* to dictate
izdržati *v* to withstand
izdržavanje *n* support
izdržavati *v* to support
izdržljiv *adj* tough
izdržljivost *f* stamina

izdupsti *v* to gouge out
izduvati *v* to blow out
izdvojiti *v* 1. to split 2. to single out
izednačiti *v* to equalize
izgarati *v* to burn
izgladiti *v* to smooth
izgladneo *adj* 1. hungry 2. starving
izgladniti, izgladnjeti *v* to starve
izglasati *v* to vote
izgled *m* 1. appearance 2. view
izgledati *v* 1. to seem 2. to appear 3. to look forward to
izgledi *mpl* odds
izglodati *v* to gnaw
izgnanstvo *n* exile
izgoreti od sunca, izgorjeti od sunca *v* to get sunburned
izgoreti, izgorjeti *v* to burn down/out
izgovarati se *v* to make excuses
izgovarati *v* to pronounce
izgovor *m* pronunciation
izgovoriti *v* pronounce
izgraditi *v* 1. to build 2. to develop
izgradnja *f* 1. building 2. development
izgrditi *v* to scold
izgredi *mpl* riots
izgristi *v* to corrode
izgubiti se *v* to become lost
izgubiti *v* to lose
izići *v* to exit
izjaloviti se *v* to fall through
izjava *f* declaration
izjaviti *v* to declare
izjesti *v* to eat away
izjuriti *v* to rush out
izjutra *f* in the morning
izlagač *m* exhibitor
izlagati *v* to exhibit
izlaz *m* 1. exit 2. solution

izlaz u slučaju nužde *m* emergency exit
izlaz za nuždu *m* emergency exit
izlazak *m* coming out
izlazna viza *f* exit visa
izlaženje *n* going out
izlet *m* excursion
izletjeti *v* to rush out
izletnik *m* tourist
izliječiti *v* to cure
izlika *f* pretence
izliti se *v* to overflow
izliti *v* to pour out
izliv krvi *m* haemorrhage
izlizan *adj* worn out
izlizati se *v* to be worn out
izlječiv *adj* curable
izljev *m* output
izlog *m* shop window
izlomiti *v* to smash
izložba *f* show
izložiti *v* 1. to exhibit 2. to present
izložiti suncu *v* to sunburn
izmak *m* expiry
izmaknuti *v* to evade
izmena *f* 1. change 2. exchange
izmeriti, izmjeriti *v* to measure
izmeriti nekome puls, izmjeriti nekome puls *v* to take someone's pulse
izmešati *v* to mix (up)
izmet, izmetina *f* faeces; feces
između *prep* 1. between 2. among
izmijeniti *v* to exchange
izmileti *v* to crawl out
izmirenje *n* reconciliation
izmiriti *v* to reconcile
izmisliti *v* 1. to fabricate 2. to invent
izmišljotina *f* 1. fabrication 2. invention
izmjena *f* exchange

izmjenjiv *adj* exchangeable
izmjeriti *v* to measure
izmlatiti *v* to beat up
izmoriti *v* to tire out
izmrcvariti *v* to mangle
izmučiti *v* 1. to torture 2. to tire
iznad *adv* above
iznajmiti *v* 1. to rent 2. to hire (out) 3. to lease (out)
iznajmljivanje *n* 1. renting 2. hiring
iz navike *n* habitual
iznemogao *adj* exhausted
iznemoglost *f* exhaustion
iznenada *adv* suddenly
iznenadan *adj* sudden
iznenaditi *v* to surprise
iznenađenje *n* surprise
izneti, iznijeti *v* 1. to bring out 2. to produce
iznevjerenje *n* betrayal
iznevjeriti *v* to betray
izniman *adj* exceptional
iznos *m* amount
iznošen *adj* worn out
iznova *adv* afresh
iznuditi *v* to extort
iznutra *adv* (from) inside
iznuđivač *m* extortioner
iznuđivanje *n* extortion
izobilje *n* abundance
izobličenost *f* distortion
izobličiti *v* to distort
izobrazba *f* training
izobraziti *v* to train
izokola *adv* 1. from all around 2. indirectly
izokrenuti *v* to turn over
izolacija *f* 1. isolation 2. insulation
izolator *m* insulator
izolirati *v* 1. to isolate 2. to insulate
izopačenost *f* perversity
izopćiti *v* to excommunicate

izoštriti *v* to sharpen
izostajanje *n*, **izostanak** *m* 1. absence 2. (ed.) truancy
izostati *v* to be absent
izostaviti *v* to omit
izostavljanje *n* omission
izozivati *v* to provoke
izrabljivati *v* to exploit
izračunati *v* to calculate
izračunavanje *n* calculation
izrada *f* 1. craftsmanship 2. manufacture
izraditi *v* 1. to make 2. to manufacture
izrasti *v* to grow up
izravan *adj* straight
izravnati *v* 1. to straighten 2. to settle an account
izraz *m* expression
izrazit *adj* distinct
izraziti *v* to express
izražajan *adj* expressive
izražavanje *n* expression
izreka *f* 1. saying 2. statement
izrez *m* slit
izrezati *v* to cut up
izreći *v* to say
izričan *adj* precise
izričit *adj* explicit
izrod *m* renegade
izroditi se *v* to degenerate
izroniti *v* to emerge
izrovati *v* to uproot
izručenje *n* 1. delivery 2. extradition
izručiti *v* 1. to deliver 2. extradite
izrugivati se *v* to ridicule
izubijati *v* to bruise
izučavanje *n* study
izučavati *v* to study
izučen *adj* trained
izučiti *v* to train
izujedati *v* to bite

izukrštati *v* to cross
izum *m* 1. invention 2. discovery
izumirati *v* to die out
izumitelj inventor
izumiti *v* to invent
izuti *v* to take off
izuzetak *m* exception
izuzetan *adj* exceptional
izuzeti *v* to exempt
izuzetno *adv* exceptionally
izuzev, izuzevši *adv/prep* except
izvadak *m* extract
izvaditi *v* to extract
izvan *adj* outside
izvanredan *adj* 1. extraordinary 2. special 3. emergency session
izvanredno *adv* extraordinarily
izvedba *f* performance
izvesno *adv* certainly
izveštačen *adj* 1. unnatural 2. artificial
izveštačenost *f* affectation
izveštaj *m* report
izvestan *adj* certain
izvesti *v* 1. to lead out 2. to perform
izvesti pred sud *v* to bring to trial
izvesti se *v* to go for a drive
izvestilac *m* 1. reporter 2. informer
izvezen *adj* embroidered
izvežban *adj* trained
izvidjeti *v* to investigate
izvidnica *f* patrol
izvidnik *adj* scout
izviđač *m* scout
izviđačka patrola *f* reconnaissance patrol

izviđanje *n* reconnaissance
izviđati *v* to reconnoitre
izvijestiti *v* to report
izviniti *v* to excuse
izvinjenje *n* apology
izvinuti *v* to twist
izvinuti se *v* to apologize
izvirati *v* to spring
izviždati *v* to boo
izvještačenost *f* affectation
izvještaj *m* report
izvjestan *adj* a certain
izvjestitelj *m* reporter
izvježban *adj* trained
izvlačiti *v* to draw out
izvod *m* 1. certificate 2. deduction 3. extract
izvođač *m* performer
izvojevati *v* 1. to win 2. to conquer
izvoljeti *v* to be pleased
izvor *m* 1. spring 2. well 3. source
izvor nafte *m* oil well
izvoran *adj* 1. original 2. authentic
izvoz *m* export
izvoziti *v* to export
izvozni *adj* export
izvoznik *adj* exporter
izvrgnuti *v* to expose
izvrnuti *v* to overturn
izvrsno *adv* very well
izvršan *adj* executive
izvršenje *n* performance
izvršiti *v* to carry out
izvrstan *adj* excellent
izvući *v* to pull out
ižeći *v* to sear

J

ja I

jablan *m* poplar

jabuka *f* 1. apple 2. apple tree

jabukovača *f* cider

jačati *v* to strengthen

jačina *f* strength

jad *m* 1. sorrow 2. distress

jadac *m* wishbone

jadan *adj* miserable

jadikovanje *n* complaining

jadikovati *v* to complain

jadnik *m*, **jadnica** *f* wretched person

jagmiti se *v* to contend (**za** for)

jagnje *n* lamb

jagnjeći *v* lamb

jagoda *f* strawberry

jagodica *f* cheekbone

jagorčevina *f* primrose

jahač *m* 1. rider 2. jockey

jahanje *n* horse riding

jahati *v* to ride

jahta *f* yacht

jaje *n* 1. egg 2. ovum 3. testicle 4. **kuhano jaje** boiled egg 5. **jaje na oko** fried egg

jaje na oko *n* fried egg

jajnik *m* ovary

jak *adj* powerful

jakna *f* jacket

jako *adv* very

jakost *f* power

jalov *adj* 1. sterile 2. useless

jama *f* hole

jamac *m* guarantee

jamačan *adj* sure

jamačno *adv* surely

jamčevina *f* 1. deposit 2. (leg.) bail

jamčiti *v* 1. to guarantee 2. to vouch (**za** for)

jamstvo *n* guarantee

janje, janjetina *f* lamb

jantar *m* amber

januar *m* January

Japan *adj* Japan

Japanac *m* Japanese

japanski *adj* Japanese

jara *f* heat

jarac *m* billy goat

jarak *m* 1. ditch 2. trench

jaram *m* yoke

jarbol *m* mast

jare *n* kid

jarebica *f* partridge

jarki *adj* bright

jarost *f* fury

jarostan *adj* furious

jaruga *f* ravine

jasan *adj* clear

jasen *adj* ash

jasika *f* aspen

jasle *fpl* 1. manger 2. nursery

jasmin *m* jasmine

jasno *adv* clearly

jasnoća *f* clarity

jašiti *v* to ride

jastog *m* lobster

jastreb *m* hawk

jastučnica *f* pillowcase

jastuk *m* pillow

jato *n* 1. flock 2. group

jauk *m* yell

jaukati *v* to yell

java *f* reality

javan *adj* public
javašluk *m* negligence
javiti *v* to notify
javno *adv* publicly
javnost *f* public
javor *m* maple
jaz *m* gap
jazavac *m* badger
jazavičar *m* terrier
jazbina *f* lair
ječam *m* barley
jecati *v* to sob
ječmenac *m* (med.) stye
jed *m* anger
jedak *adj* angry
jedan *adj* one
jedan drugoga each other
jedan po jedan one by one
jedanaest eleven
jedanaesti *adj* eleventh
jedanput *adv* once
jedar *adj* vigorous
jedaća soba *f* dining room
jedaći pribor *m* cutlery
jedinac *m* only child
jedini *adj* sole
jedinica *f* unity
jedinjenje *n* compound
jedinka *f* individual
jedino *adv* only
jedinstven *adj* 1. unique 2. united
jedinstvo *n* unity
jednačina *f* equation
jednačiti *v* to equalize
jednadžba *f* equation
jednak *m* equal
jednako *adv* equally
jednakost *f* equality
jednina *f* singular
jednjak *m* oesophagus; esophagus
jedno 1. one 2. same
jednobojan *adj* of the same colour

jednoboštvo *n* monotheism
jednobrojan *adj* plain
jednodušan *adj* unanimous
jednodušno *adv* unanimously
jednodušnost *f* unanimity
jednofazan *adj* single-phase
jednoglasno *adv* unanimously
jednogodišnji *adj* 1. yearly 2. yearling
jednokatnica *f* house
jednokratan *adj* one-time
jednoličan *adj* 1. monotonous 2. homogeneous
jednoličnost *f* 1. monotony 2. homogeneity
jednom *adv* once
jednomišljenik *m* sympathizer
jednomotorac *m* single-engine plane
jednomotorni *adj* single-engine
jednoobrazan *adj* uniform
jednoobraznost *f* uniformity
jednook *m* one-eyed
jednopartijski *adj* one-party
jednopartijski sistem *m* one-party system
jednosmeran, jednosmjeran *adj* one-way
jednosmerna ulica *f* one-way street
jednosoban *adj* one-roomed
jednospratan *adj* one-storied
jednostavan *adj* simple
jednostavno *adv* simply
jednostavnost *f* simplicity
jednostran *adj* 1. one-sided 2. unilateral
jednostrano razoružanje *n* unilateral disarmament
jednostruk *m* single
jednovrsnost *f* homogeneity
jednovrstan *adj* homogeneous

jedrenjak *m* sailing-boat
jedrenje *n* sailing
jedrilica *f* 1. yacht 2. glider
jedriličar *m* 1. yachtsman 2. glider pilot
jedriličarstvo *n* yachting
jedrina *f* vigour
jedriti *v* 1. to sail 2. to glide
jedro *n* sail
jedva *adv* hardly
jeftin *adj* cheap
jeftino *adv* cheaply
jeftinoća *f* cheapness
jegulja *f* eel
jek *m* 1. sound 2. prime
jeka *f* echo
jela *f* fir tree
jelen *m* deer
jelka *f* 1. božićna jelka Christmas tree 2. novogodišnja jelka New Year tree
jelo *n* 1. food 2. meal
jelovnik *m* menu
jemčiti *v* 1. to guarantee 2. to vouch (za for)
jemstvo *n* guarantee
jenjati *v* to abate
jer *conj* because
jeres *f* heresy
jeretik *m* heretic
jesen *f* autumn; fall
jesetra *f* sturgeon
jest: to jest i.e., that is
jeste yes
jesti *v* to eat
jestiv *adj* edible
jetra *f* liver
jetrva *f* sister-in-law
jevanđelje *n* gospel
Jevrejin *m* Jew
jevrejski *adj* Jewish
jeza *f* shudder

jezero *n* lake
jezgra *f*, **jezgro** *n* 1. stone 2. nucleus 3. essence
jezgrovit *adj* concise
jezičac *m* pointer
jezički, jezični *adj* linguistic
jezik *adj* 1. tongue 2. language 3. maternji jezik native language
jeziv *adj* 1. terrible 2. gruesome
jež *m* 1. hedgehog 2. sea-urchin
ježiti se *v* to bristle
jod *m* iodine
joga *f* yoga
jogunast *adj* mischievous
jogurt *m* yoghurt
jonizacija *f* ionization
jorgan *m* quilt; comforter
jorgovan *m* lilac
još *adv* 1. still 2. yet 3. some more 4. as late as
jubilej *m* jubilee
juče, jučer *adv* yesterday
jučerašnji *adj* yesterday's
jučerašnjica *f* yesterday
judaizam *m* Judaism
jug *m* 1. south 2. na jug southward(s)
jugo *m/n* south wind
jugoistok *m* southeast
Jugoslaven, Jugosloven *adj* Yugoslav
jugoslavenski, jugoslovenski *adj* Yugoslav
Jugoslavija *f* Yugoslavia
jugovina *f* thaw
jugzapad *m* southwest
juha *f* soup
jul, juli *m* July
jun, juni *m* June
junačan *adj* courageous
junački *adj* heroic
junak *m* hero

junakinja *f* heroine
junaštvo *n* heroism
juni *m* June
jurisdikcija *f* jurisdiction
jurisdikcija *f* jurisdiction
jurisprudencija *f* jurisprudence
juriš *m* (mil.) attack
jurišati *v* (mil.) to attack
juriti *v* 1. to rush 2. to run 3. to race
justifikacija *f* execution (of someone)

justificirati *v* to execute (someone)
jutarnji *adj* morning
jutriti, pojutriti *v* to rise early
jutro *n* 1. morning 2. **dobro jutro!** good morning!
jutros *adv* this morning
jutrošnji *adj* this morning's
juvelir *m* jeweller
južni *adj* 1. south 2. southern
južnjak *m* 1. southerner 2. south wind

K

k, ka *prep* 1. to 2. towards
kabanica *f* overcoat
kabao *m* bucket
kabast *adj* bulky
kabel *m* cable
kabina *f* 1. cabin 2. cockpit 3. booth
kabina za glasanje *f* polling booth
kabinet *m* 1. office 2. (pol.) cabinet
kabriolet *m* convertible
kaca *f* 1. tub 2. vat
kaciga *f* helmet
kačiti *v* to hang
kačket *m* cap
kad, kada *f* 1. when 2. if 3. **bilo kad** no matter when
kada *f* bathtub
kadar *m* 1. *adj* capable, able 2. *m* personnel 3. (film) take
kadet *m* cadet
kadgod *adv* ever
kadija *m* Muslim judge
kadikad sometimes
kadrovi *see* **kadar**
kadrovski *adj* 1. (mil.) regular 2. **kadrovska služba** personnel department
kadulja *f* sage
kafa *f* coffee
kafana *f* cafe
kaiš *m* belt
kaiš ventilatora *f* fanbelt
kajak *m* kayak
kajanje *n* remorse
kajati se *v* 1. to be sorry 2. to regret
kajgana *f* omelette

kajmak *m* cream
kajsija *f* apricot
kakao *m* cocoa
kakav? what kind of?
kakavgod whatever
kako to? how come?
kako-tako so-so
kako? how?
kaktus *m* cactus
kakvoća *f* quality
kalaj *m* tin
kalajni list *m* tin foil
kalati *v* to split
kalcij *m* calcium
kaldrma *f* cobbles
kalem *m* reel
kalendar *m* calendar
kalež *m* chalice
kaligrafija *f* calligraphy
kalij, kalijum *m* potassium
kaliti *v* to harden
kaljati *v* to dirty
kaljav *adj* dirty
kaljenje *n* hardening
kalkulacija *f* calculation
kalorifer *m* fan-heater
kalup *m* 1. form 2. mould; mold
kaluđer *m* monk
kaluđerica *f* nun
kamata *f*, **kamate** *fpl* (fin.) interest
kamate na stopa *fpl* interest rate
kamate na stopa *fpl* interest rate
kamatni *adj* (fin.) interest
kameja *f* cameo
kameleon *m* chameleon
kamen *m* rock
kamen spoticanja *f* stumbling block

kamenac *m* (med.) stone
kamenica *f* oyster
kamenit *adj* rocky
kamenolom *m* quarry
kamera *f* camera
kameraman *m* cameraman
kamerna muzika *f* chamber music
kamila *f* camel
kamilica *f* camomile
kamin *m* fireplace
kamion *m* lorry; truck
kamiondžija *m* truck driver
kamionet *m* van
kamo 1. where (to) 2. **a kamo li...** let alone...
kamo bilo anywhere
kamoli *see* kamo
kamp *m* 1. camp 2. campsite
kamp-kuća *f* weekend cottage
kamping *m* campsite
kampovati *v* to camp
kamuflaža *f* camouflage
kamuflirati *v* to camouflage
kanabe *n* sofa, couch
Kanada *f* Canada
Kanadanin *m* Canadian
kanadski *adj* Canadian
kanal *m* 1. canal 2. channel
kanalizacija *f* sewers
kanalizirati *v* to channel
kanap *m* string
kanape *n* divan
kanarinac *m* canary
kancelar *m* chancellor
kancelarija *f* office
kancelarijski *adj* 1. office 2. bureaucratic
kancelarijski posao *m* office work
kanda... it seems that...
kandidat *m* candidate
kandidatura *f* candidacy
kandidirati se, kandidovati se *v* (pol.) to run for office
kandidirati, kandidovati *v* to nominate
kandilo *n* sanctuary lamp
kandža *f* claw
kaniti *v* to intend
kanjon *m* canyon
kanon *m* canon
kanta *f* 1. can 2. bin
kanta za smeće *n* dustbin; trashcan
kantina *f* canteen
kanu *m* canoe
kao *conj* 1. like 2. as
kao da *conj* as if
kaolin *m* china-clay
kaos *m* chaos
kaotičan *adj* chaotic
kap *m* 1. drop 2. (med.) stroke
kapa *f* cap
kapacitet *m* capacity
kapak *m* 1. cover 2. shutter 3. eyelid
kapara *f* (fin.) deposit
kapati *v* drop
kapavac *m* gonorrhea
kapela *f* 1. chapel 2. (mus.) band
kapelan *m* chaplain
kapetan *m* captain
kapica *f* cap
kapija *f* 1. entrance 2. gate
kapilar *m* capillary
kapital *m* (fin.) capital
kapitalan *adj* 1. major 2. (fin.) capital
kapitalist(a) *m* capitalist
kapitalizam *m* capitalism
kapitel *m* capital
kapiten *m* captain
kapitulacija *f* surrender
kapitulant *m* defeatist
kapitulirati *v* to surrender

kaplar *m* (mil.) corporal
kapric *m* whim
kapricirati se *v* to prove problematic
kapsla *f* cap
kapsula *f* capsule
kapuljača *f* hood
kaput *m* coat
karabin *m* carbine
karakter *m* character
karakteran *adj* honest
karakterisati *v* to characterize
karakterističan, karakteristika *f* characteristic
karamela *f* toffee
karanfil *m* carnation
karanfilić *m* clove
karantena *f*, **karantin** *m* 1. quarantine 2. staviti u karantin to put in quarantine
karat *m* carat
karaula *f* watchtower
karavan *m* 1. caravan 2. station wagon
karburator *m* carburettor
karcinom *m* (med.) carcinoma
kardan *m* universal joint
kardinal *m* cardinal
kardinalan *adj* basic
kardiogram *m* cardiogram
kardiolog *m* cardiologist
kardiologija *f* cardiology
karfiol *m* cauliflower
karijera *f* career
karika *f* link
karikatura *f* 1. caricature 2. cartoon
kariran *adj* checked
karlica *f* pelvis
karmin *m* 1. crimson 2. lipstick
karneval *m* carnival
karoserija *f* car body
karta *f* 1. card 2. ticket 3. map

kartanje *n* card-playing
kartati se *v* to play cards
karter *m* oil-sump
kartograf *m* cartographer
karton *m* 1. card 2. cardboard
kartoteka *f* card-index
kas *m* trot
kasa *f* 1. safe 2. cash-desk 3. checkout-counter
kasač *m* trotter
kasan *adj* late
kasapin *m* butcher
kasapnica *f* butcher's
kasarna *f* barracks
kasati *v* to trot
kasati *v* to trot, gallop
kaserola *f* casserole
kaseta *f* cassette
kasina *f*, **kasino** *m* casino
kaskader *m* stuntman
kasni *adj* late
kasniji *adj* later
kasniti *v* to be late
kasno *adv* late
kaša *f* porridge
kašalj cough
kašika *f* spoon
kašljati *v* to cough
kastracija *f* castration
kastrirati *v* to castrate
kat *m* floor, storey
katalizator *m* catalyst
katalog *m* catalogue; catalog
katanac *m* padlock
katar *m* catarrh
katarakt *m* cataract
katarka *f* mast
katarza *f* catharsis
katastar *m* land register
katastrofa *f* catastrophe
katastrofalan *adj* catastrophic
katedra *f* (acad.) chair

katedrala f cathedral
kategoričan, kategorički adj categorical
kategorija f category
kategorisati v to categorize
kateter m catheter
katkad adv sometimes
katoda f cathode
katolicizam m Catholicism
katolički adj catholic
katolik m catholic
katran m tar
kauboj m 1. cowboy 2. western (film)
kaubojski film m western (film)
kauč m couch
kaucija f 1. (fin.) deposit 2. (leg.) bail
kaučuk m rubber
kauzalan adj causal
kauzalitet m causality
kava f coffee
kavalir m gentleman
kavalirski adj chivalrous
kavalirština f chivalry
kavana f cafe
kavez m cage
kavga f fight
kavijar m caviar
kazališni adj theatrical
kazalište n theatre; theater
kazaljka f 1. watch hand 2. indicator
kazalo n 1. table of contents 2. index
kazan m 1. kettle 2. (mil.) mess tin
kazati v to say
kazivati v 1. to narrate 2. to express
kazna f 1. punishment 2. penalty 3. fine 4. **telesna kazna** corporal punishment 5. **smrtna kazna**

capital punishment 6. **proći bez kazne** to get off scot-free
kaznionica f prison
kazniti v 1. to punish 2. to fine
kažiprst m index-finger
kažnjavan adj having a criminal record
kažnjavanje n punishment
kažnjenik m convict
kažnjiv adj punishable
kći, kćer f daughter
kec m ace
kecelja f apron
kečiga f sturgeon
kej m quay
keks m biscuits
keleraba f kohlrabi
kelj m kale
kelner m waiter
kelnerica f waitress
kemičar m chemist
kemija f chemistry
kemikalija f, **kemijski** adj chemical
kengur m kangaroo
kepec m dwarf
ker m dog
keramički adj ceramic
keramika f ceramics
keruša f bitch
kesa f 1. bag 2. purse
kesiti se v to grin
kesonska bolest f (mar.) bends
kesten m chestnut
kibernetika f cybernetics
kičica f brush
kičma f spine
kičmena moždina f spinal cord
kičmeni adj spinal
kičmeni stub m spinal column
kičmenjak m vertebrate
kidanje n tearing
kidati v to tear apart

kidisati *v* to attack
kidnaper *m* kidnapper
kidnapirati, kidnapovati *v* to kidnap
kidnapovanje *n* kidnapping
kidnapovati *v see* **kidnapirati**
kifla *f* croissant
kihati *v* to sneeze
kijanje *n* sneezing
kijati *v* to sneeze
kijavica *f* (med.) cold
kika *f* plait
kikiriki *m* peanuts
kiks, kikser *m* blunder
kila *f* 1. kilo 2. (med.) hernia
kilo, kilogram *m* kilogramme
kilometar *m* kilometre
kilovat *m* kilowatt
kimati *v* to nod
kiml *m* caraway seeds
kinematografija *f* cinematography
kinin *m* quinine
kino *m/n* cinema
kinomatografija *f* film industry
kinoteka *f* film library
kiosk *m* kiosk
kip *m* statue
kipar *m* sculptor
kiparstvo *n* sculpture
kipjeti *v* to boil
kipući *adj* boiling hot
kirija *f* rent
kirurg *m* surgeon
kirurgija *f* surgery
kirurški *adj* surgical
kirurški zahvat *m* surgery
kiseli kupus *m* sauerkraut
kiselina *f* 1. acid 2. pickle
kiseo *adj* 1. sour 2. **kisela voda** mineral water
kiseonik, kisik *adj* oxygen
kisnuti *v* to get soaked

kiša *f* 1. rain 2. **pada kiša** it is raining
kišica *f* drizzle
kišni ogrtač *m* raincoat
kišni *adj* rainy
kišnica *f* rain water
kišobran *adj* umbrella
kišovito vreme/vrijeme *n* wet weather
kist *m* brush
kit *m* 1. whale 2. putty
kita *f* bunch
kititi *v* to decorate
kitolovac *m* whaling boat
kitolovstvo *n* whaling
kivan *adj* resentful
kićen *adj* ornate
kićenje *n* decoration
klackalica *f* seesaw
klada *f* log
kladionica *f* betting office
kladiti se *v* to bet
kladivo *n* (spor.) hammer
klan *m* clan
klanac *m* mountain pass
klanica *f* slaughterhouse
klanjati se *v* to bow
klanje *n* slaughter
klaonica *f* slaughterhouse
klarinet *m* clarinet
klas *m* ear of corn
klasa *f* 1. class 2. **srednja klasa** middle class
klasičan *adj* 1. classical 2. classic
klasifikacija *f* classification
klasifikovati *v* to classify
klasika *f* the classics
klatež *m* scum
klati *v* to slaughter
klauzula *f* clause
klavijatura *f* keyboard
klavir *m* piano

klečanje *n* kneeling
klečati *v* to kneel
kleka *f* juniper
kleknuti *v* to kneel down
klekovača *f* gin
klepetati *v* to rattle
kler *m* clergy
klerikalac *m* clerical
klesar *m* stonemason
klesati *v* to chisel stone
klešta *npl* 1. pincers 2. pliers
kleti se *v* to swear
kleti *v* to curse
kletva *f* curse
kleveta *f* slander
klevetati *v* to slander
klevetnik *m* slanderer
klica *f* sprout
klicati *v* to cheer
kliconoša *m* (med.) carrier
klijalište *n* hotbed
klijent *m* client
klijentela *f* clientele
kliješta *npl* 1. pincers 2. pliers
klika *f* clique
kliker *m* marble
kliknuti *v* to cheer
klima *f* climate
klima-uređaj *m* air conditioner
klimaks *m* climax
klimati *v* to nod, shake
klimatizacija *f* air-conditioning
klimatiziran *adj* air-conditioned
klimatski *adj* climatic
klimav *adj* shaky
klin *m* 1. nail 2. wedge
klinčić *m* clove
klinički *adj* clinical
klinika *f* clinic
klip *m* 1. cob 2. piston
kliring *m* (fin.) 1. clearing 2. payments

kliše *m/n* cliché
klistir *m* enema
klistirati *v* to give an enema
klisura *f* cliff
klitoris *m* clitoris
klizač *m*, **klizačica** *f* skater
klizak *m* slippery
klizalište *n* skating rink
klizaljka *f* skate
klizanje na ledu *n* ice-skating
klizanje *n* skating
klizati (se) *v* 1. to skate 2. to skid
kliziti *v* to glide
klokotati *v* to murmur
kloniti se *v* to avoid
klonulost *f* collapse
klonuti *v* to collapse
klopka *f* trap
klopka za ljude *n* man-trap
klor *m* chlorine
klorirati *v* to chlorinate
klovn *m* clown
klozet *m* toilet
klozet-papir *m* toilet paper
klub *m* club
klupa *f* 1. bench 2. desk
klupko *n* ball
kljenut *f* paralysis
kljova *f* tusk
ključ *m* 1. key 2. francuski ključ spanner; wrench
ključanica *f* keyhole
ključanje *n* boiling
ključaonica *f* keyhole
kljucati *v* to peck
ključni *adj* 1. key 2. major
kljukati *v* to stuff
kljun *m* beak
kljusa *f* trap
kljuvati *v* to pick out
kmet *m* serf
knedla *f* dumpling

kneginja f princess
knez m prince
kneževina f principality
knjiga f book
knjigovezac m bookbinder
knjigovodstvo n bookkeeping
knjigovođa f bookkeeper
knjižar m bookseller
knjižara f bookshop; bookstore
knjižarstvo n book trade
književni adj literary
književnik m, **književnica** f writer
književnost f literature
knjižica f 1. booklet 2. čekovna knjižica chequebook; checkbook
knjižiti v 1. to book 2. to record
knjižnica f library
knjižničar m librarian
ko 1. who 2. ma ko anybody, whoever
koagulacija f coagulation
koalicija f coalition
koautor m co-author
kob m fate
kobac m sparrowhawk
kobalt m cobalt
koban adj 1. fateful 2. fatal
kobasica f sausage
kobila f mare
kobra f cobra
kočenje n braking
kočija f, **kočije** fpl coach
kočijaš m coach-driver
kočiti v to brake
kocka f 1. cube 2. dice
kockanje n gambling
kockar m gambler
kockarnica f gambling house
kockica leda f ice-cube
kočnica f brake
kod prep 1. at 2. by 3. near 4. with
kodeks m codex

koeficijent m coefficient
koegzistencija f 1. coexistence 2. miroljubiva koegzistencija peaceful coexistence
koegzistirati v to coexist
kofer m suitcase
kogod anybody
koh m pudding
koherencija f coherence
koherentan adj coherent
kohezija f cohesion
koincidencija f coincidence
koitus m coitus
kojegde, kojegdje here and there
kojekad adv from time to time
kojekakav adj any
kojekako somehow
kojeko, kojetko anybody, whosoever
kojekuda f anywhere, wheresoever
koješta all sorts of things
koješta! nonsense!
koji 1. who 2. which 3. that
kokain m cocaine
koketa f flirt
koketirati, koketovati v to flirt (s with)
kokice fpl popcorn
kokos, kokosov orah m coconut
kokoš f hen
koks m coke
koksara f coke plant
koktel m 1. cocktail 2. cocktail party
kola npl 1. cart 2. car; auto
kolac m pole
kolač m 1. cake 2. pastry 3. biscuit; cooky
kolanje n circulation
kolati v to circulate
kolebanje n hesitation
kolebati se v to hesitate

kolebljiv *adj* hesitant
kolebljivac *m* waverer
kolega *f* colleague
kolegijalan *adj* helpful
kolegijum *m* 1. staff 2. board
kolekcija *f* collection
kolekcionar *m* collector
kolektiv *m* 1. collective 2. staff
kolektivan *adj* collective
koleno, koljeno *n* knee
kolera *f* cholera
kolevka *f* cradle
koliba *f* hut
kolica *npl* 1. pram 2. wheelchair
kolica za bebu *npl* pram
količina *f* quantity
količinski *adj* quantitative
količnik *m* quotient
kolijevka *f* cradle
koliki 1. how large 2. **u koliko** insofar
koliko how much, how many
kolikogod no matter how much/many
koljač *m* murderer
koljeno *n* knee
kolnik *m* roadway
kolo *n* 1. dance 2. circuit 3. series
kolodvor *m* 1. railway station 2. bus station
kolokvijalan *adj* colloquial
kolokvijum *m* oral examination
kolona *f* (mil.) column
kolonija *f* colony
kolonist(a) *m* colonist
kolonizacija *f* colonization
kolonizator *m* colonizer
kolonizirati *v* to colonize
koloristčan *adj* colourful
kolorit *m* colour
kolos *m* colossus
kolosalan *adj* splendid

kolosek, kolosjek *m* rail gauge
kolotečina *f* rut
kolovoz *m* 1. August 2. road
kolovođa *m* ringleader
koludrica *f* nun
kolut *m* ring
komad *m* 1. piece 2. play
komad nameštaja/namještaja *m* piece of furniture
komadić *m* bit
komanda *f* command
komandant, komandir *m* commander
komandirati *v* to command
komandos *m* commando
komarac *m* gnat
kombajn *m* combine harvester
kombi *m* 1. pick-up truck 2. minibus
kombinacija *f* 1. combination 2. plan
kombinat *m* 1. industrial complex 2. **pamučni kombinat** cotton mill 3. **tekstilni kombinat** textile mill
kombine, kombinezon *m* slip
komedija *f* comedy
komedijaš *m* comedian, clown
komemoracija *f* commemoration
komemorirati *v* to commemorate
komentar *m* 1. comment 2. commentary
komentator *m* commentator
komentirati *v* to comment
komercijalan *adj* 1. commercial 2. business 3. **komercijalan direktor** business manager
komesar *m* commissar
komesarijat *m* commissariat
komešanje *n* commotion
kometa *f* comet
komfor *m* 1. comfort 2. conveniences

komforan *adj* 1. comfortable 2. convenient
komičan *adj* comic
komičar *m* comedian
komik *adj* comic
kominike *m* communiqué
komisija *f* 1. commission 2. board 3. panel
komitet *m* committee
komoda *f* chest of drawers
komora *f* 1. chamber 2. council
komotan *adj* comfortable
komovica *f* brandy
kompaktan *adj* compact
kompanija *f* company, firm
kompanjon *m* partner
komparativ *adj* comparative
komparirati *v* 1. to compare 2. to collate
kompas *m* compass
kompenzacija *f* compensation
kompetencija *f* competence
kompjuter *m* computer
kompleks *m* complex
kompleksaš *m* someone with a complex
komplet *m* set
kompletan *adj* complete
kompliciran *adj* complicated
komplikacija *f* complication
komplikovati *v* to complicate
kompliment *m* compliment
komponirati *v* to compose
komponist *m* composer
komponovati *v* to compose
kompot *m* stewed fruit
kompozicija *f* 1. composition 2. train
kompozicija *f* composition
kompozitor *m* composer
kompromis *m* compromise
kompromitirati *v* to compromise

komšija *f* neighbour
komšiluk *m* neighbourhood
komunalan *adj* public
komunalije *pl* public service
komunikacija *f* communication
komunikacije *fpl* communications
komunikativan *adj* communicative
komunist *m* communist
komunistički *adj* communist
komunizam *m* communism
komutator *m* switchboard
konac *m* 1. thread 2. conclusion
konačan *adj* final
konačište *n* lodgings
konačno *adv* finally
koncentracija *f* concentration
koncentričan *adj* concentric
koncepcija *f* conception, concept
koncept *m* draft
koncerat *m* concert
koncern *m* (com.) firm
koncert *m* concert
koncesija *f* concession
koncipirati *v* to draft
koncizan *adj* concise
kondenzacija *f* condensation
kondenzator *m* condenser
kondicija *f* condition
kondicionalan *adj* conditional
kondoliranje *n* condolence
kondom *m* condom
kondukter *m* conductor
konfederacija *f* confederation
konfekcija *f* 1. garments 2. garment industry
konferansje *m* master of ceremonies
konferencija *f* conference
konferencija za štampu *f* press conference
konferisati *v* to confer
konfiguracija *f* configuration
konfiskacija *f* confiscation

konflikt *m* conflict
konfrontacija *f* confrontation
konfuzija *f* confusion
kongres *m* 1. congress 2. conference
kongresmen *m* congressman
konjugacija *f* conjugation
konjunktiv *m* subjunctive
konjunktivitis *m* conjunctivitis
konjunktura *f* (fin.) favourable conditions
konkordat *m* agreement
konkretan *adj* concrete
konkurencija *f* competition
konkurent *m* 1. competitor 2. rival 3. candidate 4. applicant
konkurentan *adj* competitive
konkurisati *v* 1. to compete with 2. to be a candidate for 3. to apply for
konkurs *m* open competition
konoba *f* wine cellar
konobar *m* waiter, steward
konobarica *f* waitress, stewardess
konop *m* rope
konopac *m* cord, line rope
konoplja *f* hemp
konsignacija *f* consignment
konspekt *m* outline
konspiracija *f* 1. conspiracy 2. secrecy
konspirativan *adj* 1. conspiratorial 2. secret
konstanta *f* constant
konstantan *adj* constant
konstantnost *f* constancy
konstatacija *f* 1. statement 2. conclusion
konstatirati *v* to state
konstelacija *f* constellation
konstitucija *f* constitution
konstitutcionalan, konstitutcioni *adj* constitutional

konstruirati *v* 1. to design 2. to construct
konstrukcija *f* 1. design 2. construction
konstruktivan *adj* constructive
konstruktor *m* 1. designer 2. constructor
konstruktor *m* constructor
konsultant *m* consultant
konsultovati *v* to consult
kontakt *m* contact
kontaktno sočivo *n* contact lens
kontejner *m* container
kontekst *m* context
kontinent *m* continent
kontingent *m* 1. contingent 2. shipment
konto *m* 1. account 2. credit
kontrabas *m* double bass
kontracepcija *f* contraception
kontraceptivan *adj* contraceptive
kontraceptivno sredstvo *n* 1. contraceptive 2. **oralno kontraceptivno sredtsvo** oral contraceptive
kontradikcija *f* contradiction
kontradiktoran *adj* contradictory
kontrarevolucija *f* counter-revolution
kontrašpijunaža *f* counter-espionage
kontrast *m* contrast
kontrola *f* 1. check 2. control 3. checkpoint
kontrolirati *v* 1. to check 2. to control
kontrolni toranj *m* control tower
kontrolor *m* 1. inspector 2. controller
kontroverzan *adj* controversial
kontura *f* contour
kontuzija *f* shellshock

konvencija f convention
konvencionalan adj 1. conventional 2. formal
konvenirati v to suit
konvertibilan adj convertible
konvertibilnost f convertibility
konverzacija f conversation
konvoj m convoy
konzerva f tin, can
konzervativac m conservative
konzervator m curator
konzervatorijum m conservatory
konzervirati v to tin, to can
konzervisanje n preservation
konzilijum m consultation
konzul m consul
konzulat m consulate
konj m 1. horse 2. **na konju** on horseback
konjak m cognac
konjanik m rider
konjica f cavalry
konjska sila f horsepower
konjušar m stableboy
konjušnica f stable
kooperacija f cooperation
kooperant collaborator
koordinacija f coordination
koordinata f coordinate
koordinatna mreža karte f map grid
koordinirati v to coordinate
kop m excavation
kopač m miner
kopačka f (spor.) spikes
kopati v to dig
kopča f 1. buckle 2. (med.) stitch
kopija f copy
kopile n bastard
kopiranje n copying
kopirati v to copy
kopito n hoof

kopkati v to bother
koplje n 1. spear 2. (spor.) javelin
kopneni adj land
kopniti v to melt
kopno n land
koprcati se v to struggle
koprena f veil
kopriva f nettle
koprodukcija f co-production
kora f 1. skin 2. rind 3. bark
koračati v 1. to walk 2. to march
koračnica f march
korak m step
korak napred/naprijed m a step forward
korak po korak step by step
koral m coral
koran m the Koran
korbač m whip
korektkan adj correct
korektura f correction
koren m root
korenit adj fundamental
koreograf m choreographer
korespondencija f correspondence
korespondent m correspondent
korice fpl 1. cover 2. sheath
korida f bullfight
koridor m corridor
korigirati v to correct
korijen m root
korisnik m user
korisno adv usefully
korisnost f usefulness
korištenje n use
korist f 1. benfit 2. **Od kavke je koristi...?** What's the use of...?
koristan adj useful
koristiti v to be useful
koristljubiv adj greedy
koristoljublje n greed

koriti *v* to blame
korito *n* 1. trough 2. hull 3. river bed
korizma *f* Lent
korjenit *adj* radical
kormilar *m* (mar.) pilot
kormilariti *v* to steer
kormilo *n* rudder
kornjača *f* 1. tortoise 2. turtle
koronarni *adj* coronary
korota *f* mourning
korov *m* weed(s)
korozija *f* corrosion
korpa *f* basket
korporacija *f* corporation
korumpiran *adj* corrupt
korumpirati *v* to corrupt
korupcija *f* corruption
kos 1. *adj* sloped 2. *m* blackbird
kosa *f* 1. hair 2. scythe
kosano meso *n* minced meat
kosati *v* to chop
kosina *f* slope
kositi *v* to mow
kosmat *adj* hairy
kosmonaut *m* astronaut
kosmos *m* cosmos
kost *f* bone
kostim *m* 1. suit 2. costume
kostimograf *m* costume designer
kostur *m* skeleton
koš *m* 1. barn 2. wastepaper basket
košara *f* basket
košarka *f* basketball
košarkaš *m* basketball player
košava *f* east wind
koščat *adj* bony
košer *m* kosher food
košmar *m* nightmare
košnica *f* beehive
koštan *adj* bone
koštati *v* to cost

koštica *f* stone
košulja *f* shirt
košćat *adj* bony
kotač *m* wheel
kotao *m* 1. kettle 2. boiler
kotar *m* district
kotlet *m* cutlet
kotlina *f* valley
kotlokrpa *f* tinker
kotracepcija *f* contraception
kotrljati *v* to roll
koturaljke *fpl* roller skates
kotva *f* anchor
kotvište *n* mooring
kovač *m* blacksmith
kovačnica *f* forge
kovak *m* malleable
kovati *v* 1. to forge 2. to mint
kovčeg *m* suitcase
koverat *m*, **koverta** *f* envelope
kovina *f* metal
kovnica *f* (fin.) mint
kovrčast *adj* curly
koza *f* nanny goat
kozice *n* smallpox
kozmetičarka *f* beautician
kozmetički *adj* cosmetic
kozmetika *f* cosmetics
kozmički *adj* cosmic
koža *f* leather
kradljivac *m* thief
krafna *f* doughnut
kragna *f* collar
krah *m* disaster
kraj 1. *m* end 2. area 3. country 4. *prep* next to
krajlevski *adj* royal
krajnik *adj* tonsil
krajnji *adj* 1. extreme 2. final
krajnost *f* limit
krajolik *m* landscape
krak *m* leg

kralj *m* king
kraljevina *f* kingdom
kraljević *m* prince
kraljevski *adj* royal
kralježak *m* vertebra
kraljica *f* queen
kramp *m* pick
kran *adj* crane
krasan *adj* 1. splendid 2. good-looking
krasiti *v* to adorn
krasno *adv* nicely
krasta *f* scab
krastača *f* toad
krastavac *m* cucumber
krasti *v* to steal
krasuljak *m* daisy
kratak *adj* short
krater *m* crater
kratica *f* abbreviaton
kratka biografija *f* curriculum vitae, C.V.
kratki spoj *m* short circuit
kratki talas *m* short wave
kratko *adv* abruptly
kratkoročan *adj* short-term
kratkotalasni *adj* short wave
kratkotrajan *adj* short-lived
kratkovidan *adj* short-sighted
kratkoća *f* brevity
krava *f* cow
kravata *f* tie; necktie
krađa *f* theft
krčag *m* jug
krcat *adj* 1. full 2. crowded
krcati *v* to load
krčiti *v* to clear land
krčma *f* pub; bar
krdo *n* herd, flock
kreacija *f* design
kreativan *adj* creative
kreativnost *f* creativity

kreator *m* designer
kreč *m* lime
krečiti *v* to whitewash
krečnjak *m* limestone
kreda *f* chalk
kredenac *m* cupboard
kredit *m* credit
kreirati *v* to design
kreketati *v* to croak
krem *m*, **krema** *f* cream
kremacija *f* cremation
krematorij *m* crematory
kremen *m* flint
krenuti *v* to set off
krepak *adj* hearty
krepiti *v* to refresh
krepost *f* virtue
krepostan *adj* virtuous
kresnuti šibicu *v* to strike a match
kretanje *n* 1. movement 2. exercise 3. trend
kreten *m* cretin
kreton *m* cotton fabric
krevet *m* bed
krevet za jednog *m* single bed
krezle *fpl* tripe
krhak *adj* fragile
krhotina *f* fragment
kričav *adj* ostentatious
krigla *f* beer mug
krijepiti *v* to strengthen
krijes *m* bonfire
krijesnica *f* glow worm
krijumčar *m* smuggler
krijumčar vatrenog oružja *f* gunrunner
krijumčarenje *n* smuggling
krijumčarenje vatrenog oružja *f* gunrunning
krijumčariti puške *n* to run guns
krijumčariti *v* to smuggle
krik *m* scream

kriknuti *v* to scream
krilo *n* wing
krilo prozora *n* casement
kriminal *m* crime
kriminalac *m* criminal
kriminalan *adj* criminal
krin *m* lily
krinka *f* mask
kriška *f* slice
krišom *adv* stealthily
kristal *m* crystal
kriterij *m* criterion
kriti (se) *v* to hide
kritičan *adj* critical
kritičar *m* critic
kritika *f* criticism
kritikovati *v* to criticize
kriv *adj* 1. wrong 2. guilty
kriva *f* curve
kriva zaketva *f* perjury
krivac *m* culprit
krivica *f* 1. blame 2. fault 3. guilt
krivični *adj* penal
krivični zakonik *m* penal code
kriviti *v* to blame
krivnja *f* 1. fault 2. guilt
krivo *adv* wrongly
krivo se zakleti *v* to perjure oneself
krivo shvaćanje *n* misunderstanding
krivo tumačiti *v* to misinterpret
krivokletstvo *n* perjury
krivotvoren *adj* counterfeit
krivotvorina *f* forgery
krivotvoritelj *m* counterfeiter
krivotvoriti *v* to counterfeit
krivovjerac *m* heretic
krivudati *v* to wind
krivudav *adj* winding
krivudavo *adv* zigzag
krivulja *f* curve
kriza *f* crisis

krizma *f* (rel.) confirmation
križ *m* cross
križaljka *f* crossword
križati se *v* (rel.) to cross oneself
križati *v* to cross out
krkljanac *m* 1. bustle 2. mess 3. row
krlja *f* tick
krljušt *f* scales
krma *f* stern
krmača *f* sow
krmenadla *f* pork chop
krnj *adj* incomplete
krofna *f* doughnut
kroj *m* 1. cut 2. style
krojač *m* tailor
krojačica *f* dressmaker
krojiti *v* to cut
krokodil *m* crocodile
krom *m* chrome
kromiran *adj* chrome-plated
krompir *m* potato
kroničan *adj* chronic
kronika *f* chronicle
krošnja *f* treetop
krotak *m* tame
krotitelj *m* tamer
krotiti *v* to tame
krov *m* roof
kroz *prep* through
krpa *f* 1. rag 2. cloth
krpati *v* to mend
krpelj *m* tick
krsni list *m* birth certificate
krsno ime *n* first name
krš *m* rocky soil
kršenje *n* violation
kršiti *v* 1. to snap 2. to violate
krštenje *n* baptism
kršćanin *m* Christian
kršćanski *adj* Christian
kršćanstvo *n* Christianity
krst *m* cross

krstarenje *n* cruise
krstarica *f* cruiser
krstariti *v* to cruise
krstionica *f* baptistry
krstiti *v* to baptize
krt *adj* breakable
krtica *f* mole
krug *m* 1. circle 2. cycle 3. (spor.) lap 4. **prestići za ceo krug** to lap
kruh *m* bread
kruliti *v* to rumble
krumpir *m* potato
kruna *f* crown
krunisanje *n* coronation
krunisati *v* to crown
krupan *adj* large
kruška *f* pear
krut *adj* 1. rigid 2. solid
kružan *adj* circular
kruženje *n* circulation
kružiti *v* to circulate
kružni put *m* ring road
kružnica *f* circle
krv *f* blood
krvarenje *n* bleeding
krvariti *v* to bleed
krvav *adj* bloody
krvavica *f* black pudding
krvnik *m* executioner
krvoliptanje *n* bleeding
krvoločan *adj* bloodthirsty
krvoproliće *n* bloodshed
krvoproliće *n* bloodshed
krvotok *m* (blood) circulation
krzmati *v* to hesitate
krzno *n* fur
kržljav *adj* stunted
ksenofob *m* xenophobe
ksenofobija *f* xenophobia
ksenofobski *adj* xenophobic
kub *m* cube
kube *n* cupola

kubik *adj* cubic metre
kucanje *n* knocking
kucati *v* 1. to knock 2. to beat 3. to tick
kučka *f* bitch
kuća *f* 1. house 2. home 3. building 4. **kod kuće** at home 5. **pokretna kuća** mobile home
kućanica *f* housewife
kućanstvo *n* household
kuća za goste *n* guesthouse
kućevlasnik *m* home-owner
kućica *f* 1. house 2. shell
kućište *n* shell
kućna haljina *f* bathrobe
kućni pritvor *m* house arrest
kud, kuda where
kudelja *f* hemp
kudgod wherever
kuditi *v* to criticize
kudrav *adj* curly
kuga *f* plague
kugla *f* ball
kuglanje *n* bowling
kuglični ležaj *m* ball bearing
kuhača *f* ladle
kuhalo *n* cooker
kuhano jaje *n* boiled egg
kuhar *m*, **kuharica** *f* cook
kuhati *v* to cook
kuhinja *f* kitchen
kuja *f* bitch
kuk *m* hip
kuka *f* hook
kukac *m* insect
kukast *adj* hooked
kukasta glista *f* hookworm
kukati *v* to wail
kukavica *f* 1. coward 2. cuckoo
kukukjica *f* hood
kukurikati *v* to crow
kukuruz *m* maize; corn

kula *f* 1. tower 2. **svetilja kula** lighthouse
kulinarstvo *n* cookery
kulisa *f*, **kulise** *fpl* scenery
kuljati *v* to pour out
kulminacija *f* culmination
kult *m* cult
kultura *f* culture
kulturni *adj* cultural
kum *m* 1. godfather 2. best man
kuma *f* 1. godmother 2. maid of honour
kumče *m* godson
kumica *f* goddaughter
kumir *m* idol
kumovati *v* to be a godparent
kundak *m* rifle butt
kunić *m* rabbit
kunjati *v* to be sleepy
kup *m* pile
kupac *m* 1. buyer 2. customer
kupač *m* swimmer
kupalište *n* 1. bathing spot 2. seaside resort
kupanje *n* 1. bath 2. swim
kupaona *f* bathroom
kupati se *v* 1. to have a bath 2. to have a swim
kupati *v* to bath(e)
kupatilo *n* bathroom
kupaće gaćice *fpl* swimming trunks
kupaći kostim *m* swimsuit
kupe *n* train compartment
kupina *f* blackberry
kupiti *v* 1. to buy 2. to collect
kupke *fpl* spa
kupnja, kupovina *f* 1. purchase 2. shopping
kupola *f* 1. dome 2. (mil.) turret
kupon *m* coupon
kupoprodaja *f* buying and selling

kupovina *f* 1. buying 2. shopping
kupovna snaga *f* purchasing power
kupus *m* cabbage
kura *f* cure
kurir *m* courier
kurje oko *n* corn
kurs *m* course
kuršum *m* bullet
kurva *f* (sl.) hooker
kurziv *m* italics
kurzivan *adj* italic
kušati *v* 1. to test 2. to try
kušnja *f* test
kustos *m* custodian
kusur *m* change
kut *m* 1. corner 2. angle
kuta *f* overalls
kutija *f* box
kutlača *f* ladle
kutnjak *m* molar
kuvanje *n* cooking
kuvar *m* cook
kuvati *v* to cook
kužan *adj* infectious
kvačilo *n* clutch (of car)
kvadrat *m* square
kvaka *f* door handle
kvalificiran *adj* qualified
kvalificirati *v* 1. to qualify 2. to train
kvalifikacija *f* qualification
kvalifikacije *fpl* training
kvalifikovan *adj* qualified
kvalitativan *adj* qualitative
kvalitet *m* quality
kvalitetan *adj* of good quality
kvantitet *m* quantity
kvar *m* 1. damage 2. breakdown 3. **u kvaru** out of order
kvaran *adj* 1. bad 2. rotten
kvarc *m* quartz
kvarilac raspoloženja *m* killjoy

kvariti se *v* to go bad
kvariti *v* to spoil
kvarljiv *adj* perishable
kvart *m* area; neighborhood
kvartal *m* quarter
kvartet *m* quartet

kvasac *m* yeast
kvazi quasi
kviz *m* quiz
kvorum *m* quorum
kvota *f* quota
kvrga *f* bump

L

labav *adj* loose
labilan *adj* 1. labile 2. unstable
laboratorija *f* laboratory
labud *m* swan
lađa *f* ship, boat
lagan *adj* 1. slow 2. easy
laganje *n* lying
lagano *adv* 1. slowly 2. gently
lagodan *adj* easygoing
laguna *f* lagoon
lahor *m* breeze
laik *m* layman
lajati *v* to bark
lak 1. *adj* light 2. gentle 3. easy
   4. *m* polish 5. varnish
laka industrija *f* light industry
lakat *m* elbow
lakej *m* lackey
lakmus *m* litmus paper
lako *adv* easily
lakom *adj* greedy
lakomislen *adj* light-minded
lakomislenost *f* levity
lakomost *f* greed
lakovati *v* to varnish
lakoveran, lakovjeran *adj*
   credulous
lakoća *f* 1. lightness 2. ease
lakrdija *f* comedy
lakrdijaš *m* clown
laksativ *m* laxative
laktaš *m* pusher
lala *f* tulip
lampa *f* 1. lamp 2. torch; flash-light
lan *m* flax
lanac *m* chain
lančanik *m* bicycle chain

lančić *m* 1. chain 2. necklace
lani *adv* last year
lanjski *adj* last year's
lansirati *v* to launch
lansirati raketu *v* launch a rocket
laringitis *m* laryngitis
larma *f* noise
larmati *v* to make noise
laser *m* laser
laserski štampač *m* laser printer
lasica *f* weasel
laskanje *n* flattery
laskati *v* to flatter
laskav *adj* flattering
laskavac *m* flatterer
last *f* the good life
lasta *f* swallow
lastavica *f* 1. swallow 2. flying fish
lastika *f* elastic
lastiš *m* rubber band
laštilo *n* polish
laštiti *v* to polish
lateks *m* latex
latentan *adj* latent
latica *f* petal
latinica *f* Latin alphabet
latiti se *v* 1. to reach for 2. to take
   up
lav *m* lion
lava *f* lava
lavabo *m* washbasin
lavež *m* barking
lavica *f* lioness
lavina *f* avalanche
lavirati *v* (mar.) to tack
lavirint *m* labyrinth
lavor *m* washbasin

laž _f_ lie
lažac _m_ liar
lažan _adj_ false
lažljiv _adj_ lying
lažljivac _m_ liar
lažno se zakleti _v_ to commit perjury
lebdjeti _v_ to hover
lečenje _n_ 1. cure 2. treatment
lečilište _n_ health resort
lečiti _v_ 1. to cure 2. to treat
leća _f_ 1. lens 2. lentil
leći _v_ 1. to lay 2. to lie down 3. to go to bed
led _m_ ice
ledara _f_ icebox
leden _adj_ icy
ledeni zator _m_ ice patch
ledenjak _m_ glacier
ledina _f_ heath
ledište _n_ freezing point
lediti _v_ to freeze
lednik _m_ glacier
ledolomac _m_ ice-breaker
leđa _npl_ 1. back 2. shoulders
legalan _adj_ legal
legat _m_ legacy
legenda _f_ legend
legendaran _adj_ legendary
legija _f_ legion
legionar _m_ legionary
legitimacija _f_ I.D.
legitiman _adj_ legitimate
legitimirati se _v_ to show one's identification
leglo _n_ hotbed
legnuti _v_ to lie down
legura _f_ alloy
lek _m_ medicine
lekar _m_ doctor; physician
lekcija _f_ lesson
lekovit _adj_ medicinal

leksikografija _f_ lexicography
leksikon _m_ dictionary
lektira _f_ literature
lektira _f_ reading list
lektor _m_ lector
lem _m_ solder
lemilo _n_ soldering iron
lemiti _v_ to solder
lenčariti _v_ to be idle
lenger _m_ anchor
lengerisati _v_ to moor
lenština _m/f_ lazybones
lenj _adj_ lazy
lenjir _m_ ruler
leopard _m_ leopard
lep _adj_ beautiful, handsome
lepak _m_ glue
lepeza _f_ fan
lepiti _v_ to glue
lepljiv _adj_ adhesive
lepo _adv_ 1. beautifully 2. well
lepota _f_ beauty
lepotan _m_ handsome boy/man
lepotica _f_ beautiful girl/woman
lepršati _v_ to flutter
leptir _m_ butterfly
leptir za gas _m_ throttle
lesonit _m_ hardboard
lestve _fpl_ ladder
lestvica _f_ scale
leš _m_ corpse, carcass
lešinar _m_ vulture
lešnik _m_ hazelnut
let _m_ flight
let na međunarodnoj _m_ international flight
let na unutrašnjoj _m_ domestic flight
letač _m_ flyer
letačko osoblje _n_ flight crew
letak _m_ leaflet
letenje _n_ flying

leteti *v* to fly
leti *adv* in summer
letilica *f* aircraft
letimičan *adj* hasty
letina *f* 1. crop 2. harvest
letjeti *v* to fly
letnjikovac *m* (summer) cottage
leto *n* summer
letopis *m* chronicle
letos *adv* this summer
letovalište *n* summer resort
letovanje *n* summer holidays
levak *m* left-handed person
levi *adj* left, left-hand
levica *f* (pol.) the left
levičar *m* leftist
levoruk *m* left-handed
lezbijka *f* lesbian
lezbijska ljubav *f* lesbianism
lezbijski *adj* lesbian
ležaj *m* 1. bed 2. support
ležaljka *f* easychair
ležanje *n* lying, resting
ležarina *f* 1. storage 2. warehouse
ležati *v* to lie (down)
ležati u porođajnim mukama *v* to
  be in labour
ležeran *adj* 1. comfortable 2. light
ležeran *adj* relaxed
ležernost *f* being relaxed
ležećke *n* lying down
ležište *n* bearing
ležište *n* support
li *emphasizes a question*
libela *f* 1. level 2. dragonfly
liberalan *adj* liberal
liberalizacija *f* liberalization
liberalizam *m* liberalism
libretist(a) *m* lyricist
libreto *m* libretto
lice *n* 1. face 2. person
licemer, licemjer *m* hypocrite

licemeran, licemjeran *adj*
  hypocritical
licemerje, licemjerje *n* hypocrisy
licenca *f* 1. licence 2. concession
ličan *adj* personal
ličilac *m* painter
ličilati *v* to paint
licitacija *f* auction
lična karta *f* I.D. card
lični *adj* personal
lično *adv* personally
ličnost *f* 1. person 2. personality
liferant *m* supplier
lift *m* lift
liga *f* league
lignit *m* brown coal
lignja *f* squid
lihvar *m* usurer
lihvarstvo *n* usury
liječenje *n* 1. cure 2. treatment
liječiti *v* 1. to cure 2. to treat
liječnik *m*, **lijenica** *f* doctor;
  physician
lijeha *f* bed
lijek *m* medicine
lijen *adj* lazy
lijenčina *f* lazy person
lijenost *f* laziness
lijep *adj* 1. beautiful, handsome 2.
  nice
lijepiti *v* to stick
lijes *m* coffin
lijevak *m* 1. funnel 2. crater
lijevak *m* left-handed person
lijevati *v* to pour
lijevi *adj* left
lijev *adv* left
lik *m* figure
liker *m* liquer
likvidacija *f* liquidation
likvidan *adj* liquid
likvidirati *v* to liquidate

lila *f* violet
lim *m* sheet metal
limar *m* plumber
limen *m* tin
limenka *f* tin, can
limfa *f* lymph
limfatičan, limfni *adj* lymphatic
limun *m* lemon
limunada *f* lemonade
limuzina *f* 1. limousine 2. saloon car
linčovanje *n* lynching
linčovati *v* to lynch
linearan *adj* linear
lingvist(a) *m* linguist
lingvistika *f* linguistics
linija *f* line
linija fronta/fronte *f* (mil.) front line
linoleum *m* linoleum
lipa *f* lime tree
lipanj *m* June
lira *f* lira
liričan *adj* lyrical
lirika *f* lyrics
lirski *adj* lyrical
lisica *f* fox
lisice *fpl* handcuffs
lisnat *adj* leafy
lisnica *f* wallet
lišaj *m* (med.) eczema
lišavanje *n* deprivation
lišen *adj* deprived (of)
lišiti *v* to deprive
lišiti mandata *v* (pol.) to unseat
lišće *n* foliage
list *m* 1. leaf 2. sheet of paper 3. sole 4. calf
list čaja *f* tea leaf
lista čekanja *f* waiting list
listopad *m* October
listopadni *adj* deciduous

litar *m* litre; liter
literatura *f* literature
litica *f* cliff
litija *f* procession
litografija *f* lithography
litra *f* litre; liter
liturgija *f* liturgy
livada *f* meadow
livnica *f* foundry
lizati *v* to lick
lobanja *f* skull
lobi *m* (pol.) lobby
lobist(a) *m* (pol.) lobbyist
logaritam *m* logarithm
logika *f* logic
logički *adj* logical
logor *m* camp
logor za internice *m* internment camp
logor za izbeglice/izbjeglice *m* refugee camp
logoraš *m* 1. detainee 2. internee
logorovanje *n* camping
logorovati *v* to camp
lojalan *adj* loyal
lojalnost *f* loyalty
lokal *m* 1. premises 2. shop, restaurant, bar, club 3. telephone extension
lokalan *adj* local
lokalizovati *v* to localize
lokomotiva *f* locomotive
lokot *m* padlock
lokva *f* 1. puddle 2. pool
lokvanj *m* water lily
lom *m* 1. break 2. uproar
lomiti *v* to break
lomljava *f* crash
lomljiv *adj* fragile
lon-plej ploča *f* lp (long-playing record)
lonac *m* pot

lončar *m* potter
lončarija *f* pottery
lončarska roba, lončarstvo *n* pottery
lončič *m* cup
lopata *f* spade
lopatica *f* shoulder-blade
lopatica za smeće *f* dustpan
lopov *m* thief
lopovluk *m* dirty trick
lopta *f* ball
lord *m* lord
losion za sunčanje *m* suntan lotion
losos *m* salmon
loš *adj* 1. bad 2. evil
lotati *v* to solder
lov *m* hunt(ing)
lovac *m* hunter
loviti *v* 1. to catch 2. to hunt
lovna sezona *f* open season
lovor *m* laurel
loz *m* lottery
loza *f* 1. vine 2. origin
lozinka *f* 1. motto 2. (mil.) password
lozovača *f* grape brandy
loža *f* 1. theatre box 2. masonic lodge
ložač *m* stoker
ložiti *v* to stoke
ložnica *f* bedroom
lubanja *f* skull
lubenica *f* watermelon
lučenje *n* secretion
lucidan *adj* lucid
lučiti *v* to secrete
lučka postrojenja *npl* port facilities

lučka uprava *f* port authority
luckast *adj* crazy
lučki *adj* port
lučki grad *m* port
lučki radnik *m* docker
lud *adj* insane
ludak, luđak *m* madman
ludilo *n* insanity
ludnica *f* mental institution
ludorija *f* idiocy
ludost *f* folly
ludovati *v* to be crazy (**za** about)
lugar *m* forester; ranger
luk *m* 1. onion 2. arch 3. bow
luka *f* 1. harbour 2. port
lukav *adj* cunning
lukavost *f* cunning
lukavština *f* trick
lukavstvo *n* 1. craft 2. trick
lukobran *adj* breakwater
lukovica *f* bulb
luksuz *m* luxury
luksuzan *adj* 1. luxury 2. luxurious
lula *f* pipe
lumbalna punkcija *f* spinal tap
lumpati *v* to have a good time
lupa *f* magnifying glass
lupanje srca *f* (med.) palpitation
lupati *v* to bang
lupetati *v* to chatter
lupina *f* 1. skin 2. bark 3. shell
lupiti *v* to hit
luster *m* light
lutalica *m/f* 1. wanderer 2. tramp
lutati *v* to wander
lutka *f* 1. doll 2. puppet
lutrija *f* lottery

LJ

ljaga *f* 1. stain 2. blemish
lječilište *n* health resort
ljekovit *adj* healing
ljenčariti *v* to idle about
ljepenka *f* cardboard
ljepilo *n* glue
ljepljiv *adj* sticky
ljepljivost *f* stickiness
ljepota *f* beauty
ljepuškast *adj* pretty
lješnjak *m* hazelnut
ljestve *n* ladder
ljestvica *f* scale
ljetina *f* crops
ljetni *adj* summer
ljeto *n* summer
ljevica *f* (pol.) the left
ljevoruk *m* left-handed
ljigav *adj* slimy
ljiljan *m* lily
ljubak *adj* charming
ljubav *f* 1. love 2. sake
ljubavnik *m*, **ljubavnica** *f* lover
ljubazan *adj* 1. kind 2. nice
ljubazno *adv* 1. kindly 2. nicely
ljubaznost *f* kindness
ljubičast *m* purple

ljubičica *f* violet
ljubimac *m* 1. darling 2. favourite
ljubiti *v* 1. to love 2. to kiss
ljubljenje *n* kissing
ljubomora *f* jealousy
ljubomoran *adj* jealous
ljubopitljiv *adj* curious
ljudi *mpl* people
ljudožder *m* cannibal
ljudožderstvo *n* cannibalism
ljudski 1. *adj* human 2. *adv* humanely 3. properly
ljuljaška *f* swing
ljuljati *v* to swing
ljupko *adv* gracefully
ljupkost *f* charm
ljusdska žrtva *f* fatality
ljuska *f* 1. shell 2. skin 3. pod 4. husk
ljuskar *m* shellfish
ljuštiti *v* 1. to shell 2. to peel
ljuštura *f* shell
ljutak *m* pomegranate
ljut *adj* 1. angry 2. hot
ljutina *f* anger
ljutiti *v* to anger
ljutiti se *v* to be angry
ljuto *adv* badly

M

ma *conj* 1. but 2. any
maca *f* catkin
mač *m* sword
mačad *f* kittens
mačak *m* cat
mače *n* kitten
mačevanje *n* (spor.) fencing
mačka *f* cat
maćeha *f* stepmother
mada *conj* although
madež *m* mole
madrac *m* mattress
Madžar, Mađar *m* Hungarian
Madžarska, Mađarksa *f* Hungary
madžarski, mađarski *adj* Hungarian
mađija *f* 1. spell 2. magic
madionичar *m* magician
maestral *m* north wind
mafija *f* mafia
magacin 1. warehouse 2. depot 3. (mil.) magazine
magacioner *m* storekeeper
magarac *m* donkey
magazin *m* 1. magazine 2. *see* magacin
magistar *m* Master of Arts (M.A.)
magisterijum *m* M.A. degree
magistrala *f* main road
magistrat 1. city hall 2. town authorities
magla *f* 1. mist 2. fog
maglica *f* haze
maglovit *adj* 1. misty 2. foggy
magnet *m* magnet
magnetofon *m* tape-recorder
magnetski *adj* magnetic

magnezijum *m* magnesium
magnovenje *n* instant
mah *m* 1. moment 2. movement
mahati *v* 1. to swing 2. to be in a frenzy
mahati *v* to wave
mahinacija *f* machination
mahnit *adj* frantic
mahnitost *f* madness
mahnuti *v* to motion
mahom *adv* mostly
mahovina *f* moss
mahuna *f* pod
mahune *fpl* green beans
maj *m* May
majčin *adj* mother's
majčinski *adj* maternal
majčinstvo *n* motherhood
majdan *m* mine
majica *f* 1. T-shirt 2. vest; undershirt
majka *f* mother
majmun *m* 1. monkey 2. ape
majonez *m*, **majoneza** *f* mayonnaise
major *m* (mil.) major
majstor *m* 1. master 2. craftsman
majstorija *f* 1. skill 2. trick
majstorski 1. *adj* skilful 2. *adv* with skill
majstorstvo *n* mastery
majur *m* farmstead
mak *m* poppy
makar *m* 1. although 2. at least 3. **pa makar** even if
makar *m* although, even if, at least
makaze *fpl* scissors
Makedonac *m* Macedonian

Makedonija f Macedonia
makedonski adj Macedonian
maketa f 1. model 2. proposal
maknuti v 1. to move 2. to displace 3. to set in motion
makro m pimp
maksima f maxim
maksimalan adj maximal
maksimum m maximum
malaksalost f exhaustion
malaksao adj exhausted
malaksati v to be exhausted
malarija f malaria
malati v to paint
malen adj 1. small 2. little
malenlost f triviality
maler m misfortune
malerozan adj unfortunate
mali adj 1. small 2. little
malina f raspberry
mališan m, **mališanka** f small child
malj m 1. hammer 2. sledge
maljavost f hairiness
malje n soft hair
malkice, malko adv a little, a bit
malo adv 1. a little 2. **na malo** (com.) retail
malo-pomalo adv little by little
maločas adv recently
malodušan adj cowardly
malograđanski adj middle-class
malograđanština f middle-class mentality
malokrvan adj anaemic
maloletan, maloljetan adj 1. teenaged 2. juvenile
maloletan prestupnik, maloljetan prestupnik m juvenile delinquent
maloletnik, maloljetnik m minor, juvenile
maloposjednik m smallholder

maloprodaja f retail
maloprodajni adj retail
malter m mortar
malterisati v to plaster
maltretirati v to mistreat
malverzacija f misconduct
mama f mummy
mamac m 1. bait 2. decoy
mamiti v to lure
mamlaz m slob
mamuran adj 1. drowsy 2. hungover
mamurluk m 1. drowsiness 2. hangover
mamut m mammoth
mamuza f spur
mana f fault
manastir m monastery
mandarina f mandarin, tangerine
mandat m 1. mandate 2. **poslanički mandat** (pol.) seat
mandatni adj mandatory
mandolina f mandolin
manekanka f fashion model
maneken m mannequin
manekena f fashion model
manevar m manoeuvre; maneuver
mangup m good-for-nothing
manifest m manifesto
manifestacija f manifestation
manija f 1. mania 2. enthusiasm
manijak m 1. maniac 2. enthusiasm
manikir m manicure
manipulacija f 1. manipulation 2. managing
manipulisati v 1. to manipulate 2. to manage
manir m manner
mansarda f attic
manšeta f cuff
mantija f cloak
mantil m 1. coat 2. overalls

manjak *m* deficit
manje *conj* 1. less 2. minus
manje ako (da) *conj* unless
manji *adj* 1. smaller 2. minor
manjina *f* 1. minority 2. **nacionalna manjina** national minority 3. **voda manjine** minority leader
manjinska prava *f* minority rights
manjinski *adj* minority
manjkati *v* to lack
manjkav *adj* defective
mapa *f* 1. map 2. album
marama *f* shawl
maramica *f* handkerchief
maraton *m* marathon
marelica *f* apricot
margarin *m* margarine
marinac *m* marine
marioneta *f* marionette, puppet
marionetska vlada *f* puppet regime
mariti *v* to care for
marka *f* 1. postage stamp 2. (com.) brand
marketing *m* marketing
markirati *v* to mark
marksizam *m* Marxism
marljiv *adj* diligent
marljivost *f* diligence
marmelada *f* jam; jelly
marš *m* march
maršal *m* marshal
maršruta *f* route
mart *m* March
marva *f* 1. cattle 2. livestock
masa *f* mass
masakr *m* massacre
masakrirati *v* to massacre
masaža *f* massage
masažirati *v* to massage
maser *m* masseur
maserka *f* masseuse

masivan *adj* massive
maska *f* 1. mask 2. goggles
maska za kiseonik/kisik *f* oxygen mask
maskenbal *m* masquerade ball
maskirati *v* 1. to mask 2. to disguise
maskirati se *v* to be in disguise
maslac *m* butter
maslačak *m* dandelion
maslina *f* olive
masnica *f* bruise
masnoća *f* fat
masovan *adj* 1. massive 2. mass
masovna migracija *f* mass migration
masovna potrošnja *f* mass consumption
masovna proizvodnja *f* mass production
masovna vakcinacija *f* immunization campaign
masovno proizvoditi *v* to mass-produce
masovno streljanje/strijeljanje *n* mass execution
masovno ubijanje *n* mass murder
mašina *f* machine
mašina za pranje *f* washing machine
mašinerija *f* machinery
mašinista *f* 1. machinist 2. technician
mašinka *f* automatic rifle, submachine gun
mašinski *adj* mechanical
mašinstvo *n* mechanical engineering
mašiti se *v* to reach for
mašna *f* 1. ribbon 2. bow
mašta *f* imagination
maštati *v* to daydream

mast *f* 1. fat 2. ointment
mastan *adj* greasy
mastilo *n* ink
mat 1. *adj* dull 2. *m* (check)mate
matematičar *m* mathematician
matematika *f* mathematics
materica *f* uterus
materija *f* 1. substance 2. *see* material
materijal *m* material
materijalan *adj* material
materijalista *f* materialist
materijalizam *m* materialism
materijalno-tehnički *adj* logistic
materinski *adj* maternal
materinstvo *n* motherhood
maternica *f* womb
maternji *adj* maternal
maternji jezik *m* native language
mati *f* mother
matica *f* 1. (metal) nut 2. queen bee
matičar *m* registrar
matine *m*, **matineja** *f* matinee
matrica *f* 1. stencil 2. matrix
matrični štampač *m* dot-matrix printer
matura *f* matriculation
maturant *m* matriculating pupil
maturirati *v* to matriculate
mauzolej *m* mausoleum
mazati *v* to coat
mazga *f* mule
maziti *v* to fondle
mazivo *n* lubricant
maženje *n* petting
meč *m* (spor.) match
mećava *f* blizzard
med *m* honey
medalja *f* medal
medaljon *m* medallion
medeni mesec/mjesec *m* honeymoon

medenjak *m* honey cake
medicina *f* medicine
medicinski fakultet *m* medical school
medij *m* medium
mediokritet *m* mediocrity
meditacija *f* meditation
meditirati *v* to mediate
meduza *f* jellyfish
medved, medvjed *m* bear
međa *f* border
među *prep* 1. between 2. among
međudržavni *adj* interstate
međugradski *adj* intercity
međuigra *f* intermezzo
međukat *m* mezzanine
međumesni *adj* long-distance
Međunarodna organizacija a izbeglice/izbjeglice *n* International Refugee Organization
Međunarodna organizacija rada *f* International Labour Organization
Međunarodni fond UN za pomoć deci/djeci *m* UNICEF
Međunarodni monetarni fond *m* International Monetary Fund
Međunarodni monetarni fond *m* International Monetary Fund
Međunarodni sud pravde *m* International Court of Justice
međunarodni *adj* international
međunarodno pravo *n* international law
međuparlamentarni *adj* interparliamentary
međupartijski *adj* interparty
međuplanetarni *adj* interplanetary
međuprostor *m* space
međurasni *adj* interracial
međuratni *adj* interwar

međusklop m interface
međusoban adj mutual
međusobni adj mutual, reciprocal
međutim conj 1. however 2. meanwhile
međuvreme, međuvrijeme n 1. pause 2. interval 3. meantime
megdan m duel
mehaničar m mechanic
mehanika f mechanics
mehanizam m mechanism
mehanizovati v to mechanize
mehur m 1. blister 2. bubble
mejtef m (Isl.) religious school
mek adj 1. soft 2. tender
meka f bait
meketati v to bleat
mekinje n bran
mekoća f 1. softness 2. tenderness
mekšati v 1. to soften 2. to tenderise
mekušac m mollusc
melanholičan adj melancholic
melanholija f melancholy
melem m balsam
melez m mongrel
melodičan adj melodious, melodic
melodija f melody, tune
melos m folk music
membrana f membrane
memoari mpl memoirs
memorandum m memo, memorandum
memorija f memory
mena f change
menadžer m 1. manager 2. agent
menažerija f menagerie
mene, meni me
mengele fpl, **mengeli** mpl vice; vise
menica f 1. bill of exchange 2. (com.) draft
meningitis m meningitis

menjač m 1. money-changer 2. transmission
menjačnica f exchange
menjati v to change/exchange
menopauza f menopause
menstruacija f menstruation
menstruirati v to menstruate
mentalitet m mentality
mentalni adj mental
mentor m supervisor
menza f canteen
mera f 1. measurement 2. size
merdevine fpl ladder
meridijan m meridian
merilo n 1. standard 2. scale
meriti v to measure
mermer m marble
merodavan adj competent
mesar m butcher
mesarnica f butcher's shop
mesec m 1. moon 2. month 3. **mladi mesec** new moon 4. **puni mesec** full moon
mesečina f moonlight
mesečni adj monthly
mesečnik m monthly publication
mesija m messiah
mesing m brass
mesiti v to knead
mesnat adj meaty
mesnica f butcher's
meso n 1. meat 2. flesh
mešalica f mixer
mešati v to mix, blend
mesti v to sweep
mestimice adj sporadically
mesto 1. n place 2. prep in place of
meta f target
metabolizam m metabolism
metafizičar m metaphysics
metafora f metaphor
metak m cartridge

metal *m* metal
metalan *adj* metal, metallic
metalugrija *f* metallurgy
metamorfoza *f* metamorphosis
metan *m* methane
metar *m* metre; meter
meteor *m* meteor
meteorologija *f* meteorology
meteorološka stanica *f* weather station
meteorološki bilten *m* weather report
meteorološki biro *m* weather office; weather bureau
metež *m* 1. confusion 2. riot
metla *f* broom
metnuti *v* to put
metod *m*, **metoda** *f* method
metodičan *adj* methodical
metrički *adj* metric
metro *m* underground; subway
metropola *f* metropolis
metvica *f* mint
meze *n* snack
mezimac *m* favourite
mi we
micati *v* to move
micati *v* to move, stir, displace
midi *adj/m* midi
mig *m* wink
migati *v* to blink
migavac *m* signal
mignuti *v* to wink
migracija *f* migration
migrena *f* migraine
mijaukati *v* to meow
mijenjanje *n* change
mijenjati *v* 1. to change 2. to exchange
mijenjati se *v* to vary
miješan *adj* mixed
miješati *v* 1. to mix 2. to stir

miješati se *v* to interfere
mikrob *m* microbe
mikrofon *m* microphone
mikroprocesor *m* microprocessor
mikroskop *m* microscope
mikrotalas *m* **šporet na mikrotalase** microwave oven
mikser *m* mixer
milenij, milenijum *m* millennium
milicija *f* 1. militia 2. police
milicionar *m* policeman
milijarda *f* milliard; billion
milijardaš, milijarder *m* multi-millionaire
milijunar *m* millionaire
milimetar *m* millimetre; millimeter
milina *f* pleasure
milion *m* million
milionar, milioner *m* millionaire
militarizam *m* militarism
militarizovati *v* to militarize
milo *adv* fondly
milosrdan *adj* 1. merciful 2. charitable
milosrđe *n* 1. mercy 2. charity
milost *f* mercy
milostinja *f* charity
milostiv *adj* 1. graceful 2. merciful
milovanje *n* caress
milovati *v* to caress
milja *f* 1. mile 2. (mar.) knot
miljaža *f* mileage
miljenik *adj* favourite
miljokaz *m* milestone
mimičar *m* mimic
mimika *f* mimicry
mimo *prep* 1. past 2. except 3. without
mimogred *adv* by the way
mimoići *v* 1. to pass by 2. to overlook
mimoići se *v* to miss one other

mina *f* (mil.) **1.** mine **2. kontaktna mina** contact mine **3. magnetska mina** magnetic mine **4. mina nagaznog** pressure mine **5. mina poteznog** tripwire mine **6. plutajuća mina** floating mine **7. protivpešadijska/protupješadijska mina** antipersonnel mine **8. protivoklopna mina** antitank mine **9. rasprskavajuća mina** fragmentation mine **10. nagaziti na minu** to hit a mine **11. postaljati mine** to lay mines **12. ukloniti mine** to clear mines

minare, minaret *m* minaret

minđuša *f* earring

mineralna voda *f* mineral water

mineralogija *f* mineralogy

mini *adj* mini

minijatura *f* miniature

minimalan *adj* minimum

minirati *v* **1.** to blast **2.** to undermine **3.** (mil.) to mine

ministar *m* minister; secretary of state

ministarstvo *n* ministry

minobacač *m* (mil.) mortar

minodetektor, minoistraživač *m* mine detector

minolovac *m* (mil.) minesweeper

minolovka *f* mine sweep

minonosac, minopolagač *m* (mil.) minelayer

minsko polje *n* (mil.) minefield

minus *adj/conj* minus

minut *m* minute

minuti *v* to pass by

mio *adj* **1.** dear **2.** nice

mir *m* **1.** peace **2.** quiet

miran *adj* **1.** peaceful **2.** quiet

miraz *m* dowry

mirenje *n* reconciliation

miris *m* (nice) smell

mirisan *adj* fragrant

mirisati *v* to smell (nice)

miriti *v* to make peace

mirno doba *f* peacetime

mirnodopski *adj* peacetime

mirnoća *f* calm

mirodija *f* spice

miroljubiv *adj* peaceful

miroljubiva koegzistencija *f* peaceful coexistence

miroljubivost *f* peacefulness

mirovanje *n* rest

mirovati *v* **1.** to keep still **2.** to rest

mirovina *f* pension

mirovinski fond *m* pension fund

mirovna konferencija *f* peace conference

mirovne snage *fpl* peacekeeping forces

mirovni *adj* **1.** peace **2.** peacekeeping

mirovni pregovori *mpl* peace talks

mirovni ugovor *m* peace treaty

mirođija *f* dill

mirta *f* myrtle

mis *f* miss

misa *f* (rel.) mass

misao *f* thought

misaon *adj* thoughtful

misija *f* **1.** mission **2.** delegation

misionar *m* missionary

mislilac *m* thinker

misliti *v* **1.** to think **2.** to mean

miš *m* mouse

mišić *m* muscle

mišićav, mišićni *adj* muscular

mišljenje *n* opinion

mišljenje *n* **1.** opinion **2. po mom mišljenju** in my opinion **3.**

javno mišljenje public opinion
4. izraziti mišljenje to express
an opinion
mišolovka *f* mousetrap
misterija *f* mystery
misteriozan *adj* mysterious
mističan *adj* mystical
misticizam *m* mysticism
mistifikacija *f* mystification
mistika *f* mystique
mit *m* myth
miting *m* **1.** meeting **2.** (pol.) rally
mititi *v* to bribe
mito *n* **1.** bribe **2.** corruption
mitologija *f* mythology
mitraljez *m* machine-gun
mitropolit *m* metropolitan,
archbishop
mizeran *adj* miserable
mizerija *f* misery
mizogin *m* misogynist
mizoginija *f* misogyny
mjed *m* brass
mjehur *m* **1.** bladder **2.** bubble **3.**
blister
mjenica *f* (fin.) bill of exchange
mjenjačnica *f* (fin.) exchange
office
mjera *f* **1.** measure **2.** extent **3. po
mjeri** made to measure
mjerenje *n* measurement
mjerilo *n* criterion
mjeriti *v* to measure
mjeriti temperaturu *v* to take
someone's temperature
mjerodovan *adj* competent
mjesec *m* **1.** moon **2.** month **3.**
mladi mjesec new moon **4. puni
mjesec** full moon
mjesečina *f* moonlight
mjesečni *adj* monthly
mjesni *adj* local

mješavina *f* mixture
mješovit *adj* mixed
mještanin *m* townsman
mjestimice *adv* in places
mjesto 1. *n* place **2.** *prep* instead of
mjuzikl *m* musical
mlad *adj* **1.** young **2.** new
mlada *f* bride
mladenački *adj* youthful
mladenci *mpl* newlyweds
mladež *f* **1.** young people **2.** birth
mark
mladica *f* (plant) shoot
mladić *m* **1.** boy **2.** young man **3.**
boyfriend
mlado *adj/n* young
mladolik *adj* youthful
mladost *f* youth
mladoženja *f* bridegroom
mlađi *adj* **1.** younger **2.** junior
mlak *adj* lukewarm
mlatiti *v* to thresh
mlaz *m* **1.** jet **2.** beam
mlazni avion *m* jet plane
mleč *m* **1.** milt **2.** *see* **mleko**
mlečan *adj* **1.** milk **2.** milky
mlekadžija *f* milkman
mlekarstvo *n* dairy
mleko *n* milk
mleti *v* to grind
mliječni *adj* milk
mliječni proizvodi *pl* dairy
products
mlijeko *n* milk
mlin *m* mill
mlinac *m* grinder
mlinar *m* miller
mlitav *adj* **1.** limp **2.** slack
mljekar *m* milkman
mljekara *f* dairy
mljekarstvo *n* dairy farming
mljeti *v* to grind

mljeven *adj* ground
mlohav *adj* 1. flabby 2. loose
mnenje, mnijenje *n* opinion
mnogi *adj* many
mnogo *adv* much
mnogoboštvo *n* polytheism
mnogobrojan *adj* numerous
mnogojezički *adj* multilingual
mnogostran *adj* versatile
mnogostruk *m* 1. complex 2. varied
mnogoženstvo *n* polygamy
mnoštvo *n* crowd
množenje *n* multiplication
množina *f* plural
množiti *v* to multiply
mobilan *adj* mobile
mobilisati (se) *v* to mobilize
mobilizacija *f* mobilization
močti *v* to wet
močvara *f* marsh
močvaran *adj* marshy
moć *f* power
moćan *adj* powerful
moći 1. *fpl* (rel.) relics 2. *v* to be able
moda *f* 1. fashion 2. **u modi** in vogue
modar *m* dark blue
model *m* model, mannequin
modelar *m* model-maker
modem *m* modem
moderan *adj* modern
modernizovati *v* to modernize
modifikovati *v* to modify
modna revija *f* fashion show
modni *adj* fashion
modrica *f* bruise
modus *m* way
moguć *adj* possible
moguće *adj* possibly
mogućnost *f* possibility

moj 1. my 2. mine
moji *mpl* my family
mokar *m* 1. wet 2. damp
mokraća *f* urine
mokrenje *n* urination
mokriti *v* to urinate
mol *m* 1. embankment 2. (mus.) minor
molba *f* 1. request 2. application
molekul molecule
moler *m* house-painter
molilac *m* 1. applicant 2. claimant
moliti *v* 1. to ask 2. to request 3. to pray
molitva *f* prayer
molitvenik *n* prayer-book
moljac *m* moth
moljakati *v* to pester with questions
molo *n* jetty
momački *adj* bachelor
momak *m* 1. bachelor 2. boy
momčad *f* team
momčić *m* lad
moment, momenat *m* moment
monah *m* monk
monahinja *f* nun
monarh *m* monarch
monarhija *f* monarchy
monarhista *f* monarchist
monden *adj* 1. *adj* fashionable 2. *n* jetsetter
moneta *f* 1. money 2. currency
monetarni *adj* monetary
monitor *m* (tel.) monitor
monogamija *f* monogamy
monolog *m* monologue
monopol *m* monopoly
monopolizovati *v* to monopolize
monoteizam *m* monotheism
monoton *adj* monotonous
monotonija *f* monotony

monstrum *m* monster
monstruozan *adj* monstrous
monsun *m* monsoon
montaža *f* 1. installation 2. film/ sound editing
montažni *adj* prefabricated
monter *m* fitter
montirati *v* 1. to instal 2. to edit film/sound
monumentalan *adj* monumental
moped *m* moped
mora *f* nightmare
moral *m* 1. morals 2. morale
moralan *adj* moral
moralnost *f* morality
morati *v* must, to have to
morbidan *adj* morbid
more *n* 1. sea 2. **po moru** by sea 3. **u moru** overboard
moreplovac *m* seaman
moreuz *m* straits
morfijum *m* morphine
mornar *m* sailor
mornarica *f* 1. navy 2. fleet
mornarički *adj* naval
morska bolest *f* sea-sickness
morski *adj* 1. sea 2. maritime
morski pas *m* shark
mortalitet *m* mortality
moruna *f* sturgeon
morž *m* walrus
mošnice *n* 1. scrotum 2. testicles
mošti *v* relics
most *f* 1. bridge 2. **viseći most** suspension bridge
mostarina *f* bridge toll
mostić *m* footbridge
mostobran *adj* (mil.) bridgehead
motati se *v* to meddle
motati *v* to wind up
motati *v* to wind up, roll up
motel *m* motel

motika *f* hoe
motiv *adj* 1. motive 2. motif
motivacija *f* motivation
motka *f* pole
motocikl *m* motorcycle
motociklist *m* motor cyclist
motor *m* engine
motorni čamac *m* 1. motor boat 2. cruiser
motriti *v* to watch
mozaik *m* mosaic
mozak *m* brain
možda *adv* perhaps
moždina *f* 1. marrow 2. **leđna moždina** spinal cord 3. **koštana moždina** bone marrow
mračan *adj* dark
mrak *m* darkness
mramor *m* marble
mramorni *adj* marble
mrav *m* ant
mravinjak *m* anthill
mraz *m* 1. frost 2. **ofuren od mraza** frostbitten
mrazom oštetiti *v* to make frostbitten
mrcvariti *v* 1. to mangle 2. to torture
mrdati *v* to move, stir
mrena *f* (med.) cataract
mreškast *adj* wrinkled
mreškati se *v* to ripple
mreža *f* 1. net 2. hammock 3. bag 4. network
mrežnica, mrežnjača *f* retina
mrgoditi se *v* 1. to sulk 2. to frown
mrijestiti se *v* to spawn
mrk *adj* 1. sulky 2. gloomy 3. dark 4. brown
mrki ugalj *m* brown coal
mrko *adv* darkly
mrkva *f* carrot

mrlja *f* stain
mrljati *v* to stain
mrmljati *v* to mutter
mrsko: mrsko mi je... I hate to.....
mrskost *f* odiousness
mršav *adj* thin
mršaviti *v* to lose weight
mršavljenje *n* slimming
mrtav *adj* dead
mrtva priroda *f* still life
mrtva sezona *f* off season
mrtvac *m* dead person
mrtvačka kola *f* hearse
mrtvačka ukočenost *f* rigor
  mortis
mrtvačnica *f* morgue; mortuary
mrtvi *pl* the dead
mrtvilo *adv* lethargy
mrtvorođen *adj* stillborn
mrtvorođenče *n* stillborn child
mrtvorođenje *n* stillbirth
mrva, mrvica *f* crumb
mrviti *v* to crumble
mrzak *m* hateful
mrzeti, mrziti, mrjeti *v* to hate
mrzovoljan *adj* surly
mržnja *f* hatred
mržnja prema strancima *f*
  xenophobia
mržnja prema ženama *f* misogyny
mucanje *n* stammering
mucati *v* to stammer
mučan *adj* painful
mučenik *adj* martyr
mučeništvo *n* martyrdom
mučenje *n* 1. torture 2. **sprave za
  mučenje** torture instruments
mučilac *m* torturer
mučilište *n* torture chamber
mučiti *v* to torture
mučiti se *v* to suffer
mučki *adj* treacherously

mučnina *f* 1. nausea 2. pain
mućkati *v* to shake
mudar *adj* wise
mudo *n* testicle
mudrac *m* wise man
mudrost *f* wisdom
mudrovanje *n* speculation
mudrovati *v* to speculate
muha *f* fly
mujezin *m* muezzin
muk *m* stillness
muka *f* 1. suffering 2. torture 3.
  morning sickness
mukao *adj* 1. dull 2. hollow
mukaš *m* sponger
mukati *v* to moo
mukotrpan *adj* painstaking
mula 1. *f* mule 2. *m* mullah
mulj *m* 1. mud 2. silt
muljati grožđe *v* to press grapes
multinacionalni *adj* multinational
mumija *f* mummy
mumlati, mumljati *v* to mumble
municija *f* ammunition
municija *f* munitions
munja *f* lightning
munuti *v* to shove
muskulatura *f* musculature
Musliman *adj* Muslim
muslimanski *adj* Muslim
mušica *f* 1. midge 2. whim
muška dominicija *f* sexism
muškarac *m* 1. male 2. man
muški *adj* 1. male 2. masculine
mušterija *f* 1. customer 2. client
musti *v* to milk
mustra *f* 1. sample 2. design
mutan *adj* 1. muddy 2. vague
muta *m/f* mute
mutacija *f* mutation
mutan *adj* troubled
mutav *adj* mute

mutikasa *m/f* troublemaker
mutilica *f* mixer
mutirati *v* to mutate
mutiti *v* to trouble
muva *f* fly
muza *f* muse
muzej *m* museum
muzejski *adj* museum

muzičar *m* musician
muzicirati *v* (mus.) to play
muzika *f* music
muzikalan *adj* musical
muž *m* 1. husband 2. man
muževan *adj* virile
muževnost *f* virility
mužjak *m* male

N

na *prep* 1. on 2. at 3. with 4. for 5. **na to** after that 6. **na engleskom jeziku** in English
na! here you are!
nabaciti *v* 1. to put on 2. to throw in 3. to suggest
nabasati *v* to run into
nabava *f* 1. purchase 2. supply
nabaviti *v* to acquire
nabavljač *m* 1. buyer 2. supplier
nabavljati *v* 1. to buy 2. to supply
nabiti *v* 1. to ram 2. to hit 3. to charge 4. to load
naboj *m* 1. cartridge 2. charge
nabor *m* fold
naborati *v* to wrinkle
nabrajanje *n* listing
nabrajati *v* to list
nabrati se *v* to hope
nabreknuti *v* to swell
nabuhao *f* swelling
nabujati *v* to rise up
nabusit*adj* bad-tempered
načas *adv* 1. at once 2. for a while
nacifran *adj* dressed up
nacija *f* nation
nacionalan *adj* national
nacionalist(a) *m* nationalist
nacionalizacija *f* nationalization
nacionalizam *m* nationalism
nacionalizirati, nacionalizovati *v* to nationalize
nacionalna država *f* nation state
nacionalni park *m* national park
nacionalnost *f* nationality
nacist(a) *m* nazi
nacistički *adj* nazi

nacizam *m* nazism
nacrt *m* 1. plan 2. design 3. draft
nacrtati *v* to draw
načelan *adj* fundamental
načelnik *m* 1. head 2. mayor
načelo *n* principle
načeti *v* to cut into
način *m* 1. manner 2. **na taj način** in this way
načiniti *v* 1. to make 2. to commit
načinjen *adj* made
načisto *adv* 1. clearly 2. well
načitan *adj* well-read
načuti *v* to hear about
naći *v* to find
naći se *v* 1. to meet 2. to end up 3. to be located
nad, nada *prep* over
nada *f* hope
nadahnuti *v* to inspire
nadahnuće *n* inspiration
nadaleko *adv* 1. far 2. at a distance
nadalje *adv* 1. further 2. furthermore
nadanje *n* hope, hoping
nadaren *adj* talented
nadarenost *f* talent
nadasve *adv* above all
nadati se *v* to hope
nadbiskup *m* archbishop
nadbubrežni *adj* adrenal
nadčovječan *adj* superhuman
nadesno *adv* to the right
nadev *m* stuffing
nadglasati *v* to outvote
nadgledanje prekida vatre *n* truce supervision

nadgledati *v* 1. to inspect 2. to supervise

nadglednik *m* 1. inspector 2. supervisor

nadgradnja *f* superstructure

nadgrobni *adj* grave

nadimak *m* nickname

nadiranje *n* 1. advance 2. penetration

nadirati *v* 1. to advance 2. to penetrate

nadjenuti *v* to stuff

nadlaktica *f* (upper) arm

nadležan *adj* 1. competent 2. in charge

nadležnost *f* 1. competence 2. authority 3. jurisdiction

nadluh *adj* hard of hearing

nadmašiti *v* to excel

nadmetanje *n* competition

nadmetati se *v* 1. to compete 2. to bid

nadmoć *f* superiority

nadmoćan *adj* superior

nadmoćnost *f* superiority

nadmudriti *v* to outwit

nadmudrivati se *v* to quibble

nadnaravan *adj* supernatural

nadnica *f* (daily) wages

nadničar *m* (day) labourer

nadobudan *adj* 1. promising 2. ambitious 3. naive

nadograditi *v* to extend (a building)

nadogradnja *f* (building) extension

nadoknada *f* compensation

nadole *adv* down

nadomak *adj* near

nadomestiti *v* to replace

nadovezati *v* 1. to tie to 2. to add

nadoći *v* to rise

nadražaj *m* 1. stimulus 2. irritation

nadražiti *v* 1. to stimulate 2. to irritate

nadrealist(a) *m* surrealist

nadrealistički *adj* surreal

nadrealizam *m* surrealism

nadstojnik *m* caretaker; janitor

nadut *adj* 1. inflated 2. arrogant

naduti, naduvati *v* to inflate

nadvikivati se *v* to vie with one another

nadvisiti *v* to be be higher

nadvladati *v* to overcome

nadvoje *adv* in two

nadvožnjak *m* overpass

nadzemaljski *adj* supernatural

nadzemni *adj* overground, surface

nadzirati *v* 1. to inspect 2. to supervise

nadzor *m* 1. inspection 2. supervision

nadzorni *adj* supervisory

nadzornica *f* (med.) matron

nadzornik *m* 1. inspector 2. supervisor

nadzvučni *adj* supersonic

nadživeti *v* to outlive, survive

nadživjeti *v* to outlive

naelektrisati *v* to turn on

nafora *f* water

nafta *f* 1. oil 2. petroleum 3. **izvor nafte** oil well 4. **prosipanje nafte** oil spill

naftna mrlja *f* oil slick

naftonosan *adj* oil-bearing

naftovod *m* oil pipeline

nag *adj* naked

nagađanje *n* guesswork

nagađati *v* to guess

nagao *adj* 1. sudden 2. rash

nagaziti *v* 1. to step on, 2. to come across

nagib *m* 1. incline 2. inclination

naginjati *v* 1. to incline 2. to tend
naglas *adv* aloud
naglasak *m* stress
naglasiti *v* to stress
naglavce *n* 1. headlong 2. upside down
naglavne slušalice *fpl* earphones
naglo *adv* abruptly
nagluv *adj* hard of hearing
nagnut *adj* inclined
nagnuti *v* to incline
nagodba *f* 1. agreement 2. settlement
nagoditi se *v* to reach an agreement
nagomilati, nagomilavati *v* 1. to accumulate 2. to stockpile
nagomilavanje *n* accumulation
nagon *m* instinct
nagost *f* nudity
nagovarati *v* to persuade
nagovestiti, nagovijestiti *v* 1. to announce 2. to hint
nagovještaj *m* 1. announcement 2. hint
nagovor *m* 1. persuasion 2. address
nagovoriti *v* 1. to persuade 2. to address
nagrada *f* 1. reward 2. prize
nagraditi *v* to reward
nagradni *adj* prize
nagrditi *v* to deform
nagrizanje *n* corrosion
nagrizati *v* to corrode
nagrnuti *v* to crowd
nahraniti *v* to feed
nahuškati *v* to urge on
naime... that is to say,...
naimenovani kandidat *m* candidate
naimenovanje *n* 1. appointment 2. nomination

naimenovati *v* 1. to appoint 2. to nominate
naivan *adj* naive
naivko *m*, **naivka** *f* naive person
naizmence *adv* alternately
naizmeničan *adj* 1. alternate 2. alternating
naizmjence *see* **naizmence**
naizust *adv* by heart
naići na *v* to come across
najam *m* 1. rent 2. hire
najamnik *m* mercenary
najamnina *f* rent
najava *f* announcement
najaviti *v* to announce
najavljivač *m* announcer
najbliži *adj* nearest
najbolji *adj* the best
najdalji *adj* furthest
najdraži *adj* favourite
najedanput *adv* all at once
najednom *adv* suddenly
najesti se *v* to be full up
najezda *f* invasion
najgori *adj* worst
najgornji *adj* uppermost
najlon *m* nylon
najlon-kesica *f* plastic bag
najlonke *fpl* nylons
najmanje *adv* 1. least 2. at least 3. **ni najmanje** not at all
najmiti *v* to rent
najmodavac *m* lessor
najmoprimac *m* lessee
najniži *adj* lowest
najnovije vesti/vijesti *fpl* the latest news
najnoviji *adj* latest
najpre *adv* first of all
najpreči *adj* most important
najprije *adv* first
najradije *adv* preferably

najuriti *v* to throw out
najveća brzina *f* top speed
najveći *adj* greatest
najviše *adv* 1. most 2. at most
najzad *adv* finally
nakalemiti *v* to graft
nakaza *f* monster
nakazan *adj* monstrous
nakaznost *f* monstrosity
nakiseo *adj* sour
nakit *m* jewellery
nakiti *v* to accumulate
nakladnik *m* publisher
naklapati *v* 1. to chatter 2. to gossip
naklon *m* bow
naklonost *f* 1. favour 2. inclination
naknada *f* 1. compensation 2. reparation
naknada štete *f* (leg.) damages
naknaditi *v* to compensate
naknadno *adv* subsequently
nakon *prep* after
nakraj *prep* at the end of, extremely
nakratko *adv* briefly
nakrcati *v* 1. to load 2. pack
nakrenuti, nakriviti *v* to tilt
nakresan *adj* tipsy
nakriviti *v* to distort
nakriv, nakrivljen *adj* crooked
nakupac *m* dealer
nakupovati *v* to purchase
nalaz *m* finding
nalazač *m* finder
nalazište *n* 1. deposit 2. discovery 3. **nalažista rude** ore deposits
nalaziti se *v* to be situated
nalepiti *v* to stick on
nalepnica, naljepnica *f* 1. sticker 2. label
naletjeti *v* to crash into
nalevo *adv* to the left

naličje *n* reverse
nalijepiti *v* to stick on
nalik *adj* resembling
naliti *v* to pour
naliv-pero *n* fountain pen
naljepnica *f* sticker
naljutiti *v* to madden
nalog *m* 1. order 2. (leg.) warrant
nalog za pretres/premetačinu *m* search warrant
naložiti *v* to order
nama to/for us
namamiti *v* to entice
namena *f* purpose
nameniti *v* 1. to assign 2. to dedicate
namera *f* intention
namerno *adv* on purpose
namesnik *m* 1. deputy 2. regent
namesništvo *n* 1. deputyship 2. regency
namestiti *v* 1. to place 2. to arrange 3. to employ 4. to tune in
nameštaj *m* furniture
nameštenik *m* employee
nameštenje *n* employment
namet *m* 1. rate 2. tax
nametljivac *m* intruder
nametnik *m* parasite
nametnuti *v* to impose
nametnuti se *v* 1. to intrude 2. to arise
namignuti *v* to wink at
namijeniti *v* to intend
namirisati *v* to perfume
namiriti *v* 1. to pay 2. to settle
namirnica *f* foodstuff
namirnice *fpl* provisions
namjena *f* purpose
namjeniti *v* 1. to assign 2. to dedicate
namjera *f* intention

namjeravati *v* to intend
namjerno *adv* on purpose
namjesnik *m* 1. deputy 2. regent
namjesništvo *n* 1. deputyship 2. regency
namještaj *m* furniture
namješten *adj* 1. employed 2. irregular
namještenik *m* employee
namještenje *n* employment
namjestiti *v* 1. to place 2. to arrange 3. to employ 4. to tune in
namjestiti *v* to tune in
namjet *m* 1. rate 2. tax
namjetljivac *m* intruder
namjetnik *m* parasite
namjetnuti *v* to impose
namjetnuti se *v* 1. to intrude 2. to arise
namnožiti se *v* to multiply
namočiti *v* to dip
namotati *v* to wind up
namrgoditi se, namrštiti se *v* to frown
namršten *adj* gloomy
nana *f* mint
nanijeti *v* 1. to deposit 2. to plot a course
naniže *adv* downwards
nanos *m* deposit
nanos snega/snijega *m* snow bank, snow drift
nanula *f* sandal
nanjušiti *v* 1. to smell 2. to get wind of
naoblačen *adj* cloudy
naoblačiti se *v* to become cloudy
naobrazba *f* education
naobraziti se *v* to educate
naobražen *adj* educated
naočale, naočare *fpl* 1. glasses 2. sunglasses

naočare za sunce *fpl* sunglasses
naočarka *f* cobra
naočigled 1. *prep* in sight of 2. *adv* visibly
naočit *adj* handsome
naoko *adv* apparently
naokolo *adv* around
naopak *adj* 1. evil 2. wrong 3. upside-down 4. reversed
naopako *adv* 1. wrong 2. upside-down 3. reversed
naoružan *adj* armed
naoružanje *n* arms
naoružati *v* to arm
naoružati se *v* to arm oneself
naoštren *adj* sharpened
napad *m* 1. attack 2. air raid
napadač *m* 1. attacker 2. aggressor
napadaj *m* (med.) attack
napadan *adj* striking
napadati *v* to attack
napakostiti *v* to spite
napalm *m* napalm
napamet *adv* by heart
napasnik *m* tempter
napast *f* temptation
napasti *v* to attack
napastovati *v* 1. to tempt 2. to rape
napatiti *v* to wear out
napatiti se *v* to suffer
naperiti *v* to aim at
napet *adj* 1. tight 2. tense 3. cocked
napeti *v* 1. to tighten 2. to tense 3. to cock
napeto *adv* intently
napetost *f* 1. tension 2. strain
napipati *v* to touch
napisati *v* to write
napismeno *adv* in writing
napitak *m* drink

napiti *v* to make drunk
napiti se *v* to get drunk
naplakati se *v* to wail
naplata *f* 1. charge 2. collection
naplatiti *v* 1. to charge 2. to collect
napojiti *v* to water
napojnica *f* tip
napokon *adv* finally
napol, napola *adv* partly
napolju *adv* outside
napomena *f* remark
napomenuti *v* to remark
napon *m* 1. tension 2. voltage 3. visoki napon high tension
napor *m* effort
naporan *adj* strenuous
naporedan *adj* parallel
naporedo *adv* at the same time
naporno *adv* hard
napose *adv* separately
naposletku *adv* finally
naprasan *adj* sudden
naprasit *adj* short-tempered
naprašiti *v* to powder
naprava *f* 1. device 2. appliance
napraviti *v* 1. to make 2. to commit 3. to accomplish
naprečac *adv* suddenly
napred *adv* 1. forward 2. in front
napredak *m* 1. progress 2. growth
napredan *adj* progressive
napredovanje *n* 1. progress 2. promotion 3. (mil.) advance
napredovati *v* 1. to progress 2. to grow 3. to be promoted 4. (mil.) to advance
napredovati *v* to progress, advance, make progress
napregnut *adj* strained
naprezati *v* to exert
naprijed *adv* forward
naprosto *adv* simply

naprotiv *adj* on the contrary
napršnjak *m* bib
naprstak *m* thimble
naprtiti *v* to burden
naprtnajača *f* backpack
napuhati *v* to inflate
napukao *adj* cracked
napuklina *f* crack
napuknuti *v* to crack
napumpati *v* to pump up
napuniti *v* to fill up
napuštanje *n* 1. abandoning 2. withdrawal
napustiti *v* 1. to abandon 2. to give up 3. to withdraw from
nar *m* pomegranate
naramenica *f* suspenders
naranča, narandža *f* orange
narančast *adj* orange
naraštaj *m* generation
narasti *v* 1. to grow 2. to grow up
narav *f* nature
naravan *adj* natural
naravno *adv* naturally
narcis *m* narcissus
narečje *n* dialect
naredan *adj* next
naredba *f* order
narediti *v* to order
narednik *m* sergeant
narezak *m* cutlet
narječje *n* dialect
narkoman *m* drug addict
narkomanija *f* drug addiction
narkotik *m* narcotic
narkoza *f* drug
naročit *adj* special
naročito *adv* especially
narod *m* 1. people 2. ethnic group 3. nation
narodan *adj* national
narodna pravda *f* lynch-law

narodna vojska f militia
narodnooslobodilački adj of national liberation
narodnost f nationality
naručaj m 1. armful 2. hug
naručen adj (com.) ordered
naručiti v (com.) to order
naručje n arms
narudžba f (com.) order
narudžbenica f order form
narukvica f bracelet
narumeniti, narumjeniti v to redden
narušiti v to disturb
nas us
nasadi mpl gardens
nasamariti v to deceive
nasamariti nekoga v to pull someone's leg
nasamo adv privately
naseckati v to chop
naseliti v to settle
naselje n 1. settlement 2. housing estate
naseljen adj populated
naseljenik m 1. settler 2. bespravni naseljenik squatter
naseljenost f population
nasilan adj violent
nasilje n violence
nasilnik m 1. tyrant 2. bully
nasilno adv violently
nasip m 1. embankment 2. dyke; dike
nasipati v to fill (up)
nasititi se v to eat one's fill
nasjesti v to be deceived
naslada f delight
naslaga f layer
naslagati v to stack
naslanjati v to lean (na on)
naslađivati se v to enjoy

naslediti v 1. to inherit 2. to succeed to
naslednik m 1. heir 2. successor
nasledstvo n 1. inheritance 2. heredity
naslepo adv blindly
naslijediti v 1. to inherit 2. to succeed
naslikati v to paint
nasljedan adj hereditary
nasljednik m 1. heir 2. successor
nasljedstvo n 1. inheritance 2. heredity
naslon m 1. back 2. support
naslonjač, naslonjača f armchair
naslov m 1. title 2. headline
naslućivati v to have a premonition
nasmejan adj jolly
nasmejati v to make somebody laugh
nasmešiti se v to smile
nasmijati v to make somebody laugh
nasmijati se v to laugh
nasmiješiti se v to smile
naspavati se v to have a good sleep
nasred prep in the middle of
nasrnuti v to attack
nasrtaj m attack
nasrtljiv adj aggressive
nasrtljivost f aggression
naš 1. our 2. ours
našaliti se v to make a joke
naši mpl our people
naširoko adv 1. far and wide 2. in detail
naškoditi v 1. to harm 2. to damage
nastajati v to arise
nastamba f quarters

nastanak *m* origin
nastaniti *v* to accommodate
nastaniti se *v* 1. to find accommodation 2. to settle
nastanjen *adj* 1. populated 2. occupied
nastanjen u *m* resident of
nastati *v* to begin
nastava *f* teaching
nastavak *m* 1. continuation 2. suffix
nastaviti *v* to continue
nastavni *adj* educational
nastavni plan *adj* curriculum
nastavničko osoblje *n* teaching staff
nastavnik *m* teacher
nastavno osoblje *n* teaching staff
nastojaje *n* effort
nastojati *v* to try
nastojnik *m* caretaker; janitor
nastradati *v* to have an accident
nastran *adj* peculiar
nastranost *f* peculiarity
nastrešnica *f* eaves
nastup *m* appearance
nastupajući *adj* coming
nastupati, nastupiti *v* 1. to appear 2. to behave
nasukati *v* to strand
nasukati se *v* to run aground
nasumce *adv* at random
nasuprot *prep/adv* 1. opposite 2. vis-à-vis
nasuti *v* to cover
nat *m* seam
nataknuti *v* 1. to put on 2. to pierce
natalitet *m* birthrate
natapanje *n* 1. irrigation 2. impregnation
natapati *v* to irrigate
natašte *adv* on an empty stomach

nataći *v* to put on
natčovek *m* superman
natčulan *adj* supersensory
natečaj *m* competition
natečen *adj* swollen
nategnuti *v* to tighten
natenane *adv* 1. at leisure 2. in great detail
natezati *v* to stretch
natezati se *v* to wrangle
nateći *v* to swell
natječaj *m* 1. competition 2. application
natjecanje *n* competition
natjecatelj *m* 1. competitor 2. applicant
natjecati se *v* 1. to compete 2. to make an application
natjerati *v* to force
natmuren *adj* 1. gloomy 2. overcast
na to after that
natočiti *v* to pour out
natovariti *v* 1. to load up 2. to burden with
natpis *m* sign
natprirodan *adj* supernatural
natprosječan *adj* above average
natrag *m* back
natraške *adv* backwards
natražnjački *adj* reactionary
natražnjak *m* reactionary
natrij, natrijum *m* sodium
natrpan *adj* 1. overfilled 2. overcrowded
natrpati *v* to stuff
natucati *v* to speak badly
natuknuti *v* to hint at
natura *f* 1. nature 2. kind
naturalizacija *f* naturalization
naturalizovati *v* to naturalize
naturiti *v* to impose

natući v 1. to ram 2. to hit 3. to charge 4. to load

naučan adj 1. scientific 2. academic 3. research

naučenjak m 1. scientist 2. academic

naučiti v 1. to learn 2. to teach

naučiti v to learn, teach, instruct

naučna fantastika f science fiction

naučni rad m research

naučni radnik m researcher

naučni adj scholarly, scientific, learned

naučnik m 1. scholar 2. scientist 3. apprentice

naučno adv scientifically

nauka f 1. science 2. knowledge 3. study 4. apprenticeship

nauljiti v to oil

naušnica f earring

nautika f sailing

navala f 1. attack 2. rush

navaliti, navaljivati v 1. to attack 2. to urge

navečer m 1. in the evening 2. danas navečer tonight

naveliko adv 1. prodaja naveliko wholesale 2. prodavati naveliko to wholesale

navesti v 1. to induce 2. to specify 3. to quote

navijač m supporter

navijati v to support

navijestiti v to announce

navika f habit

navikao adj accustomed to

naviknuti v to accustom

naviknuti se v to get used to

navlaka f cover

navlažiti v to moisturize

navod m 1. statement 2. allegation

navoditi v 1. to state 2. to allege

navodni adj alleged

navodnice fpl quotation marks

navodnjavanje n irrigation

navodnjavati v to irrigate

navodno adv allegedly

navođenje n quotation

navoj m coil

navorati se v to wrinkle

navrat f time

navratiti v to drop by

navrh prep at the top of

navršiti v (med.) to recur

navrtanj m (metal) nut

navući v 1. to put on 2. to incur 3. to catch

nazad adv backward

nazadak m decline

nazadan adj 1. backward 2. reactionary

nazadnjaštvo n reaction

nazadovati v to regress

nazdraviti v to toast

nazdravlje! cheers!

nazeb m cold

nazepsti v to catch a cold

naziv m name

nazivati v to name

naznačiti v to denote

nazočan adj present

nazočnost f presence

nazor m 1. idea 2. opinion

nazovi adj 1. pseudo- 2. so-called 3. would-be

nazvati v to call

nažaliti (se) v to regret

nažao adj učiniti ... nažao to offend somebody

nažuljati v to make sore

ne 1. no 2. not

neadekvatan adj inadequate

neafirmiran adj unestablished

neaktivan *adj* inactive
neartikularan *adj* inarticulate
nebesa *f* heavens
nebeski *adj* heavenly
nebitan *adj* not essential
nebo *n* 1. sky 2. heaven 3. pod vedrim nebom outdoor
neboder *m* skyscraper
nebriga *f* indifferent
nebriga *f* indifference
nebrojen *adj* countless
nečastan *adj* dishonest
nečiji *adj* somebody's
nečist *adj* 1. dirty 2. bad 3. dishonest
nečistoća *f* dirt
nečitak, nečitljiv *adj* illegible
nečovečan *adj* brutal
nečovečno *adv* brutally
nečovek *m* brute
nečovječan *adj* brutal
nečujan *adj* inaudible
nečuven *adj* extraordinary
nećak *m* nephew
nećaka, nećinja *f* niece
nećkanje *n* reluctance
nećkati se *v* to be reluctant
nedaleko *adv* nearby
nedarovit *adj* talentless
nedavan, nedavni *adj* recent
nedavno *adv* recently
nedaća *f* 1. difficulty 2. setback
nedelja *f* 1. Sunday 2. weekend 3. week
nedeljiv *adj* indivisible
nedeljni *adj* weekly
nedelo *n* crime
nedirnut *adj* untouched
nedisciplina *f* indiscipline
nedjelja *f* 1. Sunday 2. weekend 3. week
nedjeljiv *adj* indivisible
nedjelo *n* crime

nedobronamjeran *adj* malevolent
nedogled: u nedogled as far as the eye can see
nedogledan *adj* immense
nedohvatljiv *adj* unreachable
nedokaziv *adj* not provable
nedokučiv *adj* inconceivable
nedolazak *m* absence
nedoličan *adj* indecent
nedonošče *n* 1. premature child 2. abortive attempt
nedopušten *adj* forbidden
nedopustiv *adj* inadmissible
nedorađen *adj* incomplete
nedorastao *adj* 1. immature 2. underage
nedorečen *adj* understated
nedorečenost *f* understatement
nedosledan, nedosljedan *adj* inconsistent
nedoslednost, nedosljednost *f* inconsistency
nedostajati *v* to lack
nedostatak *m* 1. lack 2. drawback
nedostatan *adj* insufficient
nedostižan *adj* 1. unattainable 2. matchless
nedostojan *adj* 1. unworthy 2. dishonest
nedoumica *f* 1. dilemma 2. hesitation
nedovoljan *adj* insufficient
nedovršen *adj* incomplete
nedozreo *adj* 1. immature 2. unripe
nedozvoljen *adj* forbidden
nedra *f* breast, bosom
nedruštven *adj* unsociable
nedužan *adj* 1. innocent 2. harmless
nedvojben *adj* certain
neefikasan *adj* ineffective
nega *f* care
negacija *f* negation

negativ *m* negative
negativan *adj* negative
negativno *adv* negatively
negde, negdje somewhere
negirati *v* 1. to deny 2. to reject
nego *conj* 1. than 2. apart from
negodovanje *n* disapproval
negodovati *v* to disapprove
negostoljubiv *adj* inhospitable
negovateljica *f* nurse
negovati *v* to nurse
nehaj *m* indifference
nehat *m* carelessness
nehatan *adj* derelict
nehotičan *adj* accidental
nehotice *n* accidentally
neidentifikovan *adj* unidentified
**neidentifikovani leteći objekt
(NLO)** *m* unidentified flying
object (UFO)
neimaština *f* poverty
neimenovan *adj* unnamed
neiscrpan *adj* inexhaustible
neishranjen *adj* malnourished
neishranjenost *f* malnutrition
neiskazan *adj* unsaid
neiskorišten *adj* unused
neiskorjenjiv *adj* ineradicable
neiskren *adj* 1. insincere 2. false
neiskusan *adj* inexperienced
neiskustvo *n* inexperience
neiskvaren *adj* unspoiled
neiskvarenost *f* 1. honest 2.
simplicity
neispavan *adj* sleepy
neispitan *adj* unexplored
neisplaćen *adj* unpaid
neispravan *adj* 1. incorrect 2.
faulty 3. improper
neispravnost *f* fault
neispunjen *adj* 1. blank 2. unused
3. unfilled 4. unfulfilled

neistina *f* falsehood
neistinit *adj* untrue
neistražen *adj* 1. unexplored 2.
uninvestigated
neizazvan *adj* unprovoked
neizbježan *adj* inevitable
neizbježnost *f* inevitability
neizbrisiv *adj* indelible
neizdržljiv *adj* unbearable
neizgrađen *adj* 1. immature 2.
crude
neizlječiv *adj* incurable
neizmenljiv *adj* irreversible
neizmeran *adj* limitless
neizmijenjen *adj* unaltered
neizmirljiv *adj* irreconcilable
neizmjenljiv *adj* irreversible
neizmjeran *adj* limitless
neizostavan *adj* 1. infallible 2.
obligatory
neizostavno *adv* infallibly
neizravan *adj* indirect
neizreciv *adj* inexpressible
neizvediv *adj* unfeasible
neizvesnost, neizvjesnost *f*
uncertainty
neizvjestan *adj* uncertain
neizvježban *adj* untrained
nejak *adj* weak
nejasan *adj* indistinct
nejednak *m* unequal
nejednakost *f* inequality
neka, nek 1. let... 2. okay...
nekada *f* formerly
nekadašnji *adj* 1. former, ex- 2.
ancient
nekakav *adj* some
nekako somehow
nekamo somewhere
nekažnjen *adj* unpunished
neki *adj* 1. a 2. some 3. any
neknjiževan *adj* non-standard

neko somebody
nekolicina f a few, several
nekoliko 1. a few 2. some 3. any
nekorektan adj incorrect
nekoristan adj useless
nekretnina f real estate
nekrolog m obituary
nekud, nekuda 1. somewhere 2. anywhere
nekulturan adj uncultured
nekvalificiran adj 1. unqualified 2. unskilled
nekvalitetan adj inferior
nelagodan adj uneasy
nelagodnost f uneasiness
neljubazan adj 1. unkind 2. unfriendly
neljudski adj inhuman
nelogičan adj illogical
nelogičnost f illogicality
nelojalan adj disloyal
nem adj 1. mute 2. silent
nema... there is no..., there are no...
Nemac m, **Nemica** f German
Nemačka f Germany
nemački adj German
neman f monster
nemar m indolence
nemaran adj indolent
nemaština f poverty
nemati v to be without
nemerljiv adj immeasurable
nemešanje n non-intervention
nemilosrdan adj cruel
nemilost f disgrace
nemilostiv adj ruthless
neminovno adv unavoidable
nemio adj deplorable
nemir m 1. unrest 2. anxiety
nemir m unrest
nemiran adj 1. restless 2. anxious
nemiri mpl riots

nemoguć adj impossible
nemogućnost f impossibility
nemoj... do not...
nemoral m immorality
nemoralan adj immoral
nemoralnost f immorality
nemoć f 1. helplessness 2. weakness
nemoćan adj helpless
nenadmašan, nenadmašiv adj unsurpassable
nenadoknadiv adj irretrievable
nenadoknadiv adj modest
nenametljiv adj modest
nenamjeran adj unintentional
nenaoružan adj unarmed
nenapadanje n non-aggression
nenaplativ adj priceless
nenaseljen adj uninhabited
nenasit adj insatiable
nenastanjen adj uninhabited
nenormalan adj 1. abnormal 2. strange
neo- neo-
neobavešten adj uninformed
neobezbeđen, neobezbijeđen adj unprotected
neobičan adj unusual
neobično adv remarkably
neobjašnjiv adj inexplicable
neobljubljen adj unpopular
neoboriv adj irrefutable
neobrađen adj 1. uncultivated 2. crude
neobrazovan adj uneducated
neobučen adj undressed
neobuven adj barefoot
neobuzdan adj unrestrained
neobvezan adj optional
neobziran adj inconsiderate
neočekivan adj unexpected
neodgojen adj rude
neodgojenost f bad manners

neodgovoran *adj* irresponsible
neodgovornost *f* irresponsibility
neodložan *adj* urgent
neodlučan *adj* indecisive
neodlučan rezultat *m* (spor.) draw
neodlučnost *f* indecision
neodobravanje *n* disapproval
neodoljiv *adj* irresistible
neodređen *adj* 1. indefinite 2. uncertain
neodrživ *adj* untenable
neogovoran *adj* irresponsible
neogovornost *f* irresponsibility
neograničen *adj* unlimited absolute
neokolonijalizam neocolonialism
neokretan *adj* awkward
neokrnjen *adj* whole
neolaljan *adj* spotless
neon *m* neon
neonski *adj* neon
neonsko svetlo/svjetlo *n* neon light
neopasan *adj* harmless
neopažen *adj* unnoticed
neophodan *adj* indispensable
neopisiv *adj* indescribable
neopravdan *adj* unjustified
neopredeljen, neopredijeljen *adj* undecided
neoprezan *adj* thoughtless
neoprostiv *adj* inexcusable
neorganski *adj* inorganic
neorporan *adj* delicate
neosetljiv *adj* insensitive
neosetno *adv* imperceptibly
neosiguran *adj* 1. not secured 2. uninsured
neosjetan *adj* imperceptible
neosjetljiv *adj* numb
neosjetljivost *f* numbness
neoskvrnjen *adj* inviolate
neosnovan *adj* groundless

neosporan *adj* indisputable
neoštećen *adj* undamaged
neostvaren *adj* unrealized
neostvariv *adj* unattainable
neosvojiv *adj* 1. inaccessible 2. unconquerable
neotesan *adj* rude
neotporan *adj* non-resistant
neotuđiv *adj* inalienable
neovlašten *adj* unauthorized
neozbiljan *adj* trivial
neozbiljnost *f* insignificance
neozleđen *adj* unharmed
neoženjen *adj* unmarried, single
neparan *adj* odd
neparan broj *m* odd number
nepatvoren *adj* genuine
nepažljiv *adj* 1. inattentive 2. inconsiderate
nepažljivost *f* 1. inattention 2. lack of consideration
nepce *n* palate
nepčan *adj* palatal
nepečen *adj* underdone
nepibitan *adj* irrefutable
nepiduzetan *adj* unenterprising
nepiduzetnost *f* lack of enterprise
nepisan *adj* unwritten
nepismen *adj* illiterate
nepismenost *f* illiteracy
neplanski *adj* unplanned
neplaćanje *n* non-payment
neplodan *adj* 1. sterile 2. infertile
neplodnost *f* 1. sterility 2. infertility
nepobediv *adj* invincible
nepobitan *adj* irrefutable
nepobjediv *adj* invincible
nepodesan *adj* inconvenient
nepodmitljiv *adj* incorruptible
nepodnosiv, nepodnošljiv *adj* unbearable

nepodoban *adj* unfit, unsuitable
nepogoda *f* bad weather
nepogodan *adj* unsuitable
nepogrešiv *adj* infallible
nepokolebljiv *adj* unshakeable
nepokoran *adj* disobedient
nepokretan *adj* immovable, fixed
nepokretnostima *f* trgovac nepokretnostima estate agent; realtor
nepomirljiv *adj* irreconcilable
neponovljiv *adj* unique
nepopravljiv *adj* irreparable
nepopularan *adj* unpopular
nepopularnost *f* unpopularity
nepopunjen *adj* vacant
nepopustljiv *adj* relentless
neposluh *m* disobedience
neposlušan *adj* disobedient
neposlušnost *f* disobedience
neposredan *adj* direct
nepošten *adj* dishonest
nepoštenje *n* dishonesty
nepoštivanje *n* disrespect
nepostojan *adj* inconsistent
nepostojeći *adj* non-existent
nepotpun *adj* 1. incomplete 2. defective
nepotreban *adj* unnecessary
nepouzdan *adj* unreliable
nepoverljiv, nepovjerljiv *adj* distrustful
nepoverenje, nepovjerenje *n* distrust
nepovoljan *adj* unfavourable
nepovrediv *adj* inviolable
nepoznat *adj* unknown
nepoznavanje *n* ignorance
nepoželjan *adj* undesirable
nepraktičan *adj* impractical
nepravda *f* injustice
nepravedan *adj* unjust

nepravilan *adj* 1. incorrect 2. irregular
nepravilnost *f* irregularity
nepredvidiv *adj* unpredictable
nepredviđen *adj* unforeseen
nepregledan *adj* 1. vast 2. uneven
nepregledan *adj* immense, vast
neprekidan *adj* continuous
neprelazan *adj* intransitive
nepremostiv *adj* insurmountable
neprenosiv *adj* untransferable
neprestan *adj* ceaseless
neprestano *adv* continuously
nepresušan *adj* inexhaustible
nepretenciozan *adj* unpretentious
neprihvatljiv *adj* unacceptable
neprijatan *adj* unpleasant
neprijatelj *m* enemy
neprijatelj stranaca *m* xenophobe
neprijateljski *adj* hostile
neprijateljstvo *n* hostility
neprijatno *adv* awkwardly
neprijatnost *f* 1. unpleasantness 2. difficulty
neprijazan *adj* unkind
neprikladan *adj* unsuitable
npriličan *adj* indecent
neprilika *f* trouble
neprimjetan *adj* imperceptible
neprirodan *adj* unnatural
nepristojan *adj* 1. rude 2. indecent
nepristojnost *f* 1. rudeness 2. indecency
nepristran *adj* impartial
nepristrasan *adj* objective
nepristupačan *adj* inaccessible
nepritajateljevi projektili *mpl* (mil.) incoming fire
neprivlačan *adj* unattractive
neprobojan *adj* 1. impenetrable 2. bulletproof
neprocenjiv *adj* invaluable

neprohodan *adj* impassable
neprolazan *adj* permanent
nepromenljiv *adj* unchangeable
neprometan *adj* quiet
nepromišljen *adj* thoughtless
nepromjenljiv *adj* unchangeable
nepromočiv *adj* waterproof
nepropisan *adj* 1. illegal 2. irregular
nepropustan *adj* hermetically-sealed
neprovediv *adj* impracticable
neprovidan *adj* non-transparent
neproziran *adj* opaque
nepunoletan, nepunoljetan *adj* underage
nepušač *m* 1. non-smoker 2. za nepušače non-smoking
nerad *m* 1. inactivity 2. idleness
nerado *adv* unwillingly
neranjiv *adj* invulnerable
neraskidiv *adj* 1. unbreakable 2. permanent
neraspoložen *adj* 1. in a bad mood 2. depressed
neraspoloženje *n* bad mood
nerast *m* boar
nerastopiv *adj* insoluble
neravan *adj* 1. uneven 2. rough 3. rugged
neravnopravan *adj* unequal
nerazborit *adj* unreasonable
nerazborit *adj* unwise
nerazdvojan *adj* inseparable
nerazgovjetan *adj* unintelligible
nerazjašnjiv *adj* inexplicable
nerazješiv *adj* insoluble
nerazoriv *adj* indestructible
nerazuman *adj* unreasonable
nerazumijevanje *n* lack of comprehension
nerazumljiv *adj* incomprehensible

nerazvijen *adj* 1. undeveloped 2. underdeveloped
nerazvijenost *f* underdevelopment
nerđajući čelik *m* stainless steel
nerđajući *v* rustproof
nerealan *adj* unreal
nerealan *adj* unrealistic
nered *m* chaos
neredan *adj* untidy
neredi *mpl* rioting
neredovan, neredovit *adj* irregular
nerentabilan *adj* unprofitable
nerešen *adj* unsolved
nerešeni rezultat *m* (spor.) draw
nerešeno, neriješeno *n* (spor.) 1. draw 2. igrati nerešeno/neriješeno (spor.) to draw
nerješiv *adj* insoluble
nerodan *adj* 1. barren 2. unfruitful
nerodica *f* crop failure
nerv *m* nerve
nervčik *m* nervous person
nervirati *v* to make nervous
nervni bojni otrov *m* nerve gas
nervoza *f* nervousness
nervozan *adj* nervous
nesagoriv *adj* non-flammable
nesalomljiv *adj* unbreakable
nesamostalan *adj* dependent
nesanica *f* insomnia
nesavestan *adj* unscrupulous, dishonest
nesavjestan *adj* unconscientious
nesavladiv *adj* insurmountable
nesavladiv *adj* invincible
nesavršen *adj* imperfect
nesavršenost *f* imperfection
nescrpan *adj* inexhaustible
nesebičan *adj* unselfish
nesebičnost *f* unselfishness
neseser *m* vanity case
neshvatanje *n* misunderstanding

neshvatljiv *adj* incomprehensible
neshvaćanje *n* incomprehension
neshvaćen *adj* 1. misunderstood 2. unrecognized
nesiguran *adj* 1. unsafe 2. uncertain
nesimpatičan *adj* unpleasant
nesklad *m* 1. discrepancy 2. discord
nesklon *adj* reluctant
neskroman *adj* immodest
nesladan *adj* 1. disproportionate 2. discordant
neslaganje *n* disagreement
neslan *adj* unsalted
neslavan *adj* infamous
nesloga *f* discord
neslomljiv *adj* unbreakable
nesložan *adj* discordant
neslućen *adj* unsuspected
nesmanjen *adj* 1. unrelenting 2. apsolutna laž an unmitigated lie
nesmiljen *adj* merciless
nesmisao *adj* absurdity
nesmotren *adj* incautious
nesmotren *adj* inconsiderate
nesnalažljiv *adj* unresourceful
nesnosan *adj* intolerable
nesnošljiv *adj* intolerant
nesolidan *adj* 1. unreliable 2. inferior
nespavanje *n* insomnia
nespojiv *adj* incompatible
nesporazum *m* misunderstanding
nesposoban *adj* incapable
nespreman *adj* unprepared
nespretan *adj* clumsy
nesrazmeran *adj* disproportionate
nesreća *f* 1. bad luck 2. accident
nesrećan *adj* unlucky
nesređen *adj* 1. disorderly 2. unbalanced 3. unregulated
nesreslučaj *m* accident

nesretan *adj* unlucky
nesretnik *m* wretch
neškodljiv *adj* harmless
neškolovan *adj* uneducated
neštedimice *adv* lavishly
nešto something
nestabilan *adj* unstable
nestalan *adj* unsteady
nestali *adj* missing
nestaluk *m* prank
nestanak *m* disappearance
nestao *adj* missing
nestao u borbi *adj* missing in action
nestašan *adj* 1. playful 2. restless 3. wild
nestašica *f* shortage
nestašluk *m* mischief
nestati *v* to disappear
nesti *v* to lay eggs
nestrpljenje *n* impatience
nestrpljiv *adj* impatient
nestrpljivost *f* impatience
nestručan *adj* non-technical
nestručnjak *m* non-professional
nesuglasica *f* disagreement
nesumnjiv *adj* certain
nesumnjiv *adj* doubtless
nesuvisao *adj* incoherent
nesuvremen *adj* old-fashioned
nesvest *f* unconsciousness
nesvestan *adj* 1. unconscious 2. unaware
nesvestica *f* dizziness
nesvijest *f* unconsciousness
nesvijestan, nesvjestan *adj* 1. unconscious 2. unaware
nesvrstan *adj* non-aligned
nesvrstane zemlje *fpl* non-aligned nations
nesvrstavanje *n* non-alignment
netačan *adj* inaccurate

netačnost *f* inaccuracy
netaknut *adj* intact
netaktičan *adj* tactless
netko someone
neto *adj* (com/fin.) net
netočan *adj* inaccurate
netolerantan *adj* intolerant
netremice *adv* fixedly
netrpeljiv *adj* intolerant
netrpeljivost *f* intolerance
neubrojiv *adj* mentally unsound
neučtiv *adj* impolite
neudata *fadj* unmarried, single
neudoban *adj* uncomfortable
neuglađen *adj* uncouth
neugledan *adj* plain
neugodan *adj* unpleasant
neujednačen *adj* uneven
neuk *adj* uneducated
neukrotiv *adj* untameable
neukusan *adj* 1. tasteless 2. unrefined
neuljepšan *adj* plain
neuljudan *adj* impolite
neumeren, neumjeren *adj* immoderate
neumestan, neumjestan *adj* inappropriate
neumjeće *n* lack of skill
neumoljiv *adj* merciless
neumoran *adj* tireless
neumrli *adj* immortal
neuništiv *adj* indestructible
neunosan *adj* unprofitable
neuporediv *adj* incomparable
neupotrebljiv *adj* unsuitable
neupotrebljiv *adj* useless
neuputan *adj* inadvisable
neupućen *adj* uninformed
neuračunljiv *adj* irresponsible
neuralgija *f* neuralgia
neuravnotežen *adj* unbalanced

neuravnoteženost *f* instability
neuredan *adj* sloppy
neurolog *m* neurologist
neurologija *f* neurology
neurotičan *adj* neurotic
neuroza *f* neurosis
neuslužan *adj* unobliging
neuspeh, neuspjeh failure
neuspešan, neuspješan *adj* unsuccessful
neusporediv *adj* incomparable
neustrašiv *adj* fearless
neutješan *adj* broken-hearted
neutralan *adj* neutral
neutralnost *f* neutrality
neutrt *adj* untrodden
neuvažanje *n* disregard
neuviđavan *adj* inconsiderate
nevaljalac *m* rascal
nevaljao *adj* bad, wicked
nevaspitan *adj* spoilt
nevažići *adj* not valid
neven *m* marigold
neveran *adj* unfaithful
nevernik *m* unbeliever
neverovatan *adj* unbelievable
nevesao *adj* sad
nevesta *f* bride
nevezan *adj* informal
nevidljiv *adj* invisible
neviđen *adj* unseen
nevin *adj* innocent
nevinost *f* innocence
nevjeran *adj* unfaithful
nevjernik *m* unbeliever
nevjerojatan *adj* incredible
nevjerojatno *adv* incredibly
nevješt *adj* unskilled
nevjesta *f* bride
nevolja *f* trouble
nevreme, nevrijeme *n* storm
nezaboravan *adj* unforgettable

nezadovoljan *adj* discontented
nezadovoljnik *m* malcontent
nezadovoljstvo *n* 1. discontent 2. dissatisfaction
nezahvalan *adj* ungrateful
nezahvalnost *f* ingratitude
nezainteresiran *adj* uninterested
nezainteresiranost *f* lack of interest
nezakonit *adj* 1. illegal 2. illegitimate
nezamjenljiv *adj* irreplaceable
nezanimljiv *adj* uninteresting
nezapaljiv *adj* non-flammable
nezapamćen *adj* unprecedented
nezapažen *adj* unnoticed
nezaposlen *adj* unemployed
nezaposlenost *f* unemployment
nezapošljiv *adj* unemployable
nezasitan *adj* insatiable
nezaštićen *adj* unprotected
nezavidan *adj* unenviable
nezavisan *adj* 1. independent 2. autonomous
nezavisnost *f* 1. independence 2. autonomy
nezbrinut *adj* neglected
nezdrav *adj* unhealthy
nezgoda *f* trouble
nezgodan *adj* inconvenient
nezgrapan *adj* awkward
neznaboštvo *n* paganism
neznalica *m/f* ignorant person
neznan *adj* unknown
neznanje *n* 1. ignorance 2. inexperience
neznatan *adj* insignificant
nezreo *adj* 1. unripe 2. immature
nezvaničan *adj* unofficial
nežan *adj* tender
neženja *m* bachelor
nežnost *f* tenderness

ni *conj* neither/either
ni... ni *conj* neither...nor
ničice *adv* prostrate
ničija zemlja *f* no man's land
ničiji *adj* no one's, (not) anyone's
nigde, nigdje nowhere, (not) anywhere
nijansa *f* 1. shade 2. nuance
nijansirati *v* to shade
nije 1. no 2. not
nijedan *adj* none, (not) any, neither, (not) either
nijednom not once
nijekanje *n* denial
nijekati *v* to deny
nijem *adj* 1. mute 2. speechless
Nijemac *m* German
nikad, nikada never, (not) ever
nikakav no, none, (not) any
nikako not at all
nikamo nowhere, (not) anywhere
nikl *m* nickel
niknuti *v* to appear
niko no one, nobody
nikotin *m* nicotine
nikud nowhere
nikuda *f see* **nikamo**
nilski konj *m* hippopotamus
nimalo *adv* not at all
nimfa *f* nymph
niokuda from nowhere
nipošto *adv* by no means
niska 1. *f* string 2. *see* **nizak**
niska žičana prepreka *f* (mil.) tripwire
nisko *see* **nizak**
niskost *f* 1. lowness 2. meanness
niša *f* niche
nišan *m* target
nišaniti *v* to aim
ništa nothing, (not) anything
ništavan *adj* trivial

ništavilo triviality
nit f 1. thread 2. connection
nitko no one, (not) any one
nitkov m villain
nivelirati v level
nivo n level
niz 1. m row 2. series 3. *prep* down 4. along
nizak adj 1. low 2. short 3. mean
nizati se v to be in sequence
nizbrdica f slope
nizbrdo adv downhill
nizija f lowland
nizina f plain
Nizozemska f the Netherlands
nizozemski adj Dutch
nizvodno adv downstream
no but
Nobelova nagrada f Nobel Prize
noć f 1. night 2. **laku noć!** good night!
noćas adv 1. last night 2. tonight
noćiti v to spend the night
noćni čuvar m night watchman
noćni lokal m night club
noga f 1. leg 2. foot
nogare fpl, **nogari** mpl tripod
nogavica f trouser leg
nogomet m football
nogometaš m footballer
noj m ostrich
nokat m fingernail
nokaut m (spor.) knockout
nokautirati v (spor.) to knock out
nokširić m potty
nominativ m nominative
norma f 1. standard 2. quota
normala f normal state, average, vertical
normalan adj normal
normirati v 1. to standardize 2. to set a quota

Norveška f Norway
norveški adj Norwegian
Norvežanin m Norwegian
nos m nose
nosač m 1. porter 2. girder 3. support
nosač aviona m aircraft carrier
nosila f stretcher
nosilac m bearer
nositi v 1. to carry 2. to support 3. to wear
nosivost f load capacity
nosorog m rhinoceros
nošnja f costume
nostalgija f 1. nostalgia 2. homesickness
nostrifikacija f validation of a diploma
nostrifikovati v to validate a diploma
nota f note
notes m notepad
notica f report
notoran adj notorious
nov adj new
Nova Godina f 1. New Year's Day 2. **Sretna Nova Godina!** Happy New Year!
nov grad m satellite city
novac m money
novajlija m beginner
novčan adj financial
novčana sredstva f finances
novčana uputnica f money order
novčanica f (fin.) note; bill
novčanik m purse, wallet
novcat adj brand new
novčić m coin
novela f short story
novembar m November
novina f 1. novelty 2. news item
novinar m journalist

novinarska agencija *f* news agency
novinarski *adj* journalistic
novinarstvo *n* journalism
novine *fpl* newpaper
novinska agencija *f* news agency
novitet *m* novelty
novogodišnji *adj* New Year's
novogradnja *f* block of flats; apartment house
novoizabran *adj* newly elected
novorođenče *n* newborn child
novost *f* 1. news 2. novelty
novotarija *f* novelty
nozdrva *f* nostril
nož *m* knife
nožić *m* **džepni nožić** penknife
nudilac *m* bidder
nudist(a) *m* nudist
nuditi *v* to make an offer
nukati *v* to encourage
nuklearan *adj* nuclear

nuklearna centrala *f* nuclear power station
nuklearna energija *f* nuclear energy
nuklearni rat *m* nuclear war
nuklearni reaktor *m* nuclear reactor
nuklearno oružje *n* nuclear weapons
nula 1. zero 2. no one
nulti zero
numera *f* 1. number 2. size
numerirati *v* to number
nusproizvod *m* by-product
nusprostorija *f* utility room
nutkati *v* to press
nužan *adj* necessary
nužda *f* 1. necessity 2. emergency
nužda, nužnost *f* necessity
nužnik *m* lavatory, toilet
nužno *adv* necessarily
nužnost *f* necessity, need

NJ

njedra *f* bosom
njega *f* 1. care 2. nursing
njegov 1. his 2. its
njegovatelj *m*, **njegovatica** *f* nurse
njegovati *v* 1. to care for 2. to nurse
Njemac *m*, **Njemica** *f* German
Njemačka *f* Germany
njemački *adj* German
njen, njezin 1. her 2. hers
njezini *mpl* her family
nježan *adj* delicate

nježnost *f* delicateness
njihalti *v* to swing
njihati se *v* to swing, rock
njihov 1. their 2. theirs
njiskati *v* to neigh
njiva *f* field
nju 1. her 2. hers
njuh *m* (sense of) smell
njušiti *v* 1. to smell 2. to sniff
njuška *f* 1. nose 2. muzzle
njuškalo *m/n* snooper
njuškati *v* to snoop

o *prep* 1. about 2. at 3. on 4. oh!
oaza *f* oasis
oba *m/n*, **obe, obje** *f* both
obala *f* 1. river bank 2. shore 3. coast
obalni *adj* coastal
obamrijeti *v* 1. to become numb 2. to become listless
obamrlost *f* 1. numbness 2. lethargy
obao *adj* round
obarač *m* trigger
obarati *v* to bring down
obariti *v* to boil
obasipati, obasuti *v* to heap
obasjati *v* to light up
obavest *f* information
obavestiti *v* to inform
obaveštajna služba *f* (mil.) intelligence
obaveštajni *adj* information
obaveštenje *n* information
obaveza *f* obligation
obavezan *adj* obliged
obavezati *v* to oblige
obavezati se *v* to be obliged
obavijati *v* to wind round
obavijest *f* information
obaviti, obavljati *v* 1. to do 2. to carry out
obaveštajac *m* intelligence officer
obavještajna služba *f* (mil.) intelligence
obavještenje *n* information
obazirati, obazreti se *v* to consider
obazriv *adj* considerate
obazrivost *f* caution

obdanište *n* kindergarten, nursery school
obdaren *adj* talented
obdornik *m* committee member
obdukcija *f* autopsy
obdukcija *f* postmortem
obe *see* **both**
obećanje *n* promise
obećati, obećavati *v* to promise
obed *m* meal
obedovati *v* to eat a meal
obeležiti *v* to mark
obeshrabriti *v* to discourage
obesiti *v* to hang up
obestan *adj* unruly
obeščastiti *v* 1. to disgrace 2. to rape
obeštetiti *v* to compensate
obezbediti *v* to ensure
obezbeđenje *n* safeguard
obezbjediti *v* to ensure
običaj *m* habit
običan *adj* usual
obično *adv* usually
obići *v* to go round
obijač *m* burglar
obijeliti *v* to whitewash
obijestan *adj* spoilt
obilan *adj* abundant
obilazak *m* tour
obilazan put *m* indirect route
obilaziti *v* to go round
obilje *n* abundance
obilježiti *v* to mark
obilježje *n* mark
obim *m* volume
obiman *adj* voluminous

obitelj *m* family
obiteljski *adj* family
obiti *v* 1. to break open 2. to pick a lock
objasniti *v* to explain
objašnjavanje *n* 1. argument 2. explanation
objašnjavati *v* to explain
objašnjavati se *v* to argue
objašnjenje *n* explanation
objava *f* 1. announcement 2. za objavu for the record
objava za štampu *f* press release
objaviti *v* 1. to announce 2. to release 3. to publish
objaviti rat *v* to declare war
objavljivanje *n* 1. announcement 2. release 3. publication
obje *see* both
objed *m* meal
objediniti *v* to unite
objekat, objekt *m* 1. topic 2. object 3. facility 4. craft
objektiv *m* 1. objective 2. lens
objektivan *adj* objective
objektivnost *f* objectivity
objelodaniti *v* to make public
objeručke *adj* wholeheartedly
objesiti *v* to hang
oblačan *adj* cloudy, overcast
oblačiti *v* to dress
oblak *m* cloud
oblanda *f* wafer
oblast *f* district
obletjeti *v* to fly around
obličje *n* shape
oblijepiti *v* to coat
oblik *m* form
oblikovati *v* to form
oblina *f* roundness
oblizati, oblizivati *v* to lick
obližnji *adj* nearby

obljernica *f* anniversary
obljesiti slušalicu *v* to ring off
obljuba *f* sexual intercourse
obljubljen *adj* popular
obljubljenost *f* popularity
oblog *m* (med.) compress
obložiti *v* to cover
oblutak *m* pebble
obmana *f* illusion
obmanuti *v* 1. to delude 2. to cheat
obnažiti *v* to bare
obnova *f* 1. reconstruction 2. revival
obnova *f* redevelopment
obnoviti *v* 1. to redevelop 2. to revive
obod *m* brim
obogatiti *v* to enrich
obogatiti se *v* to become rich
oboje, obojica *f* both
obojen *adj* coloured
oboji *m* both
obojiti *v* to paint
oboleti *v* to be ill
oboljenje *n* illness
oboljeti *v see* oboleti
obor *m* paddock
oborine *fpl* precipitation
oboriti *v* 1. to bring down 2. to overturn
oboriti *v* to subvert
obostran *adj* mutual
obospolan *adj* 1. bisexual 2. coeducational
obostran *adj* mutual
obožavalac *m see* obožavatelj
obožavanje *n* 1. admiration 2. worship
obožavatelj *m* 1. fan 2. admirer 3. supporter 4. worshipper
obožavati *v* 1. to be a fan of 2. to admire 3. to worship

obračun *m* 1. confrontation 2.
(fin.) account 3. settlement
obračunati *v* 1. to calculate 2.
(fin.) to settle up
obrada *f* 1. treatment 2. cultivation
obrada teksta *f* word processing
obradiv *adj* 1. adaptable 2. arable
obradiva zemlja *f* arable land
obradovati *v* to gladden
obradovati *v* to please
obramben *adj* defensive
obrana *f* defence
obraniti *v* to defend
obrano mleko/mlijeko *n*
skimmed milk
obrasti *v* to be overgrown
obratan *adj* reverse
obrati *v* to skim
obratiti *v* (rel.) to convert
obratiti se *v* 1. to contact 2. (rel.)
to convert
obratnik *m* tropic
obratno *adv* vice-versa
obraz *m* 1. cheek 2. honour
obrazac *m* 1. form 2. role model
obrazloženje *n* explanation
obrazložiti *v* to explain
obrazovan *adj* educated
obrazovanje, obrazovanost *f*
education
obrazovati *v* to educate
obraćenik *m* (rel.) convert
obraćenje *n* (rel.) conversion
obred *m* ritual
obredni *adj* ritualistic
obrezati *v* 1. to trim 2. to
circumcise
obrezivanje *n* circumcision
obrijan *adj* shaved
obrijati *v* to shave
obris *m* outline
obrisati *v* to wipe

obrlatiti *v* to convince
obrnut *adj* contrary
obrnuti *v* to reverse
obrok *m* 1. meal 2. instalment
obronak *m* slope
obrt *m* 1. handicraft 2. rotation 3.
(fin.) turnover
obrtnica *f* trade licence
obrtnik *m* craftsman
obrtno oružje *n* swivel gun
obrub *m* hem
obruč *m* 1. ring 2. hoop
obrukati *v* to disgrace
obrva *f* eyebrow
obučavanje *n* training
obučavati *v* to train
obučen *adj* trained
obuća *f* footwear
obućar *m* shoemaker
obući *v* to dress
obući se *v* to get dressed
obuhvaćati *v* to include
obujam *m* circumference
obuka *f* training
obuka na terenu *f* field training
obustava *f* suspension
obustaviti *v* to suspend
obuti, obuvati *v* to put on (shoes)
obuvati se *v* to put on one's shoes
obuzdati *v* to restrain
obuzdavanje *n* restraint
obuzdavati *v* to restrain
obuzdavati se *v* to restrain oneself
obuzeti *v* 1. to seize 2. to absorb
obveznica *f* obligation
obveznik *m* taxpayer
obzir *m* 1. consideration 2. bez
obzira na regardless of 3. bez
obzira na irrespective of
obziran *adj* considerate
obzirom na *adj* considering
ocariniti *v* to clear through customs

ocarinjenje *n* customs clearance

ocat *m* vinegar

ocena, ocjena *f* 1. assessment 2. grade

oceniti, ocijeniti *v* to assess

ocrniti *v* to defame

ocrtati, ocrtavati *v* to outline

očaj *m* despair

očajan *adj* desperate

očajavati *v* to despair

očajnički *adj* desperate

očaran *adj* fascinated

očarati *v* to fascinate

očekivanje *n* expectation

očekivati *v* to expect

očešljati *v* to comb, do one's hair

očetkati *v* to brush off

očevidac *m* eyewitness

očevidan *adj* evident

oči *fpl* eyes

očigledan *adj* evident

ocijeniti *v* 1. to assess 2. to mark

očinski *adj* fatherly

očinstvo *n* paternity

očistiti *v* to clean

očistiti usisivačem *v* to vacuum

očit *adj* evident

očitovati se *v* to become clear

očnjak *m* canine tooth

očuh *m* stepfather

očuvati *v* to preserve

oćelaviti *v* to lose hair

od *prep* 1. of 2. from 3. since 4. by 5. than

od sada *adv* from now on

od tada *adv* from then on

oda *f* ode

odabirati, odabrati *v* to choose

odaja *f* room

odakle 1. from where 2. **Odakle znate?** How do you know? 3. **Odakle ste?** Where are you from?

odan *adj* devoted

odan kocki hooked on gambling

odan uživanju droga hooked on drugs

odande from there

odanost *f* devotion

odapeti *v* to shoot

odašiljač *m* transmitter

odasvud from everywhere

odati, odavati *v* 1. to reveal 2. to betray

odatle from there

odavanje *n* 1. revelation 2. betrayal

odavde from here

odavna, odavno *adv* 1. a long time ago 2. for a long time

odazivati se, odazvati se *v* to respond

odbaciti *v* 1. to discard 2. to reject

odbacivanje *n* rejection

odbegao *adj* 1. runaway 2. hit-and-run

odbijanje *n* 1. refusal 2. rejection 3. subtraction

odbiti, odbijati *v* 1. to refuse 2. to reject 3. to subtract

odbiti od sise *v* to wean

odbjegao *see* **odbegao**

odblesak *m* reflection

odbojan *adj* repulsive

odbojka *f* volleyball

odbojkaš *m* volleyball player

odbor *m* 1. committee 2. board 3. council 4. **upravni odbor** steering committee

odbrana *f* defence

odčepiti *v* to uncork

odcijepiti se *v* to secede

odcijepljenje *n* secession

odeća *f* clothing

odeliti *v* to separate

odeljak *m* section
odeljenje *n* 1. department 2. division
odelo *n* clothes
oderati *v* 1. to skin 2. to peel
odevanje *n* dressing
odgađanje *n* delay
odgajati *v* to bring up
odgoda *f* delay
odgoditi *v* to delay
odgoj *m* upbringing
odgojitelj *m* kindergarten teacher
odgojiti *v* to bring up
odgonetnuti *v* to solve
odgovarajući *v* suitable
odgovarati *v* 1. to suit 2. to be responsible 3. to reply
odgovor *m* answer
odgovoran *adj* responsible
odgovoriti *v* 1. to answer 2. to discourage
odgovornost *f* responsibility
odgristi *v* to bite off
odgurnuti *v* to push away
odigrati se *v* to take place
odijeliti *v* to remove
odijelo *n* 1. suit 2. clothes
odio *m* 1. department 2. section
odista *adv* in fact
odjaviti *v* to check out
odjedanput, odjednom *adv* suddenly
odjedriti *v* to sail away
odjek *m* echo
odjel *m* section
odjeća *f* clothes
odjuriti *v* to rush off
odlagati *v* 1. to delay 2. to put aside
odlanuti *v* to feel relief
odlazak *m* departure
odlaziti *v* to go away

odlediti *v* 1. to de-ice 2. to defrost
odleteti *v* to fly away
odležati *v* to spend
odličan *adj* 1. excellent 2. cool
odlijepiti *v* to pull off
odlika *f* 1. characteristic 2. distinction
odlikovanje *n* medal
odlikovati *v* to decorate
odlikovati se *v* to distinguish oneself
odljev *m* sink
odljutiti se *v* to cool down
odlomak *m* 1. fragment 2. paragraph
odlomiti *v* to break off
odložiti *v* 1. to delay 2. to put aside
odložiti diskusiju o predlogu *v* to table a motion
odlučan *adj* determined
odlučan obračun *m* showdown
odlučiti *v* to decide
odlučnost *f* determination
odluka *f* 1. decision 2. (leg.) verdict
odlutati *v* to wander off
odmah *adv* immediately
odmaknuti se *v* to shift
odmamiti *v* to head off
odmaralište *n* 1. holiday home 2. resort 3. rest home
odmarati se *v* to rest
odmazda *f* reprisal
odmeren *adj* tactful
odmetnik *m* 1. rebel 2. outlaw
odmetnuti se *v* to rebel against
odmicati *v* 1. to pass 2. to shift
odmjeren *adj* deliberate
odmjeriti *v* to measure
odmoć *f* hindrance
odmoći *v* to hinder
odmor *m* rest

odmoran *adj* rested
odmoriti *v* to rest
odmotati *v* 1. to unwind 2. to unwrap
odnekle from somewhere
odneti, odnijeti *v* to take away
odnos *m* link
odnosan *adj* particular
odnositi se *v* to concern
odnosno *adv* 1. in other words... 2. *prep* with regard to
odnošaj *m* sexual intercourse
odobravanje *n* approval
odobravati *v* to approve
odobrenje *n* permission
odobriti *v* to permit
odojak *m* suckling pig
odoleti, odoljeti *v* to resist
odora *f* robe
odostrag, odostraga *adv* from behind
odozdo, odozdol, odozdola *adv* from below
odozgo, odozgor, odozgora *adv* from above
odračunati *v* to deduct
odraditi *v* to work off
odrasli *mpl* adults
odrastao *adj* grown-up
odrasti *v* to grow up
odraz *m* reflection
odraziti *v* to reflect
odrečan *adj* negative
odred *m* (mil.) detachment
odred za spasavanje *m* search party
odredba *f* 1. decree 2. (leg./pol.) provision
odreći *v* to give up
odreći se *v* 1. to give up 2. to waive 3. to resign
odredište *n* destination

odrediti *v* 1. to determine 2. to assign
odrednica *f* entry
određen *adj* definite
određen član *m* definite article
određivanje *n* determination
odrešenje *n* discharge
odrezak *m* 1. cutting 2. steak
odrezati *v* to cut off
odricanje *n* 1. self-sacrifice 2. denial
odriješiti *v* 1. to untie 2. to acquit
odrješit *m* bluff
odrod *m* renegade
odron *m* landslide
odrpan *adj* tattered
odrubiti glavu *v* to behead
održanje *n* 1. existence 2. survival
održati, održavati *v* 1. to hold 2. to keep
održati manevre *v* to hold manouevres
održati reč/riječ *v* to keep one's word
održati referendum *v* to hold a referendum
održati se, održavati se *v* 1. to survive 2. to take place
održavanje *n* 1. keeping 2. maintenance
održavati *v* 1. to hold 2. to keep
odsada from now on
odsečak *m* segment
odseći *v* to cut off
odsek *m* 1. department 2. section
odseliti se *v* to move
odsjaj *m* reflection
odsjeći *v* to cut off
odsjek *m* 1. department 2. section
odsjesti *v* to stay
odsjev *m* reflection
odskočiti *v* to jump out

odskok *m* ricochet
odslužiti *v* to serve (time)
odspavati *v* to sleep
odšarafiti *v* to unscrew
odšetati *v* to walk away
odštampani znakovi *mpl* print-out
odštampati *v* to print out
odšteta *f* 1. compensation 2. reparations 3. (leg.) damages
odštetiti *v* to compensate
odšuljati se *v* to sneak away
odšutjeti *v* to keep silent
odsto percent
odstojanje *n* 1. distance 2. interval
odstraniti *v* to remove
odstraniti se *v* to withdraw
odstranjenje *n* 1. removal 2. withdrawal
odstupanje *n* 1. departure 2. retreat 3. surrender
odstupati, odstupiti *v* 1. to depart 2. to surrender 3. to retreat
odstupnina *f* compensation
odsukati *v* to refloat
odsustvo *n* absence
odsutan *adj* absent
odsutati od *v* to stop short of
odsutnost *f* absence
odsvirati *v* to play
odsvuda from everywhere
odučiti *v* to give up
odudarati *v* to contrast
odugovlačiti *v* to hesitate
oduljiti se *v* to linger
odumirati *v* to die out
oduprijeti se *v* to resist
oduran *adj* repulsive
odustati *v* to give up
odustati od *v* 1. to give up 2. to waive
odustojiti *v* to vouchsafe
odušak *m* outlet

oduševiti *v* to enthuse
oduševljen *adj* enthusiastic
oduševljenje *n* enthusiasm
oduvati *v* to blow away
oduvek, oduvijek *adv* always
oduzet *adj* paralyzed
oduzeti *v* to take away
oduzetost *f* paralysis
oduzimanje *n* subtraction
odužiti se *v* 1. to repay 2. to linger
odvagnuti *v* to weigh
odvajanje *n* 1. removal 2. separation
odvaliti, odvaljivati *v* 1. to break off 2. **Baš je odvalio.** He put his foot in it.
odvažan *adj* daring
odvažiti se *v* to dare
odvažnost *f* daring
odvesti *v* 1. to take 2. to drive
odvesti se *v* to drive
odvezati *v* to undo
odvijač *m* screwdriver
odvijati *v* 1. to unwind 2. to unscrew
odvijati se *v* to be in progress
odviknuti se *v* to give up
odviše *adv* too much
odvod *m*, **odvođenje** *n* removal
odvoditi *v* to remove
odvodnjavanje *n* drainage
odvojak *m* side road
odvojiti *v* to separate
odvoz *m* 1. removal 2. transport
odvoziti *v* 1. to remove 2. to transport
odvraćanje *n* discouragement
odvratan *adj* repulsive
odvratiti *v* to discourage
odvratnost *f* disgust
odvrnuti *v* to turn off
odvrtka *f* screwdriver

odvući *v* to draw away,
odzdraviti *v* to greet
odzvanjati *v* to reverberate
odžak *m* chimney
ofanziva, ofenziva *f* (mil.) offensive
oficir *m* officer
oformiti *v* to form
ofsajd *m* offside
oftalmičan *adj* ophthalmic
oftalmolog ophthalmologist
oftalmologija *f* ophthalmology
ofuriti *v* to scald
oganj *m* fire
ogavan *adj* repulsive
ogladnjeti *v* to be hungry
oglas *m* 1. notice 2. advertisement
oglasiti *v* 1. to announce 2. to advertise
oglasna ploča *f* noticeboard
oglasni zavod *m* advertising agency
ogled *m* 1. inspection 2. trial 3. essay
ogledalo *n* mirror
ogledni *adj* experimental
ogluha *f* iz ogluhe by default
oglušiti *v* to be deaf
ognjište *n* fireplace
ogoliti *v* to bare
ogorčen *adj* bitter
ogorčenje *n* bitterness
ogorčiti *v* to embitter
ogovaranje *n* gossip
ogovarati *v* to gossip
ograda *f* fence
ograditi *v* to fence
ogranak *m* 1. branch 2. chapter
ograničen *adj* 1. limited 2. narrow-minded
ograničenje *n* 1. limitation 2. restriction

ograničiti *v* to limit
ogrebotina *f* stratch
ogrepsti *v* to scratch
ogrev *m* 1. firewood 2. fuel
ogrevno drvo *n* firewood
ogriješiti se *v* 1. to sin 2. to violate
ogrjev *m* 1. firewood 2. fuel
ogrlica *f* 1. necklace 2. collar
ogrnuti *v* 1. to cover 2. to wrap up
ogroman *adj* huge
ogrozd *m* gooseberry
ogrtač *m* 1. cloak 2. coat
oguliti *v* to peel
oguliti *v* to peel off
oho! oh!
ohladenje *n* cool relations
ohladiti *v* to cool
ohol *adj* haughty
oholost *f* haughtiness
ohrabrenje *n* encouragement
ohrabriti *v* to encourage
ohrabriti se *v* to have courage
ojačati *v* to strengthen
okačiti *v* to hang on
okajati *v* to repent
okaljati *v* to besmirch
okameniti *v* to petrify
okaniti se *v* to give up
okapanje *n* trouble
okean *m* ocean
okidač *m* trigger
okinuti *v* to pull a trigger
okititi *v* to adorn
oklada *f* bet
okladiti se *v* to bet
oklevanje, oklijevanje *n* hesitation
oklevati, oklijevati *v* to hesitate
okliznuti se *v* to slip
oklop *m* armour
oklopni *adj* armoured
oklopnjača *f* battleship

okno *n* 1. window-pane 2. porthole 3. shaft
oko 1. *n* eye 2. mesh 3. *prep* around
okolica *f* neighbourhood
okolina *f* environment
okolišati *v* to beat about the bush
okolnost *f* situation
okolo *adv/prep* around
okomica *f* perpendicular
okomit *adj* vertical
okomiti se *v* to attack
okončati *v* to end
okoreo, okorio *adj* inveterate
okosnica *f* framework
okov *m* fittings
okovati *v* 1. to shackle 2. to plate
okovi *mpl* 1. chains 2. fittings
okovratnik *m* collar
okrajak *m* 1. remnant 2. stub
okrasti *v* to rob
okrečiti *v* to whitewash
okrenuti *v* to turn
okrepa *f* refreshment
okrepiti *v* to refresh
okrepljenje *n* refreshment
okret *m* 1. turn 2. rotation
okretan *adj* agile
okretati se *v* to rotate
okretnost *f* agility
okrhnuti *v* to chip
okrijepiti *v* to refresh
okrilje *n* 1. shelter 2. patronage
okriviti *v* to accuse
okrivljeni *adj* accused, defendant
okrnjiti *v* 1. to injure 2. to infringe
okršaj *m* skirmish
okrstiti *v* to name
okrug *m* district
okrugao *adj* round
okruglica *f* dumpling
okruniti *v* to crown
okrutan *adj* cruel

okrutnost *f* cruelty
okružiti *v* to surround
okrznuti *v* to graze
oksid *m* oxide
oksidacija *f* oxidation
oksigen *m* oxygen
oktan *m* octane
oktava *f* octave
oktobar *m* October
okuka *f* curve
okupacija *f* (mil.) occupation
okupacione snage *fpl* occupying forces
okupati *v* to have a bath
okupator *m* invader
okupatorska vojska *f* occupying army
okupirati *v* (mil.) to occupy
okupirati zemlju *v* (mil.) to occupy a country
okupiti *v* to gather
okupiti se *v* to gather
okus *m* taste
okusiti *v* to taste
okušan *adj* tried
okušati se *v* to attempt
okvir *m* frame
odeset eighty
okvir *m* 1. frame 2. u okviru as part of
olabaviti (se) *v* to relax
olako *adv* easily
olakšanje *n* relief
olakšati *v* to facilitate
olakšica *f* 1. facility 2. privilege
oličenje *n* personification
olimpijada *f* Olympic Games
ološ *m* 1. rabble 2. vermin
olovka *f* pencil
olovo *n* 1. lead 2. bez olova unleaded 3. benzin bez dodatka olova unleaded petrol

oltar *m* altar
oluja *f* storm
oluja s gradom *f* hailstorm
olujni *adj* stormy
olujno vreme/vrijeme *n* rough weather
oluk *m* drain
olupina *f* wreck
omaknuti se *v* to slip up
omalovažiti, omalovažavati *v* to belittle
omama *f* daze
omamiti *v* to stun
omanji *adj* smallish
omaška *f* 1. error 2. oversight
omađijati *v* to bewitch
omaći se *v* to slip
omča *f* 1. loop 2. noose
omediti *v* to delimit
omekšati *v* to soften
ometati *v* 1. to hamper 2. to jam
omiljen *adj* favourite
omiljen *adj* popular
omiljenost *f* popularity
omjer *m* proportion
omladina *f* young people
omladinsko prenoćište *n* (youth) hostel
omlet *m* omelette
omogućiti *v* to enable
omorika *f* spruce
omot, omotač *m* 1. wrapping 2. cover
omotati *v* 1. to wrap 2. to cover
omražen *adj* hated
omršaviti *v* to lose weight
on 1. he 2. him
on sam he himself
ona sama she herself
ona 1. she 2. her
onaj that
onaj koji the one who

onakav *adj* such
onako *adv* 1. so 2. **i onako** any way
onamo there
onanija *f* masturbation
onda *adv* then
onde, ondje *adv* there
one 1. they 2. those
onemogućiti *v* 1. to frustrate 2. to disqualify
oneraspoložiti *v* to upset
oneraspoložiti se *v* to be upset
onesposobiti *v* to disable
onesposobljenost *f* disability
onesvestiti se *v* to faint
onesviješten *adj* unconscious
onesvijestiti se *v* to faint
oni 1. they 2. those
onlajn *adj* on-line
ono 1. it 2. that
onoliko so many, so much, that many, that much
onoliko so much, so many
onomad *adv* recently
onošto that which
onuda *adv* that way, in that direction
onuda *adv* there
ooperirati *v* to operate
opačina *f* atrocity
opadanje *n* decline
opadati *v* to decline
opak *adj* wicked
opaliti *v* 1. to burn 2. to tan
opaljen *adj* suntanned
opametiti *v* to bring to reason
oparati *v* to undo
opasač *m* belt
opasan *adj* dangerous
opaska *f* note
opasnost *f* danger
opasti *v* to decline

opat *m* abbot
opatica *f* abbess
opatija *f* abbey
opaziti *v* to observe
opažanje *n* observation
opčiniti *v* to fascinate
opća praksa *f* family medicine
općenit *adj* general
općenito *adv* generally
općenje *n* intercourse
opći *adj* general
općina *f* 1. district 2. borough 3. municipality 4. townhall
općinski *adj* municipal
općiti *v* to have intercourse with
opeći *v* to burn
opeka *f* brick
opeklina, opekotina *f* burn
opekotina od sunca *f* sunburn
opelo *n* requiem
opera *f* 1. opera 2. opera house
operacija *f* operation
operaciona dvorana/sala *f* operating theatre
operater *m* operator
operativan *adj* operative
operativna grupa *f* (mil.) task force
operator *m* surgeon
opereta *f* operetta
operisati *v* to operate
opet *adv* again
opetovano *adv* repeatedly
ophođenje *n* behaviour
opijen *adj* (sl.) stoned
opip *m* touch
opipati *v* to touch
opipljiv *adj* tangible
opiranje *n* resistance
opirati se *v* to resist
opis *m* description
opisati, opisavati *v* to describe

opit *m* experiment
opiti *v* to intoxicate
opiti se *v* (sl.) to get high
opjevati *v* to praise
opklada *f* bet
opkoliti *v* to surround
opkop *m* trench
oplakati, oplakivati *v* to lament
oplata *f* panelling
oplemeniti *v* to refine
opljačkati *v* to mug
opljačkati *v* to rob, ransack
opločen *adj* 1. tiled 2. panelled
oploditi *v* to fertilize
oplodnja *f* 1. fertilization 2. umjetna oplodnja artificial insemination
oploviti *v* to sail around
opmičar *m* kidnapper
opna *f* membrane
opojno sredstvo *n* drug
opomena *f* warning
opomenuti *v* to warn
oponašanje *n* imitation
oponašati *v* imitate
opor *m* 1. harsh 2. dry 3. sharp
oporavak *m* 1. recovery 2. convalescence
oporavak *m* recovery
oporaviti se *v* 1. to recover 2. to convalesce
oporezivanje *n* taxation
oporezovati *v* 1. to tax 2. to impose
oporežljiv *adj* taxable
oporuka *f* will and testament
oposliti *v* to employ
opovrgnuti *v* to deny
opovrgnuće *n* denial
opozicija *f* opposition
opoziciona partija *f* opposition party
opoziv *adj* 1. cancellation 2. repeal

opozvati *v* 1. to cancel 2. to repeal
opraštati *v* to pardon
oprati *v* to wash
opravdan *adj* justified
opravdanje *n* justification
opravdati *v* to justify
opravdavati se *v* to justify oneself
opraviti *v* to repair
opravka *f* repair
oprečan *adj* contrary
oprečka *f* contrast
opredeliti, opredijeliti *v* to determine
opredeliti se, opredijeliti se *v* to take sides
opredeljenje, opredjeljenje *n* orientation
oprema *f* 1. equipment 2. layout
opremiti *v* to equip
oprez *m* caution
oprezan *adj* cautious
opreznost *f* caution
oproban *adj* tested
oprobati *v* to try, test, try out
oproštaj *m* 1. pardon 2. farewell
oprošten *adj* exempt
oproštenje *n* pardon
oprostiti *v* to pardon
oprostiti se *v* to take one's leave
opruga *f* (metal) spring
opsada *f* 1. siege 2. blockade
opsadno stanje *n* martial law
opseg *m* extent
opsena *f* illusion
opsenar *m* illusionist
opseniti *v* 1. to delude 2. to bluff
opservator *m* watcher
opservatorij, opservatorija *f* observatory
opsesija *f* obsession
opsežan *adj* extensive
opsjedati *v* 1. to lay siege to 2. blockade

opskrba *f* 1. supply 2. supplies 3. equipment
opskrbiti, opskrbljivati *v* to supply
opskrbni centar *m* shopping centre
opsovati *v* to swear
opširan *adj* detailed
opširno *adv* in detail
opšta praksa *f* family medicine
opšti *v* common, universal
opšti izbori *mpl* general elections
opšti troškovi *mpl* overheads
opština *f* commune
opštiti *v* 1. to communicate 2. to associate with
opstanak *m* 1. survival 2. existence
opstati *v* 1. to survive 2. to exist
opteretiti *v* 1. to load 2. to strain
opterećenje *n* 1. load 2. strain
opticaj *m* circulation
optičar *m* optician
optika *f* optics
optička varka *f* optical illusion
optimist(a) *m* optimist
optužba *f* 1. accusation 2. prosecution
optuženik *m* 1. accused 2. defendant
optužiti *v* 1. to accuse 2. to impeach
optužnica *f* indictment
opunomoćenik *m* representative
opunomoćiti *v* 1. to authorize 2. to empower
opušak *m* stub
opustiti, opustiti se *v* to relax
opustošiti *v* to devastate
oraditi *v* 1. to process 2. to cultivate

orah *m* walnut
oralno kontraceptivno sredtsvo
   n oral contraceptive
oran *adj* ready
oranžada *f* orange juice
oranžerija *f* greenhouse
orao *m* eagle
orati *v* to plough; to plow
oratorijum *m* oratorio
orbita *f* orbit
orden *m* order
ordinacija *f* doctor's surgery
ordinaran *adj* ordinary
ordinirati *v* to practise
oreol *m* aureole
organ *adj* organ
organist(a) *m* organist
organizacija *f* 1. organization 2.
   association 3. syndicate
**Organizacija UN za prosvetu/
   prosvjetu** *f* UNESCO
organizam *m* organism
organizator *m*, **organizatorka** *f*
   organizer
organizovati *v* to organize
organski *adj* organic
orgazam *m* orgasm
orgije *fpl* orgy
orguljaš *m* organist
orgulje *fpl* organ
original *m* original
originalan *adj* original
originalnost *f* originality
orijentacija *f* orientation
orijentalan *adj* oriental, eastern
orijentir *m* landmark
orijentirati *v* to orientate
orijentirati se *v* to concentrate
orijentisan na korisnika *f* user-
   friendly
oriti se *v* to resound
orkan *m* hurricane

orkestar *m* orchestra
orman, ormar *m* 1. cupboard 2.
   wardrobe
ornament *m* ornament
ornitolog *m* ornithologist
ornitologija *f* ornithology
ornitološki *adj* ornithological
oronuo *adj* dilapidated
orositi se *v* 1. to condense up 2. to
   sweat
ortak *m* partner
ortakluk *m* partnership
ortodoksan *adj* orthodox
ortografija *f* spelling, orthography
ortopedski *adj* orthopaedic
oruđe *n* tool
oružane snage *fpl* armed forces
oružje *n* 1. arms 2. **bez oružja**
   unarmed 3. **vatreno oružje** firearms
orvrdnuti *v* to harden
osa *f* 1. axis 2. wasp
osakatiti *v* to cripple
osam eight
osamdeset eighty
osamljen *adj* 1. lonely 2. isolated
osamljenost *f* 1. loneliness 2.
   isolation
osamnaest eighteen
osavremeniti *v* to modernize
osamostaliti se *v* to become
   independent
oscilacija *f* oscillation
osebujan *adj* peculiar
osedlati *v* to saddle
oseka *f* low tide
osetiti *v* to sense
osetljiv *adj* sensitive
osetljivost *f* sensitivity
osećaj *m* sense
osećanje *n* feeling
osećati *v* to feel

osigurač *m* fuse
osiguranik *m* insured
osiguranje *n* insurance
osiguranje putnika *n* travel insurance
osiguranje života *n* life insurance
osigurati, osiguravati *v* 1. to insure 2. to ensure
osiguravač *m* insurer
osiguravajuće društvo *n* insurance company
osiguravajući agent *m* insurance agent
osijediti *v* to go grey
osim *conj* besides
osim toga moreover
osip *m* rash
osiromašiti *v* to become poor
osjetan *adj* substantial
osjetilo *n* sense
osjetiti *v* to feel
osjetljiv *adj* sensitive
osjetljivost *f* sensitivity
osjećaj *m* feeling
osjećajan *adj* sensitive
osjećati *v* to feel
oskudan *adj* scarce
oskudevati *v* to lack
oskudica *f* scarcity
oskvrnuti *v* to desecrate
oslabiti *v* to weaken
oslabiti *v* 1. to weaken 2. to sink
oslepeti, oslijepiti *v* to become blind
oslobodilac *m* liberator
osloboditi *v* 1. to free 2. to exempt
osloboditi se *v* 1. to become free 2. to be exempt
oslobođenje *n* 1. freedom 2. exemption 3. exception
oslonac *m* support
osloniti se *v* to rely on

osloviti *v* to address
osluškivati *v* to eavesdrop
osmatrač *m* watcher
osmatračnica *f* watchtower
osmatrati *v* to observe
osmeh, osmijeh *m* smile
osmehnuti se, osmijehnuti se *v* to smile
osmotriti *v* to take a look
osmrtnica *f* obituary
osnivač *m* founder
osnivanje *n* foundation
osnivati *v* to establish
osnivati se *v* to be based on
osnova *f* 1. basis 2. foundation 3. **u osnovi** basically 4. **na osnovu** in view of
osnovan *adj* established
osnovati *v* to establish
osnovati radnju *v* to start up a business
osnovni *adj* basic
osoba *f* person
osoban *see* osobni
osobenjak *m* 1. eccentric 2. crank
osobenost *f* peculiarity
osobina *f* characteristic
osobit *adj* special
osobito *adv* especially
osoblje *n* staff
osoblje bolnice *n* hospital staff
osobni *adj* personal
osobno *adv* personally
osoran *adj* harsh
osovina *f* 1. axis 2. axle
osovna obuka *f* (mil.) basic training
ospice *fpl* measles
osporavati, osporiti *v* 1. to challenge 2. to deny
osposobiti *v* 1. to fit 2. to train 3. to enable 4. to repair

osposobljavanje n 1. training 2. repair
osramotiti se v to be disgraced
osrednji adj average
ostali adj remaining
ostarjeti v to grow old
ostatak m remainder
ostati v to remain
ostati bez v to run out of
ostava f storeroom
ostaviti v to leave
ostavka f 1. resignation 2. dati ostavku to resign
ostavština f inheritance
ostriga f oyster
ostruga f spur
ostrugati v to scrape
ostrvljanin m islander
ostrvo n island
ostvarenje n realization
ostvariti v to accomplish
ostvariti se v to be accomplished
ostvariv adj feasible
ostve fpl harpoon
osuda f 1. condemnation 2. (leg.) sentence
osuditi v 1. to condemn 2. to sentence
osuđenik m convict
osuđivanost f (previous) conviction
osujetiti v to frustrate
osumnjičen adj under suspicion
osumnjičena osoba f suspect
osumnjičiti v to suspect
osušiti se v to dry up
osuti se v to break out in a rash
osvajač m conqueror
osvajanje n conquest
osvajati v to conquer
osveta f revenge
osvetiti v to take revenge
osvetliti v to illuminate

osvetljenje n lighting
osvetljiv adj vindictive
osvetnik m avenger
osveženje n refreshments
osvežiti v to refresh
osvijestiti se v to come to
osvijetliti v 1. to light up 2. to expose
osvit m daybreak
osvjedočiti v to convince
osvježenje n refreshment
osvježiti v to refresh
osvojiti v 1. to take over 2. to conquer
osvrnuti se v 1. to look back 2. to review
osvrt m review
ošamariti v to slap
ošinuti v to lash
ošišati se v to get a haircut
oštar adj 1. sharp 2. severe
oštećenje n damage
oštetiti v to damage
oštrač za olovke m pencil sharpener
oštrica f 1. blade 2. (sharp) edge
oštrica, oštriga f oyster
oštrilo n sharpener
oštrina f 1. sharpness 2. severity
oštriti v to sharpen
oštrouman adj shrewd
oštroumnost f shrewdness
otac m father
otada since then
otadžbina f homeland
otcepiti v to break off
otcepiti se, otcijepiti se v to secede (od from)
otcepljenje, otcjepljenje n secession
otcujepiti se v to secede
otčepiti v to open up

otegnuti se v to drag on
oteklina f swelling
oterati v to drive away
oteti v to wrench away
oteti se v to break free
otezanje n delay
otezati v to delay
otežati v to hinder
oteći v 1. to drain 2. (med.) to swell
othraniti v to bring up
othrvati se v to withstand
oticanje n drain
oticati v to swell
otimačina f robbery
otipkati v to type
otirač m doormat
otisak m 1. print 2. fingerprint 3. printer's proof
otisak prstiju m fingerprint
otisak stopala m footprint
otisnuti v to print
otisnuti se v to push off
otići v to depart
otjerati v to chase off
otkačiti v to undo
otkad? 1. since when? 2. how long?
otkako conj 1. as long as 2. since
otkaz m 1. notice 2. warning
otkazati v 1. to cancel 2. to quit 3. to warn
otkinuti v to break off
otklanjanje n 1. elimination 2. refusal
otključati v to unlock
otkloniti v 1. to eliminate 2. to refuse
otkopati v 1. to dig up 2. to mine
otkopčati v to undo
otkriće n discovery
otkriti v to discover

otkriti podatke v to leak information
otkrovenje n revelation
otkucaj m 1. stroke 2. beat
otkucati v to typewrite
otkuda from where
otkup m 1. ransom 2. purchase
otkupiti v 1. ransom 2. to purchase
otkupnina f ransom
otmen adj fine
otmica f kidnapping
otmičar m kidnapper
otmjen adj 1. elegant 2. distinguished
otmjenost f 1. elegance 2. distinction
otok m island
otomanksi adj Ottoman
otopina f solution
otopiti v 1. to melt 2. to defrost
otorinolaringolog m ear, nose and throat specialist
otorinolaringologija f ear, nose and throat medicine
otpad m waste
otpadak m, **otpaci** mpl 1. rubbish; trash 2. product
otpadanje n 1. falling-off 2. desertion 3. defection
otpadati, otpasti v 1. to fall off 2. to desert 3. to defect
otpadnik m renegade
otpasti v to fall off
otpis m deduction
otpisati v 1. to deduct 2. to write off
otplata f 1. payment 2. instalment
otplatiti v to pay off
otplaćivati, otplatiti v (fin.) to pay in instalments
otploviti v to set sail
otpor m resistance

otporan adj resistant
otpornost f resistance
otpratiti v to escort
otprema f (com.) 1. forwarding 2. shipping
otpremiti v (com.) 1. to forward 2. to ship
otpremnica f bill of lading
otpremnik m (com.) forwarding agent
otpremnina f severance pay
otpremništvo n (com.) freight forwarding
otprije from before
otprilike adv approximately
otpusnica f notice of dismissal
otpuštanje n dismissal
otpustiti v to dismiss
otputovati v to depart
otraga adv behind
otrcan adj shabby
otrčati v to run away
otresit adj curt
otresti se v 1. to get rid of 2. to be curt with
otresti v to shake down/off
otrgnuti v to break away
otrijezniti se v to sober up
otrov m poison
otrovan adj poisonous
otrovati v to poison
otrpati, otrpavati v to dig out
otuđenost f alienation
otuđiti se v to grow apart
otuda 1. from there 2. therefore
otupelost f dullness
otupjeti v to become dull
otužan adj boring
otvaranje n opening
otvor m opening
otvoren adj 1. open 2. frank 2. outdoor

otvorenje n opening
otvoreno adv 1. openly 2. frankly
otvoriti v 1. to open 2. to turn on
otvoriti radnju v to start up a business
otvoriti se v to open
otvoriti vatru v to open fire
ovacija f ovation
ovaj this
ovakav such
ovako adv thus
ovamo here
ovan m ram
ovaplođenje n incarnation
ovas m oats
ovca f sheep
ovčar m shepherd
ovčarski pas m sheepdog
ovčarstvo n sheep farming
ovčetina f mutton
ovdašnji adj local
ovde, ovdje here
overa f attestation
overiti v to attest
ovi these
ovisan adj dependent
ovisan o drugi adj hooked on drugs
ovisiti v to depend
ovisnost f dependence
oviti, ovijati v to wind round
ovjekovječiti v to immortalize
ovjera f verification
ovjeriti, ovjeroviti v to verify
ovladati v 1. to control 2. to subdue
ovladati v to master
ovlastiti v to authorize
ovlašan adj slight
ovlašćenje, ovlaštenje n authority
ovlažiti v to moisten
ovo this
ovogodišnji adj this year's

ovoj *m* bandage
ovolik, ovoliki such a large, so many, this many
ovoliko so much, so many, this many
ovratnik *m* collar
ovuda this way
ovulacija *f* ovulation
ozakoniti *v* to legalize
ozbiljan *adj* serious
ozbiljno *adv* seriously
ozbiljnost *f* seriousness
ozdraviti *v* (med.) to recover
ozdravljenje *n* (med.) recovery
ozeblina *f* chilblain
ozepsti *v* 1. to freeze 2. to catch a cold
ozlijediti *v* to injure
ozljeda *f* injury
ozloglašen *adj* disreputable
ozloglastiti *v* to bring into disrepute

ozlojediti *v* to exasperate
ozlojeđenost *f* bitterness
ozlovoljiti *v* to annoy
označiti *v* 1. to designate 2. to characterize
oznaka *f* 1. designation 2. characteristic
oznojen *adj* sweaty
oznojiti se *v* to sweat
ozon *m* ozone
ozvučiti *v* to bug
ožalošćen *adj* in mourning
ožalostiti *v* to sadden
ožbukati *v* to plaster
ožedneti, ožednjeti *v* to be thirsty
oženiti *v* to marry
oženiti se *v* to get married
oženjen *adj* married
ožigosati *v* to brand
ožiljak *m* scar
oživeti, oživiti, oživjeti *v* to revive

P

pa *prep* 1. and 2. well
pa makar *prep* even if
pačati se *v* to interfere
pače 1. *n* duckling 2. *adv* even
pacijent *m* patient
pacov *m* rat
pad *m* 1. fall 2. decline
padati *v* 1. to fall 2. to decline 3. to rain 4. **Pada kiša.** It is raining.
padavica *f* epilepsy
padavina *f* rainfall
padež *m* (grammatical) case
padina *f* slope
padobran *m* parachute
padobranac *m* 1. parachutist 2. paratrooper 3. gatecrasher
padobranske jedinice *fpl* paratroops
paganin *m* pagan
pahuljica *f* snowflake
pajac *m* clown
pak *conj* but
pakao *m* hell
paket *m* 1. packet 2. parcel
pakirati *v* to pack
paklen *adj* infernal
paklo *n* pack
pakosno *adv* maliciously
pakost *f* malice
pakostan *adj* malicious
pakovati *v* to pack
pakpapir *m* wrapping paper
pakt *m* 1. pact 2. treaty
palac *m* thumb
palača *f* palace
palačinka *f* pancake
palanački *adj* provincial

palata *f* palace
palenje *n* 1. blaze 2. ignition
palica *f* stick
palidrvce *n* match
palikuća *m* arsonist
paliti *v* 1. to burn 2. to ignite 3. to fire
paljba *f* fire
palma *f* palm
paluba *f* deck
pamet *f* 1. mind 2. intelligence
pametan *adj* 1. sensible 2. intelligent
pamflet *m* pamphlet
pamtiti *v* to remember
pamuk *m* cotton
pamćenje *n* memory
pandža *f* claw
paničar *m* scaremonger
panika *f* panic
panj *m* block
panorama *f* panorama
pansion *m* pension, guesthouse
pantalone *fpl* trousers; pants
panter *m* panther
pantljika *f* 1. tape 2. ribbon
papa *m* Pope
papagaj *m* parrot
papak *m* hoof
papar *m* pepper
paperje *n* down
papiga *f* parrot
papir *m* paper
papirnica *f* stationery shop
papnirnat novac *m* (fin.) paper currency
paprat *f* fern

papren *adj* hot, spicy
paprena metvica *f* peppermint
paprika *f* pepper
papriti *v* to pepper, to spice
papuča *f* slipper
par *m* pair
para *f* 1. steam 2. fumes 3. coin
parabola *f* parable
parada *f* parade
paradajz *m* tomato
paradoks *m* paradox
paragraf *m* paragraph
paralela *f*, **paralelan** *adj* parallel
paraliza *f* 1. paralysis 2. palsy 3. cerebralna paraliza cerebral palsy
paralizovati *v* to paralyze
paramilitaristički *adj* paramilitary
paranoičan *adj* paranoid
paranoik *m* paranoiac
paranoja *f* paranoia
parati *v* to rip
paravan *m* screen
parazit *m* parasite
parče *n* piece
parcov *m* rat
pare *fpl* money
parfem *m* perfume
parfimerija *f* perfumer's
park *m* park
parket *m* parquet
parking *m* parking
parkiralište *n* car-park; parking lot
parkirati *v* to park
parlament *m* parliament
parlamentaran *adj* parliamentary
parlamentarni imunitet *m* parliamentary immunity
parni *adj* steam
parni stroj *m* steam engine
parnica *f* lawsuit, legal case
parničar *m* litigant

parobrod *m* steamship
parodija *f* parody
paroh *m* (Orth.) priest
parohija *f* parish
parter *m* ground floor
particip *m* participle
participacija *f* participation
participirati *v* to participate
partija *f* 1. party 2. shipment 3. (spor.) game
partisan *m* partisan
partitura *f* score
partizanski rat *m* guerrilla warfare
partner *m* partner
pas *m* 1. belt 2. dog 3. **morski pas** shark
pasioniran *adj* passionate
pasiv *adj* passive
pasiva *f* liabilities
pasmina *f* 1. breed 2. race
pasoš *m* passport
pasoško odeljenje/odjeljenje *n* passport office
paša *f* pasture
pašnjak *m* pasture land
pasta *f* 1. pasta 2. paste 3. polish
pasti *v* to fall
pasti na ispitu *v* to fail an exam
pasti pod stečaj *v* to go bankrupt
pastir *m* shepherd
pastor *m* pastor
pastrmka, pastrva *f* trout
pastuh *m* stallion
pasulj *m* beans
pasus *m* 1. passage 2. paragraph
patent *m* patent
patent-brava *f* Yale lock
patent-zatvarač *m* zip
patentirati, patentovati *v* to patent
patetičan *adj* pathetic
patika *f* 1. slipper 2. shoe

patisak *m* reprint
patiti *v* to suffer
patka *f* duck
patnja *f* suffering
patologija *f* pathology
patrijarh *m* patriarch
patrijarhat *m* patriarchate
patriot *m* patriot
patrola *f* patrol
patrolirati *v* to patrol
patron *m* patron
patrona *f* cartridge
patuljak *m* dwarf
patvoren *adj* 1. forged 2. artificial
patvorina *f* forgery
patvoriti *v* to forge
paučina *f* web
pauk *m* spider
paun *m* peacock
paus-papir *m* tracing paper
paušal *m* lump sum
pauza *f* pause
paviljon *m* pavilion
pavlaka *f* cream
pazar *m* market
pazarenje *n* shopping
pazariti *v* 1. to shop 2. to do business
pazikuća *f* caretaker; janitor
paziti *v* 1. to take care of 2. to watch
pazuh *m*, **pazuho** *n* armpit
pažljiv *adj* 1. careful 2. attentive
pažnja *f* 1. care 2. attention
paćenje *n* suffering
pčela *f* bee
pčelar *m* beekeeper
pecač *m* fisherman
pecaljka *f* fishing rod
pecanje *n* fishing
pecati *v* to fish
pecivo *n* rolls

pecnuti *v* to sting
pečat *m* 1. stamp 2. seal
pečatiti *v* to seal
pečen *adj* 1. roasted 2. baked
pečenka *f* roast meat
pečurka *f* mushroom
peć *m* oven
peći *v* 1. to roast 2. to bake
pećina *f* 1. cave 2. rock
pećnica *f* oven
pedagogija *f* pedagogy
pedagoški fakultet *m* teacher training college
pedantan *adj* pedantic
pedeset fifty
pedigre *m* pedigree
pedijatar *m* paediatrician
pedijatrija *f* paediatrics
pega *f* 1. spot 2. stain
pegav *adj* spotty
pegla *f* iron
peglati *v* to iron
pehar *m* 1. cup 2. jug
pejzaž *m* landscape
pekar *m* baker
pekara *f* bakery
pekara, pekarnica *f* bakery
pekmez *m* jam
pelcovati *v* to vaccinate
pelena *f* nappy
pelikan *m* pelican
pelivan *m* acrobat
pena *f* foam
penal *m* (spor.) penalty
peni *m* penny
penicilin *m* penicillin
penis *m* penis
penjati se *v* to climb
penkalo *n* fountain pen
penzija *f* pension
penzioner *m* pensioner
penzioni fond *m* pension fund

pepeljara *f* ashtray
pepelnica *f* Ash Wednesday
pepeo *n* ash, ashes
perad *f* poultry
peraja *f*, **peraje** *n* fin
percepcija *f* perception
perčin *m* pigtail
perfekat *m* (grammatical) perfect
performans *m* performance
pergament *m* parchment
periferija *f* outskirts
perika *f* wig
period *m* period
periodičan *adj* periodic
periodika *f* periodicals
perionica *f* laundry
periš *m* penknife
perivoj *m* park
perje *n* plumage
perla *f* pearl
pero *n* feather
peron *m* platform
perorez *m* penknife
personal *m* personnel
perspektiva *f* perspective
peršin, peršun *m* parsley
pertla *f* shoelace
pertusis *m* whooping cough
perunika *f* iris
perušati *v* to pluck
perut *m* dandruff
perverzan *adj* perverse
perverzija *f* perversion
pesak *m* sand
pesimist *m* pessimist
pesimistički *adj* pessimistic
pesimizam *m* pessimism
peskovit *adj* sandy
pesma *f* poem
pesnica *f* fist
pesnik *m* poet
pesništvo *n* poetry

pešačenje *n* walking
pešačiti *v* to walk
pešadija *f* infantry
pešak *m* 1. pedestrian 2. infantryman
pešice *adv* on foot
peškir *m* towel
pest, pesnica *f* fist
pet five
peta *f* heel
petak *m* Friday
petao *m* cock; rooster
peteljka *f* stem
peti 1. *adj* fifth 2. *v* to lift 3. to go up
peticija *f* petition
petlja *f* 1. loop 2. noose
petljati *v* to fumble
petnaest fifteen
petoboj *m* pentathlon
petogodišnji plan *m* five-year plan
petougao *m* pentagon
petrohemijski, petrokemijski *adj* petrochemical
petrolej *m* 1. petroleum 2. kerosene
pevač *m* singer
pevanje *n* singing
pevati *v* to sing
pica *f* pizza
pidžama *f* pyjamas
pijaca *f* market, marketplace
pijan *adj* drunk
pijanac, pijanica *f* 1. heavy drinker 2. drunkard
pijančevati *v* to drink (alcohol)
pijanica *f* drunkard, drunk
pijanist *m* pianist
pijanstvo *n* drunkenness
pijavica *f* leech
pijesak *m* sand

pijetao *m* cock; rooster
pijuckati *v* to sip
pijuk *m* pick, pickaxe
pijukati *v* to chirp
pikantan *adj* spicy
piket *m* picket
piketirati *v* to picket
piknik *m* picnic
pila *f* saw
pilana *f* sawmill
pile, piletina *f* chicken
piliti *v* to saw
piljar *m*, **piljarica** *f* 1. greengrocer 2. hawker
piljarnica *f* greengrocer's
piljevina *f* sawdust
piljiti *v* to stare
pilna *f* sawmill
pilot *m* pilot
pilotina *f* sawdust
pilula *f* pill
pilula za spavanje *f* sleeping pill
pin-ap *f* pin-up
pinceta *f* pincers
pingvin *m* penguin
pion *m* pawn
pionir *m* pioneer
pipa *f*, **pipac** *m* tap; faucet
pipati *v* to feel
pir *m* wedding
piramida *f* pyramid
pirat *m* pirate
pire *m* mashed potatoes
pirinač *m* rice
pirjati *v* to stew
pirotehnika *f* pyrotechnics
pisac *m* writer
pisak *m* 1. whistle 2. mouthpiece
pisaljka *f* pencil
pisan *adj* written
pisanje *n* writing
pisanka *f* notebook

pisar *m* clerk
pisarna *f* office
pisati *v* to write
pisaći *adj* writing
pisaći pribor *m* stationery
pisaći stol *m* desk
pisaći stroj *m* typewriter
piskati *v* to whistle
piskutati *v* to squeak
pismen *adj* 1. written 2. literate
pismenost *f* 1. writing 2. literacy
pismo *n* 1. letter 2. handwriting
pismo s bombom *n* letter bomb
pisoar *m* urinal
pišati *v* to piss
pištaljka *f* whistle
pištati *v* to hiss
pištolj *m* pistol
pista *f* runway
pista za skijanje *f* ski slope
pita *f* pie
pitak *m* drinkable
pitalica *f* riddle
pitanje *n* question
pitati *v* to ask
piti *v* to drink
pitka voda *f* drinking water
pitom *adj* tame
piton *m* python
pivara *f* brewery
pivnica *f* 1. bar 2. wine cellar
pivo *n* beer, lager
pizma *f* 1. grudge 2. spite
piće *n* drink
pjega *f* 1. freckle 2. spot
pjegav *adj* 1. freckled 2. spotty
pjena *f* 1. foam 2. lather
pjenušac *m* champagne
pjenušav *adj* sparkling (wine)
pjesma *f* 1. poem 2. song
pješačiti *v* to walk
pješadija *f* infantry

pješak *m* 1. pedestrian 2. infantryman
pješak *m* pedestrian
pješčan *adj* sandy
pješčani brijeg *m* sand dune
pješice, pješke *adv* on foot
pjevač *m*, **pjevačica** *f* singer
pjevanje *n* singing
pjevati *v* to sing
plac *m* lot, site
plaća *f* pay
plaćanje *n* payment
plaćati *v* to pay
plaćen *adj* paid
plaćenik *m* mercenary
placenta *f* placenta
plač *m* weeping
pladanj *m* 1. plate 2. dish
plafon *m* ceiling
plagijat *m* plagiarism
plagirati *v* to plagiarize
plah *adj* 1. hot-tempered 2. shy
plahost *f* shyness
plakar *m* cupboard
plakat *m* poster
plakati *v* to cry
plamen 1. *adj* blazing 2. *m* flame 3. blaze
plamsati, plamteti, plamtjeti *v* to blaze
plan *m* plan
planeta *f* planet
planina *f* mountain
planinar *m* mountaineer
planinarenje *n* mountaineering
planinski *adj* 1. mountain 2. mountainous
planiranje porodice *n* family planning
planirati *v* to plan
plantaža *f* plantation
planuti *v* to catch fire

plasirati *v* 1. to place 2. to invest
plasman *m* 1. (spor.) place 2. (fin.) investment
plast *m* haystack
plastičan *adj* plastic
plastična bomba *f* plastic bomb
plastična hirurgija/kirurgija *f* plastic surgery
plastika *f* plastic
plašiti *v* to frighten
plašiti se *v* to be afraid (**of** od)
plašljiv *adj* scared
plašt *m* cloak
plata *f* pay
platforma *f* platform
platforma za posmorsko bušenje *f* oil rig
platina *f* platinum
platiti *v* to pay
platiti u naturi *v* to pay in kind
plativ *adj* payable
platnen *adj* linen
platni dan *m* payday
platno *n* linen
plato *m* plateau
plav *adj* 1. blue 2. fair
plavičast *adj* bluish
plaviti *v* to flood
plaviti *v* to overflow
plavook *m* blue-eyed
plavuša *f* blonde
plaziti *v* to crawl
plazma *f* plasma
plaža *f* beach
plebiscit *m* plebiscite
pleh *m* sheet metal
pleme *n* 1. clan 2. tribe
plemenit *adj* noble
plemenito *adv* nobly
plemenitost *f* nobleness
plemić *m* nobleman
plemstvo *n* nobility

plenarna sednica/sjednica *f* plenary session

plenarni *adj* plenary

pleniti *v* to loot

ples *m* dance, dancing

plesač *m*, **plesačica** *f* dancer

plesan *m* mould; mold

plesati *v* to dance

plesti *v* 1. to knit 2. to plait

pletenica *f* plait

pletenje *n* knitting

pletivo *n* 1. knitting 2. network

pleuritis *m* pleurisy

pleća *f* shoulders

pličina *f*, **pličak** *m* shallows

plijen *m* 1. loot 2. prey

plijeniti *v* to loot

plijesan *adj* mould; mold

plik *m* blister

plima *f* high tide

plimski talas/val *m* tidal wave

plimski *adj* tidal

plin *m* gas

plinara *f* gasworks

plinomod *m* gas pipe

plinska glavna cijev *m* gas main

plišan *adj* plush

plitak *m* shallow

plitica *f* plate

plivač *m* swimmer

plivački bazen *m* swimming pool

plivanje *n* swimming

plivati *v* to swim

plivaći bazen *m* swimming pool

ploča *f* 1. board 2. plate 3. disc 4. record

pločica *f* tile

pločnik *m* pavement; sidewalk

plod *m* fruit

plodan *adj* 1. fruitful 2. fertile

plodno *adv* fruitfully

plodnost *f* 1. fruitfulness 2. fertility

ploha *f* surface

plomba *f* filling

plombirati *v* to fill

plosan *adj* level surface

ploška *f* slice

plot *m* enclosure

plotun *m* (mil.) salvo

plovak *m* buoy

plovan *adj* navigable

plovidba *f* 1. navigation 2. voyage

ploviti *v* 1. to navigate 2. to sail

plovka *f* duck

pluća *f* lungs

plućni *adj* pulmonary

plug *m* plough; plow

plural *m* plural

plus *adj/conj* plus, extra

pluta *f* cork

plutača *f* buoy

plutati *v* to float

pluto *n* cork

plutonij, plutonijum *m* plutonium

plužiti *v* to plough/plow

pljačka *f* 1. robbery 2. looting

pljačkaš *m* 1. robber 2. looter

pljačkati *v* 1. to rob 2. to loot

pljesak *m*, **pljeskanje** *n* applause

pljeskati *v* to applaud

pljeskavica *f* hamburger

pljesniv *adj* mouldy

pljesnuti *v* to slap

pljosan *f* level surface

pljunuti *v* to spit

pljusak *m* shower

pljusak *m*, **pljuska** *f* slap

pljusnuti *v* to slap

pljuvačka *f* spit

pljuvanje *n* spitting

pljuvati, pljunuti *v* to spit

pneumatičan, pneumatski *adj* pneumatic

pneumonija f pneumonia
po prep 1. at 2. by 3. on 4. about 5. during 6. after 7. slightly 8. half
pobačaj m miscarriage
pobacati v to discard
pobaciti v to miscarry
pobeda f victory
pobediti v 1. to defeat 2. to win
pobednik m 1. victor 2. winner
pobesneti v to be furious
pobeći v to flee
pobijanje n refutation
pobijati v to refute
pobijediti v 1. to defeat 2. to win
pobirati v to collect
pobiti v 1. to slaughter 2. to dispute
pobjeda f victory
pobjednik m victor
pobjedonosan adj victorious
pobjesniti v to be furious
pobjeđivati v 1. to defeat 2. to win
pobjeći v to flee
pobledeti, poblijediti v to turn pale
pobliže adv in detail
pobočan adj lateral
pobočnik m adjutant
poboljšanje n improvement
poboljšati v to improve
pobornik m 1. defender 2. (leg.) advocate
pobožan adj pious
pobožan adj religious
pobožnost f piety
pobrati v to collect
pobrinuti se v to take care of
pobrkan adj mixed up
pobrkati v to mix up
pobrojiti v to count
pobuda f 1. stimulus 2. provocation

pobuditi, pobuđivati v 1. to stimulate 2. to provoke
pobuna f 1. riot 2. rebellion
pobuniti v to incite rebellion
pobuniti se v to rebel against
pobunjenik m rebel
pocrneo adj 1. blackened 2. tanned
pocrnjeti v to tan
pocrvenjeti v to blush
počasni adj honorary
počast f honours
počastiti v to honour
počekati v to wait for
počelo n element
pocepan adj ragged
počešati v to scratch
počešljati v to comb
početak m beginning
početan adj initial
početi v to begin
početnik m, **početnica** f beginner
počevši od... beginning with...
počinak m rest
počinitelj m 1. doer 2. perpetrator
počiniti v 1. to do 2. to commit
počiniti samubojstvo v to commit suicide
počinjati v to start
počinuti se v to rest
počistiti v to clear up
počivati v to rest
poći v to set off
poći po v to fetch
pod 1. prep under 2. below 3. m ground 4. floor
pod oslovom/uvjetom on condition that
pod vatrom under fire
podaleko adv rather far
podanik m 1. subject 2. citizen
podao adj 1. infamous 2. mean
podatak m 1. information 2. data

podatan *adj* flexible
podati se *v* 1. to indulge in 2. to become addicted to
podbaciti *v* 1. to fail 2. to miss
podbadati, podbosti *v* to instigate
podbočiti *v* to prop up
podbradak *m* double chin
podbuo *adj* swollen
podcijeniti, podcjenjivati *v* to underrate
podčiniti *v* to subject to
podcrtati, podcrtavati *v* to underline
podela *f* 1. division 2. distribution
podeljen *adj* divided
poderan *adj* torn
poderati *v* to tear
podesan *adj* suitable
podesiti *v* to adapt
podgradnja *f* substructure
podgrijati *v* to warm
podići *v* 1. to raise 2. to erect
podići se *v* to rise
podijeliti *v* 1. to divide 2. to distribute
podijum *m* 1. floor 2. platform
podivljati *v* to grow wild
podizanje *n* 1. raising 2. erection
podizati *v* 1. to raise 2. to erect
podjarmiti, podjarmljivati *v* to subjugate
podjarmljivanje *n* subjugation
podjednak *m* equal
podjela *f* 1. division 2. distribution
podjeljivati *v* 1. to divide 2. to distribute
podlakitca *f* forearm
podleći *v* to succumb
podlo *adv* meanly
podloga *f* 1. base 2. basis
podlost *f* meanness
podložan *adj* subordinate

podložan *adj* vulnerable
podmazati *v* to grease
podmet *m* subject
podmetnuti *v* to subject
podmiriti *v* to settle
podmiriti, podmirivati *v* to settle up
podmićivati, podmititi *v* to bribe
podmladak *m* 1. offspring 2. young people
podmladiti *v* to rejuvenate
podmlađivanje *n* rejuvenation
podmornica *f* submarine
podmorski *adj* submarine
podmuklost *f* deceit
podnajam *m* sub-lease
podnaslov *m* subtitle
podne *not declinable* 1. noon 2. at noon
podneblje *n* climate
podneti *v* to submit
podnevak *m* meridian
podnevni *adj* midday
podnijeti, podnositi *v* to bear
podnosilac *m* 1. applicant 2. complainant
podnošljiv *adj* bearable
podnožje *n* 1. base 2. foothill
podoban *adj* suitable
pododbor *m* subcommittee
podoficir *m* non-commissioned officer
podojiti *v* to suckle
podozrenje *n* suspicion
podozriv *adj* suspicious
podrazdeo, podrazdio *m* subdivision
podrazumevati *v* 1. to understand 2. to imply
podražaj *m* stimulus
podražavanje *n* imitation
podražavati *v* to imitate

podrediti, podređivati *v* to subject to
podređen *adj* subordinate
podrezati *v* to trim
podrhtavanje *n* trembling
podrigivati se *v* to burp
podrijetlo *n* origin
podriti *v* to subvert
podrivač *m* subversive
podrivačka delatnost/djelatnost *f* subversive activity
podroban *adj* detailed
podrobno *adv* in detail
podrovati *v* to undermine
podrška *f* 1. support 2. (pol.) second
podrtina *f* 1. ruin 2. wreck
područje *n* territory
podrugivati se *v* to mock
podrugljiv *adj* mocking
podrum *m* (wine) cellar
podružnica *f* 1. branch office 2. subsidiary
podsekretar *m* undersecretary
podsetnik *m* notebook
podsjećati, podsjetiti *v* to remind
podsmeh *m* mockery
podstandardan *adj* substandard
podsticaj *m* motive
podsticatelj *m* instigator
podsticati *v* to instigate
podstirati, podastrijeti *v* to submit
podstrekač *m* instigator
podstrići *v* 1. to trim 2. to crop
podsvesno *adv* subconsciously
podsvest, podsvijest *f* subconscious
podsvestan, podsvjestan *adj* subconscious
podsvojče *n* foster child
podučavanje *n* instruction

podučavati *v* to instruct
podudaran *adj* identical
podudarati se *v* to conform
podugovarač *m* subcontractor
poduhvat *m* undertaking
poduka *f* instruction
podupirač *m* strut
podupirati, poduprijeti *v* to support
podupreti *v* to support
poduzetan *adj* enterprising
poduzeti, poduzimati *v* to venture
poduzetnik *m* contractor
poduzeće *n* enterprise
podvaliti *v* to cheat
podvezica *f* garter
podvig *m* exploit
podviknuti *v* to shout
podviti *v* to turn down
podvlačiti *v* to underline
podvodač *m* procurer
podvodan *adj* marshy
podvodni *adj* underwater
podvodnik *m* pimp
podvorba *f* service
podvoriti *v* to serve
podvornik *m* attendant
podvostručiti *v* to duplicate
podvoz *m* transport
podvožnjak *m* subway; underpass
podvrći, podvrgnuti *v* to submit
podvući *v* to underline
podzeman *adj* 1. subterranean 2. underground
podzemlje *n* underground
podzemna železnica/željeznica *f* underground; subway
poema *f* poem
poen *m* (spor.) point
poenglaziti *v* to anglicize
poetičan, poetički *adj* poetic

poetika *f* poetics
poezija *f* poetry
pogađanje *n* bargaining
pogađati *v* to guess
pogađati se *v* to bargain
pogan *adj* foul
poganin *m* pagan
pogasiti *v* to extinguish
pogaziti *v* 1. to run over 2. to violate
pogibao *f* danger
pogibati *v* to perish
pogibelj *f* danger
pogibeljan *adj* dangerous
poginuli u borbi *mpl* (mil.) casualties
poginuti *v* to perish
pogladiti *v* to stroke
poglavica *f* chief
poglavije *n* chapter
poglavito *adv* mainly
poglavlje *n* chapter
pogled *m* 1. look 2. **u pogledu** in view of
pogledati *v* to look at
pognut *adj* bent over
pognuti se *v* to bend over
pogodak *m* **direktan pogodak** direct hit
pogodan *adj* suitable
pogodba *f* agreement
pogodbeni *adj* conditional
pogoditi *v* to guess
pogodnost *f* 1. convenience 2. concession
pogon *m* 1. section 2. drive 3. motive
pogonski troškovi *mpl* overheads
pogoršati *v* to aggravate
pogostiti *v* to entertain
pogotovo *adv* especially
pogovor *m* epilogue

pograbiti *v* to seize
pograničan *adj* border
pogrda *f* abuse
pogrdan *adj* abusive
pogreb *m* funeral
pogrešan *adj* 1. wrong 2. defective
pogreška *f* mistake
pogrešna presuda *f* miscarriage of justice
pogrešno *adv* by mistake
pogriješiti *v* to make a mistake
pogrom *m* pogrom
poguban *adj* dangerous
pogubiti *v* to execute
pogubljenje *n* execution
pohaban *adj* worn out
pohađati *v* 1. to vist 2. to attend
poharati *v* 1. to ravage 2. to rob
pohlepa *f* 1. greed 2. enthusiasm
pohlepan *adj* 1. greedy 2. enthusiastic
pohod *m* campaign
pohoditi *v* to visit
pohota *f* lust
pohotan *adj* lustful
pohraniti *v* to deposit
pohrliti *v* to hurry
pohvala *f* praise
pohvalan *adj* praiseworthy
poimanje *n* comprehension
poimence *adv* by name
pojačalo *n* amplifier
pojačati, pojačavati *v* to reinforce
pojam *m* idea
pojas *m* 1. belt 2. zone
pojas za spasavanje *n* lifebelt
pojava *f* 1. appearance 2. phenomenon
pojaviti se *v* to appear
pojedinac *m* individual
pojedinačno *adv* individually
pojedince *adv* one by one

pojedini, pojedinačan *adj* single
pojedinost *f* detail
pojednostaviti *v* to simplify
pojeftiniti *v* to become cheaper
pojesti *v* to consume
pojiti *v* to water
pojmiti *v* to understand
pojuriti *v* to rush
pokajati se *v* to repent
pokajnički *adj* repentant
pokapati *v* to bury
pokatkad sometimes
pokazati, pokazivati *v* 1. to demonstrate 2. to prove
poker *m* poker
pokiditi *v* to blame
pokisnuti *v* to get wet
poklade *fpl* carnival
poklanjati *v* to bow
poklati *v* 1. to slaughter 2. to massacre
pokleknuti *v* to yield
poklič, poklik *m* shout
poklisar *m* 1. envoy 2. ambassador
pokliznuti *v* to slide
poklon *m* 1. bow 2. gift
poklonik *m* 1. pilgrim 2. admirer
pokloniti *v* to present
pokloniti se *v* to bow
poklopac *m* 1. cover 2. lid
poklopiti *v* to cover
pokoj *m* rest
pokojni... *adj* the late...
pokojnik *m* deceased person
pokolenje *n* generation
pokolj *m* 1. slaughter 2. massacre
pokoljenje *n* generation
pokop *m* burial
pokopati *v* to bury
pokora *f* penitence
pokoran *adj* obedient
pokoravati, pokoriti se *v* to obey

pokornost *f* obedience
pokožica *f* epidermis
pokraj 1. *prep* close to 2. *adv* by
pokrajina *f* 1. countryside 2. province
pokrasti *v* to steal
pokratiti *v* to shorten
pokrečiti *v* to whitewash
pokrenuti *v* 1. to move 2. to start up
pokrenuti časopis *v* to launch a magazine
pokret *m* movement
pokretan *adj* moveable
pokretna kuća *f* mobile home
pokretni most *f* swing-bridge
pokriti, pokrivati *v* 1. to cover 2. to clear
pokrivač *m* 1. cover 2. blanket
pokriće *n* 1. cover 2. security
pokrovitelj *m* 1. protector 2. patron
pokroviteljstvo *n* 1. protection 2. patronage
pokroviteljstvo *n* patronage
pokrpati *v* to mend
pokrstiti *v* to baptize
pokucati *v* to knock
pokućstvo *n* furniture
pokunjen *adj* downcast
pokupiti *v* to collect
pokus *m* 1. trial 2. test
pokušaj *m* attempt
pokušati *v* 1. to try 2. to test
pokvaren *adj* 1. bad 2. corrupt 3. damaged 4. out of order
pokvarenost *f* corruption
pokvariti *v* 1. to spoil 2. to corrupt 3. to ruin
pokvarljiv *adj* perishable
pokvasiti *v* to wet
pol *m* 1. sex 2. pole 3. **Sjeverni Pol**

North Pole **4. Južni Pol** South
Pole **5.** *see* **pola**
pola *adv* half
polagan *adj* slow
polaganje *n* **1. polaganje kabla**
cable laying **2. polaganje mina**
mine laying
polagano *adv* slowly
polagati *v* **1.** to lay **2.** to deposit **3.**
to take an oath **4.** to sit an exam
polako *adv* slowly
polarizacija *f* polarization
polarni *adj* polar
polas *m* belt
polaskati *v* to flatter
polazak *m* departure
polaziti *v* to depart
polazna tačka/točka *f* starting
point
polazni *adj* initial
poleći *v* to lie down
poledica *f* glaze
poledica *f* ice
poleđina *f* back
polemika *f* polemics
polenska groznica *f* hay fever
polet *m* **1.** enthusiasm **2.** takeoff
poletan *adj* enthusiastic
poletanje *n* takeoff
poletno-sletna staza *f* runway
polica *f* shelf
policajac *m* policeman
policija *f* police
policijski čas *m* curfew
polijevati, politi *v* to water
poliklinika *f* polyclinic
poliomijelitis *m* polio
polip *m* polyp
polirati *v* to polish
polisa *f* policy
politehnički *adj* polytechnical
politički *adj* political

politika *f* **1.** politics **2.** policy
polni *adj* **1.** sexual **2.** genital
polni odnosi *mpl* sexual relations
polni organi *mpl* genitals
polno opštenje/općenje *n* sexual
intercourse
polovan *adj* **1.** used **2.** second-
hand
polovica *f* half
polovičan *adj* **1.** halfway **2.** partial
polovina *f* half
položaj *m* **1.** situation **2. pravni
položaj** (leg.) status
položaj države *m* statehood
položen *adj* situated
položiti *v* to place
položiti ispit *v* to pass an exam
polu- **1.** half- **2.** semi-
poluautomatska paljba *f* semi-
automatic fire
poluautomatski puška *f* semi-
automatic rifle
poluautomatski *adj* semi-
automatic
polubrat *m* stepbrother
polucilindar *m* bowler
poludeti, poludjeti *v* to go mad
polufinale *n* semi-final
polufinalni *adj* semi-final
poluga *f* lever
polukrug *m* semicircle
polukugla, polulopta *f*
hemisphere
polumesec, polumjesec *m*
crescent
polumer, polumjer *m* **1.** half-
measure **2.** radius
poluostrvo, poluotok *m*
peninsula
polupati *v* to smash
poluprečnik *m* radius
poluprovodnik *m* semiconductor

polusestra *f* stepsister
polutar *m* equator
poluvojni *adj* paramilitary
poluvreme, poluvrijeme *n* (spor.) half-time
poljana *f* 1. plan 2. field
polje *n* 1. field 2. line
poljepšati *v* to embellish
poljodjelac *m* farmer
poljodjelski *adj* agricultural
poljodjelstvo, poljoprivreda *f* agriculture
poljoprivredni *adj* agricultural
poljoprivrednik *m* farmer
Poljska *f* Poland
poljska bolnica *f* field hospital
poljski *adj* Polish
poljubac *m* kiss
poljubiti *v* to kiss
poljuljati *v* to weaken
pomaći *v* to move
pomada *f* face cream
pomagač *m* assistant
pomagalo *n* 1. help 2. tool
pomaganje *n* 1. help 2. relief
pomagati *v* to help
pomahnitao *adj* mad, furious
pomajka *f* fostermother
pomaknuti *v* to move
pomalo *adv* a little
pomama *f* rage
pomanjkanje *n* shortage
pomast *m* ointment
pomen *m* 1. mention 2. commemoration
pomenuti *v* to mention
pomeriti *v* to move
pomešati *v* to mix
pomesti *v* to sweep up
pometnja *f* confusion
pom frit *m* chips; french fries
pomičan *adj* 1. moveable 2. mobile

pomicati *v* to move
pomilovanje *n* (leg.) pardon
pomilovati *v* 1. to stroke 2. (leg.) to pardon
pomiriti se *v* to be reconciled
pomiriti *v* to reconcile
pomisao *f* idea
pomisliti, pomišljati *v* to imagine
pomladiti, pomlađivati *v* to rejuvenate
pomnja *f* attention
pomnjiv *adj* careful
pomno *adv* carefully
pomnožiti *v* to multiply
pomoć *f* 1. help 2. relief
pomoć pri masovnim nesrećama *f* disaster relief
pomoći *v* to help
pomoćni *adj* 1. auxiliary 2. relief
pomoćnik *m* helper
pomoću *prep* by means of
pomodan *adj* fashionable
pomodreo *adj* bluish
pomoliti se *v* 1. to appear 2. to request
pomor *m* epidemic
pomorac *m* seaman
pomorandža *f* orange
pomorski *adj* 1. marine 2. naval
pomorsko pravo *n* maritime law
pomorstvo *n* sailing
pomračenje *n* 1. eclipse 2. blackout
pomrčina *f* darkness
pomrčina *f* eclipse
pomreti *v* to die off
pomrsiti *v* 1. to entangle 2. to confuse
ponajviše *adv* chiefly
ponajviše *adv* most of all
ponaosob *adv* separately
ponašanje *n* behaviour

ponašati se *v* to behave
ponavljanje *n* 1. repetition 2. revision
ponavljati *v* 1. to repeat 2. to revise
ponedeljak, ponedjeljak *m* Monday
ponegde somewhere
ponekad sometimes
poneki *adj* some
ponešto *adv* somewhat
poneti *v* to take
poni *m* pony
ponijeti *v* to take
poništen *adj* cancelled
poništenje *n* cancellation
poništiti *v* 1. to cancel 2. (leg.) to quash
ponizan *adj* 1. humble 2. humiliated
poniziti *v* 1. to humble 2. to humiliate
poniziti se *v* 1. to be humble 2. to be humilated
poniznost *f* humility
ponižavanje, poniženje *n* humiliation
ponjava *f* sheet
ponoć *f* 1. midnight 2. at midnight
ponor *m* precipice
ponos *m* pride
ponosan *adj* proud
ponositi se *v* to be proud
ponoviti *v* to repeat
ponovo *adv* again
ponton *m* pontoon
pontonski most *f* pontoon bridge
ponuda *f* 1. offer 2. (com.) tender
ponuda i potražnja supply and demand
ponuditi *v* 1. to offer 2. (com.) to tender

ponuditi se *v* to volunteer
ponuđač *m* bidder
poočim *m* fosterfather
pooštriti *v* to intensify
pop *m* priest
popaliti *v* to burn down
popečak *m* steak
popeti se *v* to climb
popis *m* 1. list 2. inventory
popis stanovništva *f* census
popisati *v* 1. to list 2. to make an inventory
popiti *v* to drink up
poplašiti *v* to frighten
poplava *f* flood
poplaviti *v* to flood
popločiti *v* 1. to pave 2. to panel
poplun *m* quilt
popodne *n* afternoon
popravak *m* repair
popraviti, popravljati *v* to repair
popravka *f* repair
poprečan *adj* cross-
poprečni presjek *m* cross-section
popreko, poprijeko *adv* across
poprsje *n* bust
poprskati *v* to sprinkle
popularan *adj* popular
popularizacija *f* popularization
popularizovati *v* to popularize
popularnost *f* popularity
popuniti *v* 1. to fill 2. to complete
popuniti gorivom *v* to refuel
popuštanje *n* (pol.) appeasement
popust *m* 1. reduction 2. discount 3. allowance
popustiti, popuštati *v* 1. to reduce 2. to give way 3. (pol.) to appease
popustljivost *f* compliance
poput *prep* like
popuznuti *v* to slide down

pora *f* pore
poraba *f* use
poraniti *v* to get up early
porast *m* 1. growth 2. increase
porasti *v* 1. to grow 2. to increase
poratni *adj* postwar
poravnanje *n* settlement
poravnati *v* to level out
poraz *m* defeat
porazdijeliti *v* to distribute
porazgovoriti *v* to talk with
poraziti *v* to defeat
poražen *adj* defeated
porcija *f* 1. portion 2. dish
porculan *m* porcelain
poreći *v* to deny
pored *prep* 1. near 2. in spite of 3. except 4. in addition to
poredak *m* order
poredati *v* to put in order
porediti *v* to compare
poređenje *n* comparison
poreklo *n* origin
poremetiti *v* to disrupt
poremećaj *m* disruption
poremećen *adj* disrupted
poreska godina *f* tax year
poreska olakšica *f* tax break
poreska utaja *f* tax evasion
poreski *adj* tax
poreski službenik *m* tax collector
poresko oslobođenje *n* tax exemption
poresko sniženje *n* tax cut
porez *m* 1. tax 2. platiti porez to pay tax
porez na dohodak *m* income tax
porezni obaveznik *m* taxpayer
poreznik *m* tax collector
poricati *v* 1. to deny 2. to revoke
porijeklo origin
poriluk *m* leek

porinuti brod *v* to launch a ship
poriv *m* impulse
pornografija *f* pornography
pornografski *adj* pornographic
porobiti *v* to enslave
poročan *adj* bad
porod *m* 1. children 2. posterity
porodica *f* family
porodilište *n* maternity hospital
poroditi se *v* to give birth to
porođaj *m* childbirth
porođajni bolovi *mpl* labour pains
porođajni grčevi *mpl* labour contractions
porok *m* vice
porota *f* jury
porotnik *m* juror
porozan *adj* porous
poroznost *f* porosity
port-parol *m* spokesperson
portabl *m/adj* portable
portal *m* 1. doorway 2. gateway
portfelj *m* 1. briefcase 2. portfolio 3. ministar bez portfelja minister without portfolio
portir *m* doorkeeper, porter
portret *m* portrait
portretisati *v* to portray
Portugal *m* Portugal
portugiški *adj* Portuguese
porub *m* hem
poručilac *m* customer
poručiti *v* to order
poručnik *m* lieutenant
porudžbina *f* order
poruga *f* scorn
porugljiv *adj* scornful
poruka *f* message
porušiti *v* to subvert
posada *f* crew
posaditi *v* 1. to plant 2. to seat
posao *n* 1. job 2. work 3. business

posavjetovati se *v* to consult
poseban *adj* 1. separate 2. special
posebno *adv* specially
posebna emisija *f* TV special
posebno *adv* apart
posed *m* property
posednik *m* owner
posedovati *v* to own
posegnuti *v* to reach
posekotina *f* cut
posesivan *adj* possessive
posesti *v* to occupy
poseta *f* visit
posetilac *m* visitor
posetiti *v* to visit
posetnica *f* visiting card; calling card
poseći *v* to cut (down)
poseći, posegnuti *v* to seize
posijati *v* to sow
posiniti *v* to adopt
posinjenje *n* adoption
posipati *v* to scatter
posjed *m* property
posjednik *m* owner
posjedovati *v* to own
posjet *m* visit
posjetilac *m* visitor
posjetiti *v* to visit
posjetnica *f* visiting card; calling card
posjeći *v* to cut (down)
posjećivati *v* to visit
poskakivati *v* to hop
poskup *adj* pricey
poskupeti, poskupiti *v* to increase in price
poslagati *v* to order
poslanički mandat *m* seat
poslanik *m* 1. delegate 2. ambassador 3. member of parliament (MP)

poslanstvo *n* 1. delegation 2. embassy
poslastica *f* sweet
poslastičarnica *f* cake-shop
poslati *v* to send
posle 1. *prep* after 2. *adv* afterwards
posledica *f* consequence
poslednji *adj* final
poslepodne *n* afternoon
posleratni *adj* postwar
poslije 1. *prep* after 2. *adv* afterwards
posljedica *f* result
posljednji *adj* final
poslodavac *m* employer
poslovan *adj* business
poslovan čovjek *m* business man
poslovanje *n* 1. business 2. management
poslovati *v* to do business
poslovica *f* proverb
poslovni prijatelj *m* business partner
poslovni promet *m* commerce
poslovnica *f* office
poslovnik *m* rules of procedure
poslovno vrijeme *n* office hours
poslovođa *m* manager
posluga *f* 1. service 2. servants
posluh *m* obedience
poslušan *adj* obedient
poslušati *v* to obey
poslušnost *f* obedience
poslužavnik *m* tray
poslužitelj *m* attendant
poslužiti *v* to serve
poslužiti se *v* to serve oneself
posmatrač *m* observer
posmatrački status *m* observer's status
posmatranje *n* observation
posmatrati *v* to observe

posmrtni *adj* posthumous
posmrtno slovo *n* obituary
posoliti *v* to salt
pospan *adj* sleepy
pospješiti, pospješivati *v* to accelerate
posprdan *adj* ironic
pospremati *v* to tidy up
posramiti *v* to shame
posrebren *adj* silver-plated
posrebriti *v* to silver
posred *prep* in the middle of
posredan *adj* 1. indirect 2. derisive
posredna vatra *f* (mil.) indirect fire
posrednik *m* 1. agent 2. mediator
posredništvo *n* 1. agency 2. mediation
posredno *adv* indirectly
posredovanje *n* mediation
posredovati *v* to mediate
posrnuti, posrtati *v* to stumble
post restant *m* poste restante
postaja *f* 1. station 2. stop
postajati, postati *v* to become
postajkivati *v* to stop
postanak *m* origin
postanje *n* genesis
postar *adj* old
postarati se *v* 1. to age 2. to take care of
postati *v* 1. to develop 2. to become
postava *f* lining
postaviti *v* to put
postdiplomac *m* graduate student
postelja *f* bed
posteljina *f* bedding
postepen *adj* gradual
postepeno *adv* gradually
postići *v* to achieve
postići gol *v* to score a goal

postiti *v* to fast
postizati *v* to achieve
posto per cent
postojan *adj* steady
postojanje *n* existence
postojati *v* to exist
postojbina *f* homeland
postojeći *v* existing
postola *f* shoe
postolar *m* shoemaker
postolje *n* stand
postotak *m* percentage
postradati *v* to suffer damage
postrance *adv* aside
postrestant *m* poste restante
postrijeljati *v* to shoot down
postrojenje *n* 1. formation 2. factory
postupak *m* procedure
postupati, postupiti *v* to treat
posuda *f* container
posuditi *v* 1. to borrow 2. to lend
posuđe *n* dishes, plate
posuđenica *f* loanword
posuđivati *v* see **posuditi**
posumnjati *v* 1. to doubt 2. to suspect
posušiti *v* to dry
posustati *v* 1. to give up 2. to tire
posuti *v* to scatter
posvaditi se, posvađati se *v* to quarrel
posve *adv* entirely
posveta *f* dedication
posvetiti *v* see **posvećivati**
posvećen *adj* initiated
posvećivati *v* to dedicate
posvjedočiti *v* to confirm
posvojiti *v* to adopt
posvuda everywhere
pošast *m* epidemic
pošiljalac *m* sender

pošiljka f 1. package 2. shipment
poškakljati v to tickle
poškropiti v to sprinkle
pošta f 1. post 2. post office
poštanska pristojba f postage
poštanska uputnica f money order
poštanski adj post
poštanski ček m postal order
poštanski činovnik m post office clerk
poštanski pretinac m PO box (post office box)
poštanski sanduk m letterbox
poštanski ured m post office
poštar m postman; mailman
poštarina f postage
poštedeti, poštedjeti v to spare
pošten adj honest
poštenje n honesty
pošteno adv honestly
poštivati v 1. to respect 2. to estimate
pošto 1. after 2. when 3. how much?
poštovalac m admirer
poštovan adj respected
Poštovani gospodine! Dear Sir
poštovanje n 1. respect 2. s poštovanjem respectfully 3. Yours faithfully
poštovati v see **poštivati**
pošumljavanje n afforestation
potaja f secrecy
potajan adj secret
potajno adv secretly
potamneti, potamniti, potamnjeti v 1. to destroy 2. to darken
potanko adv in detail
potapati v to sink
potapšati v to tap

potaći, potaknuti v 1. to inspire 2. to stimulate
potceniti v 1. to underrate 2. underestimate
potčiniti v to subjugate
potčinjeni adj subordinate
potegnuti v to pull
potencija f power
potencijal m potential
potencirati v to emphasize
potentan adj potent
potera f pursuit
potera, potjera f manhunt
poternica f wanted notice
poteškoća f difficulty
potez m 1. line 2. move
potezati v to pull
pothranjen adj malnourished
pothranjenost f malnutrition
pothvat m undertaking
poticaj m stimulation
poticati v to stimulate
potiljak m nape
potisak m thrust
potiskivanje n pressure
potiskivati, potisnuti v to push back
potišten adj depressed
potištenost m depression
potjecati v to originate
potjera f chase
potjerati v to chase away
potkapati v to undermine
potkazati v to denounce
potkazivač m informer
potkošulja f vest; undershirt
potkova, potkovica f horseshoe
potkožan adj subcutaneous
potkradati v to creep
potkrepiti v to corroborate
potkresati v to cut off
potkrijepiti v see **potkrepiti**

potkrovlje *n* loft
potkupiti *v* to bribe
potkupljiv *adj* bribable
potlačiti *v* 1. to crush 2. to oppress
potočić *m* brook
potok *m* stream
potom *adv* afterwards
potomak *m* descendant
potomstvo *n* posterity
potonji *adj* latter
potonuti *v* to sink
potop *m* flood
potopiti *v* 1. to sink 2. to drown
potopiti brod *m* to scuttle a boat
potpaliti *v* 1. to set fire to 2. to light
potpetica *f* heel
potpis *m* signature
potpisan *adj* signed
potpisati *v* to sign
potpisati poleđinu čeka *v* to endorse a cheque
potpisnik *m* 1. signatory 2. subscriber
potplat *m* sole
potplatiti *v* to bribe
potpomagati, potpomoći, potpomognuti *v* 1. to aid 2. to support 3. to subsidise
potpora *f* 1. support 2. relief 3. subsidy
potporanj *m* 1. pillar 2. support
potporučnik *m* sub-lieutenant
potpredsednik, potpredsjednik *m* vicepresident
potpredsedništvo, potpredsjedništvo *n* vicepresidency
potpukovnik *m* lieutenant-colonel
potpun *adj* 1. full 2. complete
potpuniti *v* 1. to fill 2. to complete
potpuno *adv* completely
potpunost *f* completeness

potraga *f* 1. search 2. pursuit
potrajati *v* 1. to continue 2. to last
potratiti *v* to waste
potražiti *v* 1. to search 2. to look up
potraživanje *n* claim
potraživati *v* to claim
potražnja *f* (ec.) 1. demand 2. **ponuda i potražnja** supply and demand
potrčati *v* to run
potreba *f* need
potreban *adj* necessary
potrepštine *n* requirements
potres *m* 1. concussion 2. earthquake
potresan *adj* touching
potresti *v* to shake
potrgan *adj* torn
potrgati *v* to tear
potrošač *m* (fin.) consumer
potrošak *m* 1. expense 2. consumption
potrošiti *v* to spend
potrošnja *f* (fin.) consumption
potrostručiti *v* to triple
potruditi se *v* to take pains
potucati se *v* to wander
potući *v* to beat
potući se *v* to come to blows
potužiti se *v* to complain
potvrda *f* 1. confirmation 2. receipt 3. certificate
potvrdan *adj* affirmative
potvrditi *v* 1. to confirm 2. to certify
poubijati *v* 1. to slaughter 2. to massacre
poučan *adj* instructive
poučavanje *n* instruction
poučavati, poučiti *v* 1. to instruct 2. to coach

poučljiv *adj* teachable
pouka *f* 1. tuition 2. instruction
pouzdan *adj* reliable
pouzdanik *m* trustworthy person
pouzdanje *n* confidence
pouzdano *adv* confidently
pouzdati se *v* to trust
pouzeće *n* cash on delivery
povećalo *n* magnifying glass
povećanje *n* 1. enlargement 2. increase
povećati *v* 1. to enlarge 2. to increase
povećati se *v* 1. to become enlarged 2. to increase
povelja *f* charter
povenuti *v* to wither
poverenje *n* confidence
poverenje, povjerenje *n* 1. confidence 2. **u poverenju/ povjerenju** off the record
poverilac *m* creditor
poverljiv *adj* confidential
povesti *v* to take
povez *m* 1. bandage 2. (med.) sling
povezati *v* to bandage
povijati, poviti *v* to bind up
povijest *f* history
povijestan *adj* historical
povik *m* 1. cry 2. outcry
povikati, poviknuti *v* 1. to cry out 2. to exclaim
povinovati se *v* to obey
povisiti *v* 1. to raise 2. to heighten
povišenje *n* 1. rise 2. elevation
povišica *f* rise
poviti *v* to wrap up
povjeravati se *v* to confide in
povjerenik *m* 1. confidant 2. commissioner
povjereništvo *n* 1. commission 2. committee

povjerenje *n* 1. confidence 2. trust
povjeriti *v* 1. to entrust 2. to confide
povjerljiv *adj* 1. confidential 2. trustful
povjerovati *v* to believe
povjetarac *m* breeze
povlačenje *n* retreat
povlačiti *v* 1. to drag 2. to withdraw
povlačiti se *v* to retreat
povlađivanje *n* approval
povlađivati *v* 1. to approve 2. to applaud
povlašten *adj* privileged
povlastica *f* privilege
povod *m* 1. cause 2. motive
povodan *adj* flooded
povodanj *m* flood
povoditi se *v* to imitate
povodom *prep* on the occasion of
povoj *m* 1. bandage 2. nappy; diaper
povoljan *adj* 1. favourable 2. convenient
povoljan *adj* convenient
povoljno *adv* conveniently
povorka *f* 1. procession 2. parade
povraćaj *m* (med.) relapse
povraćanje *n* morning sickness
povraćati *v* to vomit
povratak *m* return
povratan *adj* 1. return 2. reflexive
povratiti *v* 1. to return 2. to vomit
povratiti se *v* to return
povratna karta *f* return ticket
povrće *n* vegetables
povreda *f* 1. violation 2. injury 3. trauma
povrediti *v* 1. to violate 2. to injure
povrediti vazdušni prostor, povrijediti zračni prostor *m* to violate airspace

povremen *adj* periodic
povremeno *adv* periodically
povrh *prep* 1. besides 2. over
povrijediti *v* 1. to violate 2. to injure
površan *adj* superficial
površina *f* 1. surface 2. area
površinski *adj* surface
površno *adv* superficially
površnost *f* superficiality
povučen *adj* 1. quiet 2. withdrawn
povučenost *f* 1. seclusion 2. privacy 3. reticence
povući *v* 1. to drag 2. to withdraw
poza *f* pose
pozabaviti se *v* to enjoy oneself
pozadi *adv/prep* behind
pozadina *f* background
pozadinski *adj* logistic
pozajmica *f* loan
pozajmiti *v* 1. to borrow 2. to lend
pozajmljenica *f* loanword
pozamašan *adj* large
pozdrav *m* 1. greeting 2. salute
pozdraviti *v* 1. to greet 2. to salute
pozelenti, pozelenjeti *v* to become green
pozicija *f* position
pozirati *v* to pose
pozitiv *m* (film) positive
pozitivan *adj* positive
pozitivizam *m* positivism
poziv *m* 1. call 2. invitation 3. summons
pozivati *v* 1. to call 2. to invite 3. to summon
pozivati se *v* to refer to
pozivnica *f* 1. invitation card 2. summons
pozlaćen *adj* gold-plated
pozlatiti *v* to gold-plate
pozliti *v* to feel sick

poznanik *m* acquaintance
poznanstvo *n* acquaintance
poznat *adj* well-known
poznati *v* 1. to recognize 2. to know
poznavalac *m* expert
poznavanje *n* knowledge
poznavati *v see* poznati
pozni *adj* late
pozno *adv* late
pozor *m* attention
pozoran *adj* attentive
pozorišna akademija *f* drama school
pozorište *n* theatre
pozornica *f* stage
pozornost *f* attenton
pozvati *v* to call
pozvoniti *v* to ring
požaliti *v* to regret
požar *m* fire
požderati *v* to gobble up
poželjan *adj* desirable
poželeti, poželjeti *v* to desire
požeti, požnjeti *v* to reap
poživeti, poživjeti *v* to live
požrtvovan *adj* self-sacrificing
požrtvovnost *f* 1. devotion 2. self-sacrifice
požuda *f* 1. greed 2. lust
požudan *adj* 1. lustful 2. greedy
požudno *adv* greedily
požuriti *v* to hasten
požuriti se *v* to rush
požuteti, požutjeti *v* to turn yellow
pračovek *m* primitive man
praćenje *n* tracking
praćka *f* sling
pradjed *m* great-grandfather
prag *m* 1. threshold 2. railway sleeper

prah *m* 1. powder 2. dust 3. **u prahu** powdered
praksa *f* 1. practice 2. practical work 3. use
praktičan *adj* 1. practical 2. useful
praktično *adv* virtually
praktikum *m* course
pramac *m* bow
pramen *adj* 1. lock of hair 2. patch
pramen magle *m* a patch of fog
pranje *n* washing
praonica *f* laundry
prapočetak *m* origin
praporac *m* bell
prasac *m* pig
prasak *m* 1. bang 2. explosion
prase *n* pig
prasetina *f* pork
prasica *f* sow
praskati *v* 1. bang 2. to explode
praskav *adj* explosive
praskozorje *n* dawn
prašak *m* 1. powder 2. pollen
prašan *adj* dusty
prašina *f* dust
prašnik *m* stamen
prašnjiv *adj* dusty
praštanje *n* pardon
praštati *v* to forgive
prašuma *f* 1. forest 2. jungle
prati se *v* to wash oneself
prati *v* to wash
pratilac *m* 1. companion 2. escort
pratiti *v* to accompany
pratnja *f* 1. escort 2. (mus.) accompaniment
praunučad *f* great-grandchildren
praunuk *m* great-grandson
praunuka *f* great-granddaughter
prav *adj* 1. real 2. actual 3. proper 4. just
prava *f* straight line

pravac *m* direction
pravda *f* justice
pravdanje *n* justification
pravdati *v* to justify
pravdati se *v* to quarrel
pravedan *adj* 1. just 2. fair
pravedno *adv* justly
pravednost *f* 1. justice 2. fairness
pravi *adj* 1. true 2. real
pravica *f* 1. justice 2. right
pravičan *adj* 1. just 2. right
pravično *adv* justly
pravičnost *f* justice
pravilan *adj* regular
pravilnik *m* book of regulations
pravilnost *f* regularity
pravilo *n* 1. rule 2. regulation 3. standard
praviti *v* 1. to make 2. to create 3. to manufacture
pravljen u... *adj* made in...
pravni *adj* legal
pravni položaj *m* (leg.) status
pravnički *adj* legal
pravnik *m* lawyer
pravno *adv* legally
pravo 1. *n* right 2. justice 3. law 4. *adv* straight 5. correctly
pravo azila *n* right of asylum
pravobranilac *m* lawyer; attorney
pravobranilaštvo *n* legal office
pravodoban *adj* opportune
pravodobno *adv* 1. in time 2. on time
pravo glasa *n* suffrage
pravokitan *adj* retangular
pravokut, pravokutnik *m* rectangle
pravolinijski *adj* straight
pravomoćan *adj* valid
pravopis *m* 1. spelling 2. orthography
pravopisni *adj* orthographic

pravo pristupa državnim dokumentima *f* freedom of information

pravorijek *m* (leg.) 1. verdict 2. sentence

pravoslavac *m* (rel.) Orthodox

pravoslavan *adj* (rel.) Orthodox

pravoslavlje *n* (rel.) Orthodoxy

pravosnažan *adj* in effect

pravosuđe *n* 1. jurisprudence 2. jurisdiction

pravougao *m* rectangle

pravougaoni *adj* rectangular

pravougaonik *m* rectangle

pravovernost, pravovjernost *f* orthodoxy

prazan *adj* 1. empty 2. clean 3. **prazan hod** neutral gear 4. **na prazno** in neutral

praziluk *m* leek

praznik *m* holiday

praznina *f* emptiness

prazniti *v* to vacate

prazno mesto/mjesto *n* vacancy

praznohod *m* neutral

praznovati *v* to celebrate

praznoverje, praznovjerje *n* superstition

praznoveran, praznovjeran *adj* superstitious

prčija *f* dowry

prčiti *v* to pout

prčkati *v* to fumble

pre *prep/adv* 1. before 2. ago

pre- too, very

prebaciti *v* (mil.) to redeploy

prebaciti *v* 1. to overturn 2. to overthrow

prebaciti metu *v* to overshoot a target

prebeći *v* 1. to run over 2. to desert

prebirač *m* picker

prebirati *v* 1. to pick 2. to sort

prebiti *v* to beat up

prebivalište *n* 1. home 2. residence

prebivati *v* to live

prebjeg *m*, **prebjelica** *f* 1. fugitive 2. deserter

prebjeći *v* 1. to run over 2. to desert

prebledeti *v* to turn pale

preboleti, preboljeti *v* 1. to get over 2. (med.) to recover

prebračni *adj* premarital

prebroditi *v* to overcome

prebrojati, prebrojiti *v* to count

prebrzo *adv* too quickly

prebukirati (se) *v* to overbook

prečac *m* short cut

prečaga *f* 1. rung 2. bar

preceniti *v* to overestimate

preči *adj* more important

prečica *f* short cut

precijeniti *v* to overestimate

prečistač *m* filter

prečistiti *v* 1. to purify 2. to refine

precizan *adj* precise

preciznost *f* precision

precrtati *v* 1. to copy 2. to strike out

prečka *f* bar

prečnik *m* diameter

prečuti *v* to ignore

preći *v* 1. to cross 2. to pass

prećutno *adv* by implication

pred *prep/adv* 1. before 2. ago

predah *m* rest

predahnuti *v* to have a rest

predaja *f* 1. delivery 2. surrender 3. tradition 4. extradition

predajnik *m* transmitter

predan *adj* devoted

predanje *n* tradition

predanost *f* devotion
predatelj *m* deliverer
predati *v* 1. to deliver 2. to hand over
predati se *v* to surrender
predavač *m* 1. lecturer 2. instructor
predavanje *n* lecture
predavati *v* 1. to teach 2. to lecture
predbaciti, predbacivati *v* to reproach
predbilježba *f* 1. booking 2. subscription
predbilježiti *v* 1. to book 2. to subscribe
predbračni *adj* premarital
predbrojiti se *v* to subscribe
predbrojka *f* subscription
preddodžba *f* idea
predeo *m* region
predgovor *m* introduction
predgrađe *n* 1. outskirts 2. suburbs
predigra *f* prelude
predikaonica *f* pulpit
predikat *m* predicate
predio, predjel *m* region
predionica *f* cotton-mill
predistorija *f* previous events
predivo *n* yarn
predizborna kampanja *f* election campaign
predizborni *adj* (pre-)election
predlagač *m* promoter
predlagati, predložiti *v* to propose
predlog *m* 1. proposal 2. preposition
predložiti *v* to propose
predmet *m* 1. object 2. theme
predmnijevati *v* to presume
prednjačiti *v* to lead
prednji *adj* front
prednji kraj *m* (mil.) front line

prednost *f* 1. preference 2. favour 3. advantage 4. **formalna perdnost** technical advantage
predočiti sebi *v* to imagine
predočiti *v* to produce
predodretiti *v* to predetermine
predodžba *f* notion
predohrana *f* prevention
predomisliti se *v* to change one's mind
predosećanje, predosjećanje *n* foreboding
predosećati, predosjećati *v* to have a foreboding
predostrožnost *f* precaution
predračun *m* estimate
predradnik *m* foreman
predrasuda *f* prejudice
predsedavajući, predsedavajući *adj/m* speaker of parliament
predsednik, predsjednik *m* 1. president 2. chairman
predsedništvo, predsjedništvo *n* 1. presidentship 2. chairmanship
predskazati *v* to predict
predsoblje *n* hall
predstava *f* 1. performance 2. idea
predstaviti *v* to introduce
predstavka *f* petition
predstavnik *m* representative
predstavništvo *n* representation
predstojati *v* to be imminent
predstojnik *m* 1. head 2. manager
predstraža *f* advance guard
predtakmičenje *n* (spor.) heat
predubeđenje *n* prejudice
predugo ostati *v* to overstay
preduhitriti *v* to prevent
predujam *m* advance
predumišljaj *m* 1. premeditation 2. **s predumišljajem** premeditated
preduslov *m* precondition

predusresti *v* to prevent
predusretljiv *adj* helpful
predustretljivost *f* helpfulness
preduvjet *m see* **preduslov**
preduzeti *v* to undertake
preduzeti napad *v* to launch an attack
preduzeće *n* (com.) firm
preduzimač *m* contractor
preduzimati *v* to undertake
predveče *n*, **prevečer** *f* early evening
predvečerje *n* eve
predvesti *v* to bring in
predvideti, predvidjeti *v* to anticipate
predvidiv, predvidljiv *adj* anticipated
predviđanje *n* anticipation
predviđen *adj* anticipated
predvoditi *v* 1. to lead 2. to go ahead
predvodnik *m* leader
predvorje *n* lobby
pređa *f* yarn
pređašnji *adj* former
prefabrikovati *v* to prefabricate
prefiks *m* prefix
prefinjen *adj* elegant
prefrigan *adj* clever
pregača *f* apron
pregalj *m* tick
pregaziti *v* to run over
pregibati *v* to bend
pregled *m* 1. review 2. examination
pregledan *adj* clear
pregledati *v* 1. to look over 2. to examine
pregledavač *m* 1. surveyor 2. inspector 3. examiner
pregled mrtvaca *f* post-mortem
pregledno *adv* clearly

pregovarač *m* negotiator
pregovaranje *n* negotiations
pregovarati *v* to negotiate
pregovori *mpl* 1. talks 2. negotiations 3. **voditi pregovore** to conduct talks
pregrada *f* 1. partition 2. compartment
pregraditi *v* 1. to partition 2. to reconstruct
pregršt *f* handful
pregrupisati *v* (mil.) to redeploy
prehlada *f* cold
prehladiti se *v* to catch cold
prehramben *adj* food
prehrambeni proizvodi groceries
prehrana *f* 1. food 2. feeding
prehraniti *v* to feed
preimućstvo *n* priority
preinačiti *v* 1. to alter 2. to reconstruct
preinaka *f* 1. alteration 2. reconstruction
preistorija *f* prehistory
prejesti se *v* to overeat
prejudicirati *v* to prejudice
prekapati *v* to dig up
prekasno *adv* too late
prekid *m* 1. interruption 2. **na prekide** on and off
prekid vatre *n* 1. cease-fire 2. truce
prekidač *m* switch
prekidati, prekinuti *v* to interrupt
prekipjeti *v* to boil over
prekjuče, prekjučer *adv* the day before yesterday
preklane, preklani *adv* the year before last
preklinjati *v* to implore
preklopiti *v* 1. to fold over 2. to overlap

preko *prep* 1. across 2. over 3. during 4. via
prekobaciti se *v* to somersault
prekobrojan *adj* odd
prekomeran, prekomjeran *adj* excessive
prekomjernost *f* excess
prekomorski *adj* overseas
prekonoć *adv* overnight
prekopati *v* to dig up
prekoračiti *v* 1. to overstep 2. to exceed 3. to overdraw
prekoriti *v* to blame
prekosutra *adv* the day after tomorrow
prekovremeni *adj* overtime
prekrasan *adj* wonderful
prekrcati *v* (com.) to transfer goods
prekrcavanje *n* (com.) transfer of goods
prekretnica *f* turning point
prekriti *v* to cover
prekrivač *m* 1. cover 2. blanket
prekrižiti se *v* to cross oneself
prekršaj *m* offence
prekršilac *m* offender
prekršiti *v* to break the law
preksinoć *adv* the night before last
prekupac *m* middleman
prelamanje *n* refraction
prelaz *m* 1. crossing 2. transit 3. transition
prelazan *adj* transitional
prelaziti *v* 1. to cross 2. to exceed
preleteti, preletjeti *v* to fly over
prelijevati se *v* to overflow
preliminaran *adj* preliminary
preliv *m* coating
prelom *m* 1. break 2. fracture
preloman *adj* crucial
prelomiti *v* 1. to break in two 2. to fracture

preljub *m*, **preljuba** *f* adultery
prema *prep* 1. towards 2. against 3. opposite to 4. according to
prema tome *adv* consequently
premalo *adv* too little
premašiti *v* to surpass
premašiti rekord *m* to break a record
premaz *m* coating
premazati firnajzom *v* to varnish
premazati *v* 1. to spread 2. to smear
premda *conj* although
premeriti *v* to measure
premeštaj *m* transfer
premetačina *f* search
premija *f* 1. premium 2. prize
premijer *m* 1. premier 2. prime minister
premijera *f* premiere
preminuti *v* to die
premisa *f* premise
premišljavati *v* 1. to consider 2. to hesitate
premjeravati, premjeriti *v* 1. to measure 2. to survey
premještenje *n* 1. removal 2. transferral
premjestiti *v* 1. to remove 2. to transfer
premlatiti *v* to beat up
premorenost *f* overwork
premoriti se *v* to be overworked
premotati *v* to rewind
premoć *f* superiority
premoćan *adj* superior
prenagliti (se) *v* to act rashly
prenapeti *v* to overstrain
prenapučenost *f* overpopulation
prenapučiti *v* to overpopulate
prenaseljen *adj* overpopulated
prenaseljenost *f* overpopulation

prenatovariti v to overload
prenatrpan adj overcrowded
prenatrpanost f overcrowding
prenemaganje n affectation
prenemagati se v to affect
preneraziti v to astonish
preneražen adj astonished
preneraženost f astonishment
preneti, prenijeti v 1. to carry over 2. to transfer 3. to transmit
prenoćiti v to spend the night
prenos m 1. transport 2. transfer 3. transmission
prenosilac m carrier
prenositi v see **preneti**
prenosiv adj 1. portable 2. transferable
prenuti se v to wake up
preoblačiti, preobući v to change clothes
preobražaj m transformation
preokrenuti v 1. to change 2. to turn over
preokret m 1. sudden change 2. revolution
preokupirati v to preoccupy
preomostiti v to bridge
preopterećen adj overloaded
preopteretiti v 1. to overload 2. to overcharge
preorati v to plough up
preosetljiv adj touchy
preostali adj remaining
preostati v to be left over
preoteti v 1. to snatch 2. to gain
preparat m preparation
prepariranje n preparation
prepasti v to frighten
prepatiti v to suffer
prepelica f quail
prepiliti v to saw up
prepirati se v to argue

prepirka f argument
prepis m 1. copy 2. transcript
prepisati v 1. to copy 2. to transcribe
prepiska f correspondence
preplanulost f suntan
preplanuo adj suntanned
preplanuti v to tan
preplašen adj frightened
preplašiti v to frighten
preplašiti se v to be frightened
preplatiti v to overpay
preplaviti v to overflow
prepodne n morning
prepodnevni adj morning
prepoloviti v to halve
prepona f obstacle
prepone fpl groin
preporod m 1. revival 2. renaissance
preporoditi v to revive
preporučen adj 1. recommended 2. registered
preporučiti v 1. to recommend 2. to register
preporuka f recommendation
prepotentan adj presumptuous
prepoznati v to recognize
prepoznavanje n recognition
prepraviti v to reconstruct
prepraviti v to redecorate
prepravka f alteration
prepreden adj sly
prepreka f obstacle
prepričati v to retell
preprječiti v to obstruct
preprodaja f 1. resale 2. retail
preprodavac m 1. middleman 2. retailer
preprodavati v 1. to resell 2. to retail
prepun adj overfull

prepuniti *v* to overfill
prepustiti *v* to concede
preračunati *v* (fin.) to convert
prerada, preradba *f* 1. alteration
  2. processing 3. recycling
preraditi *v* 1. to alter 2. to process
  3. to recycle
prerađevina *f* product
preran *adj* premature
prerasti *v* to outgrow
prerez *m* section
prerezati *v* to cut through
prerija *f* prairie
prerisati *v* to copy
prerušen *adj* disguised
prerušiti *v* to disguise
prerušiti se *v* to be in disguise
presa *f* press
presad *m* graft
presad kože *m* skin graft
presaditi *v* to transplant
presađen *adj* transplanted
presađivanje *n* transplant
presahnuti *v* to dry up
presan *adj* raw
presbiro *m* press bureau
presecanje *n* cutting
presedan *adj* 1. precedent 2. **bez**
  presedana without precedent
presedati *v* to change
preseliti *v* to remove
preseljenje *n* removal
presenećen *adj* astonished
preseći *v* to interrupt
presenetiti *v* to astonish
presija *f* pressure
presijecati, presjeći *v* to cross
preskočiti *v* 1. to jump over 2. to
  leapfrog
preskok *m* 1. jump 2. vault
preskup *adj* pricey
preslikati *v* to copy

preslušanje *n* 1. cross-examination
  2. interrogation 3. hearing 4. trial
preslušati *v* 1. to cross-examine 2.
  to interrogate 3. to hear
presoliti *v* to oversalt
presoljen *adj* oversalted
prespavati *v* to spend the night
presresti *v* 1. to meet 2. to
  intercept
prestanak *m* 1. break 2. **bez**
  prestanka ceaselessly
prestati *v* to stop
presti *v* 1. to spin 2. to purr
prestići *v* 1. to overtake 2. to
  surpass
prestiž *m* prestige
presto *m* throne
prestolonaslednik *m* crown
  prince
prestonica *f* capital
prestrašiti *v* to frighten
prestrašiti se *v* to be frightened
prestraviti *v* see **prestrašiti**
prestrog *adj* overstrict
prestrogo *adv* overstrictly
prestup *m* violation
prestupiti *v* to violate
prestupna godina *f* leap year
presuda *f* 1. judgement 2. verdict 3.
  pogrešna presuda miscarriage
  of justice
presudan *adj* decisive
presuditi *v* to judge
presušiti *v* to dry up
presvijetao *adj* prestigious
presvlačenje *n* changing of clothes
presvlačiti, presvući *v* to change
  clothes
preša *f* 1. press 2. hurry
prešan *adj* 1. pressed 2. urgent
prešati *v* to press
preštampati *v* to reprint

prešutjeti *v* to conceal
prešutno *adv* by implication
pretakati *v* 1. to pour 2. to bottle
preteča *m* forerunner
preteći *v* 1. to overtake 2. to surpass
preteg *m*, **pretega** *f* weight
preteganuti *v* to outweigh
pretek *m* abundance
pretendent *m* aspirant
pretendovati *v* to aspire
pretenzija *f* claim
preterati *v* to exaggerate
pretezati *v* to predominate
pretežak *adj* 1. too heavy 2. too hard
pretežan *adj* predominant
pretežno *adv* chiefly
pretežnost *f* predominance
prethodan *adj* previous
prethoditi *v* to precede
prethodnica *f* advance guard
prethodno *adv* previously
preticanje *n* passing
pretinac *m* 1. pigeonhole 2. drawer 3. locker
pretio *adj* fat
pretiskati *v* to reprint
pretiti *v* to threaten
pretjecati *v* to overtake
pretjeran *adj* exaggerated
pretjeranost *f* exaggeration
pretjerati *v* to exaggerate
pretnja *f* threat
pretočiti *v* to pour
pretovar *m* transfer of goods
pretovaren *adj* overloaded
pretovariti *v* 1. to overload 2. to transfer goods
pretplata *f* subscription
pretplatiti se *v* to subscribe
pretplatiti *v* to prepay

pretplatnik *m* subscriber
pretpoletni *adj* pre-flight
pretpostaviti *v* 1. to suppose 2. to prefer
pretpostavka *f* supposition
pretpostavljeni *adj/m* superior
pretprodaja *f* advance booking
pretraga *f* search
pretražiti *v* to search
pretrčati *v* to run across
pretres *m* 1. search 2. inspection 3. trial 4. court
pretresati, pretresti *v* 1. to discuss 2. to search
pretrpeti, pretrpjeti *v* to undergo
pretrpeti gubitke, pretrpjeti gubitke *v* to suffer losses
pretući *v* 1. to beat up 2. to beat to death
pretvaranje *n* 1. pretence 2. transformation
pretvarati se *v* to pretend
pretvoriti *v* to transform
preudati *v* to remarry
preudesiti *v* to change
preuranjen *adj* premature
preurediti *v* see preudesiti
preuređenje *n* change
preuveličati *v* to exaggerate
preuzetan *adj* presumptuous
preuzeti *v* to take over
preuzeti vlast *v* to take over power
preuzetnost *f* presumption
preuzimanje *n* taking over
preuzimanje vlasti *n* takeover
prevađati *v* 1. to translate 2. to interpret
prevaga *f* overweight
prevaliti *v* 1. to upset 2. to topple 3. to travel
prevara *f* fraud

prevarant *m* swindler
prevariti *v* to swindle
prevariti se *v* to make a mistake
prevaspitati *v* to re-educate
prevazići *v* to exceed
prevejan *adj* crafty
prevelika doza *f* overdose
preventivan *adj* preventive
prevesti *v* 1. to translate 2. to transfer
prevesti *v* 1. to take 2. to translate (s from; na into)
previjati, previti *v* 1. to fold 2. to dress
previnuti *v* to turn down
previše *adv* too much, too many
prevlačiti *v* to pull over
prevladati *v* to prevail
prevlaka *f* cover
prevlast *f* 1. prevalence 2. supremacy
prevod *m* translation
prevodilac *m* 1. translator 2. interpreter
prevoditi *v* 1. translate 2. to interprete
prevodnica *f* channel
prevođenje *n* translation
prevoj *m* 1. ridge 2. saddle
prevoz *m* 1. transport 2. freight
prevoziti *v* to transport
prevrat *m* 1. revolution 2. subversion
prevremen *adj* premature
prevrnuti, prevrtati *v* to overturn
prevrtljiv *adj* unpredictable
prevući *v* to cover
prezent *m* present
prezervativ *adj* condom
prezime *n* surname
prezimiti *v* to spend the winter
prezir *m*, **preziranje** *n* contempt

preziran *adj* contemptible
prezirati, prezreti *v* to despise
prezreo *adj* overripe
prezriv *adj* scornful (**prema** of)
preživar *m* ruminant
preživeti, preživjeti *v* to survive
prgav *adj* rash
prhak *adj* 1. crisp 2. loose
prhut *m* dandruff
pri *prep* 1. at 2. by 3. with
prianjati *v* to stick to
pribadača *f* 1. pin 2. safety pin
pribadati *v* to pin
pribaviti *v* 1. to provide 2. to obtain
pribeći sili, pribjeći sili *v* to resort to force
pribeleška *f* note
približan *adj* approximate
približavati se *v* to approach
približno *adv* approximately
pribor *m* 1. outfit 2. accessories 3. equipment 4. set
pribor za jelo *m* cutlery
pribrajati *v* to add up
pribran *adj* calm
pribrati *v* to collect
priča *f* story
pričati *v* to narrate
pričekati *v* 1. to wait a while 2. to wait for
pričiniti se *v* to seem
pričuva *f* reserve
pričuvati *v* to reserve
pričvrstiti *v* 1. to fasten 2. to attach
prići *v* to approach
pridavati 1. to add 2. to attribute
pridev, pridjev *m* adjective
pridobiti *v* to win over
pridošlica *f* newcomer
pridružiti *v* to join
pridržati *v* to reserve

prigibati se *v* to bow
prignječiti *v* 1. to press down 2. to crush
prigoda *f* opportunity
prigodan *adj* appropriate
prigodom *prep* on the occasion of
prigovarati *v* to reproach
prigovor *m* objection
prigrabiti *v* to seize
prigradski *adj* suburban
prigrliti *v* 1. to embrace 2. to adopt
prigušiti *v* to smother
prigušivač *m* silencer; muffler
prigušivati emisiju *m* to jam a broadcast
prihod *m* 1. income 2. profit
prihvatilište *n* shelter
prihvatiti *v* to accept
prihvatljiv *adj* acceptable
prijašnji *adj* former
prijatan *adj* pleasant
prijatelj *m*, **prijateljica** *f* friend
prijateljski *adj* friendly
prijateljstvo *n* friendship
prijati *v* to suit
prijatno *adv* pleasantly
prijava *f* 1. report 2. denunciation
prijaviti *v* 1. to report 2. to denounce
prijavni ured *m* registry office
prijavnica *f* 1. registration form 2. registration office
prijazan *adj* kind
prijaznost *f* kindness
prije *adv* 1. before 2. formerly 3. ago
prije ili kasnije sooner or later
prije svega first of all
priječiti *v* to prevent
prijeći *v* to cross over
prijedlog *m* suggestion
prijekor *m* reproach

prijelaz *m* 1. crossing 2. transition
prijelazan *adj* transitional
prijelom *m* break
prijem *m* 1. reception 2. admission
prijemna služba *f* hotel reception
prijemni ispit *m* entrance exam
prijemnik *m* receiver
prijenos *m* 1. transfer 2. transport
prijepis *m* 1. copy 2. transcription
prijeporan *adj* disputable
prijesto *m*, **prijestolje** *n* throne
prijestolnica *f* big city
prijetiti *v* threaten
prijetnja *f* threat
prijevara *f* fraud
prijevod *m* translation
prijevoz *m* transport
prikačiti *v* to fasten
prikaz *m* 1. account 2. description 3. review
prikazati *v* 1. to represent 2. to describe 3. to perform
prikazivanje *n* 1. representation 2. performance
prikladan *adj* suitable
priključak *m* connection
priključiti *v* to connect
prikloniti se *v* to show an inclination
prikolica *f* 1. trailer 2. caravan
prikopčati *v* to fasten
prikovati *v* to rivet
prikrajak *m* side
prikriti *v* 1. to hide 2. to shelter
prikupiti *v* to collect
prilagoditi *v* to adapt
prilagoditi se *v* to become accustomed
prilagodljiv *adj* adaptable
prilagodljivost *f* adaptability
prilagođavanje *n* adaptation
prilagođen *adj* tailor-made

prilaz *m* access
prilaziti *v* to approach
prileći *v* to lie down
prilepiti *v* to stick
priličan *adj* considerable
prilično *adv* considerably
prilijepiti *v* to stick
prilika *f* opportunity
prilike *fpl* circumstances
priliv *adj* influx
priljepčiv *adj* infectious
prilog *m* 1. contribution 2. supplement 3. adverb
priložiti *v* 1. to contribute 2. to enclose 3. to annex
primaći (se) *v* to move closer
primalac *m* recipient
primalja *f* midwife
primamiti *v* to attract
primamljiv *adj* attractive
primanje *n* 1. reception 2. acceptance
primaran *adj* primary
primati *v* to receive
primedba *f* 1. remark 2. objection
primena *f* application
primeniti *v* to apply
primenljiv *adj* applicable
primer *m* example
primerak *m* sample
primetiti *v* to notice
primijeniti *v* to apply
primijetiti *v* to notice
primirje *n* armistice
primitak *m* 1. acceptance 2. receipt
primiti *v* 1. to receive 2. to accept
primitivan *adj* primitive
primjećivati *v see* **primijetiti**
primjedba *f* comment
primjena *f* application
primjenjivati *v* to apply
primjenljiv *adj* applicable

primjer *m* 1. example 2. **na primjer** for example
primjerak *m* 1. sample 2. copy
primjeran, primjeren *adj* 1. appropriate 2. model
primjesa *f* mixture
primka *f* receipt
primorati *v* to force
primorje *n* 1. coast 2. seaside
primorski *adj* coastal
princ *m* prince
princeza *f* princess
princip *m* 1. principle 2. **iz principa** on principle
prinesti *v* to contribute
prineti *v* to bring
prinos *m* yield
prinuda *f* force
prinudan *adj* compulsory
prinuditi *v* to compel
prinudno sletanje/slijetanje *n* emergency landing, forced landing
priobalni *adj* 1. coastal 2. offshore
prionuti *v* 1. to work hard 2. to adhere
priopćenje *n* 1. announcement 2. communication
priopćiti *v* 1. to announce 2. to inform
prioritet *m* priority
prioritetni *adj* chief
pripadati, pripasati *v* to belong
pripadnik *m* 1. member 2. subject
pripajanje *n* annexation
pripaliti *v* to light
pripasti *v* 1. to fall 2. to go to 3. to belong to
pripaziti *v* to look after
pripev, pripjev *m* refrain
pripisati *v* to ascribe
pripit *adj* tipsy

pripojenje *n* annexation
pripojiti *v* to annex
pripomagati, pripomoći *v* 1. to aid 2. to assist
pripomoć *f* 1. aid 2. assistance
pripomoći *v* to assist
pripovedač *m* narrator
pripovedati *v* to narrate
pripovest, pripovjest *f* story
pripovetka *f* story
pripovijedati *v* to tell
pripovijetka, pripovijest *f* story
pripovjedač *m* narrator
priprava *f* preparation
pripravan *adj* 1. ready 2. prepared
pripraviti *v* 1. to get ready 2. to prepare
pripravljanje *n* preparation
pripravnost *f* 1. readiness 2. preparation 3. stand-by
priprema *f* preparation
pripremati *v* to prepare
pripremni rad *m* groundwork
priprost *adj* 1. simple 2. primitive
pripustiti *v* to admit
pripuštanje *n* admittance
prirast, priraštaj *m* increase
priredba *f* performance
prirediti, priredivati *v* to organize
priređivač *m* organizer
prirez *m* surtax
prirod *m* crop
priroda *f* 1. nature 2. **ljudska priroda** human nature
prirodan *adj* natural
prirodan gas *m* natural gas
prirodne znanosti *fpl* natural sciences
prirodno *adv* naturally
prirodopis *m* natural history
prirok *m* predicate
priručan *adj* handy

priručnik *m* 1. handbook 2. reference book
priručnik *m* textbook
prisan *adj* intimate
priseban *adj* calm
prisebnost *f* calmness
priseći *v* (leg.) to swear
prisega *f* oath
prisegnuti *v see* priseći
prisilan *adj* compulsory
prisiliti *v* to force
prisiljavanje *n* compulsion
prisilno *adv* forcibly
priskrbiti *v* to obtain
prisloniti se *v* to lean
prisluškivač *m* eavesdropper
prisluškivati *v* to eavesdrop
prismotra *f* 1. prismotra 2. **pod prismotru** under surveillance
prisno *adv* intimately
prispeti, prispjeti *v* to arrive
prispodoba *f* comparison
pristajanje *n* 1. fit 2. agreement
pristajati *v* 1. to fit 2. to agree with 3. to land
pristalica *f* follower
pristanak *m* consent
pristanište *n* 1. dock 2. port 3. airport
pristao *adj* 1. handsome 2. neat
pristaša *f* 1. follower 2. partisan
pristati *v* to consent
pristojan *adj* decent
pristojati se *v* to be decent
pristojba *f* 1. fees 2. duty
pristojno *adv* decently
pristojnost *f* decency
pristran, pristrasan *adj* biased
pristranost, pristrasnost *f* bias
pristup *m* access
pristup zavranjen! no entry!
pristupačan *adj* accessible

pristupačno *adv* clearly
pristupačnost *f* accessibility
pristupiti *v* 1. to enter 2. to approach 3. to set to work
pristupnica *f* application form
prisustvo *n* 1. presence 2. attendance
prisustvovati *v* 1. to be present 2. to attend
prisutan *adj* present
prisvojan *adj* possessive
prisvojiti *v* 1. to usurp 2. to appropriate
prišarafiti *v* to screw up
prišiti *v* 1. to sew on 2. to impute
prišt *m* (med.) boil
prištedjeti *v* to save
pritajiti se *v* to keep quiet
pritegnuti *v* to tighten
pritisak *m* 1. pressure 2. oppression
pritiskati, pritisnuti *v* 1. to press 2. to oppress
pritjecati *v* to flow into
pritka *f* pole
pritok *m* tributary
pritrčati *v* to run up to
pritužba *f* complaint
pritužiti se *v* to complain
pritvoriti *v* to arrest
pritvornost *f* hypocrisy
priučiti se *v* to get used (**na** to)
priušiti *v* to slap
privatan *adj* private
privatizacija *f* privatization
privatnik *m* private businessman
privatna svojina *f* private ownership
privatni sektor *m* private sector
privatno *adv* privately
privesti *v* to lead toward
privezati *v* to tie
privid *m* illusion

prividan *adj* seeming
prividno *adv* seemingly
prividnost *f* pretence
priviđenje *n* hallucination
priviknuti se *v* to get used to
privilegij *m*, **privilegija** *f* privilege
privinuti *v* to embrace
privjesak *m* 1. pendant 2. tag
privlačan *adj* attractive
privlačiti *v* to attract
privlačiv *adj* attractive
privlačivost *f* attractiveness
privola *f* consent
privoljeti *v* to consent
privreda *f* economy
privredan *adj* 1. economic 2. business
privredna reforma *f* economic reform
privredni *adj* economic
privrednik *m* businessman
privremen *adj* 1. temporary 2. provisional
privremena vlada *f* provisional government
privrijediti *v* to earn
privržen *adj* devoted
privrženost *f* devotion
privući *v* to attract
prizemlje *n* ground floor; first floor
priziv *adj* appeal
prizma *f* prism
priznanica *f* receipt
priznanje *n* 1. acknowledgement 2. confession
priznati, priznavati *v* 1. to acknowledge 2. to confess
prizor *m* scene
prizvuk *m* 1. tone 2. sound
priželjkivati *v* to long for
prkos *m* defiance

prkosan *adj* defiant
prkositi *v* to be obstinate
prljati *v* to soil
prljav *adj* dirty
prljava smicalica *f* dirty trick
prljavština *f* dirt
prnja *f* rag
prnjav *adj* ragged
proačunati *v* to calculate
proba *f* 1. test 2. trial 3. experiment 4. taste 5. rehearsal
probati *v* 1. to test 2. to try 3. to taste 4. to rehearse
probava *f* 1. digestion 2. **loša probava** indigestion
probaviti *v* digest
probavljiv *adj* digestible
probijati se *v* to fight through
probijati *v* to penetrate
probirljiv *adj* choosy
probisvet, probisvijet *m* tramp
probitačan *adj* 1. profitable 2. advantageous
probitak *m* 1. profit 2. advantage
probiti *v* to penetrate
problem *m* problem
problematičan *adj* problematic
problijediti *v* to turn pale
probni *adj* 1. test 2. trial
probni let *m* test flight
proboj *m* breakthrough
probojan *adj* 1. penetrating 2. permeable
probojnost *f* 1. penetrability 2. permeability
probosti *v* to pierce
probuditi (se) *v* to wake up
probušiti *v* to pierce
procediti *v* to filter
procedura *f* procedure
proceduralan *adj* procedural
procena *f* estimate

procenat *m* percentage
proceniti *v* to estimate
procentualan *adj* proportional
procep *m* crevice
proces *m* 1. process 2. legal action 3. trial
procesija *f* procession
procesor *m* processor
procesor za obradu reči *m* word processor
procijediti *v* to filter
procijeniti *v* to estimate
procjena *f* estimate
procuriti *v* to leak
procvasti *v* to flourish
procvat *m* bloom
pročelje *n* front
pročelnik *m* 1. head 2. chief
pročistiti *v* 1. to clean 2. to purge
pročitati *v* to read through
proći *v* 1. to pass 2. to disappear
proći na ispitu *v* to pass an exam
proći *v* to pass
proda, prodaja *f* sale
prodaja naveliko *f* wholesale
prodajni *adj* 1. selling 2. saleable
prodati *v see* prodavati
prodavač *m*, **prodavačica** *f* 1. seller 2. salesperson 3. shop assistant
prodati, prodavati *v* to sell
prodavati namalo *v* to retail
prodavati naveliko *v* to wholesale
prodavnica *f* shop; store
prodirati, prodrijeti *v* to penetrate
prodoran *adj* piercing
prodreti *v* to penetrate
prodrmati *v* to shake
produbiti *v* to deepen
producent *m* producer
producirati *v* to produce
produkcija *f* production
produkt *m* product

produktivan *adj* productive
produktivnost *f* productivity
produljiti, produžiti *v* to continue
produžiti viza *v* to extend a visa
profesija *f* profession
profesionalac *m* professional
profesionalizam professionalism
profesor *m* 1. professor 2. teacher
profil *m* profile
profit *m* profit
profiter *m* 1. profiteer 2. **ratni profiter** war profiteer
proganjanje *n* prosecution
proganjati *v* 1. to pursue 2. to persecute
proglas *m* 1. proclamation 2. manifesto
proglasiti *v* to proclaim
proglašenje *n* proclamation
prognan *adj* 1. banned 2. exiled
prognanik *m* 1. outlaw 2. exile
prognati *v* 1. to ban 2. to exile
prognostičar *m* forecaster
prognostičar *m* weather forecaster
prognosticirati *v* to forecast
prognoza *f* forecast
prognoza vremena *f* weather forecast
prognozirati *v* to forecast
progon *m* 1. pursuit 2. persecution
progoniti *v* to persecute
progonstvo *n* exile
progovarati *v see* **progovoriti**
progovor *m* objection
progovoriti *v* 1. to begin to speak 2. to object
program *m* programme; program
programer *m* programmer
programirati *v* to programme; to program
progres *m* progress
progresija *f* progression

progresivan *adj* progressive
progunđati *v* to grumble
progurati *v* to push through
progutati *v* to swallow
prohibicija *f* prohibition
prohladan *adj* cool
prohodan *adj* passable
prohodati *v* to begin to walk
prohtev *m* desire
proigrati *v* to gamble away
proizaći *v* to result from
proizvađač *m see* **proizvođač**
proizvesti *v* to produce
proizvod *m* 1. produce 2. product
proizvoditi *v see* **proizvesti**
proizvodnja *f* production
proizvođač *m* 1. producer 2. manufacturer
projekat *m* project
projekcija *f* 1. projection 2. plan
projekt *m* project
projektant *m* planner
projektil *m* missile
projektor *m* projector
projektovati, projicirati *v* 1. to project 2. to plan
projuriti *v* to rush by
proklamacija *f* proclamation
proklamovati *v* to proclaim
proklet *adj* damned
prokleti *v* to curse
prokletnik *m* damned fellow
prokletstvo *n* curse
proključati *v* to start to boil
prokockati *v* to gamble away
prokopati *v* to dig through
prokrčiti *v* to clear
prokrčiti se *v* to clear way
prokula *f* Brussel sprouts
prokule *fpl* broccoli
prokuvati *v* to boil
prolaz *m* 1. passage 2. arcade

prolazan *adj* 1. passable 2. passing
prolaziti *v* to pass by
prolaznik *m* passer-by
proleter *m* proletarian
proleće *n* spring
prolećni *adj* spring
prolijevati, proliti *v* to spill
prolistati *v* to flip through
proliti krv *v* to shed blood
proliv *m* diarrhoea
prolivati *v* to spill
proljev *m* diarrhoea
proljeće *n* spring
prolog *m* prologue
prolom *m* 1. burst 2. breach
prolongirati *v* to prolong
promaći *v* to pass by
promaja *f* draught
promaknuti *v* to promote
promašaj *m* failure
promašiti *v* 1. to fail 2. to miss 3. to make a mistake
promatrač *m* observer
promatrati *v* to observe
promećuran *adj* enterprising
promena *f* change
promenljiv *adj* changeable
promet *m* 1. traffic 2. circulation 3. business 4. (fin.) turnover
prometan *adj* busy
prometna nezgoda *f* road accident
promicati *v* to promote
promijeniti *v* to change
promiješati *v* to stir
promisliti *v* to consider
promišljen *adj* deliberate
promišljenost *f* consideration
promjena *f* change
promjenljiv *adj* unstable
promjer *m* diameter
promocija *f* graduation
promočiti *v* to soak

promrmljati *v* to mumble
promrzle ruke *fpl* frostbitten hands
promrzlina *f* frostbite
promrznuti *v* to freeze
promućkati *v* to shake
promućuran *adj* clever
promukao *adj* hoarse
promuklost *f* hoarseness
pronaći *v* 1. to discover 2. to invent
pronalazač *m* 1. inventor 2. discoverer
pronalazak *m* 1. invention 2. discovery
pronevera *f* embezzlement
proneveriti *v* to embezzle
pronevjerenje *n* embezzlement
pronevjeriti *v* to embezzle
pronicav *adj* clever
pronicavost *f* insight
pronicljiv *adj* clever
pronicljivost *f* penetration
proniknuti *v* to penetrate
pronosilac glasina *f* rumourmonger
propadanje *n* 1. decay 2. decline
propadati, propasti *v* 1. to decay 2. to decline
propaganda *f* propaganda
propagator *m* propagator
propagirati *v* to propagate
propalica *m/f* good-for-nothing
propao *adj* ruined
propast *f* ruin
propasti *v* to fall through
propeler *m* propeller
propelo *n* crucifix
propis *m* rule
propisan *adj* prescribed
propisan zakonom *adj* statutory
propisati *v* to regulate
propisno *adv* according to regulations

propište *n* 1. scene 2. battlefield
propitkivati se *v* to make enquiries
proplanak *m* glade
proporcija *f* proportion
proporcionalan *adj* proportional
propoved *m* sermon
propovedaonica *f* pulpit
propovedati *v* to preach
propovednik *m* preacher
propovijed *m* sermon
propovijedati *v* to preach
propovjednik *m* preacher
propozicija *f* 1. proposition 2. regulations
propun *m* draught
propusnica *f* 1. permit 2. pass
propust *m* omission
propustiti *v* 1. to omit 2. to miss 3. to fail to
propustljiv *adj* 1. leaky 2. porous
propustljivost *f* 1. leakiness 2. porosity
proputovanje *n* journey through
proputovati *v* to travel round
proračun *m* calculation
proračunati *v* to calculate
proreći *v* to predict
prorez *m* 1. slot 2. section
proricati *v see* **proreći**
proročanstvo *n* prophecy
proročište *n* oracle
prorok *m* prophet
prosac *m* suitor
prosečan *adj* average
prosečno *adv* on average
prosečnost *f* averageness
proseći *v* to cut through
prosek *m* 1. average 2. section
prosijati *v* to sift
prosijecati *v* to intersect
prosijed *adj* grey

prosinac *m* December
prosipanje nafte *fpl* oil spill
prosipati *v* 1. to spill 2. to waste
prositi *v* 1. to beg 2. to propose marriage
prosjačiti *v* to beg
prosjak *m* beggar
prosječan *adj* average
prosjek *m* 1. average 2. section
proslava *f* celebration
proslaviti se *v* to be famous
proslaviti *v* to celebrate
proslavljen *adj* celebrated
proslediti, proslijediti *v* to forward
proso *n* millet
prospekt *m* prospectus
prosperitet *m* prosperity
prost *adj* 1. rude 2. free (**od** from) 3. plain
prost narod *m* mob
prostački *adj* vulgar
prostak *m* rude person
prostakluk *m*, **prostaštvo** *n* vulgarity
prostata *f* prostate
prostatis *m* prostatitis
prostirač *m* 1. rug 2. mat
prostiranje *n* spread
prostirati *v* to lay out
prostirka *f* 1. cover 2. carpet
prostitucija *f* prostitution
prostitutka *f* prostitute
prosto *adv* simply, just
prostodušan *adj* 1. sincere 2. naive
prostodušnost *f* 1. sincerity 2. naivety
prostor *m* space
prostorija *f* premises
prostota *f* vulgarity
prostran *adj* spacious
prostrasan *adj* one-sided

prostreti *v* to spread
prostrijeliti *v* to shoot through
prostrijeti *v see* **prostirati**
prosuditi *v* to judge
prosuđivanje *n* judgement
prosuti *v* 1. to spill 2. to waste
prosvećen *adj* enlightened
prosvećenost *f* enlightenment
prosvećivanje *n* teaching
prosveta *f* education
prosvjećivati *v* to educate
prosvjed *m* objection
prosvjedovati *v* to protest
prosvjeta *f* education
prosvjetan *adj* educational
prošao *adj* 1. past 2. last 3. recent
prošaptati *v* to whisper
prošetati *v* to take a walk
proširene vene *fpl* varicose veins
proširiti *v* to expand
prošli *see* **prošao**
prošlogodišnji *adj* last year's
prošlost *f* past
prošnja *f* begging
prošuljati se *v* to creep through
prošupljiti *v* to puncture
prošvercovati *v* to smuggle
protagonist(a) *m* protagonist
proteći *v* 1. to pass 2. to expire 3. to flow
protegnuti se *v* to stretch
protekcionizam *m* protectionism
protektor *m* tyre tread
protektorat *m* protectorate
proterati *v* 1. to deport 2. to exile
protest *m* protest
protestant *m* 1. protester 2. Protestant
protestantizam Protestantism
protestvovati *v* to protest
protetika *f* 1. prosthetics 2. zubna protetika prosthodontics

proteza *f* 1. prosthesis 2. artificial limb 3. (dental) bridge
protezati se *v see* **protegnuti se**
protezni *adj* prosthetic
protiv *adj* against
protiv- anti-, counter-
protivan *adj* 1. opposite 2. opposed
protivavionska zaštita *f* antiaircraft defence
protiviti se *v* to oppose
protivljenje *n* opposition
protivna stranka *f* opposition
protivnapad *m* counterattank
protivnički *adj* opposing
protivnik *m* opponent
protivno *adv* 1. in opposition 2. on the contrary
protivnost *f* 1. opposite 2. opposition
protivotrov *m* antidote
protivpravni *adj* illegal
protivrečan *adj* contradictory
protivrečnost *f* contradiction
protivtelo, protivtijelo *n* antibody
protivtenkovska samohotka *f* tank destroyer
protivtenkovska klopka *f* tank trap
protivtenkovski *adj* antitank
protivtenkovski top *m* antitank gun
protivustavan *adj* unconstitutional
protivzakonit *adj* illegal
protjecati *v* 1. to pass 2. to expire
protjerati *v* 1. to exile 2. to expel 3. to deport
protkati *v* to interweave
protokol *m* protocol
proton *m* proton
protoplazma *f* protoplasm

prototip *m* prototype
protrčati *v* to run through
protrljati *v* to rub
protu- 1. re- 2. counter-
protumačiti *v* to explain
protumjera *f* 1. reprisal 2. countermeasure
protunapad *m* counterattack
protuotrov *m* antidote
protupravan *adj* unlawful
protuslovan *adj* contradictory
protusloviti *v* to contradict
protuslovlje *n* contradiction
protustaviti se *v* to resist
protuteža *f* counterbalance
protuustavan *adj* unconstitutional
protuva *f* vagabond
protuzakonit *adj* unlawful
protuzračna zaštita *f* antiaircraft defence
proučavanje *n* research
proučavati *v* 1. to research 2. to investigate
prouzročiti, prouzrokovati *v* to cause
prova *f* (mar.) bow
provala *f* 1. outburst 2. outbreak 3. break-in
provalija *f* chasm
provaliti *v* 1. to erupt 2. to break into
provalnik *m* burglar
proveravanje, provjeravanje *n* verification
proveriti, provjeriti *v* to verify
proveriti izbeglice *v* to screen refugees
provesti *v* 1. to spend 2. to carry out
provesti se *v* to have a good time
provetravanje, provjetravanje *n* ventilation
provetriti *v* to ventilate

providan *adj* transparent
providnost *f* transparency
providost *f* providence
proviđenje *n* providence
provincija *f* province
provincijalan *adj* provincial
provizija *f* (fin.) commission
provizoran *adj* provisional
provjeriti *v* 1. to check 2. to ventilate
provjeriti izbjeglice *v* to screen refugees
provocirati *v* to provoke
provod *m* fun
provodadžija *f* matchmaker
provoditi *v* 1. to spend 2. to carry out
provodnik *m* conductor
provokacija *f* provocation
provokativan *adj* provocative
proza *f* prose
prozaičan *adj* prosaic
prozebao *adj* 1. chilled 2. frozen 3. frostbitten
proziran *adj* clear
prozivanje *n*, **prozivka** *f* roll call
prozor *m* window
prozreti *v* to see through
prozvati *v* to call
proždrljiv *adj* greedy
proždrljivost *f* greed
prožet *adj* imbued
prožeti *v* to imbue
prsa *f* 1. breast 2. bust
prskalica *f* spray
prskati *v* to spray
prsluk *m* waistcoat; vest
prsluk za spasavanje *m* life jacket
prsnuti *v* 1. to crack 2. to explode
prsnuti u smeh/smijeh *v* to burst into laughter
prst *m* 1. finger 2. toe

prsten *m* ring
prstenovati *v* to ring
prstenjak *m* ring finger
pršlen, pršljen *m* vertebra
pršut *m*, **pršuta** *f* smoked ham
prtljag *m*, **prtljaga** *f* baggage
prtljati *v* to bungle
prtljažnik *m* boot; trunk
prud *m* dune
pruga *f* 1. stripe 2. line
prugast *adj* striped
prut *m* twig
pružati, pružiti *v* to offer
pružati se *v* to stretch
prvak *m* champion
prva pomoć *f* first aid
prva rata *f* down payment
prvenstvo *n* 1. priority 2.
   championship
prvi *adj* first
prvo *adv* firstly
prvobitan *adj* original
prvorazredan *adj* first-class
prvorođen *adj* firstborn
prznica *f* hothead
pržen *adj* 1. roasted 2. fried
prženje *n* 1. roasting 2. frying
pržiti *v* 1. to roast 2. to fry
pržiti na roštilju *v* to grill
pržolica *f* roast beef
psalm *m* psalm
psetance *n* puppy
pseto *n* dog
pseudonim *m* pseudonym
psiha *f* psyche
psihički *adj* psychic
psihijatar *m* psychiatrist
psihijatrija *f* psychiatry
psihijatrijski *adj* psychiatric
psihoanalitički *adj* psychoanalytic
psihoanaliza *f* psychoanalysis
psiholog *m* psychologist

psihologija *f* psychology
psihološki *adj* psychological
psihopat *m* psychopath
psihoterapija *f* psychotherapy
psihoza *f* psychosis
psovati *v* to swear (at)
psovka *f* swearword
psokve *fpl* bad language
pst! shush!
pšenica *f* wheat
ptica *f* bird
ptičar *m* pointer (dog)
pubertet *m* puberty
publicist *m* 1. publicist 2. journalist
publicistika *f* journalism
publicitet *m* publicity
publika *f* public
publikacija *f* publication
pucanj *m* shot
pucati *v* to fire
puce *n* button
pucketanje *n* crackling
pucketati *v* 1. to crack 2. to click
pucnjava *f* firing
puč *m* putsch
pučanstvo *n* population
pučina *f* high seas
pučka škola *f* primary school
pučki *adj* popular
pući *v* to fire
puder *m* powder
puding *m* pudding
pudlica *f* poodle
pudrijera *f* powder box
puhati *v* 1. to blow 2. to puff
puk *m* 1. populace 2. regiment
puki *adj* mere
puknuti *v see* **pucati**
pukotina *f* 1. gap 2. crack
pukovnija *f* regiment
pukovnik *m* colonel
pul *m* pool

pulover m pullover

puls m 1. pulse 2. **izmeriti nekome puls; izmjeriti nekome puls** to take someone's pulse

pult m stand

puma f puma

pumpa f pump

pumpati v to pump

pumpa za goriva f fuel pump

pun adj full

punica f mother-in-law

puniti v 1. to fill up 2. to load

punjenje n 1. filling 2. loading

puno adv much, many

punoglavac m tadpole

punokrvan adj thoroughbred

punoletan adj of legal age

punoletstvo n legal age

punoljetan adj of legal age

punomoć f 1. authorization 2. mandate

punovažan adj valid

pup m bud

pupak m navel

pupati v to bud

pupčana vrpca f umbilical cord

pupoljak m bud

pura f, **puran** m turkey

purgativ adj laxative

purpur m purple

pusiti v 1. to leave 2. to let

pušač m smoker

puščani adj gun

puščani prah m gunpowder

pušenje n 1. smoking 2. **Pušenje zabranjeno!** No smoking!

pušiti v to smoke

puška f 1. gun 2. rifle

puškarnica f loophole

puškomet m gun range

puškomitraljez m machine gun

puštati v 1. to leave 2. to let

pust 1. adj deserted 2. empty 3. n felt

pustara f heath

pusten adj felt

pustinja f desert

pustinjak m hermit

pustinjski adj desert

pustiti v 1. to release 2. to allow

pustolov m adventurer

pustolovan adj adventurous

pustolovina f adventure

pustoš f wasteland

pustošiti v to devastate

put m 1. way 2. journey 3. skin 4. time 5. **dva put** twice 6. **put o oba pravca** round trip

putanja f 1. path 2. orbit

putarina f toll

puten adj sensual

puter m butter

putevi dotura mpl supply lines

putni adj travel

putnica f passport

putnički adj passenger

putnički brod m 1. passenger ship 2. liner

putnički ček m traveller's cheque

putnik m 1. traveller 2. passenger

putokaz m roadsign

putopis m travel book

putovanje n 1. travel 2. trip 3. voyage 4. **grupno putovanje** package tour

putovati v to travel

puzanje n crawling

puzati v to crawl

puzavica f creeper

puž m snail

R

rabat *m* discount
rabin *m* rabbi
rabiti *v* to use
rabljen *adj* used
racija *f* raid
racionalan *adj* rational
racionalist *m* rationalist
racionalizacija *f* rationalization
racionalizam *m* rationalism
racionalizovati *v* to rationalize
racionalno *adv* rationality
racionirati *v* to ration
rackijeliti *v* 1. to divide 2. to distribute
račun *m* 1. calculation 2. bill 3. invoice 4. account
računanje *n* 1. reckoning 2. accounting
računar *m* 1. calculator 2. computer
računati *v* to calculate
računica *f* calculation
računovodstvo *n* accountancy
računovođa *m* accountant
račvanje *n* fork
račvast *adj* forked
račvati se *v* to fork
rad *m* 1. work 2. job
radar *m* radar
radi *prep* 1. because of 2. in order to
radijacija *f* radiation
radijalan *adj* radial
radijator *m* radiator
radije rather
radijum *m* radium
radijus *m* radius
radikalan *adj* radical

radikalizam *m* radicalism
radin *adj* industrious
radinost *f* industry
radio *m* radio
radioaktivan *adj* radioactive
radioaktivne padavine *fpl* nuclear fall-out
radioaktivnost *f* radioactivity
radiologija *f* radiology
radionica *f* workshop
raditi *v* to work
radna norma *f* workload
radna snaga *f* 1. manpower 2. work force
radni *adj* working
radni dan *m* working day
radnički kombinezon *m* overalls
radnički *adj* 1. working 2. labour
radnik *m* worker
radnja *f* 1. work 2. operation 3. shop; store
radno odelo/odijelo *n* (mil.) fatigues
rado, radosno *adv* gladly
radost *f* joy
radostan *adj* glad
radovati se *v* 1. to be glad 2. to look forward to
radoznalost *f* curiosity
radoznao *adj* curious
rađanje *n* childbirth
rađati *v* to give birth to
rađen rukom *adj* handmade
rafal *m* burst
rafinerija *f* refinery
rafinirati *v* to refine
ragastov *m* doorframe

ragbi *m* rugby
rahitis *m* rickets
raj *m* paradise
rajčica *f* tomato
rajsferšlus *m* zip
rajski *adj* of paradise
rak *m* 1. crab 2. (med.) cancer
raka *f* grave
raketa *f* 1. rocket 2. missile
raketa zemlja-vazduh *f* surface-to-air missile
raketa zemlja-zemlja/brod-brod *f* surface-to-surface missile
raketa srednjeg dometa *f* medium-range missiles
raketna rampa *f* launch pad
raketoplan *m* space shuttle
rakija *f* brandy
rakun *m* racoon
ralica *f*, **ralo** *n* plough; plow
ralje *fpl* jaws
ram *m* frame
rame *n* shoulder
rampa *f* ramp, barrier
ran *adj* early
rana *f* 1. sore 2. injury 3. trauma
ranac *m* rucksack
ranč *m* ranch
rančer *m* rancher
randevu *m* rendezvous
rangirati *v* to rank
rani *adj* early
ranije *adv* previously
raniti *v* 1. to hurt 2. to injure 3. to traumatize
rank *m* rank, grade
rano *adv* early
ranžiranje *n* ranging
ranjav *adj* sore
ranjavost *f* vulnerability
ranjen *adj* wounded
ranjenik *m* wounded

ranjiv *adj* vulnerable
ranjivost *f* vulnerability
raport *m* (mil.) report
raportirati *v* to report
raprskavajuća bomba *f* fragmentation bomb
rapsodija *f* rhapsody
rasa *f* race
rasaditi *v* to plant out
rasadnik *m* nursery garden
rascep *m* rift
rascijepati *v* to chop
rascvasti se, rascvetati se *v* to blossom
rasčistiti *v* to clear up
raseći *v* to cut up
rasejan *adj* absent-minded
rasejanost *f* absent-mindedness
rasejati *v* to diffuse
raselina *f* fissure
raseliti *v* 1. to displace 2. to evacuate
raseljen *adj* 1. displaced 2. evacuated
raseljeno lice *n* displaced person
rasformirati *v* to disband
rashladiti *v* to cool
rashladni *adj* cooling
rashlađen *adj* cooled
rashlađivanje *n* cooling
rashod *m* expense
rasiniti *v* to disown
rasipan *adj* 1. extravagant 2. wasteful
rasipati *v* to squander
rasipnik *m* spendthrift
rasipnost *f* extravagance
rasist(a) *m* racist
rasistički *adj* racist
rasizam *m* racism
rasjeći *v* to cut up
rasjeklina *f* rift

raskalašan, raskalašen *adj* debauched
raskid *m* break-up
raskinuti *v* to break up
rasklapanje *n* unfolding
raskliman *adj* shaky
rasklopiti *v* to unfold
raskol *m* 1. split 2. secession 3. schism
raskomadati se *v* to disintegrate
raskomotiti se *v* to make oneself comfortable
raskopati *v* to dig up
raskopčati *v* 1. to unbutton 2. to undo
raskoračen *adj* astride
raskorak *m* variance
raskoš *m* luxury
raskošan *adj* luxurious
raskrinkati *v* to expose
raskrsnica *f* crossroads
raskršće *n* 1. crossroads 2. intersection
raskrstiti se *v* to break off relations
raskužiti *v* to disinfect
raskvašen *adj* soaked
rasno mešovit/mješovit *adj* multi-racial
rasol *m* pickle
raspad *m* decay
raspadanje *n* disintegration
raspadati se *v* to decay
raspakovati *v* to unpack
raspaliti *v* to inflame
rasparati *v* 1. to rip 2. to undo
rasparen *adj* odd
raspasti se *v* to decay
raspeti *v* to crucify
raspevan *adj* joyful
raspeće *n* crucifix
raspidjela *f* distribution

raspis *m* circular
raspisati *v* to announce
raspitati se, raspitivati se *v* to make enquiries
raspitivanje *n* enquiry
raspitriti *v* to stir up
rasplakati *v* to make somebody cry
rasplakati se *v* to burst into tears
rasplet *m* outcome
rasplinjivač *m* carburettor
rasplinuti se *v* to fade
rasplod *m* breeding
rasploditi se *v* to breed
raspodela *f* distribution
raspolaganje *n* disposal
raspolagati *v* to dispose of
raspolagati *v* 1. to handle 2. to possess
raspoloviti *v* to split
raspoložen *adj* 1. good-tempered 2. loše raspoložen bad-tempered
raspoložen *adj* inclined
raspoloženje *n* mood
raspoložiti *v* to cheer up
raspoloživ *adj* available
raspon *m* range
raspored *m* 1. plan 2. programme
raspored sati *v* timetable
rasporediti *v* to arrange
rasporiti *v* to rip open
raspoznati *v* to recognize
raspoznavanje *n* recognition
raspra *f* dispute
rasprava *f* 1. discussion 2. debate 3. trial
raspraviti, raspravljati *v* to discuss
raspremiti, raspremati *v* 1. to clear away 2. to dismantle
rasprodaja *f* sale
rasprodan *adj* sold out
rasprodati *v* to sell out

rasprostirati se *v* to spread
rasprostranjen *adj* widespread
rasprostranjenost *f* spread
rasprsnuti *v* to explode
rasprsnuti se *v* 1. to split 2. to blow up
raspršiti *v* to scatter
raspucan *adj* split
raspucati, raspuknuti *v* to split
raspuklina *f* crack
raspušten *adj* 1. dispersed 2. dismissed
raspust *m* holidays
raspustiti *v* to dismiss
rasrditi se *v* to get angry
rasrditi *v* to anger
rast *m* growth
rastajanje *n* leaving
rastajati *v* to part from
rastaliti *v* to melt
rastanak *m* leaving
rastapati *v* 1. to melt 2. to smelt
rastava *f* divorce
rastaviti *v* 1. to dismantle 2. to separate
rastaviti se *v* to get divorced
rastavljen *adj* divorced
rastegljiv *adj* flexible
rastegljivost *f* flexibility
rastegnuti *v* to stretch
rasteretiti *v* to unburden
rastezati *v* to stretch
rastezljiv *adj* elastic
rasti *v* to grow
rastinje *n* vegetation
rastjerati *v* to drive off
rastojanje *n* distance
rastopiti *v* 1. to dissolve 2. to melt 3. to smelt
rastopiv *adj* soluble
rastovariti *v* to unload
rastresen *adj* distracted

rastresenost *f* distraction
rastresit *adj* loose
rastresti se *v* to relax
rastresti *v* to distract
rastrgati *v* to tear to pieces
rastrijezniti se *v* to sober up
rastrojen *adj* shattered
rastrojen *adj* upset
rastrojstvo *n* confusion
rastrošan *adj* extravagant
rastumačiti *v* to explain
rasturač droga *m* drug pusher
rasturiti *v* to distribute
rastužiti *v* to distress
rastvarati *v* to decompose
rastvor *m* solution
rastvoriti *v* 1. to dissolve 2. to open
rastvorljiv *adj* soluble
rasuđivanje *n* judgement
rasuđivati *v* to reason
rasulo *n* 1. chaos 2. dissolution
rasut *adj* scattered
rasuti *v* 1. to scatter 2. to waste
rasveta *f* lighting
rasvijetliti *v* to light up
rasvjeta *f* light
raščlaniti *v* to dismember
raširen *adj* spread
raširiti *v* to expand
rašljast *adj* forked
rašlje *fpl* fork
raštrkan *adj* dispersed
raštrkati *v* to disperse
rat *m* 1. war 2. **građanski rat** civil war 3. **hladni rat** cold war 4. **svetski rat; svjetski rat** world war 5. **objaviti rat** to declare war 6. **voditi rat to wage war**
rat za oslobođenje *m* war of liberation
rata *f* instalment

ratar *m* farmer
ratarski *adj* agricultural
ratarstvo *n* agriculture
ratifikovati *v* to ratify
ratište *n* battlefield
ratna mornarica *f* navy
ratna odšteta *f* war reparations
ratna služba *f* field manual
ratne igre *fpl* war games
ratni *adj* 1. war 2. military
ratni brod *m* warship
ratnički *see* ratni
ratni diktator *m* warlord
ratni dopisnik *m* war correspondent
ratni zarobljenik *m* prisoner of war, POW
ratni zločin *m* 1. war crime 2. izvršiti ratni zločin to commit a war crime
ratni zločinac *m* war criminal
ratnik *m* fighter, soldier
ratno stanje *n* state of war
ratno vreme/vrijeme *n* wartime
ratoboran *adj* militant
ratovanje *n* 1. campaign 2. warfare
ratovati *v* to wage war
ravan 1. *adj* flat 2. level 3. straight 4. equal 5. *f* plane
raven *m* rhubarb
ravnalo *n* ruler
ravnatelistvo *n* management
ravnatelj *m* 1. director 2. headmaster; principal
ravnati se *v* to conform
ravnati *v* 1. to level 2. to straighten
ravnica *f* plain
ravno *adv* straight
ravnodnevica *f* equinox
ravnodušan *adj* indifferent
ravnodušno *adv* indifferently
ravnodušnost *f* indifference

ravnomeran, ravnomjeran *adj* equal
ravnopravan *adj* with equal rights
ravnopravnost *f* equality
ravnoteža *f* balance
razabirati, razabrati *v* to discern
razan *adj* different
razapet *adj* stretched
razapeti, razapinjati *v* to stretch out
razarač *m* destroyer
razaranje *n* destruction
razarati *v* to destroy
razaslati *v* to send out
razbacati *v* to throw around
razbaštiniti *v* to disinherit
razbesneti *v* to enrage
razbibriga *f* pastime
razbijanje *n* smashing
razbijen *adj* smashed
razbistriti *v* to clear up
razbiti se *v* to be shipwrecked
razbiti, razbijati *v* to smash
razbjesniti *v* to enrage
razbjesniti se *v* to be enraged
razbludan *adj* immoral
razboj *m* 1. loom 2. parallel bars
razbojnik *m* robber
razbojništvo *n* robbery
razboleti se, razboljeti se *v* to be ill
razbor *m* common sense
razborit *adj* reasonable
razborito *adv* reasonably
razboritost *f see* razbor
razbuditi se *v* to wake up
razdaljina *f* distance
razdeliti *v* 1. to divide 2. to distribute
razdeoba *f* division
razderan *adj* torn
razderati *v* to tear up

razdioba *f* division
razdoblje *n* period
razdor *m* dissent
razdragan *adj* delighted
razdražen *adj* irritated
razdražiti *v* to irritate
razdražljiv *adj* irritable
razdražljivost *f* irritability
razdvajanje *n* separation
razdvajati, razdvojiti *v* to separate
razglasiti *v* to spread news
razglasni uređaj *m* public address system
razgledanje *n* sightseeing
razgledati *v* 1. to view 2. to sightsee
razgledavanje *n* sightseeing
razglednica *f* postcard
razgneviti *v* to anger
razgoropaditi se *v* to lose one's temper
razgovarati *v* to talk
razgovarati se *v* to converse
razgovetan *adj* articulate
razgovetno *adv* distinctly
razgovor *m* 1. talk 2. conversation
razgovorljiv *adj* talkative
razgranat *adj* extensive
razgranati *v* to extend
razgranati se *v* to branch out
razgraničiti *v* to determine
razići se *v* to break up
razina *f* level
razjaren *adj* furious
razjarenost *f* fury
razjariti *v* to infuriate
razjasniti *v* to explain
razjašnjenje, razlaganje *n* explanation
razjediniti *v* to separate
razkaditi se *v* to lose one's temper
razlagati *v* to explain

razlaz *m* separation
različan, različit *adj* various
različito *adv* differently
različitost *f* variety
razlijegati se *v* to reverberate
razlijevati se *see* **razliti se**
razlika *f* difference
razlikovanje *n* distinction
razlikovati se *v* to differ
razlikovati *v* to distinguish
razliti se *v* to overflow
razljutiti *v* to infuriate
razljutiti se *v* to be infuriated
razlog *m* reason
razlomak fraction
razlomiti *v* to break
razložan *adj* reasonable
razložiti *v* to explain
razložno *adv* reasonably
razlupati *v* to smash
razmak *m* interval
razmatranje *n* consideration
razmatrati *v* to consider
razmazati *v* to spread
razmaziti *v* to spoil
razmažen *adj* spoiled
razmena *f* exchange
razmeniti *v* to change
razmera *f* proportion
razmeštaj *m* arrangement
razmetati se *v* to boast
razmetljiv *adj* boastful
razmetljivac *m* boaster
razmeženo dete/dijete *n* spoilt child
razmijeniti *v* to exchange
razmimoilaženje *n* disagreement
razmirica *f* disagreement
razmisliti *v* to consider
razmišljanje *n* consideration
razmjena *f* exchange
razmjer *m* proportion

razmjeran *adj* proportional
razmnožavanje *n* propagation
razmnožiti se *v* to multiply
razmnožiti *v* to multiply
razmontirati *v* to dismantle
razmotati *v* to unpack
razmotriti *v* to consider
razmrsiti *v* to unravel
razmrskati *v* to shatter
raznobojan *adj* variegated
raznolik *adj* diverse
raznolikost *f* diversity
raznosač *m* deliverer
raznositi *v* to deliver
raznošenje *n* delivery
raznovrsnost *f* variety
raznovrstan *adj* various
razočaran *adj* disappointed
razočaran *adj* disappointed
razočarati *v* to disappoint
razočarati se *v* to be disappointed
razočarenje *n* disappointment
razonoda *f* leisure
razonoditi *v* to amuse
razoran *adj* destructive
razoriti *v* to destroy
razoružanje *n* disarmament
razoružati *v* to disarm
razotkriti *v* to expose
razraditi *v* to work out
razred *m* class
razrediti *v* to classify
razredni *adj/m* classmaster
razreden *adj* diluted
razrez *m* cut
razrezati *v* to cut up
razrijediti *v* to dilute
razriješiti *v* 1. to solve 2. to acquit
razrok *adj* cross-eyed
razrušiti *v* to demolish
razularen *adj* unrestrained
razum *m* reason

razuman *adj* reasonable
razumeti *v* 1. to understand 2. krivo razum(j)eti to misunderstand
razumevanje, razumijevanje *n* understanding
razumjeti *see* **razumeti**
razumljiv *adj* understandable
razumno *adv* reasonably
razuveriti, razuvjeriti *v* to change someone's mind
razuzdan *adj* unrestrained
razuzdano *adv* wildly
razuzdanost *f* lack of restraint
razvalina *f* ruin
razvaliti *v* to ruin
razveden *adj* divorced
razvedravanje *n* clearing up
razvedriti (se) *v* to clear up
razveseliti (se) *v* to cheer up
razvesti (se) *v* to divorce
razvezati *v* to undo
razvijanje *n* development
razvijati *v* to develop
razvijen *adj* developed
razviti *v* to develop
razvlačiti *v* to extend
razvod *m* divorce
razvodna tabla *f* switchboard
razvodniti *v* to dilute
razvoj *m* development
razvojno ometen *adj* (med.) disabled
razvrat *m* 1. vice 2. corruption
razvratan *adj* immoral
razvrći, razvrgnuti *v* 1. to dissolve 2. to cancel 3. to divorce
razvrstati *v* 1. to arrange 2. to classify
razvučen *adj* stretched
razvući *v* to stretch
raž *f* rye

ražalostiti v to sadden
ražalostiti se v to be sad
ražanj m 1. spit 2. barbecue
ražaren adj red-hot
ražestiti se v to lose one's temper
ražnjići mpl kebab
rđa f rust
rđati v to rust
rđav adj 1. rusty 2. bad
rđavo izolovanje n fault
reagovati v to react
reakcija f reaction
reaktivni adj jet
reaktor m reactor
realan adj 1. real 2. realistic
realističan adj realistic
realizacija f realization
realizam m realism
realno adv really
realnost f reality
rebrast adj ribbed
rebro n rib
recenzent m 1. critic 2. reviewer
recenzija f 1. criticism 2. review
recepcija f reception
recepcionar m receptionist
recept m 1. recipe 2. (med.) prescription
recesija f (ec.) recession
recidiv m, **recidiva** f relapse
reciklaža f recycling
reciklirati v to recycle
recipijent recipient
recipročan adj reciprocal
reciprocitet reciprocity
recitacija f recital
recitirati v to recite
reč m word
rečen adj expressed
rečenica f sentence
rečit m eloquent
rečna obala f river bank

rečni adj river
rečnik m 1. dictionary 2. vocabulary
reći v to say
red m 1. order 2. row 3. series 4. file 5. turn
redak 1. adj sparse 2. rare 3. m line
redakcija f editing
redaktor m editor
redar m 1. arranger 2. policeman
redarstvo n police
redatelj m 1. producer 2. director
redati v to line up
reditelj m see **redatelj**
rediti v to put in order
redni adj ordinal
redom adv in order
redosled m order
redov m (mil.) private
redovan, redovit regular
redovitost f regularity
redovnica f nun
redovnik m monk
redovno adv regularly
referat m report
referendum m 1. referendum 2. **održati referendum** to hold a referendum
refleks m reflex
refleksija f reflection
reflektor m 1. reflector 2. spotlight 3. searchlight
reflektovati v to aspire
reforma f reform
reformacija f reformation
reformator m reformer
reformirati, reformisati v to reform
reformist(a) m reformist
reformizam m reformism
refren m refrain
regal m shelf
regata f regatta

regeneracija *f* regeneration
regenerirati, regenerisati *v* to regenerate
regent *m* regent
regetati *v* to croak
region *m* region
regionalan *adj* regional
regionalizam *m* regionalism
registar *m* 1. index 2. register
register kasa *f* cash register
registracija *f* registration
registrirati *v* to register
regrut *m* recruit
regrutacija *f* 1. recruiting 2. (mil.) national service
regrutirati, regrutovati *v* to recruit
regulacija *f* regulation
regularan *adj* regular
regulator *m* regulator
regulirati, regulisati *v* to regulate
rehabilitacija *f* rehabilitation
rehabilitovati *v* rehabilitate
reizbor *m* reappointment
reka *f* river
reket *m* racket
reklama *f* 1. ad, advertisement 2. advertising 3. publicity
reklamacija *f* complaint
reklamirati *v* 1. to advertise 2. to make a complaint
reklamni *adj* advertising
rekonstruisati *v* to reconstruct
rekonstrukcija *f* reconstruction
rekonvalescent *adj* convalescent
rekord *m* record
rekordan *adj* record
rekorder *m* 1. recorder 2. record holder
rekreacija *f* recreation
rekreacioni *adj* recreational
rektor *m* 1. chancellor 2. rector

rektorat *m* chancellor's office
rektum *m* rectum
rekvijem *m* requiem
rekvirirati *v* to requisition
rekvizicija *f* requisitioning
rekvizit *m* equipment
relacija *f* relation
relaksacija *f* relaxation
relativan *adj* relative
relativno *adv* relatively
relativnost *f* relativity
relej *m* relay
relevantnost *f* relevance
religija *f* religion
religiozan *adj* religious
relikvija *f* relic
reljef *m* relief
remek-delo, remek-djelo *n* masterpiece
remen *m* strap
remetiti *v* to disturb
remilitarizacija *f* remilitarization
remilitarizirati *v* to remilitarize
remorker *m* tugboat
rende *n* grater
rendgen *m* 1. X-ray 2. ići na rendgen to go for an X-ray
rendgenska slika *f* X-ray
rendgenski aparat *m* X-ray machine
rendgenski snimak *m* X-ray
rendgenski *adj* X-ray
rendgenski zrak *m*, **rendgenska zraka** *f* X-ray
renesansa *f* renaissance
renome *n* reputation
renomiran *adj* famous, well-known
renovirati *v* to renovate
renovirati *v* to renovate
renta *f* 1. rent 2. fixed income
rentabilan *adj* profitable

rentabilnost *f* profitability
rentgen aparat *m* X-ray machine
rentgen *m* X-rays
rentgenizirati *v* to X-ray
rentgenske zrake *fpl* X-rays
rentgenski *adj* X-ray
reorganizacija *f* reorganization
reorganizovati *v* to reorganize
reosigurati *v* to reinsure
rep *m* 1. tail 2. queue
repa *f* turnip
reparacije *fpl* reparations
repatica *f* comet
repatrijacija *f* repatriation
repatrirac *m* repatriated person
repatrirati *v* to repatriate
reper *m* landmark
reperkusija *f* repercussion
repertoar *m* repertoire
replika *f* 1. replica 2. retort 3. line (in a play)
reporter *m* reporter
represalija *f* reprisal
represalije *fpl* reprisals
represivan *adj* repressive
reprezentacija *f* 1. representation 2. (spor.) national team
reprezentant *m* representative
reprezentirati, reprezentovati *v* to represent
repriza *f* 1. reprise 2. second half
reprodicirati *v* to reproduce
reprodukcija *f* reproduction
reprodukovati *v* to reproduce
reptil *m* reptile
republika *f* republic
republikanac *m* republican
reputacija *f* reputation
resa *f* fringe
resiti *v* to decorate
reskirati *v* to risk
resor *m* department

restauracija *f* 1. restaurant 2. restoration
restaurater, restauretor *m* restorer
restaurirati *v* to restore
restitucija *f* restitution
restoran *m* restaurant
restrikcija *f* restriction
resurs *m* resource
rešen *adj* determined
rešenje *n* 1. decision 2. solution
rešetati *v* to sift
rešetka *f* 1. lattice 2. wire-netting
rešeto *n* riddle
rešiti *v* 1. to decide 2. to solve
retina *f* retina
retko *adv* rarely
retkost *f* rarity
retorika *f* rhetoric
retorta *f* retort
retroaktivan *adj* retroactive
retrospektivan *adj* retrospective
retuširati *v* to retouch
reuma *f* rheumatism
revalorizacija *f* revaluation
revalorizovati *v* to revalue
revan *adj* keen
revanš *m* revenge
revanš-utakmica *f* (spor.) return match
revati *v* to bray
rever *m* lapel
revidirati *v* to revise
revija *f* 1. review 2. show
revir *m* 1. compound 2. mine shaft
revizija *f* revision
revnost *f* eagerness
revolt *m* revolt
revolucija *f* revolution
revolucionar *m* revolutionary
revolucionaran, revolucionarni *adj* revolutionary

revolucionirati, revolucionisati
  v to revolutionize
revolver *m* revolver
revolveraš *m* gunman
rez *m* cut
reza *f* bolt
rezak *m* sour
rezanac *m* noodle
rezanci *mpl* noodles
rezati *v* 1. to cut 2. to carve
rezbarija *f* 1. carving 2. engraving
rezbariti *v* 1. to carve 2. engrave
rezerva *f* reserve
rezervacija *f* 1. reservation 2. booking
rezervat *m* 1. reservation 2. preserve
rezervirati *v* to reserve
rezervisan *adj* reserved
rezervisati *v* 1. to reserve 2. to book
rezervna banka *f* reserve bank
rezervni fond *m* reserve fund
rezervni *adj* spare
rezervni igrač *m* (spor.) substitute
rezervoar *m* 1. reservoir 2. tank
rezervoar za gorivo *m* fuel tank
rezervoar za naftu *m* oil tank
rezidencija *f* residence
rezignacija *f* resignation
rezigniran *adj* resigned
rezime *m* summary
rezimirati *v* to summarize
rezolucija *f* resolution
rezultat *m* result
ređati *v* to line up
režati *v* to growl
režija *f* 1. overheads 2. production 3. direction
režim *m* regime
režirati *v* to direct
režiser *m* 1. director 2. producer

riba *f* fish
ribar *m* fisherman
ribarenje *n* fishing
ribarica *f* fishing boat
ribariti *v* to fish
ribarstvo *n* fishing industry
ribati *v* 1. to rub 2. to scrub
ribič *m* fisherman
ribizla *f* currant
ribolov *m* fishing
ridati *v* to sob
riđ *adj* reddish
rigati *v* 1. to burp 2. to vomit 3. to erupt
riječ *m* word
rijedak *adj* scarce
rijeka *f* river
riješiti se *v* to get rid of
riješiti *v* to resolve
rijetko *adv* seldom
rika *f* roar
rikati *v* to roar
rikošet *m* ricochet
rilo *n* trunk
rima *f* rhyme
rimokatolički *adj* (rel.) Catholic
rimokatolik *m* (rel.) Catholic
rimski *adj* Roman
ring *m* (spor.) ring
ris *m* 1. wildcat 2. ream
risač *m* 1. designer 2. draftsman
riskantan *adj* risky
risrija *f* drawing
risti *v* to draw
rit *adj* swampy
ritam *m* rhythm
ritati *v* to kick
ritati se *v* to struggle
ritmičan, ritmički *adj* rhythmic
rizičan *adj* risky
rizik *m*, **riziko** *n* risk
rizikovati *v* to risk

riznica *f* treasury
rizničar *m* treasurer
riža *f* rice
rječit *adj* eloquent
rječitost *f* eloquence
rječnik *m* dictionary
rješavati *v* to resolve
rješenje *n* solution
rob *m* slave
roba *f* goods
roba široke potrošnje *f* consumer goods
robija *f* hard labour
robijaš *m* convict
robiti *v* 1. to rob 2. to loot
robna kuća *f* department store
robovanje *n* slavery
robovati *v* to enslave
robovlasnik *m* slaver
robovska radna snaga *f* slave labour
rod *m* 1. sex 2. gender 3. relation
roda *f* stork
rodan *adj* fertile
rodbina *f* relatives, relations
rodilište *n* maternity hospital
rodislovije *fpl* genealogy
roditelj *m* parent
roditi *v* to bear
rodna zemlja *f* native country
rodni *adj* native
rodni grad *m* hometown
rodni list *m* birth certificate
rodno mesto/mjesto *n* hometown
rodoljub *m* patriot
rodoljubiv *adj* patriotic
rodoljublje *n* patriotism
rodom *m* native
rodoskrvnuće, rodoskvrnjenje *n* incest
rodoslov *m* genealogy
rođak *m*, **rođakinja** *f* relative

rođen *adj* born
rođendan *adj* birthday
rođenje *n* birth
rog *m* horn
rogoboriti *v* to rage
roj *m* swarm
rojalista *f* royalist
rok *m* 1. term 2. rock and roll
rokenrol rock and roll
rokovodilac *m* 1. top official 2. manager
roktati *v* to grunt
roletna *f* (venetian) blind
rolna *f* roll
Rom *m* Gypsy
roman *adj* novel
romanopisac *m* novelist
romansa *f* romance
romanski *adj* Romance
romantičan *adj* romantic
romantizam *m* Romanticism
rominjati *v* to drizzle
ronilac *m* diver
roniti *v* to dive
ropotarija *f* scrap
ropstvo *n* slavery
roptati *v* to grumble
rosa *n* dew
roštilj *m* grill
rotacija *f* rotation
rotkva, rotkvica *f* radish
rov *m* 1. shaft 2. trench
rovariti *v* to plot
rovaš *m* score
rovati *v* 1. to dig up 2. to undermine
rožnica *f* cornea
rt *m* cape
rub *m* edge
rubac *m* handkerchief
rubin *m* ruby
rublje *n* 1. laundry 2. underwear

rubrika *f* section
ručak *m* dinner, lunch
ručati *v* to dine
ručica, ručka *f* handle
ručna bomba, ručna granata *f* hand grenade
ručni *adj* manual
ručni rad *m* handiwork
ručni sat *m* wristwatch
ručni telefon *m* handset
ručnik *m* towel
ručno oružje *n* small arms
ruda, rudača *f* 1. mineral 2. ore
rudar *m* miner
rudarski *adj* mining
rudarstvo *n* mining
rudast *adj* curly
rudnik *m* mine
rudo *n* shaft
rudokop *m* mine
rugati se *v* to mock
ruglo *n* mockery
rugoba *f* 1. monster 2. scarecrow
ruho *n* clothes
ruina *f* 1. ruin 2. wreck
ruinirati *v* 1. to ruin 2. to wreck
rujan 1. *adj* reddish 2. *m* September
ruka *f* 1. hand 2. arm
rukav *m* sleeve
rukavica *f* glove
rukomet *m* 1. handball 2. volleyball
rukopis *m* 1. manuscript 2. handwriting
rukopoložiti *v* (rel.) to ordain
rukovalac *m* operator
rukovanje *n* 1. handling 2. operation 3. handshake
rukovati *v* 1. to handle 2. to operate
rukovati se *v* to shake hands
rukovet *f* handful

rukovodilac *m* 1. manager 2. director
rukovoditi *v* 1. to manage 2. to direct
rukovodstvo *n* 1. management 2. board
ruksak *m* rucksack
rulja *f* mob
rum *m* rum
rumen *adj* red, pink
rumeniti se *v* to blush
Rumun, Rumunj *m* Romanian
Rumunija, Rumunjska *f* Romania
rumunski, rumunjski *adj* Romanian
runda *f* round
rune *fpl* runes
runo *n* fleece
rupa *f* hole
rupčić *m* handkerchief
rupičav *adj* perforated
Rus *m* Russian
rusifikovati *v* ro russify
Rusija *f* Russian
ruski *adj* Russian
rušenje *n* demolition
ruševan *adj* demolished
ruševina *f* ruin
rušiti *v* to demolish
rušiti se *v* to fall down
rutav *adj* hairy
rutina *f* routine
rutinski *adj* routine
ruzmarin *m* rosemary
ruž *m* lipstick
ruža *f* rose
ružan *adj* ugly
ružičast *adj* pink
ružiti *v* to abuse
rvač *m* wrestler
rvanje *n* wrestling
rvati se *v* to wrestle
rzati *v* to neigh

S

s, sa *prep* **1.** with **2.** by **3.** from **4.** on

sabiljanje *n* compression

sabirač *m* collector

sabiranje *n* collection

sabirati *v* to collect

sabiti *v* to compress

sablast *f* ghost

sablastan *adj* ghostly

sablazan *f* scandal

sablazniti *v* to scandalize

sablazniti se *v* to be scandalized

sablažnjiv *adj* scandalous

sablja *f* sabre

sabor *m* **1.** parliament **2.** congress **3.** convention

sabotaža *f*, **sabotiranje** *n* sabotage

sabotirati *v* to sabotage

sabranost *f* calm

sabrati *v* to collect

sabrati se *v* to concentrate

sačinjavati *v* to consist of

sačma *f* buckshot

sačmara *f* shotgun

sačuvati *v* to keep

sačuvati datoteku *v* to save a document

saće *n* honeycomb

SAD USA

sad, sada *adv* now

sadašnji *adj* present

sadašnjost *f* present

sadist(a) *m* sadist

sadistički *adj* sadistic

saditi *v* to plant

sadizam *m* sadism

sadnica *f* seedling

sadra *f* plaster

sadreni ovoj *m* plaster cast

sadržaj *m* **1.** summary **2.** contents

sadržavati *v* **1.** to contain **2.** to include

sadržina *f* **1.** contents **2.** volume

safir *m* sapphire

sag *m* carpet

sagibati *v* to bend

saglasan *adj* agreed

saglasiti se *v* to agree

saglasnost *f* agreement

sagnjiti *v* to rot

sagnut *adj* bent

sagorevanje *n* combustion

sagraditi *v* to construct

sagriješiti *v* to sin

sahrana *f* burial

sahraniti *v* to bury

sajam *m* fair

sajla *f* cable

sakat *adj* **1.** crippled **2.** mutilated

sakatiti *v* **1.** to cripple **2.** to mutilate

sako *m* jacket

sakriti *v* to hide

saksija *f* flowerpot

saksofon *m* **1.** saxophone **2. svirati saksofon** to play the saxophone

saksonski *adj* Saxon

sakupiti, sakupljati *v* to gather

sala *f* **1.** hall **2.** auditorium

salama *f* salami

salamura *f* pickle

salata *f* **1.** salad **2.** lettuce

salata od voća *f* fruit salad

saldo *m* balance

saliven *adj* perfectly formed
salmonela *f* (med.) salmonella
salo *n* fat
salon *m* 1. drawing-room 2. saloon
salutirati *v* to salute
salva *f* salvo
salvet *m* napkin
sam *adj* 1. alone 2. only
samac *m* bachelor
samilost *f* compassion
samit *m* summit (conference)
samljeti *v* to grind
samo 1. only 2. self-
samočitač *m* word processor
samoća *f* 1. solitude 2. loneliness
samoglasnik *m* vowel
samoljublje *n* selfishness
samoobrana *f* self-defence
samoopredeljenje, samoopredjeljenje *n* self-determination
samopoštovanje *n* self-respect
samopouzdanje *n* self-confidence
samoprijegor *m* self-sacrifice
samostalan *adj* 1. self-supporting 2. independent 3. autonomous
samostalnost *f* 1. independence 2. autonomy
samostan *adj* 1. monastery 2. convent
samosvest *f* self-consciousness
samoubica *f*, **samoubistvo** *n* suicide
samoubojstvo *n* 1. suicide 2. **počiniti samubojstvo** to commit suicide
samouprava *f* home-rule, self-government
samousluga *f* 1. self-service 2. supermarket
samouveren *adj* self-confident
samovolja *f* obstinacy

samovoljan *adj* obstinate
samozadovoljstvo *n* self-satisfaction
samoživ *adj* selfish
samrtnički *adj* mortal
san *m* 1. sleep 2. dream
sanacija *f* reclamation
sanatorij *m* sanatorium
sandala *f* sandal
sanduk *m* 1. box 2. case 3. trunk
sanen *adj* sleepy
sanirati *v* 1. to improve 2. to reclaim
sanitaran *adj* sanitary
sanitarna tehnika *f* sanitary engineering
sanitet *m* health care
sanitetski *adj* medical
sankcija *f* sanction
sankcionisati *v* to sanction
sanke *fpl* sledge
santa *f* iceberg
santimetar *m* centimetre
sanjar *m* dreamer
sanjarenje *n* dream
sanjariti *v* to daydream
sanjati *v* to dream
sanjiv *adj* sleepy
sanjkati se *v* to sleigh
saobraćajac *m* traffic policeman
saobraćaj *m* 1. traffic 2. intercourse
saobraćajac *m* traffic policeman
saobraćajna pravila *f* highway code
saobraćajni znak *m* traffic sign
saobraćaj u dolasku incoming traffic
saobraziti *v* to conform
saone, saonice *fpl* sledge
saopćenje *n see* **saopštenje**
saopčiti *v see* **saopštiti**

saopštenje *n* 1. announcement 2. communication

saopštiti *v* 1. to announce 2. to communicate

saosećajan *adj* sympathetic

saosećati *v* to sympathize

sapet *adj* 1. bound 2. uncomfortable

sapeti *v* 1. to bind 2. to tighten

sapun *m* soap

sapunica *f* lather

saradnik *m* collaborator

saradnja *f* collaboration

sarađivati *v* to collaborate

sardina *f* sardine

Sardinac *m* Sardinian

Sardinija *f* Sardinia

sardinijski, sardinski *adj* Sardinian

sarkastičan *adj* sarcastic

sarkazam *m* sarcasm

sarkofag *m* sarcophagus

sarkom *m* sarcoma

sarma *f* stuffed vine leaves

saseći, sasjeći *v* to chop up

saslušanje *n* 1. audience 2. hearing 3. interrogation

saslušati *v* 1. to listen to 2. to hear 3. to interrogate

sastajati se *v* to meet

sastanak *m* appointment

sastati se *v see* **sastajati se**

sastav *adj* structure

sastavak *m* 1. composition 2. draft

sastaviti, sastavljati *v* 1. to compose 2. to draw up

sastavni *adj* integral

sastijak *m* component

sastojati se *v* to consist of

sastojina *f* component

sasuti *v* to shoot out

sasvim *adv* completely

sat *m* 1. hour 2. o'clock 3. clock 4. watch 5. period 6. **na sat** hourly

satana *m* Satan

satelit *m* 1. satellite 2. **grad-satelit** satellite city

satira *f* satire

satiričan *adj* satirical

satisfakcija *f* satisfaction

satnica *f* timetable

satrti *v* to crush

saučesnik *m* 1. participant 2. accomplice

saučešće *n* sympathy

saučestvovati *v* to participate

sauna *f* sauna

sav *adj* all

savest *f* conscience

savet *m* 1. advice 2. council

Savet bezbednosti *m* Security Council

savetnik, savetodavac *m* adviser

savetovati *v* to advise

savez *m* 1. union 2. association

savezni *adj* 1. united 2. allied

savezni *adj* federal

saveznički *adj* allied

saveznik *m* ally

savezništvo *n* alliance

savijati, saviti *v* to bend

savitljiv *adj* flexible

savitljivi disk *m* floppy disk

savjest *f* conscience

savjestan *adj* conscientious

savjet *m* 1. advice 2. council

Savjet bezbjednosti *m* Security Council

savjetnik *m* 1. adviser 2. councillor

savjetovati *v* to advise

savladati *v* to defeat

savremen *adj* contemporary

savremenik *m* contemporary

savršen *adj* perfect

savršenstvo *n* perfection
saxofonist(a) *m* saxophone player
sazidati *v* to build
sazivati, sazvati *v* to summon
saznanje *n* knowledge
saznati *v* to learn
sazreti *v* 1. to mature 2. to ripen
sazrevanje *n* ripening
sazvati *v* to convene
sazvežde *n* constellation
sažaliti *v* to pity
sažaljenje *n* pity
sažet *adj* condensed
sažeti *v* 1. to contract 2. to shrug
sažetost *f* conciseness
sažimanje *n* condensation
sažiti *v* to sew up
scena *f* 1. scene 2. stage
scenacija *f* scenery
scenarij, scenario *m* 1. scenario 2. screenplay
scenarist(a) *m* screenwriter
se, sebe 1. -self, -selves 2. each other
sebeljublje *n* selfishness
sebi to oneself
sebičan *adj* selfish
sebičnost *f* selfishness
secesija *f* secession
secirati *v* to dissect
seckati *v* to cut
sečivo *n* blade
sećanje *n* memory
seći *v* to cut down
sedam seven
sedamdeset seventy
sedamnaest seventeen
sedativ *m* sedative
sedeljka *f* party
sedenje *n* sitting
sedeti *v* to sit
sedište *n* 1. seat 2. site

sedište vlade *n* seat of government
sedlo *n* saddle
sedmi *adj* seventh
sedmica *f* week
sedmično *adv* weekly
sednica *f* meeting
sef *m* safe
segment *m* segment
segregacija *f* segregation
sejanje *n* sowing
sejati *v* to sow
sekcija *f* section
sekira *f* axe
sekirati *v* to upset
sekretar *m* secretary
sekretarica *f* secretary
sekretarijat *m* 1. department 2. secretariat
sekretarski *adj* secretarial
sekretar za štampu *m* press secretary
seks *m* sex
seksapel *m* sex appeal
seksi *adj* sexy
seksualan *adj* sexual
seksualitet *m* sexuality
seksualno maltiranje žena *f* sexual harassment
seksualnost *f* sexuality
seksualno vaspitanje *n* sex education
sekta *f* sect
sektaški *adj* sectarian
sektor *m* 1. sector 2. privatni sektor private sector 3. državni sektor public sector
sekund *m*, **sekunda** *f* second
selekcija *f* selection
selica *f* migratory
selidba *f* 1. move 2. migration
seliti *v* 1. to move 2. to migrate
selo *n* 1. village 2. the country

selotejp *m* sellotape
seljački *adj* country
seljak *m* countryman
seljakinja *f* countrywoman
seljaštvo *n* countryfolk
sem *prep/conj* except
semafor *m* traffic light
seme *n* 1. seed 2. semen
semenik *m* testicle
semenka *f* seed
semestar *m* semester
seminar *m* 1. seminar 2. (ed.)
 department 3. (rel.) seminary
senat *m* senate
senator *m* senator
sendvič *m* sandwich
senf *m* mustard
senilan *adj* senile
senilnost *f* senility
senka *f* shadow
seno *adv* hay
sentimentalan *adj* sentimental
sentimentalnost *f* sentimentality
senzacija *f* sensation
senzacionalan *adj* sensational
senzibilan *adj* sensitive
senzualan *adj* sensual
seoba *f* 1. move 2. migration
seoski *adj* 1. village 2. country
separatist(a) *m* separatist
separatizam *m* separatism
septembar *m* September
sepsa *f* sepsis
septičan *adj* septic
serenada *f* serenade
serija *f* series
serijski *adj* serial
serpentina *f* serpentine
serum *m* serum
servilan *adj* servile
servilnost *f* servility
servirati *v* to serve

servis *m* 1. service 2. service shop
 3. set
sesti *v* to sit down
sestra *f* sister
sestrinski *adj* sisterly
sestrić *m*, **sestrična** *f* cousin
seta *f* sadness
setan *adj* sad
setiti se *v* to remember
setva *f* sowing
sevati *v* to flash
sever *m* north
severac *m* north wind
severni *adj* north, northern
severno-atlanski pakt *m* NATO
severoistok *m* northeast
severozapad *m* northwest
sezati *v* to reach
sezona *f* season
sezonska karta *f* season ticket
sezonski *adj* 1. seasonal 2.
 itinerant
sezonski radnik *m* migrant worker
sfera *f* sphere
shema *f* scheme
shizofreničar *m* schizophrenic
shizofrenički *adj* schizophrenic
shizofrenija *f* schizophrenia
shodan *adj* suitable
shodno *adv* in accordance
shrvan *adj* overwhelmed
shrvati *v* to overwhelm
shvaćanje, shvatanje *n* 1.
 understanding 2. krivo
 shvaćanje misunderstanding
shvaćati, shvatiti *v* to understand
si to oneself
Sicilija *f* Sicily
Sicilijanac *m* Sicilian
siciljanski *adj* Sicilian
sići *v* to go down
sićušan *adj* tiny

sida *f* AIDS
sidrište *n* (mar.) mooring
sidro *n* anchor
siesta *f* siesta
sifilis *m* syphilis
siga *f* stalactite
signal *m* signal
signalizacija požara *f* fire alarm
signalizirati *v* to signal
signalni blok *m* signal box
siguran *adj* 1. sure 2. secure
sigurna pratnja *f* safe conduct
sigurno *adv* 1. certainly 2. safely
sigurnosni *adj* safety
sigurnosni pojas *m* seatbelt
sigurnost *f* 1. certainty 2. security
sijalica *f* 1. lamp 2. lightbulb
sijanje *n* shining
sijanje sunca *n* sunshine
sijaset *m* (large) quantity
sijati *v* 1. to sow 2. to shine
siječanj *m* January
sijed *adj* grey
sijelo *n* 1. seat 2. meeting
sijeno *adv* hay
sijevati *v* to flash
siktati *v* to hiss
sila *f* 1. force 2. violence 3. konjska sila horsepower
silan *adj* powerful
silazak *m* descent
silaziti *v* to descend
siledžija *f* skinhead
siledžija *f* tyrant
silicijum *m* silicon
siliti *v* to force
silnik *m* bully
silno *adv* 1. powerfully 2. violently
silom *adv* by force
silos *m* silo
silovanje *n* rape
silovati *v* to rape

silovit *adj* brutal
silovitost *f* brutality
silueta *f* silhouette
simbol *m* symbol
simboličan *adj* symbolic
simbolično *adv* symbolically
simbolika *f* symbolism
simbolizovati *v* to symbolize
simetričan *adj* symmetrical
simetrija *f* symmetry
simfonija *f* symphony
simfonijski *adj* symphonic
simpatičan *adj* nice
simpatija *f* 1. sympathy 2. niceness
simpatisati *v* to like
simpatizer *m* sympathizer
simpozijum *m* symposium
simptom *m* symptom
simptomatičan *adj* symptomatic
simulirati *v* to simulate
simultan *adj* simultaneous
simultano prevođenje *n* simultaneous translation
sin *m* son
sinagoga *f* synagogue
sindikalni *adj* union
sindikat *m* 1. syndicate 2. trade union
sinemaskop *m* cinemascope
sinhronizacija, sinkronizacija *f* synchronization
sinhronizovati; sinkronizirati *v* to synchronize
sinod *m* synod
sinonim *m* synonym
sinoptičar *m* weatherman, weatherwoman
sinovac *m* nephew
sinovica *f* nice
sinoć *adv* last night
sintesajzer *m* synthesizer
sintetičan *adj* synthetic

sintetizovati *v* to synthesize
sintetski, sintetičan, sintetički *adj* synthetic
sinteza *f* synthesis
sinus *m* sinus
sinuti *v* to shine
sipa *f* cuttlefish
sipati *v* 1. to pour 2. to scatter
sipljiv *adj* asthmatic
sir *m* cheese
sirće *n* vinegar
sirena *f* siren
siročad *f* orphans
siroče *n* orphan
siromah *m* 1. poor man 2. *see* sirota
siromašan *adj* 1. poor 2. wretched
siromaštvo *n* 1. poverty 2. misery
sirota, sirotica *f* poor woman
sirotinjski kvart *m* slum
sirotište *n* orphanage
sirov *adj* raw
sirovina *f* raw material
sirup *m* syrup
sisa *f* 1. nipple 2. breast 3. bust
sisaljka *f* 1. sucker 2. pump
sisanje *n* sucking
sisar *m* mammal
sisati *v* to suck
sisavac *m* mammal
sisni *adj* mammary
sistem *m*, **sistema** *f* 1. system 2. u sklopu sistema on-line
sistem-inženjer *m* system engineer
sistematičan *adj* systematic
sistematika *f* systems
sistematizacija *f* systematization
sistematizirati, sistematizovati *v* to systemize
sistematski *adj* systematic
sistemski, sistematičan *adj* systematic

sistemski softver *m* system software
sit *adj* 1. full 2. fed up
sitan *adj* 1. minute 2. trivial
sitnica *f* 1. detail 2. trifle
sitničav *adj* pedantic
sitnina *f*, **sitniš** *m* (cash) change
sito *n* sieve
sitost *f* fullness
situacija *f* situation
siv *adj* grey
sivilo *n* monotony
sivkast *adj* greyish
sjaj *m* brilliance
sjajan *adj* bright
sjati se *v* to shine
sjecište *n* junction
sjeckati *v* to mince
sjećanje *n* memory
sjećati se *v* to remember
sjeći *v* to chop
sjedalo *n* seat
sjediniti (se) *v* to unite
Sjedinjene Američke Države *fpl* United States of America
sjedište *n* 1. seat 2. headquarters 3. residence
sjediti *v* to sit
sjednica *f* 1. session 2. conference
sjekano meso *n* minced meat
sjekira *f* axe
sjeme *n* 1. seed 2. semen
sjemenik *m* testicle
sjemenište *n* seminary
sjemenje *n* seeds
sjena *f* 1. shadow 2. shade
sjenik *m* hay barn
sjenilo *n* lampshade
sjenovit *adj* shady
sjesti *v* to sit down
sjeta *f* sadness
sjetan *adj* sad

sjetilo *n* sense
sjetiti *v* to remind
sjetiti se *v* remember
sjetva *f* sowing
sjever *m* north
sjeverni *adj* north, northern
sjevernjača *f* pole star
sjeverno-atlanski pakt *m* NATO
sjeveroistočan *adj* northeastern
sjeveroistok *m* northeast
sjeverozapad northwest
sjeverozapadan *adj* northwestern
skakač *m* 1. jumper 2. diver
skakanje *n* jumping
skakati *v* to jump
skakavac *m* 1. grasshopper 2. locust
skakutati *v* to hop
skala *f* scale
skalpel *m* scalpel
skandal *m* scandal
skandalizirati, skandalizovati *v* to scandalize
skandalizirati se *v* to be scandalized
skandalozan *adj* scandalous
skandinavski *adj* Scandinavian
skandirati *v* 1. to chant 2. to scan
skanirati *v* to scan
skanjivati se *v* to hesitate
skapavati *v* to perish
skejtbord *m* skatebord
skela *f* ferry
skele *fpl* scaffolding
skelet *m* 1. skeleton 2. frame
skener *m* scanner
skeptičan *adj* sceptical
skepticizam *m* scepticism
skeptik *m* sceptic
skerletan *adj* scarlet
skica *f* 1. sketch 2. draft
skicirati *v* 1. to sketch 2. to draft

skidati, skinuti *v* to remove
skija *f* ski
skijanje *n* skiing
skijaš *m* skier
skijaški sport *m* skiing
skijati se *v* to ski
skije *fpl* skis
skinuti *v* 1. to take down 2. to undress
skitalac *m*, **skitnica** *f* tramp
skitati se *v* to roam
skitnica *m/f* vagrant
sklad *m* harmony
skladan *adj* harmonious
skladatelj *m* composer
skladati *v* to compose
skladba *f* (mus.) composition
skladište *n* warehouse
skladište goriva *n* fuel dump
skladište municije *n* ammunition dump
sklanjati *v* to decline
sklapanje *n* folding
sklapati *v* 1. to fold 2. to close 2. to make
skleroza *f* sclerosis
sklizač *m* skater
sklizak *m* slippery
sklizalište *n* skating rink
sklizaljka *f* skate
sklizanje *n* skating
sklizati (se) *v* 1. to slide 2. to skate
sklizav *adj* slippery
skliznuti *v* see **sklizati**
sklon *adj* favourable
sklonište *n* 1. shelter 2. hiding-place
skloniti *v* 1. to remove 2. to hide
skloniti se *v* to shelter
sklonost *f* inclination
sklop *m* structure
sklopac *m* tetanus

sklopiti *v* 1. to fold 2. to close 2. to make

sklopiti mir *m* to make peace

skočiti *v* to jump

skok *m* jump

skok uvis *m* (spor.) high jump

skopčati *v* to do up

skorašnji *adj* recent

skorbut *m* scurvy

skor *m* (spor.) score

skoro *adv* 1. soon 2. almost 3. recently

skorojević *m* upstart

skoroteča *f* messenger

skorup *m* cream

skraćenica *f* abbreviation

skraćenje *n* shortening

skrama *f* film

skrasiti se *v* to settle down

skraćivati, skratiti *v* to shorten

skrb *f* 1. care 2. worry

skrbiti se *v* 1. to care for 2. to worry

skrbnik *m* guardian

skrbništvo *n* guardianship

skrenuti *v* to turn

skretanje *n* turning

skretnica *f* switch

skretničarska kućica *f* signal box

skrhati *v* to smash

skrivalište *n* hiding-place

skrivanje *n* hiding

skrivati *v* to hide

skriviti *v* to blame

skrižaljka *f* schedule

skrlet *m* scarlet fever

skrojiti *v* to cut out

skroman *adj* modest

skromno *adv* modestly

skromnost *f* modesty

skrovište *n* 1. refuge 2. hiding-place

skrovit *adj* 1. hidden 2. secret

skroz *adv* 1. totally 2. through

skršen *adj* heartbroken

skršiti *v* to crush

skrupula *f* scruple

skrupulozan *adj* scrupulous

skrušen *adj* contrite

skrušenost *f* contrition

skrutiti se *v* to congeal

skučen *adj* restricted

skučiti *v* to restrict

skuhati *v* 1. to cook 2. to scheme

skulptura *f* sculpture

skulptor *m* sculptor

skup 1. *adj* expensive 2. *m* group 3. meeting

skupa *adv* together

skupan *adj* 1. joint 2. common

skupina *f* group

skupiti, skupljati *v* 1. to gather 2. to raise

skupocen, skupocjen *adj* valuable

skupoća *f* expensiveness

skupština *f* 1. meeting 2. assembly

skuša *f* mackerel

skuter *m* scooter

skver *m* square

skvrčiti se *v* 1. to shrink 2. to wrinkle

slab *adj* weak

slabašan *adj* weakly

slabina *f* 1. side 2. loins

slabiti *v* 1. to weaken 2. to lose weight

slabo *adv* 1. badly 2. slightly

slabokrvan *adj* anaemic

slabokrvnost *f* anaemia

slabost *f* weakness

slačica *f* mustard

slad *m* malt

sladak *adj* sweet

sladiti *v* to sweeten

sladoled *m* ice-cream
sladostrasan *adj* lascivious
sladostrašće *n* sensuality
slagar *m* typesetter
slagarna *f* printing-house
slagati *v* 1. to stack 2. to typeset 3. to lie
slagati se *v* to agree with
slajd *m* (film) slide
slalom *m* slalom
slam *m*, **slamovi** *mpl* slums
slama *f* straw
slamnat *adj* straw
slamka *f* straw
slan *adj* 1. salty 2. salted
slana *f* frost
slang *m* slang
slanik *m* salt-cellar
slanina *f* bacon
slap *m* waterfall
slast *f* 1. sweet; candy 2. delight
slastičarna *f* cake-shop
slati *v* to send
slatkiš *m* 1. sweet 2. cake
slatko *adv* sweetly
slatlovodan *adj* freshwater
slava *f* 1. fame 2. glory
slavan *adj* 1. famous 2. glorious
Slaven *m*, **Slavenka** *f* Slav
slavenski *adj* Slavic, Slavonic
slavina *f* tap; faucet
slaviti *v* 1. to celebrate 2. to glorify
slavlje *n* 1. celebrations 2. triumph
slavodobitan *adj* triumphant
slavohlepan, slavoljubiv *adj* ambitious
slavoljublje *n* ambition
slavuj *m* nightingale
sledbenik *m* 1. follower 2. successor
sleći *v* to shrug
sledeći *adj* next

slediti *v* to follow
sledovanje *n* ration
sledstveno *adv* consequently
sleđ *m* herring
slegnuti *v* to shrug
sleng *m* slang
slep *adj* blind
slepac *m* blind man
slepačko pismo *n* braille
slepilo *n* blindness
slepo *adv* blindly
slepoočnica *f* temple
sletanje *n* 1. landing 2. **prinudno sletanje** forced landing
sleteti, sletjeti *v* to land
slezena, slezina *f* spleen
sličan *adj* similar
sličiti *v* 1. to resemble 2. to be suitable
sličnost *f* similarity
slijed *m* sequence
slijep *adj* blind
slijepac *m* blind person
slijepiti *v* to glue
slijevati se *v* to flow into
sliječi *v* next
slijiti *v* to follow
slik *m* rhyme
slika *f* 1. picture 2. drawing 3. painting
slikanje *n* painting
slikar *m* artist
slikarska akademija *f* art school
slikarstvo *n* painting
slikati *v* 1. to paint 2. to take a picture
slikovit *adj* picturesque
slikovnica *f* picture-book
slina *f* mucus
slinav *adj* snotty
sliti se *v* to flow down
slitina *f* alloy

sliv *m* basin
sljedbenik *m* 1. follower 2. successor
sljepačko pismo *n* braille
sljepočica *f* temple
sljepoća *f* blindness
sloboda *f* 1. freedom 2. independence
sloboda govora *f* freedom of speech
slobodan *adj* 1. free 2. independent
sloboda štampe *f* freedom of the press
sloboda veroispovesti/ vjeroispovijesti *f* freedom of religion
sloboda zbora *f* freedom of assembly
slobodna trgovina *f* free trade
slobodna trgovina *f* free trade
slobodni izbori *mpl* free elections
slobodni izbori *mpl* free elections
slobodni zidar *m* freemason
slobodno *adv* freely
slog *m* 1. syllable 2. type
sloga *f* harmony
sloj *m* layer
slojevit *adj* stratified
slom *m* 1. break 2. breakdown 3. crash
slomiti *v* 1. to break 2. to crash
slomljen *adj* broken
slon *m* elephant
slonovača *f* ivory
slovački *adj* Slovak
Sloven *m* Slav
Slovenac *m* Slovene, Slovenian
slovenački, slovenski *adj* Slovenian
Slovenija *f* Slovenian
slovenski *adj* 1. Slavic 2. Slovenian

slovo *n* letter
složan *adj* 1. harmonious 2. unanimous
složen *adj* 1. complex 2. compound
složenost *f* complexity
složiti *v* 1. to stack 2. to arrange
složiti se *v* to agree
složno *adv* in harmony
slučaj *m* 1. chance 2. incident 3. accident
slučaj nužde *m* emergency
slučajan *adj* 1. incidental 2. accidental
slučajno *adv* accidentally
sluga *m/f* servant
sluh *m* 1. hearing 2. ear
slupati *v* to wreck
slušač *m* 1. listener 2. student
slušalac *m* listener
slušalica *f* 1. headphone 2. receiver
slušalica *f* telephone receiver
slušalice, naglavne slušalice *fpl* earphones
slušanje *n* listening
slušateljstvo *n* audience
slušati *v* to listen (to)
slutiti *v* to have a hunch
slutnja *f* hunch
sluz *f* 1. mucus 2. slime
sluzav *adj* slimy
služavka *f* servant
služba *f* 1. service 2. employment 3. job 4. **obaveštajna/ obavještajna služba** military intelligence
služben *adj* 1. official 2. formal
službene novine *fpl* gazette
službenik *m* 1. official 2. employee
službeno *adv* officially
službeno putovanje *n* business trip

služiti *v* to serve
služiti se *v* to use
služkinja *f* servant
služnik *m* porter
smaknuti *v* to execute
smaknuće *n* execution
smanjiti *v* to diminish
smaragd *m* emerald
smatrati *v* to consider
smeće *n* rubbish; garbage
smeđ *adj* brown
smeh *m* laughter
smejati se *v* to laugh
smekšati *v* to soften
smelo *adv* bravely
smelost *f* bravery
smena *f* shift
smeniti *v* 1. to change 2. to replace 3. to dismiss
smeo *adj* brave
smer *m* 1. direction 2. course
smeran *adj* modest
smerati *v* to intend
smernica *f* 1. trend 2. directive
smerno *adv* modestly
smernost *f* modesty
smesa *f* mixture
smesta *adv* at once
smesti *v* to confuse
smesti se *v* to get confused
smestiti *v* to place 2. to accommodate 3. to store
smešan *adj* 1. funny 2. ridiculous
smešiti se *v* to smile
smeštaj *m* accommodation
smet *m* snowdrift
smetati *v* 1. to hinder 2. to interrupt 3. to annoy
smetati *v* to disturb
smeten *adj* 1. confused 2. embarrassed
smeti *v* 1. to dare 2. to be allowed

smetište, smetlište *n* rubbish heap; trash heap
smetnja *f* 1. disturbance 2. interference
smežuran *adj* wrinkled
smežurati se *v* to wrinkle
smicalica *f* trick
smijati se *v* to laugh
smijeh *m* laughter
smiješak *m* smile
smiješan *adj* funny
smiješati *v* to mix up
smiješiti se *v* to smile
smijuckati se *v* to giggle
smilovati se *v* to pity
smion *adj* brave
smionost *f* bravery
smiren *adj* calm
smiriti *v* to calm
smisao *m* meaning
smisao za humor *m* sense of humour
smisliti *v* 1. to think out 2. to invent
smjel *adj* brave
smjelost *f* bravery
smjena *f* shift
smjer *m* direction
smjerati *v* 1. to shift 2. to aim at
smjernica *f* 1. trend 2. directive
smjesa *f* 1. mixture 2. alloy
smještaj *m* 1. situation 2. accomodation
smjesta *adv* at once
smjestiti *v* 1. to situate 2. to accommodate
smjestiti se *v* to settle
smjeti *v* 1. to dare 2. to be allowed
smočiti *v* to wet
smočnica *f* larder
smog *m* smog
smoking *m* dinner-jacket

smokva f fig
smola f 1. resin 2. pitch
smotak m roll
smotati v to roll up
smotra f inspection
smračiti se v to grow dark
smrad m stink
smrdeti, smrdjeti v to stink
smrdljiv adj smelly
smreka f juniper
smrkavati se v to become dark
smrskati v to smash
smršati v to lose weight
smrt f death
smrtan adj 1. fatal 2. deadly
smrtna kazna f capital punishment
smrtna osuda f death sentence
smrtni slučaj m casualty
smrtnik m mortal
smrtno adv mortally
smrtnost f 1. mortality 2. **stopa smrtnosti** mortality rate
smrtonosan adj 1. fatal 2. deadly
smrtonosna bolest f fatal illness
smrtovnica f death certificate
smrviti v to pound
smrzavanje n freezing
smrzavati se v to freeze
smrznut adj frozen
smrznuti v to freeze
smrznuti se v to freeze to death
smučanje n skiing
smučanje na vodi n waterskiing
smučar m skier
smučar na vodi m waterskier
smučarska staza f ski run
smučarski centar m ski resort
smučati se v to ski
smučati se na vodi v waterski
smučka f ski
smuđ m perch
smušen adj confused

smušenost f confusion
smutiti v to confuse
smutnja f intrigue
snabdeti v to supply
snabdevač m 1. supplier 2. caterer
snabdevačka jednica, snabdjevačka jednica f supply unit
snabdevački brod, snabdjevački brod m supply ship
snabdevačko skladište, snabdjevačko skladište n supply depot
snabdevanje n 1. supplying 2. catering
snabdevanje vodom, snabdijevanje vodom n water supply
snabdijevati v to supply
snaga f 1. strength 2. power
snaga volje n will power
snaha f daughter-in-law
snajper m sniper
snalažljiv adj resourceful
snast f (mar.) rigging
snažan adj strong
snebivati se v 1. to be shocked 2. to hesitate
sneg m 1. snow 2. **sneg pada** it is snowing
snek-bar, snek-bife n 1. buffet 2. snack bar
sneško belić n snowman
snesti v to lay an egg
snežni plug m snow plough/plow
snijeg m 1. snow 2. **snijeg pada** it is snowing
snijeti v see **snesti**
snimatelj m cameraman
snimati v 1. to photograph 2. to film
snimka f photograph
sniziti v to reduce

sniženje *n* reduction
snješko bjelić *n* snowman
snježni plug *m* snow plough/plow
snob *m* snob
snobizam *m* snobbery
snobovski *adj* snobbish
snop *m* bundle
snorkel *m* snorkel
snositi *v* to bear
snošaj *m* sexual intercourse
snošljiv *adj* tolerable
snošljivost *f* tolerance
snova *adv* (once) again
snovati *v* 1. to plan 2. to plot
snovi *mpl* dreams
snubiti *v* to woo
snužden *adj* depressed
snužditi se *v* to be depressed
so *f* salt
sob *m* reindeer
soba *f* room
sobarica *f* chambermaid
sobica *f* 1. small room 2. wardrobe; closet
sočan *adj* juicy
socijalan *adj* social
socijalist *m* socialist
socijalistički *adj* socialist
socijalizam *m* socialism
socijalna pomoć *f* 1. human resources 2. welfare
socijalne nauke *fpl* social sciences
socijalni *adj* social
socijalno osiguranje *n* social security
socijalno staranje *n* welfare
sociolingvistika *f* sociolinguistics
sociolog *m* sociologist
sociologija *f* sociology
sociološki *adj* sociological
sočivo *n* 1. lens 2. lentil 3. kontaktno sočivo contact lens

soda *f* soda
soda-voda *f* soda water
sofa *f* sofa
sofist *m* sophist
sofizam *m* sophism
softver *m* software
softverski paket *m* software package
soj *m* kind, type, sort
sok *m* 1. juice 2. gravy
soko, sokol *m* hawk
sokoloti *v* to encourage
sol *f* salt
solarni *adj* solar
solenka *f* salt-cellar
solidan *adj* solid
solidaran *adj* united
solidarnost *f* solidarity
solika *f* sleet
solist(a) *m* soloist
soliti *v* to salt
solo *adj/n/adv* solo
som *m* catfish
somnambul *m* sleepwalker
somot *m* velvet
sonata *f* sonata
sonda *f* probe
sonet *m* sonnet
sopran *adj* soprano
sopstven *adj* own
sopstvenik *m* owner
sorta *f* sort, type, kind
sortirati *v* to sort
SOS SOS
sos *m* sauce
sotona *f* devil
sova *f* owl
sovjet *n* soviet
sovjetski *adj* soviet
Sovjetski Savez *m* Soviet Union
spajalica *f* paper clip
spajanje *n* connecting

spajati *v see* **spojiti**
spaliti *v* 1. to burn 2. to cremate
spanać *m* spinach
sparan *adj* stuffy
spariti *v* to copulate
sparivanje *n* copulation
spas *m* 1. rescue 2. salvation
spasavanje *n* 1. rescue 2. **pojas za spasavanje** lifebelt
spasavati *v* to rescue
spasilac *m* rescuer
spasitelj *m* 1. rescuer 2. saviour
spasiti *v* to rescue
spasonosan *adj* beneficial
spavač *m* sleeper
spavanje *n* sleep
spavati *v* to sleep
spavaća kola *f* sleeping car
spavaća soba *f* bedroom
spavaći *v* to sleep
spavaćica *f* nightgown
spaziti *v* to see
specialnost *f* speciality
specifičan *adj* specific
specifijalan *adj* special
specifikacija *f* specification
specijalan *adj* special
specijalist *m* specialist
specijalitet *m* speciality
specijalizacija *f* specialization
specijalizovati se *v* to specialize (**u** in)
specijalno *adv* specially
spektar *m* spectrum
spekulirati *v* to speculate
spelovati *v* to spell
sperma *f* sperm
spev *m* epic poem
spiker *m* 1. announcer 2. newsreader
spiker *m* announcer
spilja *f* cave
spinalan *adj* spinal

spirala *f* spiral
spiralan *adj* spiral
spis *m* document
spisak *m* list
spisatelj *m* writer
spiskati *v* to waste
splasnuti *v* 1. to shrink 2. to deflate
splav *adj* raft
splesti *v* to knit
splet *m* knot
spleten *adj* confused
spletka *f* 1. intrigue 2. plot
spljoštiti, sploštiti *v* to flatten
spočitavati *v* to reproach
spodoba *f* figure
spoj *m* 1. connection 2. combination 3. **kratki spoj** short circuit
spojiti *v* 1. to connect 2. to combine
spojnica *f* 1. paper clip 2. hyphen
spokojan *adj* calm
spokojnost *f* calm
spol *m* sex
spolni *adj* 1. sexual 2. genital
spolni organi *fpl* genitals
spolja *adv* (from) outside
spoljni *adj* exterior
spoljašnost *f* exterior
spomen *adj* 1. memory 2. souvenir
spomenik *m* monument
spomenut *adj* mentioned
spomenuti, spominjati *v* to mention
spona *f* 1. link 2. buckle
spontan *adj* spontaneous
spontanost *f* spontaneity
sponzor *m* sponsor
spor 1. *adj* slow 2. *m* dispute 3. conflict
spora *f* spore
sporan *adj* controversial

sporazum *m* agreement
sporazuman *adj* in agreement
sporazumjeti se *v* to come to an agreement
sporedan *adj* secondary
sporedna ulica *f* side-street
sporiti *v* 1. to deny 2. to argue
sport *m* sport
sportaš *m* sportsman
sportista *f* sportsman
sportistkinja *f* sportswoman
sportovi na vodi *mpl* watersports
sportska odeća/odjeća *f* sportswear
sportski *adj* sport, sporting
sposoban *adj* capable
sposobnost *f* ability
spotaći se, spotaknuti se *v* to trip
spoznaja *f* 1. awareness 2. comprehension
spoznati *v* 1. to be aware 2. to comprehend
sprat *m* 1. floor 2. storey; story
sprava *f* apparatus
sprava za gašenje požara *f* fire extinguisher
sprave za mučenje *fpl* torture instruments
sprdati se *v* to ridicule
sprdnja *f* ridicule
sprečavati, sprečiti *v* 1. to prevent 2. to neutralize
spreda *adv* 1. in front of 2. before
sprega *f* team
sprema *f* 1. readiness 2. preparation 3. equipment 4. qualification
spreman *adj* 1. ready 2. prepared
spremanje *n* preparation
spremati *v* 1. to get ready 2. to prepare
spremište *n* warehouse

spremiti *v see* **spremati**
spremnost *f* readiness
spretan *adj* 1. skilful 2. clever
spretnost *f* 1. skill 2. cleverness
sprezanje *n* conjugation
sprijateljiti se *v* to beome friends
spriječiti *v see* **sprečavati**
sprijeda *adv* 1. before 2. in front of
sprint *m* sprint
sprinter *m* sprinter
sprintovati *v* to sprint
sprovesti *v* 1. to spend (time) 2. to escort
sprovesti politiku *v* to implement a policy
sprovod *m* funeral
sprovodni list *m* bill of lading
sprovodnik *m* guard, conductor
sprtljati *v* to bungle
sprud *m* dune
spržiti *v* 1. to roast 2. to burn 3. to overdo
spuštanje *n* 1. descent 2. landing
spuštati *v see* **spustiti**
spustiti se *v* 1. to drop 2. to descend 3. to sink 4. to land
spustiti (se) padobranom *v* to parachute
spustiti *v* to lower, drop
sputati, sputavati *v* 1. to bind 2. to chain
spužva *f* sponge
sračunati *v* to calculate
sram *m* shame
sraman *adj* shameful
sramežljiv *adj* 1. shamefaced 2. shy
sramežljivost *f* shyness
sramiti se *v* 1. to be ashamed 2. to be shy
sramota *f* shame
sramotan *adj* shameful

sramotiti *v* 1. to shame 2. to discredit
srasti *v* to grow together
sraz *m* 1. collision 2. crash
sraziti se *v* 1. to collide 2. to crash
srazmera *f* proportion, relation
srazmeran *adj* proportional
Srbija *f* Serbia
srbijanski *adj* Serbian
Srbin *m* Serb
srčan *adj* courageous
srčanost *f* courage
srce *n* heart
srdačan *adj* 1. affectionate 2. friendly
srdačno *adv* warmly
srdačnost *f* 1. affection 2. friendliness
srdit *adj* angry
srditi *v* to anger
srditi se *v* to get angry
srditost, srdžba *f* anger
srebrn *adj* 1. silver 2. silver-plated
srebrnast *adj* silvery
srebrnjak *m* silver coin
srebro *n* silver
sreća *f* 1. good luck 2. joy 3. **na sreću** luckily
srećan *adj* 1. happy 2. lucky
srećka *f* lottery ticket
srećnim slučajem *adv* by chance
srećom *adv* fortunately
sred *prep* in the middle of
sreda *f* Wednesday
sredina *f* middle
sredina leta/ljeta *f* midsummer
sredina sedmice *f* midweek
središnji *adv* 1. middle 2. central
središnjica *f* 1. headquarters 2. head office
središte *n* centre; center
središte pažnje *n* limelight

srediti *v* to arrange
srednja klasa *f* middle class
srednje godine *fpl* midlife
srednje godine života *fpl* middle age
srednji *adj* 1. middle 2. medium
srednji rod *m* neuter
srednji vijel *m* Middle Ages
srednjih godina *f* middle-aged
srednjoškolac *m* secondary-school pupil
srednjovekovni *adj* medieval
sredovečan, sredovječan *adj* middle-aged
sredozeman *adj* Mediterranean
Sredozemno more *n* the Mediterranean
sredstva javnog informisanja *f* mass communications, mass media
sredstvo *n* 1. means 2. resources
sredstvo za smirenje *n* tranquillizer
sređen *adj* 1. settled 2. classified 3. serious
sresti *v* to encounter
sretan *adj* 1. lucky 2. happy
sretno! good luck!
srez *m* district
srg *m* pole
sricanje *n* spelling
sricati *v* to spell
srijeda *f* Wednesday
srkati *v* to sip
srma *f* sterling silver
srna *f* doe
srndać *m* buck
srnetina *f* venison
srodan *adj* related
srodnik *m* relative, in-law
srodnost, srodstvo *n* relationship
srok *m* rhyme

srozati se *v* to collapse
srp *m* sickle
srp i čekić hammer and sickle
srpanj *m* July
srpasta anemija *f* sickle cell anaemia
srpski *adj* Serbian
srpskohrvatski *adj* Serbo-Croatian
srušiti *v* 1. to demolish 2. to overturn 3. to subvert
srušiti se *v* to collapse
srž *f* 1. core 2. marrow
stabilan *adj* stable
stabilizator *m* stabilizer
stabilizovati *v* to stabilize
stabilnost *f* stability
stabljika *f* stem
stablo *n* 1. tree 2. tree trunk
stacionirati *v* to station
stadij, stadijum *m* 1. stage 2. phase
stadion *m* stadium
stado *n* 1. herd 2. flock
stagnacija *f* 1. stagnation 2. (ec.) recession
stagnirati *v* to stagnate
staja *f* 1. stable 2. cowshed
stajalište *n* 1. standpoint 2. stop 3. station
stajanje *n* standing
stajati *v* 1. to stand 2. to cost
staklast *adj* glassy
staklen *adj* glass
staklena bašta *f*, **staklenik** *m* greenhouse
staklenina *f* glassware
stakleno vlakno *n* fibre glass
staklo *n* 1. glass 2. windscreen; windshield
staklo prozora *n* window-pane
stalak *m* stand
stalan *adj* stable

stalež *m* 1. order 2. class
staležnost *f* stability
stalno *adv* permanently
staložen *adj* steady
staložiti se *v* to settle
stambeni *adj* 1. residential 2. housing
stambeni kraj *m* residential area
stambeno naselje *n* housing estate
stan *m* 1. flat; apartment 2. residence
stanar *m* 1. tenant 2. inhabitant
stanarina *f* rental
standard *m* standard
standardan *adj* standard
stanica *f* station
staniol *m* tinfoil
stanka *f* 1. pause 2. interval
stanodavac *m* landlord
stanovanje *n* 1. residence 2. dwelling
stanovati *v* 1. to reside 2. to dwell
stanovište *n* standpoint
stanovit *adj* particular
stanovnik *m* 1. resident 2. inhabitant
stanovnik doma *m* inmate
stanovništvo *n* 1. population 2. inhabitants
stanje *n* 1. state 2. condition 3. **ratno stanje** state of war 4. **biti u stanju** to be able
stanje *n* situation
stapanje *n* merge
stapati *v* to merge
star *adj* old
starac *m* old man
starački *adj* 1. old 2. senile
starački dom *m* nursing home
stara garda *f* old guard
staranje *n* care
staratelj *m* 1. guardian 2. trustee

starateljski komitet *m* trusteeship board
starateljstvo *n* guardianship
starati se *v* to take care of
stara vremena *npl* olden times
starci *mpl* the old
starešina *f* superior officer
starešinstvo *n* rank
starica *f* old woman
stariji *adj* older, elder
starina *f* ancient times
starinar *m* 1. antique dealer 2. junk dealer
starinarnica *f* 1. antique shop 2. junk shop
starinski *adj* 1. ancient 2. antique
stariti *v* to grow old
starješina *f* 1. chief 2. senior 3. superior
staro gvožđe *n* scrap-iron
staromadan *adj* 1. old-fashioned 2. out-of-date
starosedelac, starosjedilac *m* original inhabitant
staroslavenski *adj* Old Slavonic
starosna granica *f* age limit
starost *f* old age
starstven *adj* passionate
start *m* (spor.) start
starter *m* starter
startovati *v* to start
starudija *f* old things
stas *m* 1. height 2. physique
stasit *adj* tall
stati *v* 1. to stand 2. to stop 3. to hold
statičan *adj* static
statist, statista *f* film extra
statističar *m* statistician
statistički *adj* statistical
statistika *f* statistics
stativa *f* goalpost

statua *f* statue
status *m* status
statut *m* statute
stav *m* 1. attitude 2. paragraph
staviti, stavljati *v* to put
staviti veto (na) *v* to veto
stavka *f* 1. item 2. paragraph
staza *f* 1. path 2. track
staza za sletanje *f* landing strip
stečaj *m* 1. bankruptcy 2. **pasti pod stečaj** to go bankrupt
stečen *adj* 1. vested 2. **stečena prava** vested interests
steći *v* to get
steg *m* flag
stega *f* discipline
stegno *n* thigh
stegnut *adj* tightened
stegnuti *v* 1. to tighten 2. to restrain
stena *f* 1. rock 2. cliff
stenica *f* bug
stenjati *v* to moan
stenograf *m* stenographer
stenografija *f* shorthand
stenovit *adj* rocky
stepa *f* steppe
stepen *m* degree
stepenast *adj* gradual
stepenica *f* step
stepenice *fpl* 1. stairs 2. **uz stepenice** upstairs 3. **niz stepenice** downstairs
stepenište *n* staircase
sterati se *v* to stretch
stereotip *m* stereotype
sterilan *adj* 1. sterile 2. barren
sterilitet *m* sterility
sterilizacija *f* sterilization
sterilizovati *v* to sterilize
sterlinški *adj* sterling
steroid *m* steroid

stetoskop *m* stethoscope
stezanje *n* 1. contraction 2. cramp
stezati *v see* **stegnuti**
stići *v* 1. to arrive 2. to reach 3. to happen to
stid *m* shame
stideti se *v* to be ashamed
stidljiv *adj* shy, timid
stidnica *f* vulva
stih *m* (line of) verse
stijeg *m* 1. flag 2. banner
stijena *f* cliff
stil *m* style
stilistički *adj* stylistic
stilistika *f* stylistics
stimulacija *f* stimulation
stimulans *m* stimulant
stimulirati *v* to stimulate
stipendija *f* 1. scholarship 2. grant
stipendist(a) *m* 1. scholar 2. grant holder
stiplčez *m* steeplechase
stipulacija *f* stipulation
stipulirati *v* to stipulate
stisak *m* pressure
stisak ruke *m* handshake
stiskati, stinuti *v* 1. to squeeze 2. to press
stisnut *adj* compressed
stisnuti se *v* to shrink
stišati *v* to calm
stizati *v* to arrive
stjecati *v* to get
stjuard *m* steward
stjuardesa *f* stewardess
sto 1. hundred 2. *m* table
stočar *m* cattle-farmer
stočarstvo *n* cattle farming
stog *m* stack
stog sena *f* haystack
stoga *conj* therefore
stogodišnjica *f* centenary

stojećke *n* standing
stoka *f* 1. cattle 2. livestock
stokirati *v* to stock
stol *m* table
stolac *m*, **stolica** *f* chair
stolar *m* carpenter
stolarija *f* carpenter's workshop
stoleće *n* century
stolica *f* chair
stolna crkva *f* cathedral
stolnjak *m* tablecloth
stolno suđe *n* crockery
stoljeće *n* century
stomak *m* stomach
stoni *adj* table
stoni tenis, stolni tenis table tennis
stonoga *f* centipede
stopa *f* 1. foot 2. footprint
stopa smrtnosti *v* mortality rate
stopalo *n* foot
stopiti (se) *v* 1. to melt 2. to weld
stornirati *v* to cancel
stotina hundred
stovarište *n* warehouse
stovarište đubreta *f* rubbish dump; garbage dump
stovariti *v* to unload
stožac *m* 1. stack 2. cone
stradanje *n* suffering
stradati *v* to suffer
straga *f* behind
strah *m* fear
strahopočitanje, strahopoštovanje *n* awe, respect
strahota *f* 1. terror 2. atrocity
strahovanje *n* fear
strahovati *v* to be afraid
strahovit *adj* terrible
stramputica *f* wrong way
stran *adj* 1. strange 2. alien 3. foreign

strana *f* 1. side 2. page 3. **s jedne strane... s druge strane** on the one hand... on the other
stranac *m* 1. stranger 2. alien 3. foreigner
stranica *f* 1. page 2. side
stranka *f* party
strašan *adj* terrible
strašilo *n* scarecrow
strašiti *v* to scare
strašiti se *v* to be afraid
strašljiv *adj* afraid
strast *f* passion
strastan *adj* passionate
strateg *m* strategist
strategija *f* strategics
strategija *f* strategy
stratište *n* scaffold
strava *f* horror
stravniti *v* 1. to level 2. to compare
straža *f* guard
stražar *m* 1. guard 2. policeman
stražariti *v* to be on guard
stražarnica *f* watchtower
stražarska služba *f* guard duty
stražnji *adj* rear
stražnjica *f* 1. backside 2. buttocks
strčati *v* to run down
streha *f* roof
strela *f* arrow
strelica *f* arrow
streljački vod *m* firing squad
streljana *f* rifle range
streljanje *n* shooting
streljati *v* to shoot
stremljenje *n* aspiration
strepiti *v* to worry about
strepnja *f* worry
stres *m* stress
stresati, stresti *v* to shake
stresti se *v* to shiver
strgati, strgnuti *v* to tear off

strgnuti *v* to pull off
stric *m* uncle
stričak *m* thistle
strići *v* to crop
strijela *f* arrow
strijelac *m* 1. archer 2. marksman
strijeljati *v* to shoot
strina *f* aunt
strip *m* comic strip
stripovi *mpl* comic strip(s)
strka *f* rush
strm, strmenit *adj* steep
strmina *f* slope
strn *m* stubble
strofa *f* stanza
strog *adj* strict
strogo poverljiv/povjerljiv *adj* top-secret
strogost *f* strictness
stroj *m* 1. machine 2. engine
stroj za pranje (rublja) *m* washing-machine
strojar *m* engineer
strojarnica *f* engine-room
strojiti *v* to tan
strojna puška, strojnica *f* machine-gun
strojovođa *f* engine-driver
strop *m* ceiling
strpeti se, strpjeti se *v* to be patient
strpljenje *n*, **strpljivost** *f* patience
strpljiv *adj* patient
stršiti *v* to protrude
stršljen *adj* hornet
stručak *m* stalk
stručan *adj* expert
stručnjak *m* expert
stručno *adv* expertly
struganje *n* scraping
strugara *f* sawmill
strugati *v* 1. to saw 2. to plane

strugotina *f*, **strugotine** *fpl* sawdust

struja *f* 1. current 2. electricity

strujanje *n* flow

strujati *v* to flow

strujni vod *m* power line

strujomer *m* electric meter

struk *m* 1. waist 2. stalk

struka *f* 1. occupation 2. branch 3. (com.) line

struktura *f* structure

strukturalan *adj* structural

strukturalizam *m* structuralism

struna *f* string

strunjača *f* 1. mat 2. mattress

strunuti *v* to rot,

strvina *f* carcass

strvinar *m* vulture

strvožder *m* scavenger

stub *m* 1. post 2. pillar

stub vrata *f* goalpost

stubac *m* column

stube *fpl* stairs

stubište *n* staircase

stucati, stući *v* 1. to pound 2. to bruise

studen *adj* cold

studeni *adj* November

student *m* student

studija *f* study

studije *fpl* studies

studio *m* studio

studiozan *adj* thorough

studiranje *n* study

studirati *v* to study

stup *m* 1. pillar 2. post

stupac *m* column

stupanj *m* degree

stupati *v see* stupiti

stupica *f* trap

stupiti *v* 1. to pace 2. to march

stupiti u štrajk *v* to go on strike

stvar *f* 1. thing 2. stuff 3. matter

stvaralac *m* creator

stvaralački *adj* creative

stvaralaštvo *n* creativity

stvaran *adj* real

stvaranje *n* creation

stvarati *v* 1. to make 2. to create

stvarno *adv* in fact

stvarnost *f* reality

stvor *m*, **stvornje** *n* creature

stvoritelj *m* creator

stvoriti *v see* stvarati

stvrdnuti *v* to harden

subjekat *m* subject

subjektivan *adj* subjective

subjektivnost *f* subjectivity

sublimacija *f* sublimation

sublimirati *v* to sublimate

subota *f* Saturday

subvencija *f* 1. grant 2. subsidy

subvencionirati *v* 1. to give a grant to 2. to subsidize

subverzija *f* subversion

subverzivan *adj* subversive

sučelice *prep* opposite to

sucnica *f* (leg.) court

sućut *f* sympathy

sud *m* 1. container 2. judgement 3. (leg.) court 4. **krvni sud** blood vessel

sudac *m* 1. judge 2. referee

sudar *m* 1. crash 2. conflict

sudariti se *v* to crash

sudben *adj* legal

sudbina *f* fate

sudbonosan *adj* ominous

sudelovati *v* to participate

sudija *f* judge

sudionik *m* 1. partner 2. participant

suditi *v* 1. to judge 2. (leg.) to try

sudjelovanje *n* participation

sudjelovati *v* to participate

sudnica *f* court house, court room
sudoper *m* sink
sudopera *f* 1. sink 2. dishwasher
sudska rasprava *f* (leg.) trial
sudski *adj* (leg.) court
sudski nalog *m* warrant
sudski nalog *m* writ
sudski poziv *adj* summons
suđe *n* dishes
suđenje *n* (leg.) 1. trial 2. **ponovo suđenje** retrial
suđenje ratnim zločincima *f* war crimes trial
suficit *m* surplus
sufiks *m* suffix
sugerirati *v* to suggest
sugestija *f* suggestion
sugestivan *adj* suggestive
suglasiti se *v* to consent
suglasnik *m* consonant
suglasnost *f* consent
sugrađanin *m* fellow citizen
suh *adj* 1. dry 2. smoked 3. pure 4. thin
suhomesnat *adj* delicatessen
suhoparan *adj* monotonous
sujeta *f* vanity
sujetan *adj* vain
sujeveran, sujevjeran *adj* superstitious
sujeverje, sujevjerje *n* superstition
suknja *f* skirt
sukno *adv* cloth
sukob *m* 1. collision 2. conflict
sukob generacija *f* generation gap
sukobiti se *v* 1. to collide 2. to clash
sukrivac *m* accomplice
sulica *f* spear
sulnja *f* skirt
sulud *adj* foolish
suma *f* sum

sumaran *adj* brief
suma stavke *f* subtotal
sumirati *v* to sum up
sumnja *f* 1. doubt 2. suspicion
sumnjati *v* 1. to doubt 2. to suspect
sumnjičav *adj* 1. doubtful 2. suspicious
sumnjiv *adj* 1. dubious 2. suspect
sumoran *adj* gloomy
sumornost *f* gloom
sumpor *m* sulphur
sumrak *m* dusk
sunarodnjak *m* fellow countryman
sunčan *adj* 1. sun 2. sunny 3. solar
sunčani udar *m*, **sunčanica** *f* sunstroke
sunčanje *n* sunbathing
sunčati se *v* to sunbathe
sunce *n* sun
Sunce *n* the sun
sunčev *adj* solar
sunčeva energija *f* solar energy
suncobran *adj* sunshade
suncokret *m* sunflower
sunđer *m* sponge
suočenje *n* confrontation
suočiti *v* to confront
suodgovoran *adj* jointly responsible
suoptuženik *m* codefendant
suosjećajan *adj* sympathetic
suosnivač *m* co-founder
supa *f* soup
suparištvo *n* 1. rivalry 2. hostility
suparnik *m* 1. competitor 2. rival 3. opponent 4. enemy
suparnik *m* rival
suparništvo *n* rivalry
superioran *adj* superior
superiornost *f* superiority
superlativ *adj* superlative
supermarket *m* supermarket
supersila *f* superpower

supersoničan *adj* supersonic
superstar, superzvezda, superzvijezda *m/f* superstar
supkutan *adj* hypodermic
supkutana injekcija *f* hypodermic injection
suportstaviti se *v* to oppose
supotpisati *v* to countersign
supozitorijum *m* suppository
suprotan *adj* opposite
suprotno *adv* opposite
suprotnost *f* opposite
suprotstaviti *v* to oppose
suprug *m* husband
supruga *f* wife
supsidaran *adj* subsidiary
suptilan *adj* subtle
suptilnost *f* subtlety
suputnik *m* fellow traveller
suradnik *m* collaborator
suradnja *f* collaboration
surađivati *v* to collaborate
surevnjiv *adj* envious
surevnjivost *f* envy
surla *f* trunk
surogat *m* 1. surrogate 2. substitute
surov *adj* brutal
surovost *f* brutality
surutka *f* whey
sused *m* neighbour
susedstvo *n* neighbourhood
susjed *m* neighbour
susjedan *adj* 1. next-door 2. neighbouring
susjedstvo *n* neighbourhood
suspendovati *v* to suspend
suspenzija *f* suspension
susresti *v* to encounter
susret *m* encounter
susretljiv *adj* helpful
suša *f* 1. shed 2. drought
sušan *adj* dry

sušanj *m* captive
sušanjstvo *n* captivity
sušen *adj* 1. dried 2. smoked
sušenje *n* drying
sušeno meso *n* smoked meat
sušica *f* tuberculosis
sušiti *v* 1. to dry 2. to smoke
suština *f* substance
suštinski *adj* essential
sustati *v* 1. to become tired 2. to wane
sustav *m* system
sustavan *adj* systematic
sustići *v* 1. to reach 2. to catch up with
suteren *m* basement
suton *m* dusk
sutra *adv* tomorrow
sutradan *adv* the following day
sutrašnji *adj* tomorrow's
sutrašnjica *f* tomorrow
suv *adj* 1. dry 2. dried 3. thin
suvenir *m*, **suvenira** *f* souvenir
suveren *m* sovereign
suverenitet *m* sovereignty
suvislo *adv* coherently
suvislost *f* coherence
suvišak *m* excess
suvišan *adj* superfluous
suviše *adv* excessively
suvišnost *f* excess
suvlasnik *m* joint owner
suvonjav *adj* lean
suvoparan *adj* dry
suvozeman *adj* land
suvremen *adj* modern
suvremenik *m* contemporary
suza *f* tear
suzavac *m* tear gas
suzbijati *v* *see* **suzbiti**
suzbiljanje *n* suppression
suzbiti *v* 1. to suppress 2. to resist

suziti *v* 1. to weep 2. to limit
sužanj *m* prisoner
svadba *f* wedding
svadbeno putovanje *n* honeymoon
svaditi se *v* to quarrel
svadljiv *adj* quarrelsome
svađa *f* quarrel
svađati se *v see* svaditi se
svagda *adv* always
svagdašnji *adj* everyday
svagde, svagdje everywhere
svakakav *adj* various
svakako *adv* certainly
svaki *adj* 1. each 2. every
svakidašnji *adj* everyday
svako everybody, everyone
svakodnevni *adj* daily
svakojaki *adj* various
svakuda everywhere
svaliti, svaljivati *v* to overturn
svanuti *v* to dawn
svanuće *n* dawn
svariti *v* 1. to stew 2. to brew 3. to digest 4. to endure
svarljiv *adj* digestible
svašta everything
svastika *f* sister-in-law
svat *m* wedding guest
svatko everyone
sve all
svečan *adj* festive
svečanost *f* festivity
sveća *f* candle
svećenik *m* priest
svećenstvo *n* clergy
svećica *f* spark plug
svedočanstvo *n* 1. certificate 2. testimony
svedočenje *n* testimony
svedočiti *v* to testify (**protiv** against; **u nečiju korist** on behalf of)

svedok *m* witness
svejedno *adv* nevertheless
svekar *m* father-in-law
svekrva *f* mother-in-law
svemir *m* 1. space 2. universe
svemoćan, svemoguć *adj* almighty
sveobuhvatan *adj* all-inclusive
sveopći, sveopšti *v* universal
sversdan *adj* cordial
sveska *f* 1. notebook 2. volume
svesno *adv* consciously
svesrdan *adj* hearty
sveštenik *m* priest
sveštenstvo *n* clergy
svest *f* consciousness
svestan *adj* conscious
svesti *v* 1. to bring down 2. to bring together 3. to reduce
svestran *adj* 1. versatile 2. universal
svestranost *f* 1. versatility 2. universality
svet 1. *adj* holy 2. *m* world
svetac *m* saint
svetac zaštitnik *m* patron saint
svetao *adj* bright
svetilište *n* holy place
svetiljka *f* lamp
svetina *f* mob
svetinja *f* 1. holy object 2. sacredness
svetionik *m* lighthouse
svetište *n* shrine
svetiti se *v* to take revenge
svetkovina *f* 1. holiday 2. feast day
svetlo *n* light
svetlosna godina, svjetlosna godina *f* light year
svetlucav *adj* glittering
sveto pismo *n* the Bible
svetost *f* holiness

Svetska banka *f* World Bank
Svetska zdravstvena organizacija *f* World Health Organization (WHO)
svetska sila *f* world power
svetski *adj* world
svetski putnik *m* globetrotter
sveučilište *n* university
sveukupan *adj* whole
sveza *f* connection
svezak *m* volume
svezati *v* to bind
sveznalica *f* erudite
svež *adj* 1. recent 2. fresh 3. cool
svežanj *m* pack
svežina *f* 1. freshness 2. coolness
svi 1. all 2. everybody
svibanj *m* May
svideti se, svidjeti se *v* 1. to please 2. To mi se sviđa. I like it.
svijati *v* to bend
svijeća *f* candle
svijećnjak *m* candlestick
svijest *f* consciousness
svijestan *adj* conscious
svijet *m* world
svijetao *adj* bright
svijetliti *v* to shine
svijetlo *n* light
svila *f* silk
svilen *adj* silk, silken
svinja *f* pig
svinjac *m* pigsty
svinjarija *f* filth
svinjetina *f* pork
svinuti *v* to bend
svirač *m* player
svirala *f* 1. whistle 2. flute
svirati *v* (mus.) to play
svirep *adj* cruel
svirepost *f* cruelty
Svisveti *mpl* All Saints' Day

svita *f* suite
svitac *m* firefly
svitak *m* roll
svitanje *n* daybreak
svitati *v* to dawn
sviđati se *v see* svideti se
svjedočanstvo *n* testimony
svjedočiti *v* to testify (**protiv** against; **u nečiju korist** on behalf of)
svjedodžba *f* 1. certificate 2. (ed.) report
svjedok *m* witness
svjetiljka *f* 1. lamp 2. torch; flashlight
svjetina *f* mob
svjetionik *m* lighthouse
svjetlost *f* light
svjetlucati *v* to glitter
svjetovan *adj* secular
svjetovnjak *m* layman
Svjetska banka *f* World Bank
Svjetska zdravstvena organizacija *f* World Health Organization (WHO)
svjetska sila *f* world power
svjetski *adj* 1. world 2. universal
svjetski putnik *m* globetrotter
svjež *adj* 1. recent 2. fresh 3. cool
svježina *f* 1. freshness 2. coolness
svlačenje *n* undressing
svlačionica *f* dressing-room
svlačiti (se) *v* to undress
svladati *v* 1. to conquer 2. to beat
svod *m* arch
svoj own
svoja *f* sole (fish)
svojatati *v* 1. to lay claim to 2. to usurp
svojatati se *v* to be on familiar terms with
svojeglav *adj* stubborn

svojeglavost *f* stubbornness
svojevoljan *adj* 1. voluntary 2. arbitrary
svojina *f* 1. property 2. ownership 3. **privatna svojina** private ownership
svojski *adv* thoroughly
svojstven *adj* characteristic
svojstvo *n* 1. characteristic 2. property
svota *f* sum
svrab *m* 1. scab 2. itch
svraćati *v* to divert
svrabežljiv *adj* itchy
svraka *f* magpie
svratište *n* hotel

svratiti se *v* to visit
svrbeti, svrbjeti *v* to itch
svrdlo *n* 1. bore 2. drill
svrgnuti *v* to depose
svrha *f* purpose
svrsishodan *adj* useful
svršavati *v* to complete
svršen *adj* completed
svršetak *m* completion
svršiti *v* to complete
svrstati *v* to sort
svtati *v* to dawn
svući *v* to undress
svud, svuda, svugde, svugdje, svukuda 1. everywhere 2. generally

Š

šablon *m*, **šablona** *f* 1. pattern 2. model 3. stereotype
šafran *m* saffron
šah *m* chess
šahist(a) *m* chess player
šaht *m* manhole
šaka *f* fist
šakal *m* jackal
šal *m* 1. shawl 2. scarf
šala *f* 1. joke 2. fun
šalica *f* cup
šaliti se *v* to joke
šaljiv *adj* funny
šamar *m* slap
šamariti *v* to slap
šampanjac *m* champagne
šampion *m* champion
šampionat *m* (spor.) 1. championship 2. title
šampon *m* shampoo
šanac *m* trench
šank *m* bar
šansa *f* chance
šapa *f* paw
šapat *m* whisper
šapnuti, šaptati *v* to whisper
šaptalac *m* prompter
šara *f* 1. pattern 2. hue
šaraf *m* screw
šarafiti *v* to screw
šaran *m* carp
šarati *v* 1. to colour 2. to decorate
šaren *adj* multi-coloured
šargarepa *f* carrot
šariah *m* scarlet fever
šarka *f* 1. hinge 2. viper
šarm *m* charm

šarmantan *adj* charming
šasija *f* chassis
šaš *m* reed
šašav *adj* crazy
šator *m* tent
šatrovački *adj* slang
šav *adj* 1. seam 2. (med.) stitch
šćepati *v* to seize
šćućuriti se *v* to crouch
šećer *m* sugar
šećerana *f* sugar refinery
šećerna bolest *f* diabetes
šećerna repa *f* sugar-beet
šećerna trska *f* sugar-cane
šef *m* 1. chief 2. director 3. manager
šef biroa *m* office manager
šegrt *m* apprentice
šenut *adj* insane
šenuti *v* to become insane
šepati *v* to limp
šepav *adj* lame
šepiriti se *v* to swagger
šeprtlja *f* bungler
šerpa *f* pan
šesnaest sixteen
šešir *m* hat
šest six
šestar *m*, **šestilo** *n* compasses
šesti *adj* sixth
šetač, šetalac *m* walker
šetalište *n* walk
šetanje *n* walking
šetati se *v* to walk
šetnja *f* walk
ševa *f* lark
ševar *m* reeds

ševuljica *f* zigzag
šezdeset sixty
šiba *f* rod
šibati *v* to flog
šibica *f* match
šifra *f* code
šija *f* nape
šikara *f* thicket
šiknuti *v* to gush out
šiljak *m* 1. point 2. peak
šiljast *adj* pointed
šiljiti *v* to sharpen to a point
šina *f* rail
šindra *f* shingle
šinja *f* rail
šipka *f* rod
širenje *n* expansion
širina *f* breadth
širiti, širiti se *v* to expand
širok *m* broad
širokogrudan *adj* broad-minded
širokotrupni džet *m* wide-bodied jet
širom 1. *adv* wide (open) 2. *prep* throughout
šišanje *n* 1. haircut 2. shearing
šišarka *f* cone
šišati *v* 1. to cut hair 2. to shear
šišmiš *m* bat
šištati *v* to wheeze
šiti, šivati *v* to sew
šivanje *n* sewing
šivaća igla *f* needle
šivaći *v* sewing
šivaći stroj *m* sewing-machine
škakljati *v* to tickle
škakljiv *adj* ticklish
škare *fpl* scissors
škembići *v* tripe
škiljav *adj* cross-eyed
škiljavost *f* squint
škljocati *v* to click

škoda *f* damage
škoditi *v* 1. to damage 2. to harm
škodljiv *adj* harmful
škola *f* school
školarina *f* 1. scholarship 2. tuition fees
školjka *f* shell
školovan *adj* educated
školovanje *n* schooling
školovati *v* to educate
školska vlast *f* school board
školski centar *m* training centre
školski logor *m* training camp
škopiti *v* to castrate
škorpija *f* scorpion
Škot *m* Scot
Škotska *f* Scotland
škotski *adj* Scottish
škrebetaljka *f* rattle
škrga *f* gill
škriljevac *m* slate
škrinja *f* box
škripac *m* trouble
škripati *v* to creak
škrlet *m* scarlet fever
škrob *m* starch
škrobiti *v* to starch
škropilo *n* sprinkler
škropiti *v* to spray
škrt *adj* miserly
škrtac *m* miser
škrtost *f* miserliness
škulja *f* hole
škuna *f* schooner
škver *m* shipyard
šlag *m* whipped cream
šlem *m* helmet
šlep *m* barge
šlepovati *v* to tow
šljaka *f* slag
šljam *m* rubbish
šljem *m* helmet

šljiva *f* plum
šljivovica *f* plum brandy
šljunak *m* gravel
šminka *f* make-up
šminkati *v* to make up
šmirgla *f*, **šmirglpapir** *m* sandpaper
šmrkati *v* to sniff
šminka za oči *f* eyeshadow
šnala *f* hairpin
šnicla *f* steak
šnorkl *m* snorkel
šofer *m* 1. driver 2. chauffeur
šogor *m* brother-in-law
šogorica *f* sister-in-law
šojka *f* jay
šok *m* 1. shock 2. **biti u šoku** to be in shock
šokantan *adj* shocking
šokirati *v* to shock
šolja *f* cup
šopati *v* to stuff
šorc *m* shorts
šou *m* show
šou-biznis *m* show busines
šovinizam *m* chauvinism
špaga *f* string
špageti *v* spaghetti
špalir *m* row
Španija , Španjolska *f* Spain
Španjolac *m* Spaniard
španjolski *adj* Spanish
šparga *f* asparagus
špedicija *f* shipping
špediterski *adj* shipping
špekulacija *f* 1. speculation 2. (com.) venture
špekulant *m* speculator
špekulantski *adj* speculative
špekulisati *v* to speculate
šperploča *f* plywood
špic *m* tip
špijun *m* spy

špijunaža *f* espionage
špijunski satelit *m* spy satellite
špilja *f* cave
špinat *m* spinach
šporet na mikrotalase *m* microwave oven
špric *m* syringe
špricati *v* to inject
špric za supkutane injekcije *m* hypodermic syringe
šraf *m* screw
šrafciger *m* screwdriver
šrapnel *m* shrapnel
šta *f see* što
štab *m* 1. headquarters 2. staff
štabni oficir *m* staff officer
štafeta *f* (spor.) relay race
štagalj *m* 1. barn 2. shed
štaka *f* crutch
štakor *m* rat
štala *f* 1. stable 2. cowshed
štampa *f* 1. the press 2. printing press
štampač *m* 1. printer 2. **matrični štampač** dot-matrix printer
štampani primerak *m* hard copy
štampanje *n* printing
štampar *m* printer
štamparija *f* printing house
štamparstvo *n* printing
štampati *v* to print
štand *m* stand
štap *m* stick
štapić *m* baton
štavionica *f* tannery
štaviti *v* to tan
štavljač *m* tanner
štavljenje *n* tanning
štedeti *v* to save
štedionica *f* savings bank
štediša *f* saver
štedjeti *v* to save

štedljiv *adj* economical
štedljivost *f* economizing
štedni *adj* savings
štednja *f* saving
štednjak *m* kitchen range
štek-kontakt, štekontakt *m* socket
štektati *v* to yelp
štene *n* puppy
šteta *f* 1. harm 2. Kakva šteta! What a pity!
štetan *adj* harmful
štetiti *v* to harm
štetočina *f* pest
štetočine *n* vermin
štetovati *v* to suffer harm
štihproba *f* spot check
štimung *m* atmosphere
štipaljka *f* clothes peg
štipati *v* to pinch
štirak *m*, **štirka** *f* starch
štit *m* shield
štititi *v* to protect
štivo *n* text
štićenik *m* protégé
što what
štof *m* material
štogod 1. something 2. anything
štoperica *f* stopwatch
štopovati *v* to time
štos *m* stunt
štošta *f* all kinds of things
štovalac *m* admirer
štovan *adj* respected
štovanje *n* respect
štovatelj *m* admirer
štovati *v* to respect
štrajk *m* strike
štrajkač, štrajkaš *m* striker
štrajkati, štrajkovati *v* to go on strike
štrajkbreher *m* scab, blackleg

štrcaljka *f* 1. sprinkler 2. syringe
štropot *m* noise
štučanje *n* hiccup
štucati *v* to hiccup
štucavica *f* hiccup
štuka *f* pike
štula *f* stilt
šubara *f* fur hat
šuga *f* scab
šuljati se *v* to sneak
šum *m* noise
šuma *f* 1. wood 2. forest
šumar *m* forester
šumarak *m* copse
šumarstvo *n* forestry
šumeti *v* to make a noise
šumovit kraj *m* woodland
šumovit *adj* wooded
šumski *adj* 1. wood 2. forest
šunjati se *v* to sneak
šunka *f* ham
šupa *f* shed
šupalj *m* hollow
šupljikav *adj* porous
šupljikavost *f* porosity
šupljina *f* 1. hollow 2. pit
šupljina *f* hole
šurjak *m* brother-in-law
šurjakinja *f* sister-in-law
šurovati *v* to plot
šuškati, šuštati *v* to rustle
šut *m* (spor.) shot
šutirati *v* to shoot
šutjeti *v* to be quiet
šutljiv *adj* quiet
šutnja *f* quietness
švaler *m*, **švalerka** *f* lover
švedski *adj* Swedish
Švedska *f* Sweden
Šveđanin *m* Swede
švelja *f* dressmaker
švelo *n* needlework

šverc *m* 1. smuggling 2. black-marketeering
švercer *m* 1. smuggler 2. black-marketeer
švercovati *v* to smuggle

Švicarac *m* Swiss
Švicarska *f* Switzerland
švicarski *adj* Swiss
švrljati *v* to hang around
strcati *v* 1. to sprinkle 2. to squirt

T

T macija *f* T-shirt
ta well...
tabak *m* sheet
taban *adj* sole
tabela *f* 1. list 2. table
tabla *f* 1. board 2. table
tablatura *f* tablature
tableta *f* tablet
tablica *f* table
tabor *m* camp
tabu *adj/m* taboo
tačan *adj* exact
tačka *f* 1. full stop 2. point 3.
  (spor.) event 4. **tačka i zarez**
  semi-colon 5. **dvije tačke** colon
tacna *f* saucer
tačnost *f* precision
taći *v* to touch
tad, tada *adv* then
taj this
tajac *m* silence
tajan *adj* secret
tajanstven *adj* mysterious
tajfun *m* typhoon
tajiti *v* to conceal
tajna *f* 1. secret 2. mystery 3. **vojna**
  tajna military secret
tajna služba *f* secret service
tajni agent *m* secret agent
tajni *adj* secret
tajnica, tajnik *m* secretary
tajnički *adj* secretarial
tajništvo *n* secretariate
tajno *adv* in secret
tajno pismo *n* code
tajnost *f* secrecy
takav *adj* such

takmac *m* 1. rival 2. competitor
takmičar *m* competitor
takmičenje *n* competition
takmičiti se *v* to compete
taknuti *v* to touch
tako *adv* 1. so 2. in this way
tako da so that
takođe, također as well
tako reći so to speak
takozvani *adj* so-called
taksa *f* tax
taksi *m* taxi
taksist(a) *m* taxi driver
takt *m* 1. tact 2. (mus) time
taktičan *adj* 1. tactful 2. tactical
taktičar *m* tactician
taktički *adj* tactical
taktički poraz *m* tactical reverse
taktika *f* tactics
talac *m* 1. hostage 2. **zadržati kao**
  taoca to take as hostage
talas *m* wave
talasati se *v* to undulate
talasna dužina *f* wavelength
talenat, talent *m* talent
talentiran, talentovan *adj*
  talented
talionica *f* foundry
taliti *v* 1. to melt 2. to smelt
Talijan *m* Italian
talog *m* sediment
taložiti se *v* to settle
Taljan *m* Italian
taljanski *adj* Italian
tama *f* darkness
taman 1. *adj* dark 2. *adv* just 3. just
  right

tamaniti *v* to destroy
tambler *m* tumbler
tamjan *adj* incense
tamna komora *f* dark room
tamneti, tamnjeti *v* 1. to darken 2. to tarnish
tamnica *f* jail
tamničar *m* jailer
tamnovati *v* to be in jail
tamo 1. there 2. **amo tamo** to and fro
tamo preko over there
tamošnji *adj* local
tampon *m* tampon
tanak *m* thin
tane *n* bullet
tanjir *m* plate
tanjiti *v* to thin
tanjur *m* plate
tanjurić *m* saucer
tank *m* tank
tanker *m* tanker
tankoćutan *adj* sensitive
tantijema *f* royalty
tapecirati *v* to wallpaper
tapet *m*, **tapeta** *f* wallpaper
tapija *f* deed
tapiserija *f* tapestry
tapšati *v* to clap
tara *f* tare
tarac *m* pavement
taracati *v* to pave
tarifa *f* tariff
tast *m* father-in-law
tastatura *f* keyboard
taster *m* button
tašna *f* bag
tašt *adj* vain
tašta *f* mother-in-law
taština *f* vanity
tat *m* thief
tata, tatica *m* daddy

tava *f* pan
tavan *m* attic
tavanica *f* ceiling
te *conj* 1. and 2. moreover
teča *f* uncle
tečaj *m* 1. course 2. rate of exchange
tečan *adj* tasty
tečno *adv* fluently
tečnost *f* 1. flavour 2. liquid 3. fluency
teći *v* to flow
teg *m* 1. (spor.) weight 2. **dizati tegove** to lift weights
tegla *f* jar
tegliti *v* 1. to tow 2. to drag
tegljač *m* tugboat
tegoba *f* hardship
tegoban *adj* difficult
tehničar *m* technician
tehnička obuka *f* technical training
tehnički *adj* 1. technical 2. technological
tehnički savetnik/savjetnik *m* technical advisor
tehničko uputstvo *n* technical manual
tehnika *f* 1. technique 2. technology 3. engineering
tehnokracija, tehnocratija *f* technocracy
tehnokrat *m* technocrat
tehnologija *f* technology
tehnološki *adj* technological
tek 1. *m* appetite 2. flavour 3. **bez teka** tasteless 4. *adv* only 5. just 6. not until
teklić *m* courier
teknika *f* engineering
tekovina *f* achievement
tekst *m* text

tekst pesme/pjesme *m* lyrics
tekstil *m* textiles
tekuća voda *f* running water
tekući *v* 1. flowing 2. current 3. fluent
tekući račun *m* current account
tekućina *f* liquid
telad *f* calves
tele *n* 1. calf 2. veal
telefon *m* telephone
telefonirati *v* to telephone
telefonist(a) *m*, **telefonistkinja** *f* telephone operator
telefonska centrala *f* switchboard
telefonska govornica *f* telephone booth; call-box
telefonski imenik *m* telephone book
telefonski poziv *adj* telephone call
telefonski *adj* telephone
telegraf *m* telegraph
telegrafski stub *m* telegraph pole
telegram *m* telegram
telekomunikacija *f*, **telekomunikacije** *fpl* telecommunications
teleks *m* telex
teleobjektiv *adj* telephoto lens
telepatija *f* telepathy
telepatski *adj* telepathic
teleskop *m* telescope
telesni *adj* physical
teletina *f* veal
televizija *f* television (TV)
televizor *m* television set
teleće meso *n* veal
teliti se *v* to calve
telo *n* body
telohranitelj *m* bodyguard
tema, tematika *f* theme
tematski *adj* thematic

temelj *m* 1. base 2. foundation 3. **na temelju** on the basis of
temeljan *adj* fundamental
temeljit *adj* thorough
temeljiti *v* to base upon
temeljito *adv* thoroughly
tempera *f* tempera
temperament *m* temperament
temperamentan *adj* vivacious
temperatura *f* 1. temperature 2. **mjeriti temperaturu** to take someone's temperature
tempirana bomba *f* time bomb
tempirni upaljač *m* time fuse
tempo *m* rate
tendencija *f* tendency
tenis *m* tennis
teniser *m* tennis player
tenk *m* tank
teologija *f* theology
teoretičar *m* theoretician
teoretisati *v* to theorize
teoretski *adj* theoretical
teorija *f* theory
tepati *v* 1. to babble 2. to stammer
tepih *m* carpet
terapeut *m* therapist
terapija *f* therapy
terasa *f* terrace
terati *v* to force
terazije *fpl* scales
teren *m* terrain
terenska služba *f* field work
teret *m* 1. weight 2. load 3. cargo
teretiti *v* 1. to weigh down 2. to charge
teretni brod *m* cargo boat
teretni vagon *m* freight car
teretni vlak *m* goods train
teretnjak *m* lorry; truck
teritorij *m*, **teritorija** *f* territory
teritorijalan *adj* territorial

teritorijalne pretenzijevode *fpl* territorial claims

teritorijalne vode *fpl* territorial waters

termalan *adj* thermal

termin *m* term

terminal *m* computer terminal

terminologija *f* terminology

terminološki *adj* terminological

termit *m* termite

termofor *m* hotwater bottle

termometar *m* thermomometer

termos *m* thermos

termostat *m* thermostat

teror *m* 1. terror 2. **vršiti teror nad** to terrorize

terorisati *v* to terrorize

terorist(a) *m* terrorist

teroristički *adj* terrorist

terorizam *m* terrorism

tesan *adj* tight

tesar *m* carpenter

tesati *v* to cut

teskoba *f* 1. narrowness 2. anxiety

teskoban *adj* cramped

tesnac *m* ravine

test *m* test

test za utvrđivanje trudnoće *m* pregnancy test

testamenat, testament *m* (leg.) will

testenina *f* pasta

testera *f* saw

testiranje *n* testing

testirati *v* to test

testis *m* testicle

testo *n* dough

teška industrija *f* heavy industry

teško *adv* 1. severely 2. hardly

teškoća *f* hardship

teta *f* aunt

tetak *m* uncle

tetanus *m* tetanus

tetiva *f* tendon

tetka *f* aunt

tetošiti *v* to pamper

tetovirati *v* to tattoo

tetreb, tetrijeb *m* grouse

teturati *v* to totter

teza *f* thesis

teža *f* gravity

težak *m* heavy

težina *f* 1. weight 2. **dobiti u težini** to put on weight 3. **izgubiti u težini** to lose weight

težina *f* weight

težiti *v* to weigh

ti 1. you *singular* 2. those

ticati se *v* 1. to concern 2. to adjoin 3. **što se tiče** with regard to

ticati *v* to touch

tifus *m* typhoid

tifusna groznica *f* typhoid

tiganj *m* frying pan

tigar *m* tiger

tigrica *f* tigress

tih *adj* quiet

tiho *adv* quietly

tijek *m* flow

tijelo *n* body

tijesak *m* press

tijesan *adj* narrow

tijesto *n* dough

tik *adv* close by

tikva *f* pumpkin

tikvan *m* idiot

tikvica *f* marrow

tili: u tili čas in a moment

tim 1. *m* team 2. *see* **time**

time in this way

tim više the more so

tinarnica *f* ink-pot

tinejdžer *m* teenager

tinjati *v* to smoulder

tinta *f* ink
tip *m* type, kind, sort
tipičan *adj* typical
tipično *adv* typically
tipizacija *f* standardization
tipizirati *v* to standardize
tipka *f* key
tipkač *m*, **tipkačica** *f* typist
tipkati *v* to type
tipograf *m* typesetter
tipski *adj* standard
tirada *f* tirade
tiranija *f* tyranny
tiranin *m* tyrant
tiranisati *v* to tyrannize
tiranski *adj* tyrannical
tiraž *m* printing
tirkis *m* turquoise
tisa *f* yew
tisak *m* 1. print 2. **kosi tisak** italics 3. **masni tisak** bold
tiska *f* crowd
tiskanica *f* form
tiskar *m* printer
tiskara *f* printing-house
tiskati *v* 1. to press 2. to print
tišina *f* quiet
tištati *v* 1. to press 2. to oppress
tisuća thousand
titl *m* subtitle
titlovati *v* to subtitle
titraj *m* vibration
titrati *v* to vibrate
titula *f* title
tjedan *m* 1. week 2. **dva tjedna** fortnight 3. **konac tjedna** weekend
tjednik *m* weekly
tjedno *adv* per week
tjelesan *adj* physical
tjelesna kazna *f* corporal punishment

tjelesna straža *f* bodyguard
tjelovježba *f* gymnastics
tjeme *n* top of head
tjeralica *f* arrest warrant
tjerati *v* to chase
tjeskoba *f* anxiety
tjeskoban *adj* anxious
tjesnac *m* gorge
tješiti *v* to console
tjestenina *f* pasta
tkač, tkalac *m* weaver
tkalački stan *m* loom
tkanina *f* fabric
tkati *v* to weave
tkivo *n* 1. fabric 2. tissue
tko who
tkogod whoever
tlačenje *n* oppression
tlačitelj *m* oppressor
tlačiti *v* to oppress
tlak *m* pressure
tlapnja *f* illusion
tle, tlo *n* 1. ground 2. land 3. earth
tmina *f* darkness
tmuran *adj* 1. gloomy 2. overcast
to 1. this, that 2. it 3. **k tome** moreover
to jest that is... , i.e.
toalet *m* toilet
toaleta *f* 1. toilet 2. clothes
toaletni papir *m* toilet-paper
toaletni stolić *m* dressing-table
tobdžija *m* gunner
tobogan *m* toboggan
tobolac *m* quiver
tobož, tobože *adv* ostensibly
tobožnji *adj* 1. ostensible 2. would-be
točak *m* 1. wheel 2. **panorama točak** ferris wheel
točan *adj* exact
točiti *v* to pour out

točka *f* 1. point 2. clause 3. full stop 4. (spor.) event 5. **dvije točke** colon

točka zarez *m* semicolon

točno *adv* exactly

točnost *f* exactness

tok *m* 1. flow 2. **u toku** in the course of

tokariti *v* to turn wood

tokom *prep* during

toksičan *adj* toxic

tolerancija *f* tolerance

tolerantan *adj* tolerant

tolerisati *v* to tolerate

tolik, toliki *adj* such

toliko *adv* so much, so many

toljaga *f* cosh

tom *m* volume

ton *m* tone

tona *f* ton, tonne

tonaža *f* tonnage

tonuti *v* to sink

tonzilitis *m* tonsilitis

top *m* gun

topao *adj* warm

topionica *f* foundry

topiti se *v* 1. to melt 2. to smelt 3. to thaw

toplana *f* heating plant

toples *adj/m* topless

toplice *fpl* spa

toplina, toplota *f* warmth

toplomer, toplomjer *m* thermometer

toplota *f* warmth

toplotni talas *m* heatwave

topništvo *n* artillery

topografija *f* topography

topola *f* poplar

topovnjača *f* gunboat

toptati *v* to stamp

tor *m* enclosure

tora *f* torah

toranj *m* tower

torba *f* bag

torbar *m* pedlar

torbariti *v* to peddle

torbica *f* handbag

tornado *m* tornado

tornjaj se! clear off!

torpedirati *v* to torpedo

torpedni čamac *m* torpedo boat

torpedo *m* torpedo

torpiljarka *f* torpedo-boat

torta *f* cake

tortura *f* torture

torzo *m/n* torso

tost *f* toast

totalan *adj* total

totalitaran *adj* totalitarian

totalitarizam *m* totalitarianism

tovar *m* cargo

tovariti *v* to load

tovarni list *m* bill of lading

toviti *v* to fatten

trabunjati *v* to talk incoherently

trač *m* gossip

tračak *m* ray

tračati *v* to gossip

tračnica *f* track

tradicija *f* tradition

tradicionalan *adj* traditional

tradicionalizam *m* traditionalism

trafika *f* tobacconist's

trafikant *m* tobacconist

trag *m* 1. track 2. trace

traganje *n* search

tragati *v* 1. to track 2. to trace

tragedija *f* tragedy

tragičan *adj* tragic

trajan *adj* 1. lasting 2. continual

trajanje *n* duration

trajati *v* 1. to last 2. to continue

trajekt *m* ferry

trajno *adv* permanently
trajnost *f* 1. permanence 2. constancy
trak, traka *f* 1. strip 2. tape 3. (spor.) lane
trakavica *f* tapeworm
traktor *m* tractor
traljav *adj* shabby
traljavost *f* shabbiness
tralje *fpl* rags
tram *m* beam
trambulina *f* trampoline
trampa *f* barter
tramvaj *m* tram
tramvajska kola *f* tram car
trankilizer, trankvilizant *m* tranquillizer
trans *m* trance
transakcija *f* transaction
transfer *m* (com.) transfer
transfer tehnologije *n* technology transfer
transferacija *f* (leg.) transfer
transformacija *f* transformation
transformator *m* transformer
transformisati *v* to transform
transfuzija *f* transfusion
transfuzija krvi *f* blood transfusion
transkontinentalan *adj* transcontinental
transkripcija *f* transcription
transliteracija *f* transliteration
transliterirati *v* to transliterate
transmisija *f* transmission
transplatacija *f* transplant
transport *m* transport
transporter *m* 1. conveyor belt 2. (mil) transporter
transporter za ljudstvo *m* (mil.) troop carrier
transportirati, transportovati *v* to transport

transportni brod *m* (mil.) troopship
tranšeja *f* trench
transvestit *m/f* transvestite
tranutan *adj* instantaneous
tranzistor *m* transistor
tranzit *m* transit
tranzitna čekaonica *f* transit lounge
tranzitna viza *f* transit visa
tranzitni *adj* transit
tranzitni logor *m* transit camp
trapav *adj* clumsy
trapiti se *v* to mortify
trasant *m* maker
trasirno zrno *n* tracer bullet
tratina *f* lawn
tratinčica *f* daisy
tratiti *v* to waste
trauma *f* trauma
traumatičan *adj* traumatic
trava *f* 1. grass 2. herb
travanj *m* April
travar *m* herbalist
travka *f* blade of grass
travnik *m* meadow
travnjak *m* lawn
tražen *adj* 1. looked for 2. applied for
traženje *n* 1. search 2. application
tražilac *m* 1. searcher 2. applicant
tražilo *n* viewfinder
tražiti *v* 1. to look for 2. to apply for 3. to request
tražiti viza *f* to apply for a visa
tražnja *f* demand
traćiti *v* to waste
trbuh *m* stomach
trčanje *n* race
trčati *v* to race
trebati *v* 1. to need 2. to be necessary

trebovanje *n* requisitioning
trebovati *v* to requisition
tref *m* club
trem *m* porch
trema *f* nervousness
tren, trenutak *m* moment
trend *m* trend
trener *m* trainer
trenerka *f* track suit
trening *m* training
trening-utakmica *f* (spor.) warm-up match
trenirati *v* to train
trenje *n* friction
trenutačan, trenutan *adj* instantaneous
trenuti *v* to wink
trepavica *f* eyelash
treperenje *n* 1. flickering 2. trembling
treperiti *v* 1. to flicker 2. to vibrate 3. to tremble
trepet *m* 1. fear 2. flicker
treptati *v* 1. to wink 2. to flicker
tresak *m* bang
treset *m* peat
treskati, tresnuti *v* 1. to hit 2. to slam 3. to bang
trešnja *f* 1. shaking 2. cherry
tresti se *v* to shiver
tresti *v* to shake
tretirati *v* to treat
tretman *m* treatment
trezan *adj* sober
trezor *m* safe box
trezvenjak *adj* abstinent
treće lice *n* (leg.) third party
treći *v* third
trećina *f* one third
trg *m* square
trgati *v* to pluck
trgnuti se *v* to draw back

trgnuti *v* to draw a weapon
trgovac *m* 1. shopkeeper 2. merchant 3. retailer
trgovac nepokretnostima *m* estate agent; realtor
trgovačka komora *f* chamber of commerce
trgovačka kuća *f* firm
trgovačka mornarica *f* merchant marine
trgovački *adj* 1. merchant 2. commercial
trgovački brod *m* merchant ship
trgovački pomoćnik *m* sales assistant
trgovački putnik *m* travelling salesman
trgovački ugovor *m* trade agreement
trgovati *v* to trade
trgovina *f* 1. trade 2. shop 3. **slobodna trgovina** free trade
trgovina robljem *m* slave trade
trgovinski deficit *m* trade gap
trgovište *n* market town
tri puta three times
tri three
tribina *f* 1. platform 2. grandstand
tričav *adj* insignificant
trideset thirty
trijem *m* 1. porch 2. arcade
trijeska *f* splinter
trijezan *adj* sober
trijeznost *f* sobriety
trijumf *m* triumph
trijumfalan *adj* triumphant
trijumfovati *v* to triumph
trik *m* trick
triler *m* thriller
trilogija *f* trilogy
trinaest thirteen
tripe, tripice *fpl* tripe

triplikat *m* triplicate
triumf *m* triumph
triumfalan *adj* triumphant
triumfirati *v* to triumph
trivijalan *adj* trivial
trivijalnost *f* triviality
trk *m* running
trka *f* race
trka u naoružavanju *f* arms race
trkač *m* 1. runner 2. racer
trkalište *n* race course
trljati *v* to rub
trn *m* thorn
trnci *mpl* pins and needles
trnokop *m* pick-axe
trnovit *adj* thorny
trnuti *v* to go numb
trnje *n* brambles
trodimenzionalan *adj* three-dimensional
trofej *m* trophy
trojci *mpl*, **trojke** *fpl* triplets
trojni *adj* tripartite
trojstvo *n* trinity
trokut *m* triangle
trokutan *adj* triangular
trola *f* trolley
trolejbus *m* trolley bus
trom *adj* slow
trombon *m* trombone
tromblon *m* grenade launcher
tromboza *f* thrombosis
tromesečni, tromjesečni *adj* quarterly
tromost *f* slowness
tron *m* throne
tronožac *m* tripod
tronut *adj* moved
tropi *mpl* tropics
tropski *adj* tropical
troskok *m* triple jump
trošak *m* 1. expense 2. **pogonski**

troškovi overheads
trošan *adj* 1. dilapidated 2. fragile
trošenje *n* spending
trošiti *v* 1. to spend 2. to use up
troškovnik *m* estimate
trošnost *f* dilapidation
trostruk *m* triple
trotinet *m* scooter
trotoar *m* pavement; sidewalk
trougao *m* triangle
trouglast *adj* three-cornered
trovanje *n* poisoning
trovati *v* to poison
trpak *m* bitter
trpati *v* to cram
trpeljivost *f* tolerance
trpeti *v* 1. to suffer 2. to endure
trpeza *f* table
trpezarija *f* dining room
trpjeti *v* 1. to suffer 2. to endure
trpni *adj* passive
trs *m* vine
trsiti se *v* to try hard
trska *f* reed
tršav *adj* curly
trti *v* to rub
trtica *f* rump
truba *f* trumpet
trubač *m* trumpeter
trubiti *v* to blow a trumpet
trud *m* effort
trudan *adj* tired
truditi se *v* to take pains
trudna *f* pregnant
trudnica *f* pregnant woman
trudnoća *f* pregnancy
trudovi *mpl* labour pains
trul *adj* rotten
trulež *m/f* rot
truliti *v* to rot
trun *m* bit
trunuti *v* to rot

truo *adj* rotten
trup *m* 1. trunk 2. hull
trupa *f* 1. troupe 2. *see* **trupe**
trupac *m* log
trupe *fpl* 1. troops 2. **elitne trupe** crack troops
truplo *f* corpse
trust *m* trust
trvenje *n* quarrel
trzati *v* to jerk
trzavica *f* convulsion
tržišni *adj* market
tržište *n* market place
tržnica *f* market hall
tu here
tuba *f* tube
tuberkuloza *f* tuberculosis (TB)
tucanik *m* gravel
tucati *v* 1. to crush 2. to grind
tuce, tucet *n* dozen
tuča *f* 1. brawl 2. hail
tučnjava *f* fight
tući *v* to beat
tući se *v* to fight
tuda *f* this way
tuđ *adj* 1. strange 2. foreign
tuđina *f* abroad
tuđinac *m* 1. stranger 2. foreigner
tuga *f* sorrow
tuga za zavičajem *f* homesickness
tugovati *v* to grieve
tulipan *m* tulip
tuliti *v* to yell
tuljan *m* seal
tumač *m* interpreter
tumačenje *n* interpretation
tumačiti *v* 1. to interpret 2. to explain
tumarati *v* to roam
tumor *m* tumour
tuna *f* tuna
tunel *m* tunnel

tup *adj* 1. blunt 2. stupid
tupost *f* bluntness
tur *m* backside
tura *f* tour
turati *v* to shove
turbina *f* turbine
turbulencija *f* turbulence
turbulentan *adj* turbulent
Turčin *m* Turk
turist *m* tourist
turistička agencija *f* travel agency
turistička privreda *f* travel industry
turistički *adj* tourist
turistički vodič *m* tourist guide
turiti *v* to shove
turizam *m* 1. travel 2. tourism
turneja *f* tour
turnir *m* tournament
turoban *adj* 1. sad 2. depressed
tur-operator *m* tour operator
turpija *f* file
turpijati *v* to file
Turska *f* Turkey
Turska *f* Turkish
turski *adj* Turkish
tuš *m* shower
tuširati se *v* to shower
tutanj *m* boom
tutkalo *n* glue
tutnjati, tutnjiti *v* to boom
tutor *m* tutor
tutorski *adj* tutorial
tužan *adj* unhappy
tužba *f* 1. complaint 2. accusation
tužen, tuženik *m* (leg) defendant
tužilac *m* 1. plaintiff 2. prosecutor
tužilaštvo *n* prosecutor's office
tužitelj *m* 1. plaintiff 2. prosecutor
tužiti *v* 1. to accuse 2. to prosecute
tužiti se *v* to complain about

tužno *adv* unhappily
TV-serija *f* TV series
tvar *f* 1. matter 2. stuff
tvoj *singular* 1. your 2. yours
tvor *m* skunk
tvorac *m* 1. creator 2. manufacturer
tvorba *f* 1. creation 2. manufacture
tvorevina *f* product
tvornica *f* factory
tvornički *adj* manufactured
tvrd *adj* 1. hard 2. solid
tvrdičluk *m* miserliness

tvrdi disk *m* hard disk
tvrditi *v* to assert
tvrdnja *f* assertion
tvrdo *n* solid
tvrdoglav *adj* obstinate
tvrdoglavost *f* obstinacy
tvrdokoran *adj* stubborn
tvrdokornost *f* stubbornness
tvrdoća *f* solidity
tvrđava *f* fortress
tvrđenje *n* assertion
tvrtka *f* firm

u

u *prep* 1. at 2. in 3. to 4. into 5. **u to** at that moment 6. **u principu** in general 7. **u blizini obale** offshore
ubaciti *v* to insert
ubav *adj* nice
ubediti *v* to convince
ubedljiv *adj* convincing
ubeđenje *n* conviction
ubeležiti *v* to register
ubezeknuti se *v* to be stunned
ubica *m* 1. killer 2. murderer 3. assassin
ubično *adv* generally
ubijanje *n* killing
ubistvo *n* 1. killing 2. murder 3. assassination
ubistvo bez predumišljaja *n* manslaughter
ubiti *v* 1. to kill 2. to murder 3. to assassinate
ublaženje *n* mitigation
ublažiti *v* 1. to alleviate 2. to mitigate
ubo *n* ear
ubod *m* sting
ubog *adj* poor
ubojica *f* killer
ubojit *adj* deadly
ubojstvo *n* 1. killing 2. murder 3. assassination
ubosti *v* to sting
ubrajati *v* to include
ubrati *v* to pick
ubrizgati *v* to inject
ubrojiti *v* to include
ubrus *m* towel

ubrzanje *n* accleration
ubrzati *v* to accelerate
ubrzo *adv* quickly
ubuduće *n* in future
uceniti, ucijeniti *v* to blackmail
učen *adj* scholarly
učenica *f* schoolgirl
učenik *m* schoolboy
učenjak *m* 1. scholar 2. scientist
učenje *n* study
učenost *f* learning
učesnik *m* participant
učešće *n* participation
učestalost *f* frequency
učestovati *v* to participate
učinak *m* effect
učiniti *v* to do
učiniti kompromis *v* to compromise
učiniti neplodnim *v* to sterilize
učionica *f* classroom
učitelj *m*, **uciteljica** *f* teacher
učiti *v* 1. to teach 2. to study 3. to learn
učtiv *adj* polite
učtivost *f* politeness
učvrstiti *v* to fix
ući *v* to enter
ućutkati *v* to silence
ud *m* limb
udahnuti *v* to inhale
udaja *f* marriage
udalenost *f* distance
udaljen *adj* far
udaljiti se *v* to go away
udaljiti *v* to send away
udar *m* 1. blow 2. shock 3. (med.)

heart attack **4. državni udar** coup d'état

udarac *m* **1.** blow **2.** kick

udariti *v* **1.** to hit **2.** to kick

udariti u plač *v* to burst into tears

udarna eskadra *f* naval task force

udarna grupa *f* strike force

udati *v* to marry

udaviti *v* **1.** to strangle **2.** to drown

udati se *v* to get married

udebljati se *v* to get fat

udeo *m* share

udes *m* fate

udesiti *v* to arrange

udica *f* fish hook

udijeliti *v* to grant

udio *m* share

udisanje *n* inhalation

udisati *v* to inhale

udjenuti *v* to thread

udlaga *f* splint

udo *n* limb

udoban *adj* comfortable

udobno *adv* comfortably

udobnost *f* comfort

udomaćiti *v* to domesticate

udomaćiti se *v* to feel at home

udomiti se *v* to settle down

udostojati se *v* to condescend

udova *f* widow

udovac *m* widower

udovica *f* widow

udovištvo *n* widowhood

udovoljiti *v* **1.** to satisfy **2.** to fulfil

udružen *adj* **1.** united **2.** joint **3.** associated

udruženje *n* **1.** union **2.** association **3.** syndicate

udružiti se *v* **1.** to unite **2.** to associate

udubina *f* niche

udubljenje *n* recess

udušiti *v* to suffocate

udvoran *adj* polite

udvornost *f* politeness

udvostručiti *v* to double

udžbenik *m* textbook

ufanje *n* hope

ufati se *v* to hope

ugađati *v* (mus.) to tune

ugalj *m* coal

uganuti *v* **1.** to sprain **2.** to dislocate

ugao *m* **1.** corner **2.** angle

ugasiti *v* **1.** to extinguish **2.** to turn off

ugasiti *v* to switch off

ugasiti se *v* to go out

ugaziti *v* to stamp on

uginuti *v* to die

uglađen *adj* well-mannered

uglađenost *f* good manners

uglat *adj* angular

uglaviti *v* to fix

uglavnom *adv* mainly

ugled *m* reputation

ugledan *adj* respected

ugledanje *n* imitation

ugledati *v* to see

uglen, ugljen *m* coal

ugljenik *m* carbon

ugljenokop *m* coal mine

ugljičan *adj* carbonic

ugljična kiselina *f* carbonic acid

ugljik *m* carbon

ugnjetavati *v* to oppress

ugnuti se *v* to sink

ugodan *adj* pleasant

ugoditi *v* to please

ugodno *adv* pleasantly

ugojen *adj* fat

ugojenost *f* fatness

ugojiti *v* to fatten

ugojiti se *v* to get fat

ugostiti *v* to entertain
ugovarač *m* contractor
ugovarati *v* to make an agreement
ugovor *m* 1. agreement 2. contract 3. treaty 4. pact 5. **usmeni ugovor** verbal contract 6. **mirovni ugovor** peace treaty 7. **ugovor o nenapadanju** non-aggression treaty 8. **potpisati ugovor** to sign a treaty 9. **raskinuti ugovor** to break a treaty
ugovor o nenapadanju *m* non-aggression pact
ugovoriti *v* to make an agreement
ugrabiti *v* 1. to seize 2. to kidnap
ugraditi *v* to build
ugrijati *v* to heat
ugristi *v* to bite
ugriz *m* bite
ugroziti, ugrožavati *v* 1. to threaten 2. to endanger
ugrožavanje *n* threat
ugrožena životinjska vrsta *f* endangered species
ugurati *v* to put in
ugušenje *n* suppression
ugušiti *v* 1. to choke 2. to suppress
ugušivač *m* suppressor
uhađati *v* shadow
uhapsiti *v* to arrest
uhapšenik *m* prisoner
uhobolja *f* earache
uhoda *f* spy
uhodan *adj* established
uhoditi *v* to spy
uhvatiti *v* to catch
uistinu *adv* really
ujak *m* uncle
ujed *m* bite
ujedati *v* to bite
ujediniti (se) to unite, to unify

ujedinjen *adj* united
Ujedinjene nacije *fpl*, **Ujedinjeni narodi** *mpl* United Nations
ujedinjenje *n* union
ujedljiv *adj* sarcastic
ujedljivost *f* sarcasm
ujednačiti *v* to unify
ujedno *adv* altogether
ujesti *v* to sting
ujna *f* aunt
ujutro, ujutru *adv* in the morning
ukaljati *v* to get dirty
ukaz *m* decree
ukazati *v* to point out
ukidanje *n* abolition
ukidati, ukinuti *v* 1. to cancel 2. to abolish
ukiseliti *v* to pickle
uklanjanje *n* removal
uklanjati, ukloniti *v* to remove
uklet *adj* cursed
ukloniti *v* to remove
ukloniti se *v* to avoid
uključiti *v* to include
uključivo *adv* including
uknjižiti *v* to register
ukočen *adj* stiff
ukočeno *adv* stiffly
ukočenost *f* stiffness
ukočiti *v* to stiffen
ukočiti se *v* to become stiff
ukonačiti *v* to accomodate
ukop *m* burial
ukopan *adj* burial
ukopati *v* to bury
ukor *m* blame
ukorenjen *adj* rooted
ukorijeniti *v* to take root
ukoriti *v* to blame
ukosnica *f* hairpin
ukoso *adv* at an angle
ukotviti *v* to anchor

ukotvljen *adj* anchored
ukras *m* decoration
ukrasiti *v* to decorate
ukrasni *adj* decorative
ukrasti *v* to steal
ukratko *adv* briefly
ukrcati *v* to load
ukrcati se *v* to board
ukrcavanje *n* embarkation
ukrivo *adv* at an angle
ukrotiti *v* to tame
ukrštanje *n* crossing
ukrstiti *v* to cross
ukrućen *adj* stiff
ukuhan *adj* preserved
ukuhati *v* to cook up
ukupan *adj* total
ukupna suma *f* lump sum
ukupno *adv* totally
ukus *m* 1. taste 2. **bez ukusa**
  tasteless
ukusan *adj* tasty
ukućanin *m* inmate
ulagač *m* 1. depositor 2. investor
ulaganje *n* 1. deposit 2. investment
ulagati *v* 1. to deposit 2. to invest
ulagivač *m* yes-man
ulaz, ulazak *m* entrance
ulaziti *v* to enter
ulazna viza *f* entry visa
ulaznica *f* ticket
ulaznina *f* entrance fee
ulaženje *n* entry
ulediti *v* to freeze
ulegnuće *n* subsidence
uleknuti se *v* to subside
ulepšan *adj* adorned
ulica *f* street
uličarka *f* prostitute
uličica *f* alley
ulični *adj* street
uličujak *m* vagabond

ulijeniti se *v* to grow lazy
ulijevati, uliti *v* 1. to pour in 2. to
  inspire
uliti *v* to pour into
ulizica *f* sycophant
ulizivanje *n* sycophancy
ulog *m* deposit
uloga *f* role
ulogoriti *v* to camp
ulomak *m* 1. fragment 2. passage
ulov *m* catch
uloviti *v* to catch
ulozi *mpl* gout
uložiti *v* to deposit
ultimatum *m* ultimatum
ulje *n* oil
uljepšati *v* to adorn
uljiti *v* to oil
uljudan *adj* polite
uljudno *adv* politely
uljudnost *f* politeness
uljuljati *v* to lull
ultra- ultra-
uludo *adv* in vain
um *m* 1. reason 2. mind
umak *m* sauce
umalo *adv* almost
umanjiti *v* 1. to diminish 2. to
  reduce
umanjiti se *v* to diminish
umarati *v* to exhaust
umaći, umaknuti *v* to escape
umekšati *v* to soften
umekšati se *v* to relent
umeren *adj* moderate
umerenost *f* moderation
umesno *adv* appropriately
umešan *adj* involved
umešati *v* to involve
umešnost *f* skill
umesto *prep* instead of
umetati *v* to insert

umeti v 1. to know how (to) 2. to be skilled
umetnički adj artistic
umetnički film m feature film
umetnik m artist
umetnost f art
umetnuti v to insert
umeće n skill
umijesiti v to knead
umiješati v to involve
umijeće n skill
umilan, umiljat adj lovable
umiranje n dying
umirati v to be dying
umiriti v 1. to calm down 2. to paficy
umišljati se v to be conceited
umišljen adj conceited
umišljenost f conceit
umiti v to wash
umivanje n washing
umivaonik m washbasin
umivati se v to wash onself
umjeren adj moderate
umjerenost f moderation
umjestan adj appropriate
umjesto prep instead of
umjetan adj artificial; artistic
umjeti v 1. to know how (to) 2. to be skilled
umjetnički adj artistic
umjetnički film m feature film
umjetnik m artist
umjetnost f art
umni adj intellectual
umnožavanje n multiplying
umnožiti v to multiply
umobolan adj insane
umobolnik m insane person
umobolnost f insanity
umočiti v to dip
umor m weariness

umoran adj weary
umoriti v 1. to exhaust 2. to kill
umoriti se v to become weary
umorstvo n 1. killing 2. murder 3. assassination
umotati v to wrap up
umreti, umrijeti v to die
umrli adj dead
umrlica f death certificate
umrljati v to stain
umrtviti v to deaden
umuknuti v to be speechless
unakaziti v to deform
unakrsna vatra f crossfire
unakrsno ispitivanje n cross-examination
unakrst adv crossways
unakrstan adj cross
unaokolo adv around
unapred adv in advance
unapređenje n promotion
unapređivati v to promote
unaprijed adv in advance
unaprijediti v to promote
unatoč 1. adv nevertheless 2. against 3. prep despite
unatrag adv 1. backwards 2. ago
unazad adv backwards
unca, unča f ounce
unesrećiti se v to be hurt
unificirati v to unify
uniforma f uniform
unija f union
unijeti v 1. to carry into 2. to enter
unikat m something unique
unilateralan adj unilateral
uništavanje n destruction
uništavati, uništiti v to destroy
uništenje n destruction
univerzalan adj universal
univerzalija f universal
univerzalno adv universally

univerzalnost *f* universality
univerzitet *m* university
unosan *adj* profitable
unositi *v* 1. to carry into 2. to enter
unovačiti *v* to recruit
unovčiti *v* to sell
unučad *f* grandchildren
unuče *n* grandchild
unuk *m* grandson
unuka *f* granddaughter
unutar *adv* inside
unutarnji *adj* internal
unutra *adv* inside
unutrašnji guma *f* inner tube
unutrašnji *adj* internal
unutrašnji poslovi *mpl* internal affairs
unutrašnjost *f* interior
uobičajen *adj* usual
uobličiti *v* to form
uobrazilja *f* imagination
uobraziti *v* to imagine
uobražen *adj* vain
uobraženje *n* imagination
uobraženost *f* vanity
uoči *prep* on the eve of
uočiti *v* to notice
uokviriti *v* to frame
uopštavanje *n* generalization
uopšte *adv* in general
uopštiti *v* to generalize
uopće *adv* in general
uopće ne not at all
uostalom after all
upad *m* invasion
upadan *adj* conspicuous
upadati *v* to interrupt
upadica *f* interruption
upala *f* inflammation
upala pluća *f* pneumonia
upala slijepog crijeva *f* appendicitis

upaliti *v* 1. to set fire to 2. to switch on
upaliti se *v* to catch fire
upaljač *m* lighter
upaljiv *adj* (in)flammable
upamtiti *v* to remember
upasti *v* 1. to fall into 2. to invade 3. to interrupt
upecati *v* to catch
upečatljiv *adj* impressive
upetljati se *v* to get involved in
upijanje *n* absorption
upijati *v* to absorb
upirati se *v* to lean against
upis *m* 1. registration 2. record
upisati *v* to register
upisnica *f* registration form
upisnina *f* registration fee
upit *m* inquiry
upitati *v* to inquire
upiti *v* to absorb
upitni arak *m* questionnaire
upitnik *m* question mark
uplašen *adj* frightened
uplašiti *v* to frighten
uplašiti se *v* to be frightened
uplata *f* payment
uplatiti *v* to pay in
uplatnica *f* money order
uplaćivati, uplatiti *v* to pay in
uplesti *v* to involve
upletati, uplesti se, uplitati *v* to interfere
upliv *adj* influence
uplivisati *v* to influence
uporaba *f* use
uporabiti *v* to use
uporan *adj* stubborn
uporedan *adj* 1. parallel 2. comparative
uporediti *v* to compare
uporednik *m* parallel

uporedo *adv* side by side
upoređenje, upoređivanje *n* comparison
uspoređivati *v* to compare
uporište *n* foothold
upornica *f* strut
uporno *adv* stubbornly
upornost *f* stubbornness
uposlen *adj* employed
upotpuniti *v* to complete
upotreba *f* use
upotrebiti, upotrebljavati *v* to make use of
upoznati *v* 1. to get to know 2. to meet 3. to introduce
upozorenje *n* warning
upozoriti, upozoravati *v* to warn
uprava *f* management
upravan *adj* vertical
upravitelj *m* 1. manager 2. director
upravljanje *n* 1. administration 2. management 3. rđavo upravljanje mismanagement
upravljati *v* 1. to manage 2. to govern
upravni *adj* adminstrative
upravni odbor *m* steering committee
upravo *adv* exactly
upražnjavati *v* to practise
upregnuti *v* to harness
uprijeti se *v* to make an effort
uprkos *prep* despite
uprkos tome *adv* regardless
uprljati *v* to make dirty
upropastiti *v* to wreck
uprošćen *adj* simplified
uprostiti *v* to simplify
uprtiti *v* to shoulder
uputa *f* 1. instruction 2. directions
uputan *adj* advisable
uputiti se *v* to start off

uputnica *f* money-order
uputstvo *n* directions
uputstvo *n* instruction
upućen *adj* informed
upućivati, uputiti *v* to instruct
ura *f* 1. hour 2. watch 3. clock
uračunati *v* to take into account
uraditi *v* 1. to do 2. to commit
urađen od čoveka/čovjeka *f* manmade
uragan *m* hurricane
uramiti *v* to frame
uran *m* uranium
uraniti *v* to rise early
urar *m* watchmaker
uravnotežiti *v* to balance
urbanist *m* town-planner
urbanizacija *f* urbanization
urbanizam *m* town-planning
urbanizovati *v* to urbanize
ureći *v* to fix a time
ured *m* office
uredan *adj* neat
uredba *f* regulation
urediti *v* to arrange
urednik *m* editor
uredništvo *n* editorship
uredno *adv* neatly
urednost *f* neatness
uredovno vrijeme *n* office hours
uređaj *m* 1. machine 2. arrangement
uređivati *v* 1. to arrange 2. to edit
ures *m* decoration
uresiti *v* to decorate
urezati *v* to engrave
urgirati *v* to urge
urin *m* urine
urlati *v* to howl
urma *f* date
urna *f* urn
urnebes *m* uproar

urod *m* crop
uroditi *v* to bear fruit
urođen *adj* 1. indigenous 2. native
urođenički *adj* native
urođenik *m* original inhabitant
urologija *f* urology
uroniti *v* to dive
urota *f* conspiracy
urotiti se *v* to conspire
urotnik *m* conspirator
uručenje *n* handing over
uručiti *v* to hand over
usaditi *v* to insert
usahnuti *v* to wither
usamljen *adj* lonely
usamljenost *f* loneliness
usavršavati, usavršiti *v* to improve
useknuti se *v* to blow one's nose
useliti se *v* 1. to move into 2. to immigrate
useljenik *m* immigrant
usev *m* crop
ushititi *v* to delight
ushićen *adj* delighted
ushićenje *n*, **ushit** *m* delight
usidjelica *f* spinster
usidriti *v* to anchor
usijan *adj* red-hot
usiljen *adj* forced
usiriti se *v* to set
usisati *v* to suck up
usisivač *m* vacuum cleaner
usisni *adj* intake
usitniti *v* to chop
usjev *m* crop
usjeći *v* to incise
uskladiti *v* to harmonize
uskličnik *m* exclamation mark
usklik *m* exclamation
uskliknuti *v* to exclaim
uskomešati se *v* to make a fuss

uskoro *adv* soon
uskotračan *adj* narrow-gauge
uskraćivati, uskratiti *v* to deny
Uskrs *m* Easter
uskrsnuti *v* to resurrect
uskrsnuće *n* resurrection
usled, uslijed *prep* because of
uslijed toga as a result
uslišiti *v* to grant
uslov *m* 1. condition 2. **pod oslovom** on condition that
uslovi sporazuma *mpl* terms of agreement
uslovno *adv* conditionally
usluga *f* favour
uslužan *adj* kind
uslužiti *v* to serve
usluživanje u sobama *f* room service
uslužnost *f* kindness
usmen *adj* oral
usmeni ispit *m* oral examination
usmeni ugovor *m* verbal contract
usmeno *adv* orally
usmjeriti *v* to aim
usmrtiti *v* to kill
usna, usnica *f* lip
usniti, usnuti *v* to fall asleep
usoliti *v* 1. to salt 2. to pickle
usov *m* avalanche
uspaničiti se *v* to panic
uspavanka *f* lullaby
uspeh *m* 1. success 2. **veliki uspeh** smash hit
uspešan *adj* successful
uspešno *adv* successfully
uspeti *v* to be successful
uspeti se *v* to climb up
uspijevati *v* 1. to succeed 2. to prosper
uspinjača *f* 1. funicular 2. ski-lift
uspinjati se *v* to climb

uspjeh m 1. success 2. **veliki uspjeh** smash hit
uspješan adj successful
uspješnost f efficiency
uspjeti v to succeed
usplahiren adj agitated
usplahirenost f agitation
uspomena f 1. memory 2. souvenir
uspon m climb
usporedan adj parallel
usporedba f comparison
usporediti v to compare
usporedo prep along with
usporen adj **na usporenom filmu** in slow motion
usporiti v to slow down
uspostaviti, uspostavljati v to restore
uspostavljen adj established
uspravan adj upright
uspraviti v to set upright
uspravno adv vertically
usprkos prep in spite of
usprotiviti se v to oppose
usput adv on the way
usred prep in the middle of
usredsrediti, usredotočiti se v to concentrate
usrećiti v to make happy
usta f mouth
ustaliti se v to be settled
ustaliti v to stabilize
ustaljen adj settled
ustanak m uprising
ustanik m rebel
ustanova f establishment
ustanoviti v to establish
ustati v to rise
ustav adj constitution
ustava f dam
ustavan adj constitutional
ustaviti v to block

ustavotvoran adj constituent
ustegnuti, ustezati v to take away
ustegnuti se v 1. to refrain from 2. to hesitate
ustezanje n hesitation
ustezati se v to hesitate
ustoličenje n installation
ustoličiti v to install
ustrajan adj persistent
ustrajati v to persist
ustrajnost f persistence
ustreliti, ustrijeliti v to shoot
ustrojstvo n organization
ustručavanje n hesitation
ustručavati se v to hesitate
ustuknuti v to give in
ustupak m concession
ustupati, ustupiti v to concede
usud m fate
usuditi se v to dare
ususret, u susret towards
usvajanje n adoption
usvojiti v to adopt
uš f louse
ušančiti se v to be entrenched
ušće n mouth
uškopiti v to castrate
ušljiv adj lousy
ušobolja f earache
uštap m full moon
ušteda f saving
uštedjeti v to save
uštedevina f savings
uštinuti v to pinch
uštipak m doughnut
uštrcati v to inject
uštrojiti v to castrate
ušutjeti v to be silent
ušutkati v silence
utaboriti se v to pitch camp
utajiti v to embezzle
utajivač poreza f tax dodger

utakmica *f* 1. competition 2. match
utamaniti *v* to exterminate
utamničiti *v* to imprison
utanačiti *v* to arrange
utažiti *v* 1. to satisfy 2. to soothe
uteći *v* to flee
uteg *m* weight
uteha *f* consolation
utemeljen *adj* founded
utemeljitelj, utemeljivač *m* founder
utemeljiti *v* to found
uterati, uterivati *v* 1. to drive into 2. (spor.) to throw/kick in
uticaj *m* influence
uticajan *adj* influential
uticati *v* to influence
utihnuti *v* to be still
utikač *m* plug
utirati *v* to stamp
utisak *m* impression
utisnuti *v* to impress
utišač *m* silencer; muffler
utišati *v* to silence
utjecaj *m* influence
utjecati *v* to influence
utjeha *f* consolation
utjeloviti *v* to incorporate
utjerati, utjerivati *v* to drive into 2. (spor.) to throw/kick in
utješiti *v* to comfort
utočište *n* 1. shelter 2. refuge
utoliko *adv* so much, more
utopiti se *v* to be drowned
utopiti *v* to drown
utopljenik *m* drowned person
utorak *m* Tuesday
utovar *m* loading
utovariti *v* to load
utrka *f* race
utrkivanje *n* racing
utrkivati se *v* to race

utrnuti *v* 1. to extinguish 2. to go out
utroba *f* 1. bowels 2. womb
utrošak *m* consumption
utrošiti *v* to spend
utrpati *v* to cram
utrt *adj* beaten
utrti *v* to beat down
utržak *m* proceeds
utučen *adj* depressed
utvara *f* phantom
utvarati sebi *v* to be conceited
utvrda *f* 1. fortification 2. stronghold
utvrditi, utvrdivati *v* to fortify
utvrđenje *n* 1. fortification 2. stronghold
uvala *f* 1. vale 2. bay
uvažavati, uvažiti *v* to appreciate
uveče *adv* in the evening
uvek *adv* always
uveličati *v* to enlarge
uvenuti *v* 1. to wilt 2. to fade
uveo *adj* 1. wilted 2. faded
uveravanje *n* assurance
uveren *adj* certain
uverenje *n* 1. certainty 2. certificate
uveriti *v* to convince
uvertira *f* overture
uveseljavanje *n* entertainment
uveseljavati *v* to entertain
uvesti *v* 1. to introduce 2. to import
uvez *m* binding
uvezati *v* bind
uvežban *adj* trained
uvežbati *v* to train
uvežbavanje *n* training
uvećati, uvećavati *v* to enlarge
uvid *m* insight
uvideti, uvidjeti, uviđati *v* to realize

uviđaj *m* investigation
uviđavan *adj* considerate
uviđavnost *f* consideration
uvijati *v* to wrap up
uvijek *adv* 1. always 2. još uvijek still
uvijen *adj* wrapped up
uvjeravanje *n* conviction
uvjeravati, uvjeriti *v* to convince
uvjerenje *n* 1. certainty 2. certificate
uvjerljiv *adj* reassuring
uvjet *m* 1. condition 2. pod uvjetom on condition that
uvjetan *adj* conditional
uvjetovati *v* to stipulate
uvježbati *v* to train
uvo *n* ear
uvod *m* introduction
uvoditi *v* to introduce
uvodni članak, uvodnik *m* leading article
uvođenje *n* introduction
uvojak *m* curl
uvoz *m* import
uvoziti *v* to import
uvozni *adj* imported
uvoznik *m* importer
uvreda *f* offence
uvrediti, uvrijediti *v* to offend
uvredljiv *adj* offensive
uvriježiti se *v* to take root
uvrnuti *v* to twist
uvrstiti *v* to insert
uvući *v* to involve
uz, uza *prep* 1. up 2. by 3. beside 4. near
uzajaman *adj* mutual
uzajamno *adv* mutually
uzajmiti *v* 1. to borrow 2. to lend
uzak *adj* narrow
uzalud *adv* in vain

uzaludan *adj* futile
uzaludno *adv* in vain
uzan *adj* tight
uzao *m* knot
uzastopce *n* in succession
uzavreo *adj* boiling
uzbrdica *f* slope
uzbrdo *adv* uphill
uzbuditi, uzbuđivati *v* to excite
uzbudljiv *adj* exciting
uzbuna *f* 1. alarm 2. agitation
uzbuniti *v* 1. to alarm 2. to agitate
uzburkan *adj* stormy
uzbuđen *adj* excited
uzbuđenje *n* excitement
uzda *f* rein
uzdah *m* sigh
uzdahnuti *v* to sigh
uzdati se *v* to trust
uzdisati *v* to sigh
uzdizati *v* to raise
uzdići, uzdignuti *v* to raise
uzdrmati *v* to shake
uzdržan *adj* restrained
uzdržati se *v* to be restrained
uzdržavanje *n* maintenance
uzdržavati *v* to maintain
uzdržavati se *v see* uzdržati se
uzdržljivost *f* restraint
uzduh *m* air
uzduž *prep/adv* along
uzdužni *adj* longitudinal
uzemljiti *v* to earth
uzet *adj* paralyzed
uzeti *v* to take
uzetost *f* paralysis
uzgajati *v* 1. to bring up 2. to breed 3. to grow
uzglavlje *n* pillow
uzgoj *m* 1. upbringing 2. breeding 3. cultivation
uzgred *adv* incidentally

uzgredan *adj* incidental
uzica *f* string
uzići *v* to rise
uzimanje droga *n* drug addiction
uzimati *v* to take
uzimati droge *n* to take drugs
uzjahati *v* to mount
uzlaz *m* ascent
uzlazan *adj* ascending
uzlaziti *v* to ascend
uzleteti, uzletjeti *v* to take off
uzmaći *v* to retreat
uzmak *m* retreat
uzmaknuti, uzmaći *v* to retreat
uzmanjkati *v* to run short of
uzmicati *v* to retreat
uznemiren *adj* worried
uznemiriti, uznemirivati *v* to worry
uzničar *m* jailer
uznik *m* prisoner
uznojiti se *v* to sweat
uzor *m* model
uzorak *m* 1. design 2. sample
uzoran *adj* ideal
uzorati *v* to plough
uzrast *m* 1. age 2. growth 3. stature
uzrasti *v* to grow up
uzrečica *f* proverb
uzročnik, uzrok *m* cause
uzrokovati *v* to cause
uzrujan *adj* agitated
uzrujanost *f* agitation

uzrujati *v* to agitate
uzrujati se *v* to become agitated
uzurpator *m* usurper
uzurpiranje *n* usurpation
uzurpirati *v* to usurp
uzvanik *m* guest
uzvičnik *m* exclamation mark
uzvik *m* exclamation
uzviknuti, uzvikivati *v* to exclaim
uzvišen *adj* exalted
uzvišenje *n* hill
uzvišenost *f* 1. exaltedness 2. excellency
uzvitlati *v* to stir up
uzvodni *adj* upstream
uzvrat *m* **za uzvrat** in return
uzvratiti *v* to answer back
uzvraćati *v* to repay
uzvrpoljiti se *v* to fidget
užaren *adj* red-hot
užas *m* horror
užasan *adj* horrible
užasno *adv* horribly
užasnuti se *v* to be horrified
užasnuti *v* to horrify
uže *n* rope
užežen *adj* rancid
užina *f* snack
užitak *m*, **uživanje** *n* enjoyment
uživati *v* to enjoy
užurban *adj* hasty
užurbano *adv* hastily
užurbanost *f* haste

V

vabiti *v* to tempt
vadičep *m* corkscrew
vaditi *v* to take out
vafla *f* waffle
vaga *f* balance
vagati *v* to weigh
vagina *f* vagina
vaginalan *adj* vaginal
vagon *m* carriage
vajar *m* sculptor
vajarski *adj* statuary
vajarstvo *n* sculpture
vakcina *f* vaccine
vakcinacija *f* masovna vakcinacija immunization campaign
vakcinacija *f* vaccination
vakcinisati *v* to vaccinate (**protiv** against)
vakuum *m* vacuum
val *m* 1. wave 2. dužina vala wavelength
valcer *m* waltz
valjak *m* roller
valjan *adj* 1. good 2. valid
valjanost *f* validity
valjaonica *f* rolling-mill
valjati *v* 1. to roll 2. to be good 3. to be valid
valjda *adv* probably
valjušak *m* dumpling
valovit lim *m* corrugated iron
valovit *adj* wavy
valoviti čelik *m* corrugated iron
valuta *f* currency
vam, vama you
vampir *m* vampire
van 1. *adv* outside 2. *prep* out of

van ako *conj* except
vanbračan *adj* illegitimate
vandal *m* vandal
vandalizam *m* 1. vandalism 2. izvršiti vandalizam na to vandalize
vani *adv* outside
vanila, vanilija *f* vanilla
vanredan *adj* extraordinary
vanredno *adv* extraordinarily
vanredno stanje *n* martial law
vansezonski *adj* off-season
vanjska trgovina *f* foreign trade
vanjski *adj* 1. outdoor 2. exterior
vanjština *f* 1. exterior 2. appearance
vapaj *m* cry
vapajiti *v* to cry out
vapnen *adj* chalky
vapnenac *m* limestone
vapno *n* 1. lime 2. živo vapno quicklime
varalica *m/f* 1. cheat 2. imposter
varanje *n* deception
varati *v* 1. to cheat 2. to deceive
varati se *v* to be deceived
varav *adj* deceptive
varenje *n* digestion
varijabilan *adj* variable
varijacija *f* variation
varijanta *f* variant
variti *v* 1. to boil 2. to weld 3. to digest
varivo *n* boiled vegetables
varjača *f* ladle
varka *f* trick
varljiv *adj* deceptive

varnica *f* spark
varoš *f/m* town
varvarin *m* barbarian
vas you
vasiona *f* universe
vaspitač *m* teacher
vaspitan *adj* well-behaved
vaspitanje *n* education
vaspitati *v* to educate
vaspitni *adj* educational
vaš 1. your 2. yours 3. louse
vašar *m* fair
vat *m* watt
vata *f* cotton wool
vaterpolo *m* water polo
vatra *f* 1. fire 2. **izložen vatri** under fire
vatra oruđa *f* gunfire
vatren *adj* fiery
vatreno oružje *n* firearms
vatrogasac *m* fireman
vatrogasči *mpl* fire brigade
vatrogasna kola *f* fire engine
vatromet *m* fireworks
vatrostalan *adj* fireproof
vaučer *m* voucher
vaza *f* vase
vazal *m* vassal
vazduh *m* air
vazduhoplovstvo *n* 1. aviation 2. air force
vazdušast *adj* airy
vazektomija *f* vasectomy
vazelin *m* vaseline
vazna *f* vase
važan *adj* important
važeći *v* valid
važiti *v* to be important
važnost *f* importance
ve-ce *m* toilet
večan *adj* eternal
veče *n*, **večer** *f* evening

večera *f* dinner, supper
večeras *adv* 1. this evening 2. tonight
večerati *v* to have dinner/supper
večnost *f* eternity
već *adv* already
veće *n* council
većina *f* majority
većinom *adv* mostly
većnica *f* town hall
većnik *m* councillor
vedar *adj* 1. clear 2. cheerful
vedrina *f* 1. clarity 2. cheerfulness
vedriti se *v* to clear up
vedro 1. *n* bucket 2. *adv* cheerfully
veđa *f* eyebrow
vegetacija *f* vegetation
vegetarijanac *m* vegetarian
vegetarijanski *adj* vegetarian
vegetarijanstvo *n* vegetarianism
vejavica *f* blizzard
vek *m* era
vekna *f* loaf
velegrad *m* city
veleizdaja *f* high treason
velelepan *adj* magnificent
veleposednik *m* landlord
velesila *f* great power
veletrgovački *adj* wholesale
veletrgovina *f* wholesale
veletrgovinski *adj* wholesale
veletrgovinsko preduzeće/ poduzeće *n* wholesaler
veličanstven *adj* magnificent
veličanstvo *n* majesty
veličati *v* to glorify
veličina *f* 1. size 2. dimension 3. magnitude
velik *adj* 1. big 2. great
velika zverka/zvijerka *f/m* VIP
velikaš *m* nobleman
veliki petak *m* Good Friday

veliki uspeh/uspjeh *m* smash hit
velikodušan *adj* generous
velikosdušnost *f* generosity
velo *n* veil
Vels *m* Wales
velški *adj* Welsh
veljača *f* February
vena *f* vein
venac *m* garland
venčanje *n* wedding
venčati se *v* to get married
Venecija *f* Venice
venecijanski *adj* Venetian
venerična bolest *f* venereal disease
ventil *m* valve
ventilacija *f* ventilation
ventilator *m* ventilator
ventilirati *v* to ventilate
venuti *v* to wilt
veo *m* veil
veoma *adv* very much
veoma dug maxi
vepar *m* wild boar
vera *f* faith
veran *adj* faithful
veranda *f* veranda
verati se *v* to climb
verbalan *adj* verbal
veren *adj* engaged
verenica *f* fiancée
verenik *m* fiancé
veresija *f* credit
vergl *see* **verglec**
verglaš organ grinder
verglec *m* barrel-organ
veridba *f* engagement
verifikacija *f* verification
verifikovati *v* to verify
verno *adv* faithfully
vernost *f* fidelity
verodostojan *adj* credible

verodostojnost *f* credibility
veroispoved *m*, **verovanje** *n* belief
verovatan *adj* probable
verovati *v* to believe
verovatno *adv* probably
verovatnoća *f* probability
verski *adj* religious
vertikala, vertikalan *adj* vertical
vertikalno *adv* vertically
verzija *f* version
verziran *adj* skilled
veseliti se *v* to be cheerful
veselje *n* joy
veseo *adj* cheerful
veslač *m* rower
veslati *v* to row
veslo *n* oar
vespa *f* motor scooter
vest *f* news
vestern *m* western (film)
vesternizovati *v* to westernize
vesti *v* to embroider
veš *m* laundry
vešala *f* gallows
vešalica *f* coathanger
vešati *v* to hang
vešt *adj* skilful
veštački *adj* artificial
veštački zubi *mpl* false teeth
veštačko disanje usta na usta *n* mouth-to-mouth resuscitation
veštak *m* expert
veština *f* skill
vešto *adv* skilfully
vetar *m* wind
veteran *adj* veteran
veterina *f* veterinary
veterina *f* veterinary medicine
veterinar *m* veterinary surgeon
veterinarski fakultet *m* veterinary school

veterinarski *adj* veterinary
veto *m* 1. veto 2. **staviti veto (na)** to veto 3. **podržati veto** to sustain a veto 4. **nadglasati veto** to override a veto
vetrenjača *f* windmill
vetriti *v* to ventilate
vetroban *adj* windscreen; windshield
vetrovit *adj* windy
vetrovka *f* windbreak
veverica *f* squirrel
vez *m* embroidery
veza *f* connection
vezan *adj* bound
vezati *v* 1. to bind 2. to connect
vezivni *adj* connective
vezivo *n* embroidery
veznik *m* conjunction
veža *f* doorway
vežba *f* exercise
vežbati *v* to practise
vi you
vibracija *f* vibration
vibrator *m* vibrator
vibrirati *v* to vibrate
vic *m* joke
vice- vice-
vicekonzul *m* vice-consul
vičan *adj* 1. accustomed 2. skilled
vid *m* 1. sight 2. aspect
vidan *adj* 1. visible 2. obvious
video *m* video
video-igra *f* video game
video-rekorder *m* video recorder
video-televizijski *adj* video
video-zapisivanje *n* video-recording
videotejp *m* videotape
videti *v* to see
vidik *m* view
vidjeti *v* to see

vidljiv *adj* visible
vidljivost *f* visibility
vidni *adj* visual
vidno polje *n* field officer
vidokrug *m* horizon
vidovit, vodovnjak *m* clairvoyant
vidra *f* otter
vihor *m* gale
vijadukt *m* viaduct
vijak *m* screw
vijavica *f* blizzard
vijećanje *n* consultation
vijećati *v* to confer
vijeće *n* council
Vijeće sigurnosti *n* Security Council
vijećnica *f* townhall
vijećnik *m* councillor
vijek *m* 1. century 2. **Srednji Vijek** the Middle Ages
vijenac *m* wreath
vijesnik *m* messenger
vijest *f* 1. news 2. information
vijoriti se *v* to wave
vijuga *f* curve
vijugati *v* to wind
vika *f* shouting
vikati *v* to shout
vikend *m* weekend
vila *f* 1. villa 2. cottage 3. fairy
vile *fpl* pitchfork
vilica *f* jaw
viljuška, vilica *f* fork
vime *n* udder
vinara *f* wine-shop
vinarstvo *n* wine production
vinil *m* vinyl
vinilski *adj* vinyl
vino *n* 1. wine 2. **crno vino** red wine 3. **belo/bijelo vino** white wine 4. **vrsta vina** rosé 5. **stono/stolno vino** table wine 6.

oporo vino dry wine **7. desertno vino** sweet wine **8. iskričavo vino** sparkling wine
vinograd *m* vineyard
vinogradar *m* winegrower
vinogradarstvo *n* wine growing
vinorodna godina *f* vintage (year)
vinova loza *f* grapevine
vinovnik *m* culprit
vinski *adj* wine
vinuti se *v* to soar
viola *f* viola
violina *f* violin
violinist *m* violinist
vir *m* eddy
viriti *v* to peer
virman *adj* transfer
viršla *f* hot dog
virtualan, virtuelan *adj* virtual
virtuoz *m* virtuoso
virtuoznost *f* virtuosity
virus *m* virus
vis *m* height
viseći *v* **1.** hanging **2. viseći most** suspension bridge
viseći most *f* suspension bridge
visibaba *f* snowdrop
visina *f* height
visjeti *v* to hang
viski *adj* whiskey
visok *m* **1.** high **2.** tall
visoki komesar *m* high commissioner
visoko *adv* highly
visoravan *f* plateau
vispren *adj* clever
višak *m* excess
više *adv* **1.** more **2.** more than **3. nikad više** never more
više manje more or less
višekatan *adj* multistorey; multistory

višepartijski *adj* multi-party
višespratan *adj* multistorey; multistory
višeugaonik *m* polygon
viši *adj* higher
višnja *f* sour cherry
višnjevača *f* cherry brandy
višnji *adj* omnipotent
vitak *adj* slim
vitalan *adj* vital
vitalnost *f* vitality
vitamin *m* vitamin
viteški *adj* gallant
viteštvo *n* chivalry
vitez *m* knight
viti *v* to twist
vitica *f* curl
vitkost *f* slimness
vitlati *v* to brandish
vitrina *f* cabinet
viza *f* **1.** visa **2. ulazna viza** entry visa **3. izlazna viza** exit visa
vizavi vis-à-vis
vizija *f* vision
vizir *m* viewfinder
vizita *f* visit
vizitkarta *f* visiting card; calling card
vizuelan *adj* visual
viđen *adj* visible
viđenje *n* **1.** seeing **2. do viđenja!** see you soon!
vječan *adj* eternal
vječnost *f* eternity
vjeđa *f* eyelid
vjenčan *adj* married
vjenčani list *m* marriage certificate
vjenčani prsten *adj* wedding ring
vjenčanje *n* wedding
vjenčati se *v* to get married
vjenčati *v* to marry
vjera *f* belief

vjeran *adj* faithful
vjeren *adj* engaged
vjerenica *f* fiancée
vjerenik *m* fiancé
vjeridba *f* engagement
vjeridbati se *v* to get engaged
vjernici *mpl* congregation
vjernost *f* fidelity
vjerodajnica *f* credentials,
vjerodostojan *adj* 1. authentic 2. credible
vjeroispovijest *f* faith
vjerojatan *adj* probable
vjerojatno *adv* probably
vjerojatnost *f* probability
vjeroloman *adj* faithless
vjerovati *v* to believe
vjerovnik *m* creditor
vjerski *adj* religious
vješala *f* gallows
vješalica *f* coathanger
vješati *v* to hang up
vješt *adj* 1. skilled 2. efficient
vještak *m* expert
vještica *f* witch
vještina *f* skill
vjetar *m* wind
vjetrenjača *f* windmill
vjetroban *adj* windscreen; windshield
vjetrovit *adj* windy
vjeverica *f* squirrel
vježba *f* 1. exercise 2. drill 3. training
vježbati *v* 1. to exercise 2. to drill 3. to train
vježbenica *f* 1. exercise-book 2. textbook
vlada *f* 1. government 2. administration 3. rule
vladalac, vladar *m* ruler
vladanje *n* 1. rule 2. command

vladati se *v* to behave
vladati *v* to rule
vladika *f* bishop
vlaga *f* humidity
vlak *m* 1. train 2. brzi vlak explress train 3. teretni vlak goods train
vlaknast *adj* fibrous
vlakno *adv* fibre
vlakovođa *m* train guard
vlas *m*, **vlasi** *mpl* hair
vlasac *m* chive(s)
vlasnik *m* owner
vlasnik zemlje *m* landowner
vlasništvo *n* possession
vlast *f* 1. power 2. command 3. authority
vlastela *f* landed gentry
vlastelin *m* estate-owner
vlastit *adj* own
vlastoljubiv *adj* ambitious
vlastoljublje *n* ambition
vlasulja *f* wig
vlat *f* blade
vlažan *adj* humid
vlažna boja *f* wet paint
vlažna krema *f* moisturizing cream
vlažnost *f* humidity
vo *m* ox
voajer *m* voyeur
voćarna *f* fruitier's
voćarstvo *n* fruit growing
voće *n* fruit
voćka *f* fruit tree
voćni *adj* fruit
voćnjak *m* orchard
vod *m* 1. cable 2. (mil.) squad 3. strujni vod power line
voda *f* 1. water 2. bez vode waterless
voden *adj* diluted
vodena boja *f* watercolour
vodena smučka *f* water-ski

vodeni konj *m* hippopotamus
vodeni top *m* water cannon
vodenica *f* watermill
vodeći *adj* leading
vodič *m* 1. guide 2. guidebook
vodik *m* hydrogen
voditi *v* 1. to guide 2. to lead 3. to manage,
voditi pregovore *v* to negotiate
voditi rat *v* to wage war
vodka *f* vodka
vodnik *m* sergeant
vodnjikav *adj* watery
vodo-instalater *m* plumber
vodonepropustan *adj* watertight
vodonik *m* hydrogen
vodopad *m* waterfall
vodoravan *adj* level
vodoskok *m* fountain
vodostaj *m* water level
vodovod *m* 1. plumbing 2. waterworks
vodozemac *m* amphibian
vodstvo *n* 1. guidance 2. leadership
vođa *m* leader
vođa manjine *m* minority leader
vođenje *n* 1. guiding 2. leading
vođenje rata *n* warfare
vodstvo *n* see **vodstvo**
vojarna *f* barracks
vojevati *v* to wage war
vojna akademija *f* military academy
vojna obaveza *f* national service
vojna policija *f* military police
vojni bjegunac *m* (mil) deserter
vojni, vojnički *adj* military
vojnik *m* soldier
vojnin sud *m* court martial
vojno sudstvo *n* military law
vojnopomorska baza *f* naval base

vojnopomorski *adj* naval
vojska *f* 1. army 2. **narodna vojska** militia
vojskovođa *m* commander
vojvoda *m* duke
vojvotkinja *f* duchess
vokal *m* 1. vocal 2. vowel
vokalan *adj* vocal
vokalizirati *v* to vocalize
vokalni *adj* vocal
vokativ *adj* vocative
voki-toki *adj* walkie-talkie
vol *m* ox
volan *m* steering-wheel
volej *m* (spor.) volley
voleti *v* 1. to like 2. to love
volfram *m* tungsten
volja *f* 1. will 2. mood 3. **po volji** at will
voljan *adj* 1. willing 2. ready
voljeti *v* 1. to like 2. to love
voljeti više *v* to prefer
volonter *m* volunteer
volt *m* volt
voltaža *f* voltage
voluharica *f* vole
volumen *m* volume
vonj *m* smell
vonjati *v* to smell
vosak *m*, **voštan** *adj* wax
voštanica *f* candle
voz *m* train
vozač *m* driver
vozačka dozvola *f* driving licence; driver's license
vozački ispit *m* driving test
vozarina *f* 1. fare 2. freight
vozilo *n* vehicle
voziti *v* to drive
vozna cijena *f* fare
vozni *adj* 1. transport 2. train
vozni red *m* timetable

vožnja *f* ride
vrabac *m* sparrow
vrač *m*, **vračara** *f* fortune-teller
vračati *v* to tell someone's fortune
vradžbina *f* spell
vrag *m* devil
vragolija *f* prank
vragoljast *adj* mischievous
vrana *f* crow
vraški *adj* extreme(ly)
vrat *m* neck
vrata *f* 1. door 2. gate
vratar *m* 1. doorkeeper; janitor 2. (spor.) goalkeeper
vratiti *v* to return
vratiti u otadžbinu *v* to repatriate
vratnica *f* door post
vratobolja *f* sore throat
vratoloman *adj* reckless
vražji *adj* diabolical
vraćanje *n* return
vraćati se *v* to come back
vraćati *v* to return
vrba *f* willow
vrč *m* jug
vrebati *v* to lurk
vreća *f* bag
vreća za spavanje *f* sleeping bag
vrećica *f* paper bag
vredan *adj* valuable
vrediti *v* to be worth
vrednost *f* value
vrednosti *fpl* securities
vrednovati *v* to value
vređanje *n* insult
vređati *v* to insult
vrelište *n* boiling point
vrelo *n* 1. spring 2. source 3. well
vreme *n* 1. time 2. weather 3. tense
vremenska zona *f* time zone
vremenske prilike *fpl* weather conditions

vremenski *adj* 1. time 2. weather
vremenski izvještaj *m* weather report
vremešan *adj* old
vrenje *n* boiling
vreo *adj* boiling
vreti *v* to boil
vretna *f* ferret
vreva *f* crowd
vrganj *m* mushroom
vrh *m* 1. top 2. peak
vrhnje *n* cream
vrhovna komanda *f* high command
vrhovni *adj* supreme
vrhovni sud *m* high court
vrhovni zapovjednik *m* commander-in-chief
vrhunac *m* peak
vrhunski *adj* best
vrijedan *adj* worthwhile
vrijediti *v* to be worth
vrijednost *f* 1. worth 2. bez vrijednosti worthless
vrijeme *n* 1. time 2. weather 3. tense
vrijesak *m* heather
vrijeđati *v* to offend
vrisak *m* scream
vriska *f* screaming
vriskati, vrištati *v* to scream
vrlet *f* cliff
vrletan *adj* rocky
vrli *adj* excellent
vrlina *f* virtue
vrlo *adv* very
vrpca *f* ribbon
vrpoljiti se *v* to fidget
vršak *m* tip
vršenje *n* 1. practice 2. threshing
vršidba *f* threshing
vršilica *f* thresher
vršiti *v* 1. to practise 2. to thresh

vrst, vrsta *f* kind, sort
vrsta košarke *f* netball
vrsta vina *f* rosé
vrstan *adj* excellent
vrt *m* garden
vrtati *v* to drill
vrteti, vrtjeti *v* to rotate
vrtić *m* kindergarten
vrtlar *m* gardener
vrtlarija *f* garden nursery
vrtlog *m* whirlpool
vrtoglavica *f* dizziness
vrtoglav *adj* dizzy
vrtuljak *m* merry-go-round
vruć *adj* hot
vrućica *f* fever

vrućina *f* heat
vrvjeti *v* to teem
vrzmati se *v* to move around
vuča *f* pull
vučenje *n* pulling
vucibatina *f* vagabond
vučjak *m* Alsatian
vući *v* to pull
vuk *m* wolf
vukodlak *m* werewolf
vulgaran *adj* vulgar
vulgarnost *f* vulgarity
vulkan *adj* volcano
vulkanski *m* volcanic
vuna *f* wool
vunen *adj* woollen

Z

za *prep* **1.** for **2.** to **3.** by **4.** at **5.** in **6. dan za danom** day after day

zabačen *adj* **1.** rejected **2.** remote

zabaciti *v* **1.** to reject **2.** to dismiss

zabadati *v* **1.** to pin into **2.** to tease

zabadava *f* **1.** free **2.** in vain

zabasati *v* to get lost

zabašuriti *v* to hush up

zabat *m* gable

zabava *f* **1.** party **2.** entertainment **3.** fun

zabavan *adj* **1.** amusing **2.** funny **3.** entertaining

zabavište *n* kindergarten

zabaviti *v* **1.** to amuse **2.** to entertain

zabaviti se *v* to enjoy oneself

zabavljač *m* entertainer

zabavljanje *n* **1.** fun **2.** entertainment

zabavljati *v* **1.** to amuse **2.** to entertain

zabavljati se *v* to enjoy oneself

zabavnik *m* magazine

zabeleška *f* note

zabeležiti *v* to note

zabezeknut *adj* dumbstruck

zabezeknuti *v* to dumbfound

zabijati *v* **1.** to beat **2.** to hammer

zabilježiti *v* to note

zabitan *adj* remote

zabiti *v* **1.** to beat **2.** to hammer

zablatiti *v* to soil

zabliještiti *v* **1.** to dazzle **2.** to flash

zabluda *f* **1.** mistake **2.** delusion

zabluditi *v* to get lost

zaboljeti *v* **1.** to hurt **2.** to grieve

zaborav *adj* forgetfulness

zaboravan *adj* forgetful

zaboraviti *v* to forget

zabrana *f* **1.** prohibition **2.** embargo

zabraniti, zabranjivati *v* to prohibit

zabranjen *adj* off limits

zabraviti *v* to lock

zabrinut *adj* worried

zabrinuti se *v* to be worried

zabrinutost *f* worry

zabuna *f* **1.** mistake **2.** confusion

zabuniti se *v* to make a mistake

zabunom *adv* by mistake

zabušant *m* slacker

zabušavati *v* to shirk

zabušiti se *v* to collide with

zaceliti, zacijeliti *v* to heal

zacelo, zacijelo *adv* certainly

zacrvenjeti se *v* to blush

zacrvenjeti *v* to redden

začarati *v* to bewitch

začas *adv* right away

začepiti *v* **1.** to plug **2.** to block

začepljenje *n* obstruction

začetak *m* **1.** beginning **2.** conception

začeti *v* **1.** to become pregnant **2.** to conceive

začetnik *m* creator

začeće *n* conception

začin *m* spice

začiniti *v* to spice

začinjen *adj* spiced

začuditi *v* to surprise

začuditi se *v* to be surprised

začuđen *adj* surprised
zaći *v* to go down
zadah *m* stink
zadatak *m* assignment
zadati *v* 1. to assign 2. to cause
zadaviti *v* to choke
zadaća *f*, **zadatak** *m* 1. task 2. problem 3. homework
zadesiti *v* to happen to
zadihan *adj* breathless
zadihati se *v* to gasp
zadijevati *v* to annoy
zadimiti *v* to fill with smoke
zadimljen *adj* smoky
zadirati *v* to encroach (**u** on)
zadirkivanje *n* teasing
zadirkivati *v* to tease
zadiviti *v* to amaze
zadnji *adj* 1. last 2. latest
zadnji misao *adj* ulterior
zadnjica *f* 1. bottom 2. buttocks
zadobiti *v* to get
zadocneli *adj* late
zadocniti *v* to be late
zadovoljan *adj* satisfied
zadovoljavajući *v* satisfactory
zadovoljavati *v* to satisfy
zadovoljenje *n* satisfaction
zadovoljiti *v* to satisfy
zadovoljiti se *v* to be satisfied with
zadovoljština *f* 1. satisfaction 2. compensation
zadovoljstvo *n* satisfaction
zadrhtati *v* to tremble
zadrijemati *v* to doze
zadrška *f* delay
zadruga *f* 1. community 2. co-operative
zadržati, zadržavati *v* 1. to hinder 2. to delay 3. to keep
zadubljen *adj* thoughtful
zadupsti se *v* to be thoughtful

zadušiti se *v* 1. to choke 2. to suffocate
zadužbina *f* foundation
zadužiti se *v* 1. to oblige 2. to get into debt
zadužnica *f* I.O.U. note
zađevica *f* quarrel
zagaditi *v* 1. to pollute 2. to contaminate
zagađen *adj* 1. polluted 2. contaminated
zagađenost *f*, **zagađivanje** *n* 1. pollution 2. contamination
zagasit *adj* dark
zaglavlje *n* heading
zaglušiti *v* to deafen
zagnjuriti *v* 1. to dive 2. to immerse
zagnojiti se *v* to suppurate
zagolicati *v* to tickle
zagonetan *adj* mysterious
zagonetka *f* 1. mystery 2. puzzle
zagorčiti *v* to make bitter
zagoreo *adj* burnt
zagoreti *v* to burn
zagovarati *v* to intercede
zagovor *m* intercession
zagrada *f* bracket(s)
zagraditi *v* to fence in
zagrcnuti se *v* to choke
zagrijati *v* to warm up
zagrijati se *v* to get enthusiastic about
zagristi *v* to bite
zagrižen *adj* fanatical
zagrižljiv *adj* sarcastic
zagrliti *v* to hug
zagrljaj *m* hug
zagroziti se *v* to threaten
zagušiti (se) *v* 1. to choke 2. to suffocate
zagušljiv *adj* stifling
zahladiti *v* to become cold

zahod *m* toilet
zahrđati *v* to rust
zahtev *m* 1. demand 2. requirement
zahtevati, zahtijevati *v* 1. to demand 2. require
zahtjev *m* 1. demand 2. requirement
zahvala *f* gratitude
zahvalan *adj* grateful
zahvaliti, zahvaljivati *v* to thank
zahvaljujući *prep* thanks to
zahvalnost *f* gratitude
zahvat *m* grip
zahvatiti *v* to grip
zainteresiran *adj* interested (za in)
zaista *adv* really
zajam *m* loan
zajamčiti *v* to guarantee
zajašiti *v* to mount
zajedljiv *adj* sarcastic
zajedljivo *adv* sarcastically
zajedljivost *f* sarcasm
zajednica *f* 1. community 2. society 3. union
zajednički *adj* 1. common 2. joint
zajedno *adv* altogether
zajmodavac *m* 1. lender 2. creditor
zajutrak *m* breakfast
zakačiti *v* to fasten
zakasneli *adj* late
zakasniti *v* to be late
zakašjenje *n* lateness
zakazati *v* to make an appointment
zaketva *f* 1. oath 2. kriva zaketva perjury
zakidati *v* to stint
zaklada *f* foundation
zaklati *v* to slaughter
zaklet *adj* sworn
zakleti, zakleti se *v* 1. to take an oath 2. **krivo se zakleti** to perjure oneself 3. **lažno se zakleti** to commit perjury

zaklinjati *v* to implore
zaklinjati se *v* to take an oath
zaključak *m* conclusion
zaključan *adj* 1. conclusive 2. locked up
zaključati *v* to lock up
zaključiti *v* to conclude
zaključiti mir *m* to make peace
zaključnica *f* (com.) agreement
zaključno *adv* inclusive
zaklon *m* shelter
zakloniti *v* 1. to shelter 2. to guard
zakloniti se *v* to take shelter
zaklonjen *adj* protected
zakočiti *v* to stop
zakon *m* law
zakon i red law and order
zakon rulje *m* mob rule
zakonik *m* code
zakonit *adj* legal
zakonito *adv* legally
zakonitost *f* legality
zakonodavac *m* legislator
zakonodavan *adj* legislative
zakonodavstvo *n* legislation
zakonski *adj* 1. legal 2. statutory
zakopati *v* to bury
zakopčati *v* to button up
zakoračiti *v* to step into
zakovati *v* to rivet
zakrabuljiti se *v* to disguise oneself
zakračunati *v* to bolt
zakrčen *adj* blocked
zakrčiti *v* to block
zakrenuti, zakretati *v* to turn
zakriliti *v* to protect
zakrilje *n* protection
zakrpa *f* patch
zakrpati *v* to patch
zakržljao *adj* stunted
zakucati *v* to knock

zakulisan *adj* secret
zakup *m* 1. rent 2. lease
zakupac *m* 1. tenant 2. leaseholder
zakupiti *v* 1. to rent 2. to lease
zakupnik *m* 1. tenant 2. leaseholder
zakupnina *f* rent
zakuska *f* 1. snack 2. refreshments
zakuvati *v* to boil
zakvačiti *v* to fasten
zalagaonica *f* pawnbroker's
zalagati *v* to pawn
zalagati se *v* to plead
zalaz, zalazak *m* sunset
zalaziti *v* 1. to set 2. to frequent
zalediti *v* to freeze
zaleđe *n* 1. background 2. rear 3. backing
zaleđen *adj* frozen
zalemiti *v* to solder
zalepiti *v* to glue
zaletjeti se *v* to rush forward
zaliha *f* 1. stock 2. supply
zalijeniti se *v* to get lazy
zalijepiti *v* to stick
zalijevati *v* 1. to water 2. to irrigate
zalisci *mpl* whiskers
zalistak *m* (med.) valve
zaliti *v* 1. to water 2. to lead
zaliv *m* 1. bay 2. gulf
zalivača *f* sprinkler
zaljev *m* 1. bay 2. gulf
zaljubiti se *v* to fall in love
zaljubljen *adj* in love
zalog *m* 1. pledge 2. mortgage
zaloga *f* guarantee
zalogaj *m* 1. bite 2. snack
založiti *v* 1. to pawn 2. to mortgage 3. to snack
založnica *f* pawn-ticket
zalučiti *v* to wean
zaludan *adj* useless
zaludjeti *v* to fascinate

zalupiti *v* to slam
zalutati *v* to get lost
zamah *m* swing
zamahnuti *v* to swing
zamak *m* castle
zamalo *adv* almost
zamamljiv *adj* tempting
zamašan *adj* big
zamatati *v* to wrap
zamazan *adj* dirty
zamazati *v* to make dirty
zamena *f* exchange
zamenica *f* pronoun
zamenik *m* deputy
zamenik komandanta, zamjenik komandanta *m* second-in-command
zameniti *v* to exchange
zamerka *f* objection
zametak *m* embryo
zametnuti *v* to misplace
zamijeniti *v* to exchange
zamisao *f* 1. idea 2. plan
zamisliti *v* 1. to imagine 2. to plan
zamišljen *adj* thoughtful
zamjena *f* exchange
zamjenica *f* pronoun
zamjenik *m* 1. substitute 2. deputy
zamjenjivati *v* 1. to exchange 2. to confuse
zamjeravati, zamjeriti *v* to resent
zamka *f* trap
zamoliti *v* 1. to ask 2. to beg
zamor *m* tiredness
zamoriti *v* to tire
zamotak *m* 1. parcel 2. packet
zamotati *v* to wrap up
zamotuljak *m* 1. parcel 2. packet
zamračiti *v* to dim
zamrljati *v* to stain
zamrsiti *v* to tangle up
zamršen *adj* 1. entangled 2.

complicated
zamrznut *adj* frozen
zamrznuti *v* to freeze
zamuknuti *v* to become silent
zamutiti *v* to stir up
zanat *m* craft
zanatlija *f* craftsman
zanatstvo *n* arts and crafts
zanemaren *adj* neglected
zanemariti, zanemarivati *v* 1. to neglect 2. to fail to
zanemarljiv *adj* negligible
zanemeti *v* to be quiet
zanesen *adj* 1. enthusiastic 2. fanatical
zanesenjak *m* 1. enthusiast 2. fanatic
zanesenost *f* 1. enthusiasm 2. fanaticism
zanijekati *v* to deny
zanijemiti *v* to be speechless
zanijeti *v* 1. to carry away 2. to become pregnant
zanijeti se *v* to get carried away
zanimanje *n* 1. interest 2. occupation
zanimati se *v* 1. to be interested in 2. to be occupied with
zanimljiv *adj* interesting
zanos *m* enthusiasm
zanosan *adj* fascinating
zanositi se *v* to be enthusiastic
zanovijetati *v* to grumble
zao *adj* 1. bad 2. evil
zaobilazak *m* detour
zaobići, zaobilaziti *v* 1. to go round 2. to make a detour
zaogrnuti *v* to cloak
zaokrenuti *v* to turn round
zaokret *m* turning point
zaokružiti *v* to surround
zaokupiti *v* 1. to absorb 2. to occupy

zaoštren *adj* sharpened
zaoštriti *v* to sharpen
zaostalost *f* lack of development
zaostao *adj* 1. behind 2. underdeveloped 3. retarded
zaostati *v* to lag
zaostavština *f* inheritance
zaova *f* sister-in-law
zapad *m* 1. west 2. sunset
zapadati *v* 1. to set 2. to cost
zapadni *adj* 1. west 2. western
zapadnjak *m* westerner
zapadno *adv* westwards
zapaliti *v* 1. to set fire to 2. to ignite 3. to turn on
zapaliti se *v* to catch fire
zapaliti žigicu *v* to strike a match
zapaljenje *n* inflammation
zapaljenje pluća *f* pneumonia
zapaljiv *adj* inflammable
zapaljiva bomba *f* fire bomb
zapamtiti *v* to remember
zapanjen *adj* amazed
zapanjenost *f* amazement
zapanjiti *v* to amaze
zapapriti *v* to season
zaparan *adj* sultry
zaparati *v* to scratch
zapasti *v* 1. to set 2. to cost
zapaziti *v* to notice
zapažanje *n* observation
zapažen *adj* noticeable
zapečatiti *v* to seal up
zapeti *v* 1. to be stuck 2. to try hard
zapis *m* note
zapisati *v* to note
zapisati *v* to videotape
zapisničar *m* 1. minutes taker 2. (spor.) scorer
zapisnik *m* minutes of a meeting
zapitati *v* to inquire
zapjevati *v* to burst into song

zaplakati *v* to burst into tears
zaplašen *adj* scared
zaplašiti *v* to scare
zapleniti *v* to take away
zaplesti *v* 1. to entangle 2. to confuse
zaplesti se *v* 1. to get entangled 2. to get confused
zaplet, zapletaj *m* 1. complication 2. plot
zapletati *v see* **zaplesti**
zaplijeniti *v* 1. to capture 2. to confiscate
zapljesniviti *v* to become mouldy
zaploviti *v* to set sail
započeti *v* to start
zapomagati *v* to cry for help
zapor *m* bolt
zaporka *f* bracket
zaposesti, zaposjednuti, zaposjedati, zaposjesti *v* to occupy
zaposlen *adj* employed
zaposlenje *n* job
zaposlenost *f* employment
zaposliti *v* to employ
zapostaviti, zapostavljati *v* 1. to neglect 2. to ignore
zapostavljen *adj* 1. neglected 2. ignored
zapovedati *v* to command
zapovednik *m* 1. commander 2. commander-in-chief
zapovedništvo *n* 1. command 2. authority
zapovest, zapovijed *m* order
zapovijedati, zapovjediti *v* to command
zapovjednički *adj* commanding
zapovjedni način *m* imperative
zapovjednik *m* 1. commander 2. commander-in-chief

zapovjedništvo *n* 1. command 2. authority
zaprašiti *v* to spray
zapravo *adv* in fact
zaprega *f* team
zapregnuti *v* to harness
zapreka *f* 1. obstacle 2. **utrka sa zapreka ma** (spor.) hurdles
zapremati, zapremiti *v* to occupy
zapremina *f* volume
zaprepašten *adj* panic-stricken
zaprepaštenje *n* panic
zaprepašćen *adj* panic-stricken
zaprepašćenje *n* panic
zaprepastiti (se) *v* to panic
zapriječiti *v* to obstruct
zaprijetiti se *v* to threaten
zaprljan *adj* dirty
zaprljati *v* to make dirty
zaprositi *v* to propose marriage
zapt *m* discipline
zapučak *m* buttonhole
zapušač *m* cork
zapušiti *v* to cork
zapušten *adj* 1. neglected 2. abandoned
zapustiti, zapuštati *v* 1. to neglect 2. to abandon
zapustiti se *v* 1. to be neglected 2. to be careless
zar maybe
zaračunati previše *v* to overcharge
zaračunati *v* to charge
zarada *f* earnings
zaraditi *v* to earn
zarasti *v* to heal
zaratiti se *v* to wage war
zaravan *m* plateau
zaravnati *v* to level out
zaraza *f* 1. infection 2. epidemic
zarazan *adj* 1. infectious 2. epidemic
zaraziti *v* to infect

zaraćen *adj* warring
zarđao *adj* rusty
zarđati *v* to rust
zarediti *v* to ordain
zarez *m* 1. cut 2. comma
zarezati *v* to cut into
zarobiti *v* to capture
zarobljenički logor *m* prisoner of war camp, POW camp
zarobljenički *adj* prisoner of war, POW
zarobljenik *m* captive
zarobljeništvo *n* captivity
zaroniti *v* to plunge
zaručen *adj* engaged
zaručiti se *v* to get engaged
zaručnica *f* fiancée
zaručnik *m* fiancé
zaruke *fpl* engagement
zarumenjeti se *v* to blush
zasaditi *v* to plant
zaseban *adj* separate
zasebno *adv* separately
zaseda *f* ambush
zasedanje *n* meeting
zasedati *v* to hold a meeting
zasejati *v* to sow
zaselak *m* hamlet
zaseniti *v* to impress
zasigurno *adv* without fail
zasijati *v* to sow
zasipati, zasipavati *v* to fill in
zasititi *v* to saturate
zasićen *adj* saturated
zasićenost *f* saturation
zasjati *v* 1. to brighten 2. to shine
zasjeda *f* ambush
zasjedanje *n* session
zasjedati *v* to be in session
zasjeniti *v* to screen
zaskijepiti *v* 1. to dazzle 2. to deceive

zaskočiti *v* to surprise
zasladiti *v* to sweeten
zaslepljen *adj* blinded
zaslepljenost *f* blindness
zaslon *m* screen
zasloniti *v* to screen
zasluga *f* merit
zaslužan *adj* meritorious
zaslužiti, zasluživati *v* to merit
zasnovati *v* 1. to plan 2. to found
zaspati *v* to fall asleep
zasramiti *v* to shame
zasramljen *adj* ashamed
zašarafiti *v* to screw
zašećeriti *v* to sweeten
zašiljiti *v* to sharpen
zašiti *v* to sew up
zaštedjeti *v* to save
zaštita *f* 1. protection 2. **zaštita radnika** occupational health 3. **protivavionska/protuzračna zaštita** antiaircraft defence
zaštititi *v* to protect
zaštitni znak *m* trademark
zaštitnik *m* 1. protector 2. patron 3. **svetac zaštitnik** patron saint
zaštitno pismo *n* safe conduct
zaštićen *adj* protected
zaštićivati *v* to protect
zašto? why?
zašto ne? why not?
zastareo, zastario *adj* 1. old-fashioned 2. out of date 3. expired
zastarelost, zastarjelost *f* expiry
zatareti, zastarjeti *v* 1. to be old-fashioned 2. to go out of date 3. to expire
zastati *v* to stop
zastava *f* flag
zastidjeti se *v* to be ashamed
zastirati *v* to screen

zastoj *m* 1. lull 2. standstill
zastor *m* 1. curtain 2. blind
zastraniti, zastranjivati *v* 1. to deviate 2. to stray
zastranjivanje *n* deviation
zastrašiti, zastrašivati *v* to intimidate
zastrašivanje *n* intimidation
zastrašujući *v* deterrant
zastrijeti, zastrti *v* 1. to cover 2. to screen
zastupanje *n* representation
zastupati *v* to represent
zastupnik *m* 1. representative 2. agent
zastupstvo, zastupništvo *n* 1. representation 2. agency
zasukati *v* to roll up
zasun *m* bolt
zasunuti *v* to bolt
zasušiti se *v* to dry up
zasuti *v* to bury
zasuti vatrom *v* (mil.) to shell
zasvijetliti *v* to flash
zatajiti *v* 1. to hide 2. to hush up
zataškati *v* 1. to suppress 2. (pol.) to whitewash
zataškavanje *n* 1. suppression 2. (pol.) whitewash
zategnut *adj* tight
zategnuti *v* 1. to stretch 2. to delay
zategnutost *f* tension
zatezati *v* 1. to stretch 2. to delay
zateći *v* 1. to find 2. to catch red-handed
zatiljak *m* nape
zatim *adv* afterwards
zatirati *v* to destroy
zatišje *n* calm
zato 1. *adv* therefore 2. *conj* because
zato da *conj* in order to
zatočenik *m* prisoner

zatomiti, zatomljivati *v* to suppress
zaton *m* bay
zatražiti *v* 1. to ask for 2. to apply for
zatrovati *v* to poison
zatrpati *v* to fill up
zatrti *v* to destroy
zatrudneti *v* to become pregnant
zatureti *v* to misplace
zatvarač *m* cover
zatvarati, zatvoriti *v* 1. to close 2. to turn off
zatvor *m* prison
zatvoren *adj* closed
zatvorenik *m* prisoner
zatvoriti *v* 1. to close 2. to do up
zaudarati *v* to stink
zauške *fpl* mumps
zaušnica *f* to slap
zaustaviti, zaustavljati *v* to halt
zaustavna traka *f* road verge; hard shoulder
zauvek, za uvijek, zauvijek *m* forever
zauzdati *v* to curb
zauzeti, zauzimati *v* to capture
zauzeti položaj *v* (mil.) to occupy a position
zauzeti se *v* to intercede
zauzeće *n* capture
zavada *f* 1. quarrel 2. feud
zavaditi se *v* to quarrel
zavađen *adj* variance
zavaren *adj* welded
zavariti *v* to weld
zavarivač *m* welder
zavarivanje *n* 1. welding 2. aparat za zavarivanje welding torch
zavejan *adj* snowed in
zavera *f* conspiracy
zaverenik *m* conspirator

zavesa *f* curtain
zaveštanje *n* will and testament
zaveštati *v* to bequeath
zavesti *v* to mislead
zavet *m* vow
zavetovati se *v* to vow
zavezan *adj* bound
zavezati *v* to bind
zavežljaj *m* bundle
zavičaj *m* 1. homeland 2. čežnja za zavičajem homesickness
zavidan *adj* jealous
zavideti, zavidjeti, zaviđati *v* to be jealous
zavidljiv *adj* jealous
zavidljivost *f* jealousy
zavijati *v* 1. to wrap 2. to turn 3. to howl
zavijutak *m* turn
zaviknuti *v* to shout
zaviriti, zavirivati *v* to peer
zavisan *adj* dependent
zavisiti *v* to depend on
zavisnost *f* dependence
zavist *f* jealousy
zavistan *adj* jealous
zaviti *v* to wrap up
zavitlati *v* to swing
zavjera *f* conspiracy
zavjerenik *m* conspirator
zavjeriti se *v* to conspire
zavjesa *f* 1. curtain 2. blind
zavjet *m* vow
zavjetovati se *v* to vow
zavlačiti *v* to delay
zavod *m* 1. institute 2. institution
zavod za zapošljavanje *m* employment agency/bureau
zavoditi *v* to seduce
zavodljiv *adj* seductive
zavodljivost *f* seductiveness
zavodnik *m*, **zavodnica** *f* seducer

zavođenje *n* seduction
zavoj *m* 1. turn 2. bandage 3. (med.) sling
zavojevač *m* aggressor
zavojnica *f* spiral
zavojničiti (se) *v* (mil.) to enlist
zavoleti, zavoljeti *v* to fall in love
zavor *m* brake
zavrijediti *v* to deserve
zavrnuti *v* 1. to turn 2. to roll up
završan *adj* final
završen *adj* finished
završetak *m* finish
završiti *v* to finish
zavrtanj *m* screw
zavrtati *v* 1. to turn 2. to roll up
zavrteti, zavrtjeti *v* to spin
zavući *v* to insert
zazidati *v* to wall in
zazirati *v* to abhor
zazivati *v* to invoke
zazor *m* clearance
zazoran *adj* offensive
zazvoniti *v* to ring
zaželeti *v* to wish
zbaciti *v* to discard
zbeg *m* 1. refuge 2. refugees
zbijati *v* to squeeze in
zbijen *adj* 1. compact 2. crowded
zbijenost *f* 1. compactness 2. crowding
zbilja *f* 1. reality 2. really
zbir *m* total
zbirka *f* collection
zbirni *adj* collective
zbiti se, zbivati se *v* to happen
zbiti *v* to compress
zbivanje *n* occurrence
zbjeg *m* 1. refuge 2. refugees
zbog *prep* because of
zbog toga therefore
zbogom goodbye

zbor *m* 1. meeting 2. assembly 3. convention 4. staff 5. choir

zbornik *m* 1. collection 2. code

zbrajati *v* 1. to add up 2. to total

zbrinuti *v* to take care of

zbrka *f* confusion

zbrkati *v* to confuse

zbroj *m* 1. total 2. addition

zbrojiti *v* 1. to add up 2. to total

zbuniti *v* to confuse

zbunjen *adj* confused

zbunjenost *f* confusion

zdela, zdjela *f* dish

zdenac *m* well

zdepast *adj* stocky

zdrav *adj* healthy

zdravica *f* toast

zdraviti se *v* to shake hands

zdravlje *n* 1. health 2. U vaše zdravlje! To your health!

zdravo! hello!

zdravsten *adj* health

zdravstena služba, zdravstvo *n* health services

zdravstvena nega/njega *f* healthcare

zdrobiti *v* to crush

združen *adj* united

združiti se *v* 1. to unite 2. to be allied with

zdušan *adj* eager

zdvajati *v* to be desperate

zdvojan *adj* desperate

zdvojiti *v* to be desperate

zdvojnost *f* despair

zeba *f* finch

zebnja *f* anxiety

zebra *f* zebra

zec *m* hare

zelen 1. *adj* green 2. *f* vegetables

zelenaštvo *n* usury

zelenilo *n* 1. vegetation 2. vegetables

zelenkada *f* daffodil

zelenkast *adj* greenish

zelje *n* cabbage

zemaljska kugla *f* globe

zemaljski *adj* earth

zemlja *f* 1. soil 2. land 3. country 4. earth

zemljak *m* countryman

zemljan *adj* earthen

zemljano posuđe *n* earthenware

zemljišni *adj* land

zemljište *n* 1. plot of land 2. site 3. terrain

zemljomer, zemljomjer *m* surveyor

zemljopis *m* geography

zemljoposednik, zemljoposjednik *m* land-owner

zemljoradnička zadruga *f* collective farm

zemljoradnik *m* farmer

zemljoradnja *f* agriculture

zemljotres *m* earthquake

zemljouz *m* isthmus

zemljovid *m* map

zenica *f* pupil

zenit *m* zenith

zepsti *v* 1. to freeze 2. to be cold

zeroks *m* photocopy

zeroksirati *v* to photocopy

zet *m* son-in-law

zevati *v* to yawn

zgaziti *v* to crush

zglavak, zglob *m* joint

zgnječiti *v* to crush

zgoda *f* opportunity

zgodan *adj* 1. suitable 2. amusing 3. handsome, pretty

zgoditak *m* prize

zgoditi se *v* to happen

zgodno *adv* conveniently

zgotoviti *v* 1. to prepare 2. to finish

zgrabiti *v* to catch
zgrada *f* building
zgražati se *v* to be shocked
zgrbljen *adj* bent over
zgrčen *adj* contracted
zgrčiti se *v* to be contracted
zgrčiti *v* to contract
zgrejati, zgrjati *v* to warm
zgromiti *v* to squash
zgroziti se *v* to be shocked
zgrožen *adj* disgusted
zgrtati, zgrnuti *v* 1. to shovel 2. to hoard
zgrušiti se *v* 1. to clot 2. to condense
zgusnuti se *v* to condense
zgužvati *v* to crumple
zibati *v* to rock
zid *m* wall
zidanje *n* building
zidar *m* 1. bricklayer 2. mason 3. slobodni zidar freemason
zidarstvo *n* bricklaying
zidati *v* to build
zidine *fpl* walls
zidne tapete *fpl* wallpaper
zidni *adj* wall
ziherica *f* safety-pin
zijevati *v* to yawn
zima *f* winter
zimi *adv* in winter
zimovati *v* to spend the winter
zimovnik *m* winter quarters
zimski sportovi *mpl* winter sports
zimski *adj* winter
zimzelen *adj* evergreen
zip *m* zip
zjapiti *v* to gape
zjenica *f* pupil
zlatan *adj* gold
zlatar *m* goldsmith
zlatica *f* buttercup

zlatnik *m* gold coin
zlatnina *f* jewellery
zlato *n* gold
zlikovac *m* criminal
zlikovački *adj* criminal
zlo *n* 1. evil 2. harm 3. badly
zloba *f* malice
zloban *adj* malicious
zločest *adj* wicked
zločin *m* 1. crime 2. ratni zločin war crime
zločinac *m* 1. criminal 2. ratni zločinac war criminal
zločinački *adj* criminal
zlodelo *n* crime
zloglasan *adj* notorious
zlokoban *adj* ominous
zlonameran, zlonamjeran *adj* malicious
zlopatiti se *v* to suffer
zlorabiti *v* to misuse
zloradost *f* malice
zlostavljanje *n* mistreatment
zlostavljati *v* to mistreat
zlosutan *adj* ominous, foreboding
zlotvor *m* criminal
zloupotreba *f* mistreatment
zloupotrebiti *v* to mistreat
zlovolja *f* bad temper
zlovoljan *adj* bad-tempered
zloća *f* wickedness
zloćudan *adj* malevolent
zluradost *f* malice
zmaj *m* 1. dragon 2. kite
zmija *f* snake
značaj *m* 1. character 2. significance
značajan *adj* 1. characteristic 2. significant
značajka *f* feature
značajnost *f* 1. characteristic 2. significance

značenje *n* 1. meaning 2. significance

značiti *v* 1. to mean 2. to signify

značka *f* badge

znak *m* 1. sign 2. symbol

znalac *m* expert

znamen *adj* mark

znamenit *adj* famous

znamenitost *f* 1. importance 2. place of interest

znamenitosti *fpl* places of interest

znamenje *n* sign

znamenka *f* mark

znan *adj* known

znanac, znanica *f* acquaintance

znanje *n* knowledge

znanost *f* 1. science 2. prirodne znanosti natural sciences

znanstven *adj* scientific

znanstvenik *m* scientist

znatan *adj* considerable

znati *v* to know (how)

znatiželja *f* curiosity

znatiželjan *adj* curious

znatno *adv* considerably

znoj *m* sweat

znojan, znojav *adj* sweaty

znojenje *n* sweating

znojiti se *v* to sweat

zob *f* oats

zobati *v* to peck

zodijak *m* zodiac

zona *f* 1. zone 2. zona sigurnosti safety zone

zonalan, zonski *adj* zonal

zoolog *m* zoologist

zoologija *f* zoology

zoološki vrt *m* zoo

zoološki *adj* zoological

zora *f* dawn

zov *m* call

zova *f* elder

zračan *adj* air

zračenje *n* radiation

zračiti *v* to radiate

zračna pošta *f* air mail

zračna pruga *f* airline

zračna sisaljka *f* air-pump

zračni napad *m* air-raid

zračni ventil *m* air-valve

zrak *m* 1. air 2. ray

zraka *f* 1. ray 2. rentgenske zrake X-rays

zrakoplovstvo *n* 1. aviation 2. air force

zrakoprazan prostor *m* vacuum

zrcalo *n* mirror

zrelost *f* 1. ripeness 2. maturity

zreo *adj* 1. ripe 2. mature

zreti *v* 1. to ripen 2. to mature

zrikav *adj* cross-eyed

zrnast *adj* granular

zrnce *n* 1. grain 2. cell

zrnevlje *n* grains

zrno *n* 1. grain 2. bullet

zub *m* tooth

zubac *m* 1. cog 2. prong

zubalo *n* dentures

zubar *m* dentist

zubna protetika *f* prosthodontics

zubni *adj* dental

zubno meso *n* gums

zubobolja *f* toothache

zujati *v* to hum

zum-sistem *m* zoom

zumbul *m* hyacinth

zupčanik *m* gear

zupčast *adj* indented

zupčati *v* to indent

zuriti *v* to stare at

zvanica *f* guest

zvaničan *adj* formal

zvanična izjava *f* official statement

zvaničnik *m* official

zvanično *adv* officially
zvanje *n* 1. profession 2. title 3. rank
zvati *v* to call
zvečka *f* rattle
zveckati, zvečati *v* to rattle
zveketati *v* to rattle
zver *m* beast
zverka *f* velika zverka VIP
zverski *adj* savage
zverstvo *n* atrocity
zvezda *f* star
zvijer *m* beast
zvijezda *f* star
zvinuti, zviždati *v* to whistle
zvižduk *m* whistle
zvjerinjak *m* zoo
zvjerka *f* velika zvjerka VIP
zvjerski *adj* savage
zvjerstvo *n* atrocity

zvjezdarnica *f* observatory
zvonak *adj* resonant
zvonar *m* sacristan
zvonce *n* bell
zvončić *m* bluebell
zvonik *m* bell-tower
zvoniti *v* to ring
zvonjava *f* ringing
zvono *n* bell
zvrk *m* top
zvrkast *adj* crazy
zvučan *adj* resonant
zvučati *v* to resound
zvučna traka *f* soundtrack
zvučni efekti *v* sound effects
zvučnik *m* 1. loudspeaker 2. megaphone
zvučnost *f* resonance
zvuk *m* sound

Ž

žaba *f* frog
žabica *f* cracker
žaca, žaco *m* (sl.) cop
žacati se *v* to be reluctant
žagoriti *v* to murmur
žal *m* beach
žalac *m* sting
žalba *f* 1. complaint 2. grievance
žalbiti *v* to regret
žalbiti se *v* to complain
žalfija *f* sage
žaliti *v* to regret
žaljenje *n* regret
žalosno *adv* sadly
žalost *f* sadness
žalostan *adj* sad
žalostiti *v* to sadden
žalostiti se *v* to be sad
žalovati *v* to mourn
žaluzija *f* (venetian) blind
žamoriti *v* to murmur
žandarm *m* gendarme
žandarmerija *f* gendarmerie
žanr *m* genre
žao 1. harm 2. **Žao mi je.** I am sorry.
žaoka *f* sting
žar *m* 1. embers 2. enthusiasm
žara *f* 1. urn 2. ballot-box
žarač *m* poker
žargon *m* jargon
žarište *n* focus
žariti se *v* to be red-hot
žariti *v* to sting
žarki *adj* 1. red-hot 2. enthusiastic
žarulja *f* light bulb
žbica *f* spoke

žbuka *f* plaster
žbukati *v* to plaster
žbun *m* bush
žderati *v* to scoff up
ždral *m* crane
ždrebac, ždrijebac *m* stallion
ždrebe, ždrijebe *n* foal
ždrelo, ždrijelo *n* throat
žedan *adj* thirsty
žeđ, žeđa *f* thirst
žeđati *v* to be thirsty
žega *f* heat
želeti *v* to want
železan *adj* iron
železara *f* 1. ironworks 2. ironmonger's
železarija *f* ironmonger's
železnica *f* 1. railway; railroad 2. **podzemna železnica** the underground; subway
železničar *m* railwayman
železnička stanica *f* railway station
železnički *adj* railway
železo *n* 1. iron 2. **staro železo** scrap iron
želja *f* wish
željan *adj* eager
željeti *v* 1. to want 2. to wish
željezan *adj* iron
željezara *f* 1. ironworks 2. ironmonger's
željezarija *f* ironmonger's
željeznica *f* 1. railway; railroad 2. **podzemna željeznica** the underground; subway
željezničar *m* railwayman

željeznička stanica *f* railway station
željeznički *adj* railway
željezo *n* 1. iron 2. staro željezo scrap iron
željno *adv* eagerly
želud *m* acorn
želudac *m* stomach
želudačni *adj* gastric
žemička, žemlja *f* roll
žena *f* 1. woman 2. wife
ženidba *f* marriage
ženiti se *v* to get married
ženka *f* female
ženomrzac *m* misogynist
ženski *adj* 1. female 2. feminine 3. women's
ženskinje *n* womenfolk
ženstven *adj* feminine
ženstvenost *f* femininity
žeravica *f* embers
žesta *f* alcohol
žestina *f* violence
žestiti se *v* to get angry
žestok *m* violent
žestoka pića *f* spirits
žetelac *m* reaper
žeti *v* to reap
žeton *m* chip
žetva *f* harvest
žezlo *n* sceptre
žganci *mpl* corn mush
žgaravica *f* heartburn
žica *f* 1. wire 2. string 3. bodljikava žica barbed wire
žica potezne mine *f* (mil.) trip wire
žičan *adj* wire
žičana mreža *f* wire-netting
žičara *f* cable car
židak *m* liquid
Židov *m*, **Židovka** *f* Jew

židovski *adj* Jewish
žig *m* 1. brand 2. stamp
žigica *f* match
žigosati *v* 1. to brand 2. to stamp
žila *f* 1. vein 2. artery
žilav *adj* muscular
žilavost *f* toughness
žilet *m* razor blade
žipon *m* petticoat
žir *m* acorn
žirafa *f* giraffe
žirant *m* endorser
žiri *m* jury
žirirati *v* to endorse
žiro *m* giro
žiro-konto *m* (com/fin.) 1. transfer 2. giro account
žitarica *f* cereal
žitelj *m* inhabitant
žiteljstvo *n* 1. population 2. popis žiteljstva census
žitkost *f* liquidity
žitnica *f* granary
žito *n* 1. corn 2. grain
živ *adj* 1. alive 2. live 3. lively
živa *f* mercury
živac *m* nerve
živad *f* poultry
živahan *adj* active
živahnost *f* activity
živalj *m* population
živčan *adj* nervous
živčani slom *m* nervous breakdown
živčani sustav *adj* nervous system
živeo! cheers!
živeti *v* to live
živež *m* provisions
živi pesak/pijesak *m* quicksand
živica *f* hedge
živina *f* 1. beast 2. poultry
živinski *adj* beastly

živio! cheers!
živjeti v to live
življenje n living
živo adv actively
živo vapno n quicklime
živopisan adj picturesque
živost f activity
život m life
životan adj 1. vital 2. see životni
životariti v to vegetate
životinja f animal
životinjski adj animal
životinjstvo n zoology
životni adj 1. life 2. see životan
životni standard m standard of living
životno osiguranje n life insurance
životopisv m biography
životopisac m biographer
žiža f focus
žižak m weevil
žleb m gutter
žlezda f gland
žlica f spoon
žličica f teaspoon
žlijeb m gutter
žlijezda f gland
žmarci mpl pins and needles
žmiriti v to blink
žmurka f hide-and-seek
žnjeti v to reap

žohar m cockroach
žongler m juggler
žrtva f 1. sacrifice 2. victim
žrtvovanje n sacrifice
žrtvovati v to sacrifice
žrtvovati se v to sacrifice oneself
žrvanj m grindstone
žuboriti v to murmur
žučni kamenac m gall stone
žučnost f bitterness
žudeti, žudjeti v to long for
žudnja f longing
žulj m 1. blister 2. callus
žuljevit adj callous
žuljiti v to pinch
žumance n, **žumanjak** m yolk
žuna f woodpecker
župa f parish
župnik m parish priest
žuran adj 1. hasty 2. urgent
žurba f 1. haste 2. urgency
žuriti se v to be in a hurry
žurnal m magazine
žurnalist(a) m journalist
žurnalistika f journalism
žustar adj brisk
žustrina f briskness
žut adj yellow
žutica f jaundice
žvaka f chewing gum
žvakati v to chew

ENGLISH –
SERBO-CROATIAN

A

a, an [ə, ei; ən, æn] **1.** jedan **2.** neki
abandon [əˈbændən] *v* napustiti
abate [əˈbeit] *v* smanjiti se
abattoir [ˈæbətwaː] *n* klanica
abbey [ˈæbi] *n* opatija
abbreviate [əˈbriːvieit] *v* skratiti
abbreviation [ə,briːviˈeiʃn] *n* skraćenica; kratica
ABC [eibiˈsiː] *n* azbuka
abdicate [ˈæbdikeit] *v* odreći se
abdication [,æbdiˈkeiʃn] *n* odricanje
abdomen [,æbdəmən] *n* trbuh
abdominal [,æbdɔminl] *adj* trbušni
abduct [æbˈdʌkt] *v* oteti
abduction [æbˈdʌktʃn] *n* otmica
abductor [æbˈdʌktə] *n* otmičar
abeyance [əˈbeijəns] *n* **to fall into abeyance** prestati važiti
abhor [æbˈhɔː] *v* gnušati se
abide [æˈbaid] *v* (**abode**) trpeti; trpiti
abide by *v* povinovati se
ability [əˈbiliti] *n* sposobnost
Abkhazia [æbˈkaːzijə] *n* Abhazija
ablative [ˈæblətiv] *n* ablativ
able [ˈeibl] *adj* **to be able** moći
aboard [əˈbɔːd] *adv* ukrcan
abode [əˈbəud] *n* boravište
abolish [əˈbɔliʃ] *v* ukinuti
abortion [əˈbɔːʃn] *n* pobačaj
about [əˈbaut] *prep* **1.** oko **2.** otprilike **3.** približno **4. I am about to go.** Upravo odlazim.
above [əˈbʌv] *prep* **1.** gore **2.** iznad **3.** više
above all *adv* nadasve
abreast [əˈbrest] *adj* **to keep abreast of** ići uporedo sa

abroad [əˈbrɔːd] *adv* u inostranstvu; u inozemstvu
abrogate [ˈæbrəugeit] *v* ukinuti
abrupt [əˈbrʌpt] *adj* iznenadan
abscess [ˈæbses] *n* gnojan čir
absence [ˈæbsəns] *n* odsustvo
absent [ˈæbsənt] *adj* odsutan
absolute [ˈæbsəluːt] *adj* potpun
absolutely [æbsəˈluːtli] *adv* potpuno
absolve [əbˈzɔlv] *v* oprostiti
absorb [əbˈsɔːb] *v* prigušiti
abstain [əbˈstein] *v* **to abstain from voting** uzdržati se od glasanja
abstinence [ˈæbstinəns] *n* uzdržavanje
abstract [ˈabstrækt] *adj* apstraktan
absurd [əbˈsəːd] *adj* apsurdan
abundance [əˈbʌndəns] *n* **1.** izobilje **2. in abundance** u izobilju
abundant [əˈbʌndənt] *adj* izobilan
abuse [əˈbjus] *n* **1.** zloupotreba **2.** psovanje
abuse [əˈbjuːz] *v* **1.** zloupotrebiti **2.** psovati
academic [,ækəˈdemik] **1.** *adj* akademski **2.** teorijski **3.** *n* profesor
academician [,ækədəˈmiʃn] *n* akademik
academy [əˈkædəmi] *n* akademija
accelerate [əkˈseləreit] *v* ubrzati (se)
accelerator [əkˈseləreitə] *n* pedal za gas
accent [ˈæksənt] *n* akcenat
accept [əkˈsept] *v* **1.** prihvatiti **2.** pristati

access [ˈækses] *n* 1. pristup 2. prilaz

accessible [əkˈsesəbl] *adj* pristupačan

accessory [əkˈsesəri] *n* 1. sporedna stvar 2. (leg.) saučesnik

accident [ˈæksidənt] *n* nesrećan; nesretan

accidental [ˌæksiˈdentl] *adj* slučajan

accidentally [ˌæksiˈdentli] *adv* slučajno

acclaim [əˈkleim] 1. *n* aklamacija 2. *v* aklamovati

accommodate [əˈkɔmədeit] *v* 1. smestiti; smjestiti 2. udesiti

accommodation [əˌkɔməˈdeiʃn] *n* smeštaj; smještaj

accompany [əˈkʌmpəni] *v* pratiti

accomplice [əˈkʌmplis] *n* saizvršilac

accomplish [əˈkʌmpliʃ] *v* 1. izvršiti 2. postići

accomplishment [əˈkʌmpliʃmənt] *n* dostignuće

according to [əˈkɔːdiŋ] *prep* 1. prema 2. po

accordion [əˈkɔːdijən] *n* akordeon

account [əˈkaunt] *n* 1. izveštaj; izvještaj 2. (fin.) račun 3. **on account of** zbog

accountancy [əˈkauntənsi] *n* računovodstvo

accountant [əˈkauntənt] *n* računovođa

accounting [əˈkauntiŋ] *n* računovodstvo

accumulate [əˈkjuːmuleit] *v* nagomilati

accumulation [əˌkjuːmuˈleiʃn] *n* akumulacija

accuracy [ˈækjərəsi] *n* tačnost; točnost

accurate [ˈækjərət] *adv* tačan; točan

accusation [ˌækjuːˈzeiʃn] *n* optužba

accusative [əˈkjuːzətiv] *n* akuzativ

accuse [əˈkjuːz] *v* optužiti

accused [əˈkjuːzd] *n* optuženik

accustomed [əˈkʌstəmd] *adj* **to be accustomed to** naviknuti se na

ache [eik] 1. *n* bol 2. *v* boleti; boljeti

achieve [əˈtʃiːv] *v* postići

achievement [əˈtʃiːvmənt] *n* podvig

acid [æsid] *n* kiselina

acid rain *n* kisela kiša

acknowledge [əkˈnɔlidʒ] *v* 1. priznati 2. potvrditi

acknowledgement [əkˈnɔlidʒmənt] *n* 1. priznanje 2. potvrda

acquaintance [əˈkweintəns] *n* poznanstvo

acquire [əˈkwaiə] *v* steći

acquisition [ˌækwiˈziʃn] *n* sticanje

acquit [əˈkwit] *v* osloboditi

acquittal [əˈkwitl] *n* oslobođajuća

acre [ˈeikə] *n* jutro

across [əˈkrɔs] 1. *prep* preko 2. kroz 3. *adv* unakrst

act [ækt] 1. *n* delo; djelo 2. odluka 3. čin 4. *v* postupati 5. igrati

acting [ˈæktiŋ] 1. *adj* privremen 2. *n* gluma

action [ˈækʃn] *n* 1. radnja 2. dejstvo; djejstvo 3. (leg.) postupak 4. (mil.) borba

active [ˈæktiv] *adj* aktivan

activist [ˈæktivist] *n* aktivista

activity [ækˈtivəti] *n* 1. delatnost; djelatnost 2. aktivnost

actor [ˈæktə] *n* glumac

actress [ˈæktris] *n* glumica

actual [ˈæktʃuəl] *adj* stvaran

actually [ˈæktʃuli] *adv/conj* u stvari

acute [əˈkjuːt] *adj* oštar

A.D. (Anno Domini) naše ere

adamant [ˈædəmənt] *adj* tvrd

adapt [əˈdæpt] *v* 1. podesiti 2. prilagoditi se

adapter [əˈdæptə] *n* adapter

add [æd] *v* 1. dodati 2. sabrati

addict [ˈædikt] *n* narkoman

addicted [əˈdiktid] *adj* **to be addicted to** odati se

addiction [əˈdikʃn] *n* 1. odanost 2. narkomanija

addition [əˈdiʃn] *n* 1. dodatak 2. sabiranje 3. **in addition to that** pored toga

additional [əˈdiʃənl] *adj* dodan

address [əˈdres] 1. *n* adresa 2. *v* govoriti

adequate [ˈædikwət] *adj* adekvatan

adhere to [ədˈhiə] *v* 1. lepiti se; lijepiti se 2. držati se

adherent [ədˈhiərənt] *n* sledbenik; sljedbenik

adhesive [ədˈhiːsiv] *adj* lepljiv; ljepljiv

ad hoc committee *n* ad hok komitet

adjacent [əˈdʒeisnt] *adj* susedni; susjedni

adjective [ˈædʒiktiv] *n* pridev; pridjev

adjourn [əˈdʒəːn] *v* odložiti

adjournment [əˈdʒəːnmənt] *n* odloženje

adjust [əˈdʒʌst] *v* podesiti

adjustment [əˈdʒʌstmənt] *n* podešavanje

administer [ədˈministə] *v* upravljati

administration [əd,miniˈstreiʃn] *n* 1. uprava 2. vlada

administrative [ədˈministrətiv] *adj* upravni

administrator [ədˈministreitə] *n* administrator

admiral [ˈædmərəl] *n* admiral

admiration [,ædmiˈreiʃn] *n* divljenje

admire [ədˈmaiə] *v* 1. diviti se 2. obožavati

admission [ədˈmiʃn] *n* 1. ulazak 2. priznanje

admit [ədˈmit] *v* 1. priznati 2. primiti

adolescence [,ædəˈlesns] *n* mladićke godine

adolescent [,ædəˈlesnt] *n* mladić

adopt [əˈdɔpt] *v* usvojiti

adoption [əˈdɔpʃn] *n* usvojenje

adoration [,ædəˈreiʃn] *n* obožavanje

adore [əˈdɔː] *v* obožavati

adornment [əˈdɔːnmənt] *n* ukras

adult [ˈædʌlt; əˈdʌlt] 1. *adj* odrastao 2. *n* odrasla osoba

adultery [əˈdʌltəri] *n* preljuba

advance [ədˈvaːns] 1. *adj* (mil.) isturen 2. *n* napredovanje 3. (fin.) akontacija 4. (mil) nastupanje 5. **in advance** unapred; unaprijed 6. *v* napredovati

advantage [ədˈvaːntidʒ] *n* 1. prednost 2. **to take advantage of something** iskoristiti nešto

adventure [ədˈventʃə] *n* 1. avantura 2. doživljaj

adverb [ˈædvəːb] *n* prilog

adverse [ˈædvəːs] *adj* negativan

advert [ˈædvəːt] *n* oglas

advertise [ˈædvətaiz] *v* objaviti oglas

advertisement [ædˈvəːtismənt] *n* oglas

advertising [,ædvəˈtaiziŋ] *n* reklama

advice [ədˈvais] *n* 1. savet; savjet 2. **to give advice** dati savet

advisable [ədˈvaizəbl] *adj* koristan

advise [ədˈvaiz] *v* savetovati; savjetovati

adviser, advisor [əd'vaizə] *n*
savetnik; savjetnik

advisory [əd'vaizəri] *adj*
savetodavan; savjetodavan

advisory committee *n*
savetodavni odbor

advocate [ˈædvəkət] *n* advokat

advocate [ˈædvəkeit] *v* zauzimati

Aegean Sea [iˈdʒiːənˈsiː] *n* Egejsko
more

aerial [ˈeəriəl] 1. *adj* avionski 2. *n*
antena

aeroplane [ˈeərəplein] *n* avion

affair [əˈfeə] *n* 1. posao 2. love
affair ljubavna veza 3. foreign
affairs spoljni poslovi

affect [əˈfekt] *v* uticati

affection [əˈfekʃn] *n* naklonjenost

affectionate [əˈfekʃənət] *adj*
nežan; njeæan

affidavit [ˌæfiˈdeivit] *n* pismen iskaz

afflict [əˈflikt] *v* mučiti

affirmative [əˈfəːmətiv] *adj*
affirmative action potvrdna/
pozitivna diskriminacija

affluent [ˈæfluənt] *adj* bogat

afford [əˈfɔːd] *v* priuštiti: He
cannot afford a house. On sebi
nemože da priuští kuću.

afraid [əˈfreid] *adj* 1. uplašen 2.
I'm afraid that... Na zalošt...

Africa [ˈæfrikə] *n* Afrika

African [ˈæfrikən] 1. *adj* afrički 2. *n*
Afrikanac; Afričanin

after [ˈaːftə] 1. *prep* posle; poslije
2. iza 3. po 4. *conj* pošto 5. *adv*
docnije

afterbirth [ˈaːftə,bəːθ] *n* posteljica

afternoon [ˌaːftəˈnuːn] *n*
poslepodne; poslijepodne

aftershave [ˈaːftəʃeiv] *n* losion za
posle brijanja

afterwards [ˈaːftəwədz] *adv* docnije

again [əˈgen] *adv* opet, ponovo

against [əˈgenst] *prep* 1. protiv 2.
ka 3. u, o 4. za 5. suprotno
Chelsea played against
Liverpool. Chelsea je igrao
protiv Liverpoola. 6. He put the
bicycle against the wall.
Naslonio je bicikl na zid.

age [eidʒ] *n* 1. doba 2. starost 3.
godina 4. to be under-age biti
maloletan; biti maloljetan 5. for
ages vrlo dugo

agency [ˈeidʒənsi] *n* 1. agencija 2.
društvo 3. news agency
novinska agencija

agenda [əˈdʒendə] *n* dnevni red

agent [ˈeidʒənt] *n* agent

aggravate [ˈægrəveit] *v* pogoršati

aggravating circumstances
[ˈægrə,veitiŋ] *adj* otežavajuće
okolnosti

aggravation [ˌægrəˈveiʃn] *n*
pogoršanje

aggression [əˈgreʃn] *n* agresija

aggressive [əˈgresiv] *adj* agresivan

agility [əˈdʒiləti] *n* okretnost

agitate [ˈædʒiteit] *v* 1. uzburkati 2.
agitovati (**for** za)

agitation [ˌædʒiˈteiʃn] *n* 1.
uzburkavanje 2. agitacija

agitator [ˌædʒiˈteitə] *n* agitator

ago [əˈgəu] *adv* 1. pre; prije 2. a
year ago pre godinu dana 3.
long ago u davnoj prošlosti

agony [ˈægəni] *n* agonija

agree [əˈgriː] *v* složiti se

agreed [əˈgriːd] *adj* 1. ugovoren 2.
saglasan

agreement [əˈgriːmənt] *n* 1.
sporazum 2. ugovor 3. to reach
an agreement postići sporazum

4. **in agreement with** u skladu sa

agricultural [ˌægriˈkʌltʃərəl] *adj* poljoprivredni

agriculture [ˈægrikʌltʃə] *n* poljoprivreda

ahead [əˈhed] *adv* 1. napred 2. **to get ahead** napredovati

ahead of *adj* ispred

aid [eid] 1. *n* pomoć 2. *v* pomoći

aide [eid] *n* 1. pomoćnik 2. (mil.) adutant

AIDS [eidz] *n* sida

ail [eil] *v* boleti; boljeti

aim [eim] 1. *n* nišanjenje 2. cilj 3. *v* nišaniti 4. ciljati

air [eə] *n* 1. vazduh; zrak 2. **to go on the air** početi radio-emisiju

air alert *n* vazdušna uzbuna; zračna uzbuna

air attack *n* napad iz vazduha; napad iz zraka

air base *n* vazduhoplovna baza; zrakoplovna baza

airborne [ˈeəbɔːn] *adj* vazdušnodesantni; zarčnodesantni

airconditioner [ˌeəkɔnˈdiʃənə] *n* erkondišener

airconditioning [ˌeəkɔnˈdiʃəniŋ] *n* klimatizacija

air corridor *n* vazdušni koridor; zračni koridor

air cover *n* zaštita pomoću avijacije

aircraft [ˈeəkraːft] *n* (*pl* aircraft) avion

aircraft-carrier *n* nosač aviona

airdrop *v* izbaciti iz vazduha; izbaciti iz zraka

airfield [ˈeəfiːld] *n* aerodrom

airforce [ˈeəfɔːs] *n* ratno vazduhoplovstvo; ratno zrakoplovstvo

air freight *n* avio-prevoz tereta

air hostess [ˈeəˌhəustis] *n* stjuardesa

airlift [ˈeəˌlift] *n* vazdušni most; zračni most

airline, airways [ˈeəlain; ˈeəweiz] *n* vazduhoplovna kompanija; zrakoplovna kompanija

airliner [ˈeəˌlainə] *n* putnički avion

airlinks [ˈeəliŋks] *pl* vazdušne veze

airmail [ˈeəmeil] *n* 1. avionska pošta 2. **by airmail** avionskom poštom

airplane [ˈeəplein] *n* avion

air pollution *n* aerozagađivanje

airport [ˈeəpɔːt] *n* aerodrom

air-raid *n* vazdušni napad; zračni napad

air-raid alarm *n* vazdušna uzbuna; zračna uzbuna

air-raid shelter *n* sklonište od napada iz vazduha/zraka

air route *n* vazdušni koridor

air-sea rescue *n* služba za spasavanaje avionima na moru

air show *n* aeromiting

air sickness *n* vazdušna bolest; zračna bolest

air space *n* vazdušni prostor; zračniprostor

air speed *n* brzina kroz vazduh/zrak

air strike *n* nalet avijacije

air strip *n* poletno-sletna staza

air support *n* avijacijska podrška

air terminal *n* vazduhoplovno pristanište; zrakoplovno pristanište

airtight [ˈeətait] *adj* hermetički

air-to-air missile *n* raketa vazduh-vazduh

air-to-surface missile *n* raketa vazduh-zemlja

air traffic *n* vazdušni saobraćaj; zračni saobraćaj

air-traffic control n služba kontrole letenja

airways ['eəwei] *see* **airline**

airworthy ['eəwəːði] n sposoban za letenje

alarm [ə'laːm] 1. n uzbuna 2. alarm 3. v uzbuniti 4. to give/raise the alarm zvoniti na uzbunu 5. to set off an alarm aktivirati alarm

alarm clock n budilnik

alarming [ə'laːmiŋ] *adj* koji uznemiruje

alas! [ə'læs] avaj!

Albania ['ælkəhɔl] n Albanija, Arbanija

Albanian ['ælkəhɔl] 1. *adj* albanksi, šiptarski 2. n Alabanac, Šiptar

alcohol ['ælkəhɔl] n alkohol

alcoholic [,ælkə'hɔlik] 1. *adj* alkoholni 2. n alkoholičar

alcoholism ['ælkəhɔlizm] n alkoholizam

ale [eil] n pivo

alert [ələːt] 1. *adj* budan 2. v alarmirati

algebra ['ældʒibrə] n algebra

alias ['eiliəs] n pseudonim

alien ['eiliən] *adj/n* 1. stranac 2. illegal alien ilegalni imigrant

alight [ə'lait] 1. *adj* zapaljen 2. v sići

align [ə'lain] v centrirati

alignment [ə'lainmənt] n centriranje

alike [ə'laik] 1. *adj* sličan 2. *adv* slično

alive [ə'laiv] *adj* živ

all [ɔːl] *adj/adv* 1. sve, svi 2. sav

allay [ə'lei] v umanjiti

allegation [,æli'geiʃn] n tvrđenje

allege [ə'ledʒ] v potvrditi

allegiance [ə'liːdʒəns] n vernost; vjernost

allergic ['ælədʒik] *adj* alergičan

allergy ['ælədʒi] n alergija

alley ['æli] n uličica

alliance [ə'laiəns] n savez

all over *adv* svuda

allocate ['æləkeit] v dodeliti; dodijeliti

allocation [,ælə'keiʃn] n podela; podjela

all-out [,ɔːl'aut] *adj/adv* totalan

allow [ə'lau] v 1. dozvoliti 2. dati

allowance [ə'lauəns] n popust

alloy ['ælɔi] n legura

all right [,ɔːl'rait] 1. dobro 2. u redu 3. bolje

ally ['ælai] n saveznik

ally [ə'lai] v stupiti u savez

almost ['ɔːlməust] *adv* umalo

alone [ə'ləun] *adv* 1. sam 2. let alone... a kamoli...

along [ə'lɔŋ] 1. *prep* duž 2. *adv* dajle 3. all along sve vreme; sve vrijeme

alongside [ə,lɔŋ'said] *prep/adv* pored

aloud [ə'laud] *adv* glasno

alphabet ['ælfəbet] n azbuka

Alps [alps] *pl* Alpe; Alpi

already [ɔːl'redi] *adv* već

alright [ɔːl'rait] 1. dobro 2. u redu 3. bolje

also ['ɔːlsəu] takođe; također

altar ['ɔːltə] v oltar

alter ['ɔːltə] v 1. promeniti; promijeniti 2. prepraviti

alteration [,ɔːltə'reiʃn] n 1. promena; promjena 2. popravka

alternate ['ɔːltəneit] v alternirati

alternation [,ɔːltə'neiʃn] n alternacija

alternative [ɔːl'təːnətiv] 1. *adj* alternativan 2. n alternativa

although [ɔːlˈðəu] *conj* iako
altitude [ˈæltitjuːd] *n* visina
altogether [ˌɔːltəˈgeðə] *adv* savsim
aluminium, aluminum [ˌaljuˈminjəm] *n* aluminijum
always [ˈɔːlweiz] *adv* uvek
am [æm] *see* be
a.m. *adv* pre podne; prije podne
amalgamation [əˌmælgəˈmeiʃn] *n* integracija
amass [əˈmæs] *v* nagomilati
amateur [ˈæmətjəː] 1. *adj* amaterski 2. *n* amater
amaze [əˈmeiz] *v* zadiviti
amazement [əˈmeizmənt] *n* zadivljenost
amazing [əˈmeiziŋ] *adj* neverovatno; nevjerovatno
ambassador [æmˈbæsədə] *n* ambasador
ambiguity [ˌæmbiˈgjuːəti] *n* dvosmislenost
ambiguous [æmˈbigjuəs] *adj* dvosmislen
ambition [æmˈbiʃn] *n* ambicija
ambitious [æmˈbiʃəʃ] *adj* ambiciozan
ambulance [ˈæmbjuləns] *n* 1. ambulantna kola 2. (mil.) sanitetski automobil
ambush [ˈæmbuʃ] 1. *n* zaseda; zasjeda 2. *v* napasti iz zasede/zasjede
amend [æˈmend] *v* izmeniti
amendment [æˈmendmənt] *n* amandman
amends [æˈmendz] *pl* **to make amends** dati odštetu
America [əˈmerikə] *n* Amerika,
American [əˈmerikən] 1. *adj* američki, amerikanski 2. *n* Amerikanac

amid, amidst [əˈmid; -st] *prep* u sredini
ammunition [ˌæmjuˈniʃn] *n* 1. municija 2. **live ammunition** bojeva municija
ammunition dump *n* poljsko skladište za municija
amnesty [ˈæmnəsti] *n* amnestija
Amnesty International *n* = *organizacija za zaštitu ljudskih prava*
among, amongst [əˈmʌŋ; əˈmʌŋst] *prep* 1. između 2. među
amount [əˈmaunt] *n* 1. iznos 2. **a fair amount** dosta
amount *v* 1. iznosti 2. vrediti; vrijediti
amplifier [ˈæmplifaijə] *n* pojačavač
amplify [ˈæmplifai] *v* pojačati
amputate [ˈæmpjuteit] *v* (med.) amputati
amputation [ˌæmpjuteiʃn] *n* amputacija
amuse [əˈmjuːz] *v* zabavljati
an [æn] *see* a
anaemia [əˈniːmia] *n* anemija
anaesthetic [ˌænisˈθetik] *n* anestetik
anaesthetist [ˌænisˈθetik] *n* anestetičar
anaesthetize [ˌænisˈθetik] *v* anestizirati
analogy [əˈnælədʒi] *n* 1. analogija 2. **by analogy** po analogiji
analyse [ˈænəlaiz] *v* analizirati
analysis [əˈnæləsis] *n* analiza
analyst [ˈænəlist] *n* analitičar
anarchy [ˈænəki] *n* anarhija
anatomy [əˈnætəmi] *n* anatomija
ancestor [ˈænsestə] *n* predak
anchor [ˈæŋkə] *n* sidro
anchorman [ˈæŋkəmæn] *n* glavni spiker

ancient ['einʃənt] *adj* star

and [ən; ænd] *conj* 1. i 2. da

anemia [ə'niːmia] *see* **anaemia**

anesthetic [ˌænisˈθetik] *see* anaesthetic

anesthetist [ˌænisˈθetik] *see* anaesthetist

anesthetize [ˌænisˈθetik] *see* anaesthetize

angel ['eindʒl] *n* anđeo

anger ['æŋgə] 1. *n* ljutnja 2. *v* naljutiti

angle ['æŋgl] *n* ugao; kut

Anglo-Saxon ['æŋgləuˈsæksən] *adj/n* anglosaksonski

anglophone ['æŋgləufəun] *adj* anglophone countries anglofonske zemlje

angry ['æŋgri] *adj* ljut

anguish ['æŋgwiʃ] *n* bol

animal ['æniml] *n* životinja

animate ['ænimeit] 1. *adj* živ 2. *v* oživiti

animosity [ˌæniˈmositi] *n* animoznost

ankle ['æŋkl] *n* gležanj

annex [ə'neks] *n* 1. aneks 2. *see* annexe

annex [ə'neks] *v* to annex territory prisvojiti teritoriju

annexation [ˌænekˈseiʃn] *n* aneksija

annexe ['æneks] *n* dodatak

annihilate [ə'naiəleit] *v* uništiti

anniversary [ˌæniˈvəːsəri] *n* godišnjica

announce [ə'nauns] *v* najaviti

announcement [ə'naunsmənt] *n* objava

announcer [ə'naunsə] *n* spiker

annoy [ə'nɔi] *v* dosaditi

annoying [ə'nɔijŋ] *adj* dosadan

annual ['ænjuəl] *adj* godišnji

annually ['ænjuəli] *adv* svake godine

annul [ə'nʌl] *v* ponštiti

anonymous [ə'nɔniməs] *adj* anoniman

another [ə'nʌðə] *adj* drugi

answer ['aːnsə] 1. *n* odgovor 2. *v* odgovoriti

answer back *v* odvratiti

ant [ænt] *n* mrav

antagonistic [æntægəˈnistik] *adj* antagonistički

antenatal [ˌæntiˈneitəl] *adj* antenatalni

antenna [æn'tenə] *n* antena

anthem ['ænθəm] *n* himna

anthology [ˌænθˈolodʒi] *n* antologija

anthropology [ˌænθrˈopolodʒi] *n* antropologija

anti- ['ænti] anti-

anti-aircraft gun [ˌæntiˈeəkraːft ˌgʌn] *n* protivavionsko oruđe

anti-apartheid [ˌæntiəˈpaːtait] *adj* anti-aparthejdski

antibiotics [ˌæntibaiˈɔtiks] *pl* antibiotik

antibody ['æntiˌbɔdi] *pl* antitelo; antitijelo

anticipate [æn'tisipeit] *v* 1. naslutiti 2. predvideti

anticipation [æn,tisiˈpeiʃn] *n* 1. naslućivanje 2. predviđanje

antidote ['æntidəut] *n* protivotrov; protuotrov

anti-fascism [ˌæntiˈsemitizm] *n* antifašizam

anti-fascist [ˌæntiˈsemeit] 1. *adj* antifašistički 2. *n* antifašista

antifreeze ['æntifriːz] *n* antifriz

anti-missile defence [ˌæntiˈmisail ˈdifens] *n* protivraketna odbrana/ obrana

anti-nuclear [ˌæntiˈnjuːklijə] *adj* antinuklearan

anti-personnel [ˌæntiˈpəːsənel] *adj* protivpešadijski; protupješadijski

anti-personnel mine *n* protivpešadijska mina

antique [ænˈtiːk] *adj* antički

antique [ænˈtiːk] *n* antikvitet

antique shop *n* antikvarnica

antiquity [ænˈtikwəti] *n* antika

anti-Semite [ˌæntiˈsemeit] *n* antisemit

anti-Semitic [ˌæntiseˈmitik] *adj* antisemitski

anti-Semitism [ˌæntiˈsemitizm] *n* antisemitizam

antiseptic [ˌæntiˈseptik] 1. *adj* antiseptičan 2. *n* antiseptik

anti-fascist [ˌæntiˈsemeit] 1. *adj* antifašistički 2. *n* antifašista

anti-tank [ˌæntiˈtænk] *adj* antitenkovski

anti-tank mine *n* antitenkovska mina

anti-war [ˌæntiˈwɔː] *adj* antiratni

anus [ˈeinəs] *n* čmar

anxiety [ˈæŋzaiəti] *n* zabrinutost

anxious [ˈæŋkʃəs] *adj* zabrinut

any [ˈeni] *adj* 1. neki 2. izvestan 3. jedan 4. iko 5. nešto 6. svaki

anybody [ˈenibɔdi] 1. iko, itko, ma ko, ma tko, bilo ko, ko mu drago 2. važna osoba

anyday [ˈenidei] *adv* bilo kojeg dana

anyhow [ˈenihau] *adv* u svakom slučaju

anymore [ˈenihau] *adv* nikad više

anyone [ˈeniwʌn] *see* **anybody**

anything [ˈeniθiŋ] bilo šta, išta

anytime [ˈenitaim] bilo kada, ikada

anyway [ˈeniwei] *adv* u svakom slučaju

anywhere [ˈeniweə] bilo gde/gdje

apart [əˈpaːt] *adv* odvojeno

apart from *prep* sem

apartheid [əˈpaːthait] *n* aparthajd

apartment [əˈpaːtmənt] *n* stan

apathy [ˈæpəθi] *n* apatija

ape [eip] *n* bezrei majmun

apex [ˈeipeks] *n* vrh

apiece [əˈpiːs] *adv* (za) svaki

apologize [əˈpɔlədʒaiz] *v* izviniti se

apology [əˈpɔlədʒi] *n* izvinjenje; isprika

apostrophe [əˈpɔstrəfi] *n* apostrof

appal, appall [əˈpɔːld] *v* užasnuti

appalling [əˌpɔːliŋ] *adj* užasan

apparatus [ˌæpəˈreitəs] *n* aparat

apparent [əˈpærənt] *adj* očigledan

apparently [əˈpærəntli] *adv* naizgled

appeal [əˈpiːl] 1. *n* apel 2. čar 3. (leg.) žalba 4. *v* apelovati 5. (leg.) žaliti

appealing [əˈpiːliŋ] *adj* atraktivan

appear [əˈpiə] *v* 1. pojaviti se 2. izlaziti 3. činiti se

appearance [əˈpiərəns] *n* 1. pojava 2. izgled

appease [əˈpiːz] *v* popustiti

append [əˈpend] *v* dodati

appendicitis [ˌəpendiˈsaitis] *n* apendicit

appendix [əˈpendiks] *n* dodatak

appetite [ˈæpitait] *n* apetit; tek

applaud [əˈplɔːd] *v* aplaudirati

applause [əˈplɔːz] *n* aplauz

apple [ˈæpl] *n* jabuka

appliance [əˈplaiəns] *n* uređaj

applicant [ˈæplikənt] *n* kandidat

application [ˌæpliˈkeiʃn] *n* 1. molba 2. aplikacioni program

application form *n* prijavni formular

apply [əˈplai] *v* 1. primeniti; primijeniti 2. staviti

apply for v prijaviti se za
appoint [ə'pɔint] v postaviti
appointment [ə'pɔintmənt] n 1. postavljanje 2. mesto; mjesto 3. sastanak
apportion [ə'pɔːʃn] v raspodeliti; raspodijeliti
appraisal [ə'preiʃl] n procena; procjena
appreciate [ə'priːʃieit] v ceniti; cijeniti
apprehend [æpri'hend] v uhapsiti; uhvatiti
apprehension [,æpri'henʃn] n 1. hapšenje 2. zebnja
apprentice [ə'prentis] n šegrt
approach [ə'prəutʃ] v približiti se
appropriate [ə'prəupriət] adj podesan
appropriation [ə'prəuprieiʃn] n odobravanje
approve [ə'pruːv] 1. n odobrenje 2. v odobriti
approximate [ə'prɔksimət] adj približan
approximately [ə'prɔksimətli] adv 1. približno 2. oko 3. otprilike
apricot ['eiprikɔt] n kajsija
April ['eiprəl] n april; travanj
apt [æpt] adj zgodan
aqualung ['ækwələn] n akvalung
aquatic [ə'kwætik] adj vodena biljka
Arab ['ærəb] 1. adj arapski 2. n Arapin
Arabic ['ærəbik] n aprapski jezik
arbitrate ['aːbitreit] v suditi kao arbitar
arbitration [,aːbi'treiʃn] n arbitraža
arbitrator [,aːbi'treitə] n arbitar
arcade [aː'keid] n **shopping arcade** gidan kashe ahu

arch [aːtʃ] n luk
archaeology ['aːkij'ɔlədʒi] n arheologija
archaeologist ['aːkij'ɔlədʒist] n arheolog
archbishop [aːttʃ'biʃɔp] n 1. nadbiskup 2. (Orth.) arhiepiskop
architect ['aːkitekt] n arjitekta
architecture ['aːkitektʃə] n arhitektura
archives ['aːkaivz] pl arhiva
arduous ['aːdjuəs] adj težak
are [aː] see be
area ['eəriə] n 1. oblast 2. rejon 3. površina
arena [ə'riːnə] n arena
argue ['aːgjuː] v prepirati se
argue that v dokazivati da
argument ['aːgjumənt] n 1. argumenat 2. prepirka
arid ['ærid] adj suv; suh
arise [ə'raiz] v (arose, arisen) 1. ustati 2. nastati
aristocracy [,æris'tɔkrəsi] n aristokratija
arithmetic [ə'riθmətik] n aritmetika
ark [aːk] n kovčeg
arm [aːm] 1. n ruka 2. v naoružati 3. see **arms**
armada [aː'maːdə] n armada
armament(s) ['aːməmənts] pl naoružanje
armchair ['aːmtʃeə] n fotelja
armed [aːmd] adj oružan
armed forces pl oružane snage
armed robbery n razbojnička krađa
Armenia [,aː'miːnijə] n Jermenija, Armenija
Armenian [,aː'miːnijən] 1. adj jermenski, armenski 2. n Jermenin, Armenac

armistice ['a:mistis] *n* primirje
armour ['a:mə] *n* oklop
armoured ['a:məd] *adj* oklopni
armoured car *n* borna kola
armoured column *n* kolona tenkova
armoured personnel carrier *n* oklopni transporter
armour-piercing *adj* pancirni
armpit ['a:mpit] *n* pazuho
arms [a:mz] *pl* oružje
arms build-up *n* povećanje oružja
arms race *n* trka u naoružanju
arms reduction *n* smanjenje naoružanja
army ['a:mi] 1. *adj* armijski 2. *n* vojska
aroma [ə'rəumə] *n* aroma
aromatic [,ærəu'mætik] *adj* aromatičan
around [ə'raund] *adv/prep* 1. oko 2. za 3. unaokolo 4. **all around** svuda unaokolo
arouse [ə'rauz] *v* probuditi
arrange [ə'reindʒ] *v* 1. urediti 2. spremiti
arrangement [ə'reindʒmənt] *n* uređenje
arrears [ə'ri:əs] *pl* zaostali dug
arrest [ə'rest] 1. *n* lišenje 2. **house arrest** kućni pritvor 3. *v* uhapsiti
arrival [ə'raivl] *n* dolazak
arrive [ə'raiv] *v* 1. doći 2. doneti
arrogance ['ærəgəns] *n* osionost
arrogant ['ærəgənt] *adj* osion
arrow ['ærəu] *n* strela; strijela
arsenal ['a:sinl] *n* arsenal
arson ['a:sən] *n* namerna paljevina; namjerna paljevina
art [a:t] *n* 1. umetnost; umjetnost 2. veština; vještina
artery [a:'tiəri] *n* arterija

art gallery *n* umetnička galerija; umjetnička galerija
arthritis [a:'θraitis] *n* artritis
artichoke ['a:titʃəuk] *n* artičoka
article ['a:tikl] *n* 1. predmet 2. članak
artificial [,a:ti'fiʃl] *adj* veštački; vještački, umjetan
artillery [a:'tiləri] *n* artiljerija
artisan ['a:tizæn] *n* majstor
artist ['a:tist] *n* umetnik; umjetnik
artistic [a:'tistik] *adj* umetnički; umjetnički
artistry ['a:tistri] *n* umešnost; umješnost
artwork ['a:tiwə:k] *n* crteži
as [əz; æz] 1. **They arrived as we were leaving.** Došli su baš kada smu mi odlazili. 2. **As he was late, we went without him.** Pošto je kasnio, otišli smu bez njega. 3. **Sharon is as tall as Tracey.** Sharon je visoka koliko i Tracey. 4. **Do as I do.** Radi što i ja.. 5. **The dog acted as if it were mad.** Pas se ponašao kao da je pobesneo. 6. **His brother came as well.** Došao je i njegov brat.
as soon as possible što pre; što prije
ascend [ə'send] *v* popeti se (na)
ash, ashes [æʃ; -iz] *n* pepeo
ashamed [ə'ʃeimd] *adj* postiđen
ashtray ['æʃtrei] *n* pepeljara
Asia ['eiʒə] *n* Azija
Asian ['eiʒn] 1. *adj* azijatski 2. *n* Azijat
aside [ə'said] *adv* na stranu
aside from *prep* osim
ask [a:sk] *v* 1. pitati 2. zamoliti
ask for *v* zatražiti

asleep [ə'sliːp] *adj* **to be asleep** spavati

as long as sve dok

aspect ['æspekt] *n* aspekt

aspiration [,æspə'reiʃn] *n* težnja

aspirin ['æsprin] *n* aspirin

assassin [ə'sæsin] *n* atentator

assassinate [ə'sæsineit] *v* ubiti

assassination [ə,sæsi'neiʃn] *n* atentat

assault [ə'sɔːlt] **1.** *n* juriš **2.** *v* jurišati

assemble [ə'sembl] *v* **1.** sklopiti **2.** skupiti **3.** skupiti se

assembly [ə'sembli] *n* **1.** skup **2.** House of Assembly dom

assembly plant *n* montažna fabrika; montažna tvornica

assent [ə'sent] *v* **to give one's assent** dati svoj pristanak

assert [ə'səːt] *v* afirmisati se

assess [ə'ses] *v* oceniti; ocijeniti

assessment [ə'sesmənt] *n* procena; procjena

assessor [ə'sesə] *n* asesor

assets ['æsets] *pl* aktiva

assign [ə'sain] *v* dodeliti; dodijeliti

assignment [ə'sainmənt] *n* zadatak; zadaća

assimilation [ə,simi'leiʃn] *n* asimilacija

assist [ə'sist] *v* pomoći

assistance [ə'sistəns] *n* pomoć

assistant [ə'sistənt] *n* pomoćnik

associate [ə'səuʃiət] *n* kolega

associate [ə'səuʃieit] *v* asocirati

association [ə,səusi'eiʃn] *n* asocijacija

assorted [ə'sɔːtid] *adj* raznovrstan

assume [ə'sjuːm] *v* **1.** pretpostaviti **2. to assume command** preuzeti komandu

assurance [ə'ʃɔːrəns] *n* overenje

assure [ə'ʃɔː] *v* uveriti; uvjeriti

asthma ['æsmə] *n* astma

as though [æz'ðəu] *conj* kao da

as to [æz'tuː] *prep* u pogledu

astonish [ə'stɔniʃ] *v* zadiviti

astonishing [ə'stɔniʃ] *adj* zapanjujući

astonishment [ə'stɔniʃmənt] *n* zadivljenost

astray [ə'strei] *adv* **to go astray** zalutati

astrology [ə'strɔlədʒi] *n* astrologija

astronaut ['æstrənɔːt] *n* astronaut

astronomer [ə'strɔnəmə] *n* astronom

astronomy [ə'strɔnəmi] *n* astronomija

as well as kao i

asylum [ə'sailəm] *n* **1.** ludnica **2.** (pol.) azil

at [ət; æt] *prep* **1. at school** u škola **2. at Fred's** kod Freda **3. at two o'clock** u dva sata

ate [eit] *see* eat

at first *adv* prvo

athlete ['æθliːt] *n* atletičar

athletic [æθ'letik] *adj* atletičarski

athletics [æθ'letiks] *pl* atletika

Atlantic Ocean [ət,læntik 'əuʃn] *n* Atlantski okean/ocean

atlas ['ætləs] *n* atlas

at last *adv* najzad

atmosphere ['ætməsfiə] *n* atmosfera

atom ['ætəm] *n* atom

atom bomb *n* atomska bomba

at once *adv* odmah

atrocity [ə'trɔsəti] *n* **1.** zverstvo; zvjerstvo **2. to commit an atrocity** počiniti zverstvo

attach [ə'tætʃ] *v* pričvrstiti

attache [ə'tæʃei] *n* ataše

attache case *n* aktentašna

attack [ə'tæk] 1. *n* napad 2. **heart attack** srčani udar 3. **to carry out an attack** izvršiti napad 4. **to be under attack** biti izložen napadu 5. *v* napasti

attacker [ə'tækə] *n* napadač

attain [ə'tein] *v* postići

attempt [ə'tempt] *v* 1. pokušaj 2. pokušati

attend [ə'tend] *v* 1. posetiti; posjetiti 2. prisustvovati

attendance [ə'tendəns] *n* prisustnost

attention [ə'tenʃn] *n* 1. pažnja 2. **to attract attention** privući pažnju 3. **to pay attention to** paziti na

attentive [ə'tentiv] *adj* pažljiv

attic ['ætik] *n* potkrovlje

attitude ['ætitʃuːd] *n* stav

attorney [ə'təːni] *n* advokat

attorney-general *n* vrhovni tužilac

attract [ə'trækt] *v* privući

attraction [ə'træktʃən] *n* 1. privlačanje 2. atrakcija

attractive [ə'træktiv] *adj* privlačan

attribute [ə'tribjuːt] *v* pripisati

aubergine ['əubəʒiːn] *n* plavi patlidžan

auction ['ɔkʃn] *n* licitacija

audible ['ɔkʃn] *adj* čujan

audience ['ɔːdiəns] *n* 1. audijencija 2. publika

audit ['ɔːdit] *n* 1. revizija 2. **to carry out an audit** sprovesti reviziju

auditor ['ɔːditə] *n* revizor

auditorium [,ɔːdiˈtɔːriəm] *n* sala

August ['ɔːgəst] *n* avgust, kolovoz

aunt [aːnt] *n* tetka

austerity [ɔˈsterəti] *n* štedljivost

austerity measures *pl* uštedne mere/mjere

austerity programme *n* program štednje

Australia [ɔsˈtreiljə] *n* Australija

Australian [ɔsˈtreiljən] 1. *adj* australijski, australski, australijanski 2. *n* Australijanac

Austria [ɔsˈtrijə] *n* Austrija

Austria-Hungary *n* Austro-Ugarska

Austrian [ɔsˈtrijən] 1. *adj* austrijski 2. *n* Austrijanac

authentic [ɔːˈθentik] *adj* autentičan

author ['ɔːθə] *n* autor

authorities [ɔːˈθərətiːz] *pl* vlasti

authority [ɔːˈθərəti] *n* 1. autoritet 2. vlast 3. uprava 4. **by his authority** po njegovom ovlašćenju

authorization [,ɔːθəraiˈzeiʃn] *n* ovlašćenje

authorize ['ɔːθəraiz] *v* ovlastiti

auto ['ɔːtəu] *n* auto

autobiography [,ɔːtəbaiˈɔgrəfi] *n* autobiografija

autoclave ['ɔːtəukleiv] *n* autoklav

automatic [,ɔːtəˈmætik] 1. *adj* automatski 2. *n* automatsko oružje

automatic rifle *n* automatska puška

automobile ['ɔːtəməbiːl] *n* automobil

autonomous [ɔːˈtɔnəməs] *adj* autonomski, autonoman

autonomy [ɔːˈtɔnəmi] *n* autonomija

autumn ['ɔːtəm] *n* jesen

availability [əˈveiləbiliti] *n* raspoloživost

available [əˈveiləbl] *adj* raspoloživ

avalanche ['ævəlaːntʃ] *n* lavina

avenge [əˈvendʒ] *v* osvetiti

avenue [ˈævənjuː] *n* ulica

average [ˈævərɪdʒ] *adj* 1. prosečan; prosječan 2. **on average** u proseku

aversion [əˈvəːʃn] *n* odvratnost

avert [əˈvəːt] *v* sprečiti

aviation [ˌeɪviˈeɪʃn] *n* avijacija

avoid [əˈvɔɪd] *v* izbeći; izbjeći

await [əˈweit] *v* čekati

awake [əˈweik] *adj* probuđen

award [əˈwɔːd] 1. *n* nagrada 2. *v* dodeliti; dodjeliti

aware [əˈweə] *adj* svestan; svjestan

away [əˈwei] *adv* 1. **Go away!** Odlazi! 2. **My mother is away.** Moja majka nije ovde. 3. **far away** daleko

awe [ɔː] *n* strahopoštovanje

awful [ˈɔːfl] *adj* 1. užasan 2. strašan 3. (sl.) veliki

awfully [ˈɔːfli] *adv* vrlo

awkward [ˈɔːkwəd] *adj* nezgodan

axe [æks] *n* sekira; sjekira

axis [ˈæksis] *n* osovina

axle [ˈæksl] *n* osovina

B

B.A. (bachelor's degree) *n* (acad.) diploma na drugom stepenu, fakultetska diploma

baboon [bæˈbuːn] *n* pavijan

babe [beib] *n* naivko

baby [ˈbeibi] *n* beba

babysit [ˈbeibisit] *v* (**babysat**) čuvati decu/djecu

babysitter [ˈbeibisitə] *n* lice koje čuva decu/djecu

bachelor [ˈbætʃələ] *n* neženja

back [bæk] **1.** *adj* zadnji **2.** *n* leđa **3.** *v* podržati **4.** He's back. Vratio se. **5.** He gave me the book back. Vratio mi je knjigu.

backache *n* bol u leđima

back away *v* odstupiti

backbench *n* (UK) obični članovi Parlamenta

backbiter [ˈbækbaitə] *n* ogovarati

backbone [ˈbækbəun] *n* **1.** kičma **2.** oslonac

background *n* **1.** pozadina **2.** biografija

backing [ˈbækiŋ] *n* potpora

back off *v* odstupiti

backpack [ˈbækpæk] *n* ruksak

backside [ˈbæksaid] *n* zadnjica

back up 1. *n* rezerva **2.** podrška **3.** kompjuterski pomoćni sistem **4.** *v* potpomoći **5.** voziti unazad

backward [ˈbækwəd] **1.** *adj* nazadan **2.** *adv* natraške

backwards [ˈbækwədz] *adv* natraške

backyard [ˈbeikən] *n* dvorište

bacon [ˈbeikən] *n* slanina

bacteria [bækˈtiəriə] *pl* bakterije

bad [bæd] **1.** *adj* loš, rđav **2.** *n* zlo

bade [bæd; beid] *see* **bid**

badge [bædʒ] *n* značka

badger [bædʒə] *n* jazavac

badly [ˈbædli] *adv* **1.** *see* **bad 2.** (sl.) vrlo

badminton [ˈbædmintən] *n* badminton

badness [ˈbædnis] *n* zlo

bad-tempered [ˌbædˈtempəd] *adj* loše volje

baffle [ˈbæfl] *v* zbuniti

bag [bæg] *n* torba

baggage [ˈbægidʒ] *n* prtljag; prtljaga

bail [beil] *n* (leg.) kaucija

bail out *v* **1.** izbaciti **2.** pomoći **3.** (leg.) preneti privremeno; prenijeti privremeno

bait [beit] *n* vab

bake [beik] *v* ispeći

baker [ˈbeikə] *n* pekar

bakery [ˈbeikəri] *n* pekara

balance [ˈbæləns] **1.** *n* kantar **2.** bilans; bilanca **3.** (fin.) saldo **4.** *v* balansirati **6.** uravnotežiti **7.** (fin.) saldirati

balance of payments *n* platni bilans; platna bilanca

balance of trade *n* bilans spoljne trgovine; bilans vanjske trgovine

balcony [ˈbælkəni] *n* balkon

bald [bɔːld] *adj* ćelav

balk [bɔːk] *v* odustati(**at** od)

Balkan [ˈbɔlkən] *adj* balkanski

balkanism [ˈbɔlkənizm] *n* balkanizam

balkanization [ˌbɔlkənaiˈzeiʃn] *n*
balkanizacija

Balkans [ˈbɔlkənz] *pl* Balkan

ball [bɔːl] *n* lopta

ball-bearing [ˌbɔːlˈbeəriŋ] *n* kuglični
ležaj

ballet [ˈbælei] *n* balet

balloon [bəˈluːn] *n* balon

ballot [ˈbælət] *n* glasačka kuglica

ballot box *n* glasačka kutija

ballpoint [ˈbɔːlpoint] *n* hemijska
olovka; kemijska olovka

bamboo [bæmˈbuː] *n* bambus

ban [bæn] 1. *n* zabrana 2. *v* zabraniti

banana [bəˈnaːnə] *n* banana

band [bænd] *n* 1. banda 2. vrpca 3.
(mus.) orkestar 4. **frequency
band** opseg frekvencijeuri 5.
rubber band lastiš

bandage [ˈbændidʒ] *n* zavoj

bandaid [ˈbændeid] *n* flaster

bandit [ˈbændit] *n* bandit

bang [bæŋ] 1. *n* tresak 2. **with a
bang** sa velikim uspehom/
uspjehom 3. *v* lupiti

banish [ˈbæniʃ] *v* proterati; protjerati

bank [bæŋk] *n* 1. banka 2. **river
bank** rečna obala 3. **snow bank**
nanos snega/snijega 4. **savings
bank** štedionica 5. **federal
reserve bank** federalna rezervna
banka 6. **World Bank** Svetska
banka; Svjetska banka

banker [ˈbæŋkə] *n* bankar

bank holiday *n* praznik

banking *n* [ˈbæŋkiŋ] bankarstvo

bank loan *n* bankovni kredit

banknote, (US) **bankbill**
[ˈbæŋknəut; -bil] *n* banknota

bankrupt [ˈbæŋkrʌpt] *adj* 1.
bankirotiran 2. **to go bankrupt**
bankrotirati

bankruptcy [ˈbæŋkrəpsi] *n*
bankritstvo

banner [ˈbænə] *n* zastava

banquet [ˈbæŋkwit] *n* banket

baptism [ˈbæptizəm] *n* krštenje

bar [baː] *n* 1. kafana; kavana 2.
šipka 3. **a bar of soap** komad
sapuna 4. **a bar of chocolate**
tabla čokolade 5. **behind bars**
iza rešetki

bar code [ˈbaːˌkəud] *n* elektronska
šifra

barbecue [ˈbaːbikjuː] *n* roštilj

barbed wire [ˌbaːbdˈwaiə] *n*
bodljikava žica

barber [ˈbaːbə] *n* berberin; brijač

bare [beə] 1. *adj* go; gol 2. *v*
razgoliti

barefoot [ˈbeəfut] *adj/adv* bos

barely [ˈbeəli] *adv* jedva

bargain [ˈbaːgin] 1. *n* dobar posao 2.
pogodba 3. *v* pogađati se

barge [bːdʒ] *n* barža

bark [baːk] 1. *n* kora 2. *v* lajati

barley [ˈbaːli] *n* ječam

barmaid [ˈbaːmeid] *n* kelnerica

barman [ˈbaːmən] *n* barman

barn [baːn] *n* ambar

barracks [ˈbærəks] *pl* kasarna

barrage [ˈbæraːdʒ] *n* (mil.) zaprečna
vatra

barrel [ˈbærəl] *n* bure

barren [ˈbærən] *adj* nerodan

barricade [ˌbærikˈeid] *n* barikada

barrier [ˈbæriə] *n* prepreka

barrister [ˈbæristə] *n* advokat

bartender [ˈbaːtəndə] *n* barman

barter [ˈbaːtə] *v* trampiti

base [beis] 1. *n* osnova 2. (mil.)
baza 3. *v* zasnovati

baseball [ˈbeisbɔːl] *n* bezbol;
bejzbol

baseless [ˈbeislis] *adj* bestemeljan
basement [ˈbeismənt] *n* podrum
basic [ˈbeisik] *adj* osnovi
basic training *n* osovna obuka
basin [ˈbeisn] *n* lavor
basis [ˈbeisis] *n* osnova
basket [ˈbaːskit] *n* kotarica
basketball [ˈbaːskitbɔːl] *n* košarka
bass [beis] 1. *adj* basovski 2. *n* bas
bastard [ˈbaːstəd] *n* 1. kopile 2. (sl.) kučkin sin
bat [bæt] *n* 1. šišmiš 2. (spor.) štap
bath [baːθ] *n* 1. kada 2. kupanje
bathe [beið] *v* okupati
bathing costume *n* kupaći kostim
bathroom [ˈbaːθrum] *n* kupatilo; kupaonica
battalion [bəˈtæliən] *n* bataljon
battery [ˈbætəri] *n* 1. baterija 2. **car battery** akumulator
battle [ˈbætl] 1. *n* borba 2. *v* boriti
battle casualty *n* poginuli u borbi
battlefield [ˈbætlfiːld] *n* bojište
battleship [ˈbætlʃip] *n* bojini brod
bay [bei] *n* zaliv; zaljev
bayonet [ˈbeiənit] *n* bajonet
bazaar [bəˈzaː] *n* kasuwa
B.B.C. [biːbiːˈsiː] *n* Britanska radiodifuzija
B.C. (before Christ) [biːˈsiː] pre nove ere; prije nove ere
be [biː] *v* biti
beach [biːtʃ] *n* 1. obala 2. plaža 3. **at the beach** na plaži
bead [biːd] *n* zrnce
beak [biːk] *n* kljun
beam [biːm] *n* svetlo; svjetlo
beans [biːnz] *pl* pasulj
bear [beə] 1. *n* medved; medvjed 2. *v* (**bore, borne**) nositi 3. podneti; podnijeti 4. **to bear a child** roditi dete/dijete

beard [biəd] *n* brada
bearer [ˈbeərə] *n* (fin.) imalac
beast [biːst] *n* životinja
beat [biːt] *v* (**beat, beaten**) 1. izbiti 2. potući 3. **to beat a record** nadmašiti rekord
beating [ˈbiːtiŋ] *n* bijenje
beautiful [ˈbjuːtifl] *adj* lepo; lijepo
beauty [ˈbjuːti] *n* lepota; ljepota
beauty queen *n* kraljica lepote/ ljepote
became [biˈkeim] *see* **become**
because [biˈkɔz] *conj* jer
because of *prep* zbog
beckon [ˈbekən] *v* dati znak
become [biˈkʌm] *v* (**became, become**) postati
bed [bed] *n* 1. krevet 2. **river bed** rečno korito; rječno korito 3. **to go to bed** leći u krevet
bed and board *n* pansion
bedroom [ˈbedrum] *n* spavaća soba
bee [biː] *n* pčela
beef [biːf] *n* govedina
beehive [ˈbiːhaiv] *n* košnica
beer [biə] *n* pivo
befall [biˈfɔːl] *v* zadesiti
before [biˈfɔː] 1. *prep* pre; prije 2. ispred 3. *conj* pre nego; prije nego 4. *adv* ranije
beforehand [biˈfɔːhænd] *adv* ranije
beg [beg] *v* 1. preklinjati 2. prosjačiti
began [biˈgæn] *see* **begin**
beggar [ˈbegə] *n* prosjak
begging [ˈbegiŋ] *n* prošnja
begin [biˈgin] *v* (**began, begun**) početi
beginner [biˈginə] *n* početnik
beginning [biˈginiŋ] *n* početak
begun [biˈgʌn] *see* **begin**
behalf [bˈhaːf] *n* **on behalf of** u korist

behave [bi'heiv] *v* ponašati se
behaviour [bi'heivjə] *n* ponašanje
behind [bi'haind] *prep/adv* 1. zaostao 2. za, iza
behind the scenes *adv* iza kulisa
being [·bi:iŋ] *n* 1. postojanje 2. **human being** ljudsko biće
belief [bi'li:f] *n* vera; vjera
believe [bi'li:v] *v* verovati; vjerovati
belittle [bi'litl] *v* omalovažiti
bell [bel] *n* zvono
belly [·beli] *n* trbuh
belong [bi'lɔŋ] *v* pripadati
belongings [bi'lɔŋiŋz] *pl* lične stvari
below [bi'ləu] 1. *adv* niže 2. *prep* ispod
belt [belt] *n* kaiš
bench [bentʃ] *n* klupa
bend [bend] 1. *n* luk 2. *v* (**bent**) saviti
bend down *v* nagnuti se
bends [bendz] *pl* kesonska bolest
beneath [bi'ni:θ] *prep* ispod
beneficial [,beni'fiʃl] *adj* blagotvoran
benefit [·benifit] 1. *n* korist 2. beneficija 3. *v* koristiti
bent [bent] *see* bend
bereavement [bi'ri:vmənt] *n* rashi
beside [bi'said] *prep* pored
besides [bi'saidz] 1. *prep* pored 2. *adv* uostalom
besiege [bi'si:dʒ] *v* opsesti; opsjesti
best [best] *adj* najbolji
best man [,best·mæn] *n* stari svat
bestseller [,best·selə] *n* bestseler
bet [bet] 1. *n* opklada 2. *v* (**bet**) opkladiti se
betray [bi'trei] *v* izdati
betrayal [bi'treiəl] *n* izdaja
better [·betə] *adj* 1. bolji 2. **to get better** oporaviti se 3. **We'd better go.** Bolje da idemo.

betting [·betiŋ] *n* kladilac
between [bi'twi:n] *prep* između, među
beverage [·bevəridʒ] *n* piće
beware [bi'weə] *v* čuvati se
beyond [bi'jɔnd] 1. *prep* iza 2. *adv* dalje
bias [·baijəs] *n* predrasuda
Bible [·baibl] *n* Biblija
bibliography [,bibli'ogrəfi] *n* bibliografija
bicycle [·baisikl] *n* bicikl
bid [bid] *v* (**bid**) ponuditi
big [big] *adj* veliki; velik
Big Apple *n* Njujork
bigot [·bigət] *n* bigot
bigoted [·bigətid] *adj* bigotan
bike [baik] *n* bicikl
bikini [bi'ki:ni] *n* bikini
bilingual [bai'lingwəl] *adj* dvojezični
bilingualism [bai'lingwəlizm] *n* dvojezičnost
bill [bil] *n* 1. račun 2. (pol.) zakonski nacrt 3. *see* banknote
billboard [·bilbɔ:d] *n* reklamni plakat
billion [·biliən] *n* bilion; bilijun, (US) milijarda
bill of exchange *n* menica; mjenica
bill of lading *n* tovarni list
bill of rights *n* povelja slobode
bill of sale *n* kupoprodajni ugovor
bind [baind] *v* (**bound**) vezati
binoculars [bi'nɔkjuləz] *pl* dvogled
biography [bai'ogrəfi] *n* biografija
biological warfare [,baiə·lɔdʒikl ·wɔ:feə] *n* biološki rat
biologist [bai·ɔlədʒist] *n* biolog
biology [bai·ɔlədʒi] *n* biologija
biomass fuels [·baiəu,mæs·fju:əlz] *pl* biogoriva

bipartite [baɪˈpɑːtaɪt] *adj* dvostruk
bird [bəːd] *n* prica
biro [ˈbaɪərəu] *n* hemijska olovka; kemijska olovka
birth [bəːθ] *n* 1. porođaj 2. **to give birth to a child** roditi dete/dijete
birth certificate *n* izvod iz matične knjige rođenih
birth control *n* kontrola rađanja
birthday [ˈbəːθdeɪ] *n* rođendan
birthplace [ˈbəːθpleɪs] *n* mesto rođenja; mjesto rođenja
birthrate [ˈbəːθreɪt] *n* natalitet
biscuit [ˈbɪskɪt] *n* biskvit
bisexual [ˌbaɪˈsekʃuəl] *adj/n* biseksualan
bishop [ˈbɪʃəp] *n* biskup, episkop
bit [bɪt] *n* 1. komadić 2. obol 3. **bridle bit** đem 4. *see* **bite**
bite [baɪt] 1. *n* ujed 2. **mosquito bite** ubod komarca 3. *v* (**bit**, **bitten**) ujesti
bitter [ˈbɪtə] *adj* gorak
bitterness [ˈbɪtənɪs] *n* gorčina
black [blæk] *adj* crn
black and white *adj* crnobeo; crnobijel
blackboard [ˈblækbɔːd] *n* školska tabla/ploča
blacken [ˈblækən] *v* pocrniti
blacklist [ˈblæklɪst] *n* crna lista
blackmail [ˈblækmeɪl] *v* uceniti; ucijeniti
black market *n* crna berza/burza
black marketeer *n* crnoberzijanac; crnoburzijanac
blackout [ˈblækaut] *n* 1. zamračenje 2. onesvešćenje; onesvješćenje
Black Sea *n* Crno more
bladder [ˈblædə] *n* bešika
blade [ˈbleɪd] *n* oštrica
blame [bleɪm] 1. *n* krivica 2. *v* okriviti

bland [blænd] *adj* blag
blank [blæŋk] *adj* 1. prazan 2. **blank ammunition** manevarska municija
blanket [ˈblæŋkɪt] *n* ćebe
blasphemy [ˈblæsfəmi] *n* bogohuljenje
blast [blɑːst] 1. *n* **bomb blast** eksplozija 2. *v* koristiti eksplosive
blastoff [ˈblɑːstɔf] *n* lansiranje
blaze [bleɪz] 1. *n* požar 2. *v* plamteti; plamtjeti
bleach [bliːtʃ] *n* belilo; bjelilo
bleed [bliːd] *v* (**bled**) krvariti
bleeding [ˈbliːdɪŋ] *n* krvarenje
blemish [ˈblemɪʃ] *n* mana
blend [blend] *v* pomešati; pomiješati
bless [bles] *v* blagosloviti
blew [bluː] *see* **blow**
blind [blaɪnd] 1. *adj* slep; slijep 2. *n* roletna
blindfold [ˈblaɪndfɔld] *v* povezati oči
blindness [ˈblaɪndnɪs] *n* slepilo; sljepilo
blink [blɪŋk] *v* trepnuti
blister [ˈblɪstə] *n* plik
blitz [blɪts] *n* iznenadan napad
blizzard [ˈblɪzəd] *n* mećava
bloc [blɔk] *n* (pol.) blok
block [blɔk] 1. *n* panj 2. blok 3. **block of flats** stambena zgrada 4. *v* zaprečiti; zapriječiti 5. zapušiti
blockade [blɔˈkeɪd] *n* 1. blokada 2. **to impose a blockade** zavesti blokadu 3. **to break a blockade** razbiti blokadu 4. **to lift a blockade** ukinuti blokadu
blockage [ˈblɔkɪdʒ] *n* zapušavanje
blond, blonde [blɔnd] *adj* plav/ plavuša

blood [blʌd] *n* krv
blood bank *n* skladište rezerve krvi
blood group *n* krvna grupa
blood test *n* ispitivanje krvi
bloody ['blʌdi] *adj* krvav
bloom [blu:m] 1. *n* cvet; cvijet 2. *v* cvetati; cvjetati
blouse [blauz] *n* bluza
blow [bləu] 1. *n* udar 2. *v* (blew, blown) duvati 3. trubiti
blow-out *n* eksplozija
blow up *v* 1. dići u vazduh 2. napumpati 3. povećati
blue [blu:] *adj/n* plav
blueprint ['blu:print] *n* shematski plan
blues [blu:z] *n* 1. melanholija 2. (mus.) bluz
bluff [blʌf] *v* blefirati
blunder ['blʌndə] *n* gruba greška
blunt [blʌnt] 1. *adj* tup 2. *v* zatupiti
bluntly ['blʌntli] *adv* bez uvijanja
blush [blʌʃ] *v* porumeneti; porumenjeti
board [bɔ:d] 1. *n* tabla 2. daska 3. **editorial board** uređivački odbor 4. **bed and board** pansion 5. *v* ukrcati se 6. ući
board of directors *n* upravni odbor
board of trade *n* trgovačka komora
boast [bəust] 1. *n* hvastanje 2. *v* hvastati se
boat [bəut] *n* čamac
bodily ['bɔdili] *adj* telesni; tjelesni
body ['bɔdi] *n* 1. telo; tijelo 2. **dead body** leš 3. **aircraft body** trup
bodyguard ['bɔdiga:d] *n* telesni stražar; tjelesni stražar
body search *n* lični pretres

bogus ['bəugəs] *adj* lažan
Bohemia [bəu'hi:mijа] *n* Bohemija, Češka
Bohemian [bəu'hi:mijən] 1. *adj* češki 2. *n* Čeh
boil [bɔil] 1. *n* (med.) čir 2. *v* skuvati; skuhati
bold [bəuld] *adj* hrabar
bolt [bəult] *n* 1. reza; zasun 2. bala (platna)
bomb [bɔm] 1. *n* bomba 2. *v* bombardovati
bombard [bɔm'ba:d] *v* bombardovati
bombardment [bɔm'ba:dmənt] *n* bombardovanje
bomb disposal *n* onesposobljavanje neeksplodiranih bombi
bomb disposal unit *n* četa za onesposobljavanje neeksplodiranih bombi
bomber ['bɔmə] *n* bombarder
bombing ['bɔmiŋ] *n* bombardovanje
bomb-proof ['bɔmpru:f] *adj* neprobojan za bombe
bond [bɔnd] *n* 1. veza 2. (fin.) obveznica
bondage ['bɔndidʒ] *n* ropstvo
bone [bəun] *n* kost
bonfire ['bɔnfaiə] *n* logorska vatra
bonnet ['bɔnit] *n* **car bonnet** poklopac
bonus ['bəunəs] *n* premija
boo [bu:] *v* izviždati
booby trap ['bu:bitræp] *n* mina iznenađenja
book [buk] 1. *n* knjiga 2. *v* rezervisati
bookkeeper ['buk,ki:pə] *n* knjigovođa
booklet ['buklət] *n* brošura
bookseller ['buk,selə] *n* knjižar
bookshop, bookstore ['bukʃɔp 'bukstɔ:] *n* knjižara

boom [buːm] *n* 1. tutnjava 2. (ec.) uspon, bum

boost [buːst] *v* povisiti

boot [buːt] *n* 1. čizma 2. **car boot** prtljažnik

booth [buːð; buːθ] *n* kabina

booty [ˈbuːti] *n* plen; plijen

border [ˈbɔːdə] 1. *n* granica 2. porub 3. *v* graničiti se

border crossing *n* granični prelaz

border dispute *n* granični disput

bore [bɔː] *v* 1. dosaditi 2. probiti

bored [bɔːd] *adj* dosadno

boring [ˈbɔːriŋ] *adj* dosadan

born [bɔːn] *adj* **to be born** biti rođen

borough [ˈbʌrə] *n* gradska opština

borrow [ˈbɔrəu] *v* pozajmiti

borrower [ˈbɔrəuə] *n* pozajmljivač

Bosnia [ˈbɔzniə] *n* Bosna

Bosnia and Herzegovina [ˈbɔzniə ‚ænd ‚heːtsəugəˈviːnə] *n* Bosna i Hercegovina

Bosnian [ˈbɔzniən] *adj* 1. bosanski 2. *n* Bosanac

boss [bɔs] *n* šef

botany [ˈbɔtəni] *n* botanika

both [bəuθ] *adj* oba, obe, oboje, obojica

bother [ˈbɔðə] *v* uznemiriti

bothered [ˈbɔðəd] *adj* **I couldn't be bothered to visit them.** Nije mi se išlo kodnjih.

both... and *conj* i... i

bottle [ˈbɔtl] *n* boca

bottle-opener [ˈbɔtl‚əupnə] *n* otvarač za boce

bottom [ˈbɔtəm] *n* dno

bought [bɔːt] *see* buy

bounce [bauns] *v* 1. baciti da odskoči 2. odskočiti

bound [baund] *adj* 1. na putu 2. siguran

boundary [ˈbaundri] *n* granica

bourgeois [ˈbɔːʒwaː] *adj* buržujski

bourgeoisie [‚bɔːʒwaːˈzi] *pl* buržoazija

bow [bəu] *n* 1. luk 2. pantljika

bow [bau] 1. *n* pramac 2. *v* pokloniti se

bowl [bəul] *n* činija

box [bɔks] 1. *n* kutija 2. **ballot box** glasačka kutija 3. *v* (spor.) boksovati se; boksati se

boxer [ˈbɔksə] *n* (spor.) bokser; boksač

boxing [bɔksiŋ] *n* (spor.) boks

box office *n* blagajna

boy [bɔi] *n* dečak; dječak

boycott [ˈbɔikɔt] 1. *n* bojkot 2. *v* bojkotovati

boyfriend [ˈbɔifrend] *n* dečko; dječko

boyhood [ˈbɔihud] *n* dečaštvo; dječaštvo

boy scout *n* skaut

bra [braː] *n* prslučić

bracelet [ˈbreislit] *n* narukvica

bracket [ˈbrækit] *n* **tax bracket** grupa poreznika

brackets [ˈbrækits] *pl* zagrada

braille [breil] *n* slepačko pismo; sljepačko pismo

brain [brein] *n* mozak

brain drain *n* odliv intelektualaca

brainwash [ˈbreinwɔʃ] *v* oprati mozak

brake, brakes [breik; breiks] 1. *n* kočnica 2. *v* ukočiti

bran [bræn] *n* mekinje

branch [braːntʃ] *n* grana

branch office *n* filijala

brand name [ˈbrændneim] *n* naziv marke

brand new *adj* nov novcat

brandy [ˈbrændi] n rakija
brass [braːs] n mesing
brassiere [ˈbræsiə] n prslučić
brave [breiv] adj hrabar
bravery [ˈbreivəri] n hrabost
brawl [brɔːl] n svađa
breach [briːtʃ] v probiti
breach of contract n neispunjenje ugovora
breach of the peace n narušavanje javnog reda
bread [bred] n hleb; hljeb; kruh
breadth [bretθ] n širina
break [breik] 1. n prelom 2. odmor 3. v (broke, broken) slomiti 4. to break the law prekršiti zakon
breakable [ˈbreikəbl] adj lomljiv
break away v oteti se
breakdown [ˈbreikdaun] n kvar
breakfast [brekfəst] n doručak
break in [ˈbreikin] v 1. provaliti 2. razraditi
break off v prekinuti
break out v pobeći; pobjeći
break up v rasturiti
breast [brest] n 1. grudi 2. prsa
breast-feed [ˈbrestfiːd] v dojiti
breasts [brests] see **breast**
breath [breθ] n dah
breathe [briːð] v disati
breathing [ˈbriːðiŋ] n disanje
breed [briːd] v (bred) odgajiti
breeze [briːz] n povetarac; povjetarac
brew [bruː] v variti
brewery [ˈbruəri] n pivara
bribe [braib] 1. n mito 2. v podmititi
bribery [ˈbraibəri] n podmićivanje
brick [brik] n cigla
bride [braid] n nevesta; nevjesta
bridegroom [ˈbraidgruːm] n mladoženja

bridge [bridʒ] n most
bridgehead [ˈbidʒhed] n mostobran
bridle [ˈbraidl] n oglav
brief [briːf] 1. adj kratak 2. v informisati
briefcase [ˈbriːfkeis] n aktentašna
briefly [ˈbriːfli] adv ukratko; nakratko
brigade [briˈgeid] n brigada
brigadier general [ˌbrigəˈdiə ˈdʒenrəl] n general-major
bright [brait] adj 1. svetao; svijetao 2. inteligentan
brighten [ˈbraitn] v razvedriti
brightness [ˈbraitnis] n sjajnost
brilliant [ˈbriliənt] adj briljantan
brim [brim] n ivica
bring [briŋ] v doneti; donijeti
bring about v izazvati
bring down v oboriti
bring out v izneti; iznijeti
bring to mind v podsetiti; podsjetiti
bring up v 1. doneti; donijeti 2. izneti; iznijeti
brink [briŋk] n ivica
brisk [brisk] adj živahan
Britain [ˈbritn] n Britanija
British [ˈbritiʃ] adj britanski
Briton [ˈbritn] n Britanac
brittle [ˈbritl] adj krt
broad [brɔːd] adj širok
broadcast [ˈbrɔːdkaːst] n 1. emisija 2. v (broadcast) emitovati
broad-minded [ˌbrɔːdˈmaindid] adj slobodouman
broadness [ˈbrɔːdnis] n širina
broccoli [ˈbrɔkəli] n prokule
brochure [ˈbrəuʃə] n brošura
broke, broken [brəuk; ˈbrəukən] see **break**
broker [ˈbrəukə] n posrednik

brokerage [ˈbrəukəridʒ] *n* posredništvo

bronchitis [brɔnˈkaitəs] *n* bronhitis

bronze [brɔnz] *n* bronza

broom [bruːm] *n* metla

broth [brɔθ] *n* supa

brothel [ˈbrɔθl] *n* burdelj

brother [ˈbrʌðə] *n* brat

brother-in-law [ˈbrʌðərinlɔː] *n* zet/ dever; djever/šurak

brought [brɔːt] *see* **bring**

brow [brau] *n* obrva

brown [braun] *adj* smeđ

brown coal *n* mrki ugalj

bruise [bruːz] 1. *n* modrica 2. *v* napraviti modricu (na)

brush [brʌʃ] 1. *n* četka 2. *v* očetkati

brutal [ˈbruːtl] *adj* brutalan

brutality [bruːˈtæləti] *n* brutalnost

bubble [ˈbʌbl] *n* mehur; mjehur

bucket [ˈbʌkit] *n* kofa

buckle [ˈbʌkl] *n* kopča

buckle up *v* zakopčati

bud [bʌd] *n* pupoljak

budge [bʌdʒ] *v* pomeriti; pomjeriti

budget [ˈbʌdʒit] *n* budžet

buffalo [ˈbʌfələu] *n* auna

buffer state [ˈbʌfəˈsteit] *n* tampon- država

buffet [buˈfei] *n* bife

bug [bʌg] 1. *n* insekat 2. **electronic bug** prislušni uređaj 3. **computer bug** greška 4. *v* gnjaviti 5. prisluškivati

build [bild] *v* (**built**) izgraditi

builder [ˈbildə] *n* graditelj

builder contractor *n* građevinski preduzimač

building [ˈbildiŋ] *n* 1. zgrada 2. izgradnja

building society *n* kreditno udruženje za građevinske zajmove

build-up *n* 1. raširenje 2. (mil.) koncentrija

built [bilt] *see* **build**

bulb [bʌlb] *n* 1. lukovica 2. **light bulb** sijalica; žarulja

Bulgaria [bʌlˈgeərijə] *n* Bugarska

Bulgarian [bʌlˈgeərujən] 1. *adj* bugarski 2. *n* Bugarin

bulge [bʌldʒ] *v* izbočiti se

bulk [bʌlk] 1. *adj* rasut 2. *n* veliki obim

bulky [ˈbʌlki] *adj* masivan

bull [bul] *n* bik

bulldozer [ˈbuldəuzə] *n* buldožer

bullet [ˈbulit] *n* metak

bulletin [ˈbulətin] *n* bilten

bulletproof [ˈbulitpruːf] *adj* neprobojan za zrno

bull's eye [ˈbulzai] *n* središte mete

bully [ˈbuli] *v* nasilnik

bump [bʌmp] 1. *n* čvoruga; kvrga 2. džomba 3. *v* udariti

bumper [ˈbʌmpə] *n* odbojnik

bumpy [ˈbʌmpi] *adj* džombast

bunch [bʌntʃ] *n* evenka

bundle [ˈbʌndl] *n* svežanj

bungle [ˈbʌŋgl] *v* pokvariti

buoy [bɔi] *n* boja

burden [ˈbəːdn] *n* teret

burden of proof *n* (leg.) teret dokazivanja

burdensome [ˈbəːdnsəm] *n* tegoban

bureau [ˈbjuːrəu] *n* biro

bureaucracy [ˈbjuərəkræsi] *n* birokratija; birokracija

bureaucrat [ˈbjuərəkræt] *n* birokrata

bureaucratic [ˌbjuərəˈkrætik] *adj* birokratski

bureau de change [ˈbjuːrəu də ʃɔːndʒ] *n* menjačnica

burger *n* pljeskavica

burglar [ˈbəːglə] *n* provalnik
burglary [ˈbəːgləri] *n* provalna krađa
burial [ˈberiəl] *n* pogreb
burn [bəːn] 1. *n* opekotina 2. *v* (burnt) spaliti 3. opeći 4. goreti; gorjeti
burn down *v* izgoreti; izgorjeti
burp [bəːp] 1. *n* podrigivanje 2. *v* podrignuti
burst [bəːst] *v* (burst) 1. pući 2. raskinuti
bury [ˈberi] *v* zakopati
bus [bʌs] *n* 1. autobus 2. minibus minibus
bush [buʃ] *n* 1. žbun 2. the bush divljina
business [ˈbiznis] *n* 1. posao 2. stvar 3. (com.) radnja 4. biznis 5. to go into business odati se trgovini
business card *n* podsetnica
businessman [ˈbiznismən] *n* trgovac
businesswoman [ˈbizniswumən] *n* trgovkinja
bus station *n* autobuska stanica
bus stop *n* autobuska stanica
bust [bʌst] 1. *n* grudi 2. *v* (bust) razbiti
busy [ˈbizi] *adj* 1. zauzet 2. prometan 3. The number is busy. Broj je zauzet.
but [bʌt] *conj* ali, osim, samo

butane [ˈbəutein] *n* butan
butcher [ˈbutʃə] *n* mesar
but for *prep* da nije
butt [bʌt] *v* bosti
butter [ˈbʌtə] *n* puter; maslac
butterfly [ˈbʌtəflai] *n* leptir
buttermilk [ˈbʌtəmilk] *n* mlaćenica
buttocks [ˈbʌtəks] *pl* zadnjica
button [bʌtn] *n* dugme
buttonhole [ˈbʌtnhəul] *n* rupica za dugme
buy [bai] *v* kupiti
buyer [ˈbaiə] *n* kupac
buy up *v* otkupiti
buzz [bʌz] *v* zujati
buzzer [ˈbʌzə] *n* zumer
by [bai] *prep* 1. by the house pored kuće 2. by train vozom; vlakom 3. by day podanu 4. by tomorrow do sutra 5. a book by Charles Dickens knjiga Čarlsa Dikensa
bye-bye! doviđenja!
by-election [ˈbai-e,lekʃn] *n* naknadni izbori
by-pass [ˈbaipaːs] *n* zaobilazak
bypass [ˈbaipaːs] *v* zaobići
by-product [ˈbaiprɔdʌkt] *n* sporedni proizvod
bystander [ˈbaistændə] *n* gledalac
byte [bait] *n* bajt

C

cab [kæb] *n* taxi

cabaret [ˈkæbərei] *n* kabare

cabbage [ˈkæbidʒ] *n* kupus

cabin [ˈkæbin] *n* 1. kućica 2. kabina

cabinet [ˈkæbinit] *n* 1. orman 2. the Cabinet kabinet

cable [ˈkeibl] *n* kabl

cable television *n* televizjski kabl-sistem

cadet [kəˈdet] *n* kadet

Caesarean section [səˈzeərijən ˈsektʃən] *n* carski rez

café [kæˈfei] *n* kafana; kavana

cage [keidʒ] *n* kavez

cake [keik] *n* torta

calabash [ˈkæləbæʃ] *n* vrg

calamity [kəˈlæmiti] *n* nesreća

calcium [ˈkælsiəm] *n* kalcijum

calculate [ˈkælkjuleit] *n* izračunati

calculation [ˌkælkjuˈleiʃn] *n* računanje

calculator [ˈkælkjuleitə] *n* računar

calendar [ˈkælində] *n* kalendar

calf [cɑːf] *n* (*pl* **calves**) 1. tele 2. list

call [kɔːl] *v* 1. pzvati 2. telefonirati 3. *see* **called, telephone call**

callbox [ˈkɔːlbɔks] *n* telefonska govornica

called [kɔːld] *adj* I am called Nick. Zovem se Nik.

caller [ˈkɔːlə] *n* pozivalac

call girl [ˈkɔːlgəːl] *n* prostitutka

calling card [ˈkɔːliŋkɑːd] *n* vizitkarta

call up *v* 1. telefonirati 2. (mil.) pozvati

calm [kɑːm] 1. *adj* miran 2. *n* zatišje

calm down *v* stišati

calmly [ˈkɑːmli] *adv* mirno; spokojno

calmness [ˈkɑːmnis] *see* **calm**

calves [kɑːvz] *see* **calf**

camcorder [ˈkæmkɔːdə] *n* video-kamera

came [keim] *see* **come**

camel [ˈkæml] *n* kamila

camera [ˈkæmərə] *n* kamera, foto-aparat

camouflage [ˈkæməflɑːʒ] 1. *n* maskiranje 2. *v* maskirati

camp [kæmp] 1. *n* kamping 2. logor 3. **summer camp** letovalište; ljetovalište 4. **to set up camp** podići logor 5. **training camp** (mil.) školski logor 6. **prisoner-of-war camp** zarobljenički logor 7. **concentration camp** koncentracioni logor 8. *v* kampovati

campaign [kæmˈpein] 1. *n* kampanja 2. *v* učestvovati u kampanji

campaigner [kæmˈpeinə] *n* aktivista

camping [ˈkæmpiŋ] *n* logorovanje

camp site *n* 1. kamping 2. (mil.) logorište

campus [ˈkæmpəs] *n* univerzitetsko zemljište; sveučilišno zemljište

can [kæn; kən] 1. *n* kutija 2. *v* (**could**) moći

Canada [kəˈneidə] *n* Kanada

Canadian [kəˈneidiən] 1. *adj* kanadski 2. *n* Kanađanin

canal [kəˈnæl] *n* kanal

cancel [ˈkænsl] *v* (**cancelled**) ukinuti

cancellation [ˌkænsəˈleiʃn] *n* ukinuće

cancer [ˈkænsə] *n* (med.) rak

candidate [ˈkændidət] *n* kandidat

candle [ˈkændl] *n* sveća; svijeća

candy [ˈkændi] *n* bombone

cane [kein] *n* trska

canister [ˈkænistə] *n* limena kanta

cannabis [ˈkænibis] *n* konoplja

canned food *n* u konzervi

cannon [ˈkænən] *n* top

can-opener [ˈkænəupnə] *n* otvarač za konzerve

canteen [kænˈtiːn] *n* kantina

canter [ˈkæntə] *v* lagano galopirati

cap [kæp] *n* 1. kapa 2. **sports cap** kačket

capability [ˌkeipəˈbiləti] *n* sposobnost

capable [ˈkeipəbl] *adj* sposoban

capacity [kəˈpæsəti] *n* kapacitet

cape [keip] *n* rt

capital [ˈkæpitl] *n* 1. glavni grad 2. (fin.) kapital

capitalism [ˈkæpitəlizəm] *n* kapitalizam

capitalist [ˈkæpitəlist] *n* kapitalista

capital letter *n* veliko slovo

capital punishment *n* smrtna kazna

capsize [kæpˈsaiz] *v* prevrnuti

captain [ˈkæptin] *n* 1. kapetan 2. (spor.) kapiten

caption [ˈkæpʃn] *n* naslov

captive [ˈkæptiv] *n* zarobljenik

captivity [kæpˈtivəti] *n* zarobljeništvo

captor [ˈkæptə] *n* zarobljivač

capture [ˈkæptʃə] *v* zarobiti

car [kaː] *n* automobil, kola

caravan [ˈkærəvæn] *n* stambena prikolica

car accident *n* automobilska nesreća

carbon [ˈkaːbən] *n* karbon

card [kaːd] *n* 1. karta 2. **postal card** poštanska karta 3. **to play cards** igrati karte 4. *see* **I.D. card**

cardboard [ˈkaːdbɔːd] *n* karton

cardboard box *n* kartonska kutija

care [keə] *n* 1. zaštita 2. **to take care of** pobrinuti se o

care about *v* voleti; voljeti

career [kəˈriə] *n* karijera

care for *v* mariti

careful [ˈkeəfl] *adj* oprezan

carefully [ˈkeəfəli] *adv* oprezno; pažljivo

careless [ˈkeəlis] *adj* neoprezan

carelessness [ˈkeələsnis] *n* neopreznost

caretaker [ˈkeəteikə] *n* nastojnik

cargo [ˈkaːgəu] *n* teret

cargo vessel *n* teretni brod

caricature [ˈkærikətjuə] *n* karikatura

carnival [ˈkaːnivl] *n* karneval

carol [ˈkærəl] *n* **Christmas carol** božićna pesma/pjesma

car park [ˈkaːpaːk] *n* parkiralište

carpenter [ˈkaːpintə] *n* drvodelja; drvodjelja

carpet [ˈkaːpit] *n* tepih

carphone [ˈkaːfəun] *n* telefon u automobilu

carriage [ˈkæridʒ] *n* 1. kočije 2. **train carriage** vagon

carrier [ˈkæriə] *n* 1. nosilac 2. (com.) transportno sredstvo 3. (med.) prenosilac

carrier bag *n* kesa, vrećica

carrot [ˈkærət] *n* šargarepa; mrkva

carry [ˈkæri] *v* 1. nositi 2. **to carry an election** pobediti na izborima

carry on *v* nastaviti

carry out v izvršiti
cart [ka:t] n teretna kola
carton [ka:ˈtn] n kartonska kutija
cartoon [ka:ˈtu:n] n 1. karikatura 2. crtani film
cartridge [ˈka:trɪdʒ] n 1. metak 2. **printer cartridge** kaseta za štampač
carve [ka:v] v iseći; isjeći
carve up v razdeliti; razdijeliti
case [keis] n 1. kutija 2. slučaj 3. stvar 4. (leg.) parnica 5. **in any case** u svakom slučaju
cash [kæʃ] n gotov novac
cash a cheque v onovčiti ček
cash-card n kartica za zađenje novca iz bankomata
cashier [kæˈʃiə] n blagajnik
cash-point n bankomat
cash register n registar-kasa
cash sale n prodaja za gotovo
casino [kəˈsi:nəu] n kasino
cassava [kəˈsa:və] n maniok
cassette [kəˈset] n kaseta
cassette recorder n kasetofon
cast [ka:st] 1. n glumci 2. v baciti
cast a vote v dati glas
castle [ˈka:sl] n kula
casual [ˈkæʒuəl] adj slučajan
casualties [ˈkæʒuəltiz] pl (mil.) gubici
cat [kæt] n mačka
catalogue [ˈkætəlɔg] n katalog
cataract n katarakt
catastrophe [kəˈtæstrəfi] n katastrofa
catch [kætʃ] v (**caught**) 1. uloviti 2. uhvatiti 3. **He caught a cold.** Nazebao je.
catch up v stići
categorically [ˌkætəˈgɔrikli] adv kategorično

category [ˈkætəgəri] n kategorija
caterpillar [ˈkætəpilə] n gusenica
caterpillar tractor n traktor-guseničar/gusjeničar
cathedral [kəˈθi:drəl] n 1. katedrala 2. (Orth.) saborna crkva
Catholic [ˈkæθəlik] 1. adj katolički 2. n katolik
cattle [kætl] pl stoka
caught [kɔ:t] see **catch**
cauliflower [ˈkɔliflauə] n karfiol; cvjetača
cause [kɔ:z] 1. n uzrok 2. v izazvati
caution [ˈkɔ:ʃn] n opreznost
cautious [ˈkɔ:ʃəs] adj oprezan
cautiously [ˈkɔ:ʃəsli] adv oprezno
cave [keiv] n špilja
cave in v srušiti se
cavity [ˈkæviti] n 1. duplja 2. karijes
c.d. [si:ˈdi:] see **compact disc**
cease [si:s] v prekinuti
cease-fire [ˌsi:sˈfaiə] n prekid vatre
ceaseless [ˈsi:slis] adj neprekidan
ceiling [ˈsi:liŋ] n plafon; strop
celebrate [ˈselibreit] v proslaviti
celebration [ˌseliˈbreiʃn] n proslava
celebrity [siˈlebrəti] n poznata ličnost
cell [sel] n celija; stanica
cellar [ˈselə] n podrum
cement [siˈment] n cement
cemetery [ˈsemətri] n groblje
censor [ˈsensə] v cenzurisati
censorship [ˈsensəʃip] n cenzura
census [ˈsensəs] n popis
cent [sent] n 1. cent 2. **ten per cent** deset odsto; deset posto
centimetre [ˈsentimi:tə] n santimetar; centimetar
central [ˈsentrəl] adj centralan
central government n centralna vlada

central heating *n* centralno grejanje/grijanje

central office *n* sedište; sjedište

centre ['sentə] *n* centar

centre-right *n* (pol.) desno od centra

century ['sentʃəri] *n* vek; vijek

CEO (chief executive officer) *n* (US) glavni izvršni službenik

cereal ['siəriəl] *n* žitna kaša

ceremony ['seriməni] *n* svečanost

certain ['sə:tn] *adj* 1. siguran 2. neki

certainly ['sə:tnli] *adv* sigurno

certainty ['sə:tnti] *n* sigurnost

certificate [sə'tifikət] *n* uverenje

certification [sətifi'keiʃn] *n* potvrda

certify ['sə:tifai] *v* potvrditi

chain [tʃein] *n* lanac

chair [tʃeə] *n* stolica

chair a meeting *v* predsedavati sednici/sjednici

chairman [tʃeəmən] *n* predsednik; predsjednik

chalk [tʃɔ:k] *n* kreda

challenge ['tʃælindʒ] 1. *n* izazov 2. *v* izazvati

chamber ['tʃeimbə] *n* 1. komora 2. (pol.) dom

chamber of commerce *n* trgovačka komora

chameleon [kə'mi:liən] *n* kameleon

champagne [ʃæm'pein] *n* šampanjac

champion ['tʃæmpiən] *n* šampion

championship ['tʃæmpiənʃip] *n* šampionat

chance [tʃɑ:ns] *n* 1. slučaj 2. rizik 3. prilika 4. **by chance** pukim slučajem

chancellor ['tʃɑ:nsələ] *n* 1. kancelar 2. (acad.) rektor

Chancellor of the Exchequer *n* ministar finansija/financija

change [tʃeindʒ] 1. *n* promena; promjena 2. kusur 3. *v* promeniti; promjeniti 4. preći 5. **to change one's mind** predomisliti se

channel ['tʃænl] *n* kanal

chaos ['keiɔs] *n* haos

chaotic [kei'ɔtik] *adj* haotičan

chapel ['tʃæpl] *n* kapela

chapter ['tʃæptə] *n* glava

character ['kæriktə] *n* 1. karakter 2. ličnost

characteristic [,kæriktə'ristik] *adj* karakterističan

characterize ['kæriktəraiz] *v* okarakterisati

charge [tʃɑ:dʒ] 1. *n* (com.) trošak 2. (elect.) naboj 3. (leg.) optužba 4. (mil.) juriš 5. **free of charge** besplatan 6. **to be in charge of** biti odgovoran za 7. *v* (com.) opteretiti 8. (elect.) napuniti 9. (leg.) optužiti 10. (mil.) jurišati

charity ['tʃærəti] *n* 1. milosrđe 2. dobrotvorni rad 3. dobrotvorna ustanova

charm [tʃɑ:m] *n* čarolija

chart [tʃɑ:t] *n* tabela

charter ['tʃɑ:tə] 1. *n* povelja 2. *v* zakupiti

charter flight *n* čater-let

chase [tʃeis] *v* goniti

chassis ['ʃæsi] *n* šasija

chat [tʃæt] *v* ćaskati

chatter ['tʃætə] *v* brbljati

chat up *v* udvarati se

chauffeur ['ʃəufə] *n* šofer

cheap [tʃi:p] *adj* jeftin

cheaply ['tʃi:pli] *adv* jeftino

cheat [tʃi:t] *v* 1. prevariti 2. (acad.) prepisati 3. (spor.) podvaliti

cheating ['tʃiːtiŋ] n prevara
check [tʃek] v 1. proveriti; provjeriti 2. kontrolisati 3. see cheque
checking account n (US) tekući račun
check-out ['tʃekʌp] n vreme odlaska gosta; vrijeme odlaska gosta
checkpoint ['tʃekpoint] n kontrola
check-up ['tʃekʌp] n (med.) pregled
cheek [tʃiːk] n 1. obra 2. drskost
cheeky ['tʃiːki] adj drzak
cheer [tʃiə] v bodriti
cheerful ['tʃiəfl] adj vedar
cheers! živeli!; živjeli!
cheer up v ohrabriti
cheese [tʃiːz] n sir
chef [ʃef] n glavni kuvar/kuhar
chemical ['kemikl] 1. adj hemijski; kemijski 2. n hemikalija; kemikalija
chemical warfare n hemijski rat; kemijski rat
chemical waste n hemijski otpad; kemijski otpad
chemical weapons pl hemijsko naoružanje; kemijskop oružje
chemist ['kemist] n 1. hemičar; kemičar 2. (UK) apotekar
chemistry ['kemistri] n hemija; kemija
chemist's ['kemists] n apoteka
cheque [tʃek] n ček
cheque-book n čekovna knjižica
cheque card n kartica koja garantuje pokriće čeka
cheque stub n čekovni odrezak
cherish ['tʃeriʃ] v gajiti
chess [tʃes] n šah
chest [tʃest] n 1. grudi 2. sanduk
chew [tʃuː] v sažvakati

chewing-gum ['tʃuːiŋgʌm] n guma za žvakanje
chic [ʃik] adj šik
chick [tʃik] n pilence
chicken ['tʃikin] n kokoš
chickenpox ['tʃikinpɔks] n varičela
chief [tʃiːf] 1. adj glavni 2. n šef
chiefly ['tʃiːfli] adv glavno
chief of staff n načelnik štaba
child [tʃaild] n (pl children) dete; dijete
childbirth ['tʃaildbəːθ] n porođaj
childhood ['tʃaildhud] n detinjstvo; djetinjstvo
childless ['tʃaildlis] adj bezdetan; bezdjetan
children ['tʃildrən] see child
children's ['tʃildrənz] adj dečji; dječji
chilly ['tʃili] adj hladan
chimney ['tʃimni] n (pl chimneys) dimnjak
chin [tʃin] n brađa
china, chinaware ['tʃainə] n porcelan; porculan
chip [tʃip] n 1. iver 2. chips pom frit 3. microchip čip
chocolate ['tʃɔklət] n čokolada
choice [tʃɔis] n izbor
choir ['kwaiə] n hor; kor
choke [tʃəuk] v zagušiti
cholera ['kɔlərə] n kolera
choose [tʃuːz] v (chose, chosen) izabrati
chop [tʃɔp] 1. n kotlet 2. v (chopped) seći; sjeći
chord [kɔːd] n (mus.) akord
chorus ['kɔːrəs] n hor; kor
chose, chosen [tʃuːz; 'tʃəuzən] see choose
Christian ['kristʃən] 1. adj hrišćanski; kršćanski 2. n hrišćanin; kršćanin

christian name n ime
Christianity [ˌkristiˈænəti] n hrišćanstvo; kršćanstvo
Christmas [ˌkristməs] n Božić
Christmas Eve n Badnje veče
chronic [ˈkrɔnik] adj hroničan; kroničan
chunk [tʃʌŋk] n komad
church [tʃəːtʃ] n crkva
cider [ˈsaidə] n jabukovača
cigarette [ˌsigəˈret] n cigareta
cinema [ˈsinəmə] n bioskop; kino
circle [ˈsəːkl] n krug
circuit [ˈsəːkit] n 1. kružni put 2. short circuit kratak spoj
circular [ˈsəːkjulə] adj cirkularan
circulate [ˈsəːkjuleit] v cirkulisati
circulation [ˈsəːkjuˈleiʃn] n circulacija
circumcision [ˌsəːkəmˈsiʒn] n obrezivanje
circumference [səːˈkʌmfərəns] n obim
circumstance [ˈsəːkəmstənsiz] n 1. prilika 2. **under no circumstances** ni u kom slučaju
circus [ˈsəːkəs] n cirkus
cistern [ˈsistən] n cisterna
citizen [ˈsitizn] n državljanin
citizenship [ˈsitiznʃip] n državljanstvo
city [ˈsiti] n 1. grad 2. **inner city** geto
city council n gradsko veće/vijeće
city hall n većnica; vijećnica
civic adj građanski
civil adj civilni
civil engineer n građevinski inženjer
civilian [siˈviliən] 1. adj civilni 2. n civil
civilian government n civilna vlada

civilisation [ˌsivəlaiˈzeiʃn] n civilizacija
civilised [ˈsivəlaizd] adj civilizovan
civil liberty n lično pravo
civil rights pl građanska prava
civil servant n državni činovnik
civil service n državna služba
civil war n građanski rat
claim [kleim] 1. n zahtev; zahtjev 2. v tvrditi 3. zahtevati; zahtijevati
claimant [ˈkleimənt] n tražilac
clamp-down [ˈklæmpdaun] n restrikcija
clap [klæp] v (**clapped**) pljesnuti
clapping [ˈklæpiŋ] n aplauz
clarification [ˌklærifiˈkeiʃn] n razjašnjenje
clarify [ˈklærifai] n razjasniti
clarity [ˈklærəti] n jasnoća
clash [klæʃ] v 1. sudar 2. sudariti se
class [klaːs] v 1. klasa 2. (ed.) razred
classic [ˈklæsik] 1. adj primeran; primjeran 2. n klasik
classical [ˈklæsikl] adj klasičan
classify [ˈklæsifai] v klasifikovati
classmate [ˈklaːsmeit] n školski drug
classroom [ˈklaːsrum] n učionica
clause [klɔːz] n (pol/leg.) klauzula
claw [klɔː] n kandža
clay [klei] n glina
clean [kliːn] 1. adj čist 2. v počisti
cleanse [klenz] v očistiti
cleansing [ˈklenziŋ] n **ethnic cleansing** etničko čišćenje
clear [kliə] 1. adj jasan 2. **clear waters** bistre vode 3. v očistiti 4. ukloniti 5. (leg.) opravdati 6. **to clear land** raskrčiti zemlju
clearly [ˈkliəli] adv očigledno
clear up v raščistiti

clemency [ˈklemənsi] *n* blagost
clench [klentʃ] *v* stegnuti
clergy [ˈkləːdʒi] *n* sveštenstvo; svećenstvo
clerk [klaːk] *n* trgovački pomoćnik
clever [ˈklevə] *adj* bistar
click [klik] *n* škljocanje
client [ˈklaiənt] *n* klijent
cliff [klif] *n* litica
climate [ˈklaimit] *n* klima
climax [ˈklaimæks] *n* klimaks
climb [klaim] *v* popeti se (na)
climb down *v* sići (**from** s)
climber [ˈklaimə] *n* alpinist
clinch a deal [klintʃ] *v* napraviti nagodbu
cling [kliŋ] *v* (**clung**) držati se
clinic [ˈklinik] *n* 1. klinika 2. **maternity clinic** porodilište; rodilište
clinical [ˈklinikl] *adj* klinični
clip [klip] 1. *n* **film clip** filmski insert 2. **paper clip** spajalica 3. *v* seći; sjeći
clitoris [ˈklitəris] *n* klitoris
clock [klɔk] *n* 1. časovnik, sat 2. **alarm clock** budilnik
close [kləus] 1. *adj* blizak 2. *adv* blizu
close [kləuz] *v* zatvoriti
closed [kləuzd] *adj* zatvoren
closely [ˈkləusli] *adv* 1. blisko 2. pažljivo
closet [ˈklɔzit] *n* orman
cloth [klɔθ] *n* štof
clothe [kləuð] *v* obući
clothes, clothing [kləuðz; ˈkləuðiŋ] *pl* odeća; odjeća
cloud [klaud] *n* oblak
cloudy [ˈklaudi] *n* oblačan
clown [klaun] *n* klovn
club [klʌb] 1. *n* klub 2. *v* izbatinati

clue [kluː] *n* indicija
clumsiness [ˈklʌmsinəs] *n* nezgrapnost
clumsy [ˈklʌmsi] *adj* nespretan
clung [klʌŋ] *see* **cling**
cluster [ˈklʌstə] *n* grupa
clutch [klʌtʃ] 1. *n* kvačilo 2. *v* šćepati
co. *see* **company**
coach [kəutʃ] 1. *n* autobus 2. (spor.) trener 3. *v* podučavati
coal [kəul] *n* ugalj
coalition [ˌkəuəˈliʃn] *n* koalicija
coalition government *n* koaliciona vlada
coal mine [ˈkəulmain] *n* ugljenokop
coal miner [ˈkəulmainə] *n* ugljar
coarse [kɔːs] *adj* 1. grub 2. prost
coast [kəust] *n* obala
coastal [ˈkəustl] *adj* obalski
coat [kəut] *n* kaput
coat of arms *n* grb
coax [kəuks] *v* privoleti; privoljeti
cobbler [ˈkɔblə] *n* obućar
cobra [ˈkəubrə; kɔbrə] *n* kobra
cocaine [kəuˈkein] *n* kokain
cock, cockerel [kɔk; ˈkɔkərəl] *n* petao; pijetao
cockroach [ˈkɔkrəutʃ] *n* bubašvaba
cocktail [ˈkɔkteil] *n* koktel
cocoa [ˈkəukəu] *n* kakao
coconut [ˈkəukənʌt] *n* kokos
cod [kɔd] *n* bakalar
code [kəud] *n* 1. šifra 2. **highway code** saobraćajna pravila 3. **penal code** krivični zakonik
coerce [kəuˈəːs] *v* primorati
coexistence [ˌkəuegˈzistəns] *n* 1. koegzistencija 2. **peaceful coexistence** miroljubiva koegzistencija
coffee [ˈkɔfi] *n* kafa; kava

coffin [ˈkɔfin] *n* mrtvački kovčeg
coil [kɔil] *v* kalem
coin [kɔin] *n* novčić
coincide [ˌkɔuinˈsaid] *v* podudarati se
coincidence [kɔuˈinsidəns] *n* koincidencija
cold [kəuld] 1. *adj* hladan 2. *n* hladnoća, zima 3. **He caught a cold.** Nazebao je.
cold-blooded *adj* hladnokrvan
coldness [ˈkəuldnis] *n* hladnoća
cold war *n* hladni rat
collaborate [kəˈlæbəreit] *v* sarađivati
collaboration [kəˈlæbəreitʃn] *n* 1. saradnja 2. **in collaboration with** uz saradnju s
collaborator [kəˈlæbəreitə] *n* 1. saradnik; suradnik 2. kolaboracionista
collapse [kəˈlæps] 1. *n* pad 2. (med.) slom 3. *v* srušiti se 4. (med.) doživeti slom; doživjeti slom
collar [ˈkɔlə] *n* kragna
colleague [ˈkɔliːg] *n* kolega
collect [kəˈlekt] *v* 1. skupiti 2. skupljati
collection [kəˈlekʃn] *n* 1. skupljnanje 2. zbirka
collective [kəˈlektiv] *adj* kolektivan
collective farm *n* zemljoradnička zadruga
college [ˈkɔlidʒ] *n* koledž
collide [kəˈlaid] *v* sudariti se
collision [kəˈliʒn] *n* sudar
colloquial [kəˈləukwiəl] *adj* govorni
collusion [kəˈluːʒn] *n* dosluh
colonel [ˈkəːnl] *n* pukovnik
colonial [kəˈləuniəl] *adj* kolonijalan
colonialism [kəˈləuniəlizəm] *n* kolonijalizam

colonialist [kɔˈləunijalist] *n* kolonizator
colonist [ˈkɔlənist] *n* kolonista
colonialization [ˌkɔlənaiˈzeiʃn] *n* kolonizacija
colonize [ˈkɔlənaiz] *v* kolonizovati
colony [ˈkɔləni] *n* kolonija
colour [ˈkʌlə] *n* boja
colour film *n* film u koloru
column [ˈkɔləm] *n* 1. stub 2. (mil.) kolona 3. **newspaper column** rubrika
coma [ˈkəumə] *n* koma
comb [kəum] *n* češalj
combat [ˈkɔmbæt] 1. *adj* borbeni 2. *n* borba 3. *v* boriti se (s)
combination [ˌkɔmbiˈneiʃn] *n* kombinacija
combine [kəmˈbain] *v* kombinovati
come [kʌm] *v* (**came, come**) doći
come across *v* nabasati
come back *v* vratiti se
comedian [kəˈmiːdiən] *n* komičar
come down *v* sići
come in *v* ući
comedy [kəˈmiːdi] *n* komedija
come off *v* odlomiti se
come out *v* izaći
comet [ˈkɔmet] *n* kometa
come up *v* popeti se
comfort [ˈkʌmfət] 1. *n* komfor 2. *v* utešiti; utješiti
comfortable [ˈkʌmftəbl] *adj* komotan
comic [ˈkɔmik] 1. *adj* komičan 2. *n* komik, stripovi 3. komičar
coming [ˈkʌmiŋ] 1. *adj* dolazeći 2. *n* dolazak
comma [ˈkɔmə] *n* zarez
command [kəˈmaːnd] 1. *n* naredba 2. komanda 3. *v* komandovati
commander [kəˈmaːndə] *n* komandant

commander-in-chief *n* vrhovni komandant

commando [kə·maːndəu] *n* komandos

commemoration [kə,memɔ·reiʃn] *n* komemoracija

commence [kə·mens] *v* početi

commend [kə·mend] *v* pohvaliti

comment [·kɔment] *v* komentarisati

commentary [·kɔməntri] *n* komentar

commerce [·kɔməːs] *n* trgovina

commercial [kə·məːʃl] *adj* komercijalan

commercial agency *n* trgovinsko predstavništvo

commercial bank *n* komercijalna banka

commercial centre *n* trgovački centar

commercial law *n* trgovačko pravo

commission [kə·miʃn] *n* 1. komisija 2. (mil.) oficirski čin

commissioner [kə·miʃənə] *n* komesar

commit [kə·mit] *v* (committed) 1. izvršiti 2. predati se

commitment [kə·mitmənt] *n* predaja

committee [kə·mitiː] *n* 1. odbor 2. steering committee upravni odbor

committee of inquiry *n* istražni odbor

commodity [kə·mɔdəti] *n* artikal

common [·kɔmən] *adj* opšti; opći

Common Market *n* Zajedničko tržište

commonplace [·kɔmənpleis] *adj* opšti; opći

common sense [,kɔmən·sens] *n* zdrav razum

commonwealth [·kɔmənwelθ] *n* zajednica

commotion [kə·meuʃn] *n* gungula

communal [·kɔmjunl] *adj* komunalan

communicate [kə·mjuːnikeit] *v* saopštiti; saopćiti

communication [kə,mjuːniˈkeiʃn] *n* veza

communications [kəˈmjuːniˈkeiʃnz] *pl* sredstva veze

communications network *n* telekomunikaciona mreža

communications satellite *n* telekomunikacioni satelit

communiqué [kə·mjuːnikei] *n* kominike

communism [·kɔmjunizm] *n* komunizam

communist [·kɔmjunist] 1. *adj* komunistički 2. *n* komunist

community [kə·mjuːnəti] *n* zajednica

commute [kə·mjuːt] *v* 1. redovno putovati na posao 2. (leg.) ublažiti

commuter [kə·mjuːtə] *n* osoba koja redovno putuje na posao

compact [kəm·pækt] *adj* kompaktan

compact disc *n* kompakt disk

companion [kəm·pæniən] *n* drug

company [·kʌmpəni] *n* 1. društvo 2. (com.) društvo, kompanija

comparable [·kɔmpərəbl] *adj* uporediv

comparative [kəm·pærətivl] *adj* komparativ

comparatively [kəm·pærətivli] *adv* relativno

compare [kəm·peə] *v* uporediti

comparison [kəm·pærisn] *n* upoređenje

compartment [kəm·paːtmənt] *n* 1. odeljak; odjeljak 2. **train compartment** kupe

compass [ˈkʌmpəs] *n* kompas
compassion [kəmˈpæʃn] *n* sažaljenje
compatible [kəmˈpætəbl] *adj* kompatibilan
compel [kəmˈpel] *v* prisiliti
compensate [ˈkɔmpənseit] *v* obeštetiti
compensation [ˌkɔmpənˈseiʃn] *n* odšteta
compete [kəmˈpiːt] *v* takmičiti se
competence [ˈkɔmpitəns] *n* sposobnost
competent [ˈkɔmpitənt] *adj* sposoban
competition [ˌkɔmpeˈtiʃn] *n* 1. konkurencija, takmičenje 2. free competition slobodna konkurencija
competitor [kɔmˈpetitə] *n* konkurent, takmičar
complain [kəmˈplein] *v* žaliti se
complaint [kəmˈpleint] *n* 1. žalba 2. (leg.) to lodge a complaint podneti žalbu; podnijeti žalbu
complement [ˈkɔmplimənt] *v* dopuniti
complete [kəmˈpliːt] 1. *adj* kompletan 2. *v* završiti 3. kompletirati
completely [kəmˈpliːtli] *adv* potpuno
complex [ˈkɔmpleks] *adj* kompleksan
complexion [kəmˈplekʃn] *n* ten
complicate [ˈkɔmplikeit] *v* komplikovati
complicated [ˈkɔmplikeitid] *adj* komplikovan
compliment [ˈkɔmplimənt] 1. *n* komplimenat 2. *v* komplimentovati

comply [kəmˈplai] *v* povinovati se
component [kəmˈpəunənt] *n* komponenta
compose [kəmˈpəuz] *v* 1. sastaviti 2. (mus.) komponovati
composed of [kəmˈpəuzd] *adj* sastavljen od
composer [kəmˈpəuzə] *n* kompositor
composition [ˌkɔmpəˈziʃn] *n* 1. sastav 2. (mus.) kompozicija
compound [ˈkɔmpaund] *n* 1. spoj 2. chemical compound hemijsko jedinjenje; kemijski spoj
comprehend [ˌkɔmpriˈhend] *v* shvatiti
comprehension [ˌkɔmpriˈhenʃn] *n* shvatanje
compress [kəmˈpres] *v* sabiti
compression [kəmˈpreʃn] *n* kompresija
comprise [kəmˈpraiz] *v* uključiti
compromise [ˈkɔmprəmaiz] 1. *n* kompromis 2. *v* kompromitovati
compulsory [kəmˈpʌlsəri] *adj* obavezan
compute [kəmˈpjuːt] *v* izračunati
computer [kəmˈpjuːtə] *n* računar; računalo
computer science *n* kompjuterska nauka
computing [kəmˈpjuːtiŋ] 1. *adj* računanje 2. kompjuterski 3. *n* računarstvo
comrade [ˈkɔmræd] *n* drug
concave [ˈkɔnkeiv] *adj* konkavan
conceal [kənˈsiːl] *v* sakriti
concealment [kənˈsiːlmənt] *n* skrivanje
concede [kənˈsiːd] *v* priznati
conceited [kənˈsiːtid] *adj* uobražen
conceive [kənˈsiːv] *v* 1. zamisliti 2. začeti

concentrate [ˈkɔnsntreit] *v* koncentrisati

concentration [ˌkɔnsnˈtreiʃn] *n* koncentracija

concentration camp *n* koncentracioni logor

concept [ˈkɔnsept] *n* pojam

concern [kənˈsəːn] 1. *n* briga 2. (com.) koncern 3. *v* zabrinuti

concerned [kənˈsəːnd] *adj* to be concerned biti zabrinut (**about** zbog)

concerned with, concerning [kənˈsəːniŋ] *prep* u pogledu

concert [ˈkɔnsət] *n* koncert

concession [kənˈseʃn] *n* ustupak

conciliation [kənsiliˈjeiʃn] *n* usklađenje

concise [kənˈsais] *adj* sažet

conclude [kənˈkluːd] *v* 1. završiti 2. zaključiti

conclusion [kənˈkluːʃn] *n* 1. završetak 2. zaključak 3. **in conclusion** na završetku

concrete [ˈkɔnkriːt] 1. *adj* konkretan 2. *n* beton

condemn [kənˈdem] *v* osuditi

condemnation [ˌkɔndemˈneiʃn] *n* osuda

condition [kənˈdiʃn] *n* 1. prilika 2. stanje 3. (leg.) uslov 4. **to be in good condition** biti u dobroj kondiciji 4. **on condition that** pod uslovom da

condo [ˈkɔndəu] *see* **condominium**

condolences [kənˈdəulənsiz] *pl* izjava saučešća

condom [ˈkɔndəm] *n* prezervativ

condominium [ˈkɔndəu] *n* (US) stan

condone *v* oprostiti

conduct [ˈkɔndʌkt] *n* ponašanje

conduct [kənˈdʌkt] *v* 1. voditi 2. (mus.) dirigovati

conductor [kənˈdʌctə] *n* 1. kondukter 2. (mus.) dirigent

cone [kəun] *n* kupa; stožac

confectionery [kənˈfekʃəneri] *n* poslastice; slastice

confederation [kənˌfedeˈreiʃn] *n* konfederacija

confer [kənˈfəː] *v* dodeliti; dodijeliti

conference [ˈkɔnfərəns] *n* 1. konferencija 2. **press conference** konferencija za štampu 3. **summit conference** konferencija na vrhu

confess [kənˈfes] *v* priznati

confession [kənˈfʃnl] *n* priznanje

confidence [ˈkɔnfidəns] *n* poverenje; povjerenje

confident [ˈkɔnfidəns] *adj* 1. siguran 2. samopouzdan

confidential [ˌkɔnfiˈdənʃəl] *adj* poverljiv; povjerljiv

confine [kənˈfain] *v* zatvoriti

confirm [kənˈfəːm] *v* potvrditi

confirmation [ˌkɔnfəˈmeiʃn] *n* potvrda

confirmed [kənˈfəːmd] *adj* potvrđen

confiscate [ˈkɔnfiskeit] *v* konfiskovati

conflagration [ˌkɔnfləˈgreiʃn] *n* požar

conflict [ˈkɔnflikt] *n* 1. sukob 2. (mil.) konflikt

conflict [kənˈflikt] *v* sukobiti se

conflicting [kənˈfliktiŋ] *adj* sukobljavajući

conflict resolution *n* rešenje sukoba; rješenje sukoba

conform [kənˈfɔːm] *v* povinovati se

conformist [kənˈfɔːmist] *n* konformista

confront [kən'frʌnt] v konfrontirati
confrontation [ˌkɔnfrʌn'teiʃn] n konfrontacija
confuse [kən'fju:z] v zbuniti
confused [kən'fju:zd] adj to be confused zbuniti se
confusing adj zbunjujući
confusion [kən'fju:ʒn] n zabuna
congestion [kən'dʒestʃən] n 1. zakrčenost 2. (med.) kongestija
congratulate [kən'grætʃuleit] v čestitati (on na)
congratulations [kənˌgrætʃu'leiʃnz] pl 1. čestitanje 2. congratulations on...! čestitamo na...
congregation [ˌkɔngri'geiʃn] n kongregacija
congress ['kɔngres] n 1. kongres 2. (US) Congress Kongres
congressman ['kɔngresmən] n kongresmen
conjurer ['kʌndʒərə] n mađioničar
connect [kə'nekt] v vezati
connection, connexion [kə'nekʃn] n 1. veza 2. in connection with u vezi sa
conquer ['kɔŋkə] v osvojiti
conqueror ['kɔnkərə] n osvajač
conquest ['kɔŋkwest] n osvajanje
conscience ['kɔnʃəns] n savest; savjest
conscientious [ˌkɔnʃi'enʃəs] adj savestan; savjestan
conscious ['kɔnʃəs] adj 1. svestan; svjestan 2. (med.) pri svesti/svijesti
conscript ['kənskript] n (mil.) regrut
conscription [kən'skripʃn] n vojna obaveza
consecutive [kən'sekjutiv] adj uzastopan

consensus [kən'sensəs] n konsenzus
consent [kən'sent] 1. n saglasnost 2. v pristati
consequence ['kɔnsikwens] n 1. posledica 2. in consequence of usled; uslijed
consequently ['kɔnsikwentli] conj stoga
conservation [ˌkɔnsə'veiʃn] n održanje
conservative [kən'sə:vətiv] (pol.) 1. adj konzervativan 2. n konzervativac
consider [kən'sidə] v razmotriti
considerable [kən'sidərəbl] adj znatan
considerate [kən'sidərət] adj obziran
consideration [kənˌsidə'reiʃn] n obzir
considering [kən'sidəriŋ] prep s obzirom na
consignment [kən'sainmənt] n pošiljka
consist [kən'sist] v sastojati
consistent [kən'sistənt] adj to be consistent konzistentan
consolation [ˌkɔnsə'leiʃn] n uteha; utjeha
consolidate [kən'sɔlideit] v učvrstiti
consonant ['kɔnsənənt] n suglasnik
conspicuous [kən'spikjuəs] adj upadljiv
conspiracy [kən'spirəsi] n zavera; zavjera
conspire [kən'spaiə] v konspirisati
constable ['kʌnstəbl] n policajac
constant ['kɔnstənt] adj stalan; postojan
constantly ['kɔnstəntli] adv stalnu
constipation [kən'stipeiʃn] n tvrda stolica

constituency [kən'stitjuənsi] *n*
(pol.) izborni okrug
constituent [kən'stitjuənt] *n* (pol.)
sastavni deo; sastavni dio
constitute [ˈkɔnstitjuːt] *v*
konstituisati
constitution [ˌkɔnstiˈtjuːʃn] *n* 1.
konstitucija 2. (pol.) ustav
constitutional [ˌkɔnstiˈtjuːʃənl] *adj*
ustavni
constraint [kən'streint] *n* prinuda
construct [kən'strʌkt] *v* izgraditi
construction [kən'strʌkʃn] *n*
izgradnja
construction industry *n* izgradnja
kuća
constructive [kən'strʌktiv] *adj*
konstruktivan
constructor [kən'strʌktə] *n*
konstruktor
consul [ˈkɔnsl] *n* konzul
consulate [ˈkɔnsjulət] *n* konzulat
consult [kən'sʌlt] *v* konsultovati
consultancy [kən'sʌltənsi] *n*
savetovalište; savjetovalište
consultant [kɔn'sʌltənt] *n* konsultant
consultation [ˌkɔnsʌlˈteiʃn] *n*
konsultacija
consume [kən'sjuːm] *v* 1. pojesti 2.
(ec.) potrošiti
consumer [kən'sjuːmə] *n* potrošač
consumer goods *pl* roba široke
potrošnje
consumption [kən'sʌmpʃn] *n*
potrošnja
contact [ˈkɔntækt] *n* 1. kontakt 2.
to be in contact biti u kontaktu
(**with s**) 3. **to lose contact**
izgubiti vezu 4. *v* kontaktirati
contact lens *n* kontaktno sočivo
contagious [kən'teidʒəs] *adj*
zarazan

contain [kən'tein] *v* sadržati
container [kən'teinə] *n* 1. posuda 2.
freight container kontejner
contemplate [ˈkɔntempleit] *v*
razmišljati
contemplation [ˌkɔntemˈpleiʃn] *n*
razmišljanje
contemporary [kən'tempəreri] 1.
adj savremen; suvremen 2. *n*
savremenik; suvremenik
contempt [kən'tempt] *n* prezir
contemptible [kən'temptibəl] *adj*
prezren
contemptuous [kən'temptʃuəs] *adj*
preziran
contend [kən'tend] *v* tvrditi
content [kən'tent] *adj* zadovoljan
contents [ˈkɔntents] *pl* sadržina
contest [kən'test] *n* takmičenje
contestant [kən'testənt] *n* takmičar
context [ˈkɔntekst] *n* kontekst
continent [ˈkɔntinənt] *n* 1.
kontinent 2. **the Continent**
Evropa
continental [ˌkɔntiˈnentl] *adj*
kontinentalni
contingency [kən'tindjənsi] *n* **for**
any contingency za svaku
eventualnost
continual [kən'tinjuəl] *adj* neprekidan
continually [kən'tinjuəl] *adv*
neprekidno; stalno
continue [kən'tinjuː] *v* nastaviti
continuous [kən'tinjuəs] *adj*
neprekidan
continuously [kən'tinjuəsli] *adv*
neprekidno; stalno
contour [ˈkɔntuə] *n* konturni
contraband [ˈkɔntrəbænd] 1. *adj*
krijumčaren 2. *n* kontrabanda
contraception [ˌkɔntrəˈseptʃən] *n*
kontracepcija

contraceptive [ˌkɔntrəˈseptiv] **1.** *adj* kontraceptivan **2.** *n* antikoncipijens

contract [ˈkɔntrækt] *n* ugovor

contraction [ˈkɔntræktʃən] *n* **1.** grčenje **2. labour contractions** porođajni grčevi

contractor [kənˈtræktə] *n* građevinar

contractual [kənˈtræktʃuəl] *adj* ugovorni

contradict [ˌkɔntrəˈdikt] *v* protivrečiti; protivuriječiti

contradiction [ˌkɔntrəˈdikʃn] *n* protivrečje; protivurječje

contrary [ˈkɔntrəri] *n* **on the contrary** naprotiv

contrast [ˈkɔntrɑːst] **1.** *n* supronost **2.** *v* suprotstaviti

contravene [ˌkɔntrəˈviːn] *v* prekršiti

contribute [kənˈtribjuːt] *v* priložiti

contribution [ˌkɔntriˈbjuːʃn] *n* prilog

contributor [kənˈtribjutə] *n* priložnik

contrive [kənˈtraiv] *v* skovati

control [kənˈtrəul] **1.** *n* kontrola **2. remote control** daljinsko upravljanje **3. self-control** samokontrola **4.** *v* kontrolisati

controller [kənˈtrəulə] *n* kontrolor

controversial [ˌkɔntrəˈvəːʃi] *adj* sporan

controversy [kənˈtrɔvəsi] *n* spor

convalesce [ˌkɔnvəˈles] *v* oporaviti se

convene [kənˈviːn] *v* sazvati

convenience [kənˈviːniəns] *n* **1.** zgoda **2. at your convenience** kad je vama zgodno

convenient [kənˈviːniənt] *adj* zgodan

convent [ˈkɔnvənt] *n* manastir

convention [kənˈvenʃn] *n* **1.** kongres **2.** konvencija

conventional [kənˈvenʃənl] *adj* konvencialan

conversation [ˌkɔnvəˈseiʃn] *n* razgovor

converse [kənˈvəːs] *v* razgovarati

conversion [kənˈvəːʃn] *n* **1.** pretvaranje **2.** (fin.) konverzija **3.** (rel.) preobraćanje

convert [kɔnˈvəːt] *v* **1.** pretvoriti **2.** (rel.) preobratiti

convex [ˈkɔnveks] *adj* konveksan

convey [kənˈvei] *v* **1.** preneti; prenijeti **2. to convey greetings** isporučiti pozdrave

convict [ˈkɔnvikt] *n* zatvorenik

convict [kənˈvikt] *v* osuditi

convince [kənˈvins] *v* uveriti; uvjeriti

convoy [ˈkɔnvɔi] *n* kolona

convulsion [kənˈvʌlʃn] *n* konvulzija

cook [kuk] **1.** *n* kuvar; kuhar **2.** *v* skuvati; skuhati

cookbook [ˈkukbuk] *n* kuvar; kuhar

cooker [ˈkukə] *n* peć

cool [kuːl] **1.** *adj* prohladan **2.** odličan **3.** *v* rashladiti

cool down *v* **1.** ohladiti se **2.** smiriti se

cooperate [kəuˈɔpəreit] *v* sarađivati; suradivati

cooperation [kəuˌɔpəˈreiʃn] *n* saradnja; suradnja

cooperative [kəuˈɔpərətiv] **1.** *adj* kooperativan **2.** *n* kooperativa

coordinate [kəuˈɔːdineit] *v* koordinirati

cop [kɔp] *n* (sl.) policajac

cope [kəup] *v* **to cope with something** izići s nečim na kraj

copier [ˈkɔpiə] *see* **photocopier**

copper [ˈkɔpə] *n* bakar
copulation [kɔpjuˈleiʃn] *n* snošaj
copy [ˈkɔpi] **1.** *n* kopija **2.** *v* kopirati **3.** imitirati
copyright [ˈkɔpirait] *n* autorsko pravo
coral [ˈkɔrəl] *n* koral
cord [kɔːd] *n* gajtan
cordless phone *n* bežični telefon
core [kɔː] *n* srž
cork [kɔːk] *n* čep
corkscrew [ˈkɔːkskruː] *n* vadičep
corn [kɔːn] *n* kukuruz
corner [ˈkɔːnə] *n* **1.** ugao **2.** kut
coronary [ˌkɔrəˈneri] *adj* koronarni
coronation [ˌkɔrəˈneiʃn] *n* krunisanje
coroner [ˈkɔrənə] *n* mrtvozornik, patolog
corporal [ˈkɔːpərəl] *n* kaplar
corporal punishment *n* telesna kazna
corporation [ˌkɔːpəˈreiʃn] *n* **1.** korporacija **2.** (com.) akcionarsko društvo
corps [kɔː] *n* **1.** kor **2.** (mil.) korpus
corpse [kɔːps] *n* leš
correct [kəˈrekt] **1.** *adj* tačan; točan **2.** *v* ispraviti
correction [kəˈrekʃn] *n* ispravka
correctly [kəˈrektli] *adv* tačno; točno
correspond [ˌkɔriˈspɔnd] *v* **1.** predstavljati **2.** dopisivati se
correspondence [ˌkɔriˈspɔndəns] *n* korespondencija
correspondent [ˌkɔriˈspɔndənt] *n* korespondent
corresponding [ˌkɔriˈspɔndiŋ] *adj* korespondentan
corridor [ˈkɔridɔː] *n* koridor
corrode [kəˈrəud] *v* gristi

corrugated iron [ˈkɔrəgeitidˈaiən] *n* valoviti čelik
corrupt [kəˈrʌpt] *adj* pokvaren
corruption [kəˈrʌpʃn] *n* kvarenje
cosmetic [kɔzˈmetik] **1.** *adj* kozmetički; kozmetički **2.** *n* kozmetičko sredstvo
cost [kɔst] **1.** *n* cena; cijena **2. the cost of living** životni troškovi **3.** *v* koštati
costly [ˈkɔstli] *adj* skup
costume [ˈkɔstjuːm] *n* nošnja
cottage [ˈkɔtidʒ] *n* kućica
cotton [ˈkɔtn] *n* **1.** pamuk **2.** konac
cotton wool *n* vata
couch [kautʃ] *n* kauč
cough [kɔf] **1.** *n* kašalj **2.** *v* kašaljati
could [kəd; kud] *see* **can**
council [ˈkaunsl] *n* **1.** savet; savjet **2. city council** gradsko veće
councillor [ˈkaunsələ] *n* većnik; vijećnik
Council of Europe *n* Evropski savet/savjet; Evropsko vijeće
counsel [ˈkaunsəl] *n* savet; savjet
counsellor [ˈkaunsələ] *n* savetnik; savjetnik
count [kaunt] *v* izbrojati
countdown [ˈkauntdaun] *n* odbrojavanje
counter [ˈkauntə] **1.** *n* žeton **2.** *v* odbiti
counteract [ˌkauntəˈrækt] *v* dejstvovati nasuprot; djejstvovati nasuprot
counterattack [ˌkauntəˈrættæk] *v* izvršiti protivnapad
counterfeit [ˈkauntəfit] *adj* lažan
counterfoil [ˈkauntəfɔil] *n* talon
counterpart [ˈkauntəpaːt] *n* duplikat
countless [ˈkauntlis] *adj* bezbrojan

count on v računati

country [ˈkʌntri] n 1. zamlja 2. **the country** selo

countryside [ˈkʌntrisaid] n selo

county [ˈkaunti] n okrug

coup, coup d'état [kuː; kuːdeiˈtaː] n državni udar

couple [ˈkʌpl] n 1. par 2. dva

coupon [ˈkuːpɔn] n kupon

courage [ˈkʌridʒ] n hrabrost

courageous [kəˈreidʒəs] adj hrabar

courier [ˈkuriyə] n kurir

course [kɔːs] n 1. tok 2. (ed.) kurs 3. (spor.) staza 4. **course of food** jelo 5. **in due course** blagovremeno 6. **of course!** naravno! 7. **in the course of** u toku 8. see **racecourse**

court [kɔːt] n 1. dvor 2. (spor.) igralište 3. (leg.) sud 4. **high court, supreme court** vrhovni sud

courtesy [ˈkəːtəsi] n učivost

courtesy call n kurtoazana poseta; kurtoazni posjet

court-martial [ˌkɔːtˈmaːʃl] n vojni sud

courtyard [ˈkɔːtjaːd] n dvorište

cousin [ˈkʌsin] n rođak, rođaka

covenant [ˈkʌvənənt] n svečan ogovor

cover [ˈkʌvə] 1. n pokrivač 2. **to take cover** uzeti zaklon 3. v pokriti 4. **to cover expenses** pokriti troškove

covering [ˈkʌvəriŋ] n pokrivač

covert [ˈkəuvəːt] adj prikriven

cover-up [ˈkəuvərʌp] n zataškivanje

cow [kau] n krava

coward [ˈkauəd] n kukavica

cowardice [ˈkauədis] n kukavičluk

cowboy [ˈkaubɔi] n kauboj

co-worker [ˈkəuwəːkə] n saradnik kolega; suradnik kolega

crab [kræb] n rak

crack [kræk] v razbiti

crackdown [ˈkrækdaun] n stroe kažnjavanje

crack troops pl elitne trupe

cradle [ˈkreidl] n kolevka; kolijevka

craft [kraːft] n (pl **craft**) 1. veština; vještina 2. brod 3. see **aircraft**

craftsman [ˈkraːftsmən] n majstor, obrtnik

craftsmanship [ˈkraːftsmənʃip] n umešnost; umješnost

crafty [ˈkraːfti] adj prepreden

cramp [kræmp] n grč

crane [krein] n 1. ždral 2. dizalica

crank [kræŋk] v staviti u pogon

crap [kræp] n (sl.) izmet

crash [kræʃ] 1. n sudar 2. (ec.) slom 3. v srušiti se 4. sudariti se **(into** s)

crash-helmet [ˈkræʃˌhelmit] n zaštitni šlem

crate [kreit] n koleto

crawl [krɔːl] v gmizati

crayon [ˈkreiən] n krejon, krajon

crazy [ˈkreizi] adj lud

cream [kriːm] n 1. pavlaka 2. krem

crease [kriːs] v nabrati

create [kriːˈeit] v 1. stvoriti 2. izazvati

creation [kriːˈeiʃn] n 1. stavranje 2. tvorevina

creative [kriːˈeitiv] adj stvaralački

creator [kriːˈeitə] n stvaralac

creature [ˈkriːtʃə] n stvor

credentials [kriˈdenʃlz] pl akreditivno pismo

credibility [ˌkredəˈbiləti] n verodostojnost; vjerodostojnost

credible [ˈkredəbl] adj verodostojan; vjerodostojan

credit [ˈkredit] **1.** *n* (fin.) kredit **2. to buy on credit** kupiti na kredit **4. to extend credit** dati kredit **5. to raise a credit limit** povećati kreditno ograničenje **6. to deserve credit** zaslužiti pohvalu **(for** za) **7. to give credit** pohvaliti **(for** za)

credit card *n* kreditna karta

creditor [ˈkreditə] *n* kreditor

crematorium, (US) **crematory** [ˌkreməˈtɔːriəm; kremətəri] *n* krematorijum

crescent [ˈkresnt] *n* mesečev srp; mjesečev srp

crest [krest] *n* **1. crest of a wave** breg talasa **2. crest of a mountain** vrh planine

crew [kruː] *n* posada

cricket [ˈkrikit] *n* **1.** cvrčak **2.** (spor.) kriket

crime [kraim] *n* **1.** zločin **2.** kriminalitet **3. war crime** ratni zločin **4. to commit a crime** izvršiti krivično delo

criminal [ˈkriminl] **1.** *adj* zločinački **2.** *n* zločinac

criminality [ˌkrimiˈnæləti] *n* kriminalitet

crimson [ˈkrimzn] *adj* tamnocrven

cripple [ˈkripl] **1.** *n* bogalj **2.** *v* obogaljiti

crippled [ˈkripld] *adj* osakaćen

crisis [ˈkraisis] *n* (*pl* **crises**) kriza

crisis point *n* **1.** kritična tačka/točka **2. at crisis point** na kritičnoj tački/točki

crisps [krisps] *pl* čips-krompir

critic [ˈkritik] *n* kritičar

critical [ˈkritikl] *adj* **1.** kritički **2.** (med.) kritičan **3. critical situation** kritična situacija

critically [ˈkritikli] *adv* **He is critically injured.** Teško je povreden/povrijeden.

criticism [ˈkritisizəm] *n* **1.** kritika **2. above criticism** iznad svake kritike

criticize [ˈkritisaiz] *v* kritikovati

critique [kriˈtiːk] *n* kritikovanje

croak [krəuk] *v* krekretati

crockery [ˈkrɔkəri] *n* zemljanica

crocodile [ˈkrɔkədail] *n* krokodil

crony [ˈkrəuni] *n* drug

crook [kruk] *n* lopov

crooked [ˈkrukid] **1.** *adj* kriv **2.** varalački **3.** *adv* krivo

crop, crops [krɔp; -s] *n, pl* usev; usjev

cross [krɔs] **1.** *adj* naprasit **2.** *n* krst; križ **3.** *v* preći

cross examination *n* unakrsno ispitivanje

cross-examine *v* podvrgnuti... unakrsnom ispitivanju

crossing [ˈkrɔsiŋ] *n* prelaz

crosslegged *adj/adv* prekrštenih nogu

cross out *v* precrtati

cross over *v* preći

cross-question *v* podvrgnuti... unakrsnom ispitivanju

crossroad, crossroads [ˈkrɔsrəud; -z] *n, pl* raskrsnica

cross-section *n* poprečni presek/presjek

crossword puzzle [ˈkrɔswəːd] *n* ukrštenica; križaljka

crouch [krautʃ] *v* čučnuti

crow [krəu] **1.** *n* vrana **2.** *v* kukuretnuti; kukurijetnuti

crowd [kraud] *n* gomila

crowded [ˈkraudid] *adj* prepun

crown [kraun] *n* kruna

crucial [ˈkruːʃl] *adj* preloman
crucify [ˈkruːsifai] *v* raspeti na krst/križ
crude [kruːd] *adj* 1. grub 2. sirov
crude oil *n* sirova nafta
cruel [ˈkruəl] *adj* okrutan
cruelty [ˈkruəti] *n* okrutnost
cruise [kruːz] 1. *n* krstarenje 2. *v* krstariti
cruiser [kruːz] *n* krstarica
crumb [krʌm] *n* mrva
crumble [ˈkrʌmbl] *v* izmrviti
crumple [ˈkrʌmpl] *v* izgužvati
crunchy [krʌntʃi] *adj* hrskav
crusade [kruˈseid] *n* 1. (rel.) krstaški rat 2. (pol/mil.) kampanja
crush [krʌʃ] *v* zdrobiti
crush resistance *v* slomiti otpor
crust [krʌst] *n* 1. **bread crust** komad hleba 2. **earth's crust** zemljina kora
crutch [krʌtʃ] *n* štaka
cry [krai] 1. *n* poklič 2. *v* plakati
crying [ˈkraiŋ] *n* plakanje
crystal [ˈkristl] *n* kristal
cube [kjuːb] *n* kocka
cucumber [ˈkjukʌmbə] *n* krastavac
cue [kjuː] *n* podsetnica; podsjetnica
cuisine [kwiˈziːn] *n* kuhinja
cul-de-sac [ˌkʌldiˈsæk] *n* (UK) ćorsokak
culprit [ˈkʌlprit] *adj* zločinac
cult [kʌlt] *n* kult
cultivate [ˈkʌltiveit] *v* orađivati
cultivation [ˌkʌltiˈveiʃn] *n* obrađivanje
cultivator [ˈkʌltiveitə] *n* kultivator
cultural [ˈkʌltʃərəl] *adj* kulturni
culture [ˈkʌltʃə] *n* kultura
cultured [ˈkʌltʃəd] *adj* kulturan
cunning [ˈkʌniŋ] *adj* lukav

cup [kʌp] *n* 1. šolja; šalica 2. (spor.) pehar
cupboard [ˈkʌbəd] *n* orman
curable [ˈkjuərəbl] *adj* izlečiv; izlječiv
curator [kjuˈreitə] *n* kurator
curb [kəːb] 1. *n* ivičnjak 2. *v* obuzdati
cure [kjuə] 1. *n* magani 2. *v* konzervirati 3. (med.) izlečiti; izlijeciti
curfew [ˈkəːfjuː] *n* policijski čas
curiosity [ˌkjuəriˈɔsəti] *n* radoznalost
curious [ˈkjuəriəs] *adj* 1. radoznao 2. redak; rijedak
curl [kəːl] *v* uviti
currency [ˈkʌrənsi] *n* 1. valuta 2. **foreign currency** devize
current [ˈkʌrənt] 1. *adj* tekući 2. *n* struja
current affairs *pl* aktuleni događaji
curry [ˈkʌri] *n* kari
curriculum [kəˈrikjuləm] *n* nastavni plan
curriculum vitae [kəˈrikjuləm viːtai] *n* kratka biografija
curse [kəːs] *v* 1. prokleti 2. opsovati
curtain [ˈkəːtn] *n* zavesa; zavjesa
curve [kəːv] 1. *n* krivina 2. *v* vijugati se
curved [kəːvd] *adj* kriv
cushion [ˈkuʃn] *n* jastuk
custody [ˈkʌstədi] *n* **to take into custody** zatvoriti
custom [ˈkʌstəm] *n* običaj
customary [ˈkʌstəməri] *adj* uobičajen
customer [ˈkʌstəmə] *n* kupac
customs [ˈkʌstəmz] *pl* carina
customs duties *pl* carina

customs officer, customs official n carinski službenik

cut [kʌt] **1.** n posekotina; posjekotina **2.** (ec.) smanjenje **3. short cut** prečica **4.** v (**cut**) seći; sjeći

cutback ['kʌtbæk] n smanjenje

cut down v oboriti

cute [kjuːt] adj **1.** ljubak **2.** (sl.) sladak

cutlery ['kʌtləri] n nožar

cutlet [kjuːt] n snicla

cut off v odseći; odsjeći

cuts [kʌts] pl (ec.) smanjenje

c.v. [siːviː] see **curriculum vitae**

cycle ['saikl] **1.** n ciklus **2.** v voziti bicikl

cylinder ['silində] n **1.** cilindar **2. gas cylinder** gasna komora

cynical ['sinikl] adj ciničan

Cypriot ['siprijət] **1.** adj kiparski; ciparski **2.** n Kipranin; Cipranin

Cyprus ['saiprəs] n Kipar; Cipar

Cyrillic ['siprijət] adj ćirilski

cyst [sist] n cista

cystitis [sisˈtaitis] n cistitis

Czech [tʃek] **1.** adj češki **2.** n Čeh

D

dad, daddy [dæd; ˈdædi] *n* tata
daft [dæft] *adj* šašav
dagger [ˈdægə] *n* bodež
daily [ˈdeili] 1. *n* dnevnik 2. *adj* dnevni 3. *adv* dnevno
dairy [ˈdeəri] *n* mlekarnica; mljekarnica
dale [deil] *n* dolina
dalek [ˈdaːlik] *n* robot
Dalmatia [dælˈmeiʃə] *n* Dalmacija
Dalmatian [dælˈmeiʃən] *adj* dalmatinac
dam [dæm] *n* brana
damage [ˈdæmidʒ] 1. *n* šteta 2. *v* oštetiti 3. *see* **damages**
damaged [ˈdæmidʒd] *adj* oštećen
damages [ˈdæmidʒiz] *pl* (leg.) od šteta
damn [dæm] *v* 1. prokleti 2. **damn!** do vraga!
damp [dæmp] 1. *adj* vlažan 2. *n* vlaga
dampness [ˈdæmpnis] *n* vlažnost
dam up *v* pregraditi
dance [daːns] 1. *n* igra 2. *v* igrati
dancer [ˈdaːnsə] *n* igrač
dancing [ˈdaːnsiŋ] *n* igranje
Dane [dein] *n* Danac
danger [ˈdeindʒə] *n* opasnost
dangerous [ˈdeindʒərəs] *adj* opasan
danger signal *n* znak opasnosti
dangle [ˈdæŋgl] *v* ljuljati (se)
Danish [ˈdeiniʃ] *adj* danski
dare [deə] *v* izazvati
daring [ˈdeəriŋ] *adj* smeo; smion
dark [daːk] 1. *adj* **dark colour** taman 2. **dark night** mračan 3. *n* mrak

darken [ˈdaːkən] *v* zamračiti
darkness [ˈdaːknis] *n* mrak
darling [ˈdaːliŋ] 1. *adj* omiljen 2. *n* ljubimac
dash [dæʃ] 1. *n* prepad 2. *v* poleteti; poletjeti 3. **to dash hopes** strušiti nade
data [ˈdeitə] *n* podaci
database *n* baza podataka
date [deit] *n* 1. datum 2. sastanak 3. urma; datulja 4. **out of date** zastareo; zastario 5. **up to date** moderan
date of birth *n* datum rođenja
daughter [ˈdɔːtə] *n* kći
daughter-in-law [ˈdɔːtərinlɔː] *n* snaha
dawn [dɔːn] 1. *n* zora 2. *v* svanuti
day [dei] *n* dan
day after tomorrow *n/adv* prekosutra
day before yesterday *n/adv* prekujuče
daybreak [ˈdeibreik] *n* praskozorje
daydream [ˈdeidriːm] *n* sanjarija
day in, day out *adv* iz dana u dan
daylight [ˈdeilait] *n* dnevna svetlost/svjetlost
day of remembrance *n* dan sećanja/sjećanja
daytime [ˈdeitaim] *n* dan
dazed [deizd] *adj* ošamućenost
dazzle [ˈdæzl] *v* zaslepiti; zaslijepiti
dead [ded] *adj* 1. mrtav 2. **the dead** mrtvi
dead-end *n* ćorsokak
deadline [ˈdedlain] *n* rok

deadlock [ˈdedlɔk] n zastoj
deadly [ˈdedli] adj smrtan
deaf [def] adj gluv; gluh
deafen [ˈdefən] v zaglušiti
deaf-mute n gluvonem; gluhonijem
deafness [ˈdefnis] n gluvoća; gluhoća
deal [diːl] 1. n nagodba 2. a great deal mnogo 3. v zadati 4. postupati (**with** s) 5. (com.) trgovati
dealer [ˈdiːlə] n 1. (com.) trgovac 2. drugs dealer rasturač droga
dealing [ˈdiːliŋ] n ponašanje
dear [diə] adj 1. drag 2. skup
death [deθ] n smrt
death penalty n smrtna kazna
deathrate n mortalitet
death sentence n smrtna presuda
debate [diˈbeit] 1. n debata 2. v debatovati
debit [ˈdebit] 1. n zaduženje 2. v upisati u dug
debris [ˈdeibriː] n ruševine
debt [det] n 1. dug 2. to get into debt pasti u dug 3. national debt državni dug
debtor [ˈdetə] n dužnik
decade [ˈdekeid] n dekada
decadence [ˈdekədəns] n dekadencija
decapitate [diˈkæpiteit] v odseći; odsjeći
decay [diˈkei] v raspasti se
deceased [diˈsiːsd] 1. adj pokojni 2. n the deceased pokojnik
deceit [diˈsiːt] n obmana
deceitful [diˈsiːtfl] adj obmanljiv
deceive [diˈsiːv] v obmanuti
December [diˈsembə] n decembar; prosinac

decency [ˈdiːsnsi] n pristojnost
decent [ˈdiːsnt] adj pristojan
decentralization [di,sentrəlaiˈzeiʃn] n decentralizacija
deception [diˈsepʃn] n prevara
decide [diˈsaid] v odlučiti
decimal [ˈdesiməl] adj decimalni
decipher [diˈsaifə] v dešifrovati
decision [diˈsiʒn] n 1. odluka 2. to take a decision doneti odluku; donijeti odluku
decisive [diˈsaisiv] adj presudan
deck [dek] n paluba
declaration [,dekləˈreiʃn] n deklaracija
declare [diˈkleə] n 1. objaviti 2. to declare war objaviti rat
decline [diˈklain] 1. n opadanje 2. v odbiti
decode [,diːˈkəud] v dešifrovati
decompose [,diːkəmˈpəuz] v raspasti se
decomposition [,dikɔmpəˈziʃn] n raspad
decompression [,dikɔmˈpreʃn] n dekompresija
decorate [ˈdekəreit] v 1. ukrasiti 2. (mil.) odlikovati
decoration [,dekəˈreiʃn] n 1. ukras 2. (mil.) orden
decorator [ˈdekə,reitə] n dekorater
decrease [diˈkriːs] 1. n opadanje 2. v opasti
decree [diˈkriː] n (pol.) dekret
decry [diˈkrai] v osuditi
dedicate [ˈdedikeit] v posvetiti
dedication [,dediˈkeiʃn] n posveta
deduce [diˈdʒuːs] v deducirati
deduct [diˈdʌkt] v odbiti
deduction [diˈdʌkʃn] n odbijanje
deed [diːd] n delo; djelo
deem [diːm] v smatrati

deep [di:p] 1. *adj* dubok 2. **a deep voice** dubok glas 3. *adv* duboko

deepen ['di:pən] *v* produbiti

deep-freeze *n* duboko zamrzavanje

deepness ['di:pnis] *n* dubina

deep-sea *adj* pučinski

deer [diə] *n* jelen

deface [di'feis] *v* zamrljati

defame [di'feim] *v* oklevetati

defeat [di'fi:t] 1. *n* poraz 2. *v* pobediti; pobijediti 3. (pol.) **to defeat a proposal** odbaciti predlog/prijedlog

defecate ['defəkeit] *v* isprazniti creva/crijeva

defect ['di:fekt] *n* mana

defect [di'fekt] *v* dezertirati

defection [di'fekʃn] *n* dezerterstvo

defective [di'fektiv] *adj* neispravan

defector [di'fektiə] *n* dezerter

defence [di'fens] *n* 1. odbrana; obrana 2. **self-defence** samo- odbrana; samoobrana 3. **antiaircraft defence** protiv- avionska zaštita; protuzračna zaštita

defenceless [di'fenslis] *adj* bez obrane/obrane

defend [di'fend] *v* odbraniti; obraniti

defendant [di'fendənt] *n* (leg.) tuženik

defender [di'fendə] *n* zaštitnik

defense [di'fens] *see* defence

defensive [di'fensiv] *adj* odbrambeni; obrambeni

defer [di'fə:] *v* odložiti

deferment [di'fe:mənt] *n* odlaganje

defiance [di'faiəns] *n* prkos

defiant [di'faiənt] *adj* prkosan

deficiency [di'fiʃnsi] *n* manjak

deficit ['defisit] *n* 1. manjak 2. **trade deficit** trgovinski deficit 3. **budget deficit** budžetski deficit

defile [di'fail] *v* uprljati

define ['difain] *v* 1. odrediti 2. definisati

definite ['definət] *adj* 1. određen 2. nedvomislen

definitely ['definətli] *adv* definitivno

deflate [di'fleit] *v* ispumpati

deflation [di'fleiʃn] *n* (ec.) deflacija

deflect [di'flekt] *v* skrenuti

deforest [di:'fɔrist] *v* krčiti šumu (u)

deform [di'fɔ:m] *v* deformisati

deformed [di'fɔ:md] *adj* unakažen

deformity [di'fɔ:məti] *n* deformacija

defraud [di'frɔ:d] *v* proneveriti; pronevjeriti

deft [deft] *adj* vešt; vješt

defy [di'fai] *v* 1. prkositi 2. ne dati se

degenerate [di'dʒenəreit] *v* degenerisati

degeneration [di,dʒenə'reiʃn] *n* degeneracija

degradation [,degrə'deiʃn] *n* poniženje

degrade [di'greid] *v* poniziti

degree [di'gri:] *n* 1. stepen 2. **to a degree** donekle 3. *see* **B.A.**, **M.A.**

de-ice [di:'ais] *v* odlediti

delay [di'lei] 1. *n* odgoda 2. *v* odgoditi

delayed [di'leid] *adj* odgođen

delegate ['deligət] *n* delegat

delegate ['deligeit] *v* poveriti; povjeriti

delegation [,deli'geiʃn] *n* delegacija

delete [di'li:t] *v* izbrisati

deliberate [di'libərət] *adj* nameran; namjeran

deliberately [di'libərətli] *adv* namerno; namjerno

delicate ['delikət] *adj* 1. nežan; nježan 2. **delicate situation** delikatna situacija

delicious [di'liʃəs] *adj* ukusan

delight [di'lait] *n* radost

delighted [di'laitid] *adj* ushićen

delightful [di'laitfl] *adj* divan

delinquent [di'liŋkwənt] *n* prestupnik

deliver [di'livə] *v* 1. isporučiti 2. osloboditi 3. **to deliver a baby** obaviti porođaj 4. **to deliver a speech** održati govor

deliverance [di'livərəns] *n* oslobođenje

delivery [di'livəri] *n* 1. raznošenje 2. (med.) porođaj

delude [di'lu:d] *v* prevariti

deluge ['delju:ʒ] *n* potop

delusion [di'lu:ʒn] *n* obmana

deluxe [di'lʌks] *adj* de-luks

demand [di'ma:nd] 1. *n* zahtev; zahtjev 2. **supply and demand** ponuda i potražnja 3. *v* zahtevati; zahtijevati

demarcation line [,dima:'keisnlain] *n* demarkaciona linija

demean [di'mi:n] *v* poniziti

demilitarization ['di:militərei'zeiʃn] *n* demilitarizacija

demilitarize [di:'militəraiz] *v* demilitarizovati

demilitarized zone *v* demilitarizovana zona

demobilization ['di:mobilei'zeiʃn] *n* demobilizacija

demobilize [di:'məubəlaiz] *v* demobilizovati

democracy [di'mɔkrəsi] *n* demokratija; demokracija

democrat ['deməkræt] *n* 1. demokrata 2. (US) član Demokratske stranke

democratic [,demə'krætik] *adj* demokratski

democratization ['di:mocratei'zeiʃn] *n* demokratizacija

democratize [di'mɔkrətaiz] *v* demokratizovati

demolish [di'mɔliʃ] *v* porušiti

demolition [,demə'liʃn] *n* rušenje

demon ['di:mən] *n* demon

demonstrate ['demənstreit] *v* 1. pokazati 2. (pol.) demonstrirati

demonstration [,demən'streiʃn] 1. proba 2. (pol.) demonstracija

demonstrator ['demənstreitə] *n* (pol.) demonstrant

demoralize [di'mɔrəlaiz] *v* demoralisati

demote [di'məut] *v* sniziti... čin

den [den] *n* jama

denial [di'naiəl] *n* inkari

denationalization [di,næʃənælaizei'ʃn] *n* denacionalizacija

denationalize [di,næʃnəlaiz] *v* denacionalizovati

denial [di,najəl] *n* demanti

Denmark ['denma:k] *n* Danska

denomination [di,nɔmi'neiʃn] *n* (fin.) apoen

denote [di'nəut] *v* označiti

denounce [di'nauns] *v* otkazati

dense [dens] *adj* gust

density ['densəti] *n* gustina

dent [dent] *v* ugnuće

dental ['denti] *adj* dentalni

dentifrice ['dentifris] *n* pasta za zube

dentist [ˈdentist] *n* zubar
dentures [ˈdentʃə] *pl* zubalo
denude [diˈnjuːd] *v* razgoliti
deny [diˈnai] *v* poreći
deodorant [diˈəudərənt] *n* dezodorans
depart [diˈpaːt] *v* otići
department [diˈpaːtmənt] *n* **1.** odeljenje; odjeljenje **2.** (acad.) odsek **3.** (pol.) ministarstvo
department store *n* robna kuća
departure [diˈpaːtʃə] *n* podlazak
depend [diˈpend] *v* zavisiti
dependence [diˈpendəns] *n* zavisnost
dependent [diˈpendənt] *adj* zavisan
depict [diˈpikt] *v* naslikati
deplore [diˈploː] *v* osuditi
deploy [diˈploi] *v* razviti
depopulate [diːˈpɔpjuleit] *v* smanjiti broj stanovika
deport [diˈpoːt] *v* proterati; protjerati
deportation [ˌdiːpoːˈteiʃn] *n* deportacija
deportee [ˌdiːpoːˈtiː] *n* deportirac
depose [diˈpəuz] *v* svrći
deposit [diˈpɔzit] **1.** *n* depozit **2.** *v* uložiti
depot [ˈdepəu] *n* depo
depreciate [diˈpriːʃieit] *v* opadati u vrednosti/vrijednosti
depreciation [diˌpriːʃiˈeiʃn] *n* deprecijacija
depress [diˈpres] *v* **1.** pritisnuti **2.** utući
depressed [diˈprest] *adj* utučen
depression [diˈpreʃn] *n* **1.** (med.) utučenost **2.** (ec.) depresija
deprive [diˈpraiv] *v* lišiti
depth [depθ] *n* dubina
deputy [ˈdepjuti] *n* zamenik; zamjenik

derailment [diˈreilmənt] *n* iskliznuće
derelict [ˈderəlikt] *adj* napušten
derision [diˈriʒn] *n* poruga
derive [diˈraiv] *v* izvesti
descend [diˈsend] *v* sići
descendant [diˈsendənt] *n* potomak
descent [diˈsent] *n* **1.** silaženje **2.** poreklo; porijeklo
describe [diˈskraib] *v* opisati
description [diˈskripʃn] *n* opis
desert [ˈdezət] *n* pustinja
desert [diˈzəːt] *v* napustiti
deserter [diˈzəːtə] *n* dezerter
desertification [diˌzəːtifiˈkeiʃn] *n* dezerterstvo
desertion [diˈzəːʃn] *n* napuštanje
deserve [diˈzəːv] *v* zaslužiti
design [diˈzain] **1.** *n* dezen, desen **2.** *v* nacrtati
designate [ˈdezigneit] *v* imenovan
designer [diˈzainə] *n* dizajner
desirable [diˈzaiərəbl] *adj* poželjan
desire [diˈzaiə] **1.** *n* želja **2.** *v* želeti; željeti
desist [diˈzist] *v* odustati
desk [desk] *n* **1.** pisaći sto/stol **2.** **hotel desk** recepcija
desk clerk *n* recepcionar
desktop [ˈdesktɔp] **1.** *adj* stoni; stolni **2.** *n* stoni komjuter; stolni kompjuter
desolation [ˌdesəˈleiʃn] *n* pustošenje
despair [diˈspeə] **1.** *n* očajanje **2.** *v* očajavati
despatch [disˈpætʃ] *see* **dispatch**
desperate [ˈdespərət] *adj* beznadežan
despise [diˈspaiz] *v* prezirati
despite [diˈspait] *prep* uprkos
despondency [diˈspɔndənsi] *n* utučenost

despotic [des'pɔtik] *adj* despotski

dessert [di'zə:t] *n* slatko

destabilization [di:,steibilai'zeiʃn] *n* destabilizacija

destabilize [di:'steibilaiz] *v* destabilizovati, izbaciti iz ravnoteže

destination [desti'neiʃn] *n* odredište

destine ['destin] *v* odrediti

destiny ['destini] *n* sudbina

destitute ['destitju:t] *adj* lišen

destroy [di'strɔi] *v* uništiti

destroyer [dis'trɔiə] *n* naval destroyer razarač

destruction [di'strʌkʃn] *n* uništavanje

destructive [di'strʌktiv] *adj* razoran

detach [di'tætʃ] *v* odvojiti

detail ['di:teil] *n* 1. podrobnost 2. in detail podrobno

detailed ['di:teild] *adj* detaljan

detain [di'tein] *v* zadržati

detainee [di'teini:] *n* zatočenik

detain indefinitely *v* pritvoriti na neodređeni rok

detect [di'tekt] *v* otkriti

detective [di'tektiv] *n* detektiv

detector [di'tektə] *n* detektor

détente [,dei'ta:nt] *n* detant

detention [di'tenʃn] *n* zadržavanje

deter [di'tə:] *v* zastrašiti

detergent [di'tə:dʒənt] *n* deterdžent

deteriorate [di'tiəriəreit] *v* pogoršati se

deterioration [di,tiəriə'reiʃn] *n* pogoršanje

determination [di,tə:mi'neiʃn] *n* određenje

determine [di'tə:min] *v* odrediti

determined [di'tə:mind] *adj* rešen; riješen

deterrent [di'terənt] *n* zastrašujuća

detest [di'test] *v* mrzeti; mrzjeti

detonate ['detəneit] *v* detonirati

detonator ['detəneitə] *n* detonator

detour ['di:tuə] *n* zaobilazni put

detrimental [,detri'mentl] *adj* škodljiv

deutschmark ['dɔitʃma:k] *n* marka

devaluation [,di:'vælju:'eiʃn] *n* devalvacija

devastate ['devəsteit] *v* opustošiti

devastation ['devəs'teiʃn] *n* pustoš

develop [di'veləp] *v* razviti (se)

developed [di'veləpt] *adj* developed nations razvijene zemlje

developer [di'veləpə] *n* graditelj stambenih naselja

developing [di'veləpiŋ] *adj* developing nations zemlja u razvoju

development [di'veləpmənt] *n* 1. razvoj 2. (ec.) razvitak

development project *n* razvojni projekat

development worker *n* radnik agencije za razvoj

deviate ['di:vieit] *v* odstupati

deviation [,di:vi'eiʃn] *n* odstupanje

device [di'vais] *n* naprava

devil ['devl] *n* đavo

devious ['di:viəs] *adj* zaobilazan

devise [di'vaiz] *v* smisliti

devote [di'vəut] *v* posvetiti

devotion [di'vəuʃn] *n* odanost

devour [di'vauə] *v* proždrati

devout [di'vaut] *adj* pobožan

dew [dju:] *n* rosa

dexterity [deks'terəti] *n* veština; vještina

diabetes [,daiə'bi:ti:z] *n* dijabetes

diabetic [,daiə'betik] *n* dijabetski

diagnose [ˈdaiəgnəuz] *v*
dijagnozirati

diagnosis [ˌdaiəgˈnəusis] *n* (*pl*
diagnoses) dijagnoza

diagram [ˈdaiəgræm] *n* shema

dial [daiəl] (tel.) 1. *n* brojčanik 2. *v*
okrenuti

dialect [ˈdaiəlekt] *n* narečje

dialogue [ˈdaiəlɔg] *n* dijalog

diamond [ˈdaiəmənd] *n* dijamant

diaper [ˈdaiəpə] *n* pelena

diaphragm [ˈdaiəfræm] *n*
dijafragma

diarrhoea [ˌdaiəˈriːə] *n* dijareja

diary [ˈdaiəri] *n* dnevnik

diaspora [daiˈæspərə] *n* dijaspora

dice [dais] *n* (*pl* dice) kocke

dictate [dikˈteit] *v* 1. izdiktirati 2. to
dictate terms diktirati uslove

dictation [dikˈteiʃn] *n* diktat

dictator [dikˈteitə] *n* diktator

dictatorial [ˌdiktəˈtɔːriəl] *adj*
diktatorski

dictatorship [dikˈteitəʃip] *n*
diktatura

dictionary [ˈdikʃenri] *n* rečnik;
rječnik

did [did] *see* do

didactic [diˈdæktik] *adj* didaktičan

die [dai] *v* umreti; umrijeti

die down *v* prestati

die-hard [ˈdaihaːd] *adj* nepopustljiv

die out *v* izumreti; izumrijeti

diesel [ˈdiːzl] *n* 1. diesel engine
dizel 2. diesel fuel dizel-gorivo

diet [ˈdaiət] 1. *n* dijeta 2. *v* biti na
dijeti

differ [ˈdifə] *v* 1. razlikovati 2. ne
slagati se

difference [ˈdifrəns] *n* 1. razlika 2.
nesuglasica

different [ˈdifrənt] *adj* različit

differentiate [ˌdifəˈrəntʃieit] *v*
razlikovati

difficult [ˈdifikəlt] *adj* težak

difficulty [ˈdifikəlti] *n* teškoća

difficulties [ˈdifikəltiːz] *pl* smetnje

diffuse [diˈfjuːs] *v* raširiti (se)

dig [dig] *v* (dug) kopati

digest [diˈdʒest; daiˈdʒest] *v* svariti

digestible [diˈdʒestəbl; daiˈdʒestəbl]
adj varljiv

digestion [daiˈdʒestʃən; daiˈdʒestʃən]
n varenje

digit [ˈdidʒit] *n* 1. cifra 2. prst

dignified [ˈdignifaid] *adj*
dostojanstven

dignity [ˈdignəti] *n* dostojanstvo

digress [daiˈgres] *v* udaljiti se

dike [daik] *n* nasip

dilate [daiˈleit] *v* proširiti (se)

dilemma [diˈlemə; daiˈlemə] *n* dilema

diligent [ˈdilidʒənt] *adj* marljiv

dilute [daiˈljuːt] *v* razblažiti

dim [dim] 1. *adj* bled; blijed 2. *v*
pomračiti

dimension [diˈmenʃn] *n* dimenzija

diminish [diˈminiʃ] *v* smanjiti (se)

diminutive [diˈminjutiv] *adj*
deminutiv

din [din] *n* graja

dine [dain] *v* večerati

dining room [ˈdainiŋrum] *n*
trpezarija; blagovaonica

dinner [ˈdinə] *n* večera

dinosaur [ˈdainəsɔ] *n* dinosaur

dip [dip] *v* omučiti

diphtheria [dipˈθiəriə] *n* difterija

diploma [diˈpləumə] *n* diploma

diplomacy [diˈpləuməsi] *n*
diplomatija; diplomacija

diplomat [ˈdipləmæt] *n* diplomata

diplomatic [ˌdipləˈmætik] *adj*
diplomatski

diplomatic corps n diplomatska služba

diplomatic relations pl diplomatski odnosi

diplomatic row n diplomatski sukob

direct [diˈrekt; daiˈrekt] 1. adj direktan 2. adv neposredno 3. v rukovati 4. regulisati 5. **to direct a film** režirati film

direct aid n direktna pomoć

direction [diˈrekʃn; daiˈrekʃn] n 1. pravac 2. regulisanje

directions [diˈrekʃnz; daiˈrekʃnz] pl uputstvo; uputa

directly [diˈrektli; daiˈrektli] adv 1. neposredno 2. odmah

director [diˈrektə; daiˈrektə] n 1. upravnik 2. **film director** režiser 3. **managing director** upravnik 4. **board of directors** direktorijum

directory [diˈrektəri; daiˈrektəri] n imenik

dirt [dəːt] n blato

dirty [ˈdəːti] 1. n prljav 2. v uprljati

disability [ˈdisəˈbiləti] n invaliditet

disable [disˈeibl] v onesposobiti

disabled [disˈeibld] adj invalid

disadvantage [ˌdisədˈvaːntidʒ] n nezgoda

disagree [ˌdisəˈgriː] v ne slagati se

disagreeable [ˌdisəˈgriːəbl] adj neprijatan

disagreement [ˌdisəˈgriːmənt] n nesloga

disappear [ˌdisəˈpiə] v iščeznuti

disappearance [ˌdisəˈpiərəns] n iščeznuće

disappoint [ˌdisəˈpɔint] v razočarati

disappointed [ˌdisəˈpɔintid] razočaran

disappointment [ˌdisəˈpɔintmənt] n razočarenje

disapproval [ˌdisəˈpruːvl] n osuda

disapprove [ˌdisəˈpruːv] v osuđivati

disarm [disˈaːm] v razoružati

disarmament [disˈaːməmənt] n razoružanje

disarmament talks pl pregovori o razoružanju

disaster [diˈzaːstə] n 1. katastrofa 2. **ecological disaster** ekološka nesreća

disaster relief n pomoć pri masovnim nesrećama

disastrous [diˈzaːstrəs] adj katastrofalan

disbelief [ˌdisbiˈliːf] n neverica; nevjerica

disc [disk] n disk

discard [disˈkaːd] v odbačiti

discharge [ˈdistʃaːdʒ] n 1. otpuštanje 2. ispaljivanje

discharge [disˈtʃaːdʒ] v 1. opustiti 2. opaliti

disciplinary [ˈdisiplinəri] adj disciplinski

discipline [ˈdisiplin] 1. n disciplina 2. v disciplinovati

disclose [disˈkləuz] v odati

disclosure [disˈkləuʒə] n obelodanjivanje; objelodanjivanje

disco [ˈdiskəu] n disko-klub

discomfort [disˈkʌmfət] n neudobnost

disconnect [ˌdiskəˈnekt] v isključiti

discontent [ˌdiskənˈtent] n nezadovoljstvo

discontented [ˌdiskənˈtentid] adj nezadovoljan

discontinue [ˌdiskənˈtinjuː] v ukinuti

discord [ˈdiskɔːd] n razdor

discount [ˈdiskaunt] n popust

discourage [diˈskʌridʒ] *v* obeshrabiti

discourse [ˈdiskɔːs] *n* govor

discover [disˈkʌvə] *v* otkriti

discoverer [disˈkʌvərə] *n* pronalazač

discovery [disˈkʌvəri] *n* otkriće

discredit [disˈkredit] *v* diskreditovati

discreet [disˈkriːt] *adj* diskretan

discrepancy [diˈskrepənsi] *n* protivrečnost; protivurječnost

discretion [diˈskreʃn] *n* diskrecija

discriminate [diˈskrimineit] *v* diskriminirati

discrimination [di,skrimiˈneiʃn] *n* 1. diskriminacija 2. **racial discrimination** rasna diskriminacija 3. **ethnic discrimination** etnička diskriminacija 4. **sexual discrimination** seksualna diskriminacija

discuss [disˈkʌs] *v* raspravljati

discussion [disˈkʌʃn] *n* diskusija

disdain [disˈdein] *n* prezir

disease [diˈziːz] *n* bolest

diseased [diˈziːzd] *adj* bolestan

disembark [,disimˈbaːk] *v* iskrcati se

disengage [,disinˈgeidʒ] *v* dezangažovati

disentangle [,disinˈtængl] *v* odmrsiti

disfigure [disˈfigə] *v* unakarediti

disgrace [disˈgreis] 1. *n* sramota 2. *v* osramotiti

disgraceful [disˈgreisfl] *adj* sraman

disguise [disˈgaiz] *n* prerušenje

disgust [disˈgʌst] *n* gađenje

disgusted [disˈgʌstid] *adj* odvratnošću

disgusting [disˈgʌstiŋ] *adj* odvratan

dish [diʃ] *n* zdela; zdjela

dishearten [disˈhaːtn] *v* obeshrabiti

dishonest [disˈɔnist] *adj* nepošten

dishonesty [disˈɔnisti] *n* nepoštenost

dishonour [disˈɔnə] *n* sramota

dishonourable [disˈɔnərəbl] *adj* nečastan

disillusion [,disiˈluːʒn] *v* razočarati

disinfect [,disinˈfekt] *v* dezinficirati

disinfectant [,disinˈfektənt] *n* dezinfekciono sredstvo

disinfection [,disinˈfekʃn] *n* dezinfekcija

disinformation [disˈinfəmeiʃn] *n* dezinformacija

disintegrate [disˈintigreit] *v* raspati se

disk [disk] *n* disk

diskette [disˈket] *n* disketa

dislike [disˈlaik] *v* nesklonost

dislocate [ˈdisləkeit] *v* (med.) iščasiti

dislocation [,disləˈkeiʃn] *n* (med.) iščašenje

dislodge [disˈlɔdʒ] *v* pomaći

dismal [ˈdizməl] *adj* tužan

dismantle [disˈmæntl] *v* razmontirati

dismay [disˈmei] *n* zaprepašćenje

dismiss [disˈmis] *v* 1. otpustiti 2. (leg.) obustaviti

dismissal [disˈmisl] *n* 1. otpuštanje 2. (leg.) obustava

dismount [disˈmaunt] *v* sjahati

disobedience [,disəˈbiːdiəns] *n* neposlušnost

disobedient [,disəˈbiːdiənt] *adj* neposlušan

disobey [,disəˈbei] *v* ne slušati

disorder [disˈɔːdə] *n* nemir

disorderly [disˈɔːdəli] *adj* nasilnički

disorganization [disˈɔːgənaizeiʃn] *n* dezorganizacija

disown [disˈəun] v odreći se
disparage [disˈpæridʒ] v omalovažiti
dispatch, despatch [disˈpætʃ] v otpremiti
dispel [disˈpel] v odagnati
dispensable [diˈspensəbl] adj nebitan
dispensary [diˈspensəri] n apoteka
dispenser [diˈspensər] n zidni držač
disperse [disˈpəːs] v rasturiti
displace [disˈpleis] v pomaći
displaced person [disˈpleist] n raseljeno lice
display [diˈsplei] 1. n ispoljavanje 2. **on display** izložen 3. (tel.) ekran 4. v pokazati 5. (com.) izložiti
displease [disˈpliːz] v ne sviđati se
displeasure [disˈpleʒə] n nezadovoljstvo
disposal [disˈpəusl] n 1. odstranjivanje 2. raspolaganje
dispose [disˈpəuz] v raspoložiti
disposition [ˌdispəˈziʃn] n dispozicija
dispossess [ˌdispəˈzes] v oduzeti... imanje
dispute [diˈspjuːt; ˈdispjuːt] n 1. disput 2. **border dispute** pogranični sukob
dispute [diˈspjuːt] v osporiti
disqualify [disˈkwɔlifai] v diskvalifikovati
disregard [ˌdisriˈgaːd] v ne obazirati
disrespect [ˌdisriˈspekt] n nepoštovanje
disrupt [disˈrʌpt] v prekinuti
disruption [disˈrʌpʃn] n prekid
dissatisfaction [diˌsætisˈfækʃn] n nezadovoljstvo
dissatisfied [diˈsætisfaid] adj nezadovoljan

dissect [diˈsekt] v secirati
disseminate [diˈsemineit] v raširiti
dissension [diˈsenʃn] n razdor
dissent [diˈsent] 1. n disidentstvo 2. v ne slagati se
dissertation [ˌdisəˈteiʃn] n disertacija
dissidence [ˈdisidəns] n disidentstvo
dissident [ˈdisidənt] n disident
dissimilar [diˈsimilə] adj različit
dissipate [ˈdisipeit] v rasturati se
dissociate [diˈsəuʃieit] v odvojiti
dissolve [diˈzɔlv] v 1. razmutiti 2. (pol.) raspustiti
distance [ˈdistəns] 1. n daljina 2. v **to distance oneself** držati se na odstojanju (**from** od)
distant [ˈdistənt] adj dalek
distaste [disˈteist] n nenaklonost
distend [disˈtend] v naduvati
distil [diˈstil] v destilirati
distilled water n destilovana voda
distillery [disˈtiləri] n destilacija
distinct [diˈstiŋkt] adj poseban
distinction [diˈstiŋkʃn] n 1. razlika 2. ugled
distinctive [diˈstiŋktiv] adj karakterističan
distinguish [diˈstiŋgwiʃ] v razlikovati
distinguished [diˈstiŋgwiʃt] adj proslavljen
distort [disˈtɔːt] v iskriviti
distortion [disˈtɔːʃn] n iskrivljenost
distract [disˈtrækt] v odvratiti
distracted [disˈtræktid] adj rastrojen
distraction [disˈtrækʃn] n distrakcija
distress [diˈstres] n 1. ogorčenje 2. nevolja

distressing [di·stresiŋ] *adj* tužan

distribute [di·stribju:t] *v* 1. raspodeliti; raspodijeliti 2. (com.) distribuirati

distribution [ˌdistri·bju:ʃn] *n* 1. raspodela; raspodjela 2. (com.) distribucija

distributive [di·stribjutiv] *adj* distributivan

distributor [dis·tribjutə] *n* distributer

district [·distrikt] *n* 1. distrikt 2. okrug

district court *n* okružni sud

distrust [dis·trʌst] *n* nepoverenje; nepovjerenje

disturb [di·stə:b] *v* 1. poremetiti 2. narušiti

disturbance [di·stə:bəns] *n* nemir

disturbed [di·stə:bəns] *adj* 1. poremećen 2. **mentally disturbed** duševno poremećen

disunity [dis·ju:niti] *n* razjedinjenost

disunited [ˌdisju·naitid] *adj* razjedinjen

disuse [dis·ju:s] *n* neupotreba

ditch [ditʃ] *n* jarak

dive [daiv] *v* 1. skočiti 2. obrušavati se

diver [·daivə] *n* ronilac

diverge [dai·və:dʒ] *v* divergirati

diverse [dai·və:s] *adj* raznoličan

diversion [dai·və:ʃn] *n* 1. odvraćanje 2. zaobilazni put

diversity [dai·və:səti] *n* raznolikost

divert [dai·və:t] *v* skrenuti

divide [di·vaid] *v* podeliti; podijeliti

dividend [·dividend] *n* (fin.) dividenda

divine [di·vain] *adj* božanski

diving [·daiviŋ] *n* skokovi s daske

division [di·viʒn] *n* 1. deljenje 2. (mil.) divizija 3. (spor.) liga

divorce [di·vɔ:s] 1. *n* razvod 2. *v* razvesti se (**from** od)

dizzy [·dizi] *adj* vrtoglav

do [du:] *v* (**did, done**) 1. učiniti 2. raditi

dock, docks [dɔk; dɔks] *n* dok

docker [·dɔkə] *n* lučki radnik

dockyard [·dɔkja:d] *n* brodogradilište

doctor [·dɔktə] *n* 1. (med.) lekar/ljekar; liječnik 2. (acad.) doktor

document [·dɔkjumənt] *n* dokumenat

documentary film [ˌdɔkju·mentri] *n* dokumentarni film

dodge [dɔdʒ] *v* izbeći; izbjeći

dodger [·dɔdʒə] *n* **tax dodger** utajivač porea

dog [dɔg] *n* pas

dole [daul] *n* **to be on the dole** primiti socijalnu pomoć

doll [dɔl] *n* lutka

dollar [·dɔlə] *n* dolar

dolphin [·dɔlfin] *n* delfin

dome [dəum] *n* kupola

domestic [də·mestik] 1. *adj* domaći 2. *n* sluškinja

domestic policy *n* unutrašnja politika

domicile [·dɔmisail] *n* mesto boravka

dominant [·dɔminənt] *adj* dominantan

dominate [·dɔmineit] *v* dominirati

domination [ˌdɔmi·neiʃn] *n* dominacija

domineer [ˌdɔmi·niə] *v* gospodariti

domineering [ˌdɔmi·niəriŋ] *adj* nadmen

dominion [də'miniən] *n* vlast

don [dɔn] *v* obući

donate [dəu'neit] *v* pokloniti

donation [dəu'neiʃn] *n* poklon

done [dʌn] *see* do

donkey ['dɔŋki] *n* (*pl* donkeys) magarać

donor ['dəunə] *n* **blood donor** davalac krvi

doom [du:m] *n* strašni sud

door [dɔ:] *n* vrata

doorbell ['dɔ:bel] *n* zvonce na vratima

doorman ['dɔ:mən] *n* portir

doorway ['dɔ:wei] *n* ulaz

dope [dəup] 1. *n* mazivo 2. (sl.) droga 3. *v* dopingovati

dormant ['dɔ:mənt] *adj* 1. koji spava 2. neiskorišćen

dormitory ['dɔ:mitri] *n* studentski dom

dose [dəus] *n* doza

dossier ['dɔsijə] *n* dosije

dot [dɔt] *n* tačka

dot-matrix printer *n* matrični štampač

double ['dʌbl] 1. *adj* dvostruk 2. *v* udvostručiti

doubt [daut] 1. *n* sumnja 2. **without doubt** bez sumnje 3. *v* sumnjati (u)

doubtful ['dautfl] *adj* nesiguran

doubtless ['dautlis] *adv* bez sumnje

dough [dəu] *n* testo; tijesto

doughnut ['dəunʌt] *n* krofna

dove [dʌv] *n* golub

down [daun] *adv* dole

downhill [,daun'hil] 1. *adj* nizbrdan 2. *adv* nizbrdo

download [,daun'ləud] *v* ući sa kompjuterske mreže

down payment *n* prva rata

downpour ['daunpɔ:] *n* pljusak

downstairs [,daun'steəz] *adv* dole

downward, downwards ['daunwəd; -z] *adv* silazno

dowry ['dauəri] *n* miraz

dozen ['dʌzn] *n* tuce

D.P. ['di:'pi:] *see* displaced person

Dr ['dɔktə] *see* doctor

draft [dra:ft] 1. *n* nacrt 2. (mil.) regrutovanje 3. *v* formulisati 4. (mil.) regrutovati 5. *see* draught

draft law *n* nacrt zakona

drafting committee ['dra:ftiŋ] *n* odbor za regrutaciju

drag [dræg] *v* vući

dragon ['drægən] *n* zmaj

dragonfly ['drægən,flai] *n* vilinski konjic

drain [drein] 1. *n* odvod 2. *v* isušiti

drainage ['dreinidʒ] *n* drenaža

drainpipe *n* odvodnica

drama [dra:mə] *n* drama

dramatic [drə'mætik] *adj* 1. dramski 2. dramatičan

dramatist ['dræmətist] *n* dramaturg

drank [dræŋk] *see* drink

drape [dreip] *n* zavesa; zavjesa

drastic ['dræstik] *adj* drastičan

draught [dra:ft] *n* 1. promaja 2. *see* draft

draughtsman ['dra:ftsmən] *n* tehnički crtač

draw [drɔ:] 1. *n* (spor.) nerešena igra; neriješena igra 2. *v* (drew, drawn) navući 3. (spor.) igrati nerešeno/neriješeno 4. **to draw attention** privući pažnju 5. **to draw a picture** crtati

drawback ['drɔ:bæk] *n* nezgoda

drawer [drɔ:] *n* fioka

drawing ['drɔ:iŋ] *n* crtež

drawn [drɔ:n] *see* draw

draw up v sastaviti
dread [dred] n strah
dreadful ['dredfl] adj strašan
dream [driːm] 1. n san 2. v (**dreamed/dreamt**) sanjati
drench [drentʃ] v posuti
dress [dres] 1. n haljina 2. odelo; odijelo 3. v obući (se)
dressmaker ['dresmeikə] n krojač, krojačica
dried [draid] adj 1. **dried milk** mleko u prahu; mlijeko u prahu 2. see **dry**
drift [drift] 1. n **snow drift** nanos 2. v ploviti
drill [dril] 1. n burgija 2. (mil.) vežba; vježba 3. v probušiti
drink ['driŋk] 1. n piće 2. v (**drank, drunk**) piti
drinkable ['driŋkəbl] adj pitak
drip [drip] 1. n kapanje 2. v kapati
drive [draiv] v (**drove, driven**) voziti
drive away v terati; tjerati
drive back v odbiti
drive out v isterati; istjerati
driver ['draivə] n vozač
driver's licence n vozački dozvola
driving ['draiviŋ] n vožnja
driving test n vozački ispit
driving school n škola vožnje
drizzle ['drizl] 1. n rominjanje 2. v rominjati
droop [druːp] v malaksati
drop [drɔp] 1. n kap 2. (ec.) pad 3. v (**dropped**) kapati 4. ispustiti
drop a demand v odustati od zahteva/zahtjeva
drop in v svratiti
drought [draut] n suša
drove [drəuv] see **drive**
drown [draun] v udaviti (se)

drowsy ['drauzi] adj dremljiv
drug [drʌgz] n droga
drug addict n narkoman
drug addiction n narkomanija
drugstore ['drʌgstɔː] n (US) drogerija
drum [drʌm] n 1. doboš 2. **oil drum** bure za naftu
drummer ['drʌmə] n dobošar
drunk [drʌŋk] adj 1. pijan 2. see **drink**
drunkard ['drʌŋkəd] n alkoholičar
dry [drai] 1. adj suv; suh 2. v osušiti
dryclean [draiˈkliːn] v očistiti hemijski/kemijski
dryness ['drainəs] n suvoća; suhota
dry up v presušiti
dual carriage-way ['djuːəl] n autoput
dubious ['djuːbiəs] adj dubiozan
duck [dʌk] 1. n patka 2. v pognuti
due [djuː] 1. adj dospeo; dospio 2. **due south** ka sugu 3. n priznanje 4. prep **due to** usled; uslijed
dues [djuːz] pl članarina
dug [dʌg] see **dig**
dull [dʌl] adj 1. tup 2. nezanimljiv
dumb [dʌmb] adj 1. nem; nijem 2. (sl.) glup
dummy ['dʌmi] n 1. lutka 2. lutka 3. (sl.) glupan
dump [dʌmp] 1. n **rubbish dump** stovarište dubreta 2. **ammunition dump** skladište municije 3. v svaliti
dumpster ['dʌmpstə] n (US) kontejner za đubre/smeće
dump waste v istresati đubre
dung [dʌŋ] n đubre
duo ['djuːəu] n duo
dupe [djuːp] v prevariti

duplicate ['dʒuːplikeit] 1. *n* duplikat
2. *v* kopirati
durability [,dʒuərə'biləti] *n* trajnost
durable ['dʒuːrəbl] *adj* trajan
duration [dju'reiʃn] *n* trajanje
duress [dju'res] *n* prinuda
during ['djuəriŋ] *prep* za vreme;
vrijeme
dusk [dʌsk] *n* sumrak
dust [dʌst] *n* prašina
dustbin ['dʌstbin] *n* kanta za smeće
dusty ['dʌsti] *adj* prašnjav
Dutch [dʌtʃ] *adj* holandski;
nizozemski
duty ['djuːti] *n* 1. dužnost 2. služba

3. **customs duty** carina
duty-free *adj* bescarinski
duty-free zone *n* bescarinska zona
dwarf [dwɔːf] *n* (**dwarves**) patuljak
dwell [dwel] *v* stanovati
dweller ['dwelə] *n* stanovnik
dwelling ['dweliŋ] *n* stan
dye [dai] 1. *n* boja 2. *v* ofarbati
dying ['daːjiŋ] *see* **die**
dyke [daik] *n* nasip
dynamic [dai'næmik] *adj* dinamičan
dynamite ['dainəmait] *n* dinamit
dynamo ['dainəməu] *n* dinamo
dynasty ['dinəsti] *n* dinastija
dysentery ['disəntri] *n* dizentarija

E

each [iːtʃ] 1. *adj* svaki, svaka, svako 2. *adv* po

each other *n/adv* jedan drugi, jedna druga, jedno drugo

eager [ˈiːgə] *adj* željan

eagerly [ˈiːgəli] *adv* željno

eagerness [ˈiːgənis] *n* žudnja

eagle [ˈiːgl] *n* orao

ear [iːə] *n* uvo; uho

earache [ˈiːəreik] *n* ušobolja; uhobolja

early [ˈəːli] *adj/adv* 1. rani 2. skorasnji 3. *adv* rano

earmark [ˈiːə‚maːk] *v* rezervisati

earn [əːn] *v* 1. zaraditi 2. to earn a living zarađivati za život

earnings [ˈəːniŋz] *pl* zarada

earphones [ˈiːə‚fəunz] *pl* naglavne slušalice

earring [ˈiːəriŋ] *n* minđuša

earth [əːθ] *n* zemlja

earthquake [ˈəːθkweik] *n* zemljotres

earth station *n* zemaljska stanica

earthworm [ˈəːθwəːm] *n* kišna glista

ease [iːz] 1. *n* spokojstvo 2. *v* uspokojiti

easily [ˈiːzili] *adv* 1. lako 2. bez sumnje

easiness [ˈiːzinis] *n* lakoća

east [iːst] 1. *adj* istočni 2. *adv* istočno 3. *n* istok

Easter [ˈiːstə] *n* Uskrs

eastern [ˈiːstən] *adj* itočni

easterner [ˈiːstənə] *n* istočnjak

eastwards [ˈiːstwədz] *adv* istočno

easy [ˈiːzi] *adj* lak

easy-going *adj* nemaran

eat [iːt] *v* (ate, eaten) jesti

ebony [ˈebəni] *n* abonos

eccentric [ikˈsentrik] *adj* nastran

echo [ˈekəu] *n* eho

eclipse [iˈklips] *n* pomračenje

ecological [‚iːkəˈlɔdʒikl] *adj* ekološki

ecological balance *n* ekološka ravnoteža

ecological disaster *n* ekološka katastrofa

ecology [iˈkɔlɔdʒi] *n* elologija

economic [‚iːkəˈnɔmik; ‚ekəˈnɔmik] *adj* ekonomski

economical [‚iːkəˈnɔmikl; ‚ekəˈnɔmikl] *adj* ekonomičan

economic crisis *n* ekonomska kriza

economic policy *n* ekonomska politika

economic reform *n* privredna reforma

economics [‚iːkəˈnɔmiks; ‚ekəˈnɔmiks] *n* 1. ekonomija 2. (ac.) ekonomske nauke

economize [iˈkɔnəmaiz] *v* štedeti; štedjeti

economist [iˈkɔnəmist] *n* ekonomista

economizing [iˈkɔnəmaiziŋ] *n* štednja

economy [iˈkɔnəmi] *n* 1. ekonomija 2. štednja

ecu [ˈekju] *n* eki (evropska valutna jedinica)

eczema [ˈeksmə] *n* ekcem

edge [edʒ] *n* 1. ivica 2. sečivo;
sječivo
edible ['edibl] *adj* jestiv
edit ['edit] *v* redigovati
edition [i'diʃn] *n* izdanje
editor ['editə] *n* 1. urednik 2.
redaktor
editorial [,edi'tɔːriəl] 1. *adj*
uređivački 2. *n* uvodnik
educate ['edʒukeit] *v* obrazovati
education [,edʒu'keiʃn] *n*
obrazovanje
educational [,edʒu'keiʃnl] *adj*
obrazovni
eel [iːl] *n* jegulja
effect [i'fekt] *n* 1. dejstvo; djejstvo
2. **sound effects** zvučni efekti 3.
in effect stvari 4. **to put into
effect** sprovesti u život 5. **to take
effect** imati djestva (**on** na)
effective [i'fektiv] *adj* efikasan
effectively [i'fektivli] *adv* efikasno,
efektivno
efficiency [i'fiʃnsi] *n* efikasnost
efficient [i'fiʃnt] *adj* delotvoran;
djelotvoran
effort ['efət] *n* 1. napor 2. **to make
an effort** učiniti napor 3. **to exert
great effort** uložiti napor (**in** u)
effortless ['efətlis] *adj* lak
e.g. (= **for example**) na primer
egg [eg] *n* jaje
eggplant ['egplaːnt] *n* plavi
patlidžan
egotism ['egəuizm] *n* egotizam
egotistical [,egəu'tistikl] *adj*
egotistički
eight [eit] *n/adj* osam
eighteen [ei'tiːn] *n/adj* osamnaest
eighteenth [,ei'tiːnθ] *adj* osamnaesti
eighth [eitθ] *adj* 1. osmi 2. **one
eighth** osmina

eightieth ['eitiəθ] *adj* osamdeseti
eighty ['eiti] *n/adj* osamdeset
either ['aiðə; 'iːðə] 1. *adj* jedan ili
drugi 2. *adv* ni 3. *conj* ili
either...or *conj* ili...ili
ejaculate [i'dʒækjuleit] *v* ejakulirati
ejaculation [i,dʒækju'leiʃn] *n*
ejakulacija
eject [i'dʒekt] *v* izbaciti
elaborate [i'læbəreit] *adj* detaljan
elapse [i'læps] *v* proći
elastic [i'læstik] 1. *adj* elastičan 2. *n*
lastik
elbow ['elbəu] *n* lakat
elder ['eldə] 1. *adj* stariji 2. *n* starija
osoba
elderly ['eldəli] *adj* postar
eldest ['eldist] *adj* najstariji
elect [i'lekt] *v* birati
election [i'lekʃn] *n* 1. izbori 2. **by-
election** naknadni izbori 3.
general elections opšti izbori 4.
free elections slobodni izbori
election campaign *n* predizborna
kampanja
elections [i'lekʃnz] *pl* izbori
elector [i'lektə] *n* birač
electoral [ilek'tərəl] *adj* izborni
electoral commission *n* izborna
komisija
electorate [ilek'tərət] *n* izborna
jedinica
electric [i'lektrik] *adj* električan
electrical engineer *n* inženjer
elektrotehnike
electrician [,ilek'triʃn] *n*
elektrotehničar
electricity [,ilek'trisəti] *n* 1.
elektricitet 2. **to cut off the
electricity** prekinuti struju
electrify [i'lektrifai] *v*
elektrifikovati

electrocute [iˌlektrəˈkjuːt] v pogubiti elektičnom strujom

electronic [ilekˈtrɔnik] adj elektronski

electronics [ilekˈtrɔniks] n elektronika

elegance [ˈeligəns] n elegancija

elegant [ˈeligəns] adj elegantan

element [ˈelimənt] n elemenat

elementary [ˌeliˈmentri] adj 1. početni 2. elementaran

elementary school n osnovna škola

elephant [ˈelifənt] n slon

elevate [ˈeliveit] v dići

elevation [ˌeliˈveiʃn] n elevacija

elevator [ˈeliveitə] n lift

eleven [iˈlevn] n/adj jednaest

eleventh [iˈlevnθ] adj jednaesti

eligible [ˈelidʒəbl] adj kvalifikovan

eliminate [iˈlimineit] v 1. eliminisati 2. (spor.) izbaciti

elimination [iˈlimineiʃn] n 1. eliminacija 2. (spor.) ispadanje

eloquent [ˈeləkwənt] adj rečit; rječit

else [els] 1. adj drugi 2. adv još 3. conj or else inače

elsewhere [ˌelsˈweə] adv drugde; drugdje

e-mail [ˈiːmeil] n elektronska pošta

emancipate [iˈmænsipeit] v osloboditi

embargo [imˈbaːgəu] n embargo

embark [imˈbaːk] v ukrcati (se)

embark upon v početi

embarrass [imˈbærəs] v zbuniti

embarrassing [imˈbærəsiŋ] adj neprijatan

embarrassment [imˈbærəsmənt] n zbunjenost

embassy [ˈembəsi] n ambasada

embezzle [imˈbezl] v proneveriti; pronevjeriti

embezzlement [imˈbezlmənt] n pronevera; pronevjera

emblem [ˈembləm] n simbol

embrace [imˈbreis] v zagrliti (se)

embroidery [imˈbrɔidəri] n vez

embryo [ˈembrijəu] n embrio

emerge [iˈməːdʒd] v iskrsnuti

emergency [iˈməːdʒənsi] n 1. slučaj nužde 2. **state of emergency** vanredno stanje 3. **in case of emergency** u slačaju nužde

emergency aid n hitna pomoć

emergency exit n izlaz u slučaju nužde

emergency landing n prinudno sletanje/slijetanje

emergency law n zakon o ovođenju vanrednog stanja

emergency session n hitan sastanak

emigrant [ˈemigrənt] n iseljenik

emigrate [ˈemigreit] v iseliti se

emigration [ˌemiˈgreiʃn] n iseljenje

emigre [ˈemigrei] n emigrant

eminent [ˈeminənt] adj eminentan

emir [eˈmiːə] n emir

emissary [ˈemiˌseri] n izaslanik

emit [iˈmit] v emitovati

emotion [iˈməuʃn] n emocija

emotional [iˈməuʃənl] adj emocionalan

emperor [ˈempərə] n car

emphasis [ˈemfəsis] n isticanje

emphasize [ˈemfəsaiz] v istaći

empire [ˈempaiə] n imperija

employ [imˈplɔi] v 1. zaposliti 2. upotrebiti

employee [emˈplɔiː] n službenik

employer [imˈplɔiə] n poslodavac

employment [imˈplɔimənt] n posao

employment agency n zavod za zapošljavanje

empower [im'pauə] v opunomoćiti

empress ['empris] n carica

empty ['empti] 1. adj prazan 2. **empty dream** pusti san 3. v isprazniti

empty-handed adj praznoruk

enable [i'neibl] v omogućiti

enact [i'nækt] v (leg.) doneti; donijeti

enchanting [in'tʃa:ntiŋ] adj čaroban

encircle ['ensə:kl] v okružiti

enclose [in'kləuz] v priložiti

encore! ['ɔnkɔ:] bis!

encounter [in'kauntə] v susresti

encourage [in'kʌridʒ] v ohrabiti

encouragement [in'kʌridʒmənt] n hrabrenje

encouraging [in'kʌridʒiŋ] adj ohrabrujući

encroach [in'krəutʃ] v povrediti; povrijediti

encroachment [in'krəutʃiŋ] n povreda

encyclopaedia [in,saiklə'pi:diə] n enciklopedija

end [end] 1. n kraj 2. dno 3. **in the end** najzad 4. v svršiti (se)

endanger [in'deindʒə] v ugroziti

endangered species [in'deindʒəd] n ugrožena životinjska vrsta

endeavour [in'devə] v nastojati

ending ['endiŋ] n završetak

endless ['endlis] adj beskrajan

endorse [in'dɔ:s] v indosirati

endurance [in'dʒuərəns] n izdržljivost

endure [in'dʒuə] v podneti; podnijeti

enduring [in'dʒuəriŋ] adj stalan

enema ['enəmə] n klistir

enemy ['enəmi] n neprijatelj

energetic ['enədʒetik] adj energičan

energy ['enədʒi] n energija

enforce [in'fɔ:s] v primeniti; primijeniti

engage [in'geidʒ] v 1. zaplositi 2. (mil.) uvući u borbu

engaged [in'geidʒd] adj 1. veren; vjeren 2. zauzet 3. **to get engaged** veriti; vjeriti

engagement [in'geidʒmənt] n 1. angažovanje 2. veridba; vjeridba

engine ['endʒin] n 1. motor 2. see **locomotive**

engineer [,endʒi'niə] n inženjer

engineering [,endʒi'niəriŋ] n inženjering

England ['iŋglənd] n Engleska

English ['iŋgliʃ] 1. adj engleski 2. n engleski jezik 3. **the English** Englezi

Englishman n Englez

Englishwoman n Engleskinja

engulf [in'gʌlf] v okružiti

enhance [in'ha:ns] v povećati

enjoy [in'dʒɔi] v uživati

enjoyable [in'dʒɔiəbl] adj prijatan

enjoyment [in'dʒɔimənt] n uživanje

enlarge [in'la:dʒ] v uveličati

enlist [in'list] v regrutovati

enmity ['enmiti] n neprijateljstvo

enormous [i'nɔ:məs] adj ogroman

enough [i'nʌf] 1. adj dovoljan 2. adv dosta

enquire [in'kwaiə] v raspitati se

enrich [in'ritʃ] v obogatiti

enrol [in'rəul] v upisati

en route [ɔn'ru:t] adv uz put

ensure [in'ʃɔ:] v proveriti; provjeriti

entangle [in'tæŋgəld] v upetlati

enter ['entə] v ući (u)

enterprise ['entəpraiz] n 1. inicijativa 2. (com.) preduzeće; poduzeće

entertain [,entəˈtein] v zabaviti
entertainment [,entəˈteinmənt] n zabava
enthusiasm [inˈθjuːziæzm] n oduševljenje
enthusiastic [in,θjuːziˈæstik] adj strastan
entire [inˈtaiə] adj ceo; cio
entirely [inˈtaiəli] adv potpuno
entrance [ˈentrəns] n ulaz
entrust [inˈtrʌst] v poveriti; povjeriti
entry [ˈentri] n 1. ulazak 2. (fin.) upis
entry visa n ulazna viza
envelope [ˈenvələup] n koverat
environment [inˈvaiərənmənt] n 1. okolina 2. ambijent
environmental [,invaiərənˈmentl] adj okološni
environs [ˈɔnvirɔnz] pl kewaye
envious [ˈenviəs] adj ljubomoran
envoy [ˈɔnvɔi] n izaslanik
envy [ˈenvi] 1. n zavist 2. v zavideti; zavidjeti
epidemic [,epiˈdemik] n epidemija
epilepsy [ˈepilepsi] n epilepsija
episode [ˈepisəud] n epizoda
epitaph [ˈepitaːf] n epitaf
epoch [ˈiːpɔk] n epoha
equal [ˈiːkwəl] 1. adj jednak 2. ravnopravan 3. to be equal biti ravan 4. v biti jednak (s)
equality [iˈkwɔləti] n 1. jednakost 2. ravnopravnost
equation [iˈkweiʒn] n jednačina
equator [iˈkweitə] n ekvator
equilibrium [,iːkwiˈlibriəm] n ravnoteža
equip [iˈkwip] v opremiti
equipment [iˈkwipmənt] n 1. oprema 2. (mil.) borbena tehnika

equivalent [iˈkwivələnt] 1. adj ekvivalentan 2. n ekvivalenat
era [ˈiərə] n doba
eradicate [iˈrædikeit] v iskoreniti; iskorijeniti
eradication [i,rædiˈkeiʃn] n iskorenjivanje; iskorjenjivanje
erase [iˈreiz] v izbrisati
eraser [iˈreizə] n gumica
erect [iˈrekt] 1. adj uspravan 2. adv uspravno 3. v podići
erection [iˈrekʃn] n 1. podizanje 2. erekcija
erode [iˈrəud] v oglodati
erosion [iˈrəuʒn] n erozija
erotic [iˈrɔtik] adj erotičan
err [əː] v varati se
errand [ˈerənd] n nalog
error [ˈerə] n greška
erupt [iˈrʌpt] v izbiti
eruption [iˈrʌpʃn] n erupcija
escalate [ˈeskəleit] v eskalirati
escalation [ˈeskəleiʃn] n eskalacija
escalator [ˈeskəleitə] n eskalator
escape [iˈskeip] 1. n bekstvo; bjekstvo 2. v pobeći; pobjeći (**from** iz)
escort [ˈeskɔːt] 1. n pratnja 2. **armed escort** oružana pratnja 3. v pratiti
especially [isˈpeʃəli] adv naročito
espionage [ˈespiənaːʒ] n špijunaža
essay [ˈesei] n esej
essence [ˈesns] n suština
essential [iˈsenʃl] adj 1. bitan 2. potreban
establish [iˈstæbliʃ] v 1. uspostaviti 2. **to establish a fact** utvrditi činjenicu
establishment [iˈstæbliʃmənt] n 1. smeštanje; smjestanje 2. ustanova 3. (UK) **the Establishment** državno uređenje

estate [i'steit] *n* 1. imanje 2. **real estate** nepokretna imovina 3. (UK) **housing estate** stambeno naselje

estate agent *n* trgovac nepokretnostima

esteemed [i'sti:m] *n* poštovanje

estimate ['estimət] 1. *n* procena; procjena 2. *v* proceniti; procijeniti

etc. (= et cetera) [et'setərə] i tako dalje

eternal [i'tə:nl] *adj* nešto večno/vječno

eternity [i'tə:nəti] *n* večnost; vječnost

ethical ['eθikl] *adj* etičan

ethics ['eθiks] *pl* etika

ethnic ['eθnik] *adj* etnički

ethnic cleansing *n* etničko čišćenje

ethnic minority *n* nacionalna manjina

ethnic origin *n* poreklo; porijeklo

ethnicity [eθ'nisəti] *n* etnicitet

etiquette ['etiket] *n* etiketa

eucalyptus [,ju:kə'liptəs] *n* eukaliptus

euro ['juərəp] *n* 1. evropski 2. (fin.) euro (evropska novčana jedinica)

eurocommunism [',uərəu-'komjumizm] *n* evrokomunizam

Europe ['juərəp] *n* Evropa

European [,juərə'pi:ən] 1. *adj* evropski 2. *n* Evropljanin

European Commission *n* Evropska komisija

European Community (EC) *n* Evropska zajednica

European Union (EU) *n* Evropska unija

evacuate [i'vækjueit] *v* evakuisati

evacuation [i'vækjuei∫n] *n* evakuacija

evade [i'veid] *v* izmaći

evaluate [i'væljueit] *v* oceniti; ocijeniti

evaluation [i'væljuei∫n] *n* ocena; ocjena

evaporate [i'væpəreit] *v* ispariti (se)

evaporation [i,væpə'rei∫n] *n* isparavanje

evasion [i,veiʒn] *n* isparavanje

eve [i:v] *n* predvečerje

even ['i:vn] 1. *adj* ravan 2. **even number** paran broj 3. *adv* baš

even if *conj* čak i da

evening ['i:vniŋ] *n* 1. veče 2. **good evening!** dobro veče!

event [i'vent] *n* 1. događaj 2. (spor.) tačka; točka 3. **in any event** u svakom slučaju 4. **in the event that/of** u slučaju

eventful [i'ventfl] *adj* pun događaja

even though *conj* iako

eventually [i'vent∫uəli] *adv* u svoje vreme/vrijeme

ever ['evə] *adv* 1. ikad, nikad

ever since *conj* od tada

everlasting [,evə'la:stiŋ] *adj* večit; vječit

evermore ['evə'mɔ:] *adv* zauvek; zauvijek

every ['evri] *adj* svaki, svaka, svako

everybody, everyone ['evribɔdi; 'evriwʌn] svako

every day *adv* svaki dan

everyday ['evridei] *adj* svakidašnji

every other day *adv* svaki drugi dan

everything ['evriθiŋ] sve

everywhere ['evriweə] *adv* svuda

evict [eˈvikt] v isterati; istjerati

evidence [ˈevidəns] n 1. dokaz 2. to give evidence svedočiti; svjedočiti

evident [ˈevidənt] adj očevidan

evidently [ˈevidəntli] adv očigledno

evil [ˈiːvl] 1. adj zao 2. n zlo

evolution [ˌiːvəˈluːʃn] n evolucija

evolve [iˈvɔlv] v razviti (se)

ewe [jəu] n ovca

exacerbate [eksˈæsəbeit] v pogoršati

exact [igˈzækt] adj tačan; točan

exactly [igˈzæktli] adv tačno

exaggerate [igˈzædʒəreit] v preterati; pretjerati

exaggeration [igˈzædʒəreiʃn] n preterivanje; pretjerivanje

exam [igˈzæm] see examination

examination [igˌzæmiˈneiʃn] n 1. (ed.) ispit 2. (med.) pregled

examine [igˈzæmin] v 1. (ed.) ispitati 2. (med.) pregledati

examiner [igˈzæminə] n (ed.) ispitivač

example [igˈzaːmpl] n 1. primer; primjer 2. for example na primer 3. to give an example navesti primer 4. to set an example dati primer

excavate [ˈekskəveit] v iskopati

excavation [ˌekskəˈveiʃn] n iskopavanje

exceed [ikˈsiːd] v 1. prekoračiti 2. prevazići

exceedingly [ikˈsiːdiŋli] adv veoma

excel [ikˈsel] v odlikovati se

excellence [ˈeksələns] n odlika

Excellency [ˌeksələnsi] n ekselencija

excellent [ˈeksələnt] adj odličan

except [ikˈsept] 1. prep sem 2. conj sem ško

except for prep osim

exception [ikˈsepʃn] n 1. izuzetak 2. without exception bez izuzetka 3. with the exception of s izuzetkom 4. to make an exception praviti izuzetak

exceptional [ikˈsepʃənl] adj izuzetan

excess [ikˈses] adj/n višak

excessive [ikˈsesiv] adj prekomeran; prekomjeran

excessive force [ikˈsesiv] n neprimerena sila; neprimjerena sila

exchange [iksˈtʃeindʒ] 1. n razmena; razmjena 2. foreign exchange devize 3. rate of exchange kurs razmene/razmjene 4. stock exchange berza; burza 5. telephone exchange telefonska centrala 6. v razmeniti; razmijeniti

exchange-rate n kurs

Exchequer [iksˈtʃekə] n (UK) ministarstvo finansija/financija

excite [ikˈsait] v uzbuditi

excited [ikˈsaitid] adj uzbuden

excitement [ikˈsaitmənt] n uzbuđenje

exciting [ikˈsaitiŋ] adj uzbudljiv

exclaim [ikˈskleim] v uzviknuti

exclamation [ˌeksləˈmeiʃn] n uzvik

exclamation mark n znak uzvika

exclude [ikˈskluːd] v isključiti

exclusion [ikˈskluːʒn] n isključenje

exclusive [ikˈskluːsiv] adj 1. nepristupačni 2. ekskluzivan

excrement [ˈekskrimənt] n izmet

excursion [ikˈskəːʒn] n ekskuzija

excuse [ikˈskjuːs] n izvinjenje

excuse [ikˈskjuːz] v izviniti

excuse me! izvinite!

execute [ˈeksikjuːt] v 1. pogubiti 2. (leg.) izvršiti

execution [ˌeksiˈkjuːʃn] n 1. pogubljenje 2. (leg.) izvršenje

executioner [ˌeksiˈkjuːʃənə] n krvnik

executive [igˈzekjutiv] 1. adj izvršni 2. n šef

executive director n izvršni direktor

executive power n izvršna vlast

exemplary [igˈzempləri] adj uzoran

exempt [igˈzempt] adj oslobođen

exemption [igˈzempʃn] n 1. oslobođenje 2. tax exemption poresko oslobođenje)

exercise [ˈeksəsaiz] 1. n telesno 2. (mil/ed.) vežba; vježba 3. v vršiti vežbe/vježbe

exercise book n sveska, teka

exert [igˈzəːt] v vršiti

exertion [igˈzəːʃn] n napor

exhale [eksˈheil] v izdahnuti

exhaust [igˈzɔːst] 1. n izduvni gasovi 2. v iscrpsti 3. potrošiti 4. see silencer

exhausted [igˈzɔːstid] adj 1. iscrpijen 2. Their supplies are exhausted. Ostali su bez namirnica.

exhaustion [igˈzɔːstʃən] n iscrpenost

exhibit [igˈzibit] v izložiti

exhibition [ˌeksiˈbiʃn] n izložba

exhibitor [igˈzibitə] n izlagač

exhilarate [igˈziləreit] v stimulisati

exhort [igˈzɔːt] v podstaći

exhortation [ˌegzɔːˈteiʃn] n podsticanje

exile [ˈeksail] 1. n progonstvo 2. v prognati

exist [igˈzist] v postojati

existence [igˈzistəns] n postojanje

existent [igˈzistənt] adj postojeći

existing [igˈzistiŋ] adj postojeći

exit [ˈeksit; ˈegzit] 1. n izlaz 2. v otići

exit visa n izlazna viza

exodus [ˈeksədəs] n izlazak

expand [ikˈspænd] v 1. proširiti 2. širiti se

expanse [ikˈspæns] n prostor

expansion [ikˈspænʃn] n ekspanzija

expansionism [ikˈspænʃnizəm] n ekspanzionizam

expansive [ikˈspænsiv] adj ekspanzivan

expatriate [ikˈspætriət] adj iseljenik

expect [ikˈspekt] v 1. očekivati 2. see expecting

expectant [ikˈspektənt] adj 1. koji očekuje 2. trudna

expectation [ˌekspekˈteiʃn] n očekivanje

expecting [ikˈspektiŋ] adj trudna

expedition [ˌekspiˈdiʃn] n ekspedicija

expel [ikˈspel] v isterati; istjerati (from iz)

expenditure [ikˈspenditʃə] n trošenje

expense, expenses [ikˈspens; -iz] n trošak

expensive [ikˈspensiv] adj skup

experience [ikˈspiəriəns] 1. n iskustvo 2. v doživeti; diživjeti

experienced [ikˈspiəriənst] adj iskusan

experiment [ikˈsperimənt] n eksperiment

experimental [ˌiksperiˈmentl] adj eksperimentalan

expert [ˈekspəːt] n stručnjak

expertise [ˌekspəːˈtiːz] n vičnost

expire [ikˈspaiə] v 1. isteći 2. umreti; umrijeti

explain [ikˈsplein] v objasniti

explanation [ˌekspləˈneiʃn] n objašnjenje

explicit [ik·splisit] *adj* eksplicitan
explode [ik·spləud] *v* eksplodirati
exploit ['eksplɔit] *n* podvig
exploit [ik·splɔit] *v* eksploatisati
exploitation [,eksplɔi·teiʃn] *n* eksploatacija
exploration [,eksplə·reiʃn] *n* istraživanje
explore [ik·splɔ:] *v* istraživati
explorer [ik·splɔ:rə] *n* istraživač
explosion [ik·spləuʒn] *n* eksplozija
explosive [ik·spləusiv] 1. *adj* eksplozivan 2. *n* eksploziv
explosives [ik·spləusivz] *pl* eksplozivi
expo ['ekspəu] *n* izložba
export [ik·spɔ:t] 1. *adj* izvozni 2. *n* izvoz 3. *v* izvoziti
exporter [ik·spɔ:tə] *n* izvoznik
exports ['ekspɔ:ts] *pl* izvoz
expose [ik·spəuz] *v* izložiti
exposé [ik·spəuzei] *n* ekspoze
exposure [ik·spəuʒə] *n* izloženost
express [ik·spres] 1. *adj* ekspresni 2. *n* ekspres 3. *v* izraziti
expression [ik·spreʃn] *n* 1. izraz 2. izražavanje
expressly [ik·spresli] *adv* smesta; smjesta
express train *n* ekspresni voz/vlak
express mail *n* ekspresno isporučivanje
expressway [ik·spreswei] *n* autoput
exquisite ['ekskwizit; ik·skwizit] *adj* izvrstan
extend [ik·stend] *v* 1. produžiti 2. protezati se
extension [ik·stenʃn] *n* 1. produženje 2. (tel.) lokal
extensive [ik·stensiv] *adj* 1. prostran 2. ekstenzivan
extent [ik·stent] *n* 1. veličina 2. to a

certain extent donekle
exterior [ik·stiəriə] *adj* eksterijer
exterminate [ik·stə:mineit] *v* iskoreniti
external [ik·stə:nl] *adj* spoljašnji
extinct [ik·stiŋkt] *adj* to become extinct izumreti; izumrijeti
extinction [ik·stiŋkʃn] *n* izumiranje
extinguish [ik·stiŋgwiʃ] *v* ugasiti
extinguisher [ik·stiŋgwiʃə] *n* sprava za gašenje požara
extort [ik·stɔ:t] *v* iznuditi
extortion [ik·stɔ:ʃn] *n* iznuda
extra ['ekstrə] 1. *adj* poseban 2. *adv* posebno
extract ['ekstrækt] *v* izvući
extradite ['ekstrədeit] *v* ekstradirati
extradition ['ekstrədiʃn] *n* ekstradicija
extraordinary [ik·strɔ:dnri] *adj* izvanredan
extravagance [ik·strævəgəns] *n* ekstravagancija
extravagant [ik·strævəgənt] *adj* ekstravagantan
extreme [ik·stri:m] *adj* krajnji
extremely [ik·stri:mli] *adv* krajnje
extremist [ik·stri:mist] *n* ekstremista
extremity [ik·streməti] *n* ekstremitet
eye [ai] *n* 1. oko 2. to keep an eye on pripaziti na 3. to see eye to eye potpuno se slagati (**with** s)
eyeball ['aibɔl] *n* očna jabucica
eyebrow ['aibrau] *n* obrva
eyeglasses ['aigla:siz] *pl* (US) naočari; naočale
eyelash ['ailæʃ] *n* trepavica
eyelid ['ailid] *n* očni kapak
eyeshadow ['ailʃadəu] *n* šminka za oči
eyesight ['aisait] *n* viđenje
eyewitness ['ai,witnis] *n* očevidac

F

fable [ˈfeibl] *n* basna
fabric [ˈfæbrik] *n* tkanina
fabricate [ˈfæbrikeit] *v* 1. izraditi 2. **to fabricate a charge** fabrikovati
fabulous [ˈfæbjuləs] *adj* basnoslovan
facade [fəˈsaːd] *n* fasada
face [feis] 1. *n* lice 2. **face to face** lice u lice 3. *v* biti suočen s 4. **to lose face** izgubiti obraz
face-lift *n* kozmetička hirurgija/ kirurgija na licu
face-saving *adj* koji čuva prestiž
facet [ˈfæset] *n* aspekt
facial [ˈfeiʃl] *adj* facijalan
facility [fəˈsiləti] *n* 1. veštine; vještina 2. **facilities** kapacitet i 3. **sports facilities** sportski objekti
facing [ˈfeisiŋ] *adj* pervaz
fact [fækt] *n* 1. fakat 2. **in fact** u stvari
fact-finding committee *n* istražna komisija
faction [ˈfækʃn] *n* frakcija
factor [ˈfæktə] *n* čilinac
factory [ˈfæktəri] *n* fabrika; tvornica
fact sheet *n* bilten
faculty [ˈfæklti] *n* 1. moć 2. (acad.) fakultet
fade [feid] *v* uvenuti
fail [feil] *v* 1. propustiti 2. ne moći 3. **to fail an exam** pasti na ispitu 4. **without fail** zasigurno
failure [ˈfeiljə] *n* 1. neuspeh 2. **power failure** prekid struje

faint [feint] 1. *adj* nesvestica; nesvjestica 2. *v* onesvestiti se; onesvjetiti se
fair [feə] 1. *adj* lep; lijep 2. pošten 3. *n* sajam 4. **trade fair** trgovinski sajam
fairly [ˈfeəli] *adv* prilično
fairness [ˈfeənis] *n* poštenje
fairy tale [ˈfeəri,teil] *n* bajka
faith [feiθ] *n* 1. vera; vjera 2. **to have faith** imati veru/vjeru (in u)
faithful [ˈfeiθfl] *adj* veran; vjeran
faithfully [ˈfeiθfəli] *adv* **Yours faithfully...** Vaš...
faithless [ˈfeiθlis] *adj* neveran; nevjeran
fake [feik] 1. *adj* lažan 2. *n* prevara
fall [fɔːl] 1. *n* pad 2. (US) jesen 3. *v* (**fell, fallen**) pasti
fall asleep *v* zapasti
fall ill *v* obeliti; objeliti
fall in love *v* zabljubiti se (**with** u)
fall off *v* otpasti
fall-out [ˈfɔːlaut] *n* **nuclear fall-out** radioaktivne padavine
fall short *v* ne dostići
fall through *v* propasti
false [fɔːls] *adj* lažan
falsehood [ˈfɔːlshud] *n* laž
false teeth *pl* veštački zubi
falsification [,fɔːlsifiˈkeiʃn] *n* falsifikat
falsify [ˈfɔːlsifai] *v* krivotvoriti
fame [feim] *n* slava
famed [feimd] *adj* čuven
familiar [fəˈmiliə] *adj* prisan

familiarity [ˌfəmiliˈærəti] n prisnost
familiarize [ˈfəmiliæraiz] v upoznati
family [ˈtæməli] n porodica, familija
family medicine n opšta praksa; opća praksa
family planning n planiranje porodice
famine [ˈfæmin] n glad
famous [ˈfeiməs] adj čuven
fan [fæn] n 1. ventilator 2. navijač
fanatic [fəˈnætik] n fanatik
fanbelt [ˈfænbelt] n kaiš ventilatora
fancy [ˈfænsi] 1. adj elegantan 2. v zamisliti
fantastic [fænˈtæstik] adj fantastičan
fantasy [ˈfæntəsi] n fantazija
far [faː] 1. adj dalek 2. adv daleko (from od) 3. as far as koliko 4. so far do sata
far away adv daleko (from od)
fare [feə] n cena vožnje; cijena vožnje
farewell [ˌfeəˈwel] n oproštaj
farm [faːm] 1. n gazdinstvo 2. v obraditi
farmer [ˈfaːmə] n seljak
farming [ˈfaːmiŋ] n poljoprivreda
far-sighted adj dalekovid
fart [faːt] 1. n prdež 2. v prditi
farther [ˈfaːðə] adj dalje
fascinate [ˈfæsineit] v fascinirati
fascism [ˈfæʃism] n fašizam
fascist [ˈfæʃist] 1. adj fašistički 2. n fašista
fashion [ˈfæʃn] n moda
fashionable [ˈfæʃnəbl] adj u modi
fashion show n modna revija
fast [faːst] 1. adj brz 2. stalan 3. the clock is fast sat brza 4. n post 5. v postiti
fast asleep adj u dubokom snu

fast forward n dugme za premotavanje trake unapred/unaprijed
fasten [ˈfaːsn] v pričvrstiti
fastener [ˈfaːsnə] n driker
fast-food restaurant n ekspres-retoran
fat [fæt] 1. adj mastan 2. debeo 3. n mast 4. debljina
fatal [ˈfeitl] adj smrtan
fatal illness n smrtonosna bolest
fatality [fəˈtæləti] n ljudska žrtva
fate [feit] n sudbina
father [ˈfaːðə] n otac
father-in-law [ˈfaðərinlɔː] n svekar, tast
fatigue [fəˈtiːg] n zamor
fatigue duties pl (mil.) radno odelo/odijelo
fatty [ˈfæti] n mastan
faucet [ˈfɔːset] n (US) slavina
fault [fɔːlt] n 1. mana 2. defekt 3. to find find fault with kritikovati
faultless [ˈfɔːtləs] adj besprekoran; besprijekoran
faulty [ˈfɔːlti] adj defektan
favour [ˈfeivə] 1. n milost 2. to do a favour učiniti uslugu 3. to be in favour of... biti za... 4. v favorizovati
favourite [ˈfeivərit] 1. adj omiljen 2. n ljubimac 3. (spor.) favorit
fax [fæks] 1. n telefaks, faks 2. v poslati telefaksom, faksirati
fax-modem [ˈfæksˈməudem] n faks-modem
fear [fiə] 1. n strah 2. v bojati se
fearless [ˈfiəlis] adj neustrašiv
feasible [ˈfiːzəbl] adj izvodljiv
feast [fiːst] n gozba
feat [fiːt] n podvig
feather [ˈfeðə] n pero

feature [ˈfiːtʃə] n crta
feature film n umetnički film; umjetnički film
featuring [ˈfiːtʃəriŋ] adj prikazan u glaunoj ulozi
February [ˈfebruəri] n februar; veljača
fed [ˈfedərəl] see feed
federal [ˈfedərəl] adj federalni
federal government n federalna vlada
federal republic n federativna republika
federation [ˌfedəˈreiʃn] n federacija
Federation of International Football Associations (FIFA) n Federacija međunarodnih fudbalskih udruženja
fed up [ˈfedərəl] adj to be fed up biti sit
fee [fiː] n 1. honorar 2. (ed.) školarina
feeble [ˈfiːbl] adj slab
feed [fiːd] v (fed) 1. nahraniti 2. hraniti se
feel [fiːl] v (felt) 1. osetiti; osjetiti 2. opipati
feeling [ˈfiːliŋ] n osećaj; osjećaj
feel like v biti raspoložen za
feet [fiːt] see foot
fell [fel] see fall
fellow [ˈfeləu] 1. adj fellow workers saradnici 2. n čovek; čovjek
fellowship [ˈfeləuʃip] n 1. drugarstvo 2. (ac.) stipendija
felony [ˈfeloni] n zločin
felt [felt] see feel
female [ˈfiːmeil] 1. adj ženski 2. n žena
feminine [ˈfemənin] adj ženski
femininity [ˌfeməˈniniti] n ženstvenost

femininism [ˌfeməˈninizm] n feminizam
femininist [ˌfeməˈninizt] n feministkinja
fence [fens] n ograda
fender [ˈfendə] (US) n blatobran
fend off v odbiti
ferment [fəˈment] v vreti
fermentation [ˌfəːmənˈteiʃn] n vrenje
ferocity [fəˈrɔsəti] n svirepost
fern [fəːn] n paprat
ferret [ˈferət] n vretna
ferry [ˈferi] n skela
ferryboat [ˈferibəut] n trajekt
fertile [ˈfəːtail] adj plodan
fertility [fəˈtiləti] n plodnost
fertilize [ˈfəːtəlaiz] v oploditi
fertilizer [ˈfəːtəlaizə] n 1. đubrivo 2. chemical fertilizer hemijsko đubrivo; kemijsko đubrivo
fervent [ˈfəːvənt] adj usrdan
festival [ˈfestəvl] n 1. festival 2. (rel.) praznik
festive [ˈfestiv] adj svečan
festivity [fesˈtivəti] n svečanost
fetch [fetʃ] v doneti; donijeti
fetish [ˈfetiʃ] n fetiš
fetus [ˈfiːtəs] n fetus
feud [fjuːd] n zavada
fever [ˈfiːvə] n groznica
feverish [ˈfiːvəriʃ] adj grozničav
few, a few [fjuː] 1. adj malo 2. n mali broj 3. quite a few ne malo 4. in a few days nekoliko dana
fiancé [fiˈɔnsei] n verenik; vjerenik
fiancée [fiˈɔnsei] n verenica; vjerenica
fiasco [fiˈjæskəu] n fijasko
fibre [ˈfaibə] n vlakno
fibre glass n stakleno vlakno
fiction [ˈfikʃn] n beletristika

field [fi:ld] *n* 1. polje 2. (spor.) igralište
field hospital *n* poljska bolnica
field manual *n* ratna služba
field officer *n* vidno polje
field training *n* obuka na terenu
field trip *n* grupna ekskurzija
field work *n* terenska služba
fierce [fiəs] *adj* svirep
fiery ['taiəri] *adj* 1. vatren 2. plahovit
FIFA (Federation of International Football Associations) ['fi:fə] *n* Federacija međunarodnih fudbalskih udruženja
fifteen [,fif'ti:n] *n/adj* petnaest
fifteenth [,fif'ti:nθ] *adj* petnaesti
fifth [fifθ] *adj* peti
fiftieth ['fiftiəθ] *adj* pedeseti
fifty ['fifti] *n/adj* pedeset
fig [fig] *n* figa
fight [fait] 1. *n* borba 2. *v* (**fought**) boriti se protiv (sa)
fighter ['faitə] *n* borac
fighter-plane *n* lovački avion
fighting ['faitiŋ] *n* tuča
figure ['figə] *n* 1. broj 2. linija 3. ilustracija
figure out *v* proračunati
file [fail] *n* 1. dosje 2. turpija 3. **computer file** datoteka
fill [fil] *v* napuniti
fill a form in/out *v* popuniti formular
filling ['filiŋ] *n* (med.) plomba
filling station *n* benzinska stanica
film [film] 1. *adj* filmski 2. *n* film 3. *v* filmovati
film industry *n* kinematografija
film star *n* filmska zvezda/zvijezda
filter ['filtə] 1. *n* filter, filtar 2. *v* filtrirati

filth [filθ] *n* prljavština
filthy ['filθi] *adj* prljav
final ['fainl] 1. *adj* konačan 2. definitivan 3. *n* (spor.) finale
finalist ['fainəlist] *n* finalista
finalize ['fainəlaiz] *v* završiti
finally ['fainəli] *adv* najzad
finals ['fainəlz] *see* **final**
finance ['fainæns; fi'næns] 1. *n* finansije; financije 2. *v* finansirati; financirati
finances ['fainænsiz; fi'nænsiz] *pl* novčana sredstva
Finance Secretary *n* (US) ministar finansija/financija
financial [fai'nænʃl] *adj* novčani
financial affairs *pl* finansijski poslovi; financijski poslovi
financial transactions *pl* novčani poslovi
find [faind] *v* (**found**) naći
findings ['faindiŋz] *pl* odluka
find out *v* saznati
fine [fain] 1. *adj* tanak 2. fin 3. *n* kazna 4. *v* kazniti novčano 5. *adv* dobro
finger ['fiŋgə] *n* prst
fingerprint ['fiŋgəprint] *n* otisak prstiju
finish ['finiʃ] 1. *n* kraj 2. *v* završiti
Finland ['finlənd] *n* Finska
Finn [fin] *n* Finac
Finnish ['finiʃ] *adj* finski
fir [fir] *n* jela
fire ['faiə] 1. *n* vatra 2. **to light a fire** zapaliti vatru 3. **under fire** izložen vatri 4. **to open fire** otvoriti vatru 5. *v* **to fire a gun** pucati iz puške 6. **to fire a machine-gun** opaliti mitraljez 7. **to fire someone from a job** otpustiti nekoga s posla

fire alarm n signalizacija požara
firearm [ˈfaiəraːm] n vatreno oružje
fire bomb n zapaljiva bomba
fire brigade n vatrogasna četa
fire department n (US) vatrogasna služba
fire engine n vatrogasna kola
fire escape, fire exit n požarne stepenice
firefighter n vatrogasac
firefighting n protivpožarna zaštita
firefly [ˈfaiəˌflai] n svitac
fireman [ˈfaiəmən] n vatrogasac
fireplace [ˈfaiəpleis] n kamin
fire station n vatrogasna stanica
firewood [ˈfaiwud] n drva
fireworks [ˈfaiəwəːks] pl vatromet
firing squad n streljački vod
firm [fəːm] 1. adj čvrst 2. **firm measures** stroge mere/mjere 3. n preduzeće; poduzeće, tvrtka
first [fəːst] 1. adj prvi 2. adv prvo 3. **at first** s početka 4. **first of all** pre svega
first aid n prva pomoć
first class 1. adj prvoklasan 2. n prva klasa
firstly [ˈfəːstli] adv prvo
first name n ime
fiscal [ˈfiskəl] adj budžetski
fiscal year n budžetska godina
fish [fiʃ] 1. n riba 2. v pecati (u)
fisherman [ˈfiʃəmən] n pecač
fishing [ˈfiʃiŋ] n pecanje
fist [fist] n pesnica
fit [fit] 1. adj sposoban 2. n (med.) nastup 3. v pristajati
fitness [ˈfitnis] n sposobnost
five [faiv] n/adj pet
fix [fiks] v 1. utvrditi 2. odrediti 3. opraviti
flag [flæg] n zastava

flake [fleik] n pahuljica
flame [fleim] n plamen
flap [flæp] v lepršati
flash [flæʃ] v sevnuti
flashlight [ˈflæʃlait] n džepna lampa
flask [flaːsk] n boca
flat [flæt] 1. adj ravan 2. **We had a flat tyre.** Pukla nam je guma. 3. n stan
flatter [ˈflætə] v laskati
flavour [ˈfleivə] n ukus
flaw [flɔː] n defekt
flay [flei] v oderati
flea [fliː] n buva; buha
flee [fliː] v (**fled**) pobeći; pobjeći (od)
fleet [fliːt] n flota
flesh [fleʃ] n meso
flew [fluː] see **fly**
flexibility [ˌfleksəˈbiləti] n elastičnost
flexible [ˈfleksəbl] adj savitljiv
flight [flait] n 1. let 2. bekstvo; bjekstvo
fling [fliŋ] v (**flung**) ubaciti
flip [flip] v baciti
flirt [fləːt] v flertovati (**with** s)
float [fləut] v ploviti
flock [flɔk] n stado
flood [flʌd] 1. n poplava 2. v poplaviti 3. **to flood the market** preplaviti tržište
floor [flɔː] n 1. pod 2. sprat; kat
floppy disc [ˈflɔpi ˈdisk] n fleksibilni disk
florist [ˈflɔrist] n cvećar; cvjećar
flour [ˈflauə] n brašno
flourish [ˈflʌriʃ] v cvetati; cvjetati
flout [flaut] v rugati se
flow [fləu] 1. n tečenje 2. v teći
flower [ˈflauə] n cvet; cvijet
flown [fləun] see **fly**

flu (= influenza) [flu:] *n* grip
fluctuate [flʌktʃueit] *v* fluktuirati
fluctuation [‚flʌktʃuˈeiʃn] *n* fluktuacija
fluency [ˈfluːənsi] *n* 1. tečnost 2. perfektno znanje
fluent [ˈfluːənt] *adj* 1. tečan 2. koji vlada
fluid [ˈfluːid] 1. *adj* tečan 2. *n* tečnost
fluke [fluːk] *n* by a fluke srećnim slučajem
fluorescent light tube [flɔːˈresnt] *n* fluorescentna svetiljka/ svjetiljka
flush [flʌʃ] *v* ispustiti
flute [fluːt] *n* flauta
fly [flai] 1. *n* (flies) muva; muha 2. *v* (flew, flown) leteti; ljeteti 3. to fly a plane pilotirati avionom
foal [fəul] *n* ždrebe; ždrijebe
foam [fəum] *n* pena; pjena
focus [ˈfəukəs] *v* žarište
fodder [ˈfɔdə] *n* stočna hrana
foetus [ˈfiːtəs] *n* fetus
fog [fɔg] *n* magla
foil [fɔil] *v* osujetiti
fold [fəuld] *v* presaviti
folder [ˈfəuldr] *n* fascikla
folk [fəuk] 1. *adj* narodni 2. *n* narod
folklore [ˈfəuklɔː] *n* folklor
folks [fəuks] *pl* svet; svijet
follow [ˈfɔləu] *v* 1. uslediti; uslijediti 2. pratiti
follower [ˈfɔləuə] *n* pristalica; pristaša
following [ˈfɔləuiŋ] 1. *adj* sledeći; slijedeći 2. *n* pristalice; pristaše
fond [fɔnd] *adj* to be fond of voleti; voljeti
food [fuːd] *n* jelo
food additive *n* dodatak za jelo

foodstuff [ˈfuːdstʌf] *n* namirnica
fool [fuːl] 1. *n* budala 2. *v* prevariti
foolish [ˈfuːliʃ] *adj* budalast
foolproof [ˈfuːlpruːf] *adj* siguran
foot [fut] *n* (feet) 1. noga 2. stopa 3. foot of a mountain podnožje planine 4. on foot pešice; pješice
football [ˈfutbɔːl] *n* fudbal
football pools *pl* vrsta klađenja
footballer [ˈfutbɔːlə] *n* fudbaler
footprint [ˈfutprint] *n* otisak stopala
footsoldier [ˈfutˌsəuldʒə] *n* pešak; pješak
footstep [ˈfutstep] *n* korak
footwear [ˈfutweə] *n* obuća
for [fə; fɔː] *prep* 1. za 2. radi 3. zbog 4. u 5. jer 6. iz 7. od
forbid [fəˈbid] *v* (forbade, forbidden) zabraniti
forbidden [fəˈbidn] *adj* zabranjen
force [fɔːs] 1. *n* snaga 2. sila 3. military forces oružane snage 4. in force na snazi 5. to use force primeniti silu; primijeniti silu 6. *v* prinuditi
forced [fɔːst] *adj* prinudan
forced landing *n* prinudno sletanje/slijetanje
forced retirement *n* prinudno penzionisanje
forceful [ˈfɔːsfl] *adj* snažan
forcefully [ˈfɔːsfəli] *adv* snažno, silno
ford [fɔːd] *v* preći gazom
fore [fɔː] *n* to come to the fore istaknuti se
forearm [ˈfɔːraːm] *n* podlaktica
forecast [ˈfɔːkaːst] 1. *n* prognoza 2. *v* prognozirati
forefinger [ˈfɔːfiŋgə] *n* kažiprst
forefront [ˈfɔːfrʌnt] *n* at the forefront u prvom planu

foregone [ˈfɔːgɔn] *adj* **a foregone conclusion** neminovan rezultat
forehead [ˈfɔrid; ˈfɔːhed] *n* čelo
foreign [ˈfɔrən] *adj* spoljni
foreign affairs *n* spoljni poslovi
foreigner [ˈfɔrənə] *n* stranac
foreign exchange *n* devize
foreign minister *n* ministar inostranih poslova; ministar vanuskih poslova
Foreign Office *n* (UK) ministarstvo inostranih poslova; ministarstvo vanjskih poslova
foreign policy *n* spoljna politika
foreign trade *n* spoljna trgovina
foreman [ˈfɔːmən] *n* poslovođa
foremost [ˈfɔːməust] 1. *adj* glavni 2. *adv* prvo
foresee [fɔːˈsiː] *v* predvideti; predvidjeti
foreseeable [ˌfɔːˈsiːəbl] *adj* dogledan
foresight [ˈfɔːsait] *n* predviđanje
forest [ˈfɔrist] *n* šuma
forestall [fɔːˈstɔːl] *v* predvideti; predvidjeti
forestry [ˈfɔristri] *n* šumarstvo
forever [fəˈrevə] *adv* zauvek; zauvijek
forewarn [fɔːˈwɔːn] *v* upozoriti
foreword [ˈfɔːwəːd] *n* predgovor
for example *see* e.g.
forfeit [ˈfɔːfit] *v* izgubiti
forgave [fəˈgeiv] *see* forgive
forge [fɔːdʒ] *v* 1. skovati 2. falsifikovati
forged [fɔːdʒd] 1. **forged document** lažan dokumenat 2. **a forged cheque** faslifikovan ček
forger [ˈfɔːdʒə] *n* falsifikator
forgery [ˈfɔːdʒəri] *n* falsifikat
forget [fəˈget] *v* (forgot, forgotten) zaboraviti

forgive [fəˈgiv] *v* (forgave, forgiven) oprostiti
forgive and forget oprosti i zaboravi
forgiveness [fəˈgivnis] *n* oproštaj
forgot, forgotten [fəˈgɔt; fəˈgɔtn] *see* forget
fork [fɔːk] *n* viljuška
form [fɔːm] 1. *n* forma 2. formular 3. (ed.) razred 4. *v* formirati
formal [ˈfɔːml] *adj* svečan
formality [ˈfɔːməliti] *n* formalnost
formally [ˈfɔːməli] *adv* formalno
formation [fɔːˈmeiʃn] *n* formiranje
former [ˈfɔːmə] *adj* bivši
formerly [ˈfɔːməli] *adv* ranije
formidable [ˈfɔːmidəbl] *adj* težak
formula [ˈfɔːmjulə] *n* formula
Formula One racing *n* trke formule jedan
fort [fɔːt] *n* tvrđava
forth [fɔːθ] *adv* napred; naprijed
forthcoming [ˌfɔːθˈkʌmin] *adj* predstojeći
fortify [ˈfɔːtifai] *v* utvrditi
fortnight [ˈfɔːtnait] *n* dve nedelje/dvije nedjelje; dva tjedna
fortress [ˈfɔːtris] *see* fort
fortunate [ˈfɔːtʃənət] *adj* srećan
fortunately [ˈfɔːtʃənətli] *adv* srećom
fortune [ˈfɔːtʃuːn] *n* 1. sreća 2. imovina
forty [ˈfɔːti] *n/adj* četrdeset
forum [ˈfɔːrəm] *n* forum
forward [ˈfɔːwəd] 1. *adv* napred; naprijed 2. *v* proslediti; proslijediti
fossil [ˈfɔsəl] *n* fosil
foster [ˈfɔstə] *v* gajiti
foster child *n* hranjenik
foster father *n* poočim

foster mother *n* pomajka
fought [fɔːt] *see* **fight**
foul [faul] 1. *adj* nečist 2. *n* (spor.) greška
found [faund] 1. *v* osnovati 2. *see* **find**
foundation [faunˈdeiʃn] *n* 1. fondacija 2. temelj
founder [ˈfaundə] *n* osnivač
fountain [ˈfauntin] *n* izvor
fountain pen *n* naliv-pero
four [fɔː] *n/adj* četiri
fourteen [ˌfɔːˈtiːn] *n/adj* četrnaest
fourteenth [ˌfɔːˈtiːnθ] *adj* četrnaesti
fourth [fɔːθ] 1. *adj* četvrti 2. *n* četvrt
four-wheel drive *n* automobil sa pogonom na sva četiri točka
fowl [faul] *n* živina
fox [fɔks] *n* lisica
foyer [ˈfɔjei] *see* **lobby**
fraction [ˈtrækʃn] *n* razlomak
fracture [ˈfræktʃə] 1. *n* prelom 2. *v* slomiti
fragile [ˈfrædʒail] *adj* krhak
fragment [ˈfrægmənt] *n* fragmenat
fragrance [ˈfreigrəns] *n* miris
fragrant [ˈfreigrənt] *adj* mirisav
frail [freil] *adj* krhak
frame [freim] *n* 1. sklop 2. kostur 3. **picture frame** okvir za sliku; ram za sliku
framework [ˈfreimwəːk] *n* okvir
franc [fræŋk] *n* franak
France [frɑːns] *n* Francuska
franchise [ˈfræntʃaiz] *n* 1. pravo glasa 2. licenca
frankly [ˈfræŋkli] *adv* otvoreno
frantic [ˈfræntik] *adj* pomaman
fraternal [frəˈtəːnl] *adj* bratski
fraternity [frəˈtəːnəti] *n* bratsvto
fraud [frɔːd] *n* prevara

fraudulent [ˈfrɔːdjulənt] *adj* varljiv
freak [friːk] *n* nakaza
free [friː] 1. *adj* slobodan 2. besplatan 3. **free of debt** čist od duga 4. *v* (**freed**) osloboditi
freed [friːd] *see* **free**
freedom [ˈfriːdəm] *n* sloboda
freedom of assembly *n* sloboda zbora
freedom of information *n* pravo pristupa državnim dokumentima
freedom of speech *n* sloboda govora
freedom of the press *n* sloboda štampe
free elections *n* slobodni izbori
freelance, freelancer *n* honorarac
freelancing *n* honorarni rad
free of charge *adj* besplatan
free trade *n* slobodna trgovina
free trade zone *n* zona slobodne trgovine
freeway [ˈfriːwei] *n* auto-put
freeze [friːz] *v* (**froze, frozen**) smrznuti (se)
freezer [ˈfriːzə] *n* frizer
freight [freit] *n* roba
freight car *n* teretni vagon
freighter [ˈfreitə] *n* tovarni brod
French [frentʃ] 1. *adj* francuski 2. *n* francuski jezik 3. *pl* francuski narod
French-Canadian *adj* franko-kanadski
Frenchman [ˈfrentʃmən] *n* Francuz
Frenchwoman [ˈfrentʃ,wumən] *n* Francuskinja
frequency [ˈfriːkwənsi] *n* frekvencija
frequent [ˈfriːkwənt] *adj* čest
frequently [ˈfriːkwəntli] *adv* često
fresh [freʃ] *adj* 1. nov 2. svež; sviјеž

fresh blood n sveža krv; svježa krv

freshwater [ˈfreʃˌwɔːtə] adj slatkovodni

fret [fret] v jesti se

friction [ˈfrikʃn] n trenje

Friday [ˈfraidi] n petak

fridge [fridʒ] n frižider

fried [fraid] see **fry**

friend [frend] n prijatelj

friendliness [ˈfrendlinis] n blagonaklonost

friendly [ˈfrendli] adj prijateljski

friendship [ˈfrendʃip] n prijateljstvo

frigate [ˈfrigət] n fregata

fright [frait] n strah

frighten [ˈfraitn] v uplašiti

frightened [ˈfraitənd] adj uplašen

frightful [ˈfraitfl] adj užasan

fringe [frindʒ] n 1. resa 2. (pol.) krilo

fro [frəu] adv **to and fro** napred i nazad; naprijed i nazad

frog [frɔg] n žaba

from [frɔm] prep 1. od 2. iz 3. s/sa 4. prema 5. zbog 6. **from the west** od zapada

from now on adv od sada

from then on adv od tada

front [frʌnt] n 1. prednja strana 2. **in front** ispred 3. **war front** front; fronta

frontal attack [ˈfrʌntl] n frontalan napad

frontier [ˈfrʌntiə] n granica

front line n linija fronta/fronte

front-page adj senzacionalni

frost [frɔst] n mraz

frostbite [ˈfrɔstbait] n promrzlina

frostbitten [ˈfrɔstbitn] adj **frostbitten hands** promrzle ruke

froth [frɔθ] n pena; pjena

frown [fraun] v namrštiti se

froze [frəuz] see **freeze**

frozen [ˈfrəuzn] adj 1. smrznut 2. see **freeze**

fruit [fruːt] n voće

fruitful [ˈfruːtfl] adj plodan

fruitless [ˈfruːtlis] adj besplodan

fruit salad n salata od voća

frustrate [frʌˈstreit] v osujetiti

frustrated [frʌˈstreitid] adj osujećen, isfrustriran

frustration [frʌˈstreiʃn] n frustracija

fry [frai] v (**fried**) ispržiti

frying-pan [ˈfraiiŋˌpæn] n tiganj

ft. see **foot**

fuel [ˈfjuːəl] 1. n gorivo 2. v snabdeti gorivom; snabdjeti gorivom 3. stimulisati

fuel depot/dump n skaldište goriva

fuel pump n pumpa za goriva

fuel tank n rezervoar za gorivo

fugitive [ˈfjuːdʒətiv] n begunac; bjegunac

fulfil, fulfill [fulˈfil] v ispuniti

fulfilment, fulfillment [fulˈfilmənt] n ispunjenje

full [ful] 1. adj pun 2. adv pravo

fullness [ˈfulnis] n punoća

full-scale adj potpun

full stop n tačka; točka

full-time adj neskraćen

fully [ˈfuli] adv potpuno

fully fledged adj razbuktan

fumes [fjuːm] pl dim

fun [fʌn] n 1. zabava 2. **in fun** u šali 3. **to make fun of** terati šegu s; tjerati šegu s

function [ˈfʌŋkʃn] 1. n funkcija 2. **social function** primanje 3. v funkcionisati

functional [ˈfʌnkʃənəl] *adj* funkcionalan

functionary [ˈfʌnkʃənəri] *n* funkcionar

function key *n* funkcijska tipka

fund [fʌnd] *n* 1. fond 2. relief fund sredstva za pomoć

fundamental [ˌfʌndəˈmentəl] *adj* fundamentalan

fundamentalist [ˌfʌndəˈmentəlist] *n* fundamentalista

funding [ˈfʌndiŋ] *n* finansiranje

funds [fʌndz] *pl* fondovi

funeral [ˈfjuːnərəl] *n* pogreb

funfair [ˈfʌnfeə] *n* zabavni park

fungal [ˈfʌŋgəl] *adj* gljivični

fungus [ˈfʌŋgəs] *n* gljiva

funnel [ˈfʌnl] *n* levak; ljievak

funny [ˈfʌni] *adj* 1. smešan; smiješan 2. čudan

fur [fəː] *n* krzno

furious [ˈfjuəriəs] *adj* besan; bijesan

furnace [ˈfəːnis] *n* peć

furnish [ˈfəːniʃ] *v* nemestiti; nemjestiti

furniture [ˈfəːnitʃə] *n* 1. nameštaj; namještaj 2. piece of furniture komad nameštaja/ namještaja

further [ˈfəːðə] 1. *adj* dalji(e) 2. *v* unaprediti; unaprijediti

further details *pl* dodatne pojedinosti

furthermore [ˌfəːðəˈmɔː] *adv* osim toga

fury [ˈfjuəri] *n* bes; bijes

fuse [fjuːz] *n* osigurač

fuss [fʌs] *n* larma

fussy [ˈfʌsi] *adj* cepidlački; cjepidlački

futile [ˈfjuːtail] *adj* uzaludan

future [ˈfjuːtʃə] 1. *n* budućnost 2. *adj* budući

G

gadget ['gadʒit] n naprava
gaffe [gæf] n gaf
gag [gæg] v začepiti
gage see **gauge**
gag the press v ućutkati štampu
gain [gein] 1. n dobit 2. v dobiti
gala ['ga:lə] n gala predstava
galaxy ['gæləski] n galaksija
gale [geil] n oluja
gallant ['gælənt] adj otmen
gallery ['gæləri] n 1. galerija 2. **art gallery** umetnička galerija; umjetnička galerija
gallon ['gælən] n galon
gallop ['gæləp] v galopirati
gallows ['gæləuz] n vešala; vješala
gamble ['gæmbl] v kockati se
gambler ['gæmblə] n kockar
gambling ['gæmbliŋ] n kockanje
gambling club n kockarnica
game [geim] n 1. igra 2. divljač
gang [gæŋ] n družina
gangrene ['gæŋgri:n] n gangrena
gangster ['gæŋstə] n gangster
gap [gæp] n rupa
garage ['gæra:ʒ; 'gæridʒ] n garaža
garbage ['ga:bij] n đubre
garden ['ga:dn] n vrt
gardener ['ga:dnə] n vrtlar
gardening ['ga:dniŋ] n baštovanstvo
garlic ['ga:lik] n češnjak
garment ['ga:mənt] n odevni predmet; odjevni predmet
garrison ['gærisn] n garnizon
gas [gæs] n 1. gas 2. benzin
gas line n gasovod
gasolene, gasoline ['gæsəli:n] benzin

gas station n (US) benzinska stanica
gas tank n benzinski rezervoar
gate [geit] n kapija
gatecrasher n padobranac
gather ['gæðə] v 1. skupiti (se) 2. zaključiti
gathering ['gæðəriŋ] n skup
GATT (General Agreement on Tariffs and Trade) n Opšti sporazum o carinama i trgovini
gauge [geidʒ] 1. n mera; mjera 2. v izmeriti; imjeriti
gave [geiv] see **give**
gay [gei] 1. adj veseo 2. homoseksualan 3. n homoseksualac
gaze [geiz] v piljiti (**at** u)
gazelle [gə'zel] n gazela
gazette [gə'zet] n službene novine
gear [giə] n 1. brzina 2. pribor
gearbox ['giəbɔks] n menjačka kutija; mjenjačka kutija
geese [gi:s] see **goose**
gel [dʒel] n gel
gelignite ['dʒeligneit] n gelignit
gem [dʒem] n dragulj
gendarme [dʒen'da:m] n žandarm
gendarmerie [dʒen'da:məri] n žandarmerija
gender ['dʒendə] n rod
gene [dʒi:n] n gen
genealogy [,dʒi:ni'alədʒi] n genealogija
general ['dʒenrəl] 1. adj generalni 2. n general 3. **in general** u principu

General Assembly (UN) *n* Generalna skupština

general election *n* opšti izbori; opći izbori

generalize ['dʒenrəlaiz] *v* generalizovati

generally ['dʒenrəli] *adv* uopšte; uopće

generate ['dʒenreit] *v* proizvesti

generation [,dʒenə'reiʃn] *n* generacija

generation gap *n* sukob generacija

generator [,dʒenə'reitə] *n* generator

generosity [,djenə'rɔsəti] *n* darežljivost

generous ['dʒenərəs] *adj* darežljiv

genetic [dʒi'netik] *adj* genetičan

genetics [dʒi'netiks] *pl* genetika

genial ['dʒi:niəl] *adj* ljubazan

genital ['dʒenitl] *adj* polni; spolni

genitals ['dʒenitlz] *pl* genitalije

genitive ['dʒenitiv] *n* genitiv

genius ['dʒi:niəs] *n* genije

genocidal ['dʒenəsaidl] *adj* genocidni

genocide ['dʒenəsaid] *n* 1. genocid 2. **to commit genocide** sprovesti genocid

gentle ['dʒentl] *adj* blag

gentleman ['dʒentlmən] *n* (gentlemen) gospodin

gentleness ['dʒentlnis] *n* blagost

genuine ['dʒenjuin] *adj* pravi

geography [dʒi'ɔgrəfi] *n* geografija

geologist [dʒi'ɔlədʒist] *n* geolog

geology [dʒi'ɔlədʒi] *n* geologija

geometry [dʒi'ɔmətri] *n* geometrija

Georgia ['dʒɔːrdʒə] *n* 1. Gruzija 2. Džordžija

germ [dʒəːm] *n* klica

German ['dʒəːmən] 1. *adj* nemački; njemački 2. *n* Nemac; Nijemac

Germany ['dʒəːməni] *n* Nemačka; Njemačka

gesture ['dʒestʃə] *n* gest

get [get] *v* (got, gotten) 1. dobiti 2. **to get hurt** biti povređen/povrijeđen 3. **I got measles.** Dobio sam ospice. 4. **to get better** oporaviti se 5. **They got to London by Friday.** Stigli su u London do petka.

get along *v* dovijati se

get away *v* umaći

get back *v* vratiti se

get in *v* stići

get into *v* ući

get off *v* sići

get on *v* sesti

get out *v* sići

get ready *v* spremati se

get to *v* stići do, doći do

get through to *v* dobiti vezu

get up *v* ustati

ghastly ['gaːstli] *adj* grozan

ghetto ['getəu] *n* geto

ghost [gəust] *n* duh

giant ['dʒaiənt] 1. *adj* gigantski 2. *n* div

giddy ['gidi] *adj* vrtoglav

gift [gift] *n* poklon

gifted ['giftid] *adj* darovit

gig [gig] *n* (mus.) koncert

gigantic [dʒai'gæntik] *adj* gigantski

giggle ['gigl] *n* kikotati se

gin [dʒin] *n* džin

ginger ['dʒindʒə] *n* đumbir

Gipsy ['dʒipsi] *see* Gypsy

giraffe [gi'raːf] *n* žirafa

girl ['gəːl] *n* devojka; djevojka

girlfriend ['gəːlfrend] *n* 1. devojka; djevojka 2. drugarica

give [giv] *v* (gave, given) 1. dati 2. pokloniti

give away v 1. pokloniti 2. otkriti
give back v vratiti
give birth to v roditi
give in v predati se
give up v 1. ustupiti 2. predati se 3. to give up drinking odbaciti alkohol
give way v ustupiti
glacier [ˈglæsiə] adj gleČer
glad [glæd] adj mio
gladden [ˈglædn] v obradovati
gladly [ˈglædli] adv rado
gladness [ˈglædnis] n radost
glance at [glaːns] v baciti pogled na
gland [glænd] n žlezda; žlijezda
glare [gleə] v besno gledati; bijesno gledati
glass [glaːs] n 1. staklo 2. drinking glass Čaša
glasses [ˈglaːsiz] pl naoČari; naoČale
gleam [gliːm] v sijati
glide [glaid] v planirati
glimpse [glimps] v letimice pogledati
glitter [ˈglitə] v sijati
global [ˈgləubl] adj globalan
globe [gləub] n globus
gloomy [ˈgluːmi] adj 1. mraČan 2. sumoran
glorious [ˈgloːriəs] adj slavan
glory [ˈgloːri] n slava
glossy [ˈglɔsi] 1. adj sjajan 2. n Časopis
glove [glʌv] n rukavica
glow [gləu] v bleskati se; blijeskati se
glue [gluː] 1. n lepak; lijepak 2. v zalepiti; zalijepiti
GNP see gross national product
go [gəu] v (went, gone) 1. iĆi 2. otiĆi 3. raditi
go ahead v iĆi napred/naprijed

goal [gəul] n 1. cilj 2. (sport) gol 3. to score a goal postiĆi gol 4. see goalpost
goalkeeper [ˈgəulkiːpə] n golman
goalpost [ˈgəulpəust] n stub vrata
goat [gəut] n koza
go away v otiĆi
go back v vratiti se
go bad v ukvariti se
go by v prolaziti
God, god [gɔd] n Bog, bog
godchild [ˈgɔdtʃaild] n kumČe
goddaughter [ˈgɔd,dɔtə] n kumica
goddess [ˈgɔdis] n boginja
godfather [ˈgɔdfaːθə] n kum
godless [ˈgɔdlis] adj bezbožan
godmother [ˈgɔdmʌθə] n kuma
go down v 1. siĆi 2. splasnuti
godson [ˈgɔdsən] n kumČe
godparent [ˈgɔdpeərənt] n kum
go in v uĆi
going [ˈgəuiŋ] adj the going rate tekuĆi kurs
gold [gəuld] 1. adj zlatan 2. n zlato
golden [ˈgəuldn] adj zlatan
golf [gɔlf] n golf
golf course n igralište za golf
gone [gɔn] see go
gonorrhoea [,gɔnəˈriːə] n gonoreja
good [gud] 1. adj dobar 2. n dobro 3. for good zauvek 4. see goods
goodbye [,gudˈbai] n 1. oproštaj 2. zbogom!
good deed n dobro delo/djelo
good health n dobro zdravlje
good-looking adj lep; lijep
good luck n dobra sreĆa
goodness [ˈgudnis] n dobrota
goods [gudz] n 1. roba 2. consumer goods roba široke potrošnje
goods wagon n teretni vagon
good-tempered adj blage naravi

goodwill [,gud·wil] *n* dobra volja
go off *v* 1. otići 2. opaliti
go on *v* 1. produžiti 2. dešavati se
goose [gu:s] *n* (**geese**) guska
gooseberry ['gu:sbəri] *n* ogrozd
go out *v* 1. izići 2. ugasiti se
go over *v* preći
gorge [gɔ:dʒ] *n* klisura
gorgeous ['gɔ:dʒəs] *adj* divan
gorilla [gə'rilə] *n* gorila
gospel ['gɔspl] *n* evanđelje
gossip ['gɔsip] 1. *n* torokanje 2. *v* torokati
got [gɔt] *see* **get**
go through *v* proći kroz
go to sleep *v* ići na spavanje
gouge [gaudʒ] *v* izdupsti
go up *v* skočiti
gourd ['guəd] *n* tikva
govern ['gʌvn] *v* upravljati
government ['gʌvənmənt] *n* 1. vlada 2. upravljanje
government spokesman *n* portparol vlade, predstavnik za štampu
governor ['gʌvənə] *n* guverner
governor-general *n* generalni guverner
go with *v* pratiti
gown [gaun] *n* ogrtač
grab [græb] *v* (**grabbed**) ščepati
grace [greis] *n* 1. milost 2. čar
graceful ['greisfl] *adj* graciozan
gracious ['greiʃəs] *adj* milostiv
grade [greid] *n* 1. stupanj 2. nagib 3. (ed.) razred 4. ocena; ocjena
gradual ['grædʒuəl] *adj* postepen
gradually ['grædʒuli] *adv* postepeno
graduate ['grædʒuət] *n* diplomirani student
graduate ['grædʒueit] *v* diplomirati
graffiti [grə'fi:ti] *n* zidna grafika

graft [gra:ft] (med.) 1. *n* presad 2. *v* nakalemiti; nakalamiti
grain [grein] *n* 1. žito 2. zrno
gram [græm] *n* gram
grammar ['græmə] *n* gramatika
gramme [græm] *n* gram
gramophone ['græməfəun] *n* gramofon
granary ['grænəri] *n* žitnica
grand [grænd] *adj* 1. veliki 2. glavni
grandchild ['græntʃaild] *n* unuče
granddaughter ['græn,dɔ:tə] *n* unuka
grandfather ['græn,fa:ðə] *n* ded; djed
grandmother ['grænd,mʌðə] *n* baba
grandson ['grænsʌn] *n* unuk
granite ['grænit] *n* granit
grant [gra:nt] 1. *n* stipendija 2. *v* odobriti
grape [greip] *n* zrno grožđa
grapes [greips] *pl* grožđe
grapefruit ['greipfru:t] *n* grejpfrut
graph [gra:f] *n* grafikon
graphic ['gra:fik] *adj* grafički
graphic arts *pl* grafika
graphic designer *n* grafički dizajner
grasp [gra:sp] *v* ščepati
grass [gra:s] *n* trava
grasshopper ['gra:shɔpə] *n* skakavac
grassroots [gra:s'ru:ts] *adj* narodni
grateful ['greitfl] *adj* zahvalan
gratis ['gra:tis] *adv* besplatno
gratitude ['grætitju:d] *n* zahvalnost
grave [greiv] 1. *adj* ozbiljan 2. *n* grob
gravel ['grævl] *n* šljunak
graveyard ['greivja:d] *n* groblje
gravity ['grævəti] *n* teža

gravy [ˈgreivi] n sos
gray [ˈgrei] adj siv 2. see **grey hair**
graze [greiz] v pasti
grease [griːs] n mast
greasy [ˈgriːsi] adj mastan
great [greit] adj 1. veliki 2. **a great deal** vrlo mnogo
Great Britain [ˈgreitˈbritn] n Velika Britanija
greatly [ˈgreitli] adv uveliko
greatness [ˈgreitnis] n veličina
greed [griːd] n pohlepa
greedy [ˈgriːdi] adj pohlepan
green [griːn] adj 1. zelen 2. neiskusan 3. (pol.) zelena stranka
greengrocer [ˈgriːnɡrəusə] n piljar
greenhouse [ˈgriːnhaus] n staklena bašta
greens [griːnz] pl kuhinjsko zelje
greet [griːt] v dočekati
greeting [ˈgriːtiŋ] n doček
grenade [grəˈneid] n ručna granata
grenade launcher n tromblon
grew [gruː] see **grow**
grey [grei] adj siv
grey hair n seda kosa; sijeda kosa
grid [grid] n mreža
grief [griːf] n žalost
grievance [ˈgriːvəns] n žalba
grieve [griːv] v tugovati
grievous [ˈgriːvəs] adj težak
grill [gril] v pržiti na roštilju
grim [grim] adj ljutit
grin [grin] v ceriti se
grind [graind] v (**ground**) samleti; samljeti
grinder [ˈgraində] n mlinač
grip [grip] 1. n stisak 2. v zahvatiti
groan [grəun] v ječati
grocer [ˈgrəusə] n bakalin
groceries [ˈgrəusəriːz] pl prehrambeni proizvodi

groin [grɔin] n prepone
groom [gruːm] n 1. mladoženja 2. konjušar
groove [gruːv] n žleb; žlijeb
gross income [grəus ˈinkʌm] n ukupan prihod
gross weight [grəus ˈweit] n bruto težina
gross national product (GNP) n ukupni nacionali proizvod
ground [graund] n 1. zemlja 2. see **grind, grounds**
groundnut [ˈgraundnʌt] n kikiriki
grounds [graundz] pl 1. (leg.) uzrok 2. (spor.) teren
groundwork [ˈgraundwəːk] n pripremni rad
group [gruːp] 1. n grupa 2. v grupisati
grow [grəu] v (grew, grown) 1. porasti 2. postati 3. odgajiti; uzgajiti
grower [ˈgrəuə] n odgajivač
growl [graul] v režati
grown-up [grəunˈʌp] 1. adj odrastao 2. n odrastao čovek/čovjek
growth [grəuθ] n rastenje
growth-rate n stopa rasta
grow up v odrasti
grudge [grʌdʒ] n pizma
gruesome [ˈgruːsəm] adj jeziv
grumble [ˈgrʌmbl] v gunđati
guarantee [ˌgærənˈtiː] 1. n garancija; garantija 2. v garantovati
guarantor [ˌgærənˈtɔː] n garant
guard [gaːd] 1. n čuvar 2. straža 3. **national guard** nacionalna garda 4. v čuvati
guard duty n stražarska služba
guardian [ˈgaːdiən] n stražar
guerilla, guerrilla [gəˈrilə] n partisan

guerilla warfare *n* gerilski rat

guess [ges] 1. *n* pogađanje 2. *v* pogoditi

guesswork [ˈgeswəːk] *n* nagađanje

guest [gest] *n* 1. gost 2. **hotel guest** hotelski gost

guest house *n* kuća za goste

guidance [ˈgaidəns] *n* savetovanje; savjetovanje

guide [gaid] 1. *n* vodič 2. **tourist guide** turistički vodič 3. *v* voditi

guidebook [ˈgaidbuk] *n* vodič

guided missile [ˈgaidid] *n* vođena raketa

guilt [gilt] *n* krivica

guilty [ˈgilti] *adj* 1. kriv 2. **to plead guilty** priznati krivicu 3. **to plead not guilty** odreći krivicu 4. **to find guilty** oglasiti krivim

guise [gaiz] *n* vid

guitar [giˈtaː] *n* gitara

guitarist [giˈtaː] *n* gitarista

gulf [gʌlf] *n* zaliv

gum [gʌm] *n* 1. guma 2. **chewing gum** žvakaća guma

gums [gʌmz] *pl* desni

gun [gʌn] *n* 1. puška 2. **to fire a gun** pucati iz puške 3. **to load a gun** napuniti pušku

gunboat [ˈgʌnbəut] *n* topovnjača

gunfire [ˈgʌnfajə] *n* vatra oruđa

gunman [ˈgʌnmən] *n* revolveraš

gun powder *n* barut

gunrunner [ˈgʌnˌrʌnə] *n* krijumčar vatrenog oružja

gunrunning [ˈgʌnˌrʌniŋ] *n* krijumčarenje vatrenog oružja

gunship [ˈgʌnʃip] *n* krstarica

gunshot [ˈgʌnʃɔt] *n* puškomet

gush [gʌʃ] *v* šiknuti

guts [gʌts] *pl* 1. creva; crijeva 2. hrabrost

gutter [ˈgʌtə] *n* žleb; žlijeb

guy [gai] *n* momak

gym, gymnasium [dʒim; dʒimˈneiziəm] *n* gimnastička dvorana

gymnast [dʒimˈnæst] *n* gimnastičar

gymnastics [dʒimˈnæstiks] *n* gimnastika

gynaecological [ˌgainəkɔˈlɔdʒikl] *adj* ginekološki

gynaecologist [ˌgainəˈkɔlɔdʒist] *n* ginekolog

gynaecology [ˌgainəˈkɔlɔdʒi] *n* ginekologija

gynaecological clinic *n* ginekološka klinika

Gypsy [ˈdʒipsi] 1. *adj* ciganski 2. *n* Ciganin, Rom

H

habit [ˈhæbit] *n* navika

habitable [ˈhæbitəbl] *adj* pogodan za stanovanje

habitat [ˈhæbitæt] *n* sredina

habitation [ˌhæbiˈteiʃn] *n* stanovanje

habitual [həbiˈtʃuːəl] *adj* naviknut

had [hæd] *see* **have**

hack [hæk] *v* seckati; sjeckati

hadj [hædʒ] *see* **hajj**

hadji [ˈhædʒi] *see* **haji**

haemorrhage [ˈheməridʒ] *v* naviknut

haemorrhoid [ˈhemərɔid] *n* hemeroid

hail [heil] **1.** *n* grad **2.** *v* dozvati **3.** It's hailing. Grad padati.

hair [heə] *n* kosa

hair-cut [ˈheəkʌt] *n* šišanje

hairbrush [ˈheəbrʌʃ] *n* buroshi

hairdresser [ˈheədresə] *n* frizer

hairdryer [ˈheədraiə] *n* fen za kosu

hairstyle [ˈheəstail] *n* frizura

haji [ˈhædʒi] *n* hadžija

hajj [hædʒ] *n* hadžiluk

hairy [ˈheəri] *adj* dlakav

half [haːf; haːvz] *n* (*pl* **halves**) **1.** polovina, pola **2. half past three** pola četiri

half an hour, half-hour *n* pola sata

half-price *n* pola cene/cijene

half-time *n* (spor.) poluvreme; poluvrijeme

half-way *adj/adv* na pola puta

hall [hɔːl] *n* sala

hallo [həˈləu] *see* **hello**

hall of fame *n* dvorana velikana

hallucination [həˌluːsiˈneiʃn] *n* halucinacija

hallucinatory [həˌluːsiˈneitəri] *adj* halucinantan

hallway [ˈhɔlwei] *n* hodnik

halt [hɔːlt] *v* **1.** zaustaviti (se) **2. to call a halt** obustaviti rad

halter [ˈhɔːltə] *n* ular

halve [haːv] *v* prepoloviti

halves [haːvz] *see* **half**

ham [hæm] *n* šunka

hamburger [ˈhæmbəːgə] *n* pljeskavica

hammer [ˈhæmə] **1.** *n* čekić **2.** *v* ukucati

hamper [ˈhæmpə] *v* smetati

hand [hænd] **1.** *n* ruka **2. the left hand** leva ruka **3. at hand** blizu **4. at first hand** iz prve ruke **5. at second hand** iz druga ruke **6. on the one hand... on the other** s jedne strane... s druge strane **7.** *v* predati

handbag [ˈhændbæg] *n* tašna

handball [ˈhændbɔːl] *n* rukomet

handbook [ˈhændbuk] *n* priručnik

handbrake [ˈhændbreik] *n* ručna kočnica

handcuffs [ˈhændkʌfs] *pl* lisice

handful [ˈhændful] *n* šaka

hand-grenade [ˈhændgrəˌneid] *n* ručna granata

handicap [ˈhændikæp] *n* hendikep

handicapped [ˈhændikæpt] *adj* **1.** hendikepiran **2.** (med.) razvojno ometen

hand in *v* predati

handkerchief [ˈhæŋkətʃif] *n* maramica

handle [ˈhændl] 1. *n* ručica 2. *v* rukovati 3. postupati

handlebar [ˈhændlba:] *n* upravljač

hand-made *adj* rađen rukom

hand out *v* rasturiti

hand over *v* izručiti

handset [ˈhændset] *n* ručni telefon

handshake [ˈhændʃeik] *n* rukovanje

handsome [ˈhænsəm] *adj* lep; lijep

handwriting [ˈhænd,raitiŋ] *n* rukopis

handy [ˈhændi] *adj* **to be handy** biti pri ruci

hang [hæŋ] *v* (**hung/hanged**) 1. obesiti; objesiti 2. **to get the hang of** uvežbati; uvježbati

hangar [ˈhæŋə] *n* hangar

hanger [ˈhæŋə] *n* vešalica; vješalica

hanger-on *n* muktaš

hangman [ˈhæŋmən] *n* dželat

hang on *v* 1. držati se 2. čekati

hang up *v* 1. obesiti 2. spustiti

haphazard [hæpˈhæzə:d] *adj* slučajan

happen [ˈhæpən] *v* 1. desiti se 2. zadesiti se

happily [ˈhæpili] *adv* srećom

happiness [ˈhæpinəs] *n* sreća

happy [ˈhæpi] *adj* srećan

harass [ˈhærəs] *v* uznemiriti

harassment [ˈhærəsmənt] *n* uznemiravanje

harbour, harbor [ˈha:bə] *n* luka

hard [ha:d] 1. *adj* tvrd 2. težak 3. ljut 4. *adv* teško

harden [ˈha:dn] *v* stvrdnuti (se)

hard copy *n* štampani primerak

hard disk *n* tvrdi disk

hard hat *n* šlem

hard-hitting *adj* krut

hardly [ˈha:dli] *adv* 1. jedva 2. **Hardly anyone came.** Skoro niko nije došao. 3. **I hardly ever come here.** Skoro nikada ne dolazim ovamo.

hardship [ˈha:dʃip] *n* tegoba

hardware [ˈha:dweə] *n* hardver

hard work *n* težak rad

hard-working *adj* vredan; vrijedan

hardy [ˈha:di] *adj* izdržljiv

hare [heə] *n* zec

harm [ha:m] 1. *n* povreda 2. *v* naškoditi

harmful [ˈha:mfl] *adj* štetan

harmless [ˈha:mlis] *adj* neškodljiv

harmony [ˈha:məni] *n* sklad

harness [ˈha:nis] *n* ham

harsh [ha:ʃ] *adj* surov

harvest [ˈha:vist] 1. *n* žetva 2. *v* požeti

has *see* **have**

hassle [ˈhæsl] *n* svađa

haste [heist] *n* žurba

hasten [ˈheisn] *v* ubrzati

hasty [ˈheisti] *adj* brz

hat [hæt] *n* šešir

hatch [hætʃ] *v* 1. izleći 2. **to hatch a plot** skovati zaveru/zavjeru

hate [heit] 1. *n* mržnja 2. *v* mrzeti; mrzjeti

hateful [ˌheitfl] *adj* mrzak

hatred [ˈheitrid] *n* 1. mržnja 2. **to feel hatred for** osećati mržnju prema; osjećati mržnju prema

haul [hɔ:l] *v* vući

haunt [hɔ:nt] *v* 1. obilaziti 2. *see* **haunted**

have [hæv] *v* (**had**) 1. imati 2. **to have a cold** imati kijavicu 3. **We have returned.** Vratili smo se. 4. **He has to come.** Mora da dođe.

havoc [ˈhævək] *n* opustošenje

hawk [hɔːk] 1. *n* jastreb 2. *v* raznositi

hawker [ˈhɔːkə] *n* torbar

hay [hei] *n* seno; sijeno

hay fever *n* polenska groznica

hazard [ˈhæzəd] *n* opasnost

hazardous [ˈhæzədəs] *adj* opasan

haze [heiz] *n* sumaglica

hazelnut [ˈheizəlnʌt] *n* lešnik; lješnik

he [hiː] *pro* on

head [hed] 1. *adj* glavni 2. *n* glava 3. šef 4. *v* voditi

headache [ˈhedeik] *n* glavobolja

head for *v* ići

heading [ˈhediŋ] *n* zaglavlje

headlight [ˈhedlait] *n* far

headline [hedlain] *n* naslov

headman [ˈhedmæn] *n* šef

headmaster [ˌhedˈmaːstə] *n* upravnik

headmistress [ˌhedˈmistris] *n* upravnica

headphones [ˈhedˌfəunz] *pl* naglavne slušalice

headquarters [ˈhedˈkwɔːtəz] *n* 1. štab 2. **police headquarters** policijski štab

head start [hedˈstaːt] *n* fora

heal [hiːl] *v* izlečiti (se); izliječiti (se)

health [helθ] *n* zdravlje

healthcare [ˈhelθkeə] *n* zdravstvena nega/njega

health inspector *n* sanitarni inspektor

healthy [ˈhelθi] *adj* zdrav

heap [hiːp] *n* gomila

hear [hiə] *v* (**heard**) čuti

hearing [ˈhiəriŋ] *n* 1. sluh 2. (leg.) istraga

heart [haːt] *n* 1. srce 2. **by heart** napamet

heart attack *n* srčani udar

heartbeat [ˈhaːtbiːt] *n* otkucaj srca

heartbroken [ˈhaːtˌbrəukn] *adj* skrhana srca

heartless [ˈhaːtləs] *adj* bezdušan

heat [hiːt] 1. *n* toplota 2. *v* zagrejati; zagrijati

heater [ˈhiːtə] *n* grejalica; grijalica

heated [ˈhiːtid] *adj* 1. zagrejan; zagrijan 2. buran

heating [ˈhiːtiŋ] *n* grejanje; grijanje

heat stroke [ˈhiːtstrəuk] *n* (med.) toplotni udar

heatwave [ˈhiːtweiv] *n* toplotni talas

heaven [ˈhevn] *n* nebo

heavenly [ˈhevnli] *adj* nebeski

heaviness [ˈhevinis] *n* težina

heavy [ˈhevi] *adj* težak

heavyweight [ˈheviweit] *n* (spor.) bokser teške kategorije

Hebrew [ˈhiːbruː] *n* hebrejski jezik

hectare [ˈhekteə] *n* hektar

hectic [ˈhektik] *adj* grozničav

hedge [hedʒ] *n* ograda

hedgehog [ˈhedʒhɔg] *n* jež

heed [hiːd] *v* paziti na

heel [hiːl] *n* peta

heifer [ˈhefə] *n* junica

height [hait] *n* visina

heir [eə] *n* naslednik; nasljednik

heiress [ˈeəres] *n* naslednica; nasljednica

helicopter [ˈhelikɔptə] *n* helikopter

hell [hel] *n* pakao

hello! [həˈləu] 1. alo 2. zdravo

helmet [ˈhelmit] *n* šlem

help [help] 1. *n* pomoć 2. *v* pomoći 3. **I can't help noticing...** Ne mogu a da ne primetim da... 4. **help!** upomoć!

helper [ˈhelpə] *n* pomoćnik

helpful [ˈhelpfl] *adj* koristan

helpless [ˈhelplis] *adj* bespomoćan
hemisphere [ˈhemisfiə] *n* hemisfera
hemorrhage [ˈheməridʒ] *n* izliv krvi
 v krvariti
hemorrhoid [ˈhemərɔid] *n* hemiroid
hen [hen] *n* kvočka
hence [hens] *adv* stoga
henceforth [hensˈfɔːθ] *adv* odsada
her [həː] 1. nju 2. njen
herb [həːb] *n* trava
herd [həːd] *n* stado
here [hiə] *adv* ovde; ovdje
hereabouts [ˌhiərəˈbautz] *adv* tu
 negde
hereditary [həˈreditri] *adj* nasledan;
 nasljedan
heredity [həˈrediti] *n* naslednost;
 nasljednost
heritage [ˈherətidʒ] *n* nasleđe;
 nasljeđe
hero [ˈhiərəu] *n* (*pl* **heroes**) junak
heroin [ˈherəuin] *n* heroin
heroine [ˈherəuin] *n* junakinja
heroism [ˈherəuizəm] *n* junaštvo
hers [həːz] njen
herself [həːˈself] ona sama, nju
 samu, sebi
hesitate [ˈheziteit] *v* oklevati;
 oklijevati
hesitation [ˌheziˈteiʃn] *n* oklevanje;
 oklijevanje
heterogeneous [ˌheziˈteiʃn] *n*
 heterogen
heterosexual [ˌheziˈteiʃn] *n*
 heteroseksualan
hiccough, hiccup [ˈhikʌp] 1. *n*
 štucanje 2. *v* štucati
hidden [ˈhidn] *adj* skriven
hide [haid] *v* skriti (se)
hide-and-seek [ˌhaidnˈsiːk] *n*
 žmurka
hideous [ˈhidiəs] *adj* grozan

hiding [ˈhaidiŋ] *n* skrivanje
hiding-place *n* skrivalište
high [hai] 1. *adj* visok 2. *adv* visoko
 3. (sl.) **to get high** opiti se
high commissioner *n* visoki
 komesar
high court *n* vrhovni sud
high jump *n* skok uvis
highlands [ˈhailəndz] *pl* brda
highlight [ˈhailait] 1. *n* vrhunac 2. *v*
 istaći
highly [ˈhaili] *adv* veoma
highness [ˈhainis] *n* svetlost;
 svielost
highroad [ˈhairəud] *n* glavni put
high school [ˈhaiskuːl] *n* srednja
 škola
highspeed [ˈhaiˈspiːd] *adj* ekspresni
highway [ˈhaiwei] *n* autoput
highway code *n* saobraćajna
 pravila
hijack [ˈhaidʒæk] *v* oteti
hijacker [ˈhaidʒækə] *n* otmičar
hijacking [ˈhaidʒækiŋ] *n* otmica
hike [haik] *v* pešačiti; pješačiti
hiker [ˈhaikə] *n* izletnik
hilarious [hiˈleəriəs] *adj* smešan;
 smiješan
hill [hil] *n* brdo
hilly [ˈhili] *adj* brdovit
him [him] njega, ga, njemu, njim,
 onog
himself [himˈself] on sam, sam,
 sebe, se
hind [haind] *adj* zadnji
hinder [ˈhində] *v* omesti
hindrance [ˈhindrəns] *n* smetnja
hinge [hindʒ] *n* šarka
hint [hint] 1. *n* mig 2. **to drop a**
 hint dati mig 3. *v* nagovestiti;
 nagovijestiti
hip [hip] *n* kuk

hippopotamus [ˌhipəˈpɔtəməs] *n* nilski konj

hire [ˈhaiə] **1.** *n* zakup **2. for hire** pod zakup **3.** *v* iznajmiti

hire-purchase *n* (UK) plaćanje na rate

his [hiz] njegov

hiss [his] *v* izviždati

historian [hiˈstɔːriən] *n* istoričar; historičar

historical [hiˈstɔrikl] *adj* istorijski; historijski

history [ˈhistri] *n* istorija; historija

hit [hit] *v* (**hit**) **1.** *n* pogodak **2. direct hit** direktan pogodak **3.** *v* udariti

hitch [hitʃ] *n* zapreka

hitchhike [ˈhitʃˌhaik] *v* stopirati

hitchhiker [ˈhitʃˌhaikə] *n* autostoper

hitchhiking [ˈhitʃˌhaikiŋ] *n* autostop

hitherto [ˌhiðəˈtuː] *adv* do sada

HIV virus *n* virus HIV, virus koji izaziva sidu

hive [haiv] *n* košnica

hoard [hɔːd] *v* nagomilati

hoax [həuks] **1.** *n* podvala **2.** *v* podvaliti

hobble [ˈhɔbl] *v* **1.** sapeti **2.** hramati

hobb [ˈhɔbi] *n* hobi

hockey [ˈhɔki] *n* hokej

hoe [həu] **1.** *n* motika **2.** *v* kopati motikom

hog [hɔg] *n* krmak

hold [həuld] *v* (**held**) **1.** držati **2.** sadržati **3. to hold a meeting** držati sastanak **4. to hold an inquiry** sprovoditi istragu **5. to hold elections** sprovesti izbore **6. to hold one's breath** zadržati dah

hold back *v* **1.** uzdržati se **2.** držati u rezervi

holder [ˈhəuldə] *n* **1.** držač **2.** vlasnik

hold office *v* biti na (zvaničnom) položaju

hold over *v* produžiti

hold-up *n* **1.** zadržati **2.** pljačka

hold up *v* **1.** zastoj **2.** opljačkati

hole [həul] *n* rupa

holiday [ˈhɔlədei] *n* **1.** praznik **2. to be on holiday** biti na odmoru

hollow [ˈhɔləu] *adj* šupalj

holocaust [ˈhɔləkɔːst] *n* holokaust

holy [ˈhəuli] *adj* svet

homage [ˈhɔmidʒ] *n* zakletva na vernost

home [həum] *n* kuća

homeland [ˈhəumlænd] *n* domovina

homeless [ˈhəumlis] *n* bez kuće

homemade *adj* domaći

Home Office *n* (UK) ministarstvo unutrašnjih poslova

home-sick *v* **to be home-sick** čeznuti za domovinom

home-sickness *n* nostalgija

home team *n* domaćin

hometown [ˈhəumtaun] *n* rodno mesto/mjesto

home trade *n* unutrašna trgovina

homework [ˈhəumwəːk] *n* domaći zadatak; domaća zadaća

homicide [ˈhɔmisaid] *n* ubistvo; ubojstvo

homosexual [ˌhɔməˈsekʃuəl] **1.** *adj* homoseksualan **2.** *n* homoseksualac

homosexuality [ˌhɔməsekʃuˈæləti] *n* homoseksualizam

honest [ˈɔnist] *adj* pošten

honestly [ˈɔnistli] *adv* iskreno

honesty [ˈɔnəsti] *n* poštenost

honey [ˈhʌni] *n* med

honeymoon [ˈhʌnimuːn] *n* medeni mesec/mjesec

honk [hɔŋk] *v* trubiti

honour [ˈɔnə] 1. *n* čast 2. **in honour of someone** u čast nekoga 3. *v* poštovati 4. **to honour a cheque** isplatiti ček

honourable [ˈɔnərəbl] *adj* 1. častan 2. pošten

hood [hud] *n see* **bonnet**

hoodwink [ˈhudwink] *v* prevariti

hoof [huːf] *n* kopito

hook [huk] 1. *n* kuka 2. *v* prikačiti

hooked [hukt] *adj* 1. kukast 2. **hooked on drugs** odan uživanju droga

hooker [ˈhukwə] *n* (sl.) kurva

hookworm [ˈhukwəːm] *n* kukasta glista

hooligan [ˈhuːligən] *n* mangup

hoop [huːp] *n* obruč

hoot [huːt] *v* trubiti

hoover [ˈhuːvə] *n* usisavač

hop [hɔp] *v* skakutati

hope [həup] 1. *n* nada 2. *v* nadati se 3. **to hope for the best** nadati se najboljem

hope for *v* nadati se

hopeful [ˈhəupfl] *adj* pun nade

hopeless [ˈhəuplis] *adj* benadežan

horde [hɔːd] *n* horda

horizon [həˈraizn] *n* horizont

horizontal [ˌhɔriˈzɔntl] *adj* horizontalan

horn [hɔːn] *n* 1. rog 2. truba; trublja 3. (mus.) horna

hornet [ˈhɔːnit] *n* stršljen

horrible [ˈhɔrəbl] *adj* užasan

horrid [ˈhɔrid] *adj* strašan

horrify [ˈhɔrifai] *v* užasnuti

horror [ˈhɔrə] *n* užas

horse [hɔːs] *n* konj

horseback [ˈhɔːsbæk] *n/adj* **on horseback** na konju

horseman [ˈhɔːsmæn] *n* jahač

horsepower [ˈhɔːspauə] *n* konjska snaga

horse racing *n* konjske trke

horticulture [ˈhɔːtiˌkʌltʃə] *n* hortikultura

hose [həuz] *n* crevo; crijevo

hospital [ˈhɔspitl] *n* bolnica

hospitality [ˌhɔspiˈtæləti] *n* gostoljubivost

host [həust] *n* domaćin

hostage [ˈhɔstidʒ] *n* 1. talac 2. **to take as hostage** zadržati kao taoca

hostel [ˈhɔstl] *n* omladinsko prenoćište

hostile [ˈhɔstail] *adj* neprijateljski

hostility [hɔˈstiləti] *n* neprijateljstvo

hot [hɔt] *adj* 1. vruć 2. topao

hotel [həuˈtel] *n* hotel

hour [ˈauə] *n* 1. sat 2. **working hours** radno vreme

hourly [ˈauəli] *n* na sat

house [haus] *n* kuća

house arrest *n* kućni pritvor

housebreaker [ˈhausbreikə] *n* provalnik

household [ˈhaushəuld] *n* domaćinstvo

householder [ˈhaushəuldə] *n* vlasnik kuće

House of Commons *n* (UK) Donji dom

House of Lords *n* (UK) Gornji dom

House of Representatives *n* (US) Predstavnički dom

housewife [ˈhauswaif] *n* domaćica

housing [ˈhauziŋ] *n* stambena

hover [ˈhɔvə] *v* lebdeti; lebdjeti

how [hau] 1. kako 2. **no matter how** ma kako

however [hauˈevə] *conj* 1. kako god

2. međutim
howl [haul] v urlati
how long? koliko dugo?
how many? koliko?
how much? koliko?, koliko košta?
how old? 1. koliko godina? 2.
How old are you? Koliko ti je godina?
h.p. see **horse power**
hub [hʌb] n 1. glavčina 2. čvor
hubbub [ˈhʌbʌb] n urnebes
hubcap [ˈhʌbkæp] n radkapna
huddle [ˈhʌdl] v gomila
hug [hʌg] v zagrliti
huge [hjuːdʒ] adj ogroman
hull [hʌl] n trup
hum [hʌm] 1. n zujanje 2. v zujati 3.(mus.) pevušiti; pjevušiti
human [ˈhjuːmən] 1. adj čovečiji; čovječiji 2. n čovek; čovjek
human being n ljudsko biće
humane [hjuˈmein] adj human
human error n ljudska greška, ljudski faktor
humanitarian [ˌhjuːˈmæniˈteəriən] adj humanitaran
humanitarian aid n humanitarna pomoć
humanity [hjuːˈmænəti] n 1. ljudski rod 2. humanost
human nature n ljudska priroda
human resources pl socijalna pomoć
human rights pl čovekova prava; čovjekova prava
humble [ˈhʌmbl] adj ponizan
humid [ˈhjuːmid] adj vlažan
humidity [hjuːˈmidəti] n vlažnost
humiliate [hjuːˈmilieit] v poniziti
humiliation [hjuːˌmiliˈeiʃn] n poniženje
humility [hjuːˈmiləti] n poniznost

humorous [ˈhjuːmərəs] adj humorističan
humour [ˈhjuːmə] n humor
hump [hʌmp] n grba
hunch [hʌntʃ] n **to have a hunch** slutiti
hundred [ˈhʌndrəd] n/adj sto
hundredth [ˈhʌdrədθ] adj stoti
hundredweight [ˈhʌndrədweit] n centa
hung [hʌŋ] see **hang**
hunger [ˈhʌŋgə] n glad
hungry [ˈhʌŋgri] adj gladan
hunt [hʌnt] 1. n lov 2. v loviti 3. goniti
hunt for v tražiti
hunter [ˈhʌntə] n lovac
hunting [ˈhʌntiŋ] n lov
hurdles [ˈhəːdlz] n (spor.) prepona
hurl [həːl] v baciti
hurrah!, hurray! [huˈraː; huˈrei] ura!
hurricane [ˈhʌrikən] n orkan
hurry [ˈhʌri] 1. n žurba 2. **to be in a hurry** biti u žurba 3. v žuriti se 4. **to hurry up** požuriti
hurt [həːt] 1. n bol 2. v boleti; boljeti 3. povrediti; povrijediti
husband [ˈhʌzbənd] n muž
hush [hʌʃk] n tišina
husk [hʌsk] n mahuna
hut [hʌt] n koliba
hydroelectric [ˌhaidrəuiˈlektrik] adj hidroelektričan
hydroelectric power n hidroelektrična energija
hydroelectric dam n hidrocentrala
hydrogen [ˈhaidrədʒən] n vodonik; vodik
hyena [haiˈiːnə] n hijena
hygiene [ˈhaidʒiːn] n higijena
hygienic [haiˈdʒiːnik] adj higijenski
hygienist [haiˈdʒiːnist] n higijeničar

hymn [him] *n* (rel.) himna
hypertension [ˌhaipəˈtenʃən] *n* hipertenzija
hyphen [ˈhaifn] *n* crtica
hypnosis [hipˈnəusis] *n* hipnoza
hypocrisy [hiˈpɔkrəsi] *n* hipokrizija
hypocrite [ˈhipəkrit] *n* hipokrita
hypocritical [ˌhipəˈkritikl] *adj* hipokritski

hypodermic [ˌhaipəˈdəːmik] *n* supkutan
hypodermic syringe *n* špric za supkutane injekcije
hypothesis [ˌhaiˈpoθesis] *n* hipoteza
hypothetical [ˌhaipoˈθetikl] *adj* hipotetičan
hysterical [hiˈsterikl] *adj* to become **hysterical** postati histeričan

I

I [ai] *pro* ja
ice [ais] *n* led
iceberg [ˈaisbəːg] *n* ledena santa
ice cream [ˌaisˈkriːm] *n* sladoled
ice cube [ˌaisˈkjuːb] *n* kockica leda
ice hockey *n* hokej na ledu
ice skate *v* klizati se
ice skater *n* klizač
icon [ˈaikɔn] *n* ikona
icy [ˈaisi] *adj* leden
ID card [ˈaidiːˌkaːd] *n* lična karta
idea [aiˈdiə] *n* ideja
ideal [aiˈdiəl] 1. *adj* idealan 2. *n* ideal
idealism [aiˈdiəlizəm] *n* idealizam
idealist [aiˈdiəlist] *n* idealista
identical [aiˈdentikl] *adj* identičan
identification [aiˌdentifiˈkeiʃn] 1. *n* identifikacija 2. *see* **ID card**
identify [aiˈdentifai] *v* identifikovati (se)
identity [aiˈdentəti] *n* identitet
identity card *n* lična karta
ideology [ˌaidiˈɔlədʒi] *n* ideologija
idiot [ˈidiət] *n* idiot
idle [ˈaidl] *adj* besposlen
idleness [ˈaidlnis] *n* besposlenost
idol [ˈaidl] *n* idol
idolize [ˈaidəlaiz] *v* obožavati
i.e. (*id est* = *that is*) to jest
if [if] *conj* 1. ako 2. da
ignite [igˈnait] *v* zapaliti
ignition [igˈniʃn] *n* paljenje
ignorance [ˈignərəns] *n* neznanje
ignorant [ˈignərənt] *adj* neznalički
ignore [igˈnɔː] *v* ignorisati
ill [il] *adj* bolestan
ill-advised *adj* nepromišljen

illegal [iˈliːgl] *adj* nepropisan
illegally [iˈliːgəli] *adv* ilegalno, protivzakonito
illegible [iˈledʒəbl] *adj* nečitak
illegitimate [ˌiliˈdʒitimət] *adj* vanbračan
illiteracy [iˈlitərəsi] *n* analfabetizam
illiterate [iˈlitərət] *adj* nepismen
illness [ˈilnis] *n* bolest
ill-treat *v* matretirati
illuminate [iˈluːmineit] *v* osvetliti; osvijetliti
illumination [iˌluːmiˈneiʃn] *n* osvetljenje; osvjetljenje
illusion [iˈluːʒn] *n* iluzija
illustrate [ˈiləstreit] *v* ilustrovati
illustration [ˌiləˈstreiʃn] *n* ilustracija
illustrator [ˌiləˈstreitə] *n* ilustrator
image [ˈimidʒ] *n* slika
imaginary [iˌmædʒiˈneri] *adj* imaginaran
imagination [iˌmædʒiˈneiʃn] *n* imaginacija
imagine [iˈmædʒin] *v* zamisliti
imam [iˈmaːm] *n* imam
IMF (International Monetary Fund) *n* Međunarodni monetarni fond
imitate [ˈimiteit] *v* imitirati
imitation [ˌimiˈteiʃn] 1. *adj* imitacioni 2. *n* imitacija
imitator [ˈimiteitə] *n* imitator
immaculate [iˈmækjulət] *adj* neuprljan
immeasurable [iˈmeʒərəbl] *adj* nemerljiv; nemjerljiv

immediate [i'mi:diət] *adj* neposredan
immediately [i'mi:diətli] *adv* neposredno
immense [i'mens] *adj* ogroman
immerse ['imə:s] *v* zaroniti
immigrant ['imigrənt] *n* 1. doseljenik 2. **illegal immigrant** ilegalni useljenik
immigrate ['imigreit] *v* doseliti se
immigration [,imi'greiʃn] *n* imigracija
imminent ['iminənt] *adj* blizak
immoral [i'mɔrəl] *adj* nemoralan
immorality [,imɔ'ræliti] *n* nemoralnost
immortal [i'mɔ:tl] *adj* besmrtan
immune [i'mju:n] *adj* imun
immunity [i'mju:nəti] *n* 1. imunost 2. **diplomatic immunity** diplomatski imunitet
immunize ['imjunaiz] *v* imunizovati
immunization [,imjunai'zeiʃn] *n* vakcinacija
immunization campaign *n* masovna vakcinacija
impact ['impækt] *n* 1. sudar 2. **to have an impact** imati uticaj
impair [im'peə] *v* pogoršati
impart [im'pa:t] *v* saopštiti; saopćiti
impartial [im'pa:ʃl] *adj* nepristastan; nepristran
impartiality [im,pa:ʃi'aliti] *n* nepristrasnost; nepristranost
impassable [im'pa:səbl] *adj* neprolazan
impatience [im'peiʃns] *n* nestrpljenje
impatient [im'peiʃnt] *adj* nestrpljiv
impeach [im'pi:tʃ] *v* optužiti
impede [im'pi:d] *v* smetati
impediment [im'pedimənt] *n* smetnja

impel [im'pel] *v* naterati; natjerati
impenetrable [im'penitrəbl] *adj* neprobojan
imperative [im'perətiv] 1. *adj* imperativan 2. *n* imperativ
imperfect [im'pə:fikt] 1. *adj* nesavršen 2. *n* imperfekat
imperial [im'piəriəl] *adj* imperijalni
imperialism [im'piəriəlizəm] *n* imperijalizam
impersonate [im'pə:səneit] *v* izdavati se (za), oponašati
impersonation [im,pə:sə'neiʃn] *n* igranje uloge
impersonator [im'pə:səneitə] *n* imitator
impertinence [im'pə:tinəns] *n* drskost
impertinent [im'pə:tinənt] *adj* drzak
impervious [im'pə:viəs] *adj* nepropustljiv
impetus ['impitəs] *n* podstrek
implant [im'pla:nt] *v* usaditi
implement ['implimənt] 1. *n* sredstvo 2. *v* izvršiti
implement a policy *v* sprovesti politiku
implicate ['implikeit] *v* upetljati
implication [,impli'keiʃn] *n* implikacija
implicit [im'plisit] *adj* implicitan
imply [im'plai] *v* implicirati
impolite [,impə'lait] *adj* neučtiv
import [im'pɔ:t] 1. *adj* uvozni 2. *n* uvoz 3. *v* uvesti
import duty *n* uvozna carina
importance [im'pɔ:tns] *n* važnost
important [im'pɔ:tnt] *adj* važan
import-export business *n* uvozno-izvozna firma
importing [im'pɔ:tiŋ] *n* uvoz
impose [im'pəuz] *v* 1. naturiti 2. to

impose a blockade zavesti blokadu

impossibility [im‚pɔsə'bilǝti] *n* nemogućnost

impossible [im'pɔsǝbl] *adj* nemogućan

imposter [im'pɔstǝ] *n* varalica

impotence ['impǝtǝns] *n* impotencija

impotent ['impǝtǝnt] *adj* impotentan

impoverish [im'pɔvǝriʃ] *v* osiromašiti

impractical [im'pɔvǝriʃ] *v* osiromašiti

impress [im'pres] *v* impresionirati

impression [im'preʃn] *n* 1. utisak 2. štampanje 3. **to be under the impression** imati utisak

impressive [im'presiv] *adj* upečatljiv

imprison [im'prizn] *v* zatvoriti

imprisonment [im'priznmǝnt] *n* 1. zatvaranje 2. **life imprisonment** doživotna robija, doživotna kazna zatvora

improbable [im'prɔbǝbl] *adj* neverovatan; nevjerovatan

improper [im'prɔpǝ] *adj* neprikladan

improve [im'pru:v] *v* poboljšati (se)

improvement [im'pru:vmǝnt] *n* poboljšanje

improvise ['imprǝvaiz] *v* improvizovati

imprudent [im'pru:dǝnt] *adj* nesmotren

impudence ['impjudǝns] *n* drskost

impudent [im'pjudǝnt] *adj* drzak

impulse ['impʌls] *n* impuls

impulsive [im'pʌlsiv] *adj* impulsivan

impure [im'pjuǝ] *adj* nečist

impurity [im'pjuriti] *n* nečistoća

in [in] *prep* 1. u 2. na 3. **in the country** na selu 4. **in English** na engleskom 5. **in my opinion** po mom mišljenju 6. **in the morning** jutros 7. **He will be back in a week.** Vratiće se za nedelju dana./Vratit će se za tjedan dana. 8. *see* **into**

inability ['inǝ'bilǝti] *n* nesposobnost

inaccessible [‚inæk'sesǝbl] *adj* nepristupačan

inaccurate [in'ækjǝrǝt] *adj* netačan; netočan

inaction [in'ækʃn] *n* neaktivnost

inactive [in'æktiv] *adj* neaktivan

inadequate [in'ædikwǝt] *adj* neadekvatan

inadvertently *adv* nenamerno; nenamjerno

inadvisable [in'ædveizǝbl] *adj* nepreporučljiv

inanimate [in'ænimǝt] *adj* neživ

inappropriate *adj* neprikladan

inasmuch as [‚inǝz'mʌtʃǝz] *conj* pošto

inaudible [in'ɔ:dǝbl] *adj* nečujan

inaugurate [i'nɔ:gjureit] *v* inaugurisati

inauguration [i‚nɔ:gju'reiʃn] *n* inauguracija

incalculable [in'kælkjulǝbl] *adj* neproračunljiv

incapable [in'keipǝbl] *adj* neposoban

incendiary [in'sendiǝri] *adj* 1. zapaljiv 2. podstrekački

incense ['insens] *n* tamjan

incense [in'sens] *v* razjariti

incentive [in'sentiv] *n* podstrek

incessant [in'sesnt] *adj* neprestan

incessantly [in'sesntli] *adv* neprestano

incest [ˈinsest] *n* rodoskvrnjenje
inch [intʃ] *n* inč
incidence [ˈinsidəns] *n* frekvenca
incident [ˈinsidənt] *n* događaj
incidentally *adv* slučajno
incinerator [inˈsinəreitə] *n* peć
incision [inˈsiʒn] *n* zasek; zasjek
incite [inˈsait] *v* podbosti
inclination [ˌinkliˈneiʃn] *n* inklinacija
incline [inˈklain] 1. *n* nagib 2. *v*
  inklinirati 3. *see* **inclined**
inclined [inˈklaind] *adj* **to feel
  inclined** biti naklonjen
include [inˈkluːd] *v* uključiti
including [inˈkluːdiŋ] *prep*
  uključujući
inclusion [inˈkluːʒn] *n* uključenje
inclusive [inˈkluːsiv] 1. *adj* uključan
  2. *adv* zaključno
incoherent [ˌinkəuˈhiərənt] *adj*
  inkoherentan
income [ˈinkʌm] *n* 1. dohodak 2.
  gross income bruto dohodak
income tax *n* porez na dohodak
incoming [inˈkʌmiŋ] *adj* dolazeći
incomparable [inˈkɔmprəbl] *adj* **to
  be incomparable** neuporediv;
  neusporediv
incompatible [ˌinkəmˈpætəbl] *adj*
  inkompatibilan
incompetence [inˈkɔmpitəns] *n*
  nesposobnost
incompetent [inˈkɔmpitənt] *adj*
  nesposoban
incomplete [ˌinkəmˈpliːt] *adj*
  nepotpun
i n c o m p r e h e n s i b l e
  [inˌkɔmpriˈhensəbl] *adj* nerazumljiv
inconceivable [ˌinkənˈsiːvəbl] *adj*
  nepojmljiv
inconclusive [ˌinkənˈkluːsiv] *adj*
  neubedljiv; neubjedljiv

inconsiderate [ˌinkənˈsidərət] *adj*
  bezobziran
inconsistent [ˌinkənˈsistənt] *adj*
  nedosledan; nedosljedan
inconvenience [ˌinkənˈviːniəns] *n*
  nezgodnost
inconvenient [ˌinkənˈviːniənt] *adj*
  nezgodan
incorporate [inˈkɔːpəreit] *v*
  inkorporisati
incorrect [ˌinkəˈrekt] *adj* neispravan
increase [ˈinkriːs] 1. *n* porast 2. *v*
  povećati (se)
incredible [inˈkredəbl] *adj*
  neverovatan; nevjerovatan
increment [ˈinkrimənt] *n* povećanje
incriminate [inˈkrimineit] *v*
  inkriminisati
incubate [ˈinkjubeit] *v* izleći (se)
incur [inˈkəː] *v* napraviti
incurable [inˈkjuərəbl] *adj* neizlečiv;
  neizlječiv
incursion [inˈkəːʃn] *n* (mil.) upad
indecency [inˈdiːsnsi] *n* nepristojnost
indecent [inˈdiːsnt] *adj* nepristojan
indecision [ˌindiˈsiʒn] *n* neodlučnost
indecisive [ˌindiˈsisiv] *adj* neodlučan
indeed [inˈdiːd] *adv* 1. zaista 2.
  zbilja!
indefinitely [inˈdefinətli] *adv*
  neodređeno; na neodređen rok
indemnity [inˈdemnəti] *n* obeštećenje
independence [ˌindiˈpendəns] *n*
  nezavisnost
independent [ˌindiˈpendənt] *adj*
  nezavisan
independent inquiry *n* nezavisna
  istraga
indescribable [ˌindiˈskraibəbl] *adj*
  neopisiv
indestructible [ˌindiˈstrʌktəbl] *adj*
  nerazoriv

indeterminate [ˌindiˈtəːminət] *n* neodređen

index [ˈindeks] *n* indeks

index finger *n* kažiprst

indicate [ˈindikeit] *v* 1. pokazati 2. nagovestiti; nagovijestiti

indication [ˈindiˌkeiʃn] *n* indikacija

indicator [ˈindiˌkeitə] *n* indikator

indict [inˈdait] *v* optužiti

indictment [inˈdaitmənt] *n* optužnica

indifference [inˈdifrəns] *n* ravnodušnost

indigenous [inˈdidʒinəs] *adj* urođenički

indigestion [ˌindiˈdʒestʃən] *n* loša probava

indignant [inˈdignənt] *adj* indigniran

indignation [ˌindigˈneiʃn] *n* indignacija

indigo [ˈindigəu] *n* indigo

indirect [indaiˈrekt] *adj* 1. posredan 2. **indirect route** obilazan put

indirectly [indaiˈrektli] *adv* posredno

indiscreet [ˌindiˈskriːt] *adj* nepromišljen

indiscriminate [ˌindiˈskriminət] *adj* bez selekcije

indispensable [ˌindiˈspensəbl] *adj* neophodan

individual [ˌindiˈvidʒuəl] 1. *adj* individualan 2. *n* individua

individualist [ˌindiˈvidʒuəlist] *adj* individualista

indoctrinate [inˈdɔktrineit] *v* poučavati

indoor [ˈindɔː] *adj* zatvoren

indoors [ˈindɔːz] *adv* u kući

induce [inˈdjuːs] *v* navesti

indulge [inˈdʌldʒ] *v* povlađivati

industrial [inˈdʌstriəl] *adj* industrijski

industrial estate *n* industrijska zona

industrialization [inˌdʌstriəlaiˈzeiʃn] *n* industrijalizacija

industrialize [inˈdʌstriəlaiz] *v* industrijalizovati (se)

industrialized [inˈdʌstriəlaizd] *adj* industrijalizovan

industrious [inˈdʌstriəs] *adj* vredan; vrijedan

industrial tribunal *n* privredni sud

industrial waste *n* industrijski otpad

industry [ˈindəstri] *n* 1. industrija 2. **light industry** laka industrija 3. **heavy industry** teška industrija 4. **film industry** filmska industrija

ineffective [ˌiniˈfektiv] *adj* nedelotvoran; nedjelotvoran

inefficiency [ˌiniˈfiʃnsi] *n* neefikasnost

inefficient [ˌiniˈfiʃnt] *adj* neefikasan

ineligible [inˈelidʒibl] *adj* nekvalifikovan

inequality [ˌiniˈkwɔləti] *n* nejednakost

inevitable [inˈevitəbl] *adj* neizbežan; neizbježan

inexcusable [ˌinikˈskjuːzəbl] *adj* neoprostiv

inexhaustible [ˌinigˈzɔːstəbl] *adj* nepresušan

inexpensive [ˌinikˈspensiv] *adj* jevtin

inexperience [ˌinikˈspiəriəns] *n* neiskusnost

inexperienced [ˌinikˈspiəriənst] *adj* neiskusan

inexplicable [ˌinikˈsplikəbl] *adj* neobjašnjiv

in fact [inˈfækt] u stvari

infallible [in'fæləbl] *adj* nepogrešiv

infamous ['infəməs] *adj* infaman

infancy ['infənsi] *n* detinjstvo; djetinjstvo

infant ['infənt] *n* detence; djetešce

infantry ['infəntri] *n* pešadija; pješadija

infatuation [in,fætʃu'eiʃn] *n* zaluđenost

infect [in'fekt] *v* zaraziti

infected [in'tektid] *adj* to be infected by a disease biti zaražen bolešću

infection [in'tekʃn] *n* zaraza

infectious [in'tekʃəs] *adj* zarazan

infectious disease *n* infektivna bolest

infer [in'fə:] *v* zaključiti

inferior [in'tiəriə] *adj* inferioran

inferiority [in,fiəri'ɔrəti] *n* inferiornost

infertile [in'fə:tail] *adj* neplodan

infest [in'fest] *v* pustošiti

infiltrate ['infiltreit] *v* infiltrirati

infinite ['infinət] *adj* beskrajnost

infinity [in'finəti] *n* beskrajan

infirm [in'fə:m] *adj* nemoćan

infirmary [in'fə:məri] *n* ambulanta

infirmity [in'fə:məti] *n* slabost

inflame [in'fleim] *v* raspaliti

inflamed [in'tleimd] *adj* (med.) to be inflamed zagnojiti se

inflammable ['inflæməbl] *adj* zapaljiv; upaljiv

inflammation [,inflə'meiʃn] *n* zapaljenje; upala

inflammatory [in'flæmətri] *adj* raspaljiv

inflate [in'fleit] *v* naduvati

inflation [in'fleiʃn] *n* (ec.) inflacija

inflexible [in'fleksəbl] *adj* negibak

inflict [in'flikt] *v* zadati

inflow ['infləu] *n* capital inflow priliv kapitala

influence ['influəns] 1. *n* uticaj 2. *v* uticati na

influential [,influ'enʃl] *adj* uticajan

influenza [,influ'enzə] *n* grip

influx ['inflʌks] *n* navala

inform [in'fɔ:m] *v* obavestiti; obavijestiti

informal [in'fɔ:ml] *adj* neformalan

information [,infə'meiʃn] *n* informacija

informer [in'fɔ:mə] *n* obaveštač; obavještač

infrastructure ['infrə,strʌktʃə] *n* infrastruktura

infrequently [in'fri:kwəntli] *adv* retko; rijetko

infringe [in'frindʒ] *v* posegnuti (on na)

infringement [in'frindʒmənt] *n* prekršaj

infuriate [in'fju:rieit] *v* razbesniti; razbjesniti

infusion [in'fju:ʒn] *n* infuzija

ingenious [in'dʒi:niəs] *adj* genijalan

ingratitude [in'grætitju:d] *n* nezahvalnost

ingredient [in'gri:diənt] *n* sastojak

inhabit [in'hæbit] *v* stanovati u

inhabitant [in'hæbitənt] *n* stanovnik

inhabited [in'hæbitid] *adj* naseljen

inhale [in'heil] *v* udahnuti

inherit [in'herit] *v* naslediti; naslijediti

inheritance [in'heritəns] *n* nasleđe; nasljeđe

inhibit [in'hibit] *v* inhibirati

inhospitable [,inhɔ'spitəbl] *adj* negostoljubiv

inhuman [in'hju:mən] *adj* nečovečan; nečovječan

inhumane [inhju:ˈmein] *adj* nehuman
inhumanity [ˌinhju:ˈmæniti] *n* nečovečnost; nečovječnost
initial [iˈniʃl] 1. *adj* prethodan 2. *v* napisati inicijale na
initiate [iˈniʃieit] *v* pokrenuti
initiative [iˈniʃətiv] *n* inicijativa
inject [inˈdʒekt] *v* ubrizgati
injection [inˈdʒekʃn] *n* injekcija
injunction [inˈdʒʌnkʃn] *n* nalog
injure [ˈindʒə] *v* ji wa... rauni
injured [ˈindʒəd] *adj* povređen; povrijeđen
injury [ˈindʒəri] *n* povreda
injustice [inˈdʒʌstis] *n* nepravda
ink [iŋk] *n* mastilo
inland [ˈinlənd] *adj* unutrašnji
in-law [ˈinlɔ:] *n* srodnik
inmate [ˈinmeit] *n* stanar
inn [in] *n* gostionica
inner [ˈinə] *adj* unutrašnji
inner city *n* geto
inner tube *n* unutrašnji guma
innocence [ˈinəsəns] *n* nevinost
innocent [ˈinəsnt] *adj* nevin
innovation [ˌinəˈveiʃn] *n* inovacija
innuendo [ˌinjuˈendəu] *n* insinuacija
innumerable [iˈnju:mərəbl] *adj* bezbrojan
inoculate [iˈnɔkjuleit] *v* inokulisati
inoculation [iˌnɔkjuˈleiʃn] *n* inokulacija
inoffensive [ˌinəˈfensiv] *adj* neuvredljiv
inoperable [iˌnɔpərəbl] *n* inoperabilan
input [ˈinput] 1. *n* ulaz 2. *v* (**input/ inputted**) ubaciti informacije
inquest [ˈinkwest] *n* istraga
inquire [inˈkwaiə] *v* raspitai se (**about** o)

inquire into *v* ispitivati
inquiry [inˈkwaiəri] *n* 1. pitanje 2. **an independent inquiry** nezavisna istraga
inquisitive [inˈkwizətiv] *adj* radoznao
inroad [ˈinrəud] *n* **to make inroads** zadreti; zadrijeti (**in** u)
insane [inˈsein] *adj* lud
insanity [inˈsænəti] *n* ludilo
inscription [inˈskripʃn] *n* napis
insect [ˈinsekt] *n* insekat
insecticide [inˈsektisaid] *n* insekticid
insecure [ˌinsiˈkjuə] *adj* nesiguran
insecurity [ˌinsiˈkjuəriti] *n* nesigurnost
insensitive [inˈsensitiv] *adj* neosetljiv; neosjetljiv
inseparable [inˈseprəbl] *adj* nerazdvojan
insert [ˈinsə:t] *v* umetnuti
insertion [inˈsə:ʃn] *n* 1. umetanje 2. umetak
inside [inˈsaid] 1. *adj* unutrašnji 2. *n* unutrašnjost 3. *prep* u 4. *adv* unutra
inside-out *adj* izvrnut, prevrnut
insight [ˈinsait] *n* uvid
insignia [inˈsignia] *n* insignije
insignificant [ˌinsigˈnifikənt] *adj* beznačajan
insincere [ˌinsinˈsiə] *adj* neiskren
insincerity [ˌinsinˈseriti] *n* neiskrenost
insinuate [inˈsinjueit] *v* insinuirati
insinuation [inˌsinjuˈeiʃn] *n* insinuacija
insist [inˈsist] *v* insistirati
insistent [inˈsistənt] *adj* uporan
insolence [ˈinsələns] *n* drskost
insolent [ˈinsələnt] *adj* drzak

insolvency [in·sɔlvənsi] *n* insolventnost

insomnia [in·sɔmniə] *n* nesanica

insomniac [in·sɔmniæk] *n* nespavač

inspect [in·spekt] *v* pregledati

inspection [in·spekʃn] *n* pregled

inspector [in·spektə] *n* 1. inspektor 2. **police inspector** viši oficir policije

inspector-general *n* generalni inspektor

inspiration [,inspə·reiʃn] *n* inspiracija

inspire [in·spaiə] *v* inspirisati

instability [,instə·biliti] *n* nestabilnost

install [·instɔːl] *v* postaviti

installation [,instə·leiʃn] *n* 1. instalacija 2. (mil.) ustanova

instalment, installment [in·stɔːlmənt] *n* 1. rata 2. nastavak

instance [·instəns] *n* 1. primer; primjer 2. **for instance** na primer

instant [·instənt] 1. *adj* trenutan 2. *n* **in an instant** trenutno

instantaneous [,instən·teiniəs] *adj* trenutan

instantly [·instəntli] *adv* trenutno

instead [in·sted] *adv* umesto toga; umjesto toga

instead of *prep/conj* umesto; umjesto

instigate [·instigeit] *v* podstreknuti

instigation [,insti·geiʃn] *n* **at our instigation** na naš podsticaj

instinct [·instiŋkt] *n* nagon

instinctive [in·stiŋktiv] *adj* nagonski

institute [·institjuːt] *n* institut

Institute for Strategic Studies *n* Institut za strateške studije

institution [·institjuːʃn] *n* 1. institucija 2. ustanova 3. **mental**

institution bolnica za mentalne bolesnike

instruct [in·strʌkt] *v* 1. učiti 2. narediti

instruction [in·strʌkʃn] *n* 1. nastava 2. naredba

instructions [in·strʌkʃnz] *pl* upustvo

instruction book *n* knjiga uputstava, uputsva za upotrebu

instructive [in·strʌktiv] *adj* instruktivan

instructor [in·strʌktə] *n* instruktor

instrument [·instrumənt] *n* 1. instrumenat 2. oruđe

insubordinate [,insə·bɔːdinət] *adj* neposlušan

insubordination [,insə,bɔːdiˈneiʃn] *n* neposlušnost

insufficient [·insəˈfiʃnt] *adj* nedovoljan

insulate [·insjuleit] *v* izolovati

insulation [,insjuˈleiʃn] *n* izolacija

insult [·insʌlt] *n* uvreda

insult [in·sʌlt] *v* uvrediti; uvrijediti

insurance [in·ʃɔːrəns] *n* osiguranje

insurance agent *n* osiguravajući agent

insure [in·ʃɔː] *v* osigurati

insured [in·ʃjuːd] *adj* osiguranik

insurgence [in·səːdʒəns] *n* pobuna

insurgent [in·səːdʒənt] *n* pobunjenik

insurrection [,insə·rekʃn] *n* pobuna

intact [in·tækt] *adj* intaktan

integral [·intigrəl] *adj* integralni

integrate [·intigreit] *v* integrisati

integration [,inti·greiʃn] *n* integracija

integrity [in·tegrəti] *n* integritet

intellect [in·tələkt] *n* intelekt

intellectual [,inti·lektʃuəl] *adj* intelektualan

intelligence [in'telidʒəns] *n* **1.** inteligencija **2.** (mil.) obaveštajna služba

intelligence report *n* obaveštajni izveštaj/izvještaj

intelligent [in'telidʒənt] *adj* razuman

intelligible [in'telidʒəbl] *adj* razumljiv

intend [in'tend] *v* nameravati; namjeravati

intense [in'tens] *adj* **1.** jak **2.** dubok

intensify [in'tensifai] *v* intenzivirati

intensity [in'tensəti] *n* žestina

intensive [in'tensiv] *adj* intenzivan

intensive care *n* (med.) intenzivan

intent, intention [in'tent; in'tenʃn] *n* namera; namjera

intentional [in'tenʃənl] *adj* nameran; namjeran

intentionally [in'tenʃənəli] *adv* namerno; namjerno

interact [intər'ækt] *v* međusobno delovati/djelovati

interactive [,intər'ækʃn] *adj* interaktivni

intercede [,intə'si:d] *v* založiti se

intercept [,intə'sept] *v* presresti

interchange [,intətʃeindʒ] *n* **1.** zamena; zamjena **2.** raskršće

intercontinental [,intə,kɔnti'nentəl] *adj* interkontinentalni

intercourse ['intəkɔ:s] *n* **1.** saobraćaj **2. sexual intercourse** snošaj

interdependence [,intədi'pendəns] *n* međuzavisnost

interest ['intrəst] **1.** *n* interes **2.** *v* zainteresovati **3.** *see* **interests**

interested ['intrəstid] *adj* zainsteresovan

interest-free *adj* (fin.) beskamatni

interesting ['intrəstiŋ] *adj* interesantan

interests ['intərests] *pl* krugovi

interface ['intəfeis] *n* međusklop

interfere [,intə'fiə] *v* remititi

interference [,intə'fiərəns] *n* **1.** smetnja **2. transmission interference** šumovi

interim ['intərim] *adj* međuvremeni

interior [in'tiəriə] **1.** *adj* unutrašnji **2.** *n* unutrašnjost

interlude ['intəlu:d] *n* prekid

intermarriage [,intə'mæridʒ] *n* mešoviti brak; mješoviti brak

intermediary [,intə'mi:diəri] *n* posrednik

intermediate [,intə'mi:diət] *adj* srednji

intermission [,intə'miʃn] *n* prekid

intermittent [,intə'mitənt] *adj* naizmeničan; naizmjeničan

internal [intə:nl] *adj* unutrašnji

internal affairs *pl* unutrašnji poslovi

international [,intə'næʃnəl] *adj* međunarodni

International Court of Justice *n* Međunarodni sud pravde

International Labour Organization *n* Međunarodna organizacija rada

international law *n* međunarodno pravo

International Monetary Fund (IMF) *n* Međunarodni monetarni fond

International Refugee Organization *n* Međunarodna organizacija a izbeglice/ izbjeglice

international relations *pl* međunarodni odnosi

international trade *n* međunarodna trgovina

internee [intəːni] *n* internirac

Internet [ˈintənet] *n* internet

internment [intəːnmənt] *n* internacija

internment camp *n* logor za internice

interparliamentary [intəˌpaːlə-ˈmentəri] *adj* međuparlamenterni

interparty [intəˈpaːti] *adj* međupartijski

interpret [inˈtəːprit] *v* interpretirati

interpretation [inˌtəːpriteiʃn] *n* 1. interpretacija 2. analiza

interpreter [inˈtəːpritə] *n* interpretator

interracial [inteˈreiʃl] *adj* međurasni

interrogate [inˈterəgeit] *v* saslušavati

interrogation [inˌterəˈgeiʃn] *n* saslušavanje

interrupt [ˌintəˈrʌpt] *v* prekinuti

interruption [ˌintəˈrʌpʃn] *n* prekid

intersection [ˌintəˈsekʃn] *n* 1. presek; presjek 2. raskršće

intersperse [ˈintəspəːs] *v* rasuti

interstate [ˈintəsteit] *adj* međudržavni

interval [ˈintəvl] *n* interaval

intervene [ˌintəˈviːn] *v* intervenisati

intervention [ˌintəˈvenʃn] *n* 1. intervencija 2. **armed intervention** (mil.) oružana intervencija

interview [ˈintəvjuː] 1. *n* intervju 2. *v* intervjuisati

interviewer [ˈintəvjuə] *n* intervjuist

intestines [ˈintesˌtainz] *pl* crevo; crijevo

intimacy [ˈintiməsi] *n* intimnost

intimate [ˈintimət] *adj* intiman

intimidate [inˈtimideit] *v* zastrašiti

intimidation [inˌtimiˈdeiʃn] *n* zastrašenje

into [ˈintu] *prep* 1. u 2. **to go into** ući

intolerable [inˈtɔlərəbl] *adj* nepodnošljiv

intolerance [inˈtɔlərəns] *n* netrpeljivost

intolerant [inˈtɔlərənt] *adj* netrpeljiv

intoxicated [inˈtɔksiˌkeitid] *adj* opiti

intoxication [inˌtɔksiˌkeiʃn] *n* opijanje

intransigence [inˈtrænsidʒəns] *n* beskompromis

intrepid [inˈtrepid] *adj* neustrašiv

intricate [ˈintrikət] *adj* komplikovan

intrigue [inˈtriːg] 1. *n* intriga 2. *v* intrigirati

introduce [ˌintrəˈdjuːs] *v* 1. uvesti 2. upoznati

introduce a bill *v* (pol.) izneti zakonski predlog

introduction [ˌintrəˈdʌkʃn] *n* uvod

intrude [inˈtruːd] *v* nametati se

intruder [inˈtruːdə] *n* nametnik

intrusion [inˈtruːʒən] *n* upad

intrusive [inˈtruːsiv] *adj* nemtljiv

intuition [ˌintjuˈiʃn] *n* intuicija

invade [inˈveid] *v* upasti

invader [inˈveidə] *n* upadač

invalid [inˈvælid] *adj* nevažeći

invalid [ˈinvəlid] *n* invalid

invaluable [inˈvæljuəbl] *adj* neocenljiv; neocjenljiv

invasion [inˈveiʒn] *n* upad

invent [inˈvent] *v* pronaći

invention [inˈvenʃn] *n* pronalazak

inventor [inˈventə] *n* pronalazač

inventory [inˈventəri] *n* inventar

invert [in·vəːt] v preobrnuti

invest [in·vest] v uložiti

investigate [in·vestigeit] v istražiti

investigation [in,vesti·geiʃn] n istraga

investigator [in,vesti·geitə] n 1. istraživač 2. **private investigator** privatni detektiv

investment [in·vestmənt] n ulaganje

investor [in·vestə] n ulagač

invincible [in·vinsəbl] adj nepobedan; nepobjedan

invisible [in·vizəbl] adj nevidljiv

invitation [,invi·teiʃn] n poziv

invitation card n pozivnica

invite [in·vait] v pozvati

invoice [·invɔis] 1. n faktura 2. v fakturisati

invoke [in·vəuk] v prizvati

involuntary [in·vɔləntri] adj nehotičan

involve [in·vɔlv] v 1. upetljati 2. povlačiti

involvement [in·vɔlvmənt] n upetljanost

irascible [i·rasibl] adj plah

Ireland [·aiələnd] n Irska

iris [·airis] n dužica

Irish [·aiəriʃ] 1. adj irski 2. pl Irci

Irishman [·aiəriʃmən] n Irac

Irishwoman [·aiəriʃ,wumən] n Irkinja

iron [·aiən] 1. n gvožđe 2. pegla 3. **corrugated iron** valoviti čelik 4. v ispeglati

iron discipline n gvozdena disciplina

ironic, ironical [ai·rɔnik; -əl] adj ironičan

ironing [·aiəniŋ] n peglanje

irony [·aiərəni] n ironija

irradiate [i·reidieit] v ozračiti

irrational [i·ræʃəni] adj iracionalan

irreconcilable [i,rekən·sailəbl] adj nepomirljiv

irregular [i·regjulə] 1. adj neregularan 2. n dobrovoljac

irregularity [i,regju·lærəti] n neregularnost

irrelevant [i·reləvənt] adj irelevantan

irreparable [i·repərəbl] adj nepopravljiv

irreplaceable [,iri·pleisəbl] adj nezamenljiv; nezamjenljiv

irresistible [,iri·zistəbl] adj neodoljiv

irrespective of [,iri·spektiv] prep bez obzira na

irresponsibility [,iri,spɔnsə·biləti] n neodgovornost

irresponsible [,iri·spɔnsəbl] adj neodgovoran

irreversible [,iri·vəː·səbl] adj neizmenljiv; neizmjenljiv

irrigate [·irigeit] v navodniti

irrigation [,iri·geiʃn] n navodnjavanje

irritate [·iriteit] v razdražiti

irritating [·iriteitiŋ] adj razdražujuće

irritation [,iri·teiʃn] n razdraženje

is [iz] see **be**

Islam [·izlaːm] n Islam

Islamic [iz·læmik] adj islamski

island [·ailənd] n ostrvo; otok

isolate [·aisəleit] v izolovati

isolated [·aisəleitid] adj zabačen

isolation [,aisə·leiʃn] n izolacija

issue [·iʃuː] 1. n emisija 2. odluka 3. broj 4. v izdati 5. izići

issue an order v izdati naređenja

it [it] pro 1. to 2. ono

Italian [it·ælijən] 1. adj italijanski; talijanski 2. n Italijan; Talijan

italics pl kurziv

Italy [ˈitəli] *n* Italija
itch [itʃ] 1. *n* svrab 2. *v* svrbeti; svrbjeti
itchy [ˈitʃi] *adj* svrabežljiv
item [ˈaitəm] *n* 1. stavka 2. **news item** vest; vijest

itemize [ˈaitəmaiz] *v* nabrojati
itinerary [aiˈtinərəri] *n* sezonski
its [its] njegov, svoj
itself [itˈself] ono samo, se, sebe, to
ivory [ˈaivəri] *n* slonovača
ivy [ˈaivi] *n* bršljan

J

jack [dʒæk] *n* dizalica
jackal [ˈdʒækl] *n* šakal
jacket [ˈdʒækit] *n* žaket
jackpot [ˈdʒækpɔt] *n* glavni zgoditak
jack up *v* podići
jail [dʒeil] **1.** *n* zatvor **2.** *v* zatvoriti
jailer [ˈdʒeilə] *n* tamničar
jalopy [dʒəˈlɔpi] *n* stara kola
jam [dʒæm] **1.** *n* (UK) džem **2. traffic jam** saobraćajna gužva **3.** *v* (**jammed**) pritisnuti **4.** zaglaviti se
jam a broadcast *v* prigušivati emisiju
January [ˈdʒænjuəri] *n* januar; siječanj
Japan [dʒəˈpæn] *n* Japan
Japanese [dʒəˈpæniːz] **1.** *adj* japanski **2.** *n* Japanac
jar [dʒaː] *n* tegla
jargon [ˈdʒaːgən] *n* žargon
jaundice [ˈdʒɔːndis] *n* žutica
javelin [ˈdʒævəlin] *n* (spor.) koplje
jaw [dʒɔː] *n* vilica
jazz [dʒæz] *n* džez
jealous [ˈdʒeləs] *adj* ljubomoran
jealousy [ˈdʒeləsi] *n* ljubomora
jeans [dʒiːnz] *pl* džins
jeep [dʒiːp] *n* džip
jeer [dʒiːr] **1.** *n* ruglo **2.** *v* rugati se
jelly [ˈdʒeli] *n* žele
jeopardize [ˈdʒepədaiz] *v* ugroziti
jeopardy [ˈdʒepədi] *n* opasnost
jerk [dʒəːk] *v* trgnuti
jersey [ˈdʒəːzi] *n* **1.** džemper **2.** (spor.) dres
jet [dʒet] *n* **1.** mlaz **2.** mlaznjak

jet fighter *n* mlazni lovac
jet lag [ˈdʒetlag] *n* umor od putovanja
jet plane [ˈdʒetplein] *n* mlazni avion
jetty [ˈdʒeti] *n* nasip
Jew [dʒuː] *n* Jevrejin
jewel [ˈdʒuːəl] *n* dragulj
jeweller, jeweler [ˈdʒuːələ] *n* juvelir
jewellery, jewelry [ˈdʒuːəlri] *n* nakit
Jewish [ˈdʒuːiʃ] *adj* jevrejski
job [dʒɔb] *n* posao
jockey [ˈdʒɔki] *n* džokej
jog [dʒɔg] *v* pretrčati
jogging [ˈdʒɔgiŋ] *n* trčanje
join [dʒɔin] *v* **1.** spojiti **2. to join the army** stupiti u vojsku
joint [dʒɔint] **1.** *adj* zajednički **2.** *n* zglob **3.** šav **4. joint of meat** pečenica
joint action *n* zajednička akcija
jointly [ˈdʒɔintli] *adv* zajednički
joint-venture company *n* kompanija osnovana zajedničkim vlaganjem
joke [dʒəuk] **1.** *n* šala **2.** *v* šaliti se
jolly [ˈdʒɔli] *adj* veseo
jolt [dʒɔlt] *v* drmnuti
journal [ˈdʒəːnl] *n* **1.** časopis **2.** dnevnik
journalism [ˈdʒəːnəlizəm] *n* žurnalizam
journalist [ˈdʒəːnəlist] *n* žurnalista
journey [ˈdʒəːni] **1.** *n* putovanje **2.** *v* putovati

joy [dʒɔi] *n* radost
joyful [ˈdʒɔifl] *adj* radostan
joyous [ˈdʒɔiəs] *adj* radostan
joyride [ˈdʒɔiraid] 1. *n* šetnja autom 2. *v* šetati se autom
jubilee [ˈdʒuːbili] *n* jubilej
judge [dʒʌdʒ] 1. *n* sudija; sudac 2. **chief judge** vrhovni sudija/sudac 3. *v* suditi
judgement, judgment [ˈdʒʌdʒmənt] *n* 1. sud 2. **to pass judgement** izreći presudu
judicial [ˌdʒuːˈdiʃl] *adj* sudski
judo [ˈdʒuːdəu] *n* džudo
jug [dʒʌg] *n* krčag
juggle [ˈdʒʌgl] *v* žonglirati
juggler [ˈdʒʌglə] *n* žongler
juice [dʒuːs] *n* sok
juicy [ˈdʒuːsi] *adj* sočan
juju [ˈdʒuːdʒuː] *n* fetiš
July [dʒuːˈlai] *n* jul; srpannj
jumble [ˌdʒʌmbl] *v* zbrkati
jump [dʒʌmp] 1. *n* skok 2. (spor.) **high jump** skok uvis 3. *v* skočiti
jumper [ˈdʒʌmpə] *n* 1. džemper 2. (spor.) skakač
jump over *v* preskočiti

junction [ˈdʒʌŋkʃn] *n* 1. čvor 2. raskršće
June [dʒuːn] *n* jun; lipanj
jungle [ˈdʒʌŋgl] *n* džungla
junior [ˈdʒuːniə] *adj* mlađi
junk [dʒʌŋk] *n* stara užad
junta [ˈdʒʌŋtə] *n* hunta
jurisdiction [ˌdʒuərisˈdikʃn] *n* jurisdikcija
jurisprudence [ˌdʒuərisˈpruːdəns] *n* jurisprudencija
juror [ˈdʒuərə] *n* porotnik
jury [ˈdʒuəri] *n* porota
just [dʒʌst] 1. *adj* pravedan 2. *adv* tek
just now upravo sada
just as baš kad
justice [ˈdʒʌstis] *n* 1. pravda 2. pravosuđe 3. sudija; sudac
justification [ˌdʒʌstifiˈkeiʃn] *n* opravdanje
justified [ˈdʒʌstifaid] *adj* opravdan
justify [ˈdʒʌstifai] *v* opravdati
juvenile [ˈdʒuːvənail] 1. *adj* maloletan; maloljetan 2. *n* maloletnik; maloljetnik
juvenile delinquent *n* maloletan prestupnik; maloljetan prestupnik

K

kangaroo [ˌkængəˈruː] *n* kengur
karate [kiˈbæb] *n* karate
kebab [kiˈbæb] *n* ćevapčić
keen [kiːn] *adj* 1. oštar 2. željan
keep [kiːp] *v* 1. držati 2. čuvati 3. to keep the peace održati mir 4. to keep a promise održati obećanje 5. He kept writing. Nastavlo je da piše.
keep away *v* čuvati se
keep back *v* povući se
keeper [ˈkiːpə] *n* 1. čuvar 2. *see* goalkeeper
keep on *v* nastaviti
keep out *v* ne mešati se; ne miješati se
keep quiet *v* ćutati; šutjeti
keep still *v* biti miran
keep to *v* držati se
keep up *v* držati se
kennel [ˈkenl] *n* štenara
kernel [ˈkəːnl] *n* jezgro
kerosene [ˈkerəsiːn] *n* kerozin
kettle [ˈketl] *n* 1. katao 2. electric kettle kuhalo za vodu
key [kiː] 1. *adj* osovni 2. *n* ključ 3. tipka
keyboard [ˈkiːbɔːd] *n* 1. tastatura 2. (mus.) klavijatura
keyhole [ˈkiːhəul] *n* ključaonica
key position *n* ključni položaj
kick [kik] 1. *n* udarac 2. *v* udariti
kid [kid] 1. *adj* (sl.) mlađi 2. *n* (sl.) klinac 3. *v* zavaravati
kidding [ˈkidiŋ] *n* šala
kidnap [ˈkidnæp] *v* kidnapovati
kidnapper [ˈkidnæpə] *n* kidnaper

kidnapping [ˈkidnæpiŋ] *n* kidnapovanje
kidney [ˈkidni] *n* bubreg
kill [kil] *v* ubiti
killer [ˈkilə] *n* ubica
killer disease *n* smrtonosna bolest
killing [ˈkiliŋ] *n* ubijanje
killjoy [ˈkildʒɔi] *n* kvarilac raspoloženja
kill time *v* utucati vreme/vrijeme
kiln [kiln] *n* peć
kilo, kilogramme, kilogram [ˈkiːləu; ˈkiləgræm] *n* kilogram
kilometre, kilometer [kiˈlɔmitə] *n* kilometar
kin [kin] *n* rođaci
kind [kaind] 1. *adj* dobar 2. *n* vrsta; vrst 3. to pay in kind platiti u naturi
kindergarten [ˈkindəgaːdn] *n* zabavište
kind-hearted *adj* dobrodušan
kindle [ˈkaindl] *v* zapaliti
kindly [ˈkaindli] *adv* ljubazno
kindness [ˈkaindnis] *n* dobrota
kind of *adv* malo
king [kiŋ] *n* kralj
kingdom [ˈkiŋdəm] *n* carstvo
kingship [ˈkiŋʃip] *n* kraljestvo
kinship [ˈkinʃip] *n* srodstvo
kiosk [ˈkiːɔsk] *n* kiosk
kiss [kis] 1. *n* poljubac 2. *v* poljubiti
kit [kit] *n* oprema
kitchen [ˈkitʃin] *n* kuhinja
kite [kait] *n* zmaj
kitten [ˈkitn] *n* mače
knack [næk] *n* veština; vještina

knead [niːd] *v* gnječiti
knee [niː] *n* koleno; koljeno
kneecap [ˈniːkæp] *n* čašica
kneel, kneel down [niːl] *v* kleknuti
knew [njuː] *see* **know**
knickers [ˈnikəz] *n* čakšire
knife [naif] **1.** *n* (*pl* **knives**) nož **2.** *v* udariti nožem
knight [nait] *n* vitez
knit [nit] *v* oplesti
knives [naivz] *see* **knife**
knob [nɔb] *n* **1.** čvor **2.** dugme
knock [nɔk] *v* **1.** udariti **2.** kucati
knock down *v* **1.** oboriti **2.** srušiti **3.** otresti
knocker [ˈnɔkə] *n* zvekir
knock out *v* nokautirati
knock over *v* **1.** oboriti **2.** *see* **knock down**
knot [nɔt] **1.** *n* čvor **2.** *v* vezati

know [nəu] *v* (**knew, known**) **1.** znati **2.** upoznati **3.** umeti/umjeti
know by heart *v* znati napamet
know-how [ˈnəuhau] *n* znanje
know how to *v* umeti/umjeti
knowledge [ˈnɔlidʒ] *n* **1.** znanje **2.** nauka
knowledgeable [ˈnɔlidʒəbl] *adj* dobro obavešten/obaviješten
known [nəun] *adj* **1.** poznat **2.** *see* **know**
known facts *pl* poznate činjenice
knuckle [ˈnʌkl] *n* čukalj
Koran [kɔrˈaːn] *n* koran
kosher [ˈkəuʃə] *adj* košer
kowtow [ˈkautəu; ˈkautau] *v* ulagivati se
k.p.h. (kilometres per hour; kilometers per hour) kilometara na sat

L

lab [læb] *see* **laboratory**

label [ˈleibl] 1. *n* etiketa 2. epitet 3. *v* staviti etiku na

laboratory [ləˈbɔrətri] *n* laboratorija

laborious [ləˈbɔːriəs] *adj* težak

labour, labor [ˈleibə] 1. *n* rad 2. to be in labour ležati u porođajnim mukama 5. *v* raditi

labourer, laborer [ˈleibərə] *n* radnik

Labour Party *n* laburistička stranka

labour union, labor union *n* sinidikat

lace [leis] *n* 1. čipka 2. **shoe lace** vrpca

lack [læk] 1. *n* nestašica 2. *v* oskudevati; oskudijevati

lad [læd] *n* momak

ladder [ˈlædə] *n* merdevine

ladle [ˈleidl] *n* kutlača

lady [ˈleidi] *n* gospođa

lag [læg] 1. *v* **to lag behind** zaostati 2. *see* **jet-lag**

lager [ˈlaːgə] *n* zrelo pivo

lagoon [ləˈguːn] *n* laguna

laid [leid] *see* **lay**

lain [lein] *see* **lie**

lake [leik] *n* jezero

lamb [læm] *n* jagnje; janje

lame [leim] 1. *adj* hram 2. *v* osakatiti

lament [ləˈment] *v* jadati

lamentable [ləˈmentəbl] *adj* žalostan

lamp [læmp] *n* lampa

lamp-post *n* bandera

lampshade [ˈlæmpʃeid] *n* abažur

lance [laːns] *v* koplje

land [lænd] 1. *n* kopno 2. zemlja 3. **by land** na kopnu 4. *v* sleteti; sletjeti 5. iskrcati (se)

landholder [ˈlænd,həuldə] *n* zemljoposednik; zemljoposjednik

landing [ˈlændiŋ] *n* 1. sletanje; slijetanje 2. **forced landing** prinudno sletanje

landing strip *n* staza za sletanje

landlady [ˈlændleidi] *n* gazdarica

landlord [ˈlændlɔːd] *n* 1. gazda 2. krčmar

landmark [ˈlændmaːk] 1. *adj* značajan 2. *n* orijentir

landowner [ˈlændəunə] *n* vlasnik zemlje

landscape [ˈlændskeip] *n* pejzaž

landslide [ˈlændslaid] *n* lavina

lane [lein] *n* 1. staza 2. traka

language [ˈlæŋgwidʒ] *n* 1. jezik 2. **bad language** psovke

lantern [ˈlæntən] *n* fenjer

lap [læp] 1. *n* krilo 2. (spor.) krug 3. *v* prestići za ceo krug

lapse [læps] *v* (leg.) isteći

laptop [ˈlæptɔp] *n* leptop, portabl kompjuter

larder [ˈlaːdə] *n* ostava

large [laːdʒ] *adj* veliki

large-scale *adj* velikih razmera/razmjera

laryngitis [ˈlærin,dʒaitis] *n* laringitis

larynx [ˈlæriŋks] *n* grkljan

laser [ˈleizə] *n* laser

laser printer *n* laserski štampač

lash [læʃ] *v* 1. isibati 2. vezati

lash out at v napasti

lass [læs] n devojčica; djevojčica

last [lɑːst] 1. adj poslednji; posljednji 2. **last night** sinoć 3. **last year** prošle godine 4. **at last** konačno 5. **last of all** najzad 6. adv naposlektu; naposljektu 7. v trajati

lasting [ˈlɑːstiŋ] adj trajan

lastly [ˈlɑːstli] adv na kraju

latch [lætʃ] n reza

late [leit] adj 1. kasan 2. **the late news** poslednje vesti/vijesti 3. **the late Mr...** pokojni Gospodin... 4. **to be late** zakasniti

lately [ˈleitli] adv nedavno

later [ˈleitə] 1. adv kasnije 2. see **late**

latest [ˈleitist] adj 1. najnoviji 2. **the latest news** najnovije vesti/vijesti

lather [ˈlɑːðə] n pena; pjena

Latin [ˈlætin] adj latinski

latitude [ˈlætitjuːd] n širina

latter [ˈlætə] adj drugi

latterly [ˈlætəli] adv u poslednje vreme/vrijeme

laugh [lɑːf] 1. n smeh; smijeh 2. v smejati se; smijati se

laughable [ˈlɑːfəbl] adj smešan; smiješan

laughter [ˈlɑːftə] n 1. smeh; smijeh 2. **to burst into laughter** prsnuti u smeh/smijeh

launch [lɔːntʃ] v porinuti

launch a rocket v lansirati raketu

launch a torpedo v ispaliti torpedo

launch a magazine v pokrenuti časopis

launch an attack v preduzeti napad

launch-pad n raketna rampa

launderette, laundrette [ˌlɔːndəˈret] n preionica; praonica

laundry [ˈlɔːndri] n 1. perionica 2. rublje

lava [ˈlɑːvə] n lava

lavatory [ˈlævətri] n 1. klozet 2. **public lavatory** javni klozet 3. **to go to the lavatory** ići u klozet 4. **to need to go to the lavatory** morati ići u klozet

lavish [ˈlæviʃ] adj izdašan

law [lɔː] n 1. zakon 2. pravo 3. **against the law** protiv zakona 4. **to break the law** ogrešiti se o zakon; ogriješiti se o zakon 5. **to pass a law** doneti zakon; donijeti zakon 6. see **jurisprudence**

law and order n zakon i red

law court [ˈlɔːkɔːt] n sudnica

lawful [ˈlɔːfl] adj zakonit

lawless [ˈlɔːləs] adj nezakonit

lawn [lɔːn] n travnjak

lawsuit [ˈlɔːsuːt] n parnica

lawyer [ˈlɔːjə] n 1. advokat 2. **defence lawyer** advokat odbrane, branitelj 3. **prosecuting lawyer** tužilac

lax [læks] adj labav

laxative [ˈlæksətiv] n laksativ

lay [lei] v 1. položiti 2. **to lay an egg** nositi jaja 3. see **lie**

lay down v položiti

layer [ˈleiə] n sloj

layman [ˈleimən] n laik

lay off v otpustiti s posla

layout n projekat

lay out v spremiti

laziness [ˈleizinis] n lenivost

lazy [ˈleizi] adj leniv

lead [led] n olovo

lead [liːd] 1. n vodstvo 2. **to be in**

the lead biti u vodstvu 23 *v* **(led)** voditi

leader [ˈliːdə] *n* vođa

leadership [ˈliːdəʃip] *n* vođa

leading [ˈliːdiŋ] *adj* glavni

leaf [liːf] *n* (*pl* **leaves**) list

leaflet [ˈliːflit] *n* letak

league [liːg] *n* (spor.) liga

leak [liːk] 1. *n* pukotina 2. **leak of information** curenje informacija 3. *v* propuštati 4. **to leak information** otkriti podatke

lean [liːn] 1. *adj* mršav 2. *v* (**leant/ leaned**) nasloniti (se)

leaned [liːnd] *see* **lean**

leaning [ˈliːniŋ] *n* sklonost

leant [lent] *see* **lean**

leap [liːp] 1. *n* skok 2. *v* (**leapt/ leaped**) (pre)skočiti

leapfrog [ˈliːpfrɔg] *v* preskočiti

leap-year [ˈliːpjiə] *n* prestupna godina

learn [ləːn] *v* (**learnt/ learned**) 1. učiti 2. naučiti 3. **to learn by heart** naučiti napamet

learn about/of *v* saznati za

learned [ˈləːnid] *adj* učen

learner [ləːnə] *n* učenik

learn how *v* naučiti

learning [ˈləːniŋ] *n* učenje

lease [liːs] 1. *n* zakup 2. *v* iznajmiti

least [liːst] *adj* 1. najmanji 2. **at least** u najmanju ruku

leather [ˈleðə] *n* koža

leave [liːv] 1. *n* dopuštenje 2. odsustvo 3. *v* (**left**) ostaviti 4. napustiti 5. *see* **left**

leave off *v* prestati

leaves [livz] *see* **leaf**

lecture [ˈlektʃə] 1. *n* predavanje 2. *v* ukoriti 3. (acad.) držati predavanja

lecturer [ˈlektʃərə] *n* 1. predavač 2. docent

led [led] *see* **lead**

ledge [ledʒ] *n* obod

ledger [ˈledʒə] *n* glavna knjiga

left [left] 1. *n* leva 2. (pol.) levica; ljevica 3. **on the left** s leve strane 4. *adj* levi; lijevi 5. **There is no time left. Vreme je isteklo./ Vrijeme je isteklo.** 6. *adv* levo; lijevo 7. *see* **leave**

left-handed *adj* levoruk; ljevoruk

left-luggage *n* garderoba

left over *adj* neupotrebljen; neupotrijebljen

left-wing *adj* (pol.) levičarski; ljevičarski

left wing *n* (pol.) levo krilo; lijevo krilo

left-winger *n* (pol.) levičar; ljevičar

leg [leg] *n* 1. noga 2. (spor.) etapa

legacy [ˈlegəsi] *n* legat

legal [ˈliːgl] *adj* 1. zakonit 2. sudksi

legality [liːˈgæliti] *n* legalnost

legalization [ˌliːgəlaiˈzeiʃn] *n* legalizacija

legalize [ˈliːgəlaiz] *v* legalizovati

legend [ˈledʒənd] *n* legenda

legendary [ˈledʒəndri] *adj* legendaran

legible [ˈledʒəbl] *adj* čitak

legion [ˈliːdʒən] *n* legija

legislate [ˈledʒisleit] *v* donositi zakone

legislation [ledʒisˈleiʃn] *n* zakonodavstvo

legislative [ˈledʒislətiv] *adj* zakonodavan

legislative body *n* zakonodavno telo/tijelo

legislator [ˈledʒisleitə] *n* zakonodavac

legitimacy [li·dʒitiməsi] *n* zakonitost
legitimate [li·dʒitimət] *adj* zakonit
leisure [·leʒə] *n* dokolica
leisurely [·leʒəli] 1. *adj* lagan 2. *adv* lagano
lemon [·lemən] *n* limun
lemonade [,lemə·neid] *n* limunada
lend [lend] *v* (**lent**) pozajmiti
lend a hand *v* pružiti pomoć
lender [·lendə] *n* zajmodavac
lending rate [·lendiŋ] *n* kamatna stopa
length [leŋθ] *n* 1. dužina 2. **at length** opširno
lengthen [·leŋθən] *v* produžiti; produljiti
lengthways [·leŋθweiz] *adv* po dužini
lengthy [·leŋθi] *adj* opširan
leniency [·liːniənsi] *n* blagost
lenient [·liːniənt] *adj* blag
lens [lenz] *n* (*pl* **lenses**) sočivo
lent [lent] *see* **lend**
leper [·lepə] *n* gubavac
leprosy [·leprəsi] *n* guba
lesbian [·lezbiən] 1. *adj* lezbijski 2. *n* lezbijka
lesbianism [·lezbiənizm] *n* lezbijska ljubav
less [les] *adj* 1. manje 2. **more or less** manje-više
lessen [·lesən] *v* smanjiti (se)
lesser [·lesər] *adj* manji
lesson [·lesn] *n* pouka
lest [lest] *adv* da ne bi
let [let] *v* (**let**) 1. pustiti 2. neka... 3. izdati
let alone *conj* a kamoli
let down *v* razočarati
let go *v* 1. saki 2. sàllamá
lethal [·liːθəl] *adj* smrtonosan
let in *v* pustiti

let off *v* ispustiti
let out *v* pustiti
let's... *v* hajdemo...
letter [·letə] *n* 1. pismo 2. slovo
letter bomb *n* pismo s bombom
letterbox [·letəbɔks] *n* (UK) poštansko sanduče
lettuce [·letis] *n* salata
let up *v* stišati se
level [·levl] 1. *n* nivo 2. instanca 3. **sea level** nivo mora 4. *adj* horizontalan 5. *v* izravnati
level crossing *n* ukrštanje u nivou
lever [·liːvə] *n* poluga
levy [·levi] *v* nametnuti
lewd [·ljuəd] *adj* razvratan
liability [,laiə·biləti] *n* odgovornost
liable [·laiəbl] *adj* podložan
liable to *adj* moguć
liar [·laiə] *n* lažov
libel [·laibl] 1. *n* kleveta 2. *v* oklevetati
liberal [·libərəl] 1. *adj* liberalan 2. *n* liberal
liberalism [·libərælizm] *n* liberalizam
liberalization [,libərəlai·zeiʃn] *n* liberalizacija
liberate [·libəreit] *v* osloboditi
liberation [,libə·reiʃn] *n* oslobođenje
liberator [,libə·reitə] *n* oslobodilac
liberty [·libəti] *n* sloboda
librarian [lai·breəriən] *n* bibliotekar
library [·laibrəri] *n* biblioteka
lice [lais] *see* **louse**
licence [·laisns] *n* 1. dozvola 2. **driving licence** vozačka dozvola
licence office *n* ofišin lasisi
licence plate *n* registarska tablica
license [·laisns] *v* 1. dati dozvolu 2. *see* **licence**

licensee [ˌlaisənˈsiː] n krčmar
lick [lik] v lizati
lid [lid] n poklopac
lie [lai] 1. n laž 2. v (lay, lain) ležati
3. (lied) lagati
lie down v leći
lieu [ljuː] n in lieu of umesto; umjesto
lieutenant [lefˈtenənt] n poručnik
lieutenant-colonel [lefˈtenəntˈkəːnl] n potpukovnik
life [laif] n (pl lives) 1. život 2. way of life način života
life imprisonment n doživotna robija, doživotna kazna zatvora
lifebelt n pojas za spasavanje
lifeboat n čamac za spasavanje
life insurance n osiguranje života
life jacket n prsluk za spasavanje
lifeless [ˈlaifls] adj beživotan
lifespan [ˈlaifspæn] n ljudski vek/vijek
lifestyle [ˈlaifstail] n način života
lifetime [ˈlaiftaim] n ljudski vek/vijek
lift [lift] 1. n lift 2. to give a lift povesti kolima 3. v dići 4. to lift a blockade podići blokadu
ligament [ˈligəmənt] n veza
light [lait] 1. adj lak 2. svetao; svijetao 3. n svetlo; svjetlo 4. svetlost; svjetlost 5. v (lit) upaliti
lightbulb [ˈlaitbʌlb] n sijalica; žarulja
lighten [ˈlaitn] v 1. olakšati 2. osvetliti; osvijetliti
lighter [ˈlaitə] n upaljač
lighthouse [ˈlaithaus] n svetionik; svjetionik
lightly [ˈlaitli] adv lako
lightness [ˈlaitnis] n lakoća
lightning [ˈlaitniŋ] n grom

lightning strike n (pol.) divlji štrajk
light switch n prekidač za svetlo/ svjetlo
like [laik] 1. prep/adv/conj kao 2. to feel like doing hteti 3. v voleti; voljeti
likelihood [ˈlaiklihud] n verovatnoća; vjerovatnoća
likely [ˈlaikli] adj/adv 1. verovatan; vjerovatan 2. pogodan
liken [ˈlaikn] v uporediti
likeness [ˈlaiknis] n sličnost
likewise [ˈlaikwaiz] adv isto tako
liking [ˈlaikiŋ] n simpatija
limb [lim] n ivica
lime [laim] n 1. kreč 2. vrsta limuna
limelight [ˈlaimlait] n središte pažnje
limit [ˈlimit] 1. n granica 2. age limit starosna granica 3. speed limit ograničenje brzine 4. v ograničiti
limitation [ˌlimiˈteiʃn] n ograničenje
limited [ˈlimitid] adj ograničen
limited company n društvo sa ograničenim jemstvom
limitless [ˈlimitləs] adj neograničen
limp [limp] 1. adj mlitav 2. v hramati
line [lain] n 1. crta 2. linija 3. telephone line telefonski vod
linen [ˈlinin] n laneno platno
liner [ˈlainə] n putnički brod
line up v postrojiti (se)
linger [ˈliŋgə] v zadržavati se
lingerie [ˈlɔnʒəri] n žensko donje rublje
lingua franca [ˌliŋgwəˈfræŋkə] n saobraćajni jezik
linguist [ˈliŋgwist] n lingvista
linguistic [liŋˈgwistik] adj lingvistički

linguistics [liŋ'gwistiks] *n* lingvistika
lining ['lainiŋ] *n* obloga
link [liŋk] **1.** *n* karika **2.** veza **3.** *v* povezati
link up *v* spojiti (se)
lino, linoleum ['lainəu; li'nəuliəm] *n* linoleum
lion ['laiən] *n* lav
lioness ['laiənis] *n* lavica
lip [lip] *n* usna
lip read *v* čitati s usana
lip reading *n* čitanje s usana
lip service *n* to pay lip service davati prazna obećanja u vezi (to s)
lipstick ['lipstik] *n* karmin
liquefy ['likwifai] *v* pretvoriti u tečnost
liquid ['likwid] **1.** *adj* tečan **2.** *n* tečnost
liquidate ['likwideit] *v* (fin.) likvidirati
liquidation [,likwi'deiʃn] *n* likvidacija
liquor ['likə] *n* tečnost
list [list] **1.** *n* spisak **2.** *v* popisati
listen ['lisn] *v* slušati
listen in *v* slušati emisiju
listener ['lisnə] *n* slušalac
listings ['listiŋs] *pl* spiskovi
listless ['listlis] *adj* trom
lit [lit] *see* **light**
liter ['litə] (US) *n* litar
literacy ['litərəsi] *n* pismenost
literal ['litərəl] *adj* bukvalan
literally ['litərəli] *adv* doslovce
literary ['litəreri] *adj* književni
literate ['litərəl] *adj* **1.** školovan **2.** pismen
literature ['litrətʃə] *n* književnost
litre ['litə] *n* litar
litter ['litə] *n* otpaci

little ['litl] **1.** *adj* mali **2.** *adv* malo **3. a little** malo
little by little *adv* malo-pomalo
live [laiv] **1.** *adj* živ **2. a live broadcast** direktan prenos **3.** *adv* direktno
live [liv] *v* **1.** živeti; živjeti **2.** stanovati
livelihood ['laivlihud] *n* izdržavanje
lively ['laivli] *adj* **1.** živ **2.** žustar
liver ['livə] *n* jetra
lives [laivz] *see* **life**
livestock ['laivstɔk] *n* stoka
livid ['livid] *adj* modar
living ['liviŋ] **1.** *adj* životni **2.** *n* život **3. standard of living** životni standard **4. to make a living** zarađivati za život
living-room *n* gostinska soba
lizard ['lizəd] *n* gušter
load [ləud] **1.** *n* teret **2.** *v* natovariti **3.** ukrcati **4. to load a gun** napuniti pušku
loaf [ləuf; ləuvz] *n* (*pl* **loaves**) hleb/hljeb; kruh
loan [ləun] **1.** *n* zajam **2.** *v* pozajmiti
loanword ['ləunwəːd] *n* pozajmljenica; posuđenica
loathe [ləuð] *v* gnušati se
loathsome ['ləuðsəm] *adj* gnusan
loaves [ləuvz] *see* **loaf**
lobby ['lɔbi] **1.** *n* (pol.) lobi **2. hotel lobby** foaje **3.** *v* (pol.) uticati na
lobbyist ['lɔbijist] *n* (pol.) lobista
lobe [ləub] *n* uvce
local ['ləukl] *adj* lokalni
local authority *n* lokalna vlast
local government *n* lokalna vlada
locality [ləu'kæləti] *n* mesto; mjesto
localize ['ləukəlaiz] *v* lokalizovati
locate [ləu'keit] *v* **1.** pronaći **2.** *see* **located**

located [ləuˈkeitid] *adj* to be
located biti smešten/smješten
location *n* položaj
lock [lɔk] *n* 1. *n* brava 2. *v* zaključati
locked [lɔkt] *adj* zaključan
locksmith [ˈlɔksmiθ] *n* bravar
locomotive [ˌləukəˈməutiv] *n*
lokomotiva
locust [ˈləukəst] *n* skakavac
lodge [lɔdʒ] 1. *n* kućica 2. *v*
stanovati 3. zastati 4. to lodge a
complaint uložiti žalbu
lodger [ˈlɔdʒə] *n* stanar
lodgings [ˈlɔdʒiŋz] *n* stan
loft [lɔft] *see* attic
lofty [ˈlɔfti] *adj* uzvišen
log [lɔg] *n* klada
logging [ˈlɔgiŋ] *n* seča drva; sječa
drva
logic [ˈlɔdʒik] *n* logika
logical [ˈlɔdʒikl] *adj* logičan
log in *v* ukucati šifru u kompjuter/
računar
logistic [lɔˈdʒistik] *adj* pozadinski
logo [ˈləugəu] *n* fabrički žig
loins [lɔinz] *n* slabina
loiter [ˈlɔitə] *v* zadržavati se
loneliness *n* napuštenost
lonely [ˈləunli] *adj* 1. izolovan 2.
napušten
long [lɔŋ] 1. *adj* dug 2. *adv* dugo 3.
before long uskoro 4. in the
long run na kraju 5. as long as
dokle god 6. how long? koliko
dugo? 7. *see* long for
long ago *adv* 1. u davnoj prošlosti
2. not long ago nedavno
long-distance call *n* međumesni
telefonski razgovor
longer *see* long, no longer
long for *v* čeznuti za
longing [ˈlɔŋiŋ] *n* čežnja

longitude [ˈlɔŋgitjuːd] *n* dužina
long-lasting *adj* trajan
long-range *adj* dugoročni
long-range artillery *n*
dalekometna artiljeriija
long-sighted *adj* dalekovidan
long-term *adj* dugotrajan
look [luk] 1. *n* pogled 2. *v* pogledati
3. izgledati
look after *v* starati se
look ahead *v* zagledati se
look back *v* osvrnuti se
look for *v* tražiti
look forward to *v* radovati se
looking-glass [ˈlukiŋglaːs] *n*
ogledalo
look into *v* ispitivati
look like *see* like
look-out *n* straža
look out *v* 1. gledati 2. look out!
pazi!
look over *v* pregledati
looks [luks] *pl* spoljašnjost
look up *v* potražiti
look upon *v* smatrati
look up to *v* ugledati se
loop [luːp] *n* petlja
loophole [ˈluːphəul] *n* izlaz
loose [luːs] *adj* 1. slobodan 2.
klimav 3. to break loose
osloboditi se
loosen [ˈluːsn] *v* razlabaviti (se)
lopsided [ˌlɔpˈsaidid] *adj* kos
loquacious [ləˈkweiʃəs] *adj*
govorljiv
loquacity [ləˈkwæsəti] *n* govorljivost
lord [lɔːd] *n* 1. gospodar 2. (rel.)
Our Lord Gospod
lorry [ˈlɔri] *n* (UK) kamion
lose [luːz; lɔst] *v* (lost) izgubiti
lose face *v* He has lost face.
Izgubio je obraz.

lose hope v izgubiti nadu
loser [ˈluːzə] n gubitnik
loss [lɔs] n gubitak
losses [ˈlɔsiz] pl (mil.) gubici
lost [lɔst] adj 1. to get/be lost izgubljen 2. see lose
lot [lɔt] n 1. parcela 2. ždreb 3. lots, a lot (of) mnogo 4. the whole lot u punom broju
lotion [ˈləuʃn] n losion
lots of [ˈlɔtsəv] mnogo
lottery [ˈlɔtəri] n lutrija
loud [laud] adj 1. glasan 2. to read out loud čitati glasno
loudly [ˈlaudli] adv glasno
loudness [ˈlaudnəs] n glasnost
loudspeaker [ˌlaudˈspiːkə] n glasno
lounge [laundʒ] n čekaonica
louse [laus; lais] n (pl lice) vaš
love [lʌv] 1. n ljubav 2. v voleti; voljeti 3. to make love umiljavati se 4. to fall in love zaljubiti se (with u)
love affair n ljubavna veza
lovely [ˈlʌvli] adj 1. ljubazan 2. lep; lijep
lover [ˈlʌvə] n 1. ljubavnik 2. ljubitelj
loving [ˈlʌviŋ] adj pun ljubavi
low [ləu] adj 1. nizak 2. mali 3. tih
lower [ˈləuə] 1. adj dinji 2. v sniziti
Lower House [ˈləuə] n (pol.) donji dom
low-key adj uzdržan
lowlands [ˈləulændz] pl nizina
loyal [ˈlɔiəl] adj lojalan
loyalty [ˈlɔiəlti] n lojalnost
lp (= **long-playing record**) [elˈpiː] n (mus.) long-plej ploča
ltd see **limited**
lubricant [ˈluːbrikənt] n mazivo

lubricate [ˈluːbrikeit] v pomazati
luck [lʌk] n sreća
luckily [ˈlʌkili] adv na sreću
lucky [ˈlʌki] adj srećan
lucrative [ˈluːkrətiv] adj unosan
ludicrous [ˈluːdikrəs] adj smešan; smiješan
luggage [ˈlʌgidʒ] n prtljag; prtljaga
lukewarm [ˌluːkˈwɔːm] adj mlak
lull [lʌl] n zatišje
lumber [ˈlʌmbə] n drvna građa
luminous [ˈluːminəs] adj svetao; svijetao
lump [lʌmp] n 1. grumen 2. (med.) izraslina
lump sum n ukupna suma
lunacy [ˈluːnəsi] n ludilo
lunar [ˈluːnə] adj lunarni
lunatic [ˈluːnətik] 1. adj umobolan 2. n umobolnik
lunch [lʌntʃ] 1. n ručak 2. v ručati
luncheon [ˈlʌnʃən] n svečani ručak
lunchtime [ˈlʌntʃtaim] n vreme za ručak; vrijeme za ručak
lung [lʌŋ] n pluće
lurch [ləːtʃ] v iznenada se nagnuti
lure [luə] v primamati
lurk [ləːk] v skrivati se
luscious [ˈlʌʃəs] adj sladak
lust [lʌst] n žudnja
luxurious [lʌgˈʒuəriəs] adj raskošan
luxury [ˈlʌkʃəri] n luksuz
lying [ˈlajiŋ] 1. adj lažan 2. see **lie**
lymph [limf] 1. adj limfni 2. n limfa
lymphatic [limˈfætik] adj limfatičan
lynch [lintʃ] v linčovati
lynching [ˈlintʃiŋ] n linč
lynch-law n narodna pravda
lynch mob n rulja za linčovanje
lyrics [ˈliriks] pl tekst pesme/pjesme
lyricist [ˈlirisist] n libretista

M

MA (master's degree) *n* magistar filozofije

mac *see* **macintosh**

macabre [məˈkɑːbrə] *adj* jeziv

Macedonia [ˌmæsəˈdəʊniə] *n* Makedonija

Macedonian [ˌmæsəˈdəʊniən] 1. *adj* makedonski 2. *n* Makedonac

machine [məˈʃiːn] *n* mašina

machine-gun *n* mitraljez

machinery [məˈʃiːnəri] *n* 1. mašinerija 2. (pol.) aparat

machinist [məˈʃiːnist] *n* mašinista

macintosh [ˈmækintɒʃ] *n* 1. (UK) kišni mantil 2. kompjuter

mad [mæd] *adj* 1. lud 2. ljut 3. **He's mad about football.** On je zaluđen fudbalom/nogometom.

madam [ˈmædəm] *n* gospođa

madden [ˈmædn] *v* naljutiti

made [meid] *see* **make**

madhouse [ˈmædhaus] *n* ludnica

madman [ˈmædmən] *n* ludak

madness [ˈmædnəs] *n* ludilo

magazine [ˌmægəˈziːn] *n* 1. časopis 2. (mil.) magacin

magic [ˈmædʒik] 1. *adj* čaroban 2. *n* čarolije

magical [ˈmædʒikl] *adj* magičan

magician [məˈdʒiʃn] *n* čarobnjak

magistrate [ˈmædʒistreit] *n* sudija; sudac

magistrate's court *n* sud za prekršaje

magnet [ˈmægnit] *n* magnet

magnificent [mægˈnifisnt] *adj* veličanstven

magnify [ˈmægnifai] *v* uveličati

magnifying glass [ˈmægnifaiŋ] *n* lupa

magnitude [ˈmægnitjuːd] *n* veličina

mahogany [məˈhɒgəni] *n* mahagoni

maid [meid] *n* sluškinja

maiden [ˈmeidn] *n* devojka; djevojka

maiden name *n* devojačko prezime; djevojačko prezime

mail [meil] 1. *n* pošta 2. **registered mail** preporučene pošiljke 3. **express mail** ekspreno isporučivanje 4. *v* poslati

mail-bag [ˈmeilbæg] *n* poštarska torba

mail bomb [ˈmeilbɒm] *see* **letter bomb**

mailbox [ˈmeilbɒks] *n* poštansko sanduče

mailman [ˈmeilmæn] *n* poštar

mail-order [ˈmeilɔːdə] *n* porudžbina koja se šalje poštom

maim [meim] *v* osakatiti

main [mein] *adj* glavni

mainland [ˈmeinlænd] *n* kopno

main line *n* glavna pruga

mainly [ˈmeinli] *adv* uglavnom

mainstay [ˈmeinstei] *n* glavna potpora

maintain [meinˈtein] *v* 1. održati 2. (fin.) izdržati

maintenance [ˈmeintənəns] *n* 1. održavanje 2. (fin.) izdržavanje

maize [meiz] *n* kukuruz

majestic [məˈdʒestik] *adj* veličanstven

majesty [ˈmædʒəsti] n Your Majesty Vaše veličanstvo
major [ˈmeidʒə] 1. adj glavni 2. n (mil.) major
major powers pl (pol.) velike sile
major-general n (mil.) general-potpukovnik
majority [məˈdʒɔrəti] n 1. većina 2. absolute majority apsolutna većina
majority rule n vladavina većine
make [meik; meid] 1. n tip 2. v (made) napraviti 3. spremiti 4. navesti
make a decision v doneti odluku
make fun of v terati šegu s; tjerati šegu s
make love v umiljavati se
make out v razabrati
make out a cheque v napisati ček
maker [ˌmeikə] n trasant
makeshift [ˈmeikʃift] adj improvizovan
make-up n 1. šmika 2. to put on make-up staviti šminku
make up v 1. našminkati 2. isfabrikovati 3. nadoknaditi 4. sačinjavati
make up one's mind v odlučiti se
malady [ˈmælədi] n bolets
malaria [məleəriə] n malarija
male [meil] 1. adj muško 2. n mužjak
malice [ˈmælis] n pakost
malicious [məˈliʃəs] adj pakostan
malign [məˈlain] v oklevetati
malignant [məˈlignənt] adj maligni
mall [mɔl] n trgovački centar
malnourished [mælˈnʌriʃt] adj pothranjen
malnutrition [ˌmælnjuːˈtriʃn] n pothranjenost

malpractice [mælˈpraktis] n nesavestan postupak; nesavjestan postupak
mammal [ˈmæml] n sisar
man [mæn] n (pl men) čovek; čovjek
manage [ˈmænidʒ] v 1. rukovoditi 2. doviti se 3. uspeti; uspjeti
management [ˈmænidʒmənt] n 1. rukovođenje 2. uprava
manager [ˈmænidʒə] n 1. šef 2. poslovođa 3. menadžer
managing director n upravnik
mandate [ˈmændeit] n mandat
mandatory [mænˈdeitəri] adj mandatni
mane [mein] n griva
maneuver [məˈnuːvə] see manoeuvre
mango [ˌmæŋgəu] n mango
manhood [ˈmænhud] n muškost
manhour [ˈmænæuə] n radni čas; radni sat
manhunt [ˈmænhʌnt] n potera; potjera
mania [ˈmeiniə] n manija
maniac [ˈmeiniæk] n manijak
manicure [ˈmænikjuə] v manikir
manifest [ˈmænifest] v pokazati
manifesto [ˌmæniˈfestəu] n 1. manifest 2. the Communist Manifesto Komunistički manifest
manioc [ˈmæniɔk] n maniok
manipulate [məˈnipjuleit] v manipulisati
manipulation [məˌnipjuˈleiʃn] n manipulacija
mankind [mænˈkaind] n čovečanstvo; čovječanstvo
man-made adj urađen od čoveka/čovjeka
mannequin [ˈmænikin] n maneken

manner [ˈmænə] n 1. način 2. see manners

manners [ˈmænəz] pl maniri

mannerism [ˈmænərizm] n osobina

manoeuvre [məˈnuːvə] 1. n manevar 2. **to hold manouevres** održati manevre 3. v manevrisati 4. see manoeuvres

manoeuvres [məˈnuːvəz] n (mil.) 1. manevri 2. **land manoeuvres** kopneni manevri 3. **sea manoeuvres** pomorski manevri

manor [ˈmænə] n plemićka kuća

manpower [ˈmænpauə] n radna snaga

mansion [ˈmænʃn] n zdanje

manslaughter [ˈmænslɔːtə] n ubistvo (bez predumišljaja)

mantelpiece [ˈmæntlpiːs] n okvir kamina

mantle [ˈmæntl] n ogrtač

man-trap [ˈmæntræp] n klopka za ljude

manual [ˌmænjuəl] 1. adj ručni 2. n priručnik

manufacture [ˌmænjuˈfæktʃə] 1. n fabrikat 2. v proizvoditi

manufactured [ˌmænjuˈfæktʃəd] adj proizveden

manufacturer [ˌmænjuˈfæktʃərə] n fabrikant

manufacturing [ˌmænjuˈfæktʃəriŋ] n industrijska prerada

manure [məˈnjuə] n đubre

manuscript [ˈmænjuskript] n rukopis

many [ˈmeni] adj 1. mnogi 2. **as many as** ne manje od 3. **how many?** koliko

map [mæp] n karta

map grid n koordinatna mreža karte

map out v planirati

mar [maː] v pokvariti

marathon [ˈmærəθən] n maraton

marble [ˈmaːbl] n mermer

march [maːtʃ] 1. n marš 2. v (mil.) maršovati

March n mart; ožujak

mare [meə] n kobila

margarine [ˌmaːdʒəˈriːn] n margarin

margin [ˈmaːdʒin] n 1. ivica 2. **margin of error** granica dozvoljenih grešaka

marginal [ˈmaːdʒinəl] adj 1. krajnji 2. (fin.) granični

marijuana [ˌmæriˈhwaːnə] n marihuana

marine [məˈriːn] 1. adj pomorski 2. n marinac

mariner [ˈmærinə] n pomorac

maritime [ˈmæritaim] adj pomorski

maritime law n pomorsko pravo

mark [maːk] 1. n znak 2. (acad.) ocena; ocjena 3. v obeležiti; obilježiti 4. (acad.) oceniti; ocijeniti 5. see deutschmark

marker [ˈmaːkə] n signal

market [ˈmaːkit] 1. adj tržišni 2. n tržište 3. v prodati 4. see black market

market competition n tržišna konkurencija

marketing [ˈmaːkitiŋ] n marketing

marketing board n marketinški odbor

mark out v obeležiti; obilježiti

mark up v povisiti

marmalade [ˈmaːməleid] n (UK) marmelada

marriage [ˈmæridʒ] n brak

married [ˈmærid] adj 1. **married life** bračni život 2. **a married woman** udata žena 3. **a married man** oženjen čovek/čovjek

marrow ['mærəu] *n* 1. tikva 2. srž
marry ['mæri] *v* 1. venčati; vjenčati
2. **to marry (a man)** udati se za
3. **to marry (a woman)** oženiti
se 4. **to get married** venčati se;
vjenčati se
marsh [ma:ʃ] *n* močvara
marshal ['ma:ʃl] *n* maršal
marshy ['ma:ʃi] *adj* močvara
martial ['ma:ʃl] *adj* vojni
martial law *n* opsadno stanje
martyr ['ma:tə] *n* mučenik
martyrdom ['ma:tədəm] *n*
mučeništvo
marvel ['ma:vl] *v* čuditi se
marvellous ['ma:vələs] *adj*
veličanstven
Marxism ['ma:ksizəm] *n* marksizam
masculine ['mæskjulin] *adj* muški
masculinity [,mæskju'liniti] *n*
muškost
mash [mæʃ] *v* izgnječiti
mask [ma:sk] 1. *n* maska 2. *v*
maskirati
mason ['meisn] *n* zidar
mass [mæs] 1. *adj* masovan 2. *n*
masa 3. (rel.) misa 4. *v*
koncentrisati
massacre ['mæsəkə] 1. *n* pokolj 2. *v*
masakrirati
massage ['mæsa:ʒ] 1. *n* masaža 2. *v*
masirati
mass-circulation newspaper *n*
visokotiražni list
mass communications *pl* sredstva
javnog informisanja
mass consumption *n* masovna
potrošnja
mass destruction *n* masovno
uništavanje
mass execution *n* masovno
streljanje/strijeljanje

massive ['mæsiv] *adj* masivan
mass media *n* sredstva javnog
informisanja
mass meeting *n* miting
mass migration *n* masovna
migracija
mass murder *n* masovno ubijanje
mass-produce *v* masovno
proizvoditi
mass production *n* masovna
proizvodnja
mast [ma:st] *n* jarbol
master ['ma:stə] 1. *n* gospodar 2. *v*
ovladiti 3. *see* **schoolmaster**
Master's ['ma:stəz] *n* (acad.)
magisterij
masterful ['ma:stəfəl] *adj*
zapovednički; zapovjednički
masterpiece ['ma:stəpi:s] *n* remek-
delo/djelo
mastery ['ma:stəri] *n* vladanje
mat [mæt] *n* otirač
match [mætʃ] 1. *n* šibica 2. (spor.)
utakmica 3. *v* odgovarati
matchbox *n* kutija šibica
matchstick *n* šibica
matchless ['mætʃlis] *adj* bez
premca
mate [meit] 1. *n* drug 2. *v* pariti se
material [mə'tiəriəl] *n* 1. štof 2.
materijal 3. *see* **materials**
materialize [mə'tiəriəlaiz] *v*
ostvariti (se)
materials [mə'tiəriəlz] *pl* 1.
building materials građevinski
materijal 2. **raw materials**
sirovina
materiel [mə'tiəriəl] *n* **war
materiel** borbena tehnika
maternal [mə'tə:nl] *adj* materinski
maternity [mə'tə:nəti] *n*
materinstvo

maternity clinic *n* porodilište; rodilište

maternity leave *n* porodiljsko odsustvo; porodiljni dopust

maths, mathematics [mæθs; ˌmæθəˈmætiks] *n* matematika

matinee [ˈmætinei] *n* matine

matrimonial [ˌmætriməniəl] *adj* bračni

matrimony [ˈmætriməni] *n* brak

matron [ˈmeitrən] *n* (med) nadzornica

matter [ˈmætə] 1. *n* stvar 2. materija 3. What's the matter? O čemu se radi? 4. *v* mariti 5. It doesn't matter. Ne mari.

mattress [ˈmætris] *n* dušek

mature [məˈtjuə] 1. *adj* zreo 2. *v* sazreti

maturity [məˈtjuərəti] *n* zrelost

mausoleum [ˌmɔːsəˈliːəm] *n* mauzolej

maxim [ˈmæksim] *n* maksima

maximize [ˈmæksimaiz] *v* maksimirati

maximum [ˈmæksiməm] 1. *adj* maksimalan 2. *n* maksimum

May [mei] *n* maj; svibanj

may [mei] *v* (**might**) 1. May I come with you? Mogu li poći sa vama? 2. I may come with you. Možda ću poći sa vama.

maybe [ˈmeibi] *adv* možda

mayonnaise [ˌmejəˈnaiz] *n* majonez

mayor [ˈmeə] *n* gradonačelnik

MBA [embiːˈei] *n* magistar poslovne administracije

me [miː] *pro* mene, me, meni, mi, mnom, ja

meadow [ˈmedəu] *n* livada

meagre, meager [ˈmiːgə] *adj* oskudan

meal [miːl] *n* obed; objed

meal-time *n* vreme jela; vrijeme jela

mean [miːn] 1. *adj* podao 2. bedan; bijedan 3. (fin.) srednji 4. *n* (fin.) sredina 5. *v* (**meant**) značiti 6. hteti; htjeti

meaning [ˈmiːniŋ] *n* načenje

meaningful [ˈmiːniŋfəl] *adj* značajan

meaningless [ˈmiːniŋləs] *adj* bez značenja

means [miːnz] *n* 1. sredstvo 2. način 3. **means of support** sredstva za život

meant [ment] *see* **mean**

meantime [ˈmiːntaim] *n* **in the meantime** u međuvremenu; u međuvrijemenu

meanwhile [ˈmiːnwail] *adv* u međuvremenu; u međuvrijemenu

measles [ˈmiːzlz] *n* male boginje

measurable [ˈmeʒərəbl] *adj* merljiv; mjerljiv

measure [ˈmeʒə] 1. *n* mera; mjera 2. *v* izmeriti; izmjeriti 3. *see* **measures**

measurement [ˈmeʒəmənt] *n* dimenzija

measures [ˈmeʒəz] *pl* **to take measures** preduzeti mere/mjere

meat [miːt] *n* meso

mechanic [miˈkænik] *n* mehaničar

mechanical [miˈkænikl] *adj* mašinski

mechanics [miˈkæniks] *n* mehanika

mechanism [ˈmekənizm] *n* mehanizam

mechanization [ˌmekənaiˈzeiʃn] *n* mehanizacija

mechanize [ˈmekənaiz] *v* mehanizovati

medal [ˈmedl] *n* medalja

medalist [ˈmedl] *n* dobitnik medalje

meddle [ˈmedl] *v* mešati se; miješati se

media [ˈmiːdiə] *see* **mass media**
mediaeval [ˈmiːdiə] *see* **medieval**
mediate [ˈmiːdieit] *v* posredovati
mediation [ˌmiːdiˈeiʃn] *n* posredništvo
mediator [ˈmiːdieitə] *n* posrednik
medical [ˈmedikl] *adj* lekarski; ljekarski
medical school *n* medicinski fakultet
medicate [ˈmedikeit] *v* lečiti; liječiti
medication [ˌmediˈkeiʃn] *n* lek; lijek
medicinal [məˈdisinl] *adj* lekovit; ljekovit
medicine [ˈmedsn] *n* 1. medicina 2. lek; lijek
medieval [ˌmediˈiːvl] *adj* medievalan
mediocre [ˌmiːdiˈəukə] *adj* osrednji
mediocrity [ˌmiːdiˈɔkrəti] *n* osrednjost
meditate [ˈmediteit] *v* razmišljati
meditation [ˌmediˈteiʃn] *n* razmišljanje
Mediterranean Sea [ˌmeditəˈreiniən ˈsiː] *n* Mediteran, Sredozemno more
medium [ˈmiːdiəm] 1. *adj* srednji 2. *n* sredstvo 3. (fin.) sredina
medium-range missiles *pl* rakete srednjeg dometa
medium-sized *adj* srednje veličine
meek [miːk] *adj* krotak
meekness [ˈmiːknis] *n* krotkost
meet [miːt] 1. *n* (spor.) takmičenje 2. *v* (met) sresti (se)
meeting [ˈmiːtiŋ] *n* 1. sastanak 2. miting
melancholic [ˈmelənkɔli] *adj* melanholičan
melody [ˈmelədi] *n* melodija
melon [ˈmelən] *n* dinja
melt [melt] *v* istopiti (se)

member [ˈmembə] *n* član
member of parliament *n* član parlamenta
membership [ˈmembəʃip] *n* članstvo
memo [ˈmeməu] *see* **memorandum**
memoirs [ˈmemuaːz] *pl* memoari
memorable [ˈmemərəbl] *adj* znamenit
memorandum [ˌmeməˈrændəm] *n* beleška; bilješka
memorial [məˈmɔːriəl] *n* 1. spomenik 2. komemoracija
memorize [ˈmeməraiz] *v* naučiti napamet
memory [ˈmeməri] *n* 1. pamćenje 2. memorija 3. uspomena
men [men] *see* **man**
menace [ˈmenəs] 1. *n* pretnja; prijetnja 2. *v* zapretiti; zaprijetiti
mend [mend] *v* zakrpiti
meningitis [ˌmeninˈdʒaitəs] *n* meningitis
menopause [ˌmenəˈpɔːz] *n* menopauza
menstruate [ˈmenstrueit] *v* menstruisati
menstruation [ˌmenstruˈeiʃn] *n* menstruacija
mental [ˈmentl] *adj* mentalni
mental home *n* bolnica za mentalne bolesnike
mental health *n* mentalno zdravlje
mental hospital *n* bolnica za mentalne bolesnike
mentality [menˈtæləti] *n* mentalitet
mention [ˈmenʃn] 1. *n* pomen 2. *v* pomenuti 3. **Don't mention it!** Nema na čemu!
menu [ˈmenjuː] *n* meni
mercantile [ˈməːkəntail] *adj* trgovački
mercenary [ˈməːsinəri] *n* najamnik

merchandise [ˈməːʃəndaiz] n roba
merchant [ˈməːtʃənt] n trgovac
merciful [ˈməːsifl] adj milosrdan
merciless [ˈməːsilis] adj nemilosrdan
mercury [ˈməːkjuri] n živa
mercy [ˈməːsi] n milost
mere [ˈmiə] adj čist
merely [ˈmiəli] adv samo
merge [ˈməːdʒ] v integrisati (se)
merger [ˈməːdʒə] n integracija
meridian [məˈridiən] n meridijan
merit [ˈmerit] 1. n zasluga 2. v zaslužiti
merry [ˈmeri] adj veseo
merry-making n veselje
mesh [meʃ] n mreža
mess [mes] n 1. nered 2. see **mess up**
message [ˈmesidʒ] n poruka
messenger [ˈmesindʒə] n kurir
mess up v 1. napraviti džumbus od 2. upropastiti stvari
messy [ˈmesi] adj u neredu
met [met] see **meet**
metal [ˈmetl] 1. adj metalan 2. n metal
metallic [miˈtælik] adj metalan
metallurgy [meˈtælədʒi] n metalurgija
metaphor [ˈmetəfɔː] n metafora
meteor [ˈmiːtiə] n meteor
meteoric [ˌmiːtiˈɔrik] adj meteorski
meteorologist [ˌmiːtiəˈrɔlədʒist] n meteorolog
meteorology [ˌmiːtiəˈrɔlədʒi] n meteorologija
meter [ˈmiːtə] n 1. merač; mjerač 2. (US) metar
method [ˈmeθəd] n metod
methodical [miˈθɔdikl] adj metodičan

meticulous [miˈtikjuləs] adj minuciozan
metre [ˈmiːtə] n metar
metro [ˈmetrəu] n metro
metropolis [məˈtrɔpəlis] n metropola
mice [mais] see **mouse**
microphone [ˈmaikrəfəun] n mikrofon
microprocessor [ˌmaikrəuˈprəusesə] n mikroprocesor
microscope [ˈmaikrəskəup] n mikroskop
microwave (oven) [ˈmaikrəuweiv] n šporet na mikrotalase
mid [mid] adj srednji
midday [ˌmidˈdei] n podne
middle [ˈmidl] 1. adj srednji 2. n sredina 3. **in the middle of** usred
middle-age n srednje godine života
middle-aged adj sredovečan, sredovječan
middle-class 1. adj buržoaski 2. n srednja klasa
Middle East n Bliski istok
middleman [ˈmidlmæn] n posrednik
middle school n srednja škola
midget [ˈmidʒit] n patuljak
midi [ˈmidi] adj midi
midlife [ˈmidlaif] n srednje godine
midnight [ˈmidnait] n ponoć
midst [midst] n **in the midst of** usred
midsummer [ˌmidˈsʌmə] n sredina leta/ljeta
midway [ˌmidˈwei] adv supola puta
midweek [ˌmidˈwiːk] n sredina sedmice
midwife [ˈmidwaif] n babica
midwifery [midˈwifəri] n akušerstvo
might [mait] 1. n snaga 2. see **may**
might and main iz sve snage
mighty [ˈmaiti] adj snažan

migraine [ˈmaigrein; ˈmiːgrein] *n* migrena

migrant [ˈmaigrənt] **1.** *adj* koji se seli **2.** *n* onaj koji se seli

migrant worker *n* sezonski radnik

migrate [maiˈgreit] *v* seliti se

migration [maiˈgreiʃən] *n* seoba

mild [maild] *adj* blag

mile [mail] *n* milja

mileage [ˈmailidʒ] *n* miljaža

militancy [ˈmilitənsi] *n* borbenost

militant [ˈmilitənt] *n* borbeni aktivista

militarily [ˌmiliˈterəli] *adv* vojno

militarize [ˌmiliˈteraiz] *v* militarizovati

military [ˈmilitri] **1.** *adj* vojni **2.** *n* vojska

military academy *n* vojna akademija

military affairs *n* vojna pitanja

military court *n* vojni sud

military expert *n* vojni stručnjak

military government *n* vojna vlada

military honours *pl* vojne počasti

military intelligence *n* obaveštajna služba; obavještajna služba

military law *n* vojno sudstvo

military might *n* vojna moć

military police *n* vojna policija

military regime *n* vojni režim

military rule *n* vojna vlast

military uniform *n* vojna uniforma

militia [miˈliʃə] *n* narodna vojska

milk [milk] **1.** *n* mleko; mlijeko **2. powdered milk** mleko u prahu; mlijeko u prahu **3.** *v* pomusti

milkman [ˈmilkmən] *n* mlekar; mljekar

milky [ˈmilki] *adj* mlečan; mliječan

mill [mil] *n* **1.** mlinac **2.** kombinat

millennium [miˈleniəm] *n* milenijum

millet [ˈmilit] *n* proso

million [ˈmiljən] *n* milion

millionaire [ˌmiljəˈneə] *n* milionar; milijunar

mime [maim] **1.** *n* mim **2.** *v* glumiti

mimic [ˈmimik] **1.** *n* mimičar **2.** *v* majmunisati

minaret [ˌminəˈret] *n* minaret

mince [mins] *n* iseckano meso; isjeckano meso

mind [maind] **1.** *n* um **2. to change one's mind** predomisliti se **3.** *v* čuvati **4.** imati nešto protiv **5. Never mind!** Ne brini! **6. I don't mind!** Svejedno mi je! **7. Mind your own business!** Gledaj svoja!

mind-altering *adj* halucinogen

mind-altering drugs *pl* halucinogena sredstva

mindful [ˈmaindfl] *adj* svestan; svjestan

mine [main] **1.** *pro* moj, moja, moje, moji **2.** *n* rudnik **3.** (mil.) mina **4. antipersonnel mine** protivpešadijska mina; protupješadijska mina **5. antitank mine** protivoklopna mina **6. contact mine** kontaktna mina **7. floating mine** plutajuća mina **8. fragmentation mine** rasprskavajuća mina **9. magnetic mine** magnetska mina **10. pressure mine** mina nagaznog **11. tripwire mine** mina poteznog **12. to lay mines** postaljati mine **13. to hit a mine** nagaziti na minu **14. to clear mines** ukloniti mine **15.** *v* kopati **16.** (mil.) minirati

mine detector n minodetektor
mine disposal n dezaktiviranje mina
miner ['mainə] n kopač
mine field n minsko polje
minelayer n minopolagač
mineral ['minərəl] 1. adj mineralni 2. n mineral
minerals ['minərəlz] pl osvežavajuća pića; osvježavajuća pića
mineral water n mineralna voda
mine sweep n minolovka
mine sweeper n minolovac
mingle ['miŋgl] v umešati se; umiješati se
mini ['mini] adj mini
miniature ['minətʃə] adj minijaturan
minibus ['minibʌs] n minibus
minimize ['minimaiz] v umanjiti
minimum ['miniməm] 1. adj minimalan 2. n minimum
mining ['mainiŋ] 1. adj rudarski 2. n rudarstvo
minister ['ministə] n 1. (pol.) ministar 2. (rel.) sveštenik; svećenik
minister of state n ministar
ministry ['ministri] n ministarstvo
minor ['mainə] 1. adj manji 2. n maloletnik; maloljetnik
minority [mai'nɔrəti] 1. adj manjinska 2. n manjina 3. **ethnic minority** etnička manjina 4. **national minority** nacionalna manjina
minority group n manjinska grupa
minority leader n vođa manjine
minority rights n manjinska prava
minority rule n vladavina manjine
mint [mint] 1. adj nanin 2. **mint tea** nanin čaj 3. n nana 4. kovnica 5. v kovati

minus ['mainəs] prep manje
minute [mai'njuːt] adj 1. sitan 2. detaljan
minute ['minit] n minut
minutes ['minits] pl **minutes of a meeting** zapisnik
miracle ['mirəkl] n čudo
miraculous [mi'rækjuləs] adj čudotvoran
mirror ['mirə] n ogledalo
mirth [mɔːθ] n veselje
misadventure [,misəd'ventʃə] n nezgoda
misapply ['misə'plai] v rđavo primeniti/primijeniti
misapprehension [,misapri'henʃn] n zabluda
misbehave [,misbi'heiv] v rđavo se ponašati
misbehaviour [,misbi'heiviə] n rđavo ponašanje
miscalculate [mis'kælkjuleit] v pogrešno izračuniti
miscalculation [,miskælkju'leiʃn] n pogrešan račun
miscarriage ['miskæridʒ] n (med.) pobačaj
miscarriage of justice ['miskæridʒ] n pogrešna presuda
miscarry [mis'kæri] v (med.) pobaciti
miscellaneous [,misə'leiniəs] adj raznovrstan
mischance [mis'tʃaːns] n zla sreća
mischief ['mistʃif] n šteta
mischievous ['mistʃivəs] adj štetan
misconduct [,mis'kɔndʌkt] n rđavo ponašanje
misdeed ['mis'diːd] n nedelo; nedjelo
misdemeanour [,misdəmiːnə] n prekršaj

miserable [ˈmizrəbl] *adj* 1. bedan; bijedan 2. rđav

miserly [ˈmaizəli] *adj* tvrd

misery [ˈmizəri] *n* beda; bijeda

misfire [ˌmisˈfaiəd] *v* otkazati

misfortune [ˌmisˈfɔːtʃuːn] *n* nesreća

misgivings [misˈgiviŋz] *pl* sumnje

misguide [ˌmisˈgaid] *v* dovesti u zabludu

mishap [ˈmishæp] *n* nesrećan slučaj

mishear [misˈhiːə] *v* (**misheard**) pogrešno čuti

misinterpret [ˌmisinˈtəːprit] *v* pogrešno shvatiti

misjudge [ˌmisˈdʒʌdʒ] *v* rđavo proceniti/procijeniti

mislay [ˌmisˈlei] *v* zagubiti

mislead [ˌmisˈliːd] *v* (**misled**) obmanuti

mismanagement [misˈmænidʒmənt] *n* rđavo upravljanje

misogynist [misˈɔdʒinist] *n* mizogin

misogynistic [mi,sɔdʒiˈnistik] *adj* mizoginistički

misogyny [misˈɔdʒini] *n* mizoginija

misplace [misˈplais] *v* zagubiti

misprint [ˈmisprint] *n* štamparska greška

misrule [ˌmisˈruːl] *n* loša vladavina

miss [mis] 1. *n* promašaj 2. **Miss** gospodica 3. *v* promašiti 4. propustiti 5. nedostajati 6. faliti 7. **They missed the plane.** Promašili su avion./Propustili su avion.

misshapen [ˌmisˈʃeipən] *n* unakažen

missile [ˈmisail] *n* 1. raketa 2. **guided missile** vođena raketa

missing [ˈmisiŋ] *adj* **to be missing** nestao

missing in action *adj* nestao u borbi

mission [ˈmiʃn] *n* 1. misija 2. (rel.) misionarski rad 3. **diplomatic mission** diplomatsko predstavništvo 4. **to fly a mission** izvršiti borbeni let 5. **to carry out a mission** obaviti zadatak

missionary [ˈmiʃənri] *n* (rel.) misionar

mist [mist] *n* sumaglica

mistake [misˈteik] 1. *n* greška 2. **by mistake** greškom 3. **to make a mistake** napraviti grešku 4. *v* (**mistook, mistaken**) zameniti; zamijeniti

mistaken [misˈteikn] *adj* 1. u zabludi 2. *see* **mistake**

mister [ˈmistə] *see* **Mr**

mistook [ˈmistə] *see* **mistake**

mistreat [misˈtriːt] *v* matretirati

mistreatment [misˈtriːtmənt] *n* maltretiranje

mistress [ˈmistris] *n* 1. metresa 2. *see* **Mrs**, **schoolmistress**

mistrust [ˌmisˈtrʌst] 1. *n* nepoverenje; nepovjerenje 2. *v* nemati poverenja; nemati povjerenja

mistrustful [misˈtrʌstfl] *adj* nepoverljiv; nepovjerljiv

misty [ˈmisti] *adj* maglovit

misunderstand [ˌmisʌndəˈstænd] *v* (**misunderstood**) razumeti; razumjeti

misunderstanding [ˌmisʌndəˈstændiŋ] *n* nesporazum

misuse [ˌmisˈjuːz] *v* zloupotrebiti; zloupotrijebiti

mitigate [ˈmitigeit] *v* ublažiti

mix [miks] 1. *n* mešavina; mješavina 2. *v* pomešati; pomiješati

mixed [mikst] *adj* mešovit; mješovit

mixed race *adj* mešovite rase; mješovite rase

mixed up *adj* 1. pomesati; pomijesati 2. **to be mixed up in** upetljati se u

mixer [ˈmiksə] *n* mutilica, mikser

mixture [ˈmikstʃə] *n* mešavina; mješavina

mix-up *n* 1. konfuzija 2. *see* **mixed up**

moan [məun] 1. *n* jecaj 2. *v* ječati

mob [mɔb] *n* 1. gomila 2. banda

mobile [ˈməubail] *adj* pokretan

mobile home *n* pokretna kuća

mobile phone *n* mobilni telefon

mobility [məuˈbiləti] *n* pokretljivost

mobilization [ˌməubilaiˈzeiʃn] *n* mobilizacija

mobilize [ˈməubilaiz] *v* mobilisati (se)

mob rule *n* zakon rulje

mock [mɔk] *v* rugati se

mockery [ˈmɔkəri] *n* parodija

mode [məud] *n* modalitet

model [ˈmɔdl] 1. *n* model 2. maketa 3. **fashion model** manekenka 4. *v* izvajati

modem [ˈməudem] *n* modem

moderate [ˈmɔdəret] 1. *adj* umeren; umjeren 2. srednji 3. *n* (pol.) umerenjak; umjerenjak

moderate [ˈmɔdəreit] *v* umeriti; umjeriti

moderation [ˌmɔdəˈreiʃn] *n* umerenost; umjerenost

modern [ˈmɔdn] *adj* moderan

modernize [ˈmɔdənaiz] *v* modernizovati

modest [ˈmɔdist] *adj* skroman

modesty [ˈmɔdisti] *n* skromnost

modification [ˌmɔdifiˈkeiʃn] *n* modifikacija

modify [ˈmɔdifai] *v* modifikovati

moist [mɔist] *adj* vlažan

moisten [ˈmɔisn] *v* ovlažiti

moisture [ˈmɔistʃə] *n* vlaga

moisturize [ˈmɔistʃəraiz] *v* navlažiti

moisturizing cream [ˈmɔistʃə] *n* vlažna krema

molar, molar tooth [ˈməulə] *n* kutnjak

mold [məuld] *see* **mould**

mole [məul] *n* 1. mola 2. krtica 3. špijun

molecule [ˈmɔlekjuːl] *n* molekul

molest [mɔˈlest] *v* molestirati

moment [ˈməumənt] *n* 1. momenat 2. **at the moment** sada 3. **in a moment** uskoro 4. **for the moment** za momenat

momentarily [ˌməumənˈterili] *adv* začas

momentary [ˈməuməntri] *adj* momentalan

momentous [məuˈmentəs] *adj* značajan

momentum [məuˈmentum] *n* impuls

monarch [ˈmɔnək] *n* monarh

monarchist [ˈmɔnəkist] *n* monarhista

monarchy [ˈmɔnəki] *n* monarhija

monastery [ˈmɔnəstri] *n* (rel.) manastir

Monday [ˈmʌndi] *n* ponedeljak; ponedjeljak

monetary [ˈmʌnitri] *adj* novčani

money [ˈmʌni] *n* novac

money-order *n* novčana uputnica

monitor [ˈmɔnitə] *n* (tel.) monitor

monk [mʌŋk] *n* monah

monkey [ˈmʌŋki] *n* majmun

mono- [ˈmɔnəu] *adj* mono-, jedno-

monopolize [məˈnɔpəlaiz] *v* monopolizovati

monopoly [mə'nɔpəli] *n* monopol

monotonous [mə'nɔtənəs] *adj* monoton

monotony [mə'nɔtəni] *n* monotonija

monster ['mɔnstə] *n* čudovište

monstrous ['mɔnstrəs] *adj* čudovišan

Montenegrin [,mɔntə'negrən] **1.** *adj* crnogorski **2.** *n* Crnogorac

Montenegro [,mɔntə'negrəu] *n* Crna Gora

month [mʌnθ] *n* mesec; mjesec

monthly ['mʌnθli] *adj* mesečni; mjesečni

monument ['mɔnjumənt] *n* spomenik

mood [muːd] *n* **1. to be in a good mood** biti u dobrom raspoloženju **2. to be in a bad mood** biti u rđavom raspoloženju **3. to be in the mood for** biti raspoložen za

moon [muːn] *n* Mesec; Mjesec

moonlight ['muːnlait] *n* mesečina; mjesečina

moonstruck ['muːnstrʌk] *adj* šašav

moor [mɔː] **1.** *n* vresište **2.** *v* lengerisati

mooring ['mɔːriŋ] *n* sidrište

moral ['mɔrəl] *adj* **1.** moralan **2.** *see* **morals**

morale [mə'ræl] *n* moral

morality [mə'ræləti] *n* moralnost

morals ['mɔrəlz] *n* moral

morbid ['mɔːbid] *adj* morbidan

more [mɔː] *adj/adv* **1.** više **2. more and more** sve više **3. more or less** manje-više

more than 1. više od **2. more than ever** više nego ikad

moreover [mɔː'rəuvə] *conj* osim toga

morning ['mɔːniŋ] *n* **1.** jutro **2. Good morning!** Dobro jutro!

morning sickness *n* mučnina (u trudnoći)

morsel ['mɔːsl] *n* komadić

mortal ['mɔːtl] **1.** *adj* smrtan **2. mortal wound** smrtosna rana **3.** *n* smrtnik

mortality [mɔː'tæləti] *n* **1.** smrtnost **2.** mortalitet

mortality rate *n* stopa smrtnosti

mortar ['mɔːtə] *n* **1.** stupa **2.** malter **3.** (mil.) minobacač

mortar fire *n* artiljerijska vatra, granatiranje

mortgage ['mɔːgidʒ] *n* hipoteka

mortgagee [,mɔːgə'dʒiː] *n* hipotekarni veronik/vjerovnik

mortuary ['mɔːtʃəri] *n* mrtvačnica

Moslem ['mʌzlim] **1.** *adj* muslimanski **2.** *n* Musliman

mosque [mɔsk] *n* džamija

mosquito [mɔs'kiːtəu] *n* komarac

mosquito net *n* mreža protiv komaraca

moss [mɔs] *n* mahovina

most [məust] *adj/adv* **1.** najviše **2.** vrlo **3. most of all** više od svega **4. for the most part** najvećim delom/dijelom **5. to make the most of** iskoristiti na najbolji način

mostly ['məustli] *adv* uglavnom

motel [məu'tel] *n* motel

moth [mɔθ] *n* noćni leptir, moljac

mother ['mʌðə] *n* majka

motherhood ['mʌðəhud] *n* materinstvo

mother-in-law *n* tašta, svekrva

motherland ['mʌðəlænd] *n* otadžbina

motherly ['mʌðəli] *adj* materinski

mother-tongue *n* maternji jezik

motif [məu'tiːf] *n* motiv

motion [ˈməuʃn] *n* **1.** pokret **2.** (pol.) predlog **3. to set in motion** staviti u pokret

motionless [ˈməuʃnlis] *adj* nepokretan

motion picture *n* kino-film

motivate [ˈməutiveit] *v* motivisati

motivation [ˈməutiveiʃn] *n* motivacija

motive [ˈməutiv] *n* pobuda

motor [ˈməutə] *n* motor

motor boat *n* motorni čamac

motorbike [ˈməutəbaik] *n* motocickl

motor car *n* automobil

motorcycle [ˈməutəˌsaikl] *n* motocickl

motorcyle rider *n* motociklista

motoring [ˈməutəriŋ] *n* vožnja automobilom

motorist [ˈməutərist] *n* automobilista

motor scooter *n* moped

motorway [ˈməutəwei] *n* autoput

motto [ˈmɔtəu] *n* geslo

mould [məuld] **1.** *n* kalup **2.** bud **3.** *v* ukalupiti

mouldy [ˈməuldi] *adj* buđav

mound [maund] *n* nasip

mount [maunt] **1.** *n* jahaći konj **2.** *v* uzjahati

mount an attack *v* organizovati napad

mountain [ˈmauntin] *n* planina

mountaineer [ˌmauntiˈniə] *n* alpinista

mountainous [ˈmauntinəs] *adj* planinski

mourn [mɔːn] *v* oplakati

mourner [ˈmɔːnə] *n* ožalošćeni

mourning [ˈmɔːniŋ] *n* **1.** oplakivanje **2. national mourning** narodna žalost

mouse [maus] *n* (*pl* **mice**) miš

moustache [məˈstaːʃ] *n* brkovi

mouth [mauθ] *n* usta

mouthful [ˈmauθful] *n* zalogaj

mouthpiece [ˈmauθpiːs] *see* **spokesman**

mouthwash *n* tečnost za ispiranje usta; tekućina za ispiranje usta

movable [ˈmuːvəbl] *adj* pokretan

move [muːv] **1.** *n* pokret **2.** *v* kretati se **3.** ići **4.** napredovati

move house *v* preseliti se

movement [ˈmuːvmənt] *n* **1.** pokret **2.** (com.) romet **3.** (pol.) pokret

movie, movies [ˈmuːvi; ˈmuːviz] *n* kino-film

movie theatre *n* bioskop

moving [muːviŋ] *adj* dirljiv

mow [məu] *v* (**mowed, mown**) kositi

MP (member of parliament) *n* član Parlamenta

m.p.h. (miles per hour) milja na sat

Mr (mister) [ˈmistə] gospodin

Mrs (mistress) [ˈmisiz] gospođa

Ms [məz; miz] gospođica

MSc *n* magistar prirodnih nauka/ znanosti

Mt *see* **mount**

much [mʌtʃ] *adj/adv* **1.** mnogo **2.** veći **3. much more** mnogo više **4. how much?** koliko?

mud [mʌd] *n* blato

muddle [ˈmʌdl] *n* zbrka

muddy [ˈmʌdi] *adj* blatnjav

mudguard [ˈmʌdgaːd] *n* blatobran

muezzin [muˈezin] *n* mujezin

muffler [ˈmʌflə] *n* salansa, (Nr) shamfama

mug [mʌg] **1.** *n* krigla **2.** *v* napasti i opljačkati

mugger [ˈmʌgə] *n* pljačkaš

mule [mju:l] *n* mazga
multi- [mʌlti] *adj* multi-, više-
multilingual [,mʌlti'lingwəl] *adj* mnogojezički
multilingualism [,mʌlti'lingwəlizm] *n* multilinvalnost, višejezičnost
multimedia [,mʌlti'mi:dia] *n* multimedijumi; multimediji
multinational [,mʌlti'næʃnəl] *adj* multinacionalni
multi-party [,mʌlti'pa:ti] *adj* višepartijski
multiple ['mʌltipl] *n* višestruk
multiplication [,mʌltipli'keiʃn] *n* množenje
multiply ['mʌltiplai] *v* pomnožiti
multi-racial [,mʌlti'reiʃl] *adj* rasno mešovit/mješovit
multistorey, multistory [,mʌlti'stɔ:ri] *adj* višespratan; višekatan
multitude ['mʌltitju:d] *n* bezbroj
mum [mʌm] *n* mama
mumble ['mʌmbl] *v* mrmljati
mummy ['mʌmi] *n* mama
mumps [mʌmps] *n* zauške
municipal [mju:'nisipl] *adj* gradski
municipality [mju:,nisi'pæləti] *n* grad
murder ['mə:də] 1. *n* ubistvo 2. *v* ubiti
murderer ['mə:dərə] *n* ubica
murderess ['mə:dəris] *n* (žena) ubica
murmur ['mə:mə] *v* žagoriti
muscle ['mʌsl] *n* mišić
muscular ['mʌskjulə] *adj* muskulozan
muse [mju:z] *v* razmišljati

museum [mju:'ziəm] *n* muzej
mushroom ['mʌʃrum] *n* gljiva
music ['mju:zik] *n* muzika
musical ['mju:zikl] 1. *adj* muzički 2. *n* mjuzikl
musician [mju:'ziʃn] *n* muzičar
Muslim ['mʌzlim] 1. *adj* muslimanski 2. *n* Musliman
mussel ['mʌsl] *n* mušula
must [məst; mʌst] *v* morati
mustache [mə'sta:ʃ] *n* brkovi
muster ['mʌstə] *v* formirati
mutate [mju:'teit] *v* mutirati
mutation [mju:'teiʃn] *n* mutacija
mute [mju:t] 1. *adj* mutav 2. *n* mutavac
mutilate ['mju:tileit] *v* osakatiti
mutilation [,mju:ti'leiʃn] *n* osakaćenje
mutineer [,mju:ti'niə] *n* pobunjenik
mutiny ['mju:tini] 1. *n* pobuna 2. *v* pobuniti se
mutter ['mʌtə] *v* mrmljati
mutton ['mʌtn] *n* ovčetina
mutual ['mju:tʃuəl] *adj* međusoban
muzzle ['mʌzl] 1. *n* korpa 2. *v* začepiti usta
my [mai] moj, moja, moje
myself [mai'self] ja, ja sam, sebi, sebe, meni, mene
mysterious [mi'stiəriəs] *adj* tajanstven
mystery ['mistəri] *n* misterija
mystic ['mistik] *n* mističar
mystify ['mistifai] *n* mistifikovati
myth [miθ] *n* mit
mythical ['miθikl] *adj* mitski
mythology [mi'θɔlədʒi] *n* mitologija

N

nail [neil] **1.** *n* ekser **2.** nokat **3.** *v* prikovati

naive [naiˑiːv] *adj* naivan

naivety, naivete [naiˑiːviti] *n* naivnost

naked [ˈneikid] *adj* go; gol

nakedness [ˈneikidnəs] *n* nagost

name [neim] **1.** *n* ime **2. in the name of...** u ime... **3. to call names** psovati **4.** *v* naimenovati

name day *n* imendan

nameless [ˈneimlis] *adj* bezimen

namely [ˈneimli] *adv* naime

name-plate *n* pločica sa imenom

namesake [ˈneimseik] *n* imenjak

nanny [ˈnæni] *n* dadilja

nap [næp] *n* **to take a nap** dremnuti

napkin [ˈnæpkin] *n* salvet

nappy [ˈnæpi] *n* pelena

narcotic [naːˈkɔtik] **1.** *adj* narkotičan **2.** *n* narkotik

narrate [nəˈreit] *v* pričati

narration [nəˈreiʃn] *n* pričanje

narrative [ˈnærətiv] *n* pripovest; pripovijest

narrator [nəˈreitə] *n* pripovedač; pripovjedač

narrow [ˈnærəu] *adj* **1.** uzak **2.** tesan; tijesan

narrow-minded *adj* zatucan

narrows [ˈnærəuz] *pl* moreuz

nasty [ˈnaːsti] *adj* gadan

natal [ˈneitəl] *adj* natalni

nation [ˈneiʃn] *n* narod

national [ˈnæʃnəl] **1.** *adj* narodni **2.** *n* državljanin

national anthem *n* državna himna

national dress *n* narodna nošnja

national guard *n* nacionalna garda

nationalism [ˈnæʃnəlizm] *n* nacionalizam

nationalist [ˈnæʃnəlist] **1.** *adj* nacionalistički **2.** *n* nacionalista

nationality [ˌnæʃənæliti] *n* nacionalnost

nationalization [ˌnæʃnəlaiˈzeiʃn] *n* nacionalizacija

nationalize [ˈnæʃnəlaiz] *v* nacionalizovati

national park *n* nacionalni park

national service *n* vojna obaveza

nationhood [ˈneiʃnhud] *n* nacionalnost

national state *n* nacionalna država

nationwide [ˌneiʃnˈwaid] *adv* u celoj zemlji; u cijeloj zemlji

native [ˈneitiv] **1.** *adj* rođeni **2.** *n* urođenik

native country *n* rodna zemlja

native language *n* maternji jezik

NATO (North Atlantic Treaty Organization) [ˈneitəu] *n* severno-atlanski pakt; sjeverno-atlanski pakt

natural [ˈnætʃrəl] *adj* prirodan

natural disaster *n* prirodna katastrofa

natural gas *n* prirodan gas

natural history *n* prirodna istorija

naturalization [ˌnætʃrəlaiˈzeiʃn] *n* naturalizacija

naturalize [ˈnætʃrəlaiz] *v* naturalizovati

naturally [ˈnætʃrəli] *adv* **1.** prirodno **2.** svakako

natural resources *pl* prirodna bogatstva

nature [ˈneitʃə] *n* 1. priroda 2. karakter 3. **human nature** ljudska priroda

naughty [ˈnɔːti] *adj* nestašan

nausea [ˈnɔːsiə] *n* muka

nauseous [ˈnɔːsiəs] *adj* gadan

nautical [ˈnɔːtikl] *adj* pomorski

naval [ˈneivl] *adj* vojnopomorski

naval base *n* vojnopomorska baza

navel [ˈneivl] *n* pupak

navigable [ˈnævigəbl] *adj* plovan

navigate [ˈnævigeit] *v* ploviti

navigation [ˌnæviˈgeiʃn] *n* navigacija

navigational [ˌnæviˈgeiʃnəl] *adj* navigacijski

navigator [ˈnævigeitə] *n* navigator

navy [ˈneivi] *n* ratna mornarica

nazi [ˈnɑːtsi] 1. *adj* nacistički 2. *n* nacista

nazism [ˈnɑːtsizm] *n* nacizam

near, near to [niə] 1. *adj* blizu 2. *adv* bliže 3. **to draw near** približiti se 4. *prep* blizu

nearby [ˈniəbai] *adv* blizu

Near East *n* Bliski istok

nearly [ˈniəli] *adv* 1. umalo 2. skoro

nearness [ˈniənis] *n* blizina

near-sighted *adj* kratkovid

neat [niːt] *adj* uredan

neatness [ˈniːtnis] *n* urednost

necessarily *adv* obavezno

necessary [ˈnesəsəri] *adj* 1. neophodan 2. **it is necessary that...** treba da...

necessity [niˈsesəti] *n* potreba

neck [nek] *n* vrat, šija, grlo

necklace [ˈneklis] *n* ogrlica

necktie [ˈnektai] *n* kravata

need [niːd] 1. *n* potreba 2. **in need**

u bedi 3. *v* trebati 4. **You need to do it.** Ti to moraš učiniti.

needle [ˈniːdl] *n* igla

needless [ˈniːdlis] *adj* nepotreban

needy [ˈniːdi] *adj* siromašan

negative [ˈnegətiv] 1. *adj* odrečan 2. *n* negativ

neglect [niˈglekt] 1. *n* nehat 2. *v* zanemariti

negligence [ˈneglidʒəns] *n* nemar

negligent [ˈneglidʒənt] *adj* nemaran

negotiable [niˈgəuʃiəbl] *adj* prenosiv

negotiate [niˈgəuʃieit] *v* 1. ugovoriti 2. pregovarati

negotiating table [niˈgəuʃieitiŋ] *n* pregovarački sto/stol

negotiation [niˌgəuʃiˈeiʃn] *n* 1. pregovaranje 2. *see* **negotiations**

negotiations [niˌgəuʃiˈeiʃnz] *pl* 1. pregovori 2. **to break off negotiations** prekinuti pregovore

negotiator [niˌgəuʃiˈeitə] *n* pregovarač

neigh [nei] *v* rzati

neighbour, neighbor [ˈneibə] *n* sused; susjed

neighbourhood, neighborhood [ˈneibəhud] *n* susedstvo; susjedstvo

neighbouring, neighboring [ˈneibəriŋ] *adj* susedni; susjedni

neither [ˈnaiðə; ˈniːðə] 1. nijedan 2. nijedan od dvojice

neither... nor ni... ni

neo- [ˈniːəu] *adj* neo-

neo-colonialism [ˈniːəukə-ˈləuniəlizəm] *n* neokolonijalizam

neon [ˈniːɔn] *adj* neonski

neo-nazi [ˈniːəuˈnɑːtsi] *n* neonacist(a)

neon light *n* neonsko svetlo/svjetlo

nephew [ˈnefjuː] *n* nećak, bratanac, sestrić

nerve [nə:v] *n* nerv
nerve gas *n* nervni bojni otrov
nervous [ˈnə:vəs] *adj* nervozan
nervous breakdown *n* živčani slom
nervousness [ˈnə:vəsnis] *n* nervoza
nest [nest] *n* gnezdo; gnijezdo
net [net] **1.** *adj* (fin.) čist **2.** *n* mreža
netball [ˈnetbɔːl] *n* vrsta košarke
Netherlands [ˈneðələndz] *n/pl* Holandija
network [ˈnetwə:k] **1.** *n* mreža **2.** **communications network** telekomunikaciona mreža
neuralgia [njuəˈrældʒə] *n* neuralgija
neurologist [njuəˈrɔlədʒist] *n* neurolog
neurology [njuəˈrɔlədʒi] *n* neurologija
neurosis [njuəˈrəusis] *n* neuroza
neurotic [njuəˈrɔtik] *adj* neurotičan
neuter [ˈnjuːtə] *adj* srednji
neutral [ˈnjuːtrəl] *adj* **1.** neutralan **2.** **in neutral** na prazno
neutral gear *n* prazan hod
neutrality [njuːˈtræləti] *n* neutralnost
neutralize [ˈnjuːtrəlaiz] *v* neutralizovati
never [ˈnevə] *adv* **1.** nikada **2.** **never mind!** ne brini!
never-ending *adj* beskrajan
nevermore [ˈnevəˈmɔ:] *adv* nikad više
nevertheless [ˌnevəðəˈles] *conj* ipak
new [njuː] *adj* **1.** nov **2.** **brand new** nov novcat
newborn [ˈnjuːbɔn] *adj* novoroden
newcomer [ˈnjuːˌkʌmə] *n* pridošlica
newly [ˈnjuːli] **1.** *adj* novo **2.** *adv* nevadno
news [njuːz] *n* vesti; vijesti

news agency *n* novinska agencija
newscast [ˈnjuːzcɑːst] *n* emisija vesti/vijesti
newscaster, newsreader [ˈnjuːzcɑːstə; -riːdə] *n* spiker
newspaper [ˈnjuːˌspeipə] *n* novine
newsstand [ˈnjuːzstænd] *n* kiosk (za prodaju novina)
New Year [njuːˈjiːə] *n* Nova godina
New Year's Eve *n* dan uoči Nove godine, Stara godina
New Zealand [njuːˈziːlənd] *n* Novi Zeland
next [nekst] **1.** *adj* susedni; susjedni **2.** sledeći; sleijdeći **3.** *adv* onda
next to *prep* pored
nib [nib] *n* vrh
nibble [ˈnibl] *v* grickati
nice [nais] *adj* **1.** lep; lijep **2.** simpatičan **3.** četan
niche [niːʃ] *n* niša
nick [nik] **in the nick of time** u pravom trenutku
nickname [ˈnikneim] **1.** *n* nadimak **2.** *v* dati nadimak
niece [niːs] *n* nećaka, bratanica, sestričina
night [nait] *n* **1.** noć **2.** **at night** noću **3.** **good night!** laku noć! **4.** **to spend the night** provesti noć
nightclub *n* noćni klub
nightly [ˈnaitli] **1.** *adj* noćni **2.** *adv* svake noći
nightmare [ˈnaitmeə] *n* košmar
night school *n* večernja škola
night shift *n* nočna smena/smjena
night watchman *n* noćni stražar
nil [nil] *n* ništa
nine [nain] *n/adj* devet
nineteen [ˌnainˈtiːn] *n/adj* devetnaest
nineteenth [ˌnainˈtiːnθ] *adj* devetnaesti

ninetieth [ˈnaintiəθ] adj devedeseti

ninety [ˈnainti] n /adj devedeset

ninth [nainθ] adj deveti

nip [nip] v štipnuti

nipple [ˈnipl] n bradavica

no [nəu] 1. ne 2. adj nikakav

Nobel Prize [nəuˈbel] n Nobelova nagrada

nobility [nəuˈbiləti] n 1. plemstvo 2. plemenitost

noble [ˈnəubl] adj 1. plemićki 2. plemenit

nobody [ˈnəubədi] niko

nod [nɔd] v klimnuti; kimnuti

no-go area [ˌnəugəuˈeəriə] n zabranjena zona

noise [nɔiz] n buka

noiseless [ˈnɔizlis] adj bešuman

noisy [ˈnɔizi] adj bučan

no longer [nəuˈlɔŋgə] adv He is no longer here. Više nije tu.

nomad [ˈnəumæd] n nomad

nomadic [nəuˈmædik] adj nomadski

no man's land n ničija zemlja

no matter what ma šta

nominate [ˈnɔmineit] v kandidovati

nomination [ˌnɔmiˈneiʃn] n kandidovanje

nominee [ˌnɔmiˈniː] n naimenovani kandidat

non- [nɔn] ne-

non-aggression [ˌnɔnəˈgeʃn] n nenapadanje

non-aggression pact n ugovor o nenapadanje

non-alcoholic [ˌnɔnælkəˈhɔlik] adj bezalkoholan

non-aligned adj nesvrstan

non-aligned nations [ˌnɔnəˈlaind] pl nesvrstane zemlje

non-alignment [ˌnɔnəˈlainmənt] n nesvrstavanje

non-Christian [ˌnɔnˈmʌzlim] 1. adj nehrišćanski; nekršćanski 2. n nehrišćanin; nekršćanin

non-commissioned officer [ˌnɔnkəˈmiʃnd] n podoficir

none [nʌn] 1. nijedan 2. niko 3. adv ni najmanji

nonetheless [ˌnʌnðəˈles] adv pored toga

non-fiction [ˌnɔnˈfikʃn] n dokumentarna literatura

non-intervention [ˌnɔnˌintəˈvenʃn] n nemešanje; nemiješanje

non-Muslim [ˌnɔnˈmʌzlim] adj neislamski

non-payment [ˌnɔnˈpeimənt] n neisplata

nonplus [ˈnɔnˈplʌs] v zbuniti

nonsense [ˈnɔnsns] n koješta

non-smoker [ˌnɔnˈsməukə] n nepušač

non-smoking adj za nepušače

non-stop [ˌnɔnˈstɔp] 1. adj neprekidan 2. adv neprekidno

noodles [ˈnuːdəlz] n rezanac

noon [nuːn] n podne

no one [ˈnəuwʌn] niko

noose [nuːs] n omča

nor [nɔː] see neither... nor

norm [nɔːm] n norma

normal [ˈnɔːml] adj normalan

normality [nɔːˈmæliti] v normalnost

normalize [ˈnɔːməlaiz] v normalizovati

normally [ˈnɔːməli] adv inače, obično

north [nɔːθ] 1. adj severni; sjeverni 2. n sever; sjever

northeast 1. adj severoistočan; sjeveroistočan 2. n severoistok; sjeveroistok

northern [ˈnɔːðən] adj severni; sjeverni

northerner [ˈnɔːðənə] n severnjak; sjevernjak

Northern Ireland n Severna Irska; Sjeverna Irksa

northward(s) [ˈnɔːθwədz] adv na sever

northwest 1. adj severozapadni; sjeverozapadni 2. n severozapad; sjeverozapad

Norway [ˈnɔːwei] n Norveška

Norwegian [nɔːˈwiːdʒən] 1. adj norveški 2. n Norvežanin

nose [nəuz] n 1. nos 2. **to blow one's nose** useknuti se

nosebleed [ˈnəuz] n krvarenje iz nosa

nostalgia [nɔˈstældʒə] n nostalgija

nostalgic [nɔˈstældʒik] adj nostalgičan

nostril [ˈnɔstrəl] n nozdrva

not [nɔt] ne

notable [ˈnəutəbl] adj ugledan

not at all nikako

note [nəut] 1. n beleška; bilješka 2. (mus.) nota 3. v primetiti; primjetiti 4. see **banknote**

notebook [ˈnəutbuk] n beležnica; bilježnica

noted [ˈnəutid] adj ugledan

note down v zabeležiti; zabilježiti

noteworthy [ˈnəut,wəːði] adj vredan pažnje; vrijedan pažnje

nothing [ˈnʌθiŋ] 1. ništa 2. **next to nothing** skoro ništa

nothing but ništa nego

notice [ˈnəutis] n 1. beleška; bilješka 2. **to give notice** dati otkaz 3. **until further notice** do daljnjeg 4. **to take notice of** opaziti 5. v primetiti; primijetiti

noticeable [ˈnəutisəbl] adj uočljiv

notice-board n oglasna tabla/ ploča

notification [,nəutifiˈkeiʃn] n obaveštenje; obavještenje

notify [ˈnəutifai] v obavestiti; obavjestiti

notion [ˈnəuʃn] n utisak

not only... but also ne samo... nego

notorious [nəuˈtɔːriəs] adj ozloglašen

notoriety [,nəutɔːˈrajəti] n ozloglašenost

notwithstanding [,nɔtwiθˈstændiŋ] prep uprkos

not yet adv ne još

nought [nɔːt] n nula

noun [naun] n imenica

nourish [ˈnʌriʃ] v hraniti

nourishing [ˈnʌriʃiŋ] adj hranljiv

nourishment [ˈnʌriʃmənt] n hrana

novel [ˈnɔvl] 1. adj neobičan 2. n roman

novelist [ˈnɔvəlist] n romanopisac

novelty [ˈnɔvlti] n novost

November [nəuˈvembə] n novembar; studeni

novice [ˈnɔvis] n početnik

now [nau] 1. sada 2. **just now** upravo sada

nowadays [ˈnauədeiz] adv danas

now and then adv ponekad

nowhere [ˈnəuweə] 1. nigde; nigdje 2. nikud(a)

noxious [ˈnɔkʃes] adj škodljiv

nuclear [ˈnjuːkliə] adj nuklearan

nuclear arms pl nuklearno oružje

nuclear deterrent n nuklearna zastrašujuća sila

nuclear energy n nuklearna energija

nuclear fallout n radioaktivne padavine

nuclear power n nuklearna energija

nuclear power station n nuklearna centrala

nuclear test n nuklearna proba

nuclear test site n poligon za nuklearne probe

nuclear waste n nuklearni otpad

nuclear weapons pl nuklearno oružje

nude [nju:d] adj go; gol

nudity ['nju:diti] n golost

nuisance ['nju:sns] n smetnja

null and void adj ništavan

numb [nʌm] adj **to be numb** utrnuti

number ['nʌmbə] n 1. broj 2. mnoštvo 3. v numerisati

numberplate n (UK) registarska tablica

numeral ['nju:mərəl] n broj

numerical [nju:'merikl] adj brojčani

numerous ['nju:mərəs] adj brojan

nun [nʌn] n (rel.) kaluđerica

nuptial ['nʌpʃəl] adj svadbeni

nurse [nə:s] 1. n (med.) bolničar, bolničarka 2. v dojiti 3. (med.) negovati; njegovati

nursery ['nə:səri] n obdanište

nursing ['nə:siŋ] n (med.) služba

nursing home n starački dom

nut [nʌt] n orah

nutritious [nju:'triʃəs] adj hranljiv

nylon ['nailɔn] n najlon

oak [əuk] *n* hrast
oar [ɔː] *n* veslo
oasis [əuˈeisis] (*pl* **oases**) oaza
oath [əuθ] *n* 1. zakletva 2. to take an oath položiti zakletvu 3. to break an oath prekršiti zakletvu
oats [əuts] *n* ovas
obedience [əˈbːdiəns] *n* poslušnost
obedient [əˈbiːdiənt] *adj* poslušan
obey [əˈbei] *n* slušati
obituary [əˈbitʃuəri] *n* čitulja
object [ˈɔbdʒikt] *n* 1. predmet 2. objekat
object [əbˈdʒekt] *v* protestovati (**to** protiv)
objection [əbˈdʒekʃn] *n* 1. prigovor 2. to raise an objection to staviti prigovor na
objectionable [əbˈdəʒəkʃənəbl] *adj* zamerljiv; zamjerljiv
objective [əbˈdʒəktiv] 1. *adj* objektivan 2. *n* cilj
obligate [ˌɔbliˈgeit] *v* obavezati
obligation [ˌɔbliˈgeiʃn] *n* 1. obaveza 2. to fulfil one's obligation ispuniti obavezu
obligatory [əˈbligətri] *adj* obavezan
oblige [əˈblaidʒ] *v* obavezati
obliged [əˈblaidʒd] *adj* obavezan
obliging [əˈblaidʒiŋ] *adj* ljubazan
oblique [əuˈbliːk] *adj* kos
obliterate [əˈblitəreit] *v* uništiti
oblivious [əˈbliviəs] *adj* nesvestan; nesvjestan
oblong [ˈɔblɔŋ] *adj* duguljast
obnoxious [əbˈnɔkʃəs] *adj* mrzak

obscene [ɔbˈsiːn] *adj* opscen
obscenity [ɔbˈseniti] *n* opscenost
obscure [əbˈskjuə] 1. *adj* mračan 2. *v* načiniti
observance [əbˈzəːvəns] *n* pridržavanje
observant [əbˈzəːvənt] *adj* to be observant pridržavati se
observation [ˌɔbzəˈveiʃn] *n* 1. opažanje 2. to make an observation učiniti primedba
observation station *n* osmatračnica; promatračnica
observatory [əbˈzəːvətri] *n* opservatorij
observe [əbˈzəːv] *v* 1. opažati 2. to observe the law pridržavati se zakona
observer [əbˈzəːvə] *n* 1. posmatrač; promatrač 2. political observer politički posmatrač/promatrač
observer's status *n* posmatrački status
obsess [əbˈses] *v* opsesti; opsjesti
obsessed [əbˈsest] *adj* to be obsessed biti opsednut
obsession [əbˈseʃn] *n* opsesija
obsolete [ˈɔbsəliːt] *adj* zastereo; zastario
obstacle [ˈɔbstəkl] *n* prepreka
obstinate [ˈɔbstənət] *adj* tvrdoglav
obstruct [əbˈstrʌkt] *v* omesti
obstruction [əbˈstrʌktʃən] *n* 1. ometanje 2. (med.) blokada
obstructive [əbˈstrʌktiv] *adj* opstruktivan, koji sprečava
obtain [əbˈtein] *v* dobiti

obtainable [əb·teinəbl] *adj*
dostižan, koji se može postići

obvious [·ɔbviəs] *adj* očevidan

obviously [·ɔbviəsli] *adv* očigledno

occasion [ə·keiჳn] *n* prilika

occasional [ə·keiჳənl] *adj* povremen

occasionally [ə·keiჳənli] *adv* od
vremena do vremena

occidental [ɔksi·dentl] *adj* zapadni

occupant [·ɔkjupənt] *n* 1. posednik;
posjednik 2. stanar

occupation [,ɔkju·peiʃn] *n* 1.
profesija 2. (mil.) okupacija

occupational [,ɔkju·peiʃənl] *n*
profesionalan

occupational health *n* zaštita
radnika

occupied [·ɔkjupaid] *adj* 1.
occupied territory okupirana
teritorija; okupirani teritorij 2. **to
be occupied with someone** biti
zauzet nečim

occupier [·ɔkjupaijə] *n* okupator

occupy [·ɔkjupai] *v* 1. zauzeti 2.
okupirati

occupy a country *v* (mil.)
okupirati zemlju

occupy a position *v* (mil.) zauzeti
položaj

occupying army *pl* okupatorska
vojska

occupying forces *pl* okupacione
snage

occur [ə·kə:] *v* (occurred) 1.
dogoditi se 2. doći

occurrence [ə·kʌrəns] *n* događaj

ocean [·əuʃn] *n* okean

ocean-going *adj* morski

o'clock [əu·klɔk] *adv* sat

octane [·ɔtein] *n* oktan

October [ɔk·təubə] *n* oktobar;
listopad

octopus [·ɔktəpəs] *n* hobotnica

odd [ɔd] *adj* 1. čudan 2. rasparen
3. **odd number** neparan broj

odds [ɔdz] *pl* izgledi

ode [əud] *n* oda

odious [·əudiəs] *n* odiozan

odorous [·əudərəs] *adj* mirisav

odour, odor [·əudə] *n* miris

odourless, odorless [·əudələs] *adj*
bez mirisa

of [əv] *prep* 1. **a piece of cake**
komad torte 2. od

of course naravno

off [ɔf] 1. *adj* prekinut 2. skinut 3.
a day off slobodan dan 4. *adv*
far off daleko 5. **to take off**
skinuti 6. **to set off** itići 7. **to
switch off** ugasiti 8. *prep* s
9. **off the coast** blizu obale

off duty *adj* van dužnosti

off limits *adv* zabranjen

offence [ə·fens] *n* 1. napad 2.
uvreda

offend [ə·fend] *v* uvrediti; uvrijediti

offense [ə·fens] *see* **offence**

offensive [ə·fensiv]1. *adj* uvredljiv
2. *n* (mil.) ofanziva; ofenziva

offer [·ɔfə] 1. *n* ponuda 2. **to make
an offer** podneti ponudu;
podnijeti ponudu 3. *v* ponuditi
4. raspisati

office [·ɔfis] 1. *adj* kancelarijski 1.
n kancelarija 2. ministarstvo 3.
(pol.) **to run for office**
kandidovati se

officer [·ɔfisə] *n* 1. referent 2.
(mil.) oficir

office work *n* kancelarijski posao

official [ə·fiʃl] 1. *adj* zvaničan 2. *n*
činovnik

official language *n* zvanični
jezik

official statement *n* zvanična izjava
official talks *pl* zvanični razgovori
official visit *n* zvanična poseta; zvanični posjet
officially [ə'fiʃəli] *adv* zvanično
offload [,ɔf'ləud] *v* otarasiti se
off-season [,ɔf'si:zən] *adj* mrtva sezona
offshore [,ɔf'ʃɔː] *adj/adv* u blizini obale
offside [,ɔf'ʃaid] *adv* (spor.) u ofsajdu
offspring ['ɔfspriŋ] *n* izdanak
often ['ɔfn; 'ɔftən] *adv* često
oh! [əu] oh!
oil [ɔil] *n* 1. ulje 2. nafta
oil can *n* kantica za ulje
oilfield ['ɔilfi:ld] *n* naftno polje
oil painting *n* uljana slika
oil pipeline *n* naftovod
oil producing states *pl* zamlje proizvođači nafte
oil production *n* proizvodnja nafte
oil refinery *n* rafinerija nafte
oil rig *n* platforma za posmorsko bušenje
oil rights *pl* prava na eksploataciju nafte
oil slick *n* naftna mrlja
oil spill *n* prosipanje nafte
oil tanker *n* tanker
oil well *n* izvor nafte
oily ['ɔili] *adj* uljast
ointment ['ɔintmənt] *n* mast
okay, OK [,əu'kei] 1. pristanak 2. važi!
okra ['ɔkrə] *n* okra
old [əuld] *adj* 1. star 2. *see* **how old**
old age *n* starost
olden times *pl* stara vremena
old-fashioned *adj* staromodan

old guard *n* stara garda
olive ['ɔliv] *n* maslina
olive oil *n* maslinovo ulje
olympic [ə'limpik] *adj* olimpijski
Olympics, Olympic games *pl* Olimpijski igre
omelet, omelette ['ɔmlit] *n* omlet
omen ['əumen] *n* predznak
ominous ['ɔminəs] *adj* zloslutan
omission [ə'miʃn] *n* propust
omit [ə'mit] *v* (**omitted**) propustiti
omnibus ['ɔmnibəs] *n* 1. autobus 2. antologija
on [ɔn] *prep* 1. na 2. o 3. pod 4. **on the table** na sto/stol 5. **on the radio** preko radija 6. **on foot** pešice; pješice 7. **on purpose** namerno; namjerno 8. **on his arrival...** pri njegovom dolasku... 9. **on Monday** u ponedeljak/ponedjeljak 10. **a book on Shakespeare** knjiga o Šekspiru 11. **to get on** sesti 12. **to put on** obući 13. **to put the light on** upaliti lampu 14. **What's going on?** Šta se dešava? / Što se događa?
on account of *prep* zbog
on behalf of *prep* u korist
once [wʌns] 1. *adv* jednom 2. **at once** odmah 3. **all at once** najednom 4. *conj* čim
one [wʌn] *n/adj* 1. jedan 2. neki
one another *adv* jedan drugi
one by one *adv* jedan po jedan
one-party state *n* jednopartijski
one-party system *n* jednopartijski sistem
oneself [wʌn'self] sebe, se, sam
one-sided *adj* jednostran
one-way street *n* jednosmerna ulica

one-way ticket *n* karta u jednom pravcu/smjeru

onion [ˈʌniən] *n* luk

on-line [ˈɔnˈlain] *adj* onlajn

onlooker [ˈɔnlukə] *n* gledalac

only [ˈəunli] 1. *adj* jedini 2. **an only child** jedinče 3. *adv* samo 4. **only one** samo jedan 5. **not only... but also** ne samo da... nego 6. **if only...** kad bi (bar)...

on to, onto *prep* na

on top of *prep* na

onus [ˈəunəs] *n* (leg.) teret

onward, onwards [ˈɔnwəd; ˈɔnwədz] *adv* napred; naprijed

ooze [uːz] *v* curiti

opaque [əuˈpeik] *adj* neproziran

open [ˈəupən] 1. *adj* otvoren 2. *v* otvoriti (se) 3. **to open an account** otvoriti račun 4. **to open the curtains** razvući zavese/zavjese

open-air *adj* pod vedrim nebom

opener [ˈəupənə] *n* otvarač

opening [ˈəupniŋ] 1. *adj* početni 2. *n* otvor 3. vakancija

opening night *n* premijera

openly [ˈəupənli] *adv* otvoreno

openness [ˈəupənəs] *n* otvorenost

open season *n* lovna sezona

open space *n* otvoreni prostor

opera [ˈɔprə] 1. *adj* operski 2. *n* opera

opera house *n* opera

opera singer *n* operni pevač/pjevač

operable [ˈɔpərəbl] *adj* koji se može operisati

operate [ˈɔpəreit] *v* 1. rukovati 2. (med.) operisati

operatic [ˌɔpəˈrætik] *adj* operni

operating conditions *pl* radni uslovi/uvjeti

operating frequency *n* radna frekvencija

operating theatre *n* operaciona sala

operation [ˌɔpəˈreiʃn] *n* 1. manipulacija 2. (med/mil.) operacija 3. **to put into operation** staviti u pogon

operational [ˌɔpəˈreiʃnəl] *adj* 1. operativan 2. borbeni

operations [ˌɔpəˈreiʃnz] 1. *adj* operativan 2. *pl* poslovanje

operative [ˈɔpərətiv] 1. *adj* operativan 2. *n* visokokvalifikovani radnik 3. špijun

operator [ˈɔpəreitə] *n* 1. operator 2. rukovalac 3. **telephone operator** telefonista

ophthalmic [ɔpˈθælmik] *adj* oftalmičan

ophthalmologist [ɔpˌθælˈmɔlədʒist] *n* oftalmolog

ophthalmology [ɔpˌθælˈɔlədʒi] *n* oftalmologija

opinion [əˈpiniən] *n* 1. mišljenje 2. **in my opinion** po mom mišljenju 3. **public opinion** javno mišljenje 4. **to express an opinion** izraziti mišljenje

opinionated [əˈpiniə,neitid] *adj* tvrdoglav

opinion poll *n* ispitivanje javnog mnenja

opponent [əˈpəunənt] *n* protivnik

opportunist [ˌɔpəˈtjuːnist] *n* oportunista

opportunity [ˌɔpəˈtjuːnəti] *n* prilika

oppose [əˈpəuz] *v* protiviti

opposing [əˈpəuziŋ] *adj* suprotan, protivan

opposite [ˈɔpəzit] 1. *adj* suprotan 2. *prep* prema

opposite to *adj* suprotan od
opposition [ˌɔpəˈziʃn] 1. *adj* (pol.) opozicioni 2. *n* suprotnost 3. (pol.) opozicija 4. **to put up opposition** pružati otpor
opposition party *n* opoziciona partija
oppress [əˈpres] *v* tlačiti
oppressed [əˈprest] *adj* potlačen
oppression [əˈpreʃn] *n* tlačenje
oppressive [əˈpresiv] *adj* ugnjetački
oppressor [əˈpresə] *n* tlačilac
opt [ɔpt] *v* optirati
opt for *v* odlučiti se za
optic [ˈɔptik] *adj* očni
optical [ˈɔptikl] *adj* optički
optical illusion *n* optička varka
optician [ɔpˈtiʃn] *n* optičar
optics [ˈɔptiks] *n/pl* optika
optimism [ˌɔptiˈmizm] *n* optimizam
optimist [ˌɔptiˈmiat] *n* optimista
optimistic [ˌɔptiˈmistik] *adj* optimistički
optimum [ˈɔptiməm] *n* optimum
option [ˈɔpʃn] *n* 1. izbor 2. opcija
optional [ˈɔpʃnəl] *adj* neobavezan
opulence [ˈɔpjuləns] *n* imućnost
opulent [ˈɔpjulənt] *adj* imućan
or [ɔː] *conj* 1. ili 2. **either... or ili...** ili
oral [ˈɔːrəl] *adj* oralni
oral examination *n* usmeni ispit
oral contraceptive *n* oralno kontraceptivno sredstvo
orange [ˈɔrindʒ] 1. *adj* oranžast 2. *n* pomorandža
orator [ˈɔrətə] *n* orator
orbit [ˈɔːbit] 1. *n* orbita 2. *v* kružiti
orchard [ˈɔːtʃəd] *n* voćnjak
orchestra [ˈɔːkistrə] *n* orkestar
orchestral [ɔːˈkietrəl] *adj* orkestarski

ordain [ɔːˈdein] *v* 1. narediti 2. (rel.) rukopoložiti
ordeal [ɔːˈdiːl] *n* teško iskušenje
order [ˈɔːdə] 1. *n* red 2. naredba 3. (com.) porudžbina 4. **law and order** red i mir 5. **in order** u redu 6. **out of order** van reda 7. **in order to** da bi 8. **to put in order** dovesti u red 9. **to place an order** poručiti 10. **to give an order** izdati naređenje 11. **to carry out an order** izvršiti naređenje 12. *v* narediti 13. (com.) poručiti 14. **to order a meal** poručiti ručak
orderly [ˈɔːdəli] 1. *adj* uredan 2. *n* (med.) bolničar 3. (mil.) posilni
ordinarily [ˈɔːdənrəli] *adv* obično
ordinary [ˈɔːdənri] *adj* običan
ordnance [ˈɔːdnəns] *n* (mil.) borbena tehnika
ore [ɔː] *n* ruda
organ [ˈɔːgən] *n* 1. organ 2. (mus.) orgulje 3. **sexual organs** polni organi; spolni organi
organic [ɔːˈgænik] *adj* na halitta
organism [ˈɔːgənizəm] *n* organizam
organization [ˌɔːgənaiˈzeiʃn] *n* organizacija
organize [ˈɔːgənaiz] *v* organizovati (se)
organizer [ˈɔːgənaizə] *n* organizator
orgasm [ˈɔːgæzm] *n* orgazam
oriental [ˌɔːriˈentl] *adj* istočni
orientation [ˌɔːriənˈteiʃn] *n* orientacija
orifice [ˈɔːrifis] *n* usta
origin [ˈɔridʒin] *n* 1. poreklo; porijeklo 2. **country of origin** rodna zemlja
original [əˈridʒənl] 1. *adj* originalan 2. *n* original

originality [ə,ridʒəˈnæliti] *n*
originalnost

originally [əˈridʒənəli] *adv* u
početku

originate [əˈridʒineit] *v* 1. stvoriti 2.
nastati

originator [əˈridʒineitə] *n* stvaralac

ornament [ˈɔːnəmənt] *n* ukras

ornamental [,ɔːnəˈmentl] *adj*
ukrasni

ornithological [,ɔːniθəˈlɔdʒikl] *adj*
ornitološki

ornithologist [,ɔːniˈθɔlədʒist] *n*
ornitolog

ornithology [,ɔːniˈθɔlədʒi] *n*
ornitologija

orphan [ˈɔːfn] *n* siroče

orphanage [ˈɔːfənidʒ] *n* sirotište

orthodox [ˈɔːθədɔks] *adj* 1.
ortodoksan 2. (rel.) pravoslavan

Orthodox Church *n* pravoslavna
crka

orthography [ɔːˈθɔgrəfi] *n*
ortografija

orthopaedic, **orthopedic**
[,ɔːθəˈpiːdik] *adj* ortopedski

ostracize [ˈɔstrəsaiz] *v* proterati;
protjerati

ostrich [ˈɔstritʃ] *n* noj

other [ˈʌðə] *adj/n* 1. drugi 2. each
other jedan drugi 3. the other
day onomad 4. every other day
svaki drugi dan 5. something or
other tako nešto 6. one after the
other jedan za drugim 7. on the
other hand s druge strane 8. on
the one hand..., and on the
other s jedne strane..., a s druge
strane

otherwise [ˈʌðəwaiz] *adv* inače

otter [ˈɔtə] *n* vidrica

Ottoman [ˈɔtəmən] *adj* otomanksi

ouch! [autʃ] jao!

ought [ˈɔːt] *v* trebati

ounce [auns] *n* uncija

our [aː] naš

ours [aːz] naš

ourselves [aːˈselvz] mi, mi sami,
nas, sebe, se

oust [aust] *v* isterati; istjerati

out [aut] 1. *adj* van kuće 2. *adv* van
3. way out izlaz 4. inside out
naopačke 5. to go out izići 6.
The fire's gone out. Vatra se
ugasila. 7. *see* out of

out-and-out *adj* okoreo; okorio

outbid [,autˈbid] *v* nadbiti cenom/
cijenom

outbreak [ˈautbreik] *n* 1. početak 2.
outbreak of war izbijanje rata

outburst [ˈautbəːst] *n* eksplozija

outcast [ˈautkaːst] *n* izagnanik

outcome [ˈautkʌm] *n* ishod

outcry [ˈautkrai] *n* protest

outdated [,autˈdeitid] *adj* zastereo;
zasterio

outdistance [,autˈdistəns] *v* prestići

outdo [,autˈduː] *v* (**outdid,**
outdone) nadmašiti

outdoor [,autˈdɔ] *adj* otvoren

outdoors [,autˈdɔːz] *adv* napolju

outer [ˈautə] *adj* spoljni

outer space *n* vasiona

outermost [ˈautəməust] *adj*
najudaljeniji

outfit [ˈautfit] *n* 1. oprema 2. (mil.)
jedinica

outgoing [ˈautgəuiŋ] *adj* 1. koji
odlazi 2. društven

outgrow [,autˈgrəu] *v* (**outgrew,**
outgrown) izrasti iz

outing [ˈautiŋ] *n* ekskurzija

outlast [,autˈlaːst] *v* nadživeti;
nadživjeti

outlaw ['autlɔ:] 1. *n* zločinac 2. *v* staviti van zakona

outlay ['autlei] *n* (fin.) trošak

outlet ['autlet] *n* 1. izlaz 2. oduška

outline ['autlain] 1. *n* kontura 2. *v* ocrtati

outlive ['autliv] *v* preživeti; preživjeti

outlook ['autluk] *n* perspektiva

outnumber [,aut'nʌmbə] *v* brojno nadmašiti

out of *prep* 1. van 2. od 3. iz 4. kroz 5. bez

out of date *adj* zastareo; zasterio

out of place *adj* nezgodan

out of work *adj* nezaposlen

output ['autput] *n* izlaz

outrage ['autreidʒ] 1. *n* uvreda 2. *v* uvrediti

outraged ['autreidʒd] *adj* to be outraged biti ogorčen

outrageous [aut'reidʒəs] *adj* nečuven

outright ['autrait] 1. *adj* potpun 2. *adv* potpuno

outrun [aut'rʌn] *v* (outran, outrun) nadtrčati

outsell [,aut'sel] *v* (outsold) više prodati od

outside [,aut'said] 1. *n* spolja 2. *adj* spoljni 3. *adv* napolje, napolju 4. *prep* izvan

outsider [,aut'saidə] *n* autsajder

outsize ['autsaiz] *adj* prevelik

outskirts ['autskə:ts] *pl* periferija

outsmart [,aut'sma:t] *v* nadmudriti

outspoken [,aut'spəukən] *adj* otvoren

outstanding [,aut'stændiŋ] *adj* 1. izvanredan 2. (fin.) neizmiren

outstrip [,aut'strip] *v* prestići

outward ['autwəd] *adj* spoljašnji

outwards ['autwədz] *adv* van

outweigh [,aut'wei] *v* biti važniji od

outwit [,aut'wit] *v* nadmudriti

oval ['əuvl] *adj* ovalan

ovary ['əuvəri] *n* ovarij

oven ['ʌvn] *n* peć

over ['əuvə] 1. *adj* svršen 2. *adv* preko 3. over there tamo 4. to jump over preskočiti 5. left over neupotrebljen; neupotrijebljen 6. *prep* nad

overall [,əuvər'ɔ:l] *adj* globalan

overboard [,əuvə'bɔ:d] *adv* u moru

overbook [,əuvə'buk] *v* prebukirati (se)

overcast [,əuvə'ka:st] *adj* naoblačen

overcharge [,əuvə'tʃɔ:dʒ] *v* preopteretiti

overcoat ['əuvəkəut] *n* zimski kaput

overcome [,əuvə'kʌm] *v* (overcame, overcome) savladati

overconfident [,əuvə'kɔnfidənt] *adj* previše samopouzdan

overcrowd [,əuvə'kraud] *v* pretrpati

overcrowding [,əuvə'kraudiŋ] *n* pretrpanost

overdevelop [,əuvədə'veləp] *v* previše razviti

overdo [,əuvə'du:] *v* (overdid, overdone) preterati; pretjerati

overdose ['əuvədəus] *n* prevelika doza

overdraft ['əuvədra:ft] *n* prekoračenje bankovnog računa

overdrawn [,əuvə'drɔ:n] *adj* My bank account is overdrawn. Moj bankovni račun je prekoračen.

overdue [,əuvə'dju:] *adj* istekao

overeager [,əuvə'i:gə] *adj* suviše žestok

overeagerness [,əuvə'i:gənəs] *n* suviše velika želja

overeat [ˌəuvəˈiːt] v prejesti se

overflow [ˌəuvəˈfləu] v 1. poplaviti 2. preliti se

overgrown [ˌəuvəˈgrəun] adj obrastao

overhaul [ˌəuvəˈhɔːl] 1. n remont 2. v popraviti

overhead [ˈəuvəhed] adj gornji

overheads [ˈəuvəhedz] pl opšti troškovi

overhear [ˌəuvəˈhiːə] v slučajno čuti

overheat [ˌəuvəˈhiːt] v pregrejati (se); pregrijati (se)

overjoyed [ˌəuvəˈdʒɔid] adj presrećan

overland [ˌəuvəˈlænd] 1. adj kopneni 2. adv kopnom

overlap [ˌəuvəˈlæp] v preklapati se

overload [ˌəuvəˈləud] v preopteretiti

overlook [ˌəuvəˈluk] v predvideti; previdjeti

overnight [ˌəuvəˈnait] adv prekonoć

overpay [ˌəuvəˈpei] v preplatiti

overpower [ˌəuvəˈpauə] v nadvladati

overproduction [ˌəuvəprəˈdʌkʃn] n hiperprodukcija

overrate [ˌəuvəˈreit] v preceniti; precijeniti

override [ˌəuvəˈraid] v nadglasati

overrule [ˌəuvəˈruːl] v nadglasati

overrun [ˌəuvəˈrʌn] v zauzeti

overseas [ˌəuvəˈsiːz] 1. adj prekomorski 2. adv preko mora

oversee [ˌəuvəˈsiː] v nadgledati

overseer [ˌəuvəˈsiːə] n nadglednik

overshoot [əuvəˈʃuːt] v to overshoot a target prebaciti metu

oversight [ˈəuvəsait] n omaška

oversleep [ˌəuvəˈsliːp] v uspavati se

overspend [ˌəuvəˈspend] v previše trošiti

overstay [ˌəuvəˈstei] v predugo ostati

overstep [ˌəuvəˈstep] v prekoračiti

overstock [ˌəuvəˈstɔk] v preobilno snabdeti; preobilno snabdjeti

overt [əuˈvəːt] adj otvoren

overtake [ˌəuvəˈteik] v preteći

overthrow [ˌəuvəˈθrəu] (pol.) v oboriti

overtime [ˈəuvətaim] n prekovremeni rad

overture [ˈəuvətjuə] n 1. (pol.) otvaranje 2. (mus.) uvertira

overturn [ˌəuvəˈtəːn] v 1. preturiti 2. to verturn a verdict ukinuti presudu

overuse [ˌəuvəˈjuːs] n prekomerna upotreba; prekomjerna upotreba

overuse [ˌəuvəˈjuːz] v prekomerno upotrebiti; prekomjerno upotrebiti

overvalue [ˌəuvəˈvæljuː] v preceniti; precijeniti

overweight [ˈəuvəˈvjuː] n pregled

overweight [ˌəuvəˈweit] adj pretežak

overwhelm [ˌəuvəˈwelm] v razbiti

overwhelming [ˌəuvəˈwelmiŋ] adj neodoljiv

overwork [ˌəuvəˈwəːk] n prekomeran rad; prekomjeran rad

overwrought [ˌəuvəˈrɔːt] adj uzbuđen

ovulate [ˈəuvjuleit] v ovulirati

ovulation [ˈəuvjuleiʃən] n ovulacija

owe [əu] v dugovati

owing to [ˈəuiŋ tu] prep zbog

owl [aul] n sova

own [əun] 1. svoj 2. He has his own car. On ima svoj automobil. 3. to be on one's

own biti svoj čovek/čovjek 4. *v* imati

own up to *v* priznati

owner [ˈəunə] *n* vlasnik

ownership [ˈəunəʃip] *n* 1. svojina 2. **private ownership** privatna svojina

ox [ɔks] *n* vo; vol

oxygen [ˈɔksidʒən] *n* kiseonik; kisik

oxygen mask *n* maska za kiseonik/kisik

oyster [ˈɔistə] *n* oštrica

oz. *see* **ounce**

ozone [ˈəuzəun] *n* ozon

P

PA (personal assistant) [ˌpiːˈai] *n* lični sekretar

pace [peis] **1.** *n* hod **2.** korak **3.** *v* stupati

pacifism [ˈpasiˌfizm] *n* pacifizam

pacifist [ˈpasifist] *n* pacifista

pacify [ˈpæsifai] *v* smiriti

pack [pæk] **1.** *n* svežanj **2.** paklo **3.** čopor **4.** *v* spakovati **3.** *see* **packed**

package [ˈpækidʒ] *n* pošiljka

package tour *n* grupno putovanje

packed *adj* prepun

packet [ˈpækit] *n* paket

pack up *v* spakovati se

pact [pækt] *n* pakt

pad [pæd] **1.** *n* jastuk **2.** platforma **3. paper pad** blok **4.** *v* tapacirati

paddle [ˈpædl] **1.** *n* veslo **2.** *v* veslati

padlock [ˈpædlɔk] *n* katanac

paediatrician [ˌpiːdijaˈtriʃn] *n* pedijatar

paediatrics [ˌpiːdiˈjatriks] *n* pedijatrija

pagan [ˈpeign] **1.** *adj* paganski **2.** *n* paganin

page [peidʒ] *n* strana

pager [ˈpeidʒə] *n* pejdžer

paid [peid] *see* **pay**

pail [peil] *n* vedro

pain [pein] **1.** *n* bol **2. to feel pain** osećati bol; osjećati bol **3. labour pains** porođajni bolovi **4.** *v* boleti; boljeti

painful [ˈpeinfl] *adj* bolan

painkiller [ˈpeinkilə] *n* analgetik

painless [ˈpeinləs] *adj* bezbolan

paint [peint] **1.** *n* boja **2.** *v* obojiti **3.** naslikati (sliku)

paintbrush [ˈpeintbrʌʃ] *n* četka

painter [ˈpeintə] *n* **1.** moler **2.** slikar

painting [ˈpeintiŋ] *n* slika

pair [peə] *n* par

pajamas [pəˈdʒaːməz] *pl* pidžama

palace [ˈpælis] *n* palata; palača

palate [ˈpælət] *n* nepce

pale [peil] *adj* bled; blijed

palm [paːm] *n* **1.** dlan **2.** palma

palsy [ˈpɔːlzi] *n* **1.** paraliza **2. cerebral palsy** cerebralna paraliza

paltry [ˈpɔːltri] *adj* sitan

pamphlet [ˈpæmflit] *n* pamflet

pan [pæn] *n* tiganj; tava

pancake [ˈpæŋkeik] *n* palačinka

pancreas [ˈpæŋkrəəs] *n* gušterača

pandemonium [ˌpændəˈməuniəm] *n* urnebes

pane [pein] *n* okno

panel [ˈpænl] *n* **1.** ploča **2.** komisija

panic [ˈpænik] **1.** *n* panika **2.** *v* upaničiti se

pant [pænt] *v* dahtati

panties [ˈpæntiz] *pl* ženski gaće

pantry [ˈpæntri] *n* akin abinci

pants [pænts] *pl* **1.** gaće **2.** (US) pantalone; hlače

papal [ˈpaipl] *adj* papinski

paper [ˈpeipə] *n* **1.** papir, hartija **2.** novine **3.** (acad.) referat **4. toilet paper** toaletni papir

par [paː] *n* **on a par with** jednak s

parachute [ˈpærəʃuːt] **1.** *n* padobran **2.** *v* spustiti (se) padobranom

parade [pəˈreid] *n* parada
paradise [ˈpærədais] *n* raj
paradox [ˈpærədɔks] *n* paradoks
paraffin [ˈpærəfin] *n* parafin
paragraph [ˈpærəgraːf] *n* stav
parallel [ˈpærəlel] 1. *adj* paralelan 2. *n* paralela
paralysis [pəˈræləsis] *n* paraliza
paralytic [ˌpærəˈlitik] *adj* paralitičar
paralyze [ˈpærəlaiz] *v* paralizovati
paramedic [ˌpærəˈmedik] *n* bolničar
paramilitary [ˌpærəˈmilitəri] *adj* poluvojni
paramount [ˈpærəmaunt] *adj* glavni
paranoia [ˌpærəˈnojə] *n* paranoja
paranoid [ˈpærənoid] 1. *adj* paranoičan 2. *n* paranoik
paraphrase [ˈpærəfreiz] *v* parafrazirato
parasite [ˈpærəsait] *n* parazit
paratrooper [ˈpærətruːpə] *n* padobranac
paratroops [ˈpærətruːps] *pl* padobranske jedinice
parcel [ˈpaːsl] *n* pošiljka
pardon [ˈpaːdn] 1. *n* oproštenje 2. (leg.) pomilovanje 3. **I beg your pardon!** Oprostite! 4. **I beg your pardon?** Izvol'te? 5. *v* oprostiti 6. (leg.) pomilovati
parent [ˈpeərənt] *n* roditelj
parental [pəˈrentl] *adj* roditeljski
parenthood [ˈpeərənthud] *n* roditeljstvo
parents [ˈpeərəntz] *pl* roditelji
parish [ˈpæriʃ] *n* parohija; župa
parity [ˈpæriti] *n* paritet
park [paːk] 1. *n* park 2. **car-park** parkiralište 3. **amusement park** zabavni park 4. *v* **to park a car** parkirati kola
parking [ˈpaːkiŋ] *n* parkiranje

parking lot, parking space *n* parkiralište
parliament [ˈpaːləmənt] 1. *adj* skupštinski 2. *n* skupština
parliamentary [ˌpaːləˈmentri] *adj* parlamentaran
parliamentary immunity *n* parlamentarni imunitet
parody [ˈpærɔdi] *n* parodija
parrot [ˈpærət] *n* papagaj
parsnip [ˈpaːsnip] *n* paškanat; pastrnjak
parson [ˈpaːsn] *n* (rel.) pastor
part [paːt] 1. *n* deo; dio 2. kraj 3. **spare parts** rezervni delovi 4. **for the most part** najvećim delom 5. **to take part in** učestvovati u 6. *v* razdeliti; razdijeliti 7. prekinuti
partial [ˈpaːʃl] *adj* 1. delimičan; djelimičan 2. **to be partial to** voleti; voljeti
participant [paːˈtisipənt] *n* učesnik
participate [paːˈtisipeit] *v* učestvovati (**in** u)
participation [paːˌtisiˈpeiʃn] *n* učešće (**in** u)
particle [ˈpaːtikl] *n* čestica
particular [pəˈtikjulə] 1. *adj* naročit 2. *n* **in particular** osobito 3. *see* **particulars**
particularly [pəˈtikjuləli] *adv* osobito
particulars [pəˈtikjuləz] *pl* obaveštenje; obavještenje
partition [paːˈtiʃn] 1. *n* pregrada 2. *v* pregraditi
partly [ˈpaːtli] *adv* delimično; djelimično
partner [ˈpaːtnə] *n* ortak
partnership [ˈpaːtnəʃip] *n* ortakluk
part-time 1. *adj* skraćen 2. *adv* skraćeno

party ['pa:ti] *n* 1. zabava 2. (leg.) strana 3. (pol.) partija

party member *n* (pol.) član stranke

pass [pa:s] 1. *n* propusnica 2. **mountain pass** brdski klanac 3. *v* proći 4. preteći 5. **to pass time** provesti vreme/vrijeme 6. **to pass an exam** položiti ispit 7. **to pass a law** primiti zakon

passable ['pa:səbl] *adj* prolazan

passage ['pæsidʒ] *n* 1. prolaz 2. put 3. mesto; mjesto

passage way *n* hodnik

pass away *v* umreti; umrijeti

pass by *v* proći

passenger ['pæsindʒə] *n* putnik

passer-by *n* prolaznik

passion ['pæʃn] *n* strast

passionate ['pæʃənət] *adj* strastan

passive ['pæsiv] *adj* pasivan

pass out *v* onesvestiti se; onesvijestiti se

passport ['pa:spɔ:t] *n* pasoš

passport office *n* pasoško odeljenje/odjeljenje

pass through *v* proputovati

past [pa:st] 1. *adj* prošli 2. *n* prošlost 3. *adv* **to go past** proći mimo 4. *prep* pored 5. **half past four** četiri i trideset, pola pet

pasta [pastə] *n* pasta

paste [peist] 1. *n* pasta 2. *v* zalepiti; zalijepiti

pastime ['pa:staim] *n* provod

pastor ['pa:stə] *n* (rel.) pastor

pastoral ['pa:strəl] *adj* pastoralan

pastry ['peistri] *n* kolač

pasture ['pa:stʃə] *n* paša

pat [pæt] *v* potapšati

patch [pætʃ] 1. *n* zakrpa 2. **a patch of ice** ledeni zastor 3. *v* zakrpiti

pâté ['pætei] *n* pašteta

patent ['peitnt] 1. *n* patent 2. *v* patentirati

patented ['peitəntid] *adj* patentiran

paternal [pə'tə:nl] *adj* očinski

path [pa:θ] *n* staza

pathetic [pə'θetik] *adj* patetičan

pathway ['pa:θwei] *n* staza

patience ['peiʃns] *n* strpljenje

patient ['peiʃnt] 1. *adj* strpljiv 2. *n* bolesnik

patriarch ['pætrija:k] *n* patrijarh

patriot ['pætriət] *n* rodoljub

patriotic [,pætri'ɔtik] *adj* rodoljubiv

patriotism ['pætriətizəm] *n* rodoljublje

patrol [pə'trəul] 1. *n* patrola 2. *v* patrolirati

patron ['peitrən] *n* patron

patronize ['pætrənaiz] *v* 1. štititi 2. posećivati; posjećivati 3. ophoditi se s... na snishodljiv način

patron saint *n* svetac zaštitnik

pattern ['pætn] *n* 1. uzorak 2. model

pause [pɔ:z] 1. *n* pauza 2. *v* zaustaviti se

pavement ['peivmənt] *n* (UK) trotoar

paw [pɔ:] *n* šapa

pawn [pɔ:n] *v* založiti

pay [pei] 1. *n* plata; plaća 2. *v* platiti

payable ['peijəbl] *adj* plativ

pay attention *v* obratiti paznju (**to na**)

pay a visit *v* napraviti posetu

pay back *v* 1. osvetiti se 2. (fin.) vratiti

payday *n* dan isplate

payee [pei'i:] *n* primalac nekog iznosa

payer [ˈpeijə] *n* platilac
payment [ˈpeimənt] *n* isplata
pay rise *n* povišica
p.c. [piːˈsiː] *n* personalni kompjuter
pea, peas [piː; piːz] *n, pl* grašak
peace [piːs] *n* 1. *adj* mirovni 2. *n* mir 3. **to make peace** zaključiti mir
peace conference *n* mirovna konferencija
peaceful [ˈpiːsfl] *adj* miran
peaceful coexistence *n* miroljubiva koegzistencija
peacefully [ˈpiːsfəli] *adv* mirno
peaceful means *pl* by peaceful means mirnim sredstvima
peacekeeping [ˈpiːskiːpiŋ] *adj* mirovni
peacekeeping forces *pl* mirovne snage
peace talks *pl* mirovni pregovorni
peacetime [ˈpiːstaim] 1. *adj* mirnodopski 2. *n* mirno doba
peace treaty *n* mirovni ugovor
peach [piːtʃ] *n* breskva
peak [piːk] 1. *adj* maksimalan 2. *n* vrh 3. maksimum 4. *v* dostići vrhunac
peak season *n* špic sezone
peanut [ˈpiːnʌt] *n* kikiriki
pear [peə] *n* kruška
pearl [pəːl] *n* biser
peasant [ˈpeznt] *n* seljak
peat [piːt] *n* treset
pebble [ˈpebl] *n* šljunak
peck [pek] *v* kljunuti
peculiar [piˈkjuːliə] *adj* 1. čudan 2. naročit 3. jedinstven
peculiarity [piˌkjuːliˈærəti] *n* 1. čudnost 2. naročitost 3. jedinstvenost
pedal [ˈpedl] *n* pedal

peddle [ˈpedl] *v* torbariti
peddler [ˈpedlə] *n* torbar
pedestal [ˈpedistl] *n* postolje
pedestrian [piˈdestriən] *n* pešak; pješak
pediatrician [ˌpiːdijaˈtriʃn] *n* pedijatar
pediatrics [ˌpiːdiˈjatriks] *n* pedijatrija
pedigree [ˈpedigriː] *n* pedigre
pedlar [ˈpedlə] *n* torbar
peek [piːk] *v* viriti
peel [piːl] 1. *n* kora 2. *v* oljuštiti
peep [piːp] *v* proviriti
peer [piə] 1. *n* premac 2. plemić 3. *v* gviriti
peerage [ˈpiəridʒ] *n* plemstvo
peerless [ˈpiəlis] *adj* bez premca
peg [peg] *n* 1. klin 2. kolac
pelican [ˈpelikən] *n* pelikan
pelt [pelt] *v* baciti se
pelvis [ˈpelvis] *n* karlica
pen [pen] *n* pero
penal [ˈpiːnl] *adj* krivični
penal code *n* krivični zakonik
penalize [ˈpiːnəlaiz] *v* kazniti
penalty [ˈpenlti] *n* 1. kazna 2. taksa 3. (spor.) penal
penance [ˈpenəns] *n* pokora
pence [pens] *see* **penny**
pencil [ˈpensl] *n* olovka
pencil sharpener *n* oštrač za olovke
pendant [ˈpendənt] *n* pandan
pending [ˈpendiŋ] 1. *adj* nerešen; neriješen 2. *prep* do
penetrate [ˈpenitreit] *v* 1. probiti 2. prodirati
penetrating [ˈpenitreitiŋ] *adj* 1. prodoran 2. pronicljiv
penetration [ˌpeniˈtreiʃn] *n* 1. proboj 2. pronicljivost

penguin [ˈpengwin] *n* pingvin
penicilin [penəˈsilin] *n* penicilin
peninsula [pəˈninsjulə] *n* poluostrvo
penis [ˈpiːnis] *n* penis
penitent [ˈpenitənt] *adj* pokajnički
penknife [ˈpenaif] *n* perorez
penniless [ˈpenilis] *adj* bez para/novca
penny [ˈpeni] *n* (*pl* **pence/pennies**) peni
pension [ˈpenʃn] *n* penzija
pension [pɔnsiˈjɔn] *n* pansion
pensioner [ˈpenʃnə] *n* penzioner
pensive [ˈpensiv] *adj* zamišljen
people [ˈpiːpl] *pl* 1. narod 2. ljudi
pepper [ˈpepə] *n* 1. biber 2. paprika
peppermint [ˈpepəmint] *n* nana
peptalk [ˈpeptɔːk] *n* bodrenje
per [pə; pəː] *prep* 1. po 2. za
perceive [pəˈsiːv] *v* opaziti
per cent, percent [pəˈsent] posto
percentage [pəˈsentidʒ] *n* postotak
perceptible [pəˈseptəbl] *adj* opazljiv
perception [pəˈsepʃn] *n* percepcija
perceptive [pəˈseptiv] *adj* opažljiv
percussion [pəˈkʌʃn] *n* udarac
perestroika [ˌpereˈstrɔikə] *n* perestrojka
perfect [ˈpəːfikt] *n* savršen
perfect [pəˈfekt] *v* usavršiti
perfection [pəˈfekʃn] *n* savršenstvo
perfectly [pəˈfektli] *adv* 1. savsim 2. savršeno
perforate [ˈpəːfəreit] *v* perforirati
perforation [ˌpəːfəˈreiʃn] *n* perforacija
perform [pəˈfɔːm] *v* 1. izvršiti 2. funkcionisati 3. **to perform a play** izvesti komad
performance [pəˈfɔːməns] *n* 1. performanse 2. izvođenje

perfume [ˈpəːfjuːm] *n* parfem
perhaps [pəˈhæps] *adv* možda
peril [ˈperəl] *n* opasnost
perilous [ˈperələs] *adj* opasan
period [ˈpiəriəd] *n* 1. doba 2. period 3. (ed.) čas; sat 4. menstruacija 5. **to miss a period** izostanak menstruacije
periodic [ˌpiəriˈɔdik] *adj* periodičan
perish [ˈperiʃ] *v* poginuti
perishable [ˈperiʃəbl] *adj* pokvarljiv
perjury [ˈpəːdʒəri] *n* 1. krivokletstvo 2. **to commit perjury** lažno se zakleti
perks [pəːks] *pl* posredne privilegije
perm [pəːm] *n* trajna ondulacija
permanence [ˈpəːmənəns] *n* stalnost
permanent [ˈpəmənənt] *adj* stalan
permanently [ˈpəmənəntli] *adv* stalno
permanent seat *n* (pol.) doživotni položaji stalni član
permanent secretary *n* (pol.) podsekretar (u ministarstvu)
permission [pəˈmiʃn] *n* dopuštenje
permit [ˈpəːmit] *n* dozvola
permit [pəˈmit] *v* (**permitted**) dozvoliti
perpendicular [ˌpəːpənˈdikjulə] *adj* perpendikularan
perpetrate [pəˈpetʃueit] *v* izvršiti
perpetual [pəˈpetʃuəl] *adj* večit; vječit
perpetually [pəˈpetʃuəli] *adv* večno; vječno
perpetuate [pəˈpetʃueit] *v* ovekovečiti; ovjekovječiti
perplex [pəˈpleks] *v* zbuniti
persecute [ˈpəːsikjuːt] *v* proganjati
persecution [ˌpəːsiˈkjuːʃn] *n* proganjanje

persecutor [ˈpəːsikjuːtə] *n* progonilac

perseverance [ˌpəːsiˈviərəns] *n* istrajnost

persevere [ˌpəːsiˈviə] *v* istrajati (in u)

persist [pəˈsist] *v* istrajati

persistence [pəˈsistəns] *n* istrajnost

persistent [pəˈsistənt] *adj* istrajan

person [ˈpəːsn] *n* 1. lice 2. in person lično

personal [ˈpəːsənl] *adj* ličan

personality [ˌpəːsəˈnæləti] *n* ličnost

personal life *n* lični život

personally [ˈpəːsənli] *adv* 1. lično 2. što se tiče

personal organizer *n* rokovnik

personal property *n* lična svojina

personnel [ˌpəːsəˈnel] *n* personal

perspective [pəˈspektiv] *n* perspektiva

perspiration [ˌpəːspəˈreiʃn] *n* znoj

perspire [pəˈspaiə] *v* znojiti se

persuade [pəˈsweid] *v* nagovoriti

persuaded [pəˈsweidid] *adj* to be persuaded biti ubeđen

persuasion [pəˈsweiʒn] *n* nagovaranje

persuasive [pəˈsweisiv] *adj* ubedljiv; ubjedljiv

pertinent [ˈpəːtinənt] *adj* značajan

perusal [pəˈruːzl] *n* pregled

peruse [pəˈruːz] *v* pregledati

perverse [pəˈvəːs] *adj* perverzan

pervert [ˈpəːvəːt] *n* izopačenik

pervert [pəˈvəːt] *v* izopačiti

pessimism [ˈpesimizəm] *n* pesimizam

pessimist [ˈpesimist] *n* pesimista

pessimistic [ˌpesiˈmistik] *adj* to be pessimistic pesimističan

pest [pest] *n* štetočina

pester [ˈpestə] *v* dosaditi

pesticide [ˈpestisaid] *n* pesticid

pestle [ˈpesl] *n* tučak

pet [pet] *n* zlovolja

petal [ˈpetl] *n* latica

petition [pəˈtiʃn] 1. *n* molba 2. *v* podneti molbu; podnijeti molbu

petitioner [pəˈtiʃnə] *n* molilac

petition for *v* moliti za

petrochemical [ˌpetrəuˈkemikl] *adj* petrohemijski; petrokemijski

petrol [ˈpetrəl] *n* benzin

petroleum [pəˈtrəuliəm] *n* petrolej

petrol pump *n* benzinska pumpa

petrol station *n* benzinska stanica

petticoat [ˈpetikəut] *n* podsuknja

petty [ˈpeti] *adj* sitan

petty cash *n* novac za sitne troškove

phantom [ˈfæntəm] *n* fantom

pharmaceutical [ˌfaːməˈsjuːtikl] *adj* farmaceutski

pharmacist [ˈfaːməsist] *n* apotekar

pharmacologist [ˌfaːməˈkɔlɔdʒist] *n* farmakolog

pharmacology [ˌfaːməˈkɔlɔdʒi] *n* farmakologija

pharmacy [ˈfaːməsi] *n* apoteka

phase [feiz] *n* faza

PhD [ˌpiːeitʃˈdiː] *n* doktorat

phenomenon [fəˈnɔminən] *n* (*pl* **phenomena**) pojava

philosopher [fiˈlɔsəfə] *n* filozof

philosophy [fiˈlɔsəfi] *n* filozofija

phlegm [flem] *n* flegma

phobia [ˈfəubiə] *n* fobija

phone [fəun] 1. *n* telefon 2. **car phone** telefon u automobilu 3. **cordless phone** bežični telefon 4. **mobile phone** mobilni telefon 5. *v* telefonirati

phonetic [fəˈnetik] *adj* fonetski

phonetics [fə'netiks] *n* fonetika
phonology [fə'nɔlɔdʒi] *n* fonologija
phony ['fəuni] *adj* lažan
photo ['fəutəu] 1. *n* slika 2. *v* fotografisati
photocopier ['fəutəukɔpiə] *n* aparat za fotokopiranje
photocopy ['fəutəukɔpi] 1. *n* fotokopija 2. *v* fotokopirati
photograph ['fəutəgrɑːf] 1. *n* slika 2. *v* fotografisati
photographer [fə'tɔgrəfə] *n* fotograf
photography [fə'tɔgrəfi] *n* fotografija
phrase [freiz] *n* fraza
physical ['fizikl] 1. *adj* telesni; tjelesni 2. *n* (med.) lekarski pregled; ljekarski pregled
physical education *n* fizička kultura
physical examination *n* (med.) lekarski pregled; ljekarski pregled
physical therapy *n* (med.) fizioterapija
physician [fi'ziʃn] *n* lekar/ljekar; liječnik
physicist ['fizisist] *n* fizičar
physics ['fiziks] *n* fizika
physiotherapist [,fiziəu'θerəpist] *n* fizioterapeut
physiotherapy [,fiziəu'θerəpi] *n* fizioterapija
piano, pianoforte [pi'ænəu; pi,ænəu'fɔːti] *n* klavir
pick [pik] *v* 1. kopati 2. brati 3. grickati 4. to pick a pocket džepariti 5. *see* pickaxe
pickaxe ['pikæks] *n* pijuk
picket ['pikit] 1. *n* piket 2. *v* piketirati

pickle ['pikl] *v* zakiselati
pick on *v* kinjiti
pick out *v* 1. izabrati 2. jasno opaziti
pickpocket ['pik,pɔkit] *n* džeparoš
pick-up (truck) *n* kamionet
pick up *v* 1. podići 2. prihvatiti
picnic ['piknik] *n* piknik
pictorial [pik'tɔːriəl] *adj* slikarski
picture ['piktʃə] *n* 1. slika 2. to take a picture načiniti snimak
pie [pai] *n* pita
piece [piːs] 1. *n* komad 2. delo; djelo
piece together *v* sastaviti
piecework ['piːswəːk] *n* akord
pier [piə] *n* stub
pierce [piəs] *v* probiti
piercing ['piəsiŋ] *adj* prodoran
pig [pig] *n* svinja, prase
pigeon ['pidʒin] *n* golub
pigeonhole ['pidʒinhəul] *n* pretinac
piglet ['piglit] *n* mlada svinja
pigsty ['pigstai] *n* svinjac
pike [paik] *n* štuka
pile [pail] 1. *n* gomila 2. *v* nagomilati
piles [pailz] *pl* (med.) hemoroidi
pile up *v* nagomilati
pilgrim ['pilgrim] *n* hodočasnik
pilgrimage ['pilgrimidʒ] *n* hodočašće
pill [pil] *n* 1. pilula 2. the Pill hormonska tableta 3. to take a pill uzeti pilulu
pillar ['pilə] *n* stub
pillar box *n* (UK) poštansko sanduče
pillow ['piləu] *n* jastuk
pilot ['pailət] 1. *n* pilot 2. *v* pilotirati
pimp [pimp] *n* podvodnik
pimple ['pimpl] *n* bubuljica
pin [pin] *n* čioda

pinch [pintʃ] v štipnuti
pine [pain] n bor
pineapple [ˈpainæpl] n ananas
ping-pong [ˈpiŋpɔŋ] n stoni tenis; stolni tenis
pink [piŋk] adj boje karanfila
pinnacle [ˈpinəkl] n vrhunac
pins and needles pl žmarci
pint [paint] n pinta
pin-up [ˈpinʌp] n pin-ap
pioneer [ˌpaiəˈniə] n pionir
pious [ˈpaiəs] adj pobožan
pipe [pip] n tačka; točka
pipe [paip] n 1. cev; cijev 2. lula
pipeline [ˈpaiplain] n 1. cevovod; cjevovod 2. **gas pipeline** gasovod, plinovod 3. **oil pipeline** naftovod
pirate [ˈpaiərət] 1. n pirat 2. v plagirati
pistol [ˈpistl] n pištolj
piston [ˈpistən] n klip
pit [pit] n jama
pitch [pitʃ] 1. n (mus.) visina tona 2. (spor.) teren 3. **sales pitch** reklama 4. v baciti 5. **to pitch camp** postaviti logor
pitch dark adj potpuno mračan
pitfall [ˈpitfɔːl] n zamka
pitiable [ˈpitiəbl] adj jadan
pitiful [ˈpitifəl] adj veoma loš
pitiless [ˈpitilis] adj nemilosrdan
pity [ˈpiti] 1. n sažaljenje 2. **what a pity!** kakva šteta! 3. v sažaljevati
pivot [ˈpivət] n stožer
pizza [ˈpiːtsə] n pica
placard [ˈplækaːd] n plakat
place [pleis] 1. n mesto; mjesto 2. stan 3. **in place of** umesto; umjesto 4. **out of place** neumesno; neumjesno 5. **in the first place** kao prvo 6. **to take place** desiti se 7. v staviti

placenta [pləˈsentə] n posteljica
place of residence n prebivalište
place of work n radno mesto/ mjesto
placid [ˈplæcid] adj miran
plagiarism [ˌpleidʒəˈrizm] n plagijat
plagiarize [ˈpleidʒəraiz] v plagirati
plague [pleig] n kuga
plain [plein] 1. adj jasan 2. prost 3. adv jasno 4. n ravnica
plain-clothes police [ˈpleinˈkləuðz] n policija u civilu
plainly [ˈpleinli] adv otvoreno
plaintiff [ˈpleintif] n (leg.) žalilac
plait [plæt] 1. n pletenica 2. v oplesti
plan [plæn] 1. n plan 2. projekat 3. v (**planned**) planirati
plane [plein] n 1. ravan 2. avion 3. **by plane** avionom
planet [ˈplænit] n planeta
plank [plæŋk] n debela daska
planning [ˈplæniŋ] n planiranje
plant [plaːnt] 1. n biljka 2. fabrika 3. v posaditi
plantain [ˈplaːntein] n bokvica
plantation [plænˈteiʃn] n plantaža
planting [ˈplaːntiŋ] n sđenje
plaster [ˈplaːstə] 1. n gips 2. (med.) flaster 3. v gipsovati
plasterer [ˈplaːstərə] n gipsar
plastic [ˈplæstik] 1. adj plastičan 2. n plastika
plastic bag n najlon-kesica
plastic bomb n plastična bomba
plastic surgery n plastična hirurgija/kirurgija
plate [pleit] n 1. ploča 2. tanjir 3. **gold plate** zlatna prevlaka
plateau [ˈplætəu] n visoravan
platform [ˈplætfɔːm] n platforma
platoon [pləˈtuːn] n vod

play [plei] 1. *n* igra 2. komad, drama 3. *v* (spor.) igrati (se) 4. (mus.) svirati

play back *v* ponoviti

play down *v* potceniti; potcjeniti

player ['pleiə] *n* 1. igrač 2. glumac

playground ['pleigraund] *n* igralište

playing field *n* igralište

plaza ['plɑːzə] *n* trg

plea [pliː] *n* molba

plead [pliːd] *v* zastupati

pleasant ['pleznt] *adj* prijatan

pleasantness ['plezntnis] *n* prijatnost

please [pliːz] *v* 1. zadovoljiti 2. please! molim!

pleased [pliːzd] *adj* to be pleased biti zadovoljan

pleasing ['pliːziŋ] *adj* prijatan

pleasure ['pleʒə] *n* uživanje

plebiscite ['plebisait] *n* plebiscit

pledge [pledʒ] 1. *n* zaloga 2. *v* založiti

plenary session ['pliːnəri] *n* plenarna sednica/sjednica

plentiful ['plentifl] *adj* obilan

plenty ['plenti] 1. *adj* obilan 2. *n* obilje 3. *adv* veoma

pleurisy ['pləːrisi] *n* pleuritis

pliers ['plaiəz] *pl* klešta; kliješta

plight [plait] *n* neprilika

plot [plɔt] 1. (pol.) zavera; zavjera 2. plot of land parče zemlje 3. story plot zaplet 4. *v* planirati 5. (pol.) kovati zaveru/zavjeru

plough, plow [plau] 1. *n* plug 2. *v* orati

pluck [plʌk] *v* 1. otkinuti 2. (mus.) prebirati

plug [plʌg] *n* 1. čep 2. electric plug utikač 3. spark plug svećica; svjećica 4. *v* začepiti

plug in *v* utaknuti

plug socket *n* štekontakt

plum [plʌm] *n* šljiva

plumber ['plʌmə] *n* vodo-instalater

plumbing ['plʌmiŋ] *n* vodovod

plume [pluːm] *n* pero

plummet ['plʌmit] *v* pasti

plump [plʌmp] *adj* pun

plunder ['plʌndə] *v* pljačkati

plunge [plʌndʒ] *v* 1. zariti 2. srnuti

plural [,pluərəl] 1. *adj* pluralni 2. *n* plural

plus [plʌs] *conj* plus

plus factor *n* pozitivan faktor

plush [plʌʃ] *adj* luksuzan

plywood ['plaiwud] *n* iverploča

p.m. (post meridiem) [,piː'em] popodne

pneumatic [njuː'mætik] *adj* pneumatski

pneumonia [njuː'məuniə] *n* zapaljenje pluća

PO (post office) [,piː'əu] *n* pošta

poach [pəutʃ] *v* 1. poširati 2. loviti bespravno

poacher ['pəutʃə] *n* lovokradica

PO box *n* poštanski fah

pocket ['pɔkit] *n* džep

pocket money *n* džeparac

pocketful ['pɔkitful] *n* pun džep

pod [pɔd] *n* mahuna

poem ['pəuim] *n* pesma; pjesma

poet ['pəuit] *n* pesnik; pjesnik

poetic [pəu'etik] *adj* pesnički; pjesnički

poetry ['pəuitri] *n* poezija

pogrom ['pɔgrəm] *n* pogrom

point [pɔint] 1. *n* tačka; točka 2. vrh 3. mesto; mjesto 4. (spor.) poen 5. assembly point zborno mesto/mjesto 6. at that point toga trenutka 7. to be on the

point of biti na granici **8. zero point three (0.3)** nula zarez tri **9.** *v* pokazati **10. to point a gun at** uperiti pušku na

pointed ['pɔintid] *adj* šiljast

pointless ['pɔintləs] *adj* irelevantan

point of view *n* tačka gledišta; točka gledišta

point out *v* ukazati

poise [pɔiz] *n* ravnoteža

poised ['pɔizd] *adj* **to be poised** biti spreman

poison ['pɔizn] **1.** *n* otrov **2.** *v* otrovati

poison gas *n* bojni otrov

poisonous ['pɔizənəs] *adj* otrovan

poke [pəuk] *v* gurati

poker ['pəukə] *n* **1.** žarač **2.** poker

polar ['pəulə] *adj* polarni

pole [pəul] *n* **1.** pol **2. the North Pole** Severni pol; Sjeverni pol **3. the South Pole** Južni pol

pole vault *n* (spor.) skok motkom

police [pə'liːs] *pl* **1.** policija **2. secret police** tajna policija **3. military police** vojna policija

police force *n* policija

policeman, police officer [pə'liːsmən] *n* policijac

police station *n* milicijska stanica

policewoman [pə'liːs,wumən] *n* žena policijac

policy ['pɔləsi] *n* **1.** (pol.) politika **2. insurance policy** osiguranje

polio ['pəuliəu] *n* poliomielitis

polish ['pɔliʃ] **1.** *n* poliš **2.** *v* polirati

polite [pə'lait] *adj* učtiv

politeness [pə'laitnis] *n* učtivost

political [pə'litikl] *adj* politički

political asylum *n* politički azil

political crime *n* političko krivično delo/djelo

political economy *n* politička ekonomija

political science *n* političke nauke

political scientist *n* politikolog

politician [,pɔli'tiʃn] *n* političar

politics ['pɔlətiks] *n* politika

poll [pəul] **1.** *n* anketa **2. opinion poll** ispitivanje javnog mnenja **3.** *v* anketirati **4.** *see* **polls**

polling ['pəuliŋ] *n* glasanje

polling booth *n* kabina za glasanje

polls [pəulz] *n* glasanje

poll tax *n* (UK) lični porez na glavu

pollute [pə'ljuːt] *v* zagaditi

pollution [pə'luːʃn] *n* zagađenost

polo ['pəuləu] *n* polo

polygamy [pə'ligæmi] *n* poligamija

polytechnic [,pɔli'teknik] *n* (ed.) politehnika

pomegranate ['pɔmigrænit] *n* nar

pompous ['pɔmpəs] *adj* pompezan

pond [pɔnd] *n* jezerce

ponder ['pɔndə] *v* razmisliti (o)

pontoon [pɔn'tuːn] *n* ponton

pontoon bridge *n* pontonski most

pony ['pəuni] *n* poni

ponytail ['pəuniteil] *n* kika

pool [puːl] **1.** *n* lokva **2.** (fin.) rezervni fond **3.** (spor.) bilijar **4.** *v* udružiti **5.** *see* **swimming-pool**

poor [pɔː] *adj* **1.** siromašan **2.** slab **3. the poor** siromasi

poor health *n* slabo zdravlje

poorly ['pɔːli] *adv* **1.** loše **2. to feel poorly** osećati se bolesnim; osjećati se bolesnim

poorly off *adj* u bedi/bijedi

pop [pɔp] *v* pući

popcorn ['pɔpkɔːn] *n* kokice

pope [pəup] *n* papa

pop in *v* neočekivano doći

poppy ['pɔpi] *n* mak

populace ['pɔpjuləs] *n* prost narod

popular ['pɔpjulə] *adj* 1. popularan 2. narodni

popularity [,pɔpju'lærəti] *n* popularnost

popularize ['pɔpjuləraiz] *v* popularizovati

populate ['pɔpjuleit] *v* naseliti

populated [,pɔpju'leitid] *adj* The area is densely populated. To područje je gusto naseljeno.

population [,pɔpju'leiʃn] *n* 1. stanovništvo 2. naseljenost

population control *n* demografska kontrola

population density *n* gustina naseljenosti

population explosion *n* demografska eksplozija

populous ['pɔpjuləs] *adj* gusto naseljen

pop up *v* pojaviti se

porcelain ['pɔːsəlin] *n* porcelan

porch [pɔːtʃ] *n* 1. trem; trijem 2. (US) veranda

porcupine ['pɔːkjupain] *n* dikobraz

pore over [pɔː] *v* čitati

pork [pɔːk] *n* svinjetina

porn [pɔːn] *see* **pornography**

pornographic [,pɔːnə'græfik] *adj* pornografski

pornography [pɔː'nɔgrəfi] *n* pornografija

porous ['pɔːrəs] *adj* porozan

porridge ['pɔridʒ] *n* ovsena kaša

port [pɔːt] *n* luka

port authority *n* lučka uprava

port facilities *n* lučka postrojenja

portable ['pɔːtəbl] *adj* portabl

porter ['pɔːtə] *n* 1. nosač 2. (UK) vratar

portfolio [pɔːt'fəuliəu] *n* 1. portfelj 2. **minister without portfolio** ministar bez portfelja

portion ['pɔːʃn] *n* 1. deo; dio 2. porcija

portly ['pɔːtli] *adj* gojazan

portrait ['pɔːtreit] *n* portret

portray [pɔː'trei] *v* portretisati

Portugal ['pɔtʃugl] *n* Portugalija

Portuguese [pɔtʃu'giːz] 1. *adj* portugalski 2. *n* Portugalac

pose [pəuz] 1. *n* poza 2. *v* pozirati

pose a problem *v* predstavljati problem

pose a question *v* postaviti pitanje

posh [pɔʃ] *adj* luksuzan

position [pə'ziʃn] *n* 1. položaj 2. posao 2. stav

positive ['pɔzətiv] *adj* 1. pozitivan 2. siguran

positively ['pɔzətivli] *adv* sigurno

possess [pə'zes] *v* posedovati

possession [pə'zeʃn] *n* posedovanje; posjedovanje

possessions [pə'zeʃnz] *pl* posed; posjed

possessive [pə'zesiv] *adj* posesivan

possessor [pə'zesə] *n* vlasnik, posednik; posjednik

possibility [,pɔsə'biləti] *n* mogućnost

possible ['pɔsəbl] *adj* moguć

possibly ['pɔsəbli] *adv* moguće

post [pəust] 1. *n* stub 2. služba 3. pošta 4. **guard post** stražarsko mesto/mjesto 5. *v* poslati poštom 6. postaviti

postage ['pəustidʒ] *n* poštarina

postage stamp *n* poštanksa marka

postal order *n* novčana uputnica

postbox ['pəustbɔks] *n* poštansko sanduće

postcard ['pəustkaːd] *n* dopisnica

post code n (UK) poštanski broj
poster ['pəustə] n plakat
poste restante n post restant
posterior [pɔ'stiəriə] adj zadnji
posterity [pɔ'sterəti] n potomstvo
postgraduate [pəust'grædjuət] adj postdiplomski
postman ['pəustmən] n poštar
postmortem [pəust'mɔ:təm] n obdukcija
post-office adj poštanski
post office n pošta
post office box n poštanski fah
postpone [pə'spəun] v odgoditi
postponement [pə'spəunmənt] n odgoda
postulate ['pɔstjuleit] v postulirati
posture ['pɔstʃə] n stav
postwar [pɔst'wɔ:] adj posleratni; poslijeratni
pot [pɔt] n lonac
potassium [pə'tæsijəm] n kalijum
potato [pə'teitəu] n (pl **potatoes**) krompir; krumpir
potency ['pəutnsi] n potentnost
potent ['pəutnt] adj potentan
potential [pə'tenʃl] 1. adj moguć 2. n potencijal
potentiality [pə,tenʃi'aliti] n potencijalnost
pothole ['pɔthəul] n rupa
potion ['pəuʃən] n napitak
potter ['pɔtə] n lončar
potter's wheel n lončarski točak
pottery ['pɔtəri] n 1. lončarija 2. lončarstvo
potty ['pɔti] n nokširić
pouch [pautʃ] n 1. torba 2. **diplomatic pouch** diplomatska pošta
poultry ['pəultri] pl živina
pounce [pauns] v skočiti (**on** na)

pound [paund] 1. n funta 2. v tući
pounding ['paundiŋ] n (mil.) bombardovanje
pour [pɔ:] v sipati
pouring [pɔ:riŋ] adj **It is pouring.** Lije kao iz kabla.
pout [paut] v prćiti se
poverty ['pɔvəti] n siromaštvo
poverty level n granica siromaštva
poverty-stricken adj veoma siromašan
POW [,pijəud'ʌbəlju] see **prisoner of war**
powder ['paudə] n prah
powdered ['paudəd] adj u prahu
powdered milk n mleko u prahu; mlijeko u prahu
power ['pauə] 1. n sila 2. moć 3. energija 4. **in power** na vlasti 5. **to take power** preuzeti vlast
powerboat ['pauəbəut] n motorni čamac
powerbook ['pauəbuk] n portabl kompjuter
power cut n prekid u snabdevanju električnom energijom; prekid u snabdijevanju električnom energijom
power drill n električna bušilica
powerful ['pauəfl] adj jak
powerless ['pauələs] adj nemoćan
power line n strujni vod
power loss n gubitak snage
power plant, power station n elektrana
power-sharing n deljenje vlasti; dijeljenje vlasti
power source n izvor energije
PR [,pi:'a:] see **public relations**
practical ['præktikl] adj praktičan
practically ['præktikli] adv 1. praktično 2. skoro

practice [ˈpræktis] n 1. praksa 2. vežba; vježba 3. navika 4. private practice privatna praksa 5. in practice u praksi 6. to put into practice primeniti u praksi; primijeniti u praksi 7. see practise

practise [ˈpræktis] v 1. vežbati (se); vježbati (se) 2. vršiti

practitioner [prækˈtiʃənə] n 1. praktičar 2. lekar opšte prakse; ljeknik opšte prakse

praise [preiz] 1. n pohvala 2. v pohvaliti

praiseworthy [ˈpreizwəːði] adj pohvalan

pram [præm] n kolica za bebu

prank [præŋk] n šala

prawn [prɔːn] n rak

pray [prei] v moliti se

prayer [preə] n molitva

praying mantis [ˌpreijiŋˈmæntis] n bogomoljka

preach [priːtʃ] v propovedati; propovijedati

preacher [ˈpriːtʃə] n propovednik; propovjednik

precarious [priˈkeəriəs] adj nesiguran

precaution [priˈkɔːʃn] n predostrožnost

precautionary [priˈkɔːʃənəri] n obazriv

precede [priˈsiːd] v prethoditi

precedence [ˈpresidəns] n prednost

precedent [ˈpresidənt] n presedan

preceding [priˈsiːdiŋ] adj prethodan

precept [ˈpriːsept] n pravilo

precinct [ˈpriːsiŋkt] n 1. (US) policijski okrug 2. (UK) shopping precinct trgovački centar

precious [ˈpreʃəs] adj drag

precipice [ˈpresəpis] n litica

precipitate [preˈsipiteit] v ubrzati

precipitation [preˈsipiteiʃn] n padavine

precise [priˈsais] adj precizan

precisely [priˈsaisli] adv tačno; točno, baš tako

precision [priˈsiʒn] n preciznost

preconception [ˌpriːkənˈsepʃn] n predrasuda

precondition [ˌpriːkənˈdiʃn] n preduslov

precursor [ˈpriːkəːsə] n prethodnik

predecessor [ˈpriːdisesə] n prethodnik

predicament [priˈdikəmənt] n nezgoda

predict [priˈdikt] v predskazati

predictable [priˈdiktəbl] adj predvidiv

prediction [priˈdikʃn] n predskazanje

predominant [priˈdɔminənt] adj predominantan

predominate [priˈdɔmineit] v predominirati

pre-empt [priːˈempt] v prisvojiti

prefabricate [priˈfæbrikeit] v prefabrikovati

preface [ˈprefis] n predgovor

prefer [priˈfəː] v više voleti/voljeti

preferable [ˈprefrəbl] adj bolji

preference [ˈprefrəns] n prednost

preferential [ˌprefəˈrentʃəl] adj prioritetni

preferential treatment n protekcija

pre-flight [ˈpriːflait] adj pretpoletni

pregnancy [ˈpregnənsi] n trudnoća

pregnancy test n test za utvrđivanje trudnoće

pregnant [ˈpregnənt] adj trudna

prejudice ['predʒudis] *n* 1. predrasuda 2. **racial prejudice** rasna predrasuda

prejudicial [ˌpredʒuˈdiʃl] *adj* štetan

preliminary [priˈliminəri] *adj* prethodni

premarital [priˈmæritəl] *adj* prebračni

premature ['premətjuə] *adj* 1. prevremen; prijevremen 2. **premature baby** nedonošče

premeditated [ˌpriˈmediteitid] *adj* s predumišljajem

premeditated murder *n* ubistvo s predumišljajem; ubojstvo s predumišljajem

premier ['premiə] *n* premijer

premiere ['premieə] *n* premijera

premises ['premisiz] *pl* prostorije

premium ['priːmiəm] *n* premija

premonition [ˌpreməˈniʃn] *n* predosećanje; predosjećanje

prenatal [priːˈneitəl] *adj* antenatalni

preoccupation [ˌpriːɔkjuˈpeiʃn] *n* zaokupljenost

preoccupied [priːˈɔkjupaid] *adj* zaokupljen

prepaid ['priːpeid] *adj* unapred plaćen; unaprijed plaćen

preparation [ˌprepəˈreiʃn] *n* priprema

preparatory [priˈpærətri] *adj* pripremni

prepare [priˈpeə] *v* spremiti (se)

prepared [priˈpeəd] *adj* spreman

prepay [priˈpei] *v* unapr(ij)ed platiti

preposition [prepəˈziʃn] *n* predlog; prijedlog

prescribe [priˈskraib] *v* propisati

prescription [priˈskripʃn] *n* (med.) lek; lijek

presence ['prezns] *n* prisustvo

present ['preznt] 1. *adj* sadašnji 2. **to be present** biti prisutan 3. *n* poklon 4. sadašnjica 5. **at present** sada

present [priˈzent] *v* 1. podneti; podnijeti 2. predstaviti

presentation [ˌprezn̩ˈteiʃn] *n* 1. prezentacija 2. predstavljanje

present-day ['prezntˈdei] *adj* današnji

presenter *n* komentator

presently ['prezntli] *adv* 1. sada 2. uskoro

preservation [ˌprezəˈveiʃn] *n* čuvanje

preserve [priˈzəːv] *v* sačuvati

preserves [priˈzəːvz] *pl* slatko

preside [priˈzaid] *v* predsedavati; predjedavati

presidency ['prezidənsi] *n* predsedništvo; predsjedništvo

president ['prezidənt] *n* 1. predsednik; predsjednik 2. (com.) generalni direktor

president-elect *n* izabrani predsednik/predsjednik

presidential [preziˈdənʃl] *n* predsednički; predsjednički

presidential guard *n* predsednička garda; predsjednička garda

press [pres] 1. *n* presa 2. **the press** štampa 3. *v* pritiskati

press agency *n* novinska agencija

press censorship *n* cenzura štampe

press conference *n* konferencija za štampu

press grapes *n* muljati grožđe

pressing ['presiŋ] *adj* hitan

press release *n* objava za štampu

press secretary *n* sekretar za štampu

pressure [ˈpreʃə] *n* 1. pritisak 2.
under pressure pod pritiskom
pressurize [ˈpreʃəraiz] *v* staviti pod
pritisak
prestige [preˈstiːʒ] *n* prestiž
prestigious [preˈstiːʒəs] *adj*
ugledan
presume [priˈzjuːm] *v* pretpostaviti
presumption [priˈzʌmptʃən] *n*
pretpostavka
presumptuous [priˈzʌmptʃuəs] *adj*
drzak
pretence [priˈtens] *n* izgovor
pretend [priˈtend] *v* pretvarati se
pretense [priˈtens] *see* pretence
pretension [priˈtenʃn] *n* pretenzija
pretentious [priˈtenʃəʃ] *adj*
uobražen
pretext [ˈpriːtekst] *n* izogovor
pretty [ˈpriti] 1. *adj* lepuškast;
ljepuškast 2. *adv* prilično
prevail [priˈveil] *v* preovlađivati
prevalent [ˈprevələnt] *adj*
preovlađujući
prevent [priˈvent] *v* sprečiti;
spriječiti
prevention [priˈvenʃn] *n*
sprečavanje
preventive, **preventative**
[priˈventiv; priˈventətiv] *adj*
preventivan
preview [ˈpriːvju] *n* pretpremijera
previous [ˈpriːviəs] *adj* prethodan
previously [ˈpriːviəsli] *adv* prethodno
prewar [priːˈwɔː] *adj* predratni
prey [prei] *n* plen; plijen
prey on *v* hvatati
price [prais] 1. *n* cena; cijena 2. **at
half price** u pola cene 3. *v*
odretiti cenu/cijenu
priceless [ˈpraislis] *adj*
neprocenljiv; neprocjenljiv

prick [prik] *v* nabosti
prickly [ˈprikli] *adj* bodljikav
pride [praid] *n* ponos
priest [priːst] *n* sveštenik; svećenik
primarily [praiˈmerili] *adv*
uglavnom
primary [ˈpraiməri] *adj* osovni
primary education *n* osnovo
obrazovanje
primary elections *pl* preliminarni
izbori
primary health care *n* osnovna
zdravstvena zaštita
primary school *n* osovna škola
prime [praim] *n* glavni
prime minister *n* premijer
primitive [ˈprimitiv] *adj* primitivan
prince [prins] *n* knez
princess [prinˈses] *n* kneginja
principal [ˈprinsəpl] 1. *adj* glavni 2.
n (ed.) direktor
principality [ˌprinsiˈpæləti] *n*
kneževina
principle [ˈprinsəpl] *n* 1. princip 2.
in principle u principu
print [print] 1. *n* štampa 2. otisak
3. *v* štampati 4. napraviti otisak
printer [ˈprintə] *n* 1. štampar 2.
štampač
printing [ˈprintiŋ] *n* štampanje
printing house *n* štamperija
printing press *n* štamparska
mašina
print-out [ˈprintaut] *n* odštampani
znakovi
print out *v* odštampati
priority [praiˈɔrəti] *n* prioritet
prior to [ˈpraiə] *prep* do
prism [ˈprizm] *n* prizma
prison [ˈprizn] *n* zatvor
prisoner [ˈprizinə] *n* 1. zatvorenik 2.
to take prisoner zarobiti

prisoner of war (POW) 1. *adj* zarobljenički 2. *n* ratni zarobljenik

prisoner of war camp *n* zarobljenički logor

prison riot *n* zatvorski neredi

prison sentence *n* sudska presuda

privacy [ˈprivəsi] *n* tajnost

private [ˈpraivit] 1. *adj* taj 2. privatan 3. **in private** privatno 4. *n* (mil.) redov

private detective, private investigator *n* privatni detektiv

private enterprise *n* privatna inicijativa

private parts *pl* genitalje

private property *n* privatna svojina

private visit *n* privatna poseta; privatni posjet

privately [ˈpraivitli] *adv* privatno

privatization [ˌpraivətaiˈzeiʃn] *n* privatizacija

privatize [ˈpraivətaiz] *v* privatizovati; privatizirati

privilege [ˈprivəlidʒ] *n* privilegija

privileged [ˈprivəlidʒd] *adj* privilegovan

prize [praiz] *n* nagrada

prize-winning *adj* nagrađen

prize money *n* novčana nagrada

pro [prəu] 1. *adv* za 2. *see* **professional**

probability [ˌprɔbəˈbiləti] *n* verovatnoća; vjerovatnoća

probable [ˈprɔbəbl] *adj* verovatan; vjerovatan

probably [ˈprɔbəbli] *adv* verovatno; vjerovatno

probation [prəuˈbeiʃn] *n* uslovno oslobođenje

probe [prəub] *v* ispipavati

problem [ˈprɔbləm] *n* 1. problem 2. **to solve a problem** rešiti problem; riješiti problem 3. **no problem!** nema problema!

procedural [prəˈsiːdʒurəl] *adj* proceduralan

procedure [prəˈsiːdʒə] *n* postupak

proceed [prəˈsiːd] *v* postupiti

proceedings [prəˈsiːdiŋz] *n* (leg.) postupak

proceeds [ˈprəˈsiːdz] *pl* prinos

process [ˈprəuses] 1. *n* proces 2. **in process** u toku 3. *v* obraditi

processed food *n* prerađena hrana

procession [prəˈseʃn] *n* povorka

processor [ˈprəusesʃə] *n* procesor

proclaim [prəˈkleim] *v* proglasiti

proclamation [ˌprɔkləˈmeiʃn] *n* proglas

procrastinate [prəuˈkræstineit] *v* odugovlačiti

procure [prəˈkjuə] *v* nabaviti

prod [prɔd] *v* podstaći

produce [ˈprɔdjuːs] *n* proizvod

produce [prəˈdjuːs] *v* 1. proizvesti 2. pokazati 3. navesti 4. **to produce a film** producirati

producer [prəˈdjuːsə] *n* 1. proizvođac 2. **film producer** producent filmova

product [ˈprɔdʌkt] *n* proizvod

production [prəˈdʌkʃn] *n* 1. proizvodnja 2. **film production** produkcija filmova

productive [prəˈdʌktiv] *adj* produktivan

profess [prəˈfes] *v* izjaviti

profession [prəˈfeʃn] *n* profesija

professional [prəˈfeʃnl] 1. *adj* profesionalan 2. stručni 3. *n* profesionalac

professionalism [prəˈfeʃənlizm] *n* profesionalizam

professor [prə'fesə] *n* profesor
proffer ['prɔfə] *v* ponuditi
proficiency [prə'fiʃnsi] *n* vičnost
proficient [prə'fiʃnt] *adj* vešt; vješt
profile ['prəufail] *n* profil
profit ['prɔfit] 1. *n* dobit 2. **net profit** čista dobit 3. **to make a profit** dobiti (**from** na) 4. *v* profitirati
profitability [ˌprɔfitəbiliti] *n* rentabilnost
profitable ['prɔfitəbl] *adj* rentabilan
profit and loss *n* dobitak i gubitak
profiteer [ˌprɔfi'tiə] 1. *n* profiter 2. **war profiteer** ratni profiter 3. *v* biti profiter
profiteering [ˌprɔfi'tiəriŋ] *n* profiterstvo
profound [prə'faund] *adj* dubok
profusion [prə'fjuːʒn] *n* rasipnost
programme, program ['prəugræm] *n* 1. program 2. emisija 3. *v* programirati
programmer ['prəugræmə] *n* programer
progress ['prəugres] *n* 1. napredak 2. **to make progress** postići napredak
progress [prə'gres] *v* napredovati
progression [prə'greʃn] *n* progresija
progressive [prə'gresiv] *adj* napredan
prohibit [prə'hibit] *v* zabraniti
prohibition [ˌprəuhi'biʃn] *n* zabrana
project ['prɔdʒekt] *n* projekat
project [prə'dʒekt] *v* projektovati
projection [prə'dʒekʃn] *n* projekcija
projector [prə'dʒektə] *n* projektor
proliferate [prə'lifəreit] *v* množiti se
proliferation [prə,lifə'reiʃn] *n* razmnožavanje

prolific [prə'lifik] *adj* plodan
prologue ['prəulɔg] *n* prolog
prolong [prə'lɔŋ] *v* produžiti
prominent ['prɔminənt] *adj* istaknut
promise ['prɔmis] 1. *n* obećanje 2. **to keep a promise** održati obećanje 3. *v* obećati
promising ['prɔmisiŋ] *adj* koji mnogo obećava
promote [prə'məut] *v* 1. unaprediti 2. (com.) reklamirati
promoter [prə'məutə] *n* organizator
promotion [prə'məuʃn] *n* 1. unapređenje 2. (com.) propaganda
prompt [prɔmpt] *adj* brz
pronoun ['prəunaun] *n* zamenica; zamjenica
pronounce [prə'nauns] *v* izgovoriti
pronunciation [prə,nʌnsi'eiʃn] *n* izgovor
proof [pruːf] *n* 1. dokaz 2. *see* **waterproof**
prop, prop up [prɔp] *v* podupreti
propaganda [ˌprɔpə'gændɛ] *n* propaganda
propel [prə'pel] *v* pokrenuti
propeller [prə'pelə] *n* elisa
proper ['prɔpə] *adj* pravi
properly ['prɔpəli] *adv* pravilno, ispravno
property ['prɔpəti] 1. *adj* imovinski 2. *n* svojina 3. **private property** privatna svojina 4. **government property** državna svojina
property rights *pl* pravo vlasništva
prophecy ['prɔfəsi] *n* proročanstvo
prophesy ['prɔfəsai] *v* proreći
prophet ['prɔfit] *n* prorok
proportion [prə'pɔːʃn] *n* 1. proporcija 2. **out of proportion**

nesrazmerno; nesrazmjerno **3. in proportion to** u razmeri s

proportional [prə'pɔːʃnl] *adj* proporcijalan

proportional representation *n* (pol.) proporcionalni izborni sistem

proportionate [prə'pɔːʃnət] *adj* proporcijalan

proposal [prə'pəuzl] *n* predlog

propose [prə'pəuz] *v* predložiti

proposition [,prɔpə'ziʃn] *n* propozicija

proprietor [prə'praətə] *n* vlasnik

prop up *v* podupreti; poduprijeti

prose [prəuz] *n* proza

prosecute ['prɔsikjuːt] *v* (pro)goniti

prosecution [,prɔsi'kjuːʃn] *n* **1.** gonjenje **2. to conduct the prosecution** zastupati optužnicu

prosecutor ['prɔsikjuːtə] *n* (leg.) javni tužilac

prospect ['prɔspekt] *n* izgled

prospect [prɔs'pekt] *v* tražiti

prospective [prə'spektiv] *adj* mogući

prospectus [prəs'pektəs] *n* brošura

prosper ['prɔspə] *v* cvetati; cvjetati

prosperity [prɔs'perəti] *n* blagostanje

prosperous ['prɔspərəs] *adj* uspešan; uspejšan

prostate ['prɔsteit] *n* prostata

prosthesis [prɔs'θiːsis] *n* proteza

prosthetic [prɔs'θetik] *adj* protezni

prosthetics [prɔs'θetiks] *n* protetika

prosthodontics [prɔsθə'dɔntiks] *n* zubna protetika

prostitute ['prɔstitjuːt] *n* prostitutka

prostitution [,prɔsti'tjuːʃn] *n* prostitucija

prostrate ['prɔstreit] *v* ispružen

protagonist [prəu'tægənist] *n* protagonista

protect [prə'tekt] *v* štititi

protection [prə'tekʃn] *n* zaštita

protectionism [prə'tekʃnizəm] *n* (ec.) protekcionizam

protection racket *n* ucena; ucjena

protective [prə'tektiv] *adj* zaštitni

protective measures *pl* zaštitne mere/mjere

protector [prə'tektə] *n* zaštitnik

protectorate [prə'tektərət] *n* protektorat

protein ['prəutiːn] *n* protein

protest ['prəutest] **1.** *adj* protestni **2.** *n* protest

protest [prə'test] *v* protestovati

Protestant ['prɔtistənt] **1.** *adj* protestantski **2.** *n* protestant

protester [prə'testə] *n* protestant

protest march *n* protestni skup

prototype ['prəutətaip] *n* prototip

protrude [prə'truːd] *v* strčati

proud [praud] *adj* **1.** ponosan **2.** ohol

prove [pruːv] *v* (**proved, proved/proven**) dokazati

proverb ['prɔvəːb] *n* poslovica

provide [prə'vaid] *v* snabdeti; snabdjeti

provided (that) [prə'vaidid] *conj* ako

provide for [prə'vaid] *v* **1.** starati se o **2.** predvideti; predvidjeti

provident ['prɔvidənt] *adj* štedljiv

providing [prə'vaidiŋ] *see* **provided**

province ['prɔvins] *n* provincija

provincial ['prɔvinʃəl] *adj* provincijalan

provision [prə'viʒn] *n* **1.** nabava **2.** (leg/pol.) odredba **3. on the provision that** ako

provisional [prə'viʒənl] *adj*
privremen
provisional government *n*
privremena vlada
provisions [prə'viʒnz] *n* namirnice
proviso [prə'vaizəu] *n* uslov
provocation [‚prɔvə'keʃn] *n*
provokacija
provocative [prə'vɔkətiv] *adj*
provokativan
provoke [prə'vəuk] *v* provocirati
prowl [praul] *v* krstariti
proximity [prɔk'siməti] *n* blizina
proxy ['prɔksi] *n* opunomoćenik
prudent ['pru:dnt] *adj* smotren
psalm [sa:m] *n* psalam
pseudo- [‚sju:dəu] *adj* pseudo-
pseudonym [‚sju:dənim] *n*
pseudonim
psychiatric [sai'kaiətrik] *adj*
psihijatrijski
psychiatrist [sai'kaiətrist] *n*
psihijatar
psychiatry [sai'kaiətri] *n*
psihijatrija
psycho ['saikəu] *n* psihopat
psychological [‚saikə'lɔdʒikl] *adj*
psihološki
psychologist ['sai'kɔlədʒist] *n*
psiholog
psychology ['sai'kɔlədʒi] *n*
psihologija
psychosis [sai'kəusis] *n* psihoza
pub [pʌb] *n* (UK) krčma
puberty ['pju:bəti] *n* pubertet
pubic [‚pju:bik] *adj* pubičan
pubic hair *n* bruce
public ['pʌblik] 1. *adj* javan 2.
državni 3. *n* publika 4. in public
javno
publication [‚pʌbli'keiʃn] *n*
publikacija

public health *n* zdravstvena zaštita
public holiday *n* državni praznik
public house *see* pub
publicity [pʌb'lisəti] *n* publicitet
publicize [‚pʌblisaiz] *v* dati
publicitet
publicly ['pʌblikli] *adv* javno
public opinion *n* javno mnenje
public property *n* društvena
imovina
publish ['pʌbliʃ] *v* izdati
publisher ['pʌbliʃə] *n* izdavač
publishing ['pʌbliʃiŋ] *n* izdavačka
delatnost/djelatnost
publishing house *n* izdavačka
kuća
pudding ['pudiŋ] *n* puding
puddle ['pʌdl] *n* lokva
puff [pʌf] *v* ispuštati
pull [pul] *v* 1. vući 2. to pull
someone's leg nasamariti nekoga
pull back *v* povući se
pull down *v* srušiti
pulley [‚puli] *n* kotur
pull out *v* izvaditi
pullover ['puləuvə] *n* pulover
pull through *v* izvući se
pulp [pʌlp] *n* kaša
pulsate [pʌl'seit] *v* trepteti; treptjeti
pulse [pʌls] *n* puls
pump [pʌmp] 1. *n* pumpa 2. *v*
pumpati
pumpkin ['pʌmpkin] *n* bundeva
pump up *v* napumpati
pun [pʌn] *n* kalambur
punch [pʌntʃ] 1. *n* udarac 2. *v*
udariti
punctual ['pʌŋktʃuəl] *adj* punktualan
punctuality [‚pʌŋktʃu'æləti] *n*
tačnost; točnost
punctuation [‚pʌŋktʃu'eiʃn] *n*
punktuacija

puncture [ˈpʌŋktʃə] 1. *n* rupa 2. *v* probušiti

punish [ˈpʌniʃ] *v* kazniti

punishable [ˈpʌniʃəbl] *adj* kažnjiv

punishment [ˈpʌniʃmənt] *n* 1. kazna 2. **corporal punishment** telesna kazna; tjelesna kazna 3. **capital punishment** smrtna kazna

punitive [ˈpjuːnətiv] *adj* kazneni

pupil [ˈpjuːpl] *n* 1. zenica; zjenica 2. (ed.) učenik

puppet [ˈpʌpit] *n* marioneta

puppet regime *n* (pol.) marionetska vlada

puppy [ˈpʌpi] *n* štene

purchase [ˈpəːtʃəs] 1. *n* kupovina 2. *v* kupiti

purchaser [ˈpəːtʃəsə] *n* kupac

purchasing power [ˈpəːtʃəsiŋ] *n* kupovna snaga

pure [pjuə] *adj* čist

purely [pjuə] *adv* potpuno

purge [pəːdʒ] *v* (pol.) očistiti

purify [ˈpjuərifai] *v* prečistiti

purity [ˈpjuərəti] *n* čistota

purple [ˈpəːpl] *adj* purpuran

purpose [ˈpəːpəs] *n* 1. srvha 2. **on purpose** namerno; namjerno

purposely [ˈpəːpəsli] *adv* namerno; namjerno

purr [pəː] *v* presti

purse [pəːs] *n* kesa

pursue [pəˈsjuː] *v* goniti

pursuit [pəˈsjuːt] *n* gonjenje

pus [pʌs] *n* gnoj

push [puʃ] *v* (pro)gurati

push-button *adj* automatski

push-chair *n* kolica za bebu

pusher [ˈpuʃə] *n* **drug pusher** rasturač

put [put] *v* (put) 1. staviti 2. metnuti

put aside *v* 1. ajiye 2. sa a mala

put away *v* staviti na mesto/mjesto

put back *v* vratiti na mesto/mjesto

put down *v* 1. zabeležiti; zabilježiti 2. slomiti 3. ubiti

put off *v* odložiti

put on *v* 1. obući 2. upaliti

put out *v* ugasiti

putty [ˈpʌti] *n* kit

put up with *v* trpeti

puzzle [ˈpʌzl] 1. *n* zagonetka 2. *v* zbuniti

puzzled [ˈpʌzəld] *adj* **to be puzzled** biti u nedoumici

puzzle out *v* odgonetnuti

puzzling [ˈpʌzliŋ] *adj* zbunjujući

pyjamas [pəˈdʒaːməz] *pl* pidžama

pyramid [ˈpirəmid] *n* piramida

pyrotechnics [ˌpaiərəuˈtekniks] *pl* pirotehnika

python [ˈpaiθn] *n* piton

Q

quack [kwæk] **1.** *n* kvakanje **2.** *v* kvakati

quadruple [ˈkwɔˈdruːpl] *v* učetvorostručiti (se); učetverostručiti (se)

quadruplets [kwɔˈdruːplits] *pl* četvorke

quaint [kweint] *adj* baauye

quake [kweint] *v* **1.** tresti se **2.** *see* **earthquake**

qualification [ˌkwɔlifiˈkeiʃn] *n* kvalifikacija

qualified [ˈkwɔlifaid] *adj* kvalifikovan

qualify [ˈkwɔlifai] *v* karakterisati (se)

quality [ˈkwɔləti] *n* **1.** kvalitet **2.** osobina

quantity [ˈkwɔntəti] *n* kvantitet

quarantine [ˌkwɔrəntiːn] **1.** *n* karantin **2.** *adj* staviti u karantin

quarrel [ˈkwɔrəl] **1.** *n* svađa **2.** *v* svađati se (**with** s)

quarrelsome [ˈkwɔrəlsəm] *adj* svadljiv

quarry [ˈkwɔrəl] *n* kamenolom

quarter [ˈkwɔːtə] *n* **1.** četvrtina, četvrt **2.** kvart

quarterly [ˈkwɔːtəli] *adv* tromesečni; tromjesečni

quarters [ˈkɔːtəz] *pl* **1.** (mil.) kasarna **2. at close quarters** u neposrednom dodiru

quash [kwɔʃ] *v* (leg.) poništiti

quartz [kɔːts] *n* kvarc

quay [kiː] *n* kej

queen [kwiːn] *n* kraljica

queer [kwiə] *adj* **1.** čudan **2.** homoseksualan

quell [kwel] *v* ugušiti

quench [kwentʃ] *v* utoliti

query [ˈkwiːri] **1.** *n* pitanje **2.** *v* pitati

question [ˈkwestʃən] **1.** *n* pitanje **2.** stvar **3. there's no question** nema sumnje **4.** *v* ispitivati **5.** osporiti

questionable [ˈkwestʃənəbl] *adj* problematičan

question mark *n* znak pitanja

questionnaire [ˌkwestʃəˈneə] *n* anketni listić

queue [kjuː] **1.** *n* red **2.** *v* stati u red

quick [kwik] *adj* **1.** brz **2.** *see* **quickly**

quicken [ˈkwikn] *v* ubrzati (se)

quicklime [ˈkwiklaim] *n* kalcijum-oksid

quickly [ˈkwikli] *adv* brzo

quicksand [ˈkwiksænd] *n* živi pesak/pijesak

quick-witted *adj* dovitljiv

quid [kwid] *n* (UK) funta

quiet [ˈkwaiət] **1.** *adj* miran **2.** tih **3.** *n* mir **4.** tišina

quieten down [ˈkwaiətn] *v* stišati (se)

quietly [ˈkwaiətli] *adv* mirno

quietness [ˈkwaiətnis] *n* **1.** mir **2.** tišina

quilt [kwilt] *n* jorgan

quince [kwins] *n* dunja

quinine [kwiˈniːn] *n* kinin

quit [kwit] *v* **1.** napustiti **2.** prestati

quite [kwait] *adv* 1. sasvim 2. dosta
quite a few mnogo
quite so! sasvim tako!
quiz [kwiz] 1. *n* kviz 2. *v* ispitivati
quorum [ˈkwɔːrəm] *n* kvorum

quota [ˈkwəutə] *n* kvota
quotation [kwəuˈteiʃn] *n* citat
quotation marks *pl* navodni znak
quote [kwəut] 1. *n* citat 2. *v* citirati

R

rabbi [ˈræbai] *n* (rel.) rabin
rabbit [ˈræbit] *n* kunić
rabble [ˈræbl] *n* ološ
rabies [ˈreibiːz] *n* besnilo; bjesnilo
race [reis] 1. *n* rasa 2. (spor.) trka
3. **arms race** trka u naoružavanju 4. *v* trkati se
racecourse, racetrack [ˈreiskɔːs; ˈreistrak] *n* hipodrom
race horse *n* trkački konj
race relations *pl* međurasni odnosi
race riot *n* rasni nemir
racetrack [ˈreistrak] *n* trkalište
racial [ˈreiʃl] *adj* rasni
racial discrimination *n* rasna diskriminacija
racing [ˈreisiŋ] *n* trkanje
racing car *n* trkački automobil
racism [ˈreisizəm] *n* rasizam
racist [ˈreisist] 1. *adj* rasistički 2. *n* rasista
rack [ræk] *n* 1. stalak 2. **to go to rack and ruin** raspasti se
racket [ˈrækit] *n* 1. galama 2. ucenjivanje; ucjenjivanje 3. (spor.) reket
racketeer [ˌrækiˈtiə] *n* ucenjivač; ucjenjivač
radar [ˈreidaː] *n* radar
radiant [ˈreidiənt] *adj* koji zrači
radiate [ˈreidieit] *v* zračiti
radiation [ˌreidiˈeiʃn] *n* radijacija
radiator [ˈreidieitə] *n* radijator
radical [ˈrædikl] 1. *adj* korenit; korjenit 2. *n* (pol.) radikalac
radio [ˈreidiəu] *n* radio
radio announcer *n* radio-spiker

radiologist [reidiˈɔlədʒist] *n* radiolog
radiology [reidiˈɔlədʒi] *n* radiologija
radio operator *n* radio-operator
radio programme *n* radio-emisija
radio station *n* radio-stanica
radio telephone *n* radio-telefon
radius [ˈreidiəs] *n* radijus
raft [raːft] *n* splav
rag [ræg] *n* krpa
rage [reidʒ] 1. *n* bes; bijes 2. *v* besneti; bjesnjeti
ragged [ˈrægid] *adj* dronjav
raid [reid] 1. *n* prepad 2. *v* iznenada napasti 3. izvršiti raciju
raider [reidə] *n* napadač
rail [reil] *n* 1. spojnica 2. šina
railroad [ˈreilrəud] *n* (US) železnica; željeznica
railway [ˈreilwei] *n* železnička pruga; željeznička pruga
rain [rein] 1. *n* kiša 2. *v* padati (o kiši)
rainbow [ˈreinbəu] *n* duga
raincoat [ˈreinkəut] *n* kišni mantil
raindrop [ˈreindrɔp] *n* kaplja kiše
rainfall [ˈreinfɔːl] *n* količina kiše
rainy [ˈreini] *adj* kišovit
raise [reiz] 1. *n* povišica 2. *v* dići 3. podići 4. skupiti
raise children *v* odgajiti decu/djecu
raisin [ˈreizin] *n* suvo grožđe; suho grožđe
rally [ˈræli] *n* 1. miting 2. (spor.) reli
ram [ræm] 1. *n* ovan 2. *v* probiti

RAM (random access memory) [ræm] *n* memorija sa direktnim pristupom

Ramadan [ˈræmədæn] *n* Ramazan; Ramadan

ramp [ræmp] *n* platforma

ran [ræn] *see* **run**

ranch [raːntʃ] *n* ranč

random [ˈrændəm] *adj* **at random** nasumice

rang [ræŋ] *see* **ring**

range [reindʒ] *n* **1.** domet **2.** **mountain range** planinski venac **3. out of range** izvan dometa **4. medium-range missiles** rakete srednjeg dometa **5. long-range missiles** rakete dugog dometa

range of products *n* asortiman

rank [ræŋk] *n* **1.** čin **2.** vrsta

ransack [ˈrænsæk] *v* pretražiti

ransom [ˈrænsəm] **1.** *n* otkup **2.** *v* otkupiti

rap [ræp] *v* udariti

rape [reip] **1.** *n* silovanje **2.** *v* silovati

rapid [ˈræpid] *adj* brz

rapidly [ˈræpidli] *adv* brzo

rapist [ˈreipist] *n* silovatelj

rapprochement [ræˈprɔʃmaː] *n* zbliženje

rare [reə] *adj* **1.** redak; rijedak **2.** nedopečen

rarely [ˈreəli] *adv* retko

rarity [ˈreərəti] *n* raritet

raspberry [ˈraːzberi] *n* malina

rash [ræʃ] **1.** *adj* prenagljen **2.** *n* osip

rat [ræt] *n* pacov; štakor

rate [reit] **1.** *n* stopa **2.** (fin.) kurs **3. first rate** prvoklasan **4. at any rate** u svakom slučaju **5. birth rate** natalitet **6. interest rate** kamatna stopa **7.** *v* proceniti; procijeniti

rate of exchange *n* kurs

rather [ˈraːðə] *adv* **1.** prilično **2.** radije **3.** pre; prije

ratification [ˌratifiˈkeiʃn] *n* ratifikacija

ratify [ˈrætifai] *v* ratifikovati

ratio [ˈreiʃjo] *n* razmera; razmjera

ration [ˈræʃn] *v* sledovanje; sljedovanje

rational [ˈræʃnəl] *adj* racionalan

ration book *n* knjižica za namirnice

rationing [ˈræʃəniŋ] *n* racioniranje

rattle [ˈrætl] *v* čangrljati

ravage [ˈrævidʒ] *v* opustošiti

rave [reiv] **1.** *n* zabava **2.** *v* besneti; bjesnjeti

raven [ˈreivn] *n* vran

ravine [rəˈviːn] *n* jaruga

raw [rɔː] *adj* sirov

raw material [rɔː] *n* sirovina

ray [rei] *n* **1.** zrak; zraka **2.** raja

rayon [ˈreijon] *n* rejon

raze [reiz] *v* porušiti

razor [ˈreizə] *n* brijač

razor-blade *n* nožić za brijanje

reach [riːtʃ] *v* **1.** dopreti; doprijeti **2.** ispružiti **3.** stići

reach an agreement *v* dogovoriti se

reach a verdict *v* doneti presudu; donijeti prosudu

reach out *v* ispružiti ruku

react [riˈækt] *v* reagovati

reaction [riˈækʃn] *n* reakcija

reactionary [riˈækʃənri] *n* reakcionar

read [riːd] *v* (**read** [red]) pročitati

reader [ˈriːdə] *n* čitalac

readily [ˈredili] *adv* rado

readiness [ˈredinis] *n* spremnost

reading [ˈriːdiŋ] *n* čitalački

readjust [ˌriːəˈdʒʌst] *v* opet prilagoditi

ready [ˈredi] *adj* 1. spreman 2. taman 3. **to get ready** spremati se

ready-made [ˌrediˈmeid] *adj* gotov

reaffirm [ˌriːəˈfəːm] *v* ponovo tvrditi

real [riəl] 1. *adj* realan 2. pravi 3. *adv* voma

real estate *n* nepokretna imovina

realistic [ˌriəˈlistik] *adj* realističan

reality [riˈæləti] *n* 1. realnost 2. **in reality** u stvari

realization [ˌriəlaiˈzeiʃn] *n* razumevanje; razumijevanje

realize [ˈriəlaiz] *v* 1. razumeti; razumjeti 2. realizovati

really [ˈriəli] *adv* stvarno

realm [relm] *n* carstvo

realtor [ˈriːəltə] *n* trgovac nepokretnostima

reap [riːp] *v* pokositi

reap the benefit *v* ubrati plodove

rear [riə] 1. *adj* zadnji 2. *n* pozadina 3. *v* odgajiti; odgojiti

rearrange [ˌriːəˈreindʒ] *v* ponovo urediti

reason [ˈriːzn] *n* 1. razum 2. razlog 3. **by reason of** zbog

reasonable [ˈriːznəbl] *adj* 1. razuman 2. umeren; umjeren

reassurance [ˌriːəˈʃɔːrəns] *n* umirenje

reassure [ˌriːəˈʃɔː] *v* ponovo uveriti; ponovo uvjeriti

rebel [ˈrebl] *n* ustanik, pobunjenik

rebel [riˈbel] *v* ustati (**against** protiv)

rebellion [riˈbeliən] *n* ustanak

rebellious [riˈbeliəs] *adj* buntovan

rebirth [ˌriːˈbəːθ] preporod

rebuff [riˈbʌf] *v* odbiti

rebuild [ˌriːˈbild] *v* ponovo sagraditi

rebuke [riˈbjuːk] *v* prekoriti

recall [riˈkɔːl] *v* 1. opozvati 2. setiti; sjetiti

recede [riˈsiːd] *v* opasti

receipt [riˈsiːt] *n* 1. priznanica 2. primanje

receive [riˈsiːv] *v* primiti

receiver [riˈsiːvə] *n* 1. primalac 2. slušalica

recent [ˈriːsnt] *adj* skorašnji

recently [ˈriːsəntli] *adv* nedavno

receptacle [riˈseptəkl] *n* kutija

reception [riˈsepʃn] *n* 1. prijem 2. recepcija

receptionist [riˈsepʃnist] *n* recepionar

receptive [riˈseptiv] *adj* predusretljiv (**to** prema)

recess [riˈses] *n* 1. raspust 2. niša

recession [riˈseʃn] *n* (ec.) recesija

recipe [ˈresəpi] *n* recept

recipient [reˈsipijənt] *n* primalac

reciprocate [riˈsiprəkeit] *v* uzvraćati

recital [riˈsaitl] *n* recitacija

recite [riˈsait] *v* recitovati

reckless [ˈreklis] *adj* nemaran

reckon [ˈrekən] *v* 1. izračunati 2. misliti

reckoning [ˈrekənd] *n* (pro)račun

reclaim [riˈkleim] *v* 1. meliorisati 2. popraviti

recline [riˈklain] *v* naslanjati se

recognition [ˌrekəgˈniʃn] *n* 1. prepoznavanje 2. (pol.) priznanje

recognize [ˈrekəgnaiz] *v* 1. prepoznati 2. (pol.) priznati

recoil [riˈkɔil] *v* ustuknuti

recollect [ˌrekəˈlekt] *v* setiti se; sjetiti se

recollection [,rekə'lekʃn] *n* sećanje; sjećanje

recommend [,rekə'mend] *v* preporučiti

recommendation [,rekəmen'deiʃn] *n* preporuka

recompense ['rekəmpens] 1. *n* naknada 2. *v* nadoknaditi

reconcile ['rekənsail] *v* pomoriti

reconciliation [,rekən,sili'eiʃn] *n* pomirenje

reconnaissance [ri'kɔnisns] *n* izviđanje

reconnaissance patrol *n* izviđačka patrola

reconnoitre [,rekə'nɔitə] *v* izviđati

reconsider [,riːkən'sidə] *v* ponovo razmatrati

reconsideration [ˈriːkən,sidə'reiʃn] *n* ponovo razmatranje

reconstruct [,riːkən'strʌkt] *v* rekonstruisati

reconstruction [,riːkən'strʌktʃn] *n* rekonstrukcija

record ['rekɔːd] 1. *adj* rekordan 1. *n* zapis 2. protokol 3. (leg.) sudski materijal 4. (mus.) ploča 5. **for the record** za objavu 6. **off the record** u poverenju/povjerenju 7. **world record** svetski rekord; svjetski rekord 8. **to break a record** premašiti rekord 9. *see* **records**

record [ri'kɔːd] *v* 1. registrovati 2. (mus.) snimiti

recording [ri'kɔːd] *n* (mus.) snimak

record player *n* gramofon

records ['rekɔːdz] *pl* arhiva

recover [ri'kʌvə] *v* 1. dobiti natrag 2. nadoknaditi 3. (med.) oporaviti se

recovery [ri'kʌvəri] *n* 1. dobijanje natrag 2. povratak 3. (med.) oporavak

recovery programme *n* program oporavka (privrede)

recreation [,rekri'eiʃn] *n* 1. rekreacioni 2. rekreacija

recrimination [,rekrimi'neiʃn] *n* protivoptužba; protuoptužba

recruit [re'kruːt] 1. *n* novak 2. (mil.) regrut 3. *v* vrbovati 4. (mil.) regrutovati

recruitment [rekruː'tmənt] *n* 1. vrbovka 2. (mil.) regrutacija

rectangle ['rektæŋgl] *n* pravougaonik; pravokutnik

rectify ['rektifai] *v* ispraviti

rector ['rektə] *n* rektor

rectum ['rektəm] *n* rektum

recuperate [ri'kuːpəreit] *v* oporaviti se

recuperation [ri,kuːpə'reiʃn] *n* oporavak

recur [ri'kəː] *v* vratiti se

recurrence [,ri'kʌrəns] *n* vraćanje

recurrent [,ri'kʌrənt] *adj* povratan

recycle [ri'saikl] *v* preraditi

recycling [ri'saikliŋ] *n* prerada

red [red] *adj* crven

Red Cross [,red'krɔs] *n* Crveni krst/križ

redden ['redən] *v* pocrveniti

redecorate [,riː'dekəreit] *v* prepraviti

redeem [ri'diːm] *v* iskupiti

redemption [ri'dempʃn] *n* iskup

redeploy [,riːdə'plɔi] *v* (mil.) prebaciti

redevelop [,riːdə'veləp] *v* obnoviti

redevelopment [,riːdə'veləpmənt] *v* obnova

red-handed [,red'hændid] *adj* na samom delu/djelu

red-hot *adj* usijan

red light *n* crveno svetlo/svjetlo

redness ['rednis] *n* crven

red tape *n* birokratizam

reduce [ri'dju:s] *v* smanjiti

reduced [ri'dju:st] *adj* **at reduced prices** po sniženoj ceni/cijeni

reduction [ri'dʌkʃn] *n* 1. smanjenje 2. **arms reduction** smanjenje naoružanja

redundancy [ri'dʌndənsi] *n* izlišnost

redundant [ri'dʌndənt] *adj* izlišan

reduplicate [ri'dju:plikeit] *v* ponoviti

reed [ri:d] *n* trska

reef [ri:f] *n* greben

reel [ri:l] *n* kalem

re-elect [,ri:'əlekt] *v* obnoviti mandat, ponovo izabrati

re-election [,ri:ə'lektʃən] *n* obnavljanje mandata, ponovni izbor

re-enter [,ri:'entə] *v* ponovo ući

re-establish [,ri:'estæbliʃ] *v* obnoviti

refer [ri'fə:] *v* 1. uputiti (**to** na) 2. upućivati (**to** na)

referee [,refə'ri] *n* 1. arbitar 2. (spor.) sudija; sudac

reference ['refərəns] *n* 1. upućivanje 2. primedba; primjedba 3. **with reference to...** u pogledu...

reference book *n* priručnik

referendum [,refə'rendəm] *n* 1. referendum 2. **to hold a referendum** održati referendum

refill [,ri:'fil] *v* ponovo napuniti

refine [ri'fain] *v* prečistiti

refined [ri'faind] *adj* 1. prečišćen 2. otmen

refined oil *n* rafinirana nafta

refinement [ri'fainmənt] *n* 1. prečišćavanje 2. otmenost

refinery [ri'fainəri] *n* rafinerija

refit ['ri:fit] *v* ponovo opremiti

reflect [ri'flekt] *v* 1. odraziti 2. razmišljati

reflection [ri'flekʃn] *n* 1. odraz 2. razmišljanje

reflex ['ri:fleks] *n* refleks

reflexive [ri'fleksiv] *adj* povratan

reforest [ri:'fɔrest] *v* ponovo pošumiti

reform [ri'fɔ:m] 1. *n* reforma 2. *v* reformisati (se)

reformation [,refə'meiʃn] *n* reformacija

reformer [ri'fɔ:mə] *n* reformator

refrain [ri'frein] 1. *n* refren 2. *v* uzdržati se

refresh [ri'freʃ] *v* osvežiti; osvježiti

refreshing [ri'freʃiŋ] *adj* osvežavajući; osvježavajući

refreshments [ri'freʃmənts] *pl* zakuska

refrigerate [ri'fridʒəreit] *v* držati u frižideru

refrigeration [ri'fridʒəreiʃn] *n* hlađenje

refrigerator [ri'fridʒəreitə] *n* frižider

refuel [,ri:'fjuəl] *v* popuniti gorivom

refuge ['refju:dʒ] *n* zaklon

refugee [,refju'dʒi:] *n* 1. izbeglica; izbjeglica 2. **war refugees** ratne izbeglice/izbjeglice

refugee camp *n* logor za izbeglice/izbjeglice

refund [ri'fʌnd] 1. *n* vraćanje 2. *v* vratiti

refurbish [,ri:'fə:biʃ] *v* obnoviti

refurbishment [,ri:fə:biʃmənt] *n* obnova

refusal [ri'fju:zl] *n* odbijanje

refuse ['refju:s] *n* smeće

refuse [ri·fju:z] v odbiti
refute [ri·fju:t] v pobiti
regain [ri·gein] v ponovo dobiti
regard [ri·ga:d] 1. n pogled 2. **with regard to** s pogledom na 3. **without regard to** obzir 4. v smatrati (as za) 5. ceniti; cijeniti 6. *see* regards
regarding [ri·ga:diŋ] prep u pogledu
regardless [ri·ga:dlis] adv uprkos tome
regardless of prep bez obzira na
regards [ri·ga:dz] pl 1. pozdravi 2. **as regards** s pogledom na
regenerate [ri·dʒenəreit] v regenerisati
regeneration [ri,dʒenə·reiʃn] n regeneracija
regime [rei·ʒi:m] n režim
regiment [·redʒimənt] n puk
region [·ri:dʒən] n kraj
regionalism [·ri:dʒən,lizm] n regionalizam
register [·redʒistə] 1. n spisak 2. v registrovati
registered mail/post [·redʒistəd]n preporučene pošiljke
registration [,redʒi·streiʃn] n 1. registracija 2. registrovanje
registration form n prijava
registry [·redʒistri] n registar
regress [ri·gres] v kretati se nazad
regret [ri·gret] 1. n žaljenje 2. v žaliti
regretful [ri·gretful] adj žalostan
regretfully [ri·gretfuli] adv na žalost
regrettable [ri·gretəbl] adj za žaljenje
regular [·regjulə] adj 1. redovan 2. regularan
regularity [,regju·lærəti] n redovnost
regularly [·regjuləli] adv redovno

regulate [·regjuleit] v regulisati
regulation [,regju·leiʃn] n 1. regulacija 2. propis
regulations [,regju·leiʃnz] pl propis
rehabilitate [,riha·biliteit] v rehabilitovati
rehabilitation [,riha,bili·teiʃn] n rehabilitacija
rehearsal [riha:sl] n proba
rehearse [riha:s] v probati
reign [rein] 1. n vlada 2. v vladati
reimburse [,ri:im·bə:s] v naknaditi
rein [rein] n uzda
reinforce [,ri:in·fɔ:s] v pojačati
reinforced concrete [,ri:in·fɔ:st] n armirani beton
reinforcement [,ri:in·fɔ:smənt] n pojačanje
reinforcements [,ri:in·fɔ:smənts] pl (mil.) pojačanja
reins of power pl dizgini vlasti
reinstate [,ri:in·steit] v ponovo postaviti
reinsure [,ri:in·ʃuə] v reosigurati
reissue [,ri:·iʃju] v ponovo izdati
reiterate [ri:·itəreit] v ponoviti
reject [ri·dʒekt] v odbiti
rejection [ri·dʒekʃn] n odbijanje
rejoice [ri·dʒɔis] v radovati se
rejoin [ri·dʒɔin] v ponovo se pridružiti
rejuvenate [ri·dʒu:vəneit] v podmladiti
relapse [ri·læps] n (med.) povraćaj
relate [ri·leit] v 1. ispričati 2. *see* **related**
relate to v imati veze s
related [ri·leitid] adj 1. povezan 2. srodan
relation [ri·leiʃn] n 1. srodnik 2. veza 3. **in relation to** u odnosu na 4. *see* **relations**

relations [riˈleiʃns] *pl* 1. veze 2. **friendly relations** dobrosusedski odnosi; dobrosusjedski odnosi 3. **sexual relations** polni odnosi; spolni odnosi 4. **diplomatic relations** diplomatski odnosi 5. **to establish relations** uspostaviti veze 6. **to break off relations** prekinuti veze

relationship [riˈleiʃnʃip] *n* 1. srodstvo 2. odnos 3. ljubavna veza

relative [ˈrelətiv] 1. *adj* odnosan 2. *n* rođak

relatively [ˈrelətivli] *adv* relativno

relax [riˈlæks] *v* 1. olabaviti (se) 2. popustiti

relaxation [ˌriːlækˈseiʃn] *n* 1. labavljenje 2. popuštanje

relaxed [riˈlækst] *adj* 1. olabavljen 2. ležeran

relay [ˈriːlei] 1. *n* relej 2. *v* preneti; prenijeti

relay race *n* (spor.) štafeta

release [riˈliːs] 1. *n* puštanje 2. **press release** objava za štampu 3. *v* pustiti

relegate [ˈreligeit] *v* uputiti

relent [riˈlent] *v* popustiti

relentless [riˈlentlis] *adj* nemilosrdan

relevance, relevancy [ˈreləvəns; -si] *n* relevantnost

relevant [ˈreləvənt] *adj* relevantan

reliability [riˌlaiəˈbiləti] *n* pouzdanost

reliable [riˈlaiəbl] *adj* 1. pouzdan 2. **from reliable sources** iz pouzdanih izvora

reliance [reˈlaiəns] *n* pouzdanje

reliant [reˈlaiənt] *adj* pun pouzdanja

relic [ˈrelik] *n* ostatak

relief [riˈliːf] 1. *adj* pomoćni 2. *n* olakšenje 3. pomoć 4. **to bring relief to** doneti olakšanje; donijeti olakšanje

relief agency *n* humanitarna agencija, agencija za pomoć

relief fund *n* humanitarna sredstva

relief organization *n* humanitarna organizacija

relieve [riˈliːv] *v* 1. olakšati 2. oslabiti 3. **to relieve from duty** razrešiti dužnosti

relieved [riˈliːvd] *adj* **to be relieved** osjećati olakšanje

religion [riˈlidʒən] *n* religija

religious [riˈlidʒəs] *adj* religiozan

religious fundamentalist *n* verski fundamentalista;   vjerski fundamentalista

relinquish [riˈliŋkwiʃ] *v* odreći se

relish [ˈreliʃ] *v* uživati u

relocate [riːləuˈkeit] *v* preseliti (se)

reluctance [riˈlʌktəns] *n* protivljenje

reluctant [riˈlʌktənt] *adj* protiv volje

rely [riˈlai] *v* osloniti se (**on** na)

remain [riˈmein] *v* ostati

remainder [riˈmeində] *n* ostatak

remains [riˈmeinz] *pl* 1. ostaci 2. **human remains** posmrtni ostaci

remake [ˌriːˈmeik] *v* prepraviti

remark [riˈmaːk] 1. *n* primedba; primjedba 2. *v* komentarisati

remarkable [riˈmaːkəbl] *n* verdan; vrijedan

remedy [ˈremədi] *n* lek; lijek

remember [riˈmembə] *v* setiti se; sjetiti se

remembrance [riˈmembrəns] *n* sećanje

remind [ri'maind] v podsetiti; podsjetiti

reminder [ri'maində] n opomena

remnant ['remnənt] n ostatak

remorse [ri'mɔ:s] n pokajanje

remorseful [ri'mɔ:sfl] adj pokajnički

remote [ri'məut] adj udajlen

removal [ri'mu:vl] n uklanjanje

remove [ri'mu:v] v 1. ukloniti 2. skinuti

renaissance [ri'neisəns] n renesansa

renal ['ri:nəl] adj bubrežni

render ['rendə] v dati

rendezvous ['rendeivu:] n randevu

renegade ['renəgeid] n otpadnik

renege [ri'neg] v ne držati

renew [ri'nju:] v 1. obnoviti 2. produžiti

renewal [ri'nju:wəl] n obnova

renounce [ri'nauns] v odreći se

renovate ['renəveit] v obnoviti

renown [ri'naun] n slava

renowned [ri'naund] adj slavan

rent [rent] 1. n zakup 2. v uzeti u zakup 3. dati pod zakup

rental ['rentl] n iznajmljivanje

rent-free n bez kirije

renting ['rentiŋ] n iznajmljivanje

reopen ['ri:'əupn] v ponovo otvoriti

reorganization ['ri:,ɔ:gənai'zeiʃn] n reorganizacija

reorganize ['ri:'ɔ:gənaiz] v reorganizovati

repair [ri'peə] 1. n opravka 2. v opraviti

reparations [,repə'reiʃnz] pl reparacije

repatriate [ri:'pætrieit] v repatrirati

repatriation [ri:,pætri'eiʃn] n repatrijacija

repay [ri:'pei] v odužiti (se)

repayment [ri:'peimənt] n vraćanje novca

repeal [ri'pi:l] v ukinuti

repeat [ri'pi:t] v ponoviti

repeatedly [ri'pi:tidli] adv ponovo

repel [ri'pel] v odbiti

repent [ri'pent] v pokajati se (**of** za)

repentance [ri'pəntəns] n pokajanje

repercussion [,repə'kʌʃn] n reperkusija

repetition [,repi'tiʃn] n ponavljanje

replace [ri'pleis] v 1. vratiti 2. zameniti; zamijeniti

replacement [ri'pleismənt] n zamena; zamjena

replenish [ri'pleniʃ] v popuniti

reply [ri'plai] 1. n odgovor 2. v odgovoriti (**to** na)

report [ri'pɔ:t] 1. n izveštaj 2. dopis 3. **annual report** godišnji izveštaj/izvještaj 4. v podneti izveštaj o; podnijeti izvještaj o 5. poslati dopis o

reporter [ri'pɔ:tə] n 1. izveštač 2. reporter

repossess [ri'pəzes] v ponovo uzeti u posed/posjed

represent [,repri'zent] v predstavljati

representation [,reprizen'teiʃn] n predstavljanje

representative [,repri'zentətiv] 1. adj predstavnički 2. n predstavnik 3. see **House of Representatives**, **sales representative**

repress [ri'pres] v 1. suzbiti 2. **to repress a revolt** ugušiti pobunu

repression [ri'preʃn] n 1. represija 2. gušenje

repressive [ri'presiv] adj represivan

reprieve [ri'pri:v] v (leg.) odložiti izvršenje kazne

reprimand [ˈreprimɑːnd] 1. *n* ukor
2. *v* ukoriti

reprint [ˌriːˈprint] *v* preštampati

reprisal [riˈpraizl] *n* represalija

reproach [riˈprəutʃ] *v* prekoriti

reproachful [riˈprəutʃfl] *adj* pun
prekora

reproduce [ˌriːprəˈdjuːs] *v* 1.
reprodukovati 2. množiti se

reproduction [ˌriːprəˈdʌkʃn] *n* 1.
reprodukcija 2. množenje

reptile [ˈreptail] *n* reptil

republic [riˈpʌblik] *n* republika

republican [riˈpʌblikən] 1. *adj*
republikanski 2. *n* republikanac

republicanism [riˈpʌblikənizm] *n*
republikanizam

republish [ˈriːˈpʌbliʃ] *v* ponovo
izdati

repudiate [riˈpjuːdieit] *v* odreći se

repugnant [riˈpʌgnənt] *adj* oduran

repulse [riˈpʌls] *v* odbiti

repulsion [riˈpʌlʃən] *n* odurnost

repulsive [riˈpʌlsiv] *adj* oduran

reputable [ˈrepjutəbl] *adj* uvažen

reputation [ˌrepjuˈteiʃn] *n* 1.
reputacija 2. **to have a
reputation** uživati glas

repute [riˈpjuːt] *n* ugled

request [riˈkwest] 1. *n* molba 2. *v*
zamoliti

require [riˈkwaiə] *v* zahtevati,
zahtijevati

required [riˈkwaiəd] *adj* **to be
required to...** tražiti

requirement [riˈkwaiəmənt] *n*
zahtev; zahtjev

resale [ˈriːˈseil] *n* ponovna prodaja

reschedule a debt [riˈʃedjul;
riːˈskedjul] *v* reprogramirati dug

rescue [ˈreskjuː] 1. *adj* za spasavanje
2. *n* spasavanje 3. *v* spasti; spasiti

rescue [ˈreskjuːə] *n* spasilac

research [riˈsəːtʃ] 1. *adj*
istraživački 2. *n* istraživački rad
3. *v* istraživati

research into *v* ispitivati

researcher [riˈsəːtʃə] *n* istraživač

research institute *n* istraživački
institut

resell [ˈriːˈsel] *v* preprodati

resemblance [riˈzembləns] *n* sličnost

resemble [riˈzembl] *v* ličiti na

resent [riˈzent] *v* vređati se;
vrijeđati se

resentful [riˈzentfl] *adj* ozloeđen

resentment [riˈzentmənt] *n*
ozloeđenost

reservation [ˌrezəˈveiʃn] *n* 1.
rezervacija 2. **without
reservation** bez ograde 3. **to
make a reservation** izvršiti
rezervaciju

reserve [riˈzəːv] 1. *adj* rezervni 2. *n*
rezerva 3. **game reserve**
branjevina za divljač 4. **in
reserve** u rezervi 5. *v* rezervisati
6. *see* **reserves**

reserve bank *n* rezervna banka

reserved [riˈzəːvd] *adj* rezervisan

reserve fund *n* rezervni fond

reserves [riˈsəːvz] *pl* 1. **bank
reserves** bankovne rezerve 2. **oil
reserves** naftne rezerve 3.
military reserves rezerva

reservoir [ˈrezəvwaː] *n* rezervoar

reset [riːˈset] *v* ponovo namestiti/
namjestiti

reshuffle [ˈriːˈʃʌfl] *v* (pol.)
reorganizovati; reorganizirati

reside [riˈzaid] *v* stanovati

residence [ˈrezidəns] *n* 1. stan 2.
country of residence zemlja
boravka

residence permit n dozvola boravka
residency [ˈrezidənsi] n rezidencija
resident [ˈrezidənt] n stanovnik
residential [ˌreziˈdenʃl] adj stambeni
residential area n stambeni kraj
resign [riˈzain] v dati ostavku
resignation [ˌrezigˈneiʃn] n ostavka
resigned [riˈzaind] adj rezigniran
resist [riˈzist] v 1. odolevati 2. pružati otpor
resistance [riˈzistəns] n otpor
resistant [riˈzistənt] adj otporan (to na)
resolute [ˈrezəluːt] adj odlučan
resolution [ˌrezəˈluːʃn] n 1. odlučnost 2. (pol.) predlog; prijedlog
resolve [riˈzɔlv] 1. n odlučnost 2. v odlučiti
resort [riˈzɔːt] 1. n odmaralište 2. **ski resort** smučarski centar 3. **as a last resort** u krajnjoj nuždi 4. v **to resort to force** pribeći sili; pribjeći sili
resource [riˈsɔːsfl] n 1. sredstvo 2. see resources
resourceful [riˈsɔːsfl] adj snalažljiv
resources [riˈsɔːsis] pl 1. bogatstva 2. **natural resources** prirodna bogatstva
respect [riˈspekt] 1. n poštovanje 2. **with respect to** s obzirom na 3. **to show respect to someone** ukazati poštovanje nekome 4. **to pay one's respects** odati poštovanje 5. v poštovati
respectability [riˌspektəˈbiləti] n poštovanost
respectable [riˈspektəbl] adj poštovan

respectful [riˈspektfl] adj učtiv
respective [riˈspektiv] adj odnosni
respectively [riˈspektivli] adv odnosno
respects [riˈspekts] pl poštovanje; štovanje
respiration [ˌrespəˈreiʃn] n disanje
respite [ˈrespait] n predah
respond [riˈspɔnd] v ragovati (to na)
response [riˈspɔns] n odgovor
responsibility [riˌspɔnsəˈbiləti] n 1. odgovornost 2. **to accept responsibility** preuzeti odgovornost
responsible [riˈspɔnsəbl] adj odgovoran
responsive [riˈspɔnsiv] adj osećajan; osjećajan
rest [rest] 1. n odmor 2. ostatak 3. v odmoriti
rest and recuperation (R&R) n odmor i oporavak
restaurant [ˈrestrɔnt] n restoran
restitution [ˌrestiˈtjuːʃn] n restitucija
restless [ˈrestlis] adj nemiran
restoration [ˌrestəˈreiʃn] n 1. vraćanje 2. restauracija
restore [riˈstɔː] v 1. vratiti 2. ponovo uspostaviti 3. restaurirati
restrain [riˈstrein] v uzdržati
restraint [riˈstreint] n 1. uzržavanje 2. **without restraint** bez ograničenja
restrict [riˈstrikt] v ograničiti
restricted [riˈstriktid] adj ograničen
restriction [riˈstrikʃn] n restrikcija
result [riˈzʌlt] n 1. rezultat 2. **as a result of** kao rezultat
result in v rezultirati
resulting from [riˈzʌltiŋ] proizilaziti od

resume [ri·zju:m] *v* ponovo se latiti
resumé [,rezu·mei] *n* rezime
resuscitate [ri·sʌsiteit] *v* oživiti
resuscitation [ri·sʌsitei∫n] *n* 1. oživljenje 2. **mouth-to-mouth resuscitation** veštačko disanje usta na usta
retail [·ri:teil] 1. *adj* maloprodajni 2. *n* maloprodaja 3. *v* prodavati namalo
retailer [·ri:teilə] *n* trgovac na malo
retail price [·ri:teil] *n* maloprodajna cena/cijena
retain [ri·tein] *v* zadržati
retake [ri·teik] *v* ponovo uzeti
retaliate [ri·tælieit] *v* osvetiti se
retaliation [ri,tæli·ei∫n] *n* osveta
retard [re·ta:d] *v* usporiti
retarded [ri·ta:did] *adj* **mentally retarded** mentalno zaostao
rethink [,ri:·θiŋk] *v* ponovo razmotriti
retina [·retinə] *n* retina
retinue [·retinju:] *n* pratnja
retire [ri·taiə] *v* 1. povući se 2. penzionisati
retired [ri·taiəd] *adj* u penziji
retirement [ri·taiəmənt] *n* 1. penzionisanje 2. **voluntary retirement** dobrovoljno penzionisanje 3. **forced retirement** prinudno penzionisanje
retrace [ri:·treis] *v* vratiti se
retract [ri·trækt] *v* poreći
retreat [ri·tri:t] 1. *n* povlačenje 2. *v* povući se
retrench [ri·trent∫] *v* smanjiti
retrial [·ri:trajəl] *n* ponovo suđenje
retribution [,retri·bju:∫n] *n* kazna
retrieve [ri·tri:v] *v* povratiti
retroactive [,retrə·æktiv] *adj* retroaktivan

retrogression [,retrə·gre∫n] *n* nazadovanje
retrospective [,retrə·spektiv] *adj* retrospektivan
retry [,ri:·trai] *v* ponovo suditi
return [ri·tə:n] 1. *adj* povratan 2. (spor.) revanš- 3. *n* povratak 4. **in return for** u zamenu za; u zamjenu za 5. *v* vratiti (se)
return ticket *n* povratna karta
reunion [ri·ju:njən] *n* sastanak
reunite [ri·ju:nait] *v* ponovo (se) sjediniti
Rev. [·revərənd] *see* **Reverend**
reveal [ri·vi:l] *v* otkriti
revel [·revl] *v* uživati (**in** u)
revelation [,revə·lei∫n] *n* otkrivanje
revenge [ri·vend3] *n* 1. osveta 2. **to take revenge** osvetiti se (**for** za)
revenue [·revənju:] *n* 1. prihod 2. **Inland Revenue** poreska administracija
revere [ri·viə] *v* poštovati
reverence [·revərəns] *n* poštovanje
reverend [·revərənd] *n* (rel.) sveštenik; svećenik
reversal [ri·və:sl] *n* preokret
reverse [ri·və:s] 1. *adj* obrnut 2. *n* supronost 3. rikverc 4. poraz 5. *v* preokrenuti
reversible [ri·və:səbl] *adj* koji se može poništiti
revert [ri·və:t] *v* vratiti se
review [ri·vju:] 1. *v* recenzija 2. razmotriti 3. prikazati
reviewer [ri·vju:ə] *n* recenzent
revise [ri·vaiz] *v* 1. promeniti; promijeniti 2. (ed.) ponoviti
revision [ri·vi3n] *n* 1. revizija 2. (ed.) ponavljanje
revival [ri·vaivl] *n* obnova

revive [ri·vaiv] v 1. obnoviti 2. oživeti; oživjeti

revoke [ri·vəuk] v opozvati

revolt [ri·vəult] 1. n pobuna 2. v pobuniti se

revolting [ri·vəultiŋ] adj odvratan

revolution [,revə·lu:ʃn] n 1. revolucija 2. obrtaj

revolutionary [,revə·lu:ʃənəri] 1. adj revolucionarni 2. n revolucionar

revolutionize [,revə·lu:ʃənaiz] v revolucionisati

revolve [ri·volv] v obrtati se

revolver [ri·volvə] n revolver

revulsion [ri·vʌlʃn] n odvratnost

reward [ri·wɔ:d] 1. n ucena; ucjena 2. v nagraditi (for za)

rewind [,ri:·waind] v premotati

rewrite [,ri:·rait] v prepisati

rheumatism [·ru:mətizəm] n reumatizam

rhinoceros [rai·nɔsərəs] n nosorog

rhubarb [·ru:ba:b] n raven

rhyme [raim] n slik

rhythm [·riðəm] n ritam

rib [rib] n rebro

ribbon [·ribən] n vrpca

rice [rais] n pirinač; riža

rich [ritʃ] adj 1. bogat 2. mastan

riches [·ritʃiz] pl bogatstvo

ricochet [·rikəuʃai] n rikošet

rid [rid] v 1. otarasiti 2. **to get rid of something** otarasiti se nečega

ridden [·ridn] see **ride**

riddle [·ridl] n rešeto

ride [raid] 1. n jahanje 2. vožnja 3. v (**rode, ridden**) jahati 4. voziti se

rider [·raidə] n jahač

ridge [ridʒ] n 1. greben 2. sleme; sljeme

ridicule [·ridikju:l] 1. n poruga 2. v porugati se

ridiculous [ri·dikjuləs] adj smešan; smiješan

riding [·raidiŋ] n jahanje

rifle [·raifl] n puška

rift [rift] n pukotina

rig [rig] see **oil rig**

rig an election v montirati izbori

right [rait] 1. adj prav 2. pravilan 3. desni 4. (pol.) desničarski 5. n pravo 6. desnica 7. adv upravo 8. desno 9. **right away** odmah 10. v ispraviti 11. see **rights**

righteous [·raitʃəs] adj pravedan

right-hand adj desni

right-handed adj desnoruk

right-hand man n desna ruka

right of asylum n pravo azila

rights [raits] pl 1. prava 2. **human rights** ljudska prava 3. **legal rights** zakonska prava 4. **civil rights** gradanska prava 5. **constitutional rights** ustavna prava 6. **oil rights** pravo na eksploataciju nafte

right to vote n biračko pravo

right-wing adj (pol.) desničarski

right wing n (pol.) desno krilo

right-winger n (pol.) desničar

rigid [·ridʒid] adj krut

rigor mortis [,rigə·mɔ:tis] n mrtvačka ukočenost

rigorous [·rigərəs] adj rigorozan

rigour [·rigə] n strogost

rim [rim] n obod

rind [raind] n kora

ring [riŋ] 1. n prsten 2. zvonjenje 3. **boxing ring** ring 4. v (**rang, rung**) zvoniti u 5. telefonirati 6. opkoliti

ring a bell v podsetiti; podsjetiti

ringleader [ˈriŋŋliːdə] *n* kolovođa

ring road *n* kružni put

ring up *v* telefonirati

rink [riŋk] *n* klizalište

rinse [rins] *v* isprati

riot [ˈraiət] 1. *n* pobuna 2. *v* pobuniti se

rioter [ˈraiətə] *n* buntovnik

riot police *pl* specijalne policijske snage

rip [rip] 1. *n* poderotina 2. *v* razderati

ripe [raip] *n* zreo

ripen [ˈraipən] *v* sazreti

ripeness [ˈraipnis] *n* zrelost

rip-off *n* prevara

ripple [ˈripl] *n* mreškanje

rise [raiz] 1. *n* uspon 2. (fin.) porast 3. **pay rise** povišica 4. **sunrise** izlazak sunca 5. **to give rise to** izazvati 6. *v* (**rose, risen**) dići se 7. rasti 8. penjati se

rising [ˈraiziŋ] *adj* penjanje

risk [risk] 1. *n* rizik 2. *v* rizikovati

risky [ˈriski] *adj* rizičan

ritual [ˈritjul] 1. *adj* ritualan 2. *n* obred

rival [ˈraivl] 1. *adj* rivalski 2. *n* rival 3. *v* rivalizovati

rivalry [ˈraivlri] *n* rivalitet

river [ˈrivə] *n* reka; rijeka

river bank *n* rečna obala

river bed *n* korita reke/rijeke

riverside [ˈrivəsaid] *n* rečna obala

road [rəud] 1. *n* put 2. **by road** kopnenim putem

roadblock [ˈrəudblɔk] *n* barikada na putu

road map *n* putna karta

road sign *n* putokaz

roadway [ˈrəudwei] *n* kolovoz

roam [rəum] *v* tumarati

roar [rɔ:] 1. *n* rika 2. *v* rikati

roast [rəust] 1. *adj* pečen 2. *v* peći

rob [rɔb] *v* (**robbed**) ukrasti

robber [ˈrɔbə] *n* lopov

robbery [ˈrɔbəri] *n* 1. krađa 2. **armed robbery** razbojnička krađa

robe [rəub] *n* 1. odora 2. **bathrobe** bademantil

robot [ˈrəubɔt] *n* robot

robust [rəuˈbʌst] *adj* robustan

rock [rɔk] 1. *n* stena; stijena 2. *v* ljuljati

rocket [ˈrɔkit] *n* raketa

rock'n'roll [ˌrɔkənˈrɔl] *n* (mus.) rok

rocky [ˈrɔki] *adj* stenovit; stjenovit

rod [rɔd] *n* 1. šiba 2. **fishing rod** pecaljka

rode [rəud] *see* **ride**

rodent [ˈrəudənt] *n* glodar

rogue [rəug] *n* nevaljalac

role [rəul] *n* 1. uloga 2. **to play a role** igrati ulogu

role model *n* obrazac

roll [rəul] 1. *n* rolna 2. valjak 3. *v* valjati 4. saviti

roll call *n* prozivka

roll up *v* posuvratiti

romance [rəuˈmæns] *n* 1. romansa 2. romantičnost

Romania [ruˈmainiə] *n* Rumunija; Rumunjska

Romanian [ruˈmainiə] 1. *adj* rumunski; rumunjski 2. *n* Rumun; Rumunj

romantic [rəuˈmæntik] *adj* romantičan

roof [ru:f] *n* krov

room [ru:m; rum] *n* 1. soba 2. mesto; mjesto

roommate *n* sobni drug

room service *n* usluživanje u sobama

rooster [ˈruːstə] n (US) petao; pijetao

root [ruːt] n 1. koren; korijen 2. **to take root** pustiti koren 3. see **roots**

rootless [ˈruːtləs] adj bez korena/korijena

roots [ruːts] pl koreni; korjeni

rope [rəup] n uže

rose [rəuz] 1. n ruža 2. see **rise**

rosé [rəuˈzei] n vrsta vina

rosy [ˈrəuzi] adj ružičast

rot [rɔt] 1. n trulež 2. v (**rotted**) istruliti

rota [ˈrəutə] n spisak imena

rotary [ˈrəutəri] adj rotacioni

rotate [rəuˈteit] v 1. okretati se 2. rotirati

rotation [rəuˈteiʃn] n rotacija

rotten [ˈrɔtn] adj 1. truo 2. loš

rough [rʌf] adj 1. hrapav 2. neravan 3. grub 4. **rough weather** olujno vreme/vrijeme

roughly [ˈrʌfli] adv grubo

roughneck [ˈrʌfnek] n siledžija

round [raund] 1. adj okrugao 2. ravan 3. n (spor.) runda 4. adv **all year round** preko cele godine; preko cijele godine 5. see **around**

roundabout [ˈraundəbaut] n kružni tok

round table discussion n diskusija za okruglim stolom

round trip n povratno putovanje

round up v pohapsiti

rouse [rauz] v probuditi (se)

rout [raut] v razbiti

route [ruːt; raut] n put

routine [ruːˈtiːn] 1. adj rutinski 2. n rutina

row [rau] n svađa

row [rəu] 1. n red 2. v veslom terati/tjerati

rower [ˈrəuə] n veslač

rowing boat [ˈrəuiŋ] n čamac

royal [ˈrɔiəl] adj krajlevski

royalist [ˈrɔiəl] 1. adj rojalistički 2. n rojalista

royalty [ˈrɔiəlti] n 1. kraljevstvo 2. (fin.) honorar

rub [rʌb] v trljati

rubber [ˈrʌbə] 1. adj gumen 2. n kaučuk 3. guma

rubber band n lastiš

rubber stamp n gumeni pečat

rubbish [ˈrʌbiʃ] 1. adj loš 2. n smeće

rubbish bin n kanta za smeće/đubre, korpa za otpatke

rucksack [ˈrʌksæk] n ruksak

rudder [ˈrʌdə] n kormilo

rude [ruːd] adj grub

rudeness [ˈruːdnis] n grubost

rudimentary [ˌruːdiˈməntri] adj rudimentaran

rudiments [ˈruːdimənts] pl osovni elementi

rug [rʌg] n tepih

rugby [ˈrʌgbi] n ragbi

rugged [ˈrʌgid] adj grebenast

ruin [ˈruːin] 1. n propast 2. v upropastiti 3. see **ruins**

ruined [ˈruːind] adj uništen

ruins [ˈruːinz] pl ruševine

rule [ruːl] 1. n pravilo 2. vlada 3. **as a rule** po pravilu 4. v vladati

rule over v vladati

ruler [ˈruːlə] n 1. vladar 2. lenjir; ravnalo

ruling [ˈruːliŋ] 1. adj vladajući 2. n (leg.) odluka

rum [rʌm] n rum

rumble [ˈrʌmbl] v tutnjiti

ruminant [ˈruːminənt] *n* preživar

rumour, rumor [ˈruːmə] *n* 1. glas 2.
to spread **rumours** širiti glasine

rumourmonger, rumormonger
[ˈruːməmʌŋgə] *n* pronosilac glasina

rump [rʌmp] *n* ruža

run [rʌn] 1. *n* trčanje 2.
ski run smučarska staza 3. *v*
(**ran, run**) trčati 4. ići 5.
teći 6. raditi 7. to **run a
school** upravljati školom 8.
to **run guns** krijumčariti
puške 9. to **run for office**
skandidovati se

run aground *v* nasukati se

run away *v* pobeći; pobjeći

runaway [ˈrʌnəwei] *n* odbeglica;
odbjeglica

run down *v* 1. trčati niz 2. oboriti

run dry *v* osušiti se

run into *v* 1. naići 2. sudariti se

runner [ˈrʌnə] *n* trkač

runner-up [ˌrʌnəˈʌp] *n*
drugoplasirani

running [ˈrʌnin] *adj/adv* **four days
running** četiri dana uzastopce

running water *n* tekuća voda

run out *v* potrošiti

run over *v* 1. pregaziti 2. *see*
overflow

run short *v* He has run short of
money. Ostao je bez novca.

run through *v* brzo probati

rung [rʌŋ] *see* **ring**

runway [ˈrʌnwei] *n* poletno-sletna
staza

rupture [ˈrʌptʃə] 1. *n* raskid 2. *v*
raskinuti 3. pući

rural [ˈruərəl] *adj* seoski

ruse [ˈruːz] *n* prevara

rush [rʌʃ] 1. *n* žurba 2. *v* žuriti se

rush hour *n* vreme najživljeg
saobraćaja; vrijeme najživljeg
saobraćaja

rush through *v* (pol.) to **rush
through a bill** usvojiti predlog
zakona po ubrzanom postupku;
usvojiti prijedlog zakona po
ubrzanom postupku;

Russia [ˈrʌʃə] *n* Rusija

Russian [ˈrʌʃən] 1. *adj* ruski 2. *n*
Rus

rust [rʌst] 1. *n* rđa 2. *v* zarđati

rustic [ˈrʌstik] 1. *adj* seljački 2. *n*
seljak

rustproof [ˈrʌstpruːf] *adj* nerđajući

rusty [ˈrʌsti] *adj* zarđao

rut [rʌt] *n* kolosek; kolosijek

ruthless [ˈruːθlis] *adj* nemilostiv

rye [rai] *n* raž

S

sabbath [ˈsæbəθ] *n* subota

sabotage [ˈsæbətaːʒ] **1.** *n* sabotaža
2. to commit sabotage obaviti
diverzantske akcije **3.** *v* sabotirati

sabre [ˈseibə] *n* sablja

sachet [ˈsæʃei] *n* vrećica

sack [sæk] **1.** *n* džak **2.** *v* otpustiti s
posla

sacred [ˈseikrid] *adj* svet

sacrifice [ˈsækrifais] **1.** *n* žrtvovanje
2. žrtva **3.** *v* žrtvovati

sacrilege [ˈsækrilidʒ] *n* svetogrđe

sad [sæd] *adj* tužan

sadden [ˈsædn] *v* rastužiti

saddle [ˈsædl] *n* sedlo

sadism [ˈseidizm] *n* sadizam

sadist [səˈdist] *n* sadista

sadistic [səˈdistik] *adj* sadistički

sadness [ˈsædnis] *n* tuga

safari [səˈfaːri] *n* safari

safe [seif] **1.** *adj* siguran **2.** čitav **3.**
n sef

safe conduct [ˈseifgaːd] *n* sigurna
pratnja

safeguard [ˈseifgaːd] *v* osigurati

safely [ˈseifli] *adv* bezbedno;
bezbjedno, sigurno

safe sex *n* bezbedan seks; siguran
seks

safety [ˈseifti] *n* **1.** bezbednost;
bezbjednost **2.** spas

safety pin *n* pribadača

safety zone *n* zona sigurnosti

said [sed] *see* **say**

sail [seil] **1.** *n* jedro **2.** *v* jedriti **3. to
set sail** razapeti jedra

sailing [ˈseiliŋ] *n* navigacija

sailing-boat, sailing-ship
[ˈseiliŋˌbəut; -ʃip] *n* jedrilica

sailor [ˈseilə] *n* mornar

saint [seint] *n* svetac

sake [seik] *n* **1. for the sake of** radi
2. for my sake radi mene

salad [ˈsæləd] *n* salata

salami [səˈlaːmi] *n* salama

salary [ˈsæləri] *n* plata

salary increase *n* povišica

salary scale *n* platna skala

sale [seil] *n* **1.** prodaja **2.** rasprodaja
3. for sale za prodaju

saleable [ˈseiləbl] *adj* koji se može
prodati

salesclerk [ˈseilzklaːk] *n* prodavac

salesman, salesperson [seilzmən;
ˈseilzˌpəːsn] *n* **1.** prodavac **2.
travelling salesman** trgovački
putnik

saleswoman [ˈseilzwumən] *n*
prodavačica

saline [ˈseilain] *adj* slan

saliva [səˈlaivə] *n* pljuvačka

salmon [ˈsæmən] *n* losos

salmonella [ˈsælmənelə] *n* (med.)
salmonele

saloon [səˈluːn] *n* **1.** (UK) limuzina
2. (US) kafana; kavana

salt [sɔːlt] *n* so; sol

saltwater *adj* slanovodni

salt water *n* slana voda

salty [ˈsɔːlti] *adj* slan

salute [səˈluːt] **1.** *n* pozdrav **2.** *v*
pozdraviti (po)

salvage [ˈsælvidʒ] *v* spasti

salvation [sælˈveiʃn] *n* spas

same [seim] 1. *adj* isti 2. *n* isto 3.
  all the same na isti način
sample [ˈsaːmpl] *n* uzorak
sanction [ˈsæŋkʃn] 1. *n* sankcija 2.
  v odobriti
sanctuary [ˈsæŋktʃuəri] *n* svetilište
sand [sænd] *n* pesak; pijesak
sandal [ˈsændl] *n* sandala
sand dune *n* dina
sandpaper [ˈsænd,peipə] *n* šmirgla
sandwich [ˈsænwidʒ] *n* sendvič
sandy [ˈsændi] *adj* peščan; pješčan
sane [sein] *adj* duševno zdrav
sang [sæŋ] *see* **sing**
sanitary [ˈsænitri] *adj* sanitetski
sanitary engineering *n* sanitarna
  tehnika
sanitary towel, sanitary napkin
  n higijenski uložak
sanitation [ˌsæniˈteiʃn] *n* sanitarni
  uređaji
sanitation department *n* gradska
  čistoća
sanity [ˈsæniti] *n* duševno zdravlje
sank [sæŋk] *see* **sink**
sap [sæp] *n* biljni sok
sarcasm [ˈsaːkæzəm] *n* sarkazam
sarcastic [saːˈkæstik] *adj*
  sarkastičan
sarcoma [saːˈkəumə] *n* sarkom
sardine [saːˈdiːn] *n* sardina
Sardinia [saːˈdiniə] *n* Sardinija
Sardinian [saːˈdiːnijən] 1. *adj*
  sardinijski, sardinski 2. *n*
  Sardinac
sat [sæt] *see* **sit**
Satan [ˈseitn] *n* satana
satchel [ˈsætʃəl] *n* torba
satellite [ˈsætəlait] *n* 1. satelit 2.
  communications satellite
  telekomunikacioni satelit,
  telekomunikacijski satelit

satellite city *n* grad-satelit
satellite dish *n* satelitska antena
satire [ˈsætaiə] *n* satira
satirical [səˈtirikl] *adj* satiričan
satirist [ˈsætərist] *n* satiričar
satirize [ˈsætəraiz] *v* satirizirati
satisfaction [ˌsætisˈfækʃn] *n* 1.
  zadovoljenost 2. zadovoljenje
satisfactory [ˌsætiˈfæktəri] *adj*
  zadovoljavajući
satisfied [ˈsætisfaid] *adj* **to be**
  satisfied zadovoljan (**with** s)
satisfy [ˈsætisfai] *v* zadovoljiti
saturate [ˈsætʃəreit] *v* zasititi
Saturday [ˈsætədi] *n* subota
sauce [sɔːs] *n* umak
saucepan [ˈsɔːspən] *n* tiganj
saucer [ˈsɔːsə] *n* tacna
sauna [ˈsɔːnə] *n* sauna
sausage [ˈsɔsidʒ] *n* kobasica
savage [ˈsævidʒ] *adj* divlji
savannah [səˈvaːnə] *n* savana
save [seiv] 1. *prep* osim 2. *v* spasti;
  spasiti 3. **to save money** uštedeti
  novac; uštedjeti novac 4. **to save**
  a document sačuvati datoteku
saver [ˈseivə] *n* štediša
savings [ˈseiviŋz] 1. *adj* štedni 2. *pl*
  ušteđevina
savings account *n* štedni ulog
savings and loans *pl* kreditno
  udruženje za građevinske zajmove
savings bank *n* štedionica
saviour, savior [ˈseiviə] *n* spasitelj
savoir-faire [ˈsævwaːˈfeə] *n* vičnost
savour, savor [ˈseivə] *v* uživati u
savoury, savory [ˈseivəri] *adj*
  ukusan
saw [sɔː] 1. *n* testera 2. *v* (**sawed**,
  sawn/sawed) testerisati 3. *see*
  see
sawdust [ˈsɔːdʌst] *n* strugotine

sawmill [ˈsɔːmil] n strugara
sawn [sɔːn] see saw
saxophone [ˈsæksəfəun] n saksofon
saxophone player n saksofonista
say [sei; sed] v (**said**) 1. reći 2. kazati 3. govoriti 4. **that is to say** što znači
saying [ˈsejiŋ] n izreka
scab [skæb] n 1. krasta 2. (pol.) štrajkbreher
scaffold, scaffolding [ˈskæfɔld; -iŋ] n skele
scald [skɔːld] v opariti
scale [skeil] 1. n vaga 2. skala 3. v skinuti
scales [skeilz] pl 1. vaga 2. **fish scales** krljušt ; škrljut
scalpel [ˈskælpl] n skalpel
scan [skæn] 1. n osmotranje 2. skan 3. v osmatrati 4. skanirati
scandal [ˈskændl] n skandal
scandalize [ˈskændəlaiz] v skandalalizovati
scandalous [ˈskændələs] adj skandalozan
scanner [ˈskænə] n skener
scanty [ˈskænti] adj oskudan
scapegoat [ˈskeipgəut] n grešni jarac
scar [skaː] n ožiljak
scarce [skeəs] adj oskudan
scarcely [ˈskeəsli] adv jedva
scarcity [ˈskeəsəti] n oskudica
scare [skeə] 1. v strah 2. v uplašiti
scarecrow [ˈskeəkrəu] n strašilo
scared [ˈskeəd] adj uplašen
scaremonger [ˈskeəmʌŋgə] n paničar
scarf [skaːf] n 1. šal 2. rubac
scarlet [ˈskaːlət] adj skerletan
scarred [skaːd] adj pun brazgotina
scary [ˈskeəri] adj strahovit

scathing [ˈskeiθiŋ] adj oštar
scatter [ˈskætə] v 1. rasuti 2. rasturiti (se)
scavenger [ˈskævendʒə] n strvožder
scene [siːn] n 1. scena 2. **behind the scenes** iza kulisa
scenery [ˈsiːnəri] n 1. pejzaž 2. inscenacija
scent [sent] n 1. miris 2. (UK) parfem
sceptic [ˈskeptik] n skeptik
sceptical [ˈskeptikl] adj skeptičan
scepticism [ˈskeptisizəm] n skepticizam
sceptre [ˈseptə] n skiptar
schedule [ˈʃedjuːl; ˈskedjuːl] 1. n raspored 2. v planirati
scheduled flight [ˈʃedjuːld] adj redovni let
scheme [skiːm] 1. n šema 2. plan 3. intriga 4. v intrigovati
schizophrenia [ˌskitsoˈfriːnijə] n shizofrenija
schizophrenic [ˌskitsoˈfriːnijə] 1. adj shizofrenički 2. n shizofreničar
scholar [ˈskɔlə] n naučnik; učenjak
scholarship [ˈskɔləʃip] n 1. naučnost 2. stipendija 3. **to award a scholarship** dodeliti stipendiju; dodijeliti stipendiju
school [skuːl] 1. adj školski 2. n škola 3. (US) fakultet
school board n školska vlast
schoolboy [ˈskuːlbɔi] n učenik
schoolgirl [ˈskuːlgəːl] n učenica
schooling [ˈskuːliŋ] n školovanje
school-leaving certificate n potvrda o završenoj školi
schoolmaster n učitelj
schoolmistress n učiteljica
schoolteacher n učitelj, učiteljica

school uniform *n* školska uniforma

schooner [ˈsaiəns] *n* škuna

science [ˈsaiəns] *n* nauka

science and technology *n* nauka i tehnologija; znanost i tehnologija

science fiction *n* naučna fantastika

scientific [ˌsaiənˈtifik] *adj* naučan

scientist [ˈsaiəntist] *n* naučnik

scissors [ˈsizəz] *pl* makaze; škare

scoff [skɔf] *v* rugati se

scold [skəuld] *v* izgrditi

scoop [skuːp] *v* zagrabiti

scooter [ˈskuːtə] *n* skuter

scope [skəup] *n* obim

scorch [skɔːt] *n* spržiti (se)

scorched [skɔːtʃt] *adj* spaljen

score [skɔː] 1. (ed.) rezultat 2. (spor.) zapisnik 3. *v* dati gol

scorer [skɔːrə] *n* zapisničar

scorn [skɔːn] 1. *n* prezir; prijezir 2. *v* prezirati

scornful [skɔːnfl] *adj* prezriv (**of** prema)

scorpion [ˈskɔːpiən] *n* škorpija

Scot [skɔt] *n* Škotlanđanin, Škot

Scotch [skɔtʃ] *adj* škotski

scotch tape *n* selotejp

scot-free [ˈskɔtˌfriː] *adj* **to get off scot-free** proći bez kazne

Scotland [ˈskɔtlənd] *n* Škotska

Scotsman [ˈskɔtsmən] *n* Škotlanđanin, Škot

Scottish [ˈskɔtiʃ] *adj* škotski

scout [skaut] 1. (mil.) izviđač 2. *see* **boy scout**

scrabble [ˈskræbl] *v* škrabati

scramble [ˈskræmbl] *v* 1. jagmiti se (**for** oko) 2. slupati 3. šifrovati

scrambled eggs *pl* kajgana

scrap [skræp] 1. *n* komadić 2. *v* raskomadati

scrape [skreip] *v* strugati

scratch [skrætʃ] *v* ogrepsti

scream [skriːm] 1. *n* vrisak 2. *v* vrisnuti

screen [skriːn] 1. *n* zaklon 2. (tel.) ekran 3. *v* zakloniti 4. **to screen refugees** proveriti izbeglice; provjeriti izbjeglice

screenplay [ˈskriːnplei] *n* scenarij

screw [skruː] 1. *n* šraf 2. *v* zavrtnuti

screwdriver [ˈskruːˌdraivə] *n* šrafciger

scribble [ˈskribl] *v* škrabati

script [skript] *n* 1. pisana slova 2. knjiga snimanja

scripture [ˈskriptʃə] *n* Sveto pismo

scrotum [ˈskrəutm] *n* mošnice

scrounger [ˈskraundʒə] *n* žicaroš

scrub [skrʌb] *v* oribati

scruple [ˈskruːpl] *n* skrupula

scrupulous [ˈskruːpjuləs] *adj* skrupulozan

scrutinize [ˈskruːtinaiz] *v* proučiti

scrutiny [ˈskruːtini] *n* pregled

scuba-diver [ˈskuːbəˌdaivə] *n* ronilac, gnjurac (s aparatom za disanje)

scuffle [ˈskʌfl] *n* tuča

sculpt [skʌlpt] *v* izvajati

sculptor [ˈskʌlptə] *n* skulptor

sculpture [ˈskʌlptʃə] *n* skulptura

scum [skʌm] *n* kora

scuttle [ˈskʌtl] *v* potopiti brod

scythe [saiθ] *n* kosa

sea [siː] 1. *adj* pomorski 2. *n* more 3. **by sea** morem 4. **at sea** na moru 5. **on the high seas** na pučini

seacoast [ˈsiːkəust] *n* primorje

seafood [ˈsiːfuːd] *n* ribe

seagull [ˈsiːgʌl] *n* galeb

seal [siːl] 1. *n* pečat 2. foka 3. *v* zapečatiti

sea-level ['si:levl] *n* nivo mora

seal off *v* izolovati

seaman ['si:mən] *n* mornar

search [sə:tʃ] 1. *n* traganje 2. police search pretres 3. *v* pretresti 4. to search for tragati za

searchlight ['sə:tʃlait] *n* reflektor

search party *n* odred za spasavanje

search warrant *n* dozvola za pretres

seashell ['si:ʃel] *n* morska školjka

seashore ['si:ʃɔ:] *n* morska obala

seasick ['si:sik] *n* bolestan od morske bolesti

seasickness ['si:siknis] *n* morska bolest

seaside ['si:said] *n* at the seaside na moru

season ['si:zn] *n* 1. sezona 2. in season u sezoni 3. out of season van sezoni

seasonal ['si:zənəl] *adj* sezonski

seasoning ['si:zəniŋ] *n* začin

season ticket *n* sezonska karta

seat [si:t] 1. *n* sedište 2. poslanički mandat 3. *v* posaditi

seatbelt ['si:tbelt] *n* sigurnosni pojas

seat of government *n* sedište vlade

seaweed ['si:wi:d] *n* alge

secede [sə'si:d] *v* otcepiti se; otcijepiti se (from od)

secession [sə'seʃn] *n* secesija

secluded [si'klu:did] *adj* odvojen

second ['sekənd] 1. *adj* drugi 2. *n* sekund 3. (pol.) podrška

secondary ['sekəndri] *adj* sekundaran

secondary school *n* srednja škola

second-class *adj* drugorazredan

second class *n* druga klasa

second-hand *adj* polovan

second-in-command *n* zamenik komandanta; zamjenik komandanta

second-rate *adj* drugorazredan

secrecy ['si:krəsi] *n* tajnost

secret ['si:krit] 1. *adj* tajan 2. *n* tajna 3. military secret vojna tajna 4. in secret tajno

secret agent *n* tajni agent

secretarial [,sekrə'teəriəl] *adj* sekretarski

secretariat [,sekrə'teəriət] *n* sekretarijat

secretary ['sekrətri] *n* sekretar, sekretarica

secretary general *n* generalni sekretar

secretary of state *n* ministar

secret police *pl* tajna policija

secret service *n* tajna služba

secret talks *pl* tajni pregovori

secretly ['si:kritli] *adv* tajno

sect [sekt] *n* sekta

sectarian [sek'terijən] *adj* sektaški

section ['sekʃn] *n* presek; presjek

sector ['sektə] *n* 1. sektor 2. private sector privatni sektor 3. public sector državni sektor

secular ['sekjulə] *adj* sekularan

secure [si'kjuə] 1. *adj* bezbedan; bezbjedan 2. *v* obezbediti; obezbijediti

securely [si'kjuəli] *adv* bezbedno; bezbjedno

security [si'kjuərəti] *n* 1. sigurnost 2. (fin.) zalog

Security Council *n* Savet bezbednosti, Savjet bezbjednosti; Vijeće sigurnosti

security forces *pl* snage bezbednosti; snage sigurnosti

sedative ['sədətiv] *n* sedativ

sedentary [ˈsedntri] *adj* sedentaran
sediment [ˈsedimənt] *n* talog
sedition [siˈdiʃn] *n* neprijateljska agitacija
seduce [siˈdjuːs] *v* zavesti
seduction [siˈdʌktʃən] *n* zavođenje
see [siː] *v* (**saw, seen**) videti; vidjeti
seed [siːd] *n* seme; sjeme
seeing that *conj* budući da
seek [siːk] *v* (**sought**) tražiti
seek opinion *v* tražiti mišljenje
seem [siːm] *v* učiniti se
seemingly [ˈsiːmiŋli] *adv* kako se čini
seen [siːn] *see* see
see off *v* ispratiti
see through *v* 1. sprovesti do 2. prozreti
segment [ˈsegmənt] *n* segment
segregate [ˈsegrigeit] *v* odvojiti
segregation [ˌsegriˈgeiʃn] *n* segregacija
seize [siːz] *v* uhvatiti
seizure [ˈsiːʒə] *n* 1. (leg.) konfiskacija 2. (med.) napad
seldom [ˈseldəm] *adv* retko
select [siˈlekt] *v* izabrati
selection [siˈlektʃn] *n* selekcija
selective [siˈlektiv] *adj* selektivan
self [self] *n/pro* (*pl* selves) sam
self-centred, self-centered [ˌselfˈsentəd] *adj* sebičan
self-confidence [ˌselfˈkɔnfindəns] *n* samopouzdanje
self-control [ˌselfkənˈtrəul] *n* vladanje sobom
self-criticism [ˌselfˈkritisizəm] *n* samokritika
self-deception [ˌselfdiˈsepʃn] *n* samoodmana
self-defence, self-defense [ˌselfdiˈfens] *n* samoodbrana; samoobrana

self-destruction [ˌselfdiˈstrʌkʃn] *n* samouništenje
self-determination [ˌselfdiˌtəːmiˈneiʃn] *n* samoopredeljenje; samoopredjeljenje
self-governing [ˌselfˈgʌvniŋ] *adj* samoupravni
self-government [ˌselfˈgʌvnmənt] *n* samouprava
self-interest [ˌselfˈintrist] *n* lični interes
selfish [ˈselfiʃ] *adj* sebičan
selfishness [ˈselfiʃnis] *n* sebičnost
selfless [ˈselfləs] *n* nesebičan
self-reliant [ˌselfriˈlaːjənt] *n* samopouzdan
self-respect [ˌselfriˈspekt] *n* samopoštovanje
self-rule [ˌselfruːl] *n* samouprava
self-sufficient [ˌselfsəˈfiʃənt] *adj* samodovoljan
self-supporting [ˌselfsəˈpɔtiŋ] *adj* materijalno nezavisan
self-taught [ˌselfˈtɔːt] *adj* samouk
sell [sel] *v* (**sold**) prodati
seller [ˈselə] *n* 1. prodavac 2. best-seller bestseler
sellotape *n* selotejp
sell out *v* rasprodati
semblance [ˈsembləns] *n* izgled
semen [ˈsiːmən] *n* seme; sjeme
semi- [ˈsemi] *adj* polu-
semi-automatic [ˌsemiˌɔːtəuˈmætik] *n* poluautomatski
semi-automatic rifle *n* poluautomatski puška
semi-final [ˌsemiˈfainl] *n* polufinale
seminar [ˈseminaː] *n* seminar
senate [ˈsenit] *n* senat
senator [ˈsenətə] *n* senator
send [send] *v* (**sent**) (po)slati
send back *v* vratiti

sender [´sendə] *n* 1. pošiljalac 2. adresant

senile [´si:naıl] *adj* senilan

senior [´si:nıə] 1. *adj* stariji 2. viši 3. *n* stariji

senior citizen *n* penzioner

senior official *n* viši oficir

sensation [sen´seıʃn] *n* 1. osećaj; osjećaj 2. senzacija

sensational [sen´seıʃənl] *adj* senzacionalan

sense [sens] 1. *n* smisao 2. čulo 3. razum 4. *v* naslutiti

senseless [´senslis] *adj* besmislen

sensibility [‚sensı´bılətı] *n* osetljivost; osjetljivost

sensible [´sensəbl] *n* razuman

sensitive [´sensətıv] *adj* osetljiv; osjetljiv

sensitivity [‚sensə´tıvıtı] *n* osetljivost; osjetljivost

sensor [´sensə] *n* davač

sensual [´senʃuəl] *adj* senzualan

sent [sent] *see* send

sentence [´sentəns] 1. *n* rečenica 2. (leg.) presuda 3. **death sentence** smrtna presuda 4. *v* (leg.) izreći... kaznu

sentiment [´sentımənt] *n* osećanje; osjećanje

sentinel [´sentınl] *see* sentry

sentry [´sentrı] *n* stražar

separate [´seprət] *adj* 1. odvojen 2. poseban

separate [´sepəreıt] *v* 1. odvojiti (se) 2. razići se

separately [´sepəreıtlı] *adv* odvojeno

separation [‚sepə´reıʃn] *n* odvajanje

separatism [´seprə‚tızm] *n* separatizam

separatist [´seprə‚tıst] *n* separatista

separator [´sepəreıtə] *n* separator

September [sep´tembə] *n* septembar; rujan

septic [´septık] *adj* septičan

sequel [´si:kwəl] *n* nastavak

sequence [´si:kwəns] *n* 1. sekvenca 2. **in sequence** po redu

sequential [sı´kwenʃı] *adj* sledeći; slijedeći

sequestrate [sı´kwestreıt] *v* konfiskovati

Serb [sə:b] *n* Srbin

Serbian [´sə:bıjən] 1. *adj* srpski 2. *n* Srbin

Serbo-Croat, Serbo-Croatian [´sə:bıjən] 1. *adj* srpskohrvatski, hrvatskosrpski 2. *n* srpskohrvatski jezik, hrvatskosrpski jezik

serene [sı´ri:n] *adj* spokojan

sergeant [´sa:dʒənt] *n* vodnik

sergeant-major [‚sa:dʒənt ´meıdʒə] *n* stariji vodnik

serial [´sıərıəl] 1. *adj* serijski 2. *n* emisija

serial killer *n* masovni ubica; masovni ubojica

series [´sıərı:z] *n* 1. serija 2. **tv series** TV-serija

serious [´sıərıəs] *adj* ozbiljan

sermon [´sə:mən] *n* propoved; propovijed

serpent [´sə:pənt] *n* zmija

serum [´sıərəm] *n* serum

servant [´sə:vənt] *n* 1. sluga 2. **civil servant** državni činovnik

serve [sə:v] *v* 1. služiti 2. poslužiti 3. servirati

service [´sə:vıs] 1. *adj* servisni 2. (mil.) vojni 3. *n* služba 4. usluga 5. (spor.) servis 6.**military service** vojna služba 7. **secret service** obaveštajna služba; obavještajna služba

service station *n* pumpna stanica

session ['seʃn] *n* **1.** sednica; sjednica **2. joint session** zajednička sednica/sjednica **3. closed session** zatvorena sednica/sjednica **4. in session** zasedati; zasjedati

set [set] **1.** *adj* određen **2.** utvrđen **3.** *n* komplet **4. tea set** servis za čaj **5. television set** televizor **6.** *v* (set) staviti **7.** postaviti **8. to set a time** odrediti vreme/vrijeme **9. to set an example** dati primer/primjer **10.** *see* **sunset**

set aside *v* odvojiti

setback ['setbæk] *n* neuspeh; neuspjeh

set down *v* spustiti

set fire to *v* zapaliti

set free *v* pustiti na slobodu

set off, set out *v* krenuti

set sail *v* razapeti jedra

settee [se'ti:] *n* mali divan

setting ['setiŋ] *n* okolina

settle ['setl] *v* **1.** srediti **2.** naseliti (se) **3.** odlučiti **4.** poravnati (se)

settlement ['setlmənt] *n* **1.** naselje **2.** (leg/fin.) sporazum

settler ['setlə] *n* naseljenik

settle up *v* obračunati se

set up *v* **1.** postaviti **2.** osnovati **3.** prevariti

seven ['sevn] *n/adj* sedam

seventeen [,sevn'ti:n] *n/adj* sedamnaest

seventeenth [,sevn'ti:nθ] *adj* sedamnaesti

seventh ['sevnθ] *adj* sedmi

seventy ['sevnti] *n/adj* sedamdeset

sever ['sevə] *v* odvojiti (se)

several ['sevrəl] *adj* **1.** nekoliko **2.** razni

severe [si'viə] *adj* **1.** jak **2.** strog

severity [si'verəti] *n* **1.** jačina **2.** strogost

sew [səu] *v* (sewed, sewn/sewed) (sa)šiti

sewage ['su:widʒ] *n* otpaci

sewer ['su:ə] *n* šivač

sewing ['səuiŋ] *n* šivenje

sewing machine *n* šivaća mašina; šivaći stroj

sex [seks; 'seksiz] **1.** *adj* polni; spolni **2.** *n* (*pl* sexes)pol; spol **3.** snošaj

sex appeal *n* seksapel

sex education *n* sex education

sexism ['seksizm] *n* seksualni šovinizam

sexist ['seksist] **1.** *adj* seksistički **2.** *n* seksualni šovinista

sexual ['sekʃuəl] *adj* **1.** seksualan **2.** polni; spolni

sexual harassment *n* seksualno maltiranje

sexual intercourse *n* polno opštenje/općenje

sexuality [,seksju'æliti] *n* seksualnost

sexual relations *n* polni odnosi

sexy ['seksi] *adj* seksi

shabby ['ʃæbi] *adj* otrcan

shade [ʃeid] *n* **1.** hlad **2. a shade of blue** nijansa plave boje

shadow ['ʃædəu] *n* senka; sjenka

shadowy ['ʃædəui] *adj* senovit; sjenovit

shady ['ʃeidi] **1.** *adj* senovit; sjenovit **2.** sumnjiv

shaft [ʃa:ft] *n* **1.** vratilo **2. mining shaft** okno

shaggy ['ʃægi] *adj* rutav

shake [ʃeik] *v* (shook, shaken) **1.** drmati **2.** tresti se **3.** promućkati

shake hands v rukovati se
shaken ['ʃeikən] see shake
shake-up n reorganizacija
shaky ['ʃeiki] adj 1. drhtav 2. nesiguran
shall [ʃəl; ʃæl] see be
shallow ['ʃæləu] adj plitak
sham [ʃæm] n varka
shame [ʃeim] 1. n stid 2. **what a shame!** kakva šteta! 3. v osramotiti
shamefaced ['ʃeimfeist] adj zastiđen
shameful ['ʃeimfəl] adj postiđen
shameless ['ʃeimlis] adj besraman
shampoo [ʃæm'pu:] n šampon
shape [ʃeip] 1. n oblik 2. **in good shape** u dobroj kondiciji 3. v uobličiti
shapeless ['ʃeiplis] adj bezobličan
shapely ['ʃeipli] adj 1. simetričan 2. lep; lijep
share [ʃeə] 1. n udeo; udio 2. (fin.) akcija 3. v deliti; djeliti
shareholder ['ʃeə,həuldə] n akcionar
shark [ʃɑ:k] n ajkula
sharp [ʃɑ:p] adj oštar
sharpen ['ʃɑ:pən] v naoštriti
sharpener ['ʃɑ:pnə] n oštrač
sharpness ['ʃɑ:pnis] n oštrina
shatter ['ʃætə] v slomiti (se)
shave [ʃeiv] v obrijati (se)
shaving ['ʃeiviŋ] n brijanje
shawl [ʃɔ:l] n šal
she [ʃi:] pro ona
sheath [ʃi:θ] n 1. korice 2. see condom
shed [ʃed] 1. n šupa 2. v skinuti
shed blood v proliti krv
sheep [ʃi:p] n (pl sheep) ovca
sheepdog ['ʃi:pdɔg] n ovčarski pas

sheer [ʃiə] adj 1. čist 2. strm
sheet [ʃi:t] n 1. čaršav 2. ploča 3. **a sheet of paper** tabak papira
shelf [ʃelf; ʃelvz] n (pl **shelves**) polica
shell [ʃel] 1. n ljuska 2. kućica 3. (mil.) granata 4. v (mil.) zasuti vatrom
shellfish ['ʃelfiʃ] n ljuskar
shelling ['ʃeliŋ] n (mil.) artilerijsko gađanje
shellshock ['ʃelʃɔk] n kontuzija
shelter ['ʃeltə] 1. n sklonište 2. krov 3. **to take shelter** skloniti se 4. v prikriti
shelve [ʃelv] v metnuti na policu
shelves [ʃelvz] see shelf
shepherd ['ʃepəd] n ovčar
sheriff ['ʃerif] n (US) šerif
shield [ʃi:ld] 1. n štit 2. v štititi
shift [ʃift] 1. n promena; promjena 2. v promeniti; promijeniti
shilling ['ʃiliŋ] n šiling
shin [ʃin] n gnjat
shine [ʃain; ʃɔn] 1. n sjaj 2. v (**shone**) sijati
shiny ['ʃaini] adj sjajan
ship [ʃip] 1. n brod 2. v poslati
shipment ['ʃipmənt] n partija
shipping ['ʃipiŋ] 1. adj špediterski 2. n špedicija 3. brodovlje
shipwreck ['ʃiprek] n brodolom
shipyard ['ʃipjɑ:d] n brodogradilište
shire ['ʃaiə] n (UK) grofovija
shirt [ʃə:t] n košulja
shit [ʃit] n (sl.) izmet
shiver ['ʃivə] n drhtati
shivery ['ʃivəri] adj drhtav
shock [ʃɔk] 1. n sudar 2. šok 3. **electric shock** električni šok 4. **to be in shock** biti u šoku 5. v šokirati

shock absorber *n* amortizer
shocked [ʃɔkt] *adj* **to be shocked** biti šokiran
shocking [·ʃɔkiŋ] *adj* 1. šokantan 2. užasan
shoddy [·ʃɔdi] *adj* loš
shoe [ʃuː] *n* cipela
shoelace [·ʃuːleis] *n* pertla
shoemaker [·ʃuːˌmeikə] *n* obućar
shoestring [·ʃuːstriŋ] *n* (US) pertla
shone [ʃɔn] *see* **shine**
shook [ʃuk] *see* **shake**
shoot [ʃuːt] 1. *n* izdanak 2. *v* (**shot**) ustreliti; ustrijeliti 3. pucati
shoot down *v* oboriti
shooting [·ʃuːtiŋ] *n* pucanje
shooting star *n* meteor
shoot-out [·ʃuːtaut] *n* obračun vatrenim oružjem
shop [ʃɔp] 1. *n* radnja 2. *v* kupovati
shopkeeper [·ʃɔpˌkiːpə] *n* vlasnik radnje
shoplifting [·ʃɔpˌliftiŋ] *n* krađa po radnjama
shopping [·ʃɔpiŋ] *n* pazarenje
shopping centre, shopping mall *n* trgovački centar
shop window *n* izlog
shore [ʃɔː] *n* 1. obala 2. primorje
short [ʃɔːt] 1. *adj* kratak 2. malog rasta 3. **to be short of** oskudan 4. **in short** ukratko 5. *adv* kratko
shortage [·ʃɔːtidʒ] *n* oskudica
shortchange [ˌʃɔːtˈtʃeindʒ] *v* prevariti u kusuru
short circuit [ˌʃɔːtˈsəːkit] *n* kratki spoj
shortcoming [·ʃɔːtkʌmiŋ] *n* mana
short cut *n* prečica
shorten [·ʃɔːtn] *v* skratiti
shorthand [·ʃɔːthænd] *n* stenografija

shortly [·ʃɔːtli] *adv* uskoro
shortness [·ʃɔːtnis] *n* 1. kratkoća 2. nizak rast
short of *prep* bez
shorts [ʃɔːts] *pl* 1. (UK) šorc 2. (US) *see* **underwear**
short-sighted [ˌʃɔːtˈsaitid] *adj* kratkovid
short-term [ˌʃɔːtˈtəːm] *adj* kratkoročan
short-wave [·ʃɔːtweiv] *adj* kratkotalasni
shot [ʃɔt] 1. *n* pucanj 2. (med.) injekcija 3. (spor.) šut 4. *see* **shoot**
shotgun [·ʃɔtgʌn] *n* sačmara
should [ʃud] *v* trebati
shoulder [·ʃəuldə] *n* rame
shout [ʃaut] 1. *n* vika 2. *v* uzviknuti
shout at *v* viknuti na
shout for help *v* viknuti u pomoć
shouting [·ʃautiŋ] *n* vikanje
shove [ʃʌv] *v* gurnuti
shovel [·ʃʌvl] *n* lopata
show [ʃəu] 1. *n* izložba 2. demonstracija 3. šou 4. *v* (**showed, shown**) pokazati 5. prikazati
show business *n* šou-biznis
showcase [·ʃəukeis] *n* stakleni ormar
showdown [·ʃəudaun] *n* odlučan obračun
shower [·ʃauə] *n* 1. tuš 2. pljusak
shown [ʃəun] *see* **show**
show off *v* razmetati se
showroom [·ʃəurum] *n* salon
shrank [ʃræŋk] *see* **shrink**
shrapnel [·ʃræpnəl] *n* šrapnel
shrewd [ʃruːd] *adj* prepreden
shriek [ʃriːk] *v* vrisak
shrimp [ʃrimp] *n* račić

shrine [ʃrain] *n* svetište
shrink [ʃriŋk] *v* (**shrank, shrunk**) skupiti (se)
shrivel [·ʃrivl] *v* osušiti (se)
shroud [ʃraud] *n* mrtvački pokrov
shrub [ʃrʌb] *n* žbun
shrug [ʃrʌg] *v* sleći
shrunk [ʃrʌŋk] *see* **shrink**
shudder [·ʃʌdə] *v* ježiti se
shuffle [·ʃʌfl] *v* 1. vući 2. (pol.) mijenjati položaj
shun [ʃʌn] *v* izbegavati; izbjegavati
shunt [ʃʌnt] *v* manevrisati
shut [ʃʌt] 1. *adj* zatvoren 2. *v* (**shut**) zatvoriti (se)
shutdown [·ʃʌtdaun] *n* zatvaranje
shutter [·ʃʌtə] *n* kapak
shuttle [·ʃʌtl] *n* šatl
shut up! ćuti!
shy [ʃai] *adj* snebivljiv
shyness [·ʃainis] *n* snebivljivost
sibling [·sibliŋ] *n* brat, sestra
sick [sik] *adj* 1. bolestan 2. morbidan 3. sit
sicken [·sikən] *v* zgaditi
sickle [·sikl] *n* srp
sickle call anaemia *n* srpasta anemija
sickly [·sikli] *adj* bolešljiv
sickness [·siknis] *n* bolest
side [said] 1. *n* strana 2. obala 3. stranka 4. bok 5. (pol/spor.) stranka 6. **side by side** bok uz bok 7. **to change sides** preći na drugu stranu 8. *v* pristati (**with** uz)
sideline [·saidlain] *v* uzgredna roba
side-splitting [·said‚splitiŋ] *adj* grohotan
side street *n* sporedna ulica
sidetrack [·saidtræk] *v* skrenuti
sidewalk [·saidwɔ:k] *n* (US) trotoar

sideways [·saidweiz] *adv* sa strane
siege [si:dʒ] *n* 1. ospoda 2. **to lay/set siege** opsesti; opsjesti
siesta [si:·estə] *n* siesta
sieve [siv] *n* sito
sift [sift] *v* prosejati; prosijati
sigh [sai] 1. *n* uzdah 2. *v* uzdahnuti
sight [sait] 1. *n* vid 2. znamenitost 3. prizor 4. *v* ugledati
sightless [·saitlis] *adj* bez vida
sightseeing [·sait‚si:iŋ] *n* razgladenje znamenitosti
sign [sain] 1. *n* znak 2. firma 3. plakat 4. **road sign** saobraćajni znak 6. *v* potpisati
signal [·signəl] 1. *n* signal 2. *v* signalizovati
signal-box [·signəlbɔks] *n* skretničarska kućica
signaller [·signələ] *n* skretničar
signatory [·signətri] *n* potpisnik
signature [·signətʃə] *n* potpis
signboard [·sainbɔ:d] *n* oglasna tabla/ploča
significance [sig·nifikəns] *n* značaj
significant [sig·nifikənt] *adj* značajan
signify [·signifai] *v* značiti
sign language *n* govor prstima
signpost [·sainpəust] *n* putokaz
silence [·sailəns] *n* ćutanje; šutnja
silencer [·sailənsə] *n* prigušivač
silent [·sailənt] *adj* ćutljiv; šutljiv
silhouette [silju·wet] *n* silueta
silicon [·silikən] *n* silicijum
silk [silk] *n* svila
silken [·silkn] *adj* svilen
silliness [·silinis] *n* budalaština
silly [·sili] *adj* budalast
silo [·sailəu] *n* silos
silver [·silvə] 1. *adj* srebrn 2. *n* srebro

similar [ˈsimilə] *adj* sličan

similarity [ˌsiməˈlærəti] *n* sličnost

simple [ˈsimpl] *adj* 1. jednostavan 2. prost

simplicity [simˈplisəti] *n* 1. jednostavnost 2. prostota

simplify [ˈsimplifai] *v* uprostiti

simply [ˈsimpli] *adv* prosto

simulate [ˈsimjuleit] *v* simularoti

simulation [ˌsimjuˈleiʃn] *n* simuliranje

simultaneous [ˌsimlˈteiniəs] *adj* simultan

simultaneous translation *n* simultano prevođenje

simultaneously [ˌsimlˈteiniəsli] *adv* simultano

sin [sin] 1. *n* greh; grijeh 2. *v* zgrešiti; zgriješiti

since [sins] 1. *adv* otada 2. davno 3. *prep* od 4. *conj* (ot)kako

sincere [sinˈsiə] *adj* iskren

sincerely [sinˈserəti] *adv* iskreno

sincerity [sinˈserəti] *n* iskrenost

sing [siŋ] *v* (**sang, sung**) pevati; pjevati

singe [sindʒ] *v* oprljiti

singer [ˈsiŋə] *n* pevač; pjevač

singing [ˈsiŋiŋ] *n* pevanje; pjevanje

single [ˈsiŋgl] 1. *adj* jedan jedini 2. samački 3. *n* samac, samica 4. (mus.) singl ploča

single bed *n* krevet za jednog

single out *v* izdvojiti

single ticket *n* karta u jednom smeru/smjeru

singular [ˈsiŋgjulə] *n* jednina

sinister [ˈsinistə] *adj* zlokoban

sink [siŋk] 1. *n* lavabo 2. *v* (**sank, sunk**) potopiti 3. potonuti 4. pasti

sinner [ˈsinə] *n* grešnik

sip [sip] *v* srkati

sir [sə:] *n* gospodin

siren [ˈsaiərən] *n* sirena

sister [ˈsistə] *n* 1. sestra 2. (rel.) kaluđerica

sister-in-law [ˈsistərinlɔ:] *n* svastika, zaova, snaha

sit [sit] *v* (**sat**) sedeti; sjedjeti (**in/on** u; **on** na; **at** za)

sit down *v* sesti; sjesti (**on** na; **at** za)

sit-down protest *n* sedenje u znak protesta; sjedenje u znak protesta

sit-in [ˈsit,in] *n* mirna okupacija

site [sait] *n* 1. položaj 2. gradilište

sitting [ˈsitiŋ] *n* sednica; sjednica

sitting-room *n* gostinska soba

situate [ˈsitjueit] *v* postaviti

situated [ˈsitjueitid] *adj* The theatre is situated in the town centre. Pozorište se nalazi u centru grada.

situation [ˌsitʃuˈeiʃn] *n* 1. situacija 2. radno mesto/mjesto

six [siks] *n/adj* sest

sixteen [sikˈsti:n] *n/adj* šesnaest

sixteenth [sikˈsti:nθ] *adj* šesnaesti

sixth [siksθ] *adj* šesti

sixty [ˈsiksti] *n/adj* šezdeset

size [saiz] *n* 1. veličina 2. broj

skate [skeit] 1. *n* klizaljka 2. *v* klizati se

skateboard [ˈskeitbɔ:d] *n* skejtbord

skater [ˈskeitə] *n* klizač; sklizač

skating [ˈskeitiŋ] *n* klizanje; sklizanje

skating-rink [ˈskeitiŋ,rink] *n* klizalište; sklizalište

skeleton [ˈskelitn] *n* skelet

skeptic, skeptical, skepticism *see* **sceptic, sceptical, scepticism**

sketch [sketʃ] 1. *n* skica 2. *v* skicirati

ski [ski:] **1.** *adj* skijaški **2.** *n* skija **3.** *v* skijati se

skid [skid] *v* zaneti se; zanijeti se

skier [ˈski:ə] *n* skijaš

skiing [ˈski:iŋ] *n* skijaški sport

skilful, skillful [ˈskilfl] *adj* vešt; viješt

skill [skil] *n* veština; vještina

skilled [ˈskild] *adj* **1.** vešt; vješt **2.** kvalifikovan

skim [skim] *v* obrati

skimmed milk, skim milk [skimd-milk; skimˈmilk] *n* obrano mleko/mlijeko

skin [skin] **1.** *n* koža **2.** *v* oderati

skin-deep *adj* površan

skinhead [ˈskin,hed] *n* siledžija

skinny [ˈskini] *adj* mršav

skip [skip] **1.** *n* (UK) gvozdena korpa **2.** *v* preskočiti **3.** odmagliti

skip over *v* kliznuti

skirmish [ˈskə:miʃ] *n* čarka

skirt [skə:t] *n* suknja

ski slope *n* pista za skijanje

skull [skʌl] *n* lobanja

sky [skai] *n* nebo

sky-blue *adj* nebesko plavetnilo

skyscraper [ˈskai,skreipə] *n* oblakoder

slab [slæb] *n* ploča

slack [slæk] *adj* **1.** labav **2.** slab

slacken [ˈslækən] *v* oslabiti

slacker [ˈslækə] *n* zabušant

slackness [ˈslæknis] *n* labavost

slain [slein] *see* **slay**

slalom [ˈsla:ləm] *n* slalom

slam [slæm] *v* (**slammed**) zalupiti

slander [ˈsla:ndə] **1.** *n* kleveta **2.** *v* oklevetati

slanderer [ˈsla:ndərə] *n* klevetnik

slanderous [ˈsla:ndrəs] *adj* klevetnički

slang [slæŋ] *n* sleng

slant [sla:nt] **1.** *n* nagib **2.** *v* nagnuti

slanted, slanting [ˈsla:ntid; ˈsla:ntiŋ] *adj* sklon

slap [slæp] **1.** *n* pluska **2.** *v* (**slapped**) ošamariti

slash [slæʃ] *v* **1.** probušiti **2.** (fin.) smanjiti

slate [slæt] *n* škriljac

slaughter [ˈslɔ:tə] **1.** *n* klanje **2.** pokolj **3.** *v* zaklati

slaughterhouse [ˈslɔ:təhaus] *n* klanica; klaonica

Slav [sla:v] *n* Sloven; Slaven

slave [sleiv] *n* rob

slave labour *n* robovska radna snaga

slavery [ˈsleivəri] *n* ropstvo

slave trade *n* trgovina robljem

Slavic [ˈsla:vik] *adj* slovenski; slavenski

slay [slei] *v* (**slew, slain**) ubiti

sled, sledge [sled; sledʒ] *n* sanke

sleek [sli:k] *adj* sladak

sleep [sli:p] **1.** *n* san **2.** *v* (**slept**) spavati

sleeper [ˈsli:pə] *see* **sleeper car**

sleepiness [ˈsli:pinis] *n* pospanost

sleeping bag *n* vreća za spavanje

sleeping car *n* spavaća kola

sleeping pill *n* tableta za spavanje

sleeping sickness *n* bolest spavanje

sleepless [ˈsli:plis] *adj* besan

sleeplessness [ˈsliplisnis] *n* nesanica

sleepwalker [ˈsl:p,wɔ:kə] *n* somnambul

sleep with *v* imati snošaj s

sleepy [ˈsli:pi] *adj* sanjiv

sleet [sli:t] **1.** *n* susnežica; susnježica **2.** *v* padati o susnežici/ susnježici

sleeve [sliːv] *n* rukav
sleigh [slei] *see* **sled**
slender [ˈslendə] *adj* vitak
slept [slept] *see* **sleep**
slew [sluː] *see* **slay**
slice [slais] 1. *n* porcija 2. *v* seći; sjeći
sliced bread [slaisd] *n* isečen hleb; isječen kruh
slick [slik] *n* oil slick naftna mrlja
slide [slaid] 1. *n* klizaljka 2. slajd, dijapozitiv 3. *v* (**slid**) kliznuti
slight [slait] *adj* lak
slightly [ˈslaitli] *adv* malo
slim [slim] 1. *adj* vitak 2. *v* izgubiti (u težini)
slimy [ˈslaimi] *adj* muljav
sling [slin] 1. *n* (med.) zavoj 2. *v* baciti
slip [slip] 1. *n* slip of paper parče papira 2. to make a slip napraviti grešku 3. *v* (**slipped**) okliznuti se
slip away *v* umaći
slip into *v* uvući se kroz
slip of the tongue *n* gaf
slipper [ˈslipə] *n* patika
slippery [ˈslipəri] *adj* klizav
slit [slit] 1. *n* prorez 2. *v* prorezati
slogan [ˈsləugən] *n* parola
slope [sləup] 1. *n* nagib 2. *v* biti kos
sloping [ˈsləupiŋ] *adj* kos
sloppy [ˈslɔpi] *adj* aljkav
slot [slɔt] *n* otvor
Slovene [sləˈviːn] 1. *adj* slovenački; slovenski 2. *n* Slovenac
Slovenia [sləˈviːniə] *n* Slovenija
Slovenian [sləˈviːniən] 1. *adj* slovenački; slovenski 2. *n* Slovenac
slow [sləu] 1. *adj* spor 2. This clock is slow. Ovaj sat kasni. 3. *adv* polako

slow down *v* 1. usporiti 2. smanjiti brzinu
slow-motion [sləuˈməuʃn] *n* in slow motion na usporenom filmu
slowly [ˈsləuli] *adv* polako
slowness [ˈsləunis] *n* sporost
slum [slʌmə] *n* sirotinjski kvart
slumber [ˈslʌmbə] 1. *n* dremež 2. *v* dremati
slump [slʌmp] 1. *n* (ec.) recesija 2. *v* srozati se
slums [slʌmz] *see* **slum**
sly [slai] *adj* lukav
smack [smæk] 1. *n* udar 2. *v* udariti
small [smɔːl] *adj* 1. mali 2. sitan
small arms *pl* ručno oružje
small-minded [ˌsmɔːlˈmaindid] *adj* sitničav
smallpox [ˈsmɔːlpɔks] *n* variole
smart [smaːt] *adj* 1. pametan 2. lukav 3. elegantan
smash [smæʃ] *v* razbiti
smash hit *n* veliki uspeh/uspjeh
smashing [ˈsmæʃiŋ] *adj* izvanredan
smear [smiə] *v* 1. zamazati 2. (pol.) oklevetati
smear test *n* bris
smell [smel] 1. *n* miris 2. nice smell aromat 3. bad smell smrad 4. *v* (**smelt/smelled**) mirisati 5. pomirisati
smelt [smelt] *v* 1. istopiti 2. *see* **smell**
smile [smail] 1. *n* osmeh; osmjeh 2. *v* osmehnuti; osmjehnuti
smith [smiθ] *n* metalski radnik
smog [smɔg] *n* smog
smoke [sməuk] 1. *n* dim 2. *v* pušiti 3. nadimiti
smoker [ˈsməukə] *n* pušač
smoking [ˈsməukiŋ] *n* 1. pušenje 2. No smoking! Pušenje zabranjeno!

smoky [ˈsməuki] *adj* dimljiv
smooth [smuːð] 1. *adj* gladak 2. tih 3. *v* ugladiti
smoothly [ˈsmuːðli] *adv* glatko
smoothness [ˈsmuːðnəs] *n* 1. glatkost 2. ugladenost
smuggle [ˈsmʌgl] *v* prokrijumčariti
smuggler [ˈsmʌglə] *n* krijumčar
smuggling [ˈsmʌgliŋ] *n* krijumčarenje
snack [snæk] *n* užina
snack bar *n* snek-bar
snag [snæg] *n* prepreka
snail [sneil] *n* puž
snake [sneik] *n* zmija
snap [snæp] *v* (**snapped**) 1. pući 2. fotografisati
snapshot [ˈsnæpʃɔt] *n* snimak
snare [sneə] *v* zamka
snarl [snaːl] *v* režati
snatch [snætʃ] *v* zgrabiti
sneak [sniːk] *v* šunjati se
sneakers [ˈsniːkəz] *pl* (US) patike
sneaky [ˈsniːki] *adj* skriven
sneer [sniə] *v* podsmehivati se; podsmjehivati se
sneeze [sniːz] 1. *n* kijanje 2. *v* kinuti
sniff [snif] *v* 1. šmrkati 2. pronjušiti
snip [snip] *v* ostrići
snob [snɔb] *n* snob
snobbery [ˈsnɔbəri] *n* snobizam
snoop [snuːp] *v* njuškalo
snooze [snuːz] *v* dremati
snore [snɔː] *v* hrkanje
snorkel [ˈsnɔːkl] *n* snorkel
snort [snɔːt] *v* frkati
snow [snəu] 1. *n* sneg; snijeg 2. *v* It's snowing. Pada sneg/snijeg.
snow-flake *n* snežna pahuljica; snježna pahuljica

snowman [ˈsnəumæn] *n* sneško belić; snješko bjelić
snow-plough *n* snežni plug; snježni plug
snow-storm *n* mećava
snub [snʌb] *v* dati korpu
snug [snʌg] *adj* tesan; tijesan
so [səu] 1. *adv* tako 2. *conj* (and) so pa 3. so (that) da 4. so what? pa šta/što?
soak [səuk] *v* potopiti
so-and-so [ˈsəuən,səu] *n* taj i taj
soap [səup] *n* sapun
soap opera *n* sapunska opera
soar [sɔː] *v* jedriti
sob [sɔb] *v* jecati
sober [ˈsəubə] *adj* 1. trezan; trijezan 2. racionalan
sober up *v* otrezniti (se); otrijezniti (se)
so-called [səuˈkɔːld] *adj* nazovi-
soccer [ˈsɔkə] *n* fudbal
sociable [ˈsəuʃəbl] *adj* druželjubiv
social [ˈsəuʃl] *adj* društveni
social-democrat *n* socijal demokrata; socijal demokrat
socialism [ˈsəuʃəlizəm] *n* socijalizam
socialist [ˈsəuʃəlist] 1. *adj* socijalistički 2. socijalista
socialize [ˈsəuʃəlaiz] *v* kretati se u društvu
social sciences *pl* društvene nauke
social security, social welfare *n* socijalno osiguranje
society [səˈsaiəti] *n* društvo
socioeconomic [ˌsəusiəuˈkənɔmik] *adj* društveno-ekonomski
sociolinguistics [ˌsəusiəulinˈgwistiks] *n* sociolingvistika
sociologist [ˌsəusiˈɔlədʒist] *n* sociolog

sociology [ˌsəusiˈɔlɔdʒi] *n* sociologija

sociopolitical [ˌsəusiəupəˈlitikl] *adj* društveno-politički

sock [sɔk] *n* čarapa

socket [ˈsɔkit] *n* 1. čašica 2. **power socket** štekontakt

soda water *n* soda-voda

sofa [ˈsəufa] *n* sofa

soft [sɔft] *adj* mek

soft drink *n* bezalkoholno piće

soften [ˈsɔfn] *v* razmekšati

softly [ˈsɔftli] *adv* meko

softness [ˈsɔftnis] *n* mekoća

software [ˈsɔftweə] *n* softver

software package *n* softverski paket

soggy [ˈsɔgi] *adj* raskvašen

soil [sɔil] 1. *n* tle 2. *v* ukaljati

solar [ˈsəulə] *adj* sunčani

solar energy *n* Sunčeva energija

sold [səuld] *see* **sell**

solder [ˈsəuldə] 1. *n* slem 2. *v* zalemiti

soldering iron *n* alat za lemljenje

soldier [ˈsəuldʒə] *n* vojnik

sold out [səuldˈaut] *adj* rasprodat; rasprodan

sole [səul] 1. *adj* jedini 2. *n* taban 3. đon

sole agent *n* isključivi agent, isključivi zastupnik

solely [ˈsəuli] *adv* jedino

solemn [ˈsɔləm] *adj* svečan

solicit [səˈlisit] *v* tražiti

solicitor [səˈlisitə] *n* (UK) advokat

solid [ˈsɔlid] 1. *adj* solidno 2. pun 3. *n* čvrsto telo/tijelo

solidarity [ˌsɔliˈdærəti] *n* solidarnost

solidify [səˈlidifai] *v* očvrsnuti

solitary [ˈsɔlitri] *adj* usamljen

solitude [ˈsɔlitjuːd] *n* usamljenost

solo [ˈsəuləu] *adj/n/adv* solo

so long as *conj* sve dok

so long! doviđenja!

solution [səˈluːʃn] *n* 1. rešenje; rješenje 2. rastvor

solve [sɔlv] *v* rešiti; riješiti

solvency [ˈsɔlvənsi] *n* solventnost

solvent [ˈsɔlvənt] *adj* solventan

some [səm; sʌm] 1. *pro/adj* neki, nekakav 2. malo 3. *adv* otprilike

somebody [ˈsʌmbədi] neko

someday [ˈsʌmdei] *adv* jednog dana

somehow [ˈsʌmhau] *adv* nekako

someone [ˈsʌmwʌn] neko

someplace [ˈsʌmpleis] *adv* negde; negdje

somersault [ˈsʌməsɔlt] 1. *n* kolut 2. *v* napraviti kolut

something [ˈsʌmθiŋ] nešto

sometime [ˈsʌmtaim] *adv* jednom

sometimes [ˈsʌmtaimz] *adv* ponekad

someway [ˈsʌmwei] *adv* nekako

somewhat [ˈsʌmwɔt] *adv* nešto

somewhere [ˈsʌmweə] *adv* negde; negdje

son [sʌn] *n* sin

song [sɔŋ] *n* pesma; pjesma

songwriter [ˈsɔŋraitə] *n* kompozitor

son-in-law [ˈsʌninlɔː] *n* zet, kćerin muž

soon [suːn] *adv* 1. uskoro 2. **as soon as** čim 3. **how soon?** kad?

soon after *conj* uskoro posle/ poslije

soon afterwards *adv* malo zatim

sooner or later [ˈsuːnə] *adv* pre ili kasnije; prije ili kasnije

soothe [suːð] *v* ublažiti

sophisticated [səˈfistikeitid] *adj* prefinjen

sophistication [səˌfistiˈkeiʃn] *n* prefinjenost

sorcerer [ˈsɔːsərə] *n* vračar

sorcery [ˈsɔːsəri] *n* vračanje

sordid [ˈsɔːdid] *adj* prljav

sore [sɔː] 1. *adj* ranjav 2. *n* rana

sore throat *n* upala grla, grlobolja

soreness [ˈsɔːnis] *n* bolnost, osetljivost; osjetljivost

sorrow [ˈsɔrəu] *n* žalost

sorry [ˈsɔri] *adj* 1. žao 2. sorry! izvini!

sort [sɔːt] 1. *n* vrsta 2. *v* sortirati

sort out *v* 1. odvojiti 2. razmrsiti

SOS [ˌesəuˈes] *n* SOS

so-so [səu səu] *adv* osrednje

so that *conj* da

sought [sɔːt] *see* seek

soul [səul] *n* duša

sound [saund] 1. *adj* čvrst 2. *adv* čvrsto 3. *n* zvuk 4. *v* zvučati 5. zvoniti

soundless [ˈsaundlis] *adj* bez svuka

soundness [ˈsaundnis] *n* čvrstoća

soundproof [ˈsaundpruːf] *adj* otporan na zvuk

soundtrack [ˈsaundtræk] *n* zvučna traka

soup [suːp] *n* čorba, supa

sour [sauə] 1. *adj* kiseo 2. **The milk's sour.** Mleko je proskislo. 3. *v* zakiseliti

source [sɔːs] *n* izvor

source of income *n* izvor prihoda

source of information *n* izvor informacija

south [sauθ] 1. *adj* južni 2. *n* jug

southeast [ˌsauθˈiːst] 1. *adj* jugoistočan 2. *n* jugoistok

southerly [ˈsʌðəli] *adj* južni

southern [ˈsʌðən] *adj* južni

southerner [ˈsʌðənə] *n* južnjak

southwards [ˈsauθwəːds] *adv* na jug

southwest [ˌsauθˈwest] 1. *adj* jugozapadan 2. *n* jugozapad

souvenir [ˌsuːvəˈniə] *n* suvenir

sovereign [ˈsɔvrin] *n* monarh

sovereign state *n* suverena država

sovereignty [ˈsɔvrənti] *n* suverenitet

soviet [ˈsəuviət] *adj* sovjet

sow [sau] *n* krmača

sow [səu] *v* (**sowed, sown**) posejati; posijati

spa [spaː] *n* banja

space [speis] 1. *adj* vasionski 2. *n* prostor 3. razmak 4. **outer space** vasiona

spacecraft [ˈspeiskraːft] *n* kosmički brod

spacelab [ˈspeislæb] *n* istraživačka vasionska stanica

spaceman [ˈspeismæn] *n* astronaut

spaceship [ˈspeisʃip] *n* kosmički brod

space shuttle [ˈspeisʃʌtl] *n* šatl

spacious [ˈspeiʃes] *adj* prostran

spade [speid] *n* ašov

spaghetti [spəˈgeti] *n* špageti

spade [speid] *n* ašov

Spain [spein] *n* Španija; Španjolska

span [spæn] *n* raspon

Spanish [ˈspæniʃ] *adj* španski

spanner [ˈspænə] *n* ključ

spar [spaː] 1. *n* greda 2. *v* boksovati 3. debatovati

spare [speə] 1. *adj* rezervni 2. oskudan 3. *v* poštedeti; poštedjeti 4. dati

spare a life *v* poštedeti život

spare no effort *v* ne žaliti truda

spare parts *pl* rezervni delovi/ dijelovi

spare ribs *pl* suva rebra

spare time *n* slobodno vreme/
vrijeme
spare tyre, spare tire *n* rezervna
guma
spark [spa:k] *n* varnica
sparkle [ˈspa:kl] *v* bleštati; blještati
sparkling [ˈspa:kliŋ] *adj* iskričav
sparkling wine *n* iskričavo vino
spark plug *n* svećica; svjećica
sparrow [ˈspærəu] *n* vrabac
spasm [ˈspæzəm] *n* spazma
spat [spæt] *see* **spit**
spate [speit] *n* bujica
speak [spi:k] *v* (**spoke, spoken**) 1.
govoriti 2. **to speak English**
govoriti engleski
speaker [ˈspi:kə] 1. govornik 2. *see*
loudspeaker
speaker of parliament *n*
predsedavajući; predsjedavajući
speak out *v* govoriti otvoreno
speak up *v* govoriti glasnije
spear [spiə] *n* koplje
spearhead [ˈspi:əhed] *v* voditi
special [ˈspeʃl] 1. *adj* specijalan 2.
n posebna (TV) emisija
specialist [ˈspeʃəlist] *n* specijalista
specialty, speciality [ˈspeʃəlti;
ˌspeʃiˈæləti] *n* specijalnost
specialization [ˌspeʃəlaiˈzeiʃn] *n*
specijalizacija
specialize [ˈspeʃəlaiz] *v*
specijalizovati se (**in** u)
specially [ˈspeʃəli] *adv* osobito,
napose
species [ˈspi:ʃi:z] *n* vrsta
specific [spəˈsifik] *adj* specifičan
specifically [spəˈsifikli] *adv*
specifično, određeno
specification [ˌspəsifiˈkeiʃn] *n*
specifikacija
specify [ˈspesifai] *v* specifikovati

specimen [ˈspesimən] *n* uzorak
speck [spek] *n* mrljica
specs [speks] *see* **spectacles**
spectacle [ˈspektəkl] *n* prizor
spectacles [ˈspektəklz] *pl* naočari;
naočale
spectacular [spekˈtækjulə] *adj*
spektakularan
spectator [spekˈteitə] *n* gledalac
spectrum [ˈspektrəm] *n* spektar
speculate [ˈspekjuleit] *v* 1.
razmišljati 2. (fin.) špekulisati
speculation [spekjuˈleiʃn] *n* 1.
razmišljanje 2. (fin.) špekulacija
speculative [ˈspekjulətiv] *adj* (fin.)
špekulantski
speculator [ˈspekjuleitə] *n* (fin.)
špekulant
speech [spi:tʃ] *n* 1. govor 2. reč;
riječ 3. **to make a speech** održati
govor
speech defect *n* govorna mana
speechless [ˈspi:tʃlis] *adj* zanemo;
zanijemo
speed [spi:d] 1. *n* brzina 2. **at top
speed** najvećom brzinom 3. *v*
prebrzo voziti
speeding [ˈspi:diŋ] *n* prebrza vožnja
speed limit *n* ograničenje brzine
speedometer [spiˈdɔmitə] *n*
brzinomer; brzinomjer
speed up *v* 1. ubrzati 2. povećati
brzinu
speedy [ˈspi:di] *adj* brz
spell [spel] 1. *n* kratko
vreme/vrijeme 2. čini 3. *v*
(**spelt/spelled**) pisati, spelovati
spellbound [ˈspelbaund] *adj*
opčaran
spelling [ˈspeliŋ] *n* 1. pravopis 2.
spelovanje
spend [spend] *v* (**spent**) 1. potrošiti

2. yi lokaci 3. **to spend the day** provesti dan

spendthrift [ˈspendθrift] *n* rasipnik

spent [spent] *see* **spend**

sperm [spəːm] *n* sperma

sphere [sfiə] *n* sfera

spice [spais] *n* začin

spicy [ˈspaisi] *adj* 1. začinjen 2. pikantan

spider [ˈspaidə] *n* pauk

spike [spaik] *n* klin

spill [spil] 1. *n* **oil spill** prosipanje nafte 2. *v* (**split/spilled**) prosuti (se)

spin [spin] *v* (**spun**) 1. presti 2. vrteti se; vrtjeti se

spinach [ˈspinidʒ] *n* spanć; špinat

spinal [ˈspainl] *adj* spinalan

spinal column *n* kičmeni stub

spinal cord *n* kičmena moždina

spine [spain] *n* 1. kičma 2. bodlja

spinning [ˈspiniŋ] *n* predenje

spinster [ˈspinstə] *n* usedelica; usidjelica

spiny [ˈspaini] *adj* bodljikav

spiral [ˈspairəl] *adj* spiralan

spirit [ˈspirit] *n* 1. duh 2. temperament 3. *see* **spirits**

spirited [ˈspiritid] *adj* vatren

spirits [ˈspirits] *pl* 1. alkoholna pića 2. **to be in good spirits** biti u dobrom raspoloženju

spiritual [ˈspiritʃuəl] *adj* duhovni

spit [spit] 1. *n* pljuvačka 2. *v* ((UK) **spat**; (US) **spit**) ispljuvati

spite [spait] 1. *n* inat 2. **in spite of** uprkos 3. *v* terati inat; tjerati inat

spiteful [spaitfl] *adj* pakostan

spit out *v* ispljuvati

spittle [ˈspitl] *n* ispljuvak

splash [splæʃ] 1. *n* prskanje 2. *v* poprskati

splendid [ˈsplendid] *adj* divan

splendour, splendor [ˈsplendə] *n* divota

splint [splint] *n* udlaga

splinter [ˈsplintə] *n* cepka; cjepka

splinter group *n* (pol.) frakcija

split [split] 1. *n* rascep; rascjep 2. *v* (**split**) rascepiti (se); rascijepiti (se) 3. podeliti; podijeliti

spoil [spɔil] *v* (**spoilt/spoiled**) 1. pokvariti 2. upropastiti 3. *see* **spoils**

spoiled [spɔild] *adj* **a spoiled child** razmeženo dete/dijete

spoils [spɔilz] *pl* plen, plijen

spoilsport [ˈspɔilspɔːt] *n* kvarilac raspoloženja

spoilt [spɔilt] *see* **spoil, spoiled**

spoke, spoken [spəuk; ˈspəukən] *see* **speak**

spokesman, spokesperson, spokeswoman [ˈspəuksmən; -pəːsən; -wumən] *n* port-parol

sponge [spʌndʒ] *n* sunđer

sponsor [ˈsponsə] 1. *n* pokrovitelj 2. (pol.) predlagač 3. *v* finansirati; financirati 4. predložiti

spontaneous [spɔnˈteiniəs] *adj* spontan

spool [spuːl] *n* kalem

spoon [spuːn] *n* kašika

spoonful [ˈspuːnfl] *n* puna kašika

sport, sports [spɔːt; -s] 1. *adj* sportski 2. *n* sport

sportsman [ˈspɔːtsmən] *n* sportista

sportswear [ˈspɔːtsweə] *n* sportska odeća/odjeća

sportswoman [ˈspɔːtswumən] *n* sportistkinja

spot [spɔt] 1. fleka 2. mesto; mjesto 3. bubuljica 4. **on the spot** na udaru 5. *v* (**spotted**) ugledati

spot check *n* štihproba
spotless [ˈspɔtlis] *adj* neumrljan
spotlight [ˈspɔtlait] *n* **1.** reflektor **2.** prominentnost
spouse [spaus] *n* suprug, supruga
spout [spaut] *n* pisak
sprain [sprein] *v* iščašiti
sprang [spræŋ] *see* **spring**
sprawl [sprɔ:l] *v* pružiti se
spray [sprei] **1.** *n* sprej **2.** *v* zaprašiti
spray-gun *n* pištolj
spraying [ˈsprejiŋ] *n* prskanje
spread [spred] **1.** *n* širenje **2.** reportaža **3.** *v* (**spread**) širiti se **4.** raširiti
spread the table *v* postaviti sto/stol
sprightly [ˈspraitli] *adj* čio
spring [spriŋ] **1.** *n* izvor **2.** proleće; proljeće **3.** **metal spring** opruga **4.** *v* (**sprang, sprung**) skočiti
sprinkle [ˈspriŋkl] *v* poprskati
sprinkler [ˈspriŋklə] *n* prskalica
sprint [sprint] *v* sprintovati
sprinter [ˈsprintə] *n* sprinter
sprout [spraut] **1.** *n* mladica **2.** *v* izniknuti
sprung [sprʌŋ] *see* **spring**
spur [spə:] *n* mamuza
spurn [spə:n] *v* s preziranjem odbiti
spurt [spə:t] *v* napregnuti se
spy [spai] **1.** *n* špijun **2.** **industrial spy** industrijski špijun **3.** *v* špijunirati
spying [ˈspa:jiŋ] *n* špijuniranje
spy plane *n* špijunski avion
spy satellite *n* špijunski satelit
squad [skwɔd] *n* **1.** grupa **2.** (mil.) odeljenje; odjeljenje
squad car *n* policijski automobil
squadron [ˈskwɔdrən] *n* **1.** eskadrila **2.** divizion

squalid [ˈskwɔlid] *adj* prljav
squalor [ˈskwɔlə] *n* prljavština
squander [ˈskwɔndə] *v* rasuti
square [skweə] **1.** *adj* kvadratni **2.** *n* kvadrat **3.** **town square** trg
square metre, square meter *n* kvadratni metar
square kilometre, square kilometer *n* kvadratni kilometar
squash [skwɔʃ] **1.** bundeva **2.** kaša **3.** (spor.) skvoš **4.** *v* zgnječiti
squat [skwɔt] *v* čučati
squatter [skwɔtə] *n* bespravni naseljenik
squeak [skwi:k] *v* škripeti
squeeze [skwi:z] *v* stisnuti
squeeze through *v* probiti se
squid [skwid] *v* kratak dopis
squint [skwint] *v* škiljiti
squirrel [ˈskwirəl] *n* veverica; vjeverica
squirt [skə:t] *v* briznuti
SS (= **steamship**) *n* parobrod
St. *see* **saint, street**
stab [stæb] *v* (**stabbed**) ubosti
stability [stəˈbiləti] *n* stabilnost
stabilization [ˌsteibəlaiˈzeiʃn] *n* stabilizacija
stabilize [ˈsteibəlaiz] *v* stabilizovati
stable [ˈsteibl] **1.** *adj* stabilan **2.** ustaljen **3.** *n* štala
stable economy *n* stabilna privreda
stack [stæk] **1.** *n* stog **2.** *v* složiti
stadium [ˈsteidiəm] *n* stadion
staff [sta:f] *n* **1.** palica **2.** štab **3.** **hospital staff** osoblje bolnice
staff officer *n* štabni oficir
stage [steidʒ] **1.** *adj* pozornišni; kazališni **2.** *n* pozornica **3.** etapa **4.** *v* **to stage an invasion** izvršiti desant

stage-manage [ˈsteidʒˌmænidʒ] v režirati

stagger [ˈstægə] v teturati se

stagnant [ˈstægnənt] adj stagnatan

stagnate [stægˈneit] v stagnirati

stain [stein] 1. n mrlja 2. v umrljati

stainless [ˈsteinlis] adj bez mrlje

stainless steel n nerđajući čelik

stair [steə] n stepenik

staircase [ˈsteəkeis] n stepenište

stairs [steəz] pl stepenice

stairway [ˈsteəwei] see **stairs**

stake [steik] n 1. kolac 2. at stake na kocki

stale [steil] adj bajat

stalemate [ˈsteilmeit] n pat

stalk [stɔːk] 1. n stabljika 2. v kebati

stall [stɔːl] 1. n tezga 2. v ugušiti 3. odugovlačiti

stallion [ˈstæliən] n ždrebac; ždrijebac

stamina [ˈstæminə] n izdržljivost

stammer [ˈstæmə] 1. n mucanje 2. v (pro)mucati

stamp [stæmp] 1. n žig 2. **postage stamp** poštanska marka 3. v zapečatiti 4. udariti

stampede [stæmˈpiːd] n divlje bekstvo/bjekstvo

stamp out v suzbiti

stance [stæns] n stav

stand [stænd] 1. n otpor 2. stalak 3. v (**stood**) stajati 4. izdržati

standard [ˈstændəd] 1. adj standardan 2. normalan 3. n standard

standardization [ˌstændədaiˈzeiʃn] n standardizacija

standardize [ˈstændədaiz] v standardizovati

stand-by [ˈstændbai] n pripravnost

stand by v 1. pomoći 2. ispuniti 3. biti u stanju pripravnosti

stand down v povući se

stand for v simbolizovati

stand for election v kandidovati se; kandidirati se

stand out v odudarati

standpoint [ˈstændpɔint] n gledište

standstill [ˈstændstil] n zastoj

stand up v ustati

stand up for v založiti se za

stank [stæŋk] see **stink**

staple [ˈsteipl] 1. adj glavni 2. n glavni proizvod 3. spajalica 4. v spojiti spajalicama

stapler [ˈsteiplə] n heftalica

star [staː] n zvezda; zvijezda

starch [ˈstaːtʃ] n skrob

stare [steə] v piljiti (at u)

stars and stripes pl američka zastava

start [staːt] 1. n početak 2. v početi

start a fire v podložiti vatru

starter [ˈstaːtə] n starter

starting point n polazna tačka/ točka

startle [ˈstaːtl] v trgnuti

start up a business v osnovati radnju

starvation [staːˈveiʃn] n gladovanje

starve [staːv] v umirati od gladi

state [steit] 1. adj državni 2. svečan 3. n država 4. stanje 5. **federal state** savezna država 6. v izjaviti

State Department (US) n (pol.) ministarstvo inostranih poslova; ministarstvo vanjskih poslova

statehood [ˈsteithud] n položaj države

state house n gidan gwamnati

stately [ˈsteitli] adj svečan

statement [ˈsteitmənt] *n* **1.** izjava **2.**
bank statement izvod iz banke **3.**
to make a statement dati izjavu

state of emergency *n* vanredno
stanje

state of war *n* ratno stanje

States [steits] *pl* **the States**
Sjedinjene Američke Države

stateside [ˈsteitsaid] *adj/adv*
u SAD

statesman [ˈsteitsmən] *n* državnik

state visit *n* državna poseta;
državni posjet

static [ˈstætik] *adj* nepokretan

station [ˈsteiʃn] **1.** *n* stanica **2.**
položaj **3.** *v* stacionirati

stationary [ˈsteiʃənri] *adj*
nepokretan

stationer's [ˈsteiʃnəz] *n* papirnica

stationery [ˈsteiʃənri] *n* pisaći
pribor

station wagon *n* karavan (vrsta
automobila)

statistical [stəˈtistikl] *adj* statistički

statistician [ˌstætisˈtiʃn] *n*
statističar

statistics [stəˈtistiks] *pl* statistika

statue [ˈstætʃuː] *n* statua

stature [ˈstætʃə] *n* stas

status [ˈsteitəs] *n* **1.** ugled **2.** (leg.)
pravni položaj

statute [ˈstætʃuːt] *n* zakon

statutory [ˈstætʃuːtəri] *adj* propisan
zakonom

stay [stei] **1.** *n* zaustavljanje **2.** *v*
zaustaviti **3.** ostati

stead [sted] *n* **in his stead** na
njegovom mestu/mjestu

steadfast [ˈstedfəst] *adj* čvrst

steadiness [ˈstedinis] *n* čvrstoća

steady [ˈstedi] **1.** *adj* čvrst **2.** stalan
3. *adv* čvrsto

steak [steik] *n* biftek

steal [stiːl] *v* **(stole, stolen)** ukrasti
(from od)

stealing [ˈstiːliŋ] *n* krađa

stealth [stelθ] *n* potaja

stealthy [ˈstelθi] *adj* potajan

steam [stiːm] *n* para

steam engine *n* parna mašina

steamer, steamship [ˈstiːmə;
ˈstiːmʃip] *n* parobrod

steel [stiːl] *n* čelik

steel mill *n* čeličana

steep [stiːp] *adj* strm

steeple [ˈstiːpl] *n* toranj

steer [stiə] *v* upravljati

steering [ˈstiəriŋ] *n* upravljački
sistem

steering committee *n* upravni
odbor

steering wheel *n* volan

stem [stem] **1.** *n* stabljika **2.** *v*
zaustaviti **3.** poticati **(from** iz)

stench [stentʃ] *n* smrad

stencil [ˈstensl] *n* matrica

step [step] **1.** *n* korak **2.** stepenik **3.**
a step forward korak napred/
naprijed **4. step by step** korak po
korak **5.** *v* **(stepped)** stupiti

step forward *v* stupiti napred/
naprijed

stepchild [ˈsteptʃaild] *n* postorče

step up *v* (ec.) povećati

stereo [ˈsteriəu] **1.** *adj* stereofonski
2. *n* stereo-uređaj

stereotype [ˈsteriəutaip] *n* stereotip

sterile [ˈsterail] *adj* **1.** neplodan
2. sterilan

sterility [steˈriliti] *n* **1.** neplodnost
2. sterilitet

sterilization [ˌsterəlaiˈzeiʃn] *n*
sterilizacija

sterilize [ˈsterəlaiz] *v* **1.** učiniti

neplodnim **2.** sterilizovati

sterling [ˈstəːliŋ] *adj* (fin.) sterlinški

stern [stəːn] **1.** *adj* strog **2.** *n* krmeni

steroid [ˈsterɔid] *n* steroid

stethoscope [ˈsteθəskəup] *n* stetoskop

stew [stjuː] *n* paprikaš

steward [ˈstjuəd] *n* stjuard

stewardess [ˌstjuəˈdes] *n* stjuardesa

stick [stik] **1.** *n* štap **2.** *v* (**stuck**) zabosti (**into** u) **3.** metnuti **4.** lepiti; lijepiti

stick to *v* to stick to a diet držati dijetu

sticker [ˈstikə] *n* nalepnica; naljepnica

sticking-plaster [ˈstikiŋˌplaːstə] *n* flaster

stick out *v* strčati

sticky [ˈstiki] *adj* lepljiv; ljepljiv

stiff [stif] *adj* krut

stiffen [ˈstifn] *v* ukrutiti (se)

still [stil] **1.** *adj* tih **2.** *adv* tiho **3.** još **4.** *conj* međutim

stillbirth [ˈstimjulənt] *n* mrtvorođenje

stillborn [ˈstimjulənt] *n* mrtvorođen

stimulant [ˈstimjulənt] *n* stimulans

stimulate [ˌstimjuˈleit] *v* stimulisati

stimulating [ˈstimjuleitiŋ] *adj* stimulativan

stimulation [ˌstimjuˈleiʃn] *n* stimulacija

sting [stiŋ] *v* (**stung**) ubosti

stingy [ˈstindʒi] *adj* škrt

stink [stiŋk;] **1.** *n* smrad **2.** *v* (**stank, stunk**) smrdeti; smrdjeti

stipulate [ˈstipjuleit] *v* stipulirati

stipulation [ˌstipjuˈleiʃn] *n* stipulacija

stir [stəː] *v* (**stirred**) **1.** promešati; promiješati **2.** micati se

stirrup [ˈstirəp] *n* stremen

stir up *v* **1.** pobuniti **2.** zapodenuti; zapodjenuti

stitch [stitʃ] **1.** *n* petlja **2.** (med.) šav **3.** *v* (pro)šiti

stoat [stəut] *n* hermelin

stock [stɔk] **1.** *n* zalihya **2.** (fin.) akcije **3. livestock** stoka **4.** *v* snabdeti; snabdjeti

stockbroker [ˈstɔkˌbrəukə] *n* posrednik na berzi/burzi

stock exchange *n* bera; burza

stockholder [ˈstɔkhəuldə] *n* akcionar

stockings [ˈstɔkiŋ] *pl* čarape

stock market *n* bera; burza

stockpile [ˈstɔkˌpail] **1.** *n* zaliha **2.** *v* nagomilati

stock-take [ˈstɔkˌteik] *v* inventarisati robu

stocky [ˈstɔki] *adj* zdepast

stoke a fire *v* podstaći vatru

stole, stolen [ˈstəul; ˈstəulən] *see* **steal**

stomach [ˈstʌmək] *n* želudac

stomach ache *n* bol u stomaku

stone [stəun] **1.** *n* kamen **2.** *v* kamenovati

stoned [stəund] *adj* (sl.) opijen

stonemason [ˈstəunˌmeisn] *n* kamenar

stony [ˈstəuni] *adj* kamen

stood [stud] *see* **stand**

stool [stuːl] *n* hoklica

stop [stɔp] **1.** *n* zadržanje **2. bus-stop** autobuska stanica **3. to bring to a stop** zaustaviti **4.** *v* (**stopped**) zaustaviti se **5.** obustaviti **6. The rain has stopped.** Prestala je kiša.

stop dead *v* stati kao ukopan

stop gap *n* privremeno sredstvo

stop-over [ˈstɔp‚əuvə] *n* zadržanje

stoppage [ˈstɔpidʒ] *n* obustava

stopper [ˈstɔpə] *n* zapušač

stop short of *v* odsutati od

stop up *v* zapušiti

stopwatch [ˈstɔpwɔtʃ] *n* štoperica

storage [ˈstɔːridʒ] *n* skladište

store [stɔː] 1. *n* zaliha 2. radnja 3. *v* uskladištiti

storekeeper [ˈstɔːˌkiːpə] *n* vlasnik radnje

storeroom [ˈstɔːrum] *n* skladišni prostor

storey [ˈstɔːri] *n* (*pl* storeys) sprat; kat

stork [stɔːk] *n* roda

storm [stɔːm] 1. *n* oluja 2. *v* (mil.) jurišati

stormy [ˈstɔːmi] *adj* buran

story [ˈstɔːri] *n* 1. istorija 2. **to tell a story** ispričati priču 3. *see* storey

stout [staut] *adj* debeo

stove [stəuv] *n* peć

stowaway [ˈstəuəwei] *n* slepi putnik; slijepi putnik

straight [streit] 1. *adj* prav 2. *adv* pravo

straightaway [ˈstreitəˈwei] *adv* odmah

straighten [ˈstreitnd] *v* ispraviti

straighten out *v* odmrsiti

straightforward [ˌstreitˈfɔːwəd] *adj* iskren

strain [strein] 1. *n* pritisak 2. *v* istegnuti 3. zategnuti 4. procediti; procijediti

strained [streind] *adj* 1. usiljen 2. proceden; procijeden 3. napet

straits [streits] *n* moreuz

strand [strænd] *n* struka

strange [streindʒ] *adj* 1. stran 2. čudan

stranger [ˈstreindʒə] *n* stranac

strangle [ˈstræŋgl] *v* ugušiti

strap [stræp] *n* kaiš

strategic [strəˈtiːdʒik] *adj* strategijski

strategy [ˈstrætədʒi] *n* strateg

straw [strɔː] *n* 1. slama 2. slamka

strawberry [ˈstrɔːbri] *n* jagoda

stray [strei] *v* zalutati

streak [striːk] *n* pruga

stream [striːm] 1. *n* potok 2. *v* teći

streamlined [ˈstriːmlaind] *adj* aerodinamički

street [striːt] *n* ulica

streetcar [ˈstriːtkaː] *n* tramvaj

streetlamp, streetlight *n* ulična svetiljka/svjetiljka

streetsign *n* putokaz

strength [streŋθ] *n* 1. snaga 2. moć

strengthen [ˈstreŋθən] *v* ojačati

strenuous [ˈstrenjuəs] *adj* naporan

stress [stres] 1. *n* nagłasak 2. stres 3. *v* naglasiti

stretch [stretʃ] *v* 1. rastegnuti (se) 2. pružiti se

stretcher [ˈstretʃə] *n* nosila

stretch out *v* ispružiti

stricken [ˈstrikn] *adj* pogođen

strict [strikt] *adj* strog

stride [straid] 1. *n* dug korak 2. *v* koračati

strike [straik] 1. *n* štrajk 2. (mil.) udar 3. *v* (**struck**) udariti 4. stupiti u štrajk

strike a match *v* kresnuti šibicu

strike force *n* udarna grupa

striker [ˈstraikə] *n* štrajkaš

striking [ˈstraikiŋ] *adj* upadljiv

string [striŋ] *n* vrpca

stringent [ˈstrindʒənt] *adj* strog

strip [strip] 1. *n* pruga 2. parče 3. *v* svući se

stripe [straip] *n* pruga
striped [straipt] *adj* prugast
strive [straiv] *v* težiti
stroke [strəuk] 1. *n* udar 2. (med.) kap 3. *v* gladiti
stroll [strəul] 1. *n* šetnja 2. *v* šetati se
strong [strɔŋ] *adj* 1. jak 2. oštar
strongbox ['strɔŋbɔks] *n* kasa
stronghold ['strɔŋhəuld] *n* uporište
struck [strʌk] *see* **strike**
structural ['strʌktʃərəl] *adj* strukturalan
structure ['strʌktʃə] *n* struktura
struggle ['strʌgl] 1. *n* borba 2. *v* boriti se
strut [strʌt] 1. *n* podupirač 2. *v* šepuriti se
stub [stʌb] *n* panj
stubborn ['stʌbən] *adj* tvrdoglav
stubbornness ['stʌbənnis] *n* tvrdoglavost
stuck [stʌk] *see* **stick**
stud [stʌd] *n* klinac
student ['stjuːdnt] *n* student
stud farm *n* ergela
studio ['stuːdiəu] *n* studio
study ['stʌdi] 1. *n* studija 2. učenje 3. *v* učiti 4. studirati
studying ['stʌdjiŋ] *n* studiranje
stuff [stʌf] 1. *n* materijal 2. *v* natrpati
stuffed [stʌft] *adj* punjen
stumble ['stʌmbl] *v* spotaći se
stumbling block *n* kamen spoticanja
stump [stʌmp] *n* 1. panj 2. patrljak
stun [stʌn] *v* ošamutiti
stung [stʌŋ] *see* **sting**
stunk [stʌŋk] *see* **stink**
stunt [stʌnt] *n* 1. akrobacija 2. štos
stunted ['stʌntid] *adj* zakržljao
stuntman ['stʌntmæn] *n* kaskader

stupid ['stjuːpid] *adj* glup
stupidity [stjuːpidəti] *n* glupost
sturdy ['stəːdi] *adj* snažan
stutter ['stʌtə] 1. *n* mucanje 2. *v* mucati
sty [stai] *n* obor
style [stail] 1. *n* stil 2. *v* nazvati
stylish ['stailiʃ] *adj* pomodan
sub-committee ['sʌbkəˌmiti] *n* pododbor
subsonscious [ˌsʌbˈkɔnʃəs] 1. *adj* podsvestan; podsvjestan 2. *n* podsvest; podsvijest
subcontractor [ˌsʌbkənˈtræktə] *n* podugovarač
subdivide [ˌsʌbdiˈvaid] *v* dalje podeliti/podijeliti
subdivision [ˈsʌbdiˌviʒn] *n* podrazdeo; podrazdio
subdue [səbˈdjuː] *v* savladati
subject ['sʌbdʒikt] *n* 1. predmet 2. subjekt 3. sadržaj
subject [sʌbˈdʒikt] *v* podvrći
subject to *adj* podložan
subjugate ['sʌbdʒəgeit] *v* potčiniti
submachine gun ['sʌbməˈʃiːngʌn] *n* automat
submarine [ˌsʌbməˈriːn] 1. *adj* pomorski 2. *n* podmornica
submerge [səbˈməːdʒ] *v* zagnjuriti (se)
submission [səbˈmiʃn] *n* 1. potčinjenje 2. potčinjenost
submissive [səbˈmisiv] *adj* pokoran
submit [səbˈmit] *v* 1. podneti; podnijeti 2. potčiniti (se)
submit a proposal *v* podneti predlog; podnijeti predlog
subordinate [səˈbɔːdinət] *adj* podređen
subscribe [səbˈskraib] *v* pretplatiti se

subscriber [səbˈskraibə] *n* pretplatnik

subscription [səbˈskripʃn] *n* pretplata

subsequent [ˈsʌbsikwənt] *adj* sledeći; slijedići

subsequently [ˈsʌbsikwəntli] *adv* zatim

subsequent to *prep* posle; poslije

subservient [ˈsʌbsəˈvjənt] *adj* pokoran

subside [səbˈsaid] *v* 1. opasti 2. sleći se

subsidiary [səbˈsidiəri] *adj* supsidaran

subsidiary company *n* podružnica

subsidize [ˈsʌbsidaiz] *n* subvencionisati

subsidy [ˈsʌbsidi] *n* subvencija

subsistence [səbˈsistəns] *n* život

substance [ˈsʌbstəns] *n* 1. supstancija 2. čvrstina

substandard [ˈsʌb,stændəd] *adj* podstandardan

substantial [səbˈstænʃl] *adj* 1. supstancijalan 2. znatan

substitute [ˈsʌbstitjuːt] 1. *n* zamena; zamjena 2. (spor.) rezervni igrač 3. *v* zameniti; zamijeniti

substitution [ˌsʌbstiˈtjuːʃn] *n* 1. zamena; zamjena 2. (spor.) izmena igrač; izmjena igrač

substructure [ˈsʌb,strəktʃə] *n* podgradnja

subterfuge [ˈsʌbtəfjuːdʒ] *n* vrdanje

subterranean [ˌsʌbtəˈreiniən] *adj* podzemni

subtitle [ˈsʌbtaitl] 1. *n* titl 2. *v* titlovati

subtle [ˈsʌtl] *adj* suptilan

subtlety [ˈsʌtlti] *n* suptilnost

subtotal [ˈsʌbtəutl] *n* suma stavke

subtract [səbˈtrækt] *v* oduzeti

subtraction [səbˈtrækʃn] *n* oduzimanje

suburbs [ˈsʌbəːbs] *pl* predgrađe

suburban [səˈbəːbən] *adj* prigradski

subversion [səbˈvəːʒn] *n* subverzija

subversive [səbˈvəːsiv] *adj* podrivač

subversive activity *n* podrivačka delatnost/djelatnost

subvert [sʌbˈvəːt] *v* podriti

subway [ˈsʌbwei] *n* 1. (UK) podvožnjak 2. (US) metro

succeed [səkˈsiːd] *v* 1. uspeti; uspjeti 2. naslediti; naslijediti

success [səkˈses] *n* uspeh; uspjeh

successful [səkˈsesfl] *adj* uspeo; uspio

succession [səkˈseʃn] *n* 1. nasleđe; nasljeđe 2. **in succession** uzastopce

successive [səkˈsesiv] *adj* uzastopni

successor [səkˈsesə] *n* naslednik; nasljednik

succumb [səˈkʌm] *v* podleći

such [sʌtʃ] 1. *pro/adj* takav 2. *adv* tako

such and such *adj* taj i taj

such as takav kao

suck [sʌk] *v* sisati

suckle [ˈsʌkl] *v* dojiti

suction [ˈsʌkʃn] *n* sisanje

sudden [ˈsʌdn] *adj* nagao

suddenly [ˈsʌdnli] *adv* iznenada

sue [suː] *v* tužiti

suffer [ˈsʌfə] *v* trpeti; trpjeti

suffer losses *v* pretrpeti gubitke; pretrpjeti gubitke

sufferer [ˈsʌfərə] *n* stradalac

suffering [ˈsʌfəriŋ] *n* patnja

suffice [səˈfais] *v* biti dosta

sufficiency [səˈfiʃntli] *n* dovoljnost

sufficient [sə'fiʃnt] *adj* dovoljan
suffix ['sʌfiks] *v* sufiks
suffocate ['sʌfəkeit] *v* ugušiti (se)
suffrage ['sʌfridʒ] *n* pravo glasa
sugar ['ʃugə] *n* šećer
sugar beet *n* šećerna repa
sugar cube *n* kocka šećera
suggest [se'dʒest] *v* sugerisati
suggestion [sə'dʒestʃən] *n* sugestija
suicide ['su:isaid] *n* 1. samoubistvo; samoubojstvo 2. **to commit suicide** izvršiti samoubistvo/samoubojstvo
suit [su:t] 1. *n* odelo; odijelo 2. (leg.) parnica 3. *v* odgovarati 4. svideti se; svidjeti se
suitable ['su:təbl] *adj* podesan
suitcase ['su:tkeis] *n* kofer
suite [swi:t] *n* apartman
sulk [sʌlk] *v* pućiti se
sullen ['sʌlən] *adj* zlovoljan
sum [sʌm] *n* suma
summarize ['sʌməraiz] *v* rezimirati
summary ['sʌməri] *n* rezime
summary trial *n* suđenje po skraćenom postupku
summer ['sʌmə] *n* leto; ljeto
summit ['sʌmit] *n* vrh
summit conference *n* samit
summon ['sʌmən] *v* pozvati
summons ['sʌmənz] *n* sudski poziv
sums [sʌmz] *pl* računanje
sum up *v* rezimirati
sun [sʌn] *n* Sunce
sunbathe ['sʌnbeið] *v* sunčati se
sunbeam ['sʌnbi:m] *n* zraka sunca
sunburn ['sʌnbə:n] *n* opekotina od sunca
sunburnt ['sʌnbə:nt] *adj* **to be sunburnt** izgoreti od sunca, izgorjeti od sunca
Sunday ['sʌndi] *n* nedelja; nedjelja

sundown ['sʌndaun] *n* sunčev zalazak
sung [sʌŋ] *see* **sing**
sunglasses ['sʌn,gla:siz] *pl* naočare za sunce
sunk ['sʌŋk] *see* **sink**
sunken ['sʌŋkən] *adj* upao
sunlight ['sʌnlait] *n* sunčana svetlost/svjetlost
sunny ['sʌni] *adj* sunčan
sunrise ['sʌnraiz] *n* izlazak sunca
sunset ['sʌnset] *n* zalazak sunca
sunshade ['sʌnʃeid] *n* suncobran
sunshine ['sʌnʃain] *n* sijanje sunca
sunstroke ['sʌnstəuk] *n* sunčani udar
suntan ['sʌntæn] *n* preplanulost
suntan lotion *n* losion za sunčanje
super ['su:pə] *adj* 1. super- 2. izvanredan
superb [su:'pə:b] *adj* izvanredan
supercilious [su:'pəsiljəs] *adj* ohol
superficial [,su:pə'fiʃl] *adj* površan
superficiality [,su:pə,fiʃi'aliti] *n* površnost
superficially [,su:pə'fiʃəli] *adv* površno
superfluous [su:'pə:fluəs] *adj* suvišan
superhighway ['su:pə'haiwei] *n* (US) autostrada
superhuman [,su:pə'hju:mən] *adj* natčovečanski; natčovječanski
superior [su:'piəriə] 1. *adj* bolji 2. pretpostavljen 3. *n* pretpostavljeni
superiority [su:,piəri'ɔrəti] *n* nadmoćnost
supermarket ['su:pəma:kit] *n* supermarket
supernatural ['su:pənætʃrəl] *adj* natprirodan

superpower [ˈsuːpəpauə] *n* supersila

supersede [suːpəˈsiːd] *v* zameniti; zamijeniti

superstar [ˌsuːpəˈstaː] *n* superstar

superstition [ˌsuːpəˈstiʃn] *n* sujeverje; sujevjerje

superstitious [ˌsuːpəˈstiʃəs] *adj* sujeveran; sujevjeran

supervise [ˈsuːpəvaiz] *v* nadzirati

supervision [ˌsuːpəˈviʒn] *n* nadzor

supervisor [ˌsuːpəˈviʒə] *n* nadzornik

supper [ˈsʌpə] *n* 1. večera 2. **to eat supper** večerati

supplant [səˈplaːnt] *v* istisnuti

supple [ˈsʌpl] *adj* gibak

supplement [ˈsʌplimənt] 1. *n* dopuna 2. *v* dopuniti

supplementary [ˌsʌpliˈmentri] *adj* dopunski

supplier [səˈplaiə] *n* snabdevač; snabdjevač

supplies [səˈplaiz] *pl* pribor

supply [səˈplai] 1. *n* snabdevanje; snabdijevanje 2. zaliha 3. *v* snabdeti; snabdjeti 4. *see* **supplies**

supply and demand *n* ponuda i potražnja

supply base *n* snabdevački baza; snabdjevački baza

supply depot *n* snabdevačko skladište; snabdjevačko skladište

supply lines *n* putevi dotura

supply ship *n* snabdevački brod

support [səˈpɔːt] 1. *n* podrška 2. (leg.) izdržavanje 3. *v* podržati 4. (leg.) izdržavati

supportable [sʌˈpɔːtəbl] *adj* podošljiv

supporter [səˈpɔːtə] *n* 1. pristalica; pritaša 2. podupirač

supporting [səˈpɔːtiŋ] *adj* 1. koji podržava 2. **a supporting role** epizodna uloga

suppose [səˈpəuz] *v* 1. pretpostaviti 2. trebati

supposition [ˌsʌpəˈziʃn] *n* pretpostavka

suppository [ˌsʌpəˈzitɔri] *n* supozitorijum

suppress [səˈpres] *v* 1. ugušiti 2. zataškati

suppression [səˈpreʃn] *n* 1. ugušenje 2. zataškavanje

suppressor [səˈpresə] *n* ugušivač

supremacy [suːˈpreməsi] *n* 1. prevlast 2. najviša vlast

supreme [suːˈpriːm] *adj* vrhovni

supreme commander *n* vrhovni komandant

Supreme Court *n* vrhovni sud

sure [ʃɔː] 1. *adj* siguran 2. *adv* sigurno 3. **for sure** sigurno 4. **to make sure** proveriti; provjeriti

surely [ˈʃɔːli] *adv* sigurno

surety [ˈʃɔːrəti] *n* jemstvo; jamstvo

surface [ˈsəːfis] *n* površina

surface mail *n* kopnena pošta

surface-to-air missile *n* raketa zemlja-vazduh

surface-to-surface missile *n* 1. raketa zemlja-zemlja 2. raketa brod-brod

surge [səːdʒ] *v* uzburkati se

surgeon [ˈsəːdʒən] *n* hirurg; kirurg

surgery [ˈsəːdʒəri] *n* 1. hirurgija; kirurgija 2. lekareva ordinacija

surgical [ˈsəːdʒikl] *adj* hirurški; kirurški

surmise [ˈsəːmaiz] *v* pretpostavka

surname [ˈsəːneim] *n* prezime

surpass [səˈpaːs] *v* nadmašiti

surplus [ˈsəːpləs] *n* višak
surprise [səˈpraiz] 1. *adj* iznenadan 2. *n* iznenađenje 3. *v* iznenaditi
surprising [səˈpraiziŋ] *adj* iznenadan
surrender [səˈrendə] 1. *n* predaja 2. **unconditional surrender** bezuslovna predaja 3. *v* predati (se)
surrogate [ˈsʌrəgeit] 1. *adj* zamenički; zamjenički 2. *n* surogat
surround [səˈraund] *v* opkoliti
surroundings [səˈraundiŋz] *pl* okolina
surveillance [səˈveiləns] *n* 1. prismotra 2. **under surveillance** pod prismotru
survey [səˈvei] 1. *n* pregled 2. premer; premjer 3. *v* pregledati 4. premeriti; premjeriti
surveyor [səˈveiə] *n* zemljomer; zemljomjer
survival [səˈvaivl] *n* opstanak
survive [səˈvaiv] *v* preživeti; preživjeti
survivor [səˈvaivə] *n* 1. preživeli; preživjeli 2. **sole survivor** jedini preživeli; jedini preživjeli
susceptible [səˈseptəbl] *adj* osetljiv; osjetljiv
suspect [ˈsʌspekt] *n* osumnjičena osoba
suspect [səˈspekt] *v* sumnjičiti
suspend [səˈspend] *v* 1. obesiti; objesiti 2. (ed.) udaljiti iz škole 3. (leg.) oduzeti 4. **to suspend from duty** udaljiti sa službe
suspended sentence [səˈspendid] *n* (leg.) uslovna osuda; uvjetna osuda

suspense [səˈspens] *n* 1. neizvesnost; neizvjesnost 2. **to keep in suspense** držati u neizvesnosti
suspension [səˈspenʃn] *n* 1. udaljenje 2. (ed.) suspenzija 3. (leg.) oduzimanje 4. **car suspension** amortizeri
suspicion [səˈspiʃn] *n* sumnja
suspicious [səˈspiʃəs] *adj* 1. sumnjiv 2. sumnjičav
sustain [səˈstein] *v* podržati
sustenance [ˈsʌstinəns] *n* izdržavanje
suture [ˈsjuːtʃə] *n* (med.) šav
swab [swɔb] *n* (med.) tampon
swallow [ˈswɔləu] 1. *n* lasta 2. *v* progutati
swam [swæm] *see* swim
swamp [swɔmp] *n* močvara
swan [swɔn] *n* labud
swap [swɔp] *v* (**swapped**) trampiti
swarm [swɔːm] *n* roj
sway [swei] *v* uticati se
swear [sweə] *v* 1. kleti se 2. opsovati
swear in/into *v* zakleti
swearword [ˈsweəwəːd] *n* psovka
sweat [swet] 1. *n* znoj 2. *v* znojiti se
sweater [ˈswetə] *n* džemper
Swede [swiːd] *n* šveđanin
Sweden [ˈswiːdən] *n* Švedska
Swedish [ˈswiːdiʃ] *adj* švedski
sweep [swiːp] *v* (**swept**) pomesti
sweeper [ˈswiːpə] *n* čistač
sweeping [ˈswiːpiŋ] *adj* dalekosežan
sweet [swiːt] 1. *adj* sladak 2. *n* slatkiš
sweeten [ˈswiːtn] *v* zasladiti
sweetheart [ˈswiːthaːt] *n* dragan; dragana

sweetness [ˈswiːtnis] *n* slatkoća
sweet potato [ˌswiːtpəˈteitəu] *n* batata
sweets [swiːtz] *pl* bombone
swell [swəl] *v* (**swelled, swollen/ swelled**) oteći
swelling [ˈsweliŋ] *n* oteklina
swept [swept] *see* **sweep**
swerve [swəːv] *v* skrenuti
swift [swift] *adj* brz
swim [swim] 1. *n* plivanje 2. *v* (**swam, swum**) (pre)plivati
swimmer [ˈswimə] *n* plivač
swimming [ˈswimiŋ] *n* plivanje
swimming pool [ˈswimiŋpuːl] *n* plivački bazen
swimsuit [ˈswimsuːt] *n* kupaći kostim
swindle [ˈswindl] *v* prevariti
swindler [ˈswindlə] *n* varalica
swindling [ˈswindliŋ] *n* prevara
swine [swain] *pl* svinje
swing [swiŋ] 1. *n* ljuljaška 2. *v* njihati (se)
Swiss [swis] 1. *adj* švajcarski; švicarski 2. *n* Švajcarac; Švicarac
switch [switʃ] 1. *n* prekidač 2. *v* preći
switchboard [ˈswitʃbɔːd] *n* telefonska centrala
switchboard operator *n* telefonista, telefonistkinja
switch off *v* ugasiti
switch on *v* upaliti
switch over *v* obrnuti
Switzerland [ˈswitsələnd] *n* Švajcarska; Švicarska
swollen [ˈswəulən] *adj* 1. otekao 2. *see* **swell**
swoop [swuːp] *v* nasrnuti
sword [sɔːd] *n* mač

swum [swʌm] *see* **swim**
sycophancy [ˈsikəfansi] *n* ulizivanje
sycophant [ˈsikəfant] *n* ulizica
syllable [ˈsiləbl] *n* slog
syllabus [ˈsiləbəs] *n* program
symbol [ˈsimbl] *n* simbol
symbolic [simˈbɔlik] *adj* simboličan
symbolize [ˈsimbɔlaiz] *v* simbolizovati
symmetrical [siˈmetrikl] *adj* simetričan
symmetry [ˈsimətri] *n* simetrija
sympathetic [ˌsimpəˈθetik] *adj* saosećajan; suosjećajan
sympathize [ˈsimpəθaiz] *v* saosećati; suosjećati
sympathizer [ˈsimpə,θaizə] *n* simpatizer
sympathy [ˈsimpəθi] *n* saosećaj; suosjećaj
symphony [ˈsimfəni] *n* simfonija
symphony orchestra *n* simfonijski orkestar
symposium [ˈsimpəuziəm] *n* simpozijum
symptom [ˈsimptəm] *n* simptom
synagogue [ˈsinəgɔg] *n* sinagoga
synchronization [siŋkrənaiˈzeiʃn] *n* sinhronizacija; sinkronizacija
synchronize [ˈsiŋkrənaiz] *v* sinhronizovati; sinkronizirati
syndicate [ˈsindikət] 1. *n* sindikat 2. *v* organizovati
syndrome [ˈsindrəum] *n* sindrom
synonym [ˈsinɔnim] *n* sinonim
synonymous [siˈnɔniməs] *adj* sinoniman
synonymous with *adj* sličan po značenju s
synopsis [siˈnɔpsis] *n* rezime

syntax [ˈsintæks] *n* sintaksa
synthesis [ˈsinθəsis] *n* sinteza
synthesize [ˈsinθəsaiz] *v* sintetizovati
synthesizer [ˈsinθəsaizə] *n* sintesajzer
synthetic [sinˈθetik] *adj* sintetski
syphilis [ˈsifilis] *n* sifilis

syringe [siˈrindʒ] *n* špric
syrup [ˈsirəp] *n* sirup
system [ˈsistəm] *n* sistem
systematic [ˌsistəˈmætik] *adj* sistemski
system engineer *n* sistem-inženjer
system software *n* sistemski softver

T

ta! [taː] (UK) hvala!

table [ˈteibl] 1. *n* sto; stol 2. *v* to **table a motion** odložiti diskusiju o predlogu

tablecloth [ˈteiblklɔθ] *n* stolnjak

tablespoon [ˈteiblspuːn] *n* stona kašika; stolna zlica

tablet [ˈtæblit] *n* tableta

table tennis [ˈteibl,tenis] *n* stoni tenis; stolni tenis

tabloid [ˈtæblɔːid] *n* tabloid

taboo [təˈbuː] *adj/n* tabu

tacit [ˈtæsit] *adj* prećutan

tack [tæk] *n* ekserčić

tackle [ˈtækl] 1. *n* pribor 2. latiti se 3. (spor.) *v* oboriti na zemlju

tact [tækt] *n* takt

tactful [ˈtæktfəl] *adj* taktičan

tactic [ˈtæktik] *n* manevar

tactical [ˈtæktikl] *adj* taktički

tactical weapons *pl* taktičko naoružanje

tactician [tækˈtiʃən] *n* taktičar

tactless [ˈtæktləs] *adj* to be tactless yi katoara

tadpole [ˈtædpəul] *n* punoglavac

tag [tæg] 1. *n* etiketa 2. *v* staviti etiketu (**on** na)

tail [teil] *n* rep

tailor [ˈteilə] *n* krojač

tailor-made [ˌteiləˈmeid] *adj* prilagođen

taint [teint] *v* pokvariti

take [teik] *v* (**took, taken**) 1. uzeti 2. zauzeti 3. povesti 4. to take someone's pulse izmeriti nekome puls; izmjeriti nekome puls

takeaway [ˈteikəwei] *adj* (UK) za poneti/ponijeti

take away *v* odneti; odnijeti

take back *v* vratiti

take care! *v* pazi!

take care of *v* pobrinuti se o

take notice of *v* obratiti pažnju na

take off *v* 1. skinuti 2. uzletati; uzletjeti 3. ne raditi

take-out [ˈteikəwei] *adj* (US) za poneti/ponijeti

take-over [ˈteikəuvə] *n* preuzimanje vlasti

take over [teikˈəuvə] *v* preuziti

take over power *v* preuzeti vlast

take out *v* izvaditi

take place *v* desiti se

take up *v* 1. nastaviti 2. odati se 3. oduzeti

tale [teil] *n* priča

talent [ˈtælənt] *n* talenat

talented [ˈtæləntid] *adj* talentovan

talk [tɔːk] 1. *n* razgovor 2. govor 3. *v* govoriti 4. *see* talks

talkative [ˈtɔːkətiv] *adj* govorljiv

talk over *v* raspravljati

talks [tɔːks] *pl* pregovori

tall [tɔːl] *adj* visok

tame [teim] 1. *adj* pitom 2. *v* ukrotiti

tampon [ˈtæmpɔn] *n* čep, tampon

tan [tæn] 1. *n* sun tan preplanulost od sunca 2. *v* uštaviti 3. preplanuti

tangerine [tændʒəˈriːn] *n* mandarina

tangible [ˈtændʒəbl] *adj* opipljiv

tangle [ˈtæŋgl] *v* zamrsiti (se)

tank [tæŋk] *n* 1. tank 2. (mil.) tenk
tanker [ˈtæŋkə] *n* tanker
tanner [ˈtænər] *n* štavljač
tannery [ˈtænəri] *n* štavionica
tanning [ˈtæniŋ] *n* štavljenje
tantalize [ˈtæntəlaiz] *v* mučiti
tantrum [ˈtæntrəm] *n* bes; bijes
tap [tæp] 1. *n* slavina 2. *v* potapšati
tape [teip] 1. *n* traka 2. kaseta 3. *v* snimiti
tape recorder [ˈteiprikɔːdə] *n* magnetofon
tapestry [ˈtæpəstri] *n* tapiserija
tapeworm [ˈteipwəːm] *n* pantljičara
tar [taː] *n* katran
tardy [ˈtaːdi] *adj* spor
tare [teə] *n* tara
target [ˈtaːgit] *n* meta
tariff [ˈtærif] *n* carina
tarnish [ˈtaːniʃ] *v* tamneti; tamnjeti
tart [taːt] *n* voćni kolač
task [taːsk] *n* zadatak
task force *n* (mil.) operativna grupa
taste [teist] 1. *n* ukus 2. *v* probati 3. osećati se; osjećati se
tasteful [ˈteistfəl] *adj* ukusan
tasteless [ˈteistlis] *adj* bezukusan
tasty [ˈteisti] *adj* ukusan
tattered [ˈtætəd] *adj* dronjav
tatters [ˈtætəz] *pl* **in tatters** u dronjcima
tattoo [təˈtuː] 1. *n* tetoviranje 2. *v* istetovirati
taught [tɔːt] *see* **teach**
taunt [tɔːnt] *v* narugati se
taut [tɔːt] *adj* zategnut
tavern [ˈtævən] *n* krčma
tax [tæks] 1. *adj* poreski 2. *n* (*pl* **taxes**) porez 3. **value added tax** (**VAT**) dodatak porezu na promet 4. **to pay tax** platiti porez

5. *v* oporezovati 6. opteretiti
taxable [ˈtæksi] *n* oporežljiv
taxation [ˈtæksi] *n* oporezivanje
tax collector *n* poreski olakšica
tax evasion *n* poreska utaja
tax-free *n* oslobođen poreza
taxi [ˈtæksi] *n* taksi
taxi driver *n* taksista
TB [tiːbiː] *see* **tuberculosis**
tea [tiː] 1. *n* čaj 2. čajanka
teabag [ˈtiːbæg] *n* čaj u kesici
teach [tiːtʃ] *v* (**taught**) 1. naučiti 2. predavati
teacher [ˈtiːtʃə] *n* nastavnik
teacher training college *n* pedagoški fakultet
teaching [ˈtiːtʃiŋ] *n* nastava
team [tiːm] 1. *n* ekipa 2. (spor.) tim
team-leader [tiːmˈliːdə] *n* vođa ekipe
team mate [ˈtiːm‚meit] *n* saigrač
teamwork [ˈtiːmwəːk] *n* timski rad
teapot [ˈtiːpɔt] *n* čajnik
tear [tiə] *n* suza
tear [teə] 1. *n* pocepotina; pocjepotina 2. *v* (**tore**, **torn**) pocepati; pocijepati
tear apart *v* razjediniti
tear down *v* porušiti
tear gas [ˈtiəgas] *n* suzavac
tear off *v* otkinuti (se)
tears [tiəz] *pl* **in tears** u suzama
tear up *v* pocepati; pocijepati
tease [tiːz] *v* dražiti
teasing [ˈtiːziŋ] *n* zadirkivanje
teaspoon [ˈtiːspuːn] *n* kafena kašičica/žličica
teat [tiːt] *n* 1. sisa 2. bradavica
technical [ˈteknikl] *adj* 1. tehnički 2. keae
technical adviser *n* tehnički savetnik/savjetnik

technical college *n* tehnička škola
technical manual *n* tehničko uputstvo
technical training *n* tehnička obuka
technician [tekˈniʃn] *n* tehničar
technique [tekˈniːk] *n* tehnika
technological [ˌteknəˈlɔdʒikl] *adj* tehnološki
technology [tekˈnɔlədʒi] *n* tehnologija
tedious [ˈtiːdiəs] *adj* dosadan
teenager [ˈtiːneidʒə] *n* tinejdžer
teens [tiːnz] *pl* godine starosti od 13 do 19
tee-shirt [ˈtiːʃəːt] *n* T majica
teeth [tiːθ] *see* tooth
telecommunications [ˌtelikəˌmjuːniˈkeiʃnz] *n* telekomunikacije
telegram [ˈteligræm] *n* telegram
telegraph pole [ˈteligraːf] *n* telegrafski stub
telepathic [ˌteləˈpæθik] *n* telepatski
telephone [ˈtelifəun] 1. *adj* telefonski 2. *n* telefon 3. *v* telefonirati
telephone book *n* telefonski imenik
telephone booth *n* telefonska govornica
telephone call *n* telefonski poziv
telephoto lens *n* teleobjektiv
telescope [ˈteliskəup] *n* teleskop
teletext [ˈtelitekst] *n* teletekst
televise [ˈteliviaʒ] *v* emitovati (preko televizije)
television [ˈteliviʒn] *n* 1. televizija 2. **to watch television** gledati televiziju
television set *n* televizor
telex [ˈteleks] *n* teleks

tell [tel] *v* (**told**) reći, kazati
teller [ˈtelə] *n* blagajnik
tell time *v* videti koliko je časova; vidjeti koliko je sati
temp [temp] *see* **temporary worker**
temper [ˈtempə] *n* 1. mirnoća 2. **to lose one's temper** razljutiti se
tempera [ˈtempərə] *n* tempera
temperament [ˈtemprəmənt] *n* temperamenat
temperate [ˈtempərət] *adj* umeren; umjeren
temperature [ˈtemprətʃə] *n* 1. temperatura 2. groznica
tempest [ˈtempist] *n* oluja
temple [ˈtempl] *n* hram
temporary [ˈtemprəri] *adj* privremen
temporary work *n* privremeno zaposlenje
temporary worker *n* privremeni radnik
tempt [tempt] *v* iskušavati
temptation [tempˈteiʃn] *n* iskušenje
ten [ten] *n/adj* deset
tenacious [tiˈneiʃəs] *adj* uporan
tenacity [tiˈnæsəti] *n* upornost
tenant [ˈtenənt] *n* 1. zakupac 2. stanar
tend [tend] *v* 1. čuvati 2. naginjati
tendency [ˈtendənsi] *n* tendencija
tender [ˈtendə] 1. *adj* nežan; nježan 2. *n* (com.) ponuda 3. *v* (com.) ponuditi
tenderness [ˈtendənis] *n* nežnost; nježnost
tendon [ˈtendən] *n* tetiva
tenement [ˈtenəmənt] *n* stambena zgrada
tennis [ˈtenis] *n* tenis
tennis shoes *pl* sportske patike

tense [tens] 1. *adj* zategnut 2. *n* vreme; vrijeme

tension ['tenʃn] *n* 1. napon 2. napetost 3. (pol.) zategnutost

tent [tent] *n* šator

tenth [tenθ] *adj* deseti

tenuous ['tenjuəs] *adj* slab

tepid ['tepid] *adj* mlak

term [təːm] 1. *n* rok 2. termin 3. (ed.) semestar 4. **short-term** kratkoročan 5. **long-term** dugotrajan 6. *v* označiti 7. *see* **terms**

terminal ['təːminl] 1. *adj* (med.) koji umire 2. *n* krajnja stanica 3. **computer terminal** terminal

terminate ['təːmineit] *v* okončati

termination [,təːmi'neiʃn] *n* okončanje

terminology [,təːmi'nolodʒi] *n* terminologija

terminus ['təːminəs] *n* krajnja stanica

termite ['təːmait] *n* termit

terms [təːmz] *pl* 1. uslovi 2. **to be on good terms** biti u dobrim odnosima (**with** s)

terms of agreement *pl* uslovi sporazuma

terrace ['terəs] *n* terasa

terrible ['terəbl] *adj* strašan

terribly ['terəbli] *adv* veoma

terrific [tə'rifik] *adj* strahovit

terrify ['terifai] *v* prestraviti

terrifying ['terifajiŋ] *adj* užasavajući

territorial [terə'toːriəl] *adj* teritorijalan

Territorial Army *n* (UK) Teritorijalna odbrana/obrana

territorial claims *pl* teritorijalne pretenzije

territorial waters *pl* teritorijalne vode

territory ['terətri] *n* teritorija

terror ['terə] *n* 1. teror 2. **state of terror** strahovlada

terrorism ['terərizəm] *n* 1. terorizam 2. **to commit an act of terrorism** vršiti terorističkih napada

terrorist ['terərist] *n* terorista

test [test] 1. *n* ispit 2. *v* ispitati

testicle *n* testis

testify ['testifai] *v* svedočiti; svjedočiti (**against** protiv; **on behalf of** u nečiju korist)

testimonial [,testi'məuniəl] *n* uverenje

testimony ['testiməni] *n* svedočanstvo; svjedočanstvo

test-tube ['testjuːb] *n* epruveta

tetanus ['tetənəs] *n* sarewar haora

text [tekst] *n* tekst

textbook ['teksbuk] *n* udžbenik

textile ['tekstail] *n* tekstil

textile industry *n* tekstilna industrija

texture ['tekstʃə] *n* 1. tkanje 2. sastav

than [ðən] *conj* nego, od

thank [θæŋk] *v* zahvaliti (se)

thank you! hvala!

thankful ['θæŋkfl] *adj* zahvalan

thankless ['θæŋklis] *adj* nezahvalan

thanks ['θæŋks] *pl* 1. zahvalnost 2. hvala!

thanks to *prep* blagodareći

that [ðət; ðæt] 1. (*pl* those) taj, onaj 2. to 3. koji 4. *adv* tako 5. *conj* da 6. **so that/in order that** da

thatch [θætʃ] *v* pokriti krovinom

that is (=i.e.) to jest

thaw [θɔ:] 1. *n* topljenje 2. *v* topiti se

the [ðə; ði; ði:] *određen član*

theatre [ˈθiətə] *n* 1. pozorište; kazalište 2. **movie theatre** bioskop; kino 3. **operating theatre** operaciona sala

theft [θeft] *n* krađa

their [ðeə] njihov, njihova, njihovo

theirs [ðeəz] njihov, njihova, njihovo

them [ðəm; ðem] *pro* njih, njima

theme [θi:m] *n* tema

themselves [ðəmˈselvz] sami, sebe, sebi, se

then [ðen] 1. *adv* onda 2. **by then** dotada 3. **now and then** vremena na vreme

theologian [ˌθiəˈləudʒən] *n* teolog

theology [θiˈɔlədʒi] *n* teologija

theoretical [ˌθiəˈretikl] *adj* teorijski

theory [ˈθiəri] *n* teorija

therapist [ˈθerəpist] *n* terapeut

therapy [ˈθerəpi] *n* terapija

there [ðeə] tamo

there is/are... ima...

thereafter [ˌðeərˈa:ftə] *adv* posle toga; poslije toga

therefore [ˈðeəfɔ:] *adv* stoga

thereupon [ˌðeərəˈpɔn] *adv* na tome

thermometer [θəˈmɔmitə] *n* termometar

these [ði:z] *see* **this**

thesis [ˈθi:sis] *n* teza

they [ðei] *pro* oni, one, ona

thick [θik] *adj* 1. debeo 2. gust

thicken [ˈθikən] *v* zgusnuti

thicket [ˈθikit] *n* čestar

thickness [ˈθiknis] *n* 1. debljina 2. gustoća

thief [θi:f] *n* (*pl* **thieves**) lopov

thieve [θi:v] *v* ukrasti

thigh [θai] *n* but

thin [θin] *adj* 1. tanak 2. mršav 3. redak

thing [θiŋ] *n* stvar

think [θiŋk] *v* (**thought**) misliti

thinking [ˈθiŋkiŋ] *n* mišljenje

think of *v* setiti se; sjetiti se

think out/through *v* razmisliti se o

think over *v* razmisliti o

Third World *n* nesvrstane zemlje

third [θə:d] 1. *adj* treći 2. *n* trećina

thirst [θə:st] *n* žeđ

thirsty [ˈθə:sti] *adj* žedan

thirteen [ˌθə:ˈti:n] *n/adj* trinaest

thirteenth [ˌθə:ˈti:nθ] *adj* trinaesti

thirtieth [ˈθə:tiəθ] *adj* trideseti

thirty [ˈθə:ti] *n/adj* trideset

this [ðis] (*pl* **these**) ovaj, ovo

thorn [θɔ:n] *n* trn

thorny [ˈθɔ:ni] *adj* trnovit

thorough [ˈθʌrə] *adj* pravi

thoroughbred [ˈθʌrəbred] *adj* čistokrvan

thoroughfare [ˈθʌrəfeə] *n* prolaz

thoroughly [ˈθʌrəli] *adv* pravo

those [ðəuz] *see* **that**

though [ðəu] *adv* 1. iako 2. **as though** kao da

thought [θɔ:t] *n* 1. misao 2. *see* **think**

thoughtful [ˈθɔ:tfl] *adj* 1. misaon 2. pažljiv

thoughtfulness [ˈθɔ:tflnis] *n* misaonost

thoughtless [ˈθɔ:tlis] *adj* lakomislen

thought-provoking *adj* koji podstiče na razmišljanje

thousand [ˈθauznd] *n/adj* hiljada; tisuća

thousandth [ˈθauznθ] *adj* hiljaditi; tisući

thrash [θræʃ] *v* izbiti

thread [θred] *n* konac

threat [θret] *n* pretnja; prijetnja

threaten [ˈθretn] *v* zapretiti; zaprijetiti

threatening [ˈθretnin] *adj* preteći; prijeteći

three [θri:] *n/adj* tri

three-dimensional [ˌθri:daimenʃənəl] *adj* trodimenzionalan

thresh [ˈθreʃ] *v* ovrći

threshold [ˈθreʃhəuld] *n* prag

threw [θru:] *see* throw

thrift [θrift] *n* štedljivost

thrifty [ˈθrifti] *adj* štedljiv

thrill [θril] 1. *n* uzbuđenje 2. *v* uzbuditi

thriller [ˈθrilə] *n* triler

thrive [θraiv] *v* napredovati

throat [θrəut] *n* grlo

throb [θrɔb] *v* udarati

throne [θrəun] *n* presto; prijesto

throng [θrɔŋ] *n* gomila

throttle [ˈθrɔtl] 1. *n* leptir za gas 2. *v* ugušiti

through [θru:] 1. *prep* kroz 2. preko 3. po 4. *adv* skroz

throughout [θru:ˈaut] 1. *prep* kroz 2. *adv* do kraja

throw [θrəu] *v* (throw, thrown) baciti

throw away *v* baciti

throw out *v* izbaciti

throw up *v* povratiti

thrust [θrʌst] 1. *n* (mil.) napad 2. *v* zabosti

thug [θʌg] *n* siledžija

thumb [θʌm] *n* palac

thump [θʌmp] *v* udariti

thunder [ˈθʌndə] *n* grom

thunderstorm [ˈθʌndəstɔ:m] *n* pljusak s grmljavinom

Thursday [ˈθə:zdi] *n* četvrtak

thus [ðʌs] *adv* prema tome

tick [tik] 1. *n* otkucaj 2. krlja 3. *v* otkucavati 4. kucati

ticket [ˈtikit] *n* karta

ticket inspector *n* kondukter

ticket office *n* šalter za prodaju karata

tickle [ˈtikl] *v* golicati

tidal [ˈtaidl] *adj* plimski

tidal wave *n* plimski talas/val

tide [taid] *n* 1. morska mena; mijena 2. **high tide** plima 3. **low tide** oseka

tidings [ˈtaidiŋz] *pl* vesti; vijesti

tidy [ˈtaidi] 1. *adj* uredan 2. *v* urediti

tie [tai] 1. *n* veza 2. kravata 3. (spor.) nerešeni rezultat 4. *v* vezati 5. (spor.) igrati nerešeno/neriješeno

tier [tiə] *n* red

tie up *v* 1. vezati 2. zauzeti 3. obustaviti

tiger [ˈtaigə] *n* tigar

tight [tait] 1. *adj* tesan; tijesan 2. *adv* čvrsto

tighten [ˈtaitn] *v* stegnuti

tightly *adv* čvrsto

tights [taits] *pl* hula-hopke

'til [til] *see* until

tile [tail] *n* 1. crep; crijep 2. pločica

till [til] 1. *n* **cash till** fioka za novac 2. *v* obrađivati 3. *see* until

tilt [tilt] *v* nagnuti (se)

timber [ˈtimbə] *n* drvena građa

time [taim] 1. *n* vreme; vrijeme 2. **on time** na vreme/vrijeme 3. **at that time** u ono vreme 4. **at the**

same time u isto vreme **5. from time to time** s vremena a vreme **6. to waste time** gubiti vreme **7. to spend time** provoditi vreme **8. to tell time** videti koliko je časova; vidjeti kolio je sati **9.** *v* odmeriti vreme; odmijeriti vrijeme

time bomb *n* tempirana bomba

timekeeper ['taim,ki:pə] *n* merilac vremena; mjerilac vremena

time limit *n* rok

timely ['taimli] *adj* blagovremen

times [taimz] *prep* puta

timetable ['taim,teibl] *n* raspored

time zone *n* vremenska zona

timid ['timid] *adj* plašljiv

tin [tin] *n* **1.** kutija **2. tin-ore** kalaj

tin foil *n* kalajni list

tin-opener ['tinəupnə] *n* otvarač za konzerve

tinned food [tind] *n* konzervisana hrana; konzervirana hrana

tint [tint] **1.** *n* boja **2.** *v* zasenčiti; zasjenčiti

tiny ['taini] *adj* majušan

tip [tip] **1.** *n* vrh **2.** napojnica **3. rubbish tip** đubrište **4.** *v* prevrnuti **5.** dati napojnicu

tip-off *n* informacije

tip over *v* prevrnuti (se)

tipsy ['tipsi] *adj* u pripitom stanju

tiptoe ['tiptəu] **1.** *n* **on tiptoe** na vrhovima prstiju **2.** *v* ići na vrhovima prstiju

tire ['taiə] *v* **1.** umoriti (se) **2.** *see* **tyre**

tired ['taiəd] *adj* umoran

tiresome ['taiəsəm] *adj* zamoran

tissue ['tiʃu:] *n* **1.** tkivo **2.** papirna maramica

tissue paper *n* svileni papir

title ['taitl] *n* **1.** naslov **2.** titula **3.** (spor.) šampionat

to [tə; tu; tu:] *prep* **1.** u **2.** za **3. to sentence to death** osuditi na smrt

toad [təud] *n* krastava žaba

toast [təust] **1.** *n* tost **2.** zdravica **3.** *v* pržiti **4.** nazdraviti

tobacco [tə'bækəu] *n* duvan; duhan

tobacconist [tə'bækənist] *n* duvandžija; duhandžija

today [tə'dei] *adv* danas

today's [tə'deiz] *adj* današnji

toe [təu] *n* nožni prst

toenail ['təuneil] *n* nokat nonog prsta

toffee ['tɔfi] *n* vrsta karamele

together [tə'geðə] *adv* **1.** zajednički **2. all together** zajedno

toil [tɔil] **1.** *n* težak rad **2.** *v* teško raditi

toilet ['tɔilit] *n* **1.** nužnik **2. public toilets** javni klozet **3. to go to the toilet** ići u klozet

toilet paper *n* toaletni papir

token ['təukən] *n* **1.** znak **2.** bon

told [təuld] *see* **tell**

tolerable ['tɔlərəbl] *adj* podnošljiv

tolerance ['tɔlərəns] *n* tolerancija

tolerant ['tɔlərənt] *adj* tolerantan

tolerate ['tɔləreit] *v* tolerisati

toleration [,tɔlə'reiʃn] *n* tolerancija

toll [təul] *n* **1.** putarina **2. death toll** broj mrtvih **3.** *v* zvoniti u

tomato [tə'ma:təu] *n* (*pl* **tomatoes**) paradajz; rajčica

tomb [tu:m] *n* grob

tombstone ['tu:mstəun] *n* nadgrobni spomenik

tomorrow [tə'mɔrəu] *adv* **1.** sutra **2. the day after tomorrow** prekosutra

ton [tʌn] n tona
tone [təun] n ton
tongs [tɒŋz] pl klešta; kliješta
tongue [tʌŋ] n jezik
tonic ['tɒnik] n okrepa
tonight [tə'nait] adv večeras, noćas
tonnage ['tʌnidʒ] n tonaža
tonne [tʌn] n metrička tona
too [tu:] adv 1. i, takođe 2. suviše 3. baš
took [tuk] see take
tool [tu:l] n alatka
tool kit n alat, torba za alat
tooth [tu:θ] n 1. zub 2. to brush one's teeth čistiti zube
toothache ['tu:θeik] n zubobolja
toothbrush ['tu:θbrʌʃ] n četkica za zube
toothless ['tu:θlis] adj bezub
toothpaste ['tu:θpeist] n pasta za zube
top [tɒp] 1. adj gornji 2. n vrh 3. krov 4. on top of na
top speed n najveća brzina
topic ['tɒpik] n tema
topical ['tɒpikl] adj tematski
topple ['tɒpl] v oboriti
topple over v srušiti se
top-secret adj strogo poverljiv/povjerljiv
torah ['tɔrə] n tora
torch [tɔ:tʃ] n džepna lampa
tore, torn [tɔ:; tɔ:n] see tear
torment ['tɔ:ment] n muka
torment [,tɔ:'ment] v mučiti
tornado [tɔ:'neidəu] n tornado
torpedo [tɔ:'pi:dəu] 1. n (pl torpedoes) torpedo 2. v torpedirati
torpedo boat n torpedni čamac
torrent ['tɒrent] n bujica
tortoise ['tɔ:təs] n kornjača

torture ['tɔ:tʃə] 1. n mučenje 2. v mučiti
torture chamber n mučilište
torturer ['tɔ:tʃərə] n mučilac
toss [tɒs] v baciti
total ['təutl] 1. adj totalan 2. n suma 3. v sabrati
total up v sabrati
totalitarian [,təutæli'ta:riən] adj totalitaran
totalitarianism [,təutæli'ta:riənizm] n totalitarizam
totter ['tɒtə] v teturati se
touch [tʌtʃ] 1. n opip 2. v dirati
touch down ['tʌtʃdaun] v sleteti; sletjeti
touching ['tʌtʃiŋ] adj dirljiv
tough [tʌf] adj 1. tvrd 2. jak 3. težak
toughness ['tʌfnis] n tvrdoća
tour [tuə] 1. n putovanje 2. official tour obilazak 3. v putovati (po)
tour guide n turistički vodič
tourism ['tuərizəm] n turizam
tourist ['tuərist] n turista
tourist industry n turistička industrija
tourist season n turistička sezona
tournament ['tɔ:nəmənt] n turnir
tour operator n tur-operator
tow [teu] v vući
toward, towards [tə'wɔ:d; -z] prep 1. k 2. prema
tow away v odvući
towel ['tauəl] n peškir
tower ['tauə] n toranj
towering ['tauəriŋ] adj veoma visok
town [taun] n grad
town council n gradsko veće/vijeće
town hall n gradska većnica/vijećnica

town planning *n* urbanizam

toxic [ˈtɔksik] *adj* otrovan

toy [tɔi] *n* igračka

trace [treis] 1. *n* trag 2. *v* pronaći

tracer bullet *n* trasirno zrno

track [træk] 1. *n* trag 2. (spor.) staza 3. **railtrack** pruga 4. **to keep track** voditi evidenciju (of o) 5. **to lose track** izgubiti vezu (of s) 6. *v* pratiti

track suit *n* trenerka

tractor [ˈtræktə] *n* traktor

trade [treid] 1. *n* zanat 2. trgovina 3. **foreign trade** trgovina sa inostranstvom/inozemstvom 4. **retail trade** trgovina na malo 5. **wholesale trade** trgovina na veliko 6. **free trade** slobodna trgovina 7. **balance of trade** trgovinski bilans 8. **to lower trade barriers** sniziti trgovinske barijere 9. *v* trgovati 10. rarazmeniti; razmijeniti

trade agreement *n* trgovinski sporazum

trade barrier *n* trgovinska barijera

trade centre *n* trgovinski centar

trade delegation *n* privredna delegacija

trade embargo *n* trgovinski embargo

trade fair *n* trgovinski sajam

trade gap *n* trgovinski deficit

trademark [ˈtreidmaːk] *n* zaštitni žig/znak

trade prisoners *v* razmeniti zarobljenike; razmijeniti zarobljenike

trader [ˈtreidə] *n* trgovac

trade relations *pl* trgovinski odnosi

trade sanctions *pl* trgovinske sankcije

trade surplus *n* trgovinski suficit

trade union, trades union *n* sindikat

tradition [trəˈdiʃn] *n* tradicija

traditional [trəˈdiʃənl] *adj* tradicionalan

traffic [ˈtræfik] 1. *n* saobraćaj 2. (com.) trgovina 3. *v* (com.) trgovati

traffic jam *n* zatoj saobraćaja

traffic lights *pl* semafor

tragedy [ˈtrædʒədi] *n* tragedija

tragic [ˈtrædʒik] *adj* tragičan

trail [treil] 1. *n* trag 2. staza 3. *v* vući (se)

trailer [ˈtreilə] *n* prikolica

train [trein] 1. *n* voz; vlak 2. **by train** vozom; vlakom 3. *v* trenirati

trainer [ˈtreinə] *n* trener

trainers [ˈtreinəz] *pl* sportske patike

training [ˈtreiniŋ] *n* onbuka

training camp *n* školski logor

training college *n* teacher training college pedagoška škola

trait [treit] *n* crta

traitor [ˈtreitə] *n* izdajnik

tram [træm] *n* tramvaj

tramp [træmp] *n* skitnica

trample [ˈtræmpl] *v* zgaziti

tramway [ˈtræmwei] *n* tramvajska linija

trance [traːns] *n* trans

tranquil [ˈtræŋkwil] *adj* miran

tranquillity, tranquility [træŋˈkwiləti] *n* mirnoća

tranquillizer, tranquilizer [træŋˈkwilaizə] *n* trankilizer

transaction [trænˈzækʃn] *n* obavljanje

transcribe [trænˈskraib] *v* prepisati

transcript [trænˈskript] *n* prepis

transcription [træn'skrɪptʃən] *n* transkripcija

transfer [træns'fə:] 1. *n* prenos; prijenos 2. *v* preneti; prenijeti

transferable [træns'fə:rəbl] *adj* prenosiv

transform [træns'fɔ:m] *v* preobratiti

transformation [,trænsfə'meiʃn] *n* preobražaj

transformer [træns'fɔ:mə] *n* transformator

transfusion [træns'fju:ʒn] *n* **blood transfusion** transfuzija krvi

transient ['trænziənt] *adj* prolazan

transistor [træn'zistə] *n* tranzistor

transit ['trænzit] 1. *adj* tranzitni 2. *n* tranzit

transit camp *n* tranzitni logor

transit lounge *n* tranzitna čekaonica

transit visa *n* tranzitna viza

transition [træn'ziʃn] *n* prelaz; prijelaz

transitional [træn'ziʃnəl] *adj* prelazan; prijelazan

translate [trænz'leit] *v* prevesti (**from** s; **into** na)

translation [trænz'leiʃn] *n* prevod

translator [trænz'leitə] *n* prevodilac

transliterate [trænz'litəreit] *v* transliterirati

transliteration [trænz,litə'reiʃn] *n* transliteracija

transmission [trænz'miʃn] *n* prenos; prijenos

transmit [trænz'mit] *v* preneti; prenijeti

transmitter [trænz'mitə] *n* predajnik

transparency [træns'pærənsi] *n* slajd

transparent [træns'pærənt] *adj* providan

transpire [træns'paiə] *v* ispariti se

transplant [træns'pla:nt] 1. *n* presađivanje 2. *v* presaditi

transport ['trænspɔ:t] *n* transport

transport [træns'pɔ:t] *v* transportovati

transportation [,trænspɔ:'teiʃn] *n* saobraćaj

transporter [træns'pɔ:tə] *n* transporter

transvestite [træns'vestait] *n* transvestit

trap [træp] 1. *n* klopka 2. *v* (**trapped**) uhvatiti u klopku

trash [træʃ] *n* otpaci

trash can *n* kanta za smeće

trauma ['trɔ:mə] *n* povreda

traumatic [trɔ:'mætik] *adj* traumatičan

traumatize ['trɔ:mətaiz] *v* raniti

travel ['trævl] 1. *n* turizam 2. *v* (**travelled**) putovati

travel agency *n* turistička agencija

travel industry *n* turistička privreda

travel insurance *n* osigurannje putnika

traveller ['trævlə] *n* putnik

traveller's cheque *n* putnički ček

travel sickness *n* mučnina izazvana vožnjom

trawler [trɔ:lə] *n* koča

tray [trei] *n* poslužavnik

treacherous ['tretʃərəs] *adj* 1. izdajnički 2. opasan

treachery ['tretʃəri] *n* izdaja

tread [tred] 1. *n* **tyre tread** gazeća površina 2. *v* (**trod, trodden**) stupati 3. gaziti

treason ['tri:zn] *n* izdaja

treasure ['treʒə] *n* blago

treasurer ['treʒərə] *n* rizničar

treasury [ˈtreʒəri] *n* 1. riznica 2. ministarstvo finansija/financija
treasury department *n* ministarstvo finansija/financija
treasury secretary *n* ministar finansija/financija
treat [tri:t] *v* 1. postupiti s 2. (med.) lečiti; liječiti
treatise [ˈtri:tiz] *n* rasprava
treatment [ˈtri:tmənt] *n* 1. postupak 2. (med.) lečenje; liječenje
treaty [ˈtri:ti] *n* 1. ugovor 2. **peace treaty** mirovni ugovor 3. **to sign a treaty** potpisati ugovor 4. **to break a treaty** raskinuti ugovor
treble [ˈtrebl] *v* utrostručiti (se)
tree [tri:] *n* drvo
tremble [ˈtrembl] *v* drhtati
tremendous [triˈmendəs] *adj* ogroman
tremor [ˈtremə] *n* potres
trench [trentʃ] *n* rov
trend [trend] *n* trend
trespass [ˈtrespəs] *v* nezakonito stupiti
trial [ˈtraiəl] *n* 1. proba 2. (leg.) suđenje 3. **war crimes trial** suđenje ratnim zločincima 4. **to bring to trial** izvesti pred sud
triangle [ˈtraiæŋgl] *n* trougao; trokut
tribal [ˈtraibl] *adj* plemenski
tribalism [ˈtraibəlizəm] *n* tribalizam
tribe [traib] *n* pleme
tribunal [traiˈbju:nl] *n* 1. sud 2. **industrial tribunal** privredni sud
tribute [ˈtribju:t] *n* **to pay tribute to someone** odati nekome priznanje
trick [trik] *n* 1. trik 2. iluzija 3. **dirty trick** prljava smicalica 4.

to play a trick on someone napraviti smicalicu nekome 5. *v* prevariti
trickery [ˈtrikəri] *n* varanje
trickle [ˈtrikl] *v* kapati
tricky [ˈtriki] *adj* varalički
trigger [ˈtrigə] 1. *n* obarač 2. *v* izazvati
trigger off *v* izazvati
trim [trim] *v* skresati
trip [trip] 1. *n* putovanje 2. **business trip** službeno putovanje 3. **round trip** put o oba pravca 4. **to go on a trip** ići na put 5. (sl.) halucinacija 6. *v* (**tripped**) saplesti (se)
trip up *v* saplesti (se)
tripartite [ˈtraipa:tait] *adj* trojni
tripe [traip] *n* škembići
triple [ˈtripl] *v* utrostručiti (se)
triplets [ˈtriplits] *pl* trojke
triplicate [ˈtriplikət] *n* triplikat
tripod [ˈtraipɔd] *n* tronožac
tripper [ˈtripə] *n* turista
triumph [ˈtraiʌmf] 1. *n* trijumf 2. *v* trijumfovati
triumphant [traiˈʌmfnt] *n* pobednički; pobjednički
trivial [ˈtriviəl] *adj* sitan
trod, trodden [trɔd; trɔdn] *see* **tread**
trolley bus *n* trolejbus
troop [tru:p] *n* grupa
troop carrier *n* (mil.) transporter za ljudstvo
troopship [ˈtru:pʃip] *n* (mil.) transportni brod
troops [tru:ps] *pl* trupe
trophy [ˈtrəufi] *n* (spor.) trofej
tropical [ˈtrɔpik] *adj* tropski
tropics [ˈtrɔpikl] *pl* tropi
trot [trɔt] *v* kasati

trouble [ˈtrʌbl] 1. *n* nezgoda 2. trud 3. *v* uznemiriti

troubled [ˈtrʌbld] *adj* mutan

troublemaker [ˈtrʌbl,meikə] *n* smutljivac

troublesome [ˈtrʌblsəm] *adj* mučan

trough [trof] *n* korito

trousers [ˈtrauzəz] *pl* pantalone; hlače

truancy [ˈtruːənsi] *n* (ed.) izostanak

truce [truːs] *n* prekida vatre

truck [trʌk] *n* kamion

true [truː] *adj* istinit

truly [ˈtruːli] *adv* zaista

trumpet [ˈtrʌmpit] *n* truba

trunk [trʌŋk] *n* 1. sanduk 2. stablo 3. surla 4. prtljažnik

trust [trʌst] 1. *n* poverenje; povjerenje 2. **on trust** na veru 3. *v* verovati; vjerovati

trustee [trʌˈstiː] *n* (leg.) staratelj

trusteeship council [trʌˈstiːʃip] *n* starateljski komitet

trust territory *n* starateljska teritorija

trustworthy [ˈtrʌst,wəːði] *adj* dostojan poverenja/povjerenja

truth [truːθ] *n* istina

truthful [ˈtruːθfl] *adj* istinoljubiv

truthfully [ˈtruːθfuli] *adv* iskreno

try [trai] *v* 1. pokušati 2. probati 3. (leg.) suditi

try on *v* probati

try out *v* oprobati

T-shirt *n* T macija

tub [tʌb] *n* 1. kada 2. *see* **bathtub**

tube [tjuːb] *n* 1. tuba 2. **inner tube** unutrašna guma 3. (UK) **the Tube** metro

tuberculosis [tjuː,bəːkjuˈləusis] *n* tuberkuloza

tuck [tʌk] *v* uvući

Tuesday [ˈtjuːzdi] *n* utorak

tug [tʌg] *v* izvući

tuition [tjuːˈiʃn] *n* školarina

tumble [ˈtʌmbl] *v* pasti

tumbler [ˈtʌmblə] *n* čaša

tumour [ˈtjuːmə] *n* tumor

tumult [ˈtjuːmʌlt] *n* buka

tuna [ˈtjuːnə] *n* tunj

tune [tjuːn] 1. *n* melodija 2. **to be out of tune** biti nenaštimovan, falširati 3. *v* nastimovati

tune in *v* namestiti; namjestiti

tunnel [ˈtʌnl] *n* tunel

turban [ˈtəːbən] *n* turban

turbine [ˈtəːbain] *n* turbina

turbulence [ˈtəːbjuləns] *n* turbulencija

turbulent [ˈtəːbjulənt] *adj* turbulentan

turf [təːf] *n* busen

Turk [təːk] *n* Turčin

turkey [ˈtəːki] *n* (*pl* **turkeys**) ćuran

Turkey *n* Turska

Turkish [ˈtəːkiʃ] *adj* turski

turmoil [ˈtəːmoil] *n* nemir

turn [təːn] 1. *n* skretanje 2. red 3. **in turn** po redu 4. **It's your turn.** Na tebe je red. 5. **to take turns** smenjivati; smjenjivati 6. *v* okrenuti (se) 7. pretvoriti se

turn against *v* pobuniti se protiv

turn around *v* okrenuti (se)

turn back *v* 1. ići natrag 2. odbiti

turn down *v* odbiti

turning [ˈtəːniŋ] *n* skretanje

turning-point *n* prekretnica

turn into *v* 1. pretvoriti u 2. izvrnuti u

turnip [ˈtəːnip] *n* repa

turn off *v* 1. ugasiti 2. isključiti 3. zavrnuti

turn on *v* 1. upaliti 2. naelektrisati

turn-out n poseta; posjet
turn out v 1. ugasiti 2. ispasti 3. ispostaviti 4. skupiti se
turnover ['tə:n,əuvə] n (fin.) obrt
turn round see **turn around**
turn up v 1. zavrnuti 2. pojaviti se 3. pojačati
turtle ['tə:tl] n kornjača
tusk [tʌsk] n zub
tutor ['tju:tə] n privatni učitelj
TV [ti:'vi:] n televizija
tweezers ['twi:zəz] pl pinceta
twelfth [twelfθ] adj dvanaesti
twelve [twelv] n/adj dvanaest
twentieth ['twentiəθ] adj dvadeseti
twenty ['twenti] n/adj dvadeset
twice [twais] adv dvaput
twig [twig] n grančica
twilight ['twailait] n sumrak, suton
twin [twin] n blizanac
twinkle ['twiŋkl] v svetlucati; svjetlucati
twins [twinz] pl blizanci

twist [twist] v 1. upresti (se) 2. izvrnuti 3. see **sprain**
two [tu:] n/adj dva
two-faced [,tu:'feist] adj dvoličan
two-party system n dvopartijski sistem
two-way [,tu:'wei] adj dvosmerni; dvosmjerni
tycoon [tai'ku:n] n bogat industrijalac
type [taip] 1. n tip 2. v otkucati
typewriter ['taip,raitə] n pisaća mašina; pisaći stroj
typhoid ['taifɔid] n tifusna groznica
typhoon [tai'fu:n] n typhoon
typical ['tipikl] adj tipičan
typically ['tipikli] adv tipično
typist ['taipist] n daktilograf(kinja)
tyrannical [ti'rænikl] adj tiranski
tyrannize ['tirənaiz] v tiranisati
tyranny ['tirəni] n tiranija
tyrant ['taiərənt] n tiranin
tyre ['taiə] n guma

u

ugliness ['ʌglinis] *n* ružnoća

ugly ['ʌgli] *adj* 1. ružan 2. nemio

UK [, juːˈkei] *see* **United Kingdom**

ulcer ['ʌlsə] *n* grizlica

ulterior [ʌlˈtiəriə] *adj* **ulterior motive** zadnja misao

ultimate ['ʌltimət] *adj* krajnji

ultimately ['ʌltimətli] *adv* konačno

ultimatum [,ʌltiˈmeitəm] *n* ultimatum

ultra- [,ʌltrə] *adj* 1. ultra 2. (pol.) ekstremistički

umbilical cord ['ʌmbilikl,kɔːd] *n* pupčana vrpca

umbrella [ʌmˈbrelə] *n* kišobran

umpire ['ʌmpaiə] *n* sudija

unable [ʌnˈeibl] *adj* nesposoban

unacceptable ['ʌnəkˈseptəbl] *adj* neprihvatljiv (**to** za)

unaccompanied ['ʌnəˈkʌmpənid] *adj* bez pratioca

unaccustomed to ['ʌnəˈkʌstəmd] *adj* nenaviknut

unaffected ['ʌnəˈfektid] *adj* neizveštačen; neizvještačen

unanimous [juːˈnæniməs] *adj* jednoglasan

unarmed ['ʌnˈaːmd] *adj* nenaoružan

unattractive ['ʌnəˈtræktiv] *adj* neprivlačan

unauthorized ['ʌnˈɔːθəraizd] *adj* neovlašćen

unavoidable [,ʌnəˈvɔidəbl] *adj* neizbežan: neizbježan

unaware ['ʌnəˈweə] *adj* nesvestan; nesvjestan

unawares ['ʌnəˈweəz] *adv* iznenada

unbearable [ʌnˈbeərəbl] *adj* nepodnošljiv

unbelievable [,ʌnbiˈliːvəbl] *adj* neverovatan; nevjerovatan

unbroken ['ʌnˈbrəukən] *adj* 1. čitav 2. nenadmašen

unbutton ['ʌnˈbʌtn] *v* raskopčati

uncertain [ʌnˈsəːtn] *adj* neizvestan; neizvjestan

uncertainty [ʌnˈsəːtənti] *n* neizvesnost; neizvjesnost

uncle ['ʌŋkl] *n* ujak, stric

unclear [,ʌnˈkliə] *adj* 1. nejasan

uncomfortable [ʌnˈkʌmftəbl] *adj* 1. neudoban 2. nelagodan

uncommon [ʌnˈkɔmən] *adj* neobičan

unconcerned ['ʌnkənˈsəːnd] *adj* ravnodušan

unconditional ['ʌnkənˈdiʃənl] *n* bezuslovan; bezuvjetan

unconditional surrender *n* bezuslovna predaja; bezuvjetna predaja

unconditionally ['ʌnkənˈdiʃənli] *adv* bezuslovno; bezuvjetno

unconscious [ʌnˈkɔnʃəs] *adj* nesvestan; nesvjestan

unconsciously [ʌnˈkɔnʃəsli] *adv* nesvesno; nesvjesno

unconstitutional ['ʌn,kɔnsti-ˈtjuːʃənl] *adj* protivustavan; protuustavan

uncontrollable [,ʌnkənˈtrəuləbl] *adj* neobuzdan

uncooperative [,ʌnkəuˈɔpərətiv] *adj* nespreman na saradnju/suradnju

uncover [ʌnˈkʌvə] v razotkriti

undamaged [ʌnˈdæmidʒd] adj neoštećen

undaunted [ʌnˈdɔːntid] adj nezastrašen

undecided [ˌʌndiˈsaidid] adj neodlučen

undeclared [ˌʌndiˈkleːd] adj bez objave

undefeated [ˌʌndiˈfiːtid] adj neporažen

undeniable [ˌʌndiˈnaiəbl] adj neosporan

under [ˈʌndə] prep 1. ispod, pod 2. **under fire** pod vatrom 2. **under 20 years old** ispod 20 godina

underage [ˈʌndeidʒ] adj nepunoletan; nepunoljetan

undercover [ˈʌndəkʌvə] adj tajni

undercut [ˈʌndəkʌt] v (fin.) potkopati

underdeveloped [ˈʌndədiˈveləpt] n nerazvijen

underdeveloped nations pl nerazvijene zemlje

underestimate [ˌʌndərˈestimeit] v potceniti; potcijeniti

undergo [ˈʌndəˈgəu] v pretrpeti; pretrpjeti

undergraduate [ˈʌndəˈgrædʒuət] n redovni student

underground [ˈʌndəgraund] adj/adv 1. podzemni 2. ilegalan 3. (UK) **the Underground** metro

underground organization n ilegalna organizacija

undergrowth [ˈʌndəgrəuθ] n žbunje

underhand, underhanded [ˈʌndəhænd; -id] adj podmukao

underline [ˌʌndəˈlain] v potcrtati

undermine [ˌʌndəˈmain] v potkopati

underneath [ˌʌndəˈniːθ] 1. prep pod, ispod 2. adv dole; dolje

underpants, undershorts [ˈʌndəpænts; ˈʌndəʃɔːts] pl gaće

under-secretary [ˈʌndəˈsekreteri] n podsekretar

underside [ˈʌndəˈsaid] n donja površina

understand [ˌʌndəˈstænd] v razumeti; razumjeti

understandable [ˌʌndəˈstændəbl] adj razumljiv

understanding 1. adj pun razumevanja; pun razumijevanja 2. n razumevanje; razumijevanje 3. **to come to an understanding** doći do sporazuma

undertake [ˌʌndəˈteik] v preduzeti; poduzeti

under-the-counter [ˈʌndəθəˈkauntə] adj potajan

underwater [ˈʌndəˈwɔːtə] adj podvodni

underway [ˈʌndəˈwei] adv u toku

underwear [ˈʌndəweə] n donje rublje

undid [ʌnˈdid] see **undo**

undo [ʌnˈduː] v (**undid, undone**) raspakovati

undoubtedly [ʌnˈdautidli] adv nesumnjivo

undress [ʌnˈdres] v svući (se)

unearth [ʌnˈəːθ] v iskopati

uneasiness [ʌnˈiːzinis] n uznemirenost

uneasy [ʌnˈiːzi] adj uznemiren

uneducated [ʌnˈedjukeitid] adj neškolovan

unemployable [ˈʌnimˈplɔijəbl] adj nezapošljiv

unemployed [ˈʌnimˈplɔid] adj 1. nezaposlen 2. **the unemployed** nezaposleni

unemployment [ˈʌnimˈplɔimənt] *n* nezposlenost; nezpošljenost

unequal [ˈʌnˈiːkwəl] *adj* nejednak

unequivocal [ˈʌniˈkwivəkəli] *adj* nedvosmislen

UNESCO [juːˈneskəu] *n* Organizacija UN za prosvetu/prosvjetu

uneven [ˈʌnˈiːvn] *adj* neravan

unexpected [ˈʌnikˈspektid] *adj* neočekivan

unexpectedly [ˈʌnikˈspektili] *adv* neočekivano

unfair [ˈʌnˈfeə] *adj* nepravedan

unfasten [ˈʌnˈfaːsn] *v* odvezati

unfinished [ˈʌnˈfiniʃt] *adj* nesvršen

unfit [ˈʌnˈfit] *adj* nesposoban

unfold [ʌnˈfəuld] *v* odviti (se)

unfortunate [ʌnˈfɔːtʃənət] *adj* nepovoljan

unfortunately [ʌnˈfɔːtʃənətli] *adv* na žalost

unfriendly [ʌnˈfrendli] *adj* neprijateljski

ungrateful [ʌnˈgreitfl] *adj* nezahvalan

unhappiness [ʌnˈhæpinis] *n* nesreća

unhappy [ʌnˈhæpi] *adj* nesrećan

unhealthy [ʌnˈhelθi] *adj* nezdrav

unhindered [ˈʌnˈhindəd] *adj* nesmetan

unhurt [ˈʌnˈhəːt] *adj* nepovređen; neozlijeđen

UNICEF [ˈjuːnesef] *n* Međunarodni fond UN za pomoć deci/djeci

unidentified [ˌjuːnifiˈkeid] *adj* neidentifikovan

unidentified flying object (UFO) *n* neidentifikovani leteći objekt (NLO)

unification [ˌjuːnifiˈkeiʃn] *n* unifikacija

unified [ˈjuːnifaid] *adj* objedinjen

uniform [ˈjuːnifɔːm] **1.** *adj* jednolik **2.** *n* uniforma **3. school uniform** školska uniforma

uniformity [ˌjuːnifɔːmiti] *n* jednolikost

unify [ˈjuːnifai] *v* ujediniti (se)

unilateral step [juːniˈlætrəl] *n* unilateralan

unilateral disarmamaent *n* jednostrano razoružanje

unimportant [ˈʌnimˈpɔːtənt] *adj* nevažan

uninhabited [ˌʌninˈhæbitid] *adj* nenaseljen

uninjured [ˈʌnˈindʒəd] *adj* nepovređen; neozlijeđen

unintentional [ˈʌninˈtenʃənl] *adj* nenameran; nenamjeran

uninteresting [ʌnˈintərestiŋ] *adj* neinteresantan

uninterrupted [ˈʌnˌintəˈrʌptid] *adj* neprekinut

union [ˈjuːnjən] **1.** *adj* sindikalni **2.** *n* unija **3.** savez **4. trade union** sindikat

Union Jack [ˈjuːnjənˈdʒæk] *n* zavasta Velike Britanije

unique [juːˈniːk] *adj* jedini

unit [ˈjuːnit] *n* jedinica

unite [juːˈnait] *v* ujediniti (se)

united [juːˈnaitid] *adj* ujedinjen

United Kingdom [juːˌnaitid ˈkiŋdəm] *n* Ujedinjeno Kraljevstvo

United Nations (UN) *n* Ujedinjene nacije

United States of America *n* Sjedinjene Američke Države

unity [ˈjuːnəti] *n* jedinstvo

universal [ˌjuːniˈvəːsl] *adj* **1.** univerzalan **2.** opšti; opći

universally [ˌjuːniˈvəːsəli] *adv* **1.** univerzalno **2.** opšte; opće

universe [ˈjuːnivəːs] *n* svemir
university [ˌjuːniˈvəːsəti] *n* univerzitet; sveučilište
unjust [ʌnˈdʒʌst] *adj* nepravedan
unkind [ʌnˈkaind] *adj* neljubazan
unknown [ˌʌnˈnəun] 1. *adj* nepoznat 2. *n* nepoznata
unlawful [ʌnˈlɔːfəl] *adj* nezakonit
unleaded [ənˈledid] *adj* bez olova
unleaded petrol, unleaded gasoline *n* benzin bez dodatka olova
unless [ənˈles] *conj* ako (ne)
unlike [ʌnˈlaik] 1. *adj* nesličan 2. *adv* suprotno
unlikely [ʌnˈlaikli] *adv* neverovatan
unlimited [ʌnˈlimitid] *adj* neograničen
unload [ʌnˈləud] *v* istovariti
unlock [ʌnˈlɔk] *v* otključati
unlucky [ʌnˈlʌki] *adj* nesrećan
unmanageable [ʌnˈmænidʒəbl] *adj* neukrotiv
unmanned [ʌnˈmænd] *adj* bez posade
unmarried [ʌnˈmærid] *adj* neoženjen, neudata
unmistakable [ʌnmisˈteikəbl] *adj* očevidan
unmitigated [ʌnˈmitigeitid] *adj* 1. nesmanjen 2. apsolutan
unnatural [ʌnˈnætʃrəl] *adj* 1. nenormalan 2. neprirodan
unnecessary [ʌnˈnesəsri] *adj* nepotreban
unofficial [ʌnəˈfiʃl] *adj* neslužben
unpack [ʌnˈpæk] *v* raspakovati
unpaid [ʌnˈpeid] *adj* neisplaćen
unpalatable [ʌnˈpælitəbl] *adj* 1. neukusan 2. neugodan
unparalleled [ʌnˈpærəleld] *adj* nenadmašan
unplanned [ʌnˈplænd] *adj* neplanski

unpleasant [ʌnˈpleznt] *adj* neprijatan
unplug [ʌnˈplʌg] *v* isključiti
unpopular [ʌnˈpɔpjulə] *adj* nepopularan
unpopularity [ʌnˌpɔpjuˈlærəti] *n* nepopularnost
unprecedented [ʌnˈpresidentid] *adj* bez presedana
unpredictable [ʌnpriˈdiktəbl] *adj* nepredvidiv
unprepared [ʌnpriˈpeəd] *adj* nepripremljen
unprincipled [ʌnˈprinsipəld] *adj* nemoralan
unproductive [ʌnprəˈdʌktiv] *adj* neproduktivan
unprofitable [ʌnˈprɔfitəbl] *adj* nerentabilan
unprotected [ʌnprəˈtektid] *adj* neobezbeden; neobezbijeden
unprovoked [ʌnprəˈvəukt] *adj* neizazvan
unravel [ʌnˈrævl] *v* rasplesti
unreal [ʌnˈriːjəl] *adj* nestvaran
unrealistic [ʌnˌriːjəˈlistik] *adj* nerealan
unreasonable [ʌnˈriːznəbl] *adj* neumeren; neumjeren
unrelated [ʌnriˈleitid] *adj* 1. koji nije u rodu 2. nevezan
unreliable [ˈʌnriˈlaiəbl] *adj* nepouzdan
unrest [ʌnˈrest] *n* nemir
unripe [ʌnˈraip] *adj* nezreo
unroll [ʌnˈrɔl] *v* odviti (se)
unruly [ʌnˈruːli] *adj* nepokoran
unsafe [ˈʌnˈseif] *adj* nesiguran
unsaid [ˈʌnˈsed] *adj* neizrečen
unsatisfactory [ˈʌnˌsætisˈfæktri] *adj* nezadovoljavajući
unsatisfied [ˌʌnˈsætisfaid] *adj* nezadovoljen

unscrew [ˈʌnˈskruː] v odvrnuti
unscrupulous [ʌnˈskruːpjuləs] adj beskrupulozan
unseat [ˈʌnˈsiːt] v (pol.) lišiti mandata
unseen [ˈʌnˈsiːn] adj neviđen
unselfish [ˈʌnˈselfiʃ] adj nesebičan
unsettle [ˈʌnˈsetl] v uznemiriti
unskilled [ˈʌnˈskild] adj nekvalifikovan
unsolved [ʌnˈsɔlvd] adj nerešen; neriješen
unsophisticated [ʌnsɔˈfistikeitid] adj naivan
unsound [ˈʌnˈsaund] adj pogrešan
unstable [ˈʌnˈsteibl] adj nestabilan
unsteady [ˈʌnˈstedi] adj nestalan
unsuccessful [ʌnsʌkˈsesfəl] adj neuspešan; neuspješan
unsuitable [ˈʌnˈsuːtəbl] adj neprikladan
unthinkable [ʌnˈθiŋkəbl] adj nezamišljiv
untidy [ʌnˈtaidi] adj neuredan
untie [ˈʌnˈtai] v odvezati
until [ənˈtil] 1. prep do 2. conj dok (ne)
untouched [ˈʌnˈtʌtʃt] adj netaknut
untrue [ˈʌnˈtruː] adj neistinit
unusual [ʌnˈjuːʒl] adj neobičan
unveil [ʌnˈveil] v otkriti
unwelcome [ʌnˈwelkəm] adj nemio
unwell [ʌnˈwel] adj bolestan
unwilling [ʌnˈwiliŋ] adj nerad
unwillingness [ʌnˈwiliŋnis] n nespremnost
unwind [ʌnˈwaind] v odmotati (se)
unwise [ʌnˈwaiz] adj nepametan
unworthy [ʌnˈwəːði] adj nedostojan
unwrap [ʌnˈræp] v odmotati
up [ʌp] 1. adv gore 1. prep uz 2. see up to

upbringing [ˈʌpbriŋiŋ] n vaspitanje
update [ˈʌpdeit] n ažuriranje
update [ʌpˈdeit] v ažurirati
uphill [ʌpˈhil] adj uzbrdo
uphold [ʌpˈhəuld] v potvrditi
upon [əˈpɔn] prep na
upper [ˈʌpə] adj gornji
upper house n (pol.) gornji dom
uppermost [ˈʌpəməust] adj najviši
upright [ˈʌprait] 1. adj uspravan 2. adv uspravno
uprising [ˈʌpreiziŋ] n ustanak
uproar [ˈʌprɔː] n buka
uproot [ˌʌpˈruːt] v iščupati
upset [ˌʌpˈset] 1. adj to be upset biti oneraspoložen (about zbog) 2. v (upset) prevrnuti 3. osujetiti 4. potresti
upside down [ˌʌpsaidˈdaun] adv naopako
upstairs [ˌʌpˈsteəz] adv gore
upswing [ˈʌpswiŋ] n porast
up to [ʌp] prep 1. do 2. zavisan od
up-to-date [ˌʌptuˈdeit] adj aktuelan
upward, upwards [ˈʌpwəd; -z] adv gore
uranium [juəˈreinijəm] n uran
urban [ˈəːbən] adj gradski
urban development n urbani razvoj
urbanization [ˌəːbənaiˈzeiʃn] n urbanizacija
urbanize [ˈəːbənaiz] v urbanizovati
urge [əːdʒ] 1. n nagon 2. v saleteti; saletjeti
urgency [ˈəːdʒənsi] n hitnost
urgent [ˈəːdʒənt] adj hitan
urgently [ˈəːdʒəntli] adv hitno
urge on v terati; tjerati
urinal [juəˈrainl] n pisoar
urinate [ˈjuərineit] v mokriti
urine [ˈjuərin] n mokraća

us [əs; ʌs] nama, nas sebe, mi
US, USA *see* **United States (of America)**
usage [ˈjuːsidʒ] *n* upotreba
use [juːs] *n* 1. upotreba 2. uživanje 3. **What's the use of...?** Od kavke je koristi...?
use [juːz] *v* 1. upotrebiti; upotrijebiti 2. potrošiti
used [juːzd] *adj* polovan
used to [ˈjuːstu] 1. **to get used to** naviknuti se na 2. **We used to live in Sydney.** Nekada smo živjeli u Sidneju.
useful [ˈjuːsfl] *adj* koristan
usefulness [ˈjuːsfəlnis] *n* korisnost
useless [ˈjuːslis] *adj* beskoristan

uselessness [ˈjuːslisnis] *n* beskorisnost
user [ˈjuːzə] *n* korisnik
user-friendly [ˈjuːzə,frendli] *adj* blizak korisniku
usual [ˈjuːʒl] *adj* uobičajen
usually [ˈjuːʒəli] *adv* obično
use up *v* potrošiti
utensil [juːˈtensil] *n* pribor
uterus [ˈjuːtərəs] *n* materica
utility [juːˈtiliti] *n* **public utility** komunalna usluga
utilize [ˈjuːtilaiz] *v* iskoristiti
utmost [ˈʌtməust] *adj* krajnji
utter [ˈʌtə] 1. *adj* apsolutan 2. *v* izustiti
utterance [ˈʌtərəns] *n* izraz

V

v., vs. *see* **versus**
vacancy [ˈveɪkənsi] *n* vakancija
vacant [ˈveɪkənt] *adj* prazan
vacation [vəˈkeɪʃn] *n* raspust, odmor
vaccinate [ˈvæksɪneɪt] *v* vakcinisati
(**protiv** against)
vaccination [ˌvæksɪˈneɪʃn] *n* vakcinacija
vaccine [ˈvækˈsiːn] *n* vakcina
vacuum [ˈvækjuəm] **1.** *n* vakuum **2.** *v* očistiti usisivačem
vacuum cleaner *n* usisuvač
vagabond [ˈvægəbɒnd] *n* skitnica
vagina [vəˈdʒaɪnə] *n* vagina
vaginal [vəˈdʒaɪnəl] *adj* vaginalan
vagrant [ˈveɪgrənt] *n* skitnica
vague [veɪg] *adj* nejasan
vain [veɪn] *adj* **1.** tašt **2.** **in vain** uzaludno
vale [veɪl] *n* dolina
valiant [ˈvælɪənt] *adj* hrabar
valid [ˈvælɪd] *adj* **1.** opravdan **2.** (leg.) punovažan
validate [vəˈlɪdeɪt] *v* nostrifikovati
validity [vəˈlɪdəti] *n* **1.** opravdanost **2.** (leg.) punovažnost
valley [ˈvæli] *n* dolina
valour, valor [ˈvælə] *n* hrabrost
valuable [ˈvæljuəbl] *adj* vredan; vrijedan
valuables [ˈvæljuəblz] *pl* dragocenosti; dragocjenosti
value [ˈvæljuː] **1.** *n* vrednost; vrijednost **2.** korist **3.** *v* ceniti; cijeniti
value-added tax (VAT) *n* porez na promet

valve [vælv] *n* ventil
vampire [ˈvæmpaɪə] *n* vampir
van [væn] *n* kamion
vandal [ˈvændl] *n* vandal
vandalism [ˈvændəlɪzm] *n* vandalizam
vandalize [ˈvændəlaɪz] *v* izvršiti vandalizam (na)
vanilla [vəˈnɪlə] *n* vanila
vanish [ˈvænɪʃ] *v* nestati
vanity [ˈvænəti] *n* taština
vaporize [ˈveɪpəraɪz] *v* ispariti
vapour [ˈveɪpə] *n* para
variable [ˈveərɪəbl] *adj* promenljiv; promjenljiv
variant [ˈveərɪənt] *n* alternativni
variation [ˌveərɪˈeɪʃn] *n* varijacija
varicose veins [ˌværɪkəus ˈveɪnz] *pl* proširene vene
variety [vəˈraɪəti] *n* **1.** raznolikost **2.** varijetet
various [ˈveərɪəs] *adj* razni
varnish [ˈvaːnɪʃ] *n* firnajz
vary [ˈveəri] *v* **1.** menjati (se); mijenjati (se) **2.** razlikovati se
vase [vaːz] *n* vazna
vaseline [ˈvæzəliːn] *n* vazelin
vast [vaːst] *adj* ogroman
vastly [ˈvaːstli] *adv* mnogo
vastness [ˈvaːstnəs] *n* ogromnost
VAT *see* **value-added tax**
vault [vɔːlt] **1.** *n* trezor **2.** *v* zasvoditi
V.D. [ˈviːˈdiː] *see* **venereal disease**
veal [viːl] *n* teletina
vegetables [ˈvedʒtəbəlz] *pl* povrće
vegetarian [ˌvedʒɪˈteərɪən] **1.** *adj* vegetarijanski **2.** *n* vegetarijanac

vegetarianism [,vedʒiˈteərijə,nizm] *n* vegetarijanstvo

vegetation [,vedʒiˈteiʃn] *n* vegetacija

vehement [ˈviːəmənt] *adj* žestok

vehicle [ˈviəkl] *n* vozilo

veil [veil] *n* veo

vein [vein] *n* vena

velocity [viˈlɒsəti] *n* brzina

velvet [ˈvelvət] *n* somot

vender, vendor [ˈvendə] *n* prodavac

vending machine [ˈvendiŋ məˈʃiːn] *n* automat

venereal disease [vəˈniəriəl] *n* venerična bolest

vengeance [ˈvendʒəns] *n* osveta

venom [ˈvenəm] *n* 1. otrov 2. zloba

venomous [ˈvenəməs] *adj* 1. otrovan 2. zloban

ventilation [,ventiˈleiʃn] *n* ventilacija

ventilator [ˈventileitə] *n* ventilator

venture [ˈventʃə] 1. *n* opasan poduhvat 2. (com.) špekulacija 3. *v* rizikovati

venue [ˈvenju] *n* mesto događaja; mjesto događaja

veranda [vəˈrændə] *n* veranda

verb [vəːb] *n* glagol

verbal [ˈvəːbl] *adj* verbalan

verbal contract *n* usmeni ugovor

verbatim [vəːˈbeitim] 1. *adj* doslovan 2. *adv* doslovno

verdict [ˈvəːdikt] *n* presuda

verge [vəːdʒ] *n* 1. **road verge** bankina 2. **on the verge of** na ivici

verification [,verifiˈkeiʃn] *n* proveravanje; provjeravanje

verify [ˈverifai] *v* proveriti; provjeriti

vermin [ˈvəːmin] *n* gamad

verse [vəːs] *n* stih

version [ˈvəːʃn] *n* verzija

versus [ˈvəːsəs] (spor.) **Scotland versus England** Škostka protiv Engleske

vertebra [ˈvəːtəbrə] *n* pršljen

vertebrate [ˈvəːtəbreit] *n* kičmenjak

vertical [ˈvəːtikl] 1. *adj* vertikalan 2. *n* vertikala

vertigo [ˈvəːtigəu] *n* vrtoglavica

very [ˈveri] 1. *adj* sam 2. *adv* veoma, mnogo, vrlo

very much *adv* veoma

vessel [ˈvesl] *n* 1. sud 2. (mar.) brod 3. **blood vessel** krvni sud

vest [vest] *n* 1. potkošulja 2. (US) prsluk

vested interests [ˈvestid] *pl* stečena prava

vet [vet] *n* veterinar

veteran [ˈvetərən] *n* veteran

veterinarian [ˈvetinerijən] *n* veterinar

veterinary [ˈvetineri] *adj* veterinarski

veterinary clinic *n* veterinarska klinika

veterinary medicine *n* veterina

veterinary school *n* veterinarski fakultet

veterinary surgeon *n* veterinar

veto [ˈviːtəu] 1. *n* (*pl* **vetoes**) veto 2. *v* staviti veto (na)

vex [veks] *v* uznemiriti

vexed [vekst] *adj* uznemiren

via [ˈvaiə] *prep* preko

vibrant [ˈvaibrənt] *adj* živ

vibrate [vaiˈbreit] *v* vibrirati

vibration [vaiˈbreiʃn] *n* vibracija

vibrator [vaiˈbreitə] *n* vibrator

vicar [ˈvikə] *n* sveštenik; svećenik

vice [vais] 1. *adj* vice- 2. *n* porok

vice chairman *n* potpredsednik; potpredsjednik

vice consul *n* vicekonzul

vice-presidency *n* potpredsedništvo, potpredsjedništvo

vice president *n* potpredsednik; potpredsjednik

vice versa [ˌvaisiˈvəːsə] obrnuto

vicinity [viˈsinəti] *n* 1. susedstvo; susjedstvo 2. in the vicinity u blizini

vicious [ˈviʃəs] *adj* 1. žestok 2. opasan 3. nemoralan

victim [ˈviktim] *n* žrtva

victor [ˈviktə] *n* pobednik; pobjednik

victorious [vikˈtɔːriəs] *adj* pobedonosan; pobjedonosan

victory [ˈviktəri] *n* pobeda; pobjeda

video [ˈvidiəu] 1. *n* video 2. *v* zapisati

video game *n* video-igra

video recorder *n* video-rekorder

video-recording *n* video-zapisivanje

video tape *n* videotejp

video-tape *v* zapisati

vie [vai] *v* otimati se (**for** o)

view [vjuː] 1. *n* pogled 2. point of view gledište 3. *v* gledati

viewer [ˈvjuːə] *n* gledalac

viewpoint [ˈvjuːpɔint] *n* gledište

vigilant [ˈvidʒilənt] *adj* budan

vigorous [ˈvigərəs] *adj* snažan

vigour, vigor [ˈvigə] *n* snaga

vile [vail] *adj* gadan

villa [ˈvilə] *n* vila

village [ˈvilidʒ] *n* selo

villager [ˈvilidʒə] *n* stanovik sela

villain [ˈvilən] *n* 1. zlikovac 2. protivnik junaka

vindicate [ˈvindikeit] *v* osloboditi

vindication [vindiˈkeiʃn] *v* oslobođenje

vinegar [ˈvinigə] *n* sirće

vineyard [ˈvinyaːd] *n* vinograd

viniculture [ˌviniˈkʌltʃə] *n* vinogradarstvo

vintage [ˈvintidʒ] 1. *adj* odličan 2. *n* berba grožđa

vinyl [ˈvainəl] *n* vinl

violate [ˈvaiəleit] *v* 1. prekršiti 2. silovati 3. to violate airspace *v* povrediti vazdušni prostor; povrijediti zračni prostor

violation [vaiəˈleiʃn] *n* 1. prekršaj 2. povreda

violence [ˈvaiələns] *n* 1. nasilje 2. silovitost

violent [ˈvaiələnt] *adj* 1. nasilan 2. silovit

violin [ˌvaiəˈlin] *n* violina

VIP [ˌviːaiˈpiː] *n* velika zverka/ zvijerka

viper [ˈvaipə] *n* šarka

virgin [ˈvəːdʒin] *n* devica; djevica

virility [viˈriləti] *n* virilnost

virtual [ˈvəːtʃuəl] *adj* virtualan

virtually [ˈvəːtʃuəli] *adv* praktično

virtue [ˈvəːtʃuː] *n* vrlina

virus [ˈvairəs] *n* virus

visa [ˈviːzə] *n* 1. viza 2. entry visa ulazna viza 3. exit visa izlazna viza

vis-à-vis [ˌviːzaˈviː] *prep* nasuprot

visibility [ˌvizəˈbiləti] *n* vidljivost

visible [ˈvizəbl] *adj* vidljiv

vision [ˈviʒn] *n* 1. vid 2. (rel.) vizija

visit [ˈvizit] 1. *n* poseta; posjet 2. *v* posetiti; posjetiti

visiting card [ˈvizitiŋkaːd] *n* vizitkarta

visitor [ˈvizitə] *n* 1. posetilac; posjetilac 2. gost

visual [ˈviʒuəl] *adj* vidni
vital [ˈvaitl] *adj* vitalan
vitality [vaiˈtæləti] *n* vitalitet
vitalitize [vaiˈtæləti] *v* oživiti
vitamin [ˈvitəmin] *n* vitamin
vivid [ˈvivid] *adj* živ
vocabulary [vəuˈkæbjuləri] *n* rečnik; rječnik
vocal [ˈvəukl] *adj* vokalni
vocalist [ˈvəukəlist] *n* pevač; pjevač
vocalize [ˈvəukəlaiz] *v* vokalizirati
vocation [vəuˈkeiʃn] *n* poziv
vodka [ˈvɔdkə] *n* vodka
vogue [vəug] *n* **in vogue** u modi
voice [vɔis] *n* glas
volatile [ˈvɔlətail] *adj* isparljiv
volatility [ˌvɔləˈtiləti] *n* isparljivost
volcano [vəulˈkeinəu] *n* (*pl* **volcanoes**) vulkan
volley [ˈvɔli] *n* (mil.) plotun
volleyball [ˈvɔlibɔːl] *n* odbojka
volt [vəult] *n* volt
voltage [ˈvəultidʒ] *n* voltaža
volume [ˈvɔljuːm] *n* **1.** sveska **2.** obim **3.** tonska jačina
voluntarily [ˌvɔlənˈtrəli] *adv* dobrovoljno
voluntary [ˈvɔləntri] *adj* dobrovoljan
voluntary organization *n* humanitarna organizacija
voluntary worker *n* dobrovoljan radnik
volunteer [vɔlənˈtiə] **1.** *n* dobrovoljac

2. *v* dobrovoljno se javiti
vomit [ˈvɔmit] **1.** *n* povraćanje **2.** *v* povraćati
vote [vəut] **1.** *n* glas **2. secret vote** tajno glasanje **3. unanimous vote** jednoglasno glasanje **4. vote of confidence** glasanje o poverenju/povjerenju **5. vote of no-confidence** glasanje o nepoverenju/nepovjerenju **6. to cast a vote** glasati (**for** za) **7.** *v* glasati (**for** za; **on** na) **8. to vote into office** izabrati
voter [ˈvəutə] *n* glasač, birač
voting [ˈvəutiŋ] *n* glasanje
voting-booth [ˈvəutiŋˌbuːθ] *n* glasačka kabina
vouch [vautʃ] *v* jemčiti; jamčiti (**for** za)
voucher [ˈvautʃə] *n* vaučer
vouchsafe [ˌvautʃˈseif] *v* odustojiti
vow [vau] **1.** *n* zavet; zavjet **2.** *v* obećati
vowel [ˈvauəl] *n* samoglasnik
voyage [ˈvɔjidʒ] *n* putovanje
vs. *see* **versus**
vulgar [ˈvʌlgər] *adj* vulgaran
vulnerability [ˈvʌlnərəbiliti] *n* ranjivost
vulnerable [ˈvʌlnərəbl] *adj* ranji
vulture [ˈvʌltʃə] *n* strvinar; lešinar
vulva [ˈvʌlvə] *n* stidnica
vying [ˈvʌltʃə] *see* **vie**

W

wad [wɔd] *n* svežanj

wade [weid] *v* (**across** kroz; **through** po)

wafer [ˈweifə] *n* oblanda

wag [wæg] *v* mahati

wage [weidʒ] *n* 1. plata 2. *see* **wage war**

wage earner *n* primalac plate/plaće

wage freeze *n* zamrzavanje plata/plaće

wage rise *n* povišica

wage war *v* voditi rat

wages [ˈweidʒiz] *n* plata

waggon, wagon [ˈwægən] *n* kola

wail [weil] *v* cvileti; cvilijeti

waist [weist] *n* struk

waistcoat [ˈweiskəut] *n* prsluk

wait [weit] *v* čekati (**for** na)

waiter [ˈweitə] *n* kelner

waiting list [ˈweitiŋlist] *n* lista čekanja

waiting room [ˈweitiŋruːm] *n* čekaonica

waitress [ˈweitris] *n* kelnerica

waive [weiv] *v* odustati (od)

wake [weik] *n* (mar.) brazda

wake, wake up [weik] *v* (**woke/waked, woken/waked**) probuditi (se)

waken [ˈweikən] *see* **wake**

Wales [weilz] *n* Vels

walk [wɔːk] 1. *n* šetnja 1. **to go for a walk** ići u šetnju 2. *v* šetati

walking stick [ˈwɔːkiŋstik] *n* štap za šetnju

walkman [ˈwɔːkmən] *n* vokmen

walk out (of) [ˈwɔːkaut] *v* 1. napustiti 2. stupiti u štrajk

walkway [ˈwɔːkwei] *n* hodnik

wall [wɔːl] *n* zid

wallet [ˈwɔlit] *n* novčanik

wallpaper [ˈwɔlpeipə] *n* zidne tapete

walnut [ˈwɔlnʌt] *n* orah

wand [wɔnd] *n* štap

wander [ˈwɔndə] *v* lutati

wanderer [ˈwɔndərə] *n* lutalica

wane [wein] *v* 1. opasti 2. jesti se

want [wɔnt] 1. *n* potreba 2. oskudica 3. *v* hteti; htjeti

war [wɔː] 1. *adj* ratni 2. *n* rat 3. **civil war** građanski rat 4. **cold war** hladni rat 5. *see* **wage war**

war crime *n* 1. ratni zločin 2. **to commit a war crime** izvršiti ratni zločin

war criminal *n* ratni zločinac

ward [wɔːd] *n* 1. kvart 2. (med.) bolnička dvorana 3. *see* **ward off**

warden [ˈwɔːdən] *n* upravnik zatvora

warder [ˈwɔːdə] *n* čuvar

ward off *v* odbiti

wardrobe [ˈwɔːdrəub] *n* garderoba

warehouse [ˈweəhaus] *n* stovarište

wares [weə] *pl* roba

warfare [ˈwɔːfeə] *n* vođenje rata

war games *pl* ratne igre

warhead [ˈwɔːhed] *n* bojeva glava

warlord [ˈwɔːlɔːd] *n* ratni diktator

warm [wɔːm] *adj* 1. topao 2. *see* **warm up**

warmth [wɔːmθ] *n* toplota

warm up v grejati (se); grijati (se)

warn [wɔːn] v upozoriti

warning [ˈwɔːniŋ] n upozorenje

warp [wɔːp] v iskriviti (se)

warplane [ˈwɔːplein] n borbeni avion

warrant [ˈwɔrənt] 1. n (leg.) naredba 2. **search warrant** nalog za pretres 3. v ovlastiti

warranty [ˈwɔrənti] n garancija; garantija

war reparations pl ratna odšteta

warring [ˈwɔriŋ] adj zaraćen

warrior [ˈwɔriə] n ratnik

wartime [ˈwɔrtaim] 1. adj ratni 2. n ratno vreme/vrijeme

war zone n ratna zona

was [wəz; wɔz] see **be**

wash [wɔʃ] v oprati (se)

washing [ˈwɔʃiŋ] n pranje

washing machine n mašina za pranje; stroj za pranje

washing powder n deterdžent

washing up n pranje sudova

washroom [ˈwɔʃrum] n ve-ce

wash up v oprati (se)

wasp [wɔsp] n osa

waste [weist] 1. n rasipanje 2. **industrial waste** industrijski otpad 3. v proćerdati

wastebasket, wastebin [ˈweistbaːskit; -bin] n korpa za otpatke

wasteful [ˈweistfəl] adj rasipan

wasteland [ˈweistlənd] n pustoš

waste paper [ˈweist,peipə] n otpaci hartije

waste product n otpadak

watch [wɔtʃ] 1. n sat 2. v gledati

watcher [ˈwɔtʃə] n opservator

watchman [ˈwɔtʃmən] n stražar

watchtower [ˈwɔtʃtauə] n stražarnica

water [ˈwɔːtə] 1. n voda 2. v politi

waterbottle [ˈwɔːtə,bɔtl] n boca za vodu

water buffalo [ˈwɔːtə,bʌfələu] n bivol

water cannon [ˈwɔːtə,kænən] n vodeni top

waterfall [ˈwɔːtəfɔːl] n vodopad

watering can [ˈwɔːtəriŋkæn] n kanta za zalivanje

waterless [ˈwɔːtələs] adj bezvodan

water level n vodostaj

watermelon [ˈwɔːtəmelən] n lubenica

waterproof [ˈwɔːtəpruːf] adj nepromočiv

water ski [ˈwɔːtəskiː] n vodena smučka

waterski [ˈwɔːtəskiː] v smučati se na vodi

waterskier [ˈwɔːtə,skiːə] n smučar na vodi

waterskiing [ˈwɔːtəskiː] n smučanje na vodi

watersports [ˈwɔːtəspɔːts] pl sportovi na vodi

water supply n snabdevanje vodom; snabdijevanje vodom

watertank [ˈwɔːtətæŋk] n tank za vodu

watertight [ˈwɔːtətait] adj vodonepropustan

watery [ˈwɔːtəri] adj vodnjikav

watt [wɔt] n vat

wave [weiv] 1. n talas 2. v mahati

wavelength [ˈweivleŋθ] n talasna dužina; duljina vala

waver [ˈweivə] v pokolebati se

wax [wæks] n vosak

way [wei] 1. n put 2. način 3. **way of life** način života 4. **by way of** preko 5. **this way** ovuda 6. **on**

the **way** usput 7. **by the way** uzgred 8. **under way** u toku 9. **to give way** ustupiti 10. **to make way** načiniti mesta/mjesta 11. *adv* veoma

way in *n* ulazak

way out *n* izlaz

wayside ['weisaid] *n* strana puta

we [wi:] *pro* mi

weak [wi:k] *adj* slab

weaken ['wi:kən] *v* oslabiti

weakness ['wi:knis] *n* slabost

wealth [welθ] *n* 1. bogatstvo 2. **mineral wealth** rudno bogatstvo

wealthy ['welθi] *adj* bogat

wean [wi:n] *v* odbiti od sise

weapon ['wepən] *n* oružje

weaponry ['wepənri] *n* oružje

wear [weə] *v* (**wore, worn**) 1. nositi 2. *see* wear out

wear off *v* ugasiti se

wear out *v* iznositi (se)

weary ['wiəri] *adj* umoran

weasel ['wi:zəl] *n* lasica

weather ['weðə] 1. *n* vreme; vrijeme 2. *v* izdržati

weather bureau/office *n* meteorološki biro

weather conditions *n* vremenske prilike

weather forecast *n* prognoza vremena

weather report *n* meteorološki bilten

weather station *n* meteorološka stanica

weave [wi:v] *v* (**wove, woven**) satkati

web [web] *n* paukova mreža

wed [wed] *v* 1. venčati; vjenčati 2. **to wed (a man)** udati se za 3. **to wed (a woman)** oženiti se

wedding ['wediŋ] *n* venčanje; vjenčanje

wedding ring *n* burma

wedge [wedʒ] 1. *n* klin 2. *v* učvrstiti klinom

Wednesday ['wenzdi] *n* sreda; srijeda

weed(s) [wi:d] *n* korov

week [wi:k] *n* nedelja; nedjelja

weekday ['wi:kdei] *n* radni dan

weekend [,wi:k'end] *n* vikend

weekly ['wi:kli] 1. *adj* nedeljni; nedjeljni 2. **a weekly newspaper** nedeljni časopis; nedjeljni časopis 3. *adv* nedeljno; nedjeljno

weep [wi:p] *v* (**wept**) plakati

weevil [wi:p] *n* žižak

weigh [wei] *v* 1. izmeriti; izmjeriti 2. biti težak

weight [weit] *n* 1. težina 2. **to put on weight** dobiti u težini 3. **to lose weight** izgubiti u težini 4. **to lift weights** dizati tegove

weightless ['weitlis] *adj* bestežinski

weightlifter ['weit,liftə] *n* dizač tegova/utega

weightlifting ['weit,liftiŋ] *n* dizanje tegova/utega

weight watching *n* mršavljenje

weird ['wi:əd] *adj* čudan

welcome ['welkəm] 1. *adj* dobrodošao 2. *n* dobrodošlica 3. *v* primiti

weld [weld] *v* zavariti

welded [weldəd] *n* zavaren

welder [weldə] *n* zavarivač

welding ['weldiŋ] *n* zavarivanje

welfare ['welfeə] *n* 1. blagostanje 2. socijalno staranje

well [wel] 1. *adj* zdrav 2. *n* bunar 3. **oil well** izvor nafte 4. *adv* dobro 5. **as well as** kao i 6. **well!** pa!

well-being

well-being [wel·bi:jiŋ] *n* blagostanje
well-known [wel·nəun] *adj* dobro
  poznat
well-off [wel·ɔf] *adj* imućan
well-to-do [weltə·du:] *adj* imućan
Welsh [welʃ] *adj* velški
went [went] *see* **go**
wept [wept] *see* **weep**
were [wə:] *see* **be**
werewolf [weəwulf] *n* vukodlak
west [west] 1. *adj* zapadni 2. *n*
  zapad
western [·westən] 1. *adj* zapadni 2.
  n kaubojski film
westerner [·westənə] *n* zapadnjak
westernize [·westən] *v*
  vesternizovati
westward(s) [·westwəd] *adv*
  zapadno
wet [wet] 1. *adj* mokar 2. *v*
  pomokriti
wet paint *n* vlažna boja
wet weather *n* kišovito vreme/
  vrijeme
whale [weil] *n* kit
whaling [·weiliŋ] *n* kitolovstvo
wharf [wɔ:f] *n* pristanište
what [wɔt] 1. šta; što 2. koji 3.
  kakav
whatever [wɔt·evə] 1. ma šta 2. ma
  koji
what for? zašto?
whatsoever [·wɔtsəu·evə] *see*
  whatever
wheat [wi:t] *n* pšenica
wheel [wi:l] *n* 1. točak 2. *see*
  steering wheel
wheelbarrow [·wi:l,bærəu] *n* tačke
wheelchair [·wi:l,tʃeə] *n* invalidska
  kolica
when [wen] 1. kad, kada 2. **since**
  when otkad

whenever [wen·evə] ma kad
where [weə] 1. gde; gdje 2.
  kud/kuda? 3. **from where?**
  odakle
whereabouts [·weərəbauts] 1. *n*
  boravište 2. *adv* gde; gdje
whereas [,weər·æz] *conj* a
whereby [,weər·ba:i] *conj* po čemu
whereupon [·weərəpɔn] *adv* posle
  čega; poslije čega
wherever [,weər·evə] 1. ma
  gde/gdje 2. ma kuda
whether [·weθə] *conj* 1. da li 2.
  bilo da
which [witʃ] koji
whichever [,witʃ·evə] ma koji
while [wail] 1. *n* neko vreme/
  vrijeme 2. *prep* pri 3. *conj* dok
  4. iako 5. **for a while** za neko
  vreme/vrijeme 6. **once in a while**
  od vremena do vremena
whip [wip] 1. *n* bič 2. *v* bičevati
whirl [wə:l] *v* kovitlati (se)
whirlwind [·wə:lwind] *n* vihor
whisker [·wiskə] *n* dlaka
whiskey, whisky [·wiski] *n* viski
whisper [·wispə] *v* šaputati
whistle [·wisl] 1. *n* pištaljka 2. *v*
  zviždati
white [wait] *adj* beo; bijel
whiten [·waitn] *v* obeliti; obijeliti
whiteness [·waitnis] *n* belina;
  bjelina
whitewash [·waitwɔʃ] 1. *n* kreč 2.
  (pol.) zataškavanje 3. *v* okrečiti
  4. (pol.) zataškati
white wine *n* belo vino; bijelo
  vino
WHO (World Health
Organization) *n* Svetska
  zdravstvena organizacija;
  Svjetska zdravstvena organizacija

who [hu:] 1. ko; tko 2. koji
whoever [hu:'evə] ko god
whole [həul] 1. *n* celina; cjelina 2. *adj* ceo; cio 3. **on the whole** u celini/cjelini
whole-hearted [ˌhəul'ha:tid] *adj* sversdan
wholesale [ˈhəulseil] 1. *adj* veletrgovinski 2. *n* veletrgovina 3. *v* prodavati naveliko
wholesaler [ˈhəulseilə] *n* veletrgovinsko preduzeće/poduzeće
wholesale trade [ˈhəulseil] *n* veletrgovina
wholesome [ˈhəulsəm] *adj* zdrav
whom [hu:m] *see* **who**
whooping cough [ˈhu:piŋkɔf] *n* pertusis
whose [hu:z] čiji
whoever, whosoever [ˌhu:'evə; ˌhu:'səu'evə] ma čiji
why [wai] zašto
why not? zašto da ne?
wicked [ˈwikid] *adj* poročan
wide [waid] 1. *adj* širok 2. *adv* široko
wide awake *adj* sasvim budan
widen [ˈwaidn] *v* proširiti
wide-open [ˈwaidˈeəpən] *adj* širom otvoren
widespread [ˈwaidspred] *adj* rasprostranjen
widow [ˈwidəu] *n* udovica
widower [ˈwidəuə] *n* udovac
width [widθ] *n* širina
wield [wi:ld] *v* imati
wife [waif] *n* (*pl* **wives**) supruga, žena
wild [waild] *adj* divlji
wild animal *n* divlja životinja
wilderness [ˈwildənis] *n* divljina

will [wil] 1. *n* volja 2. (leg.) testamenat 3. *see* **be**
willing [ˈwiliŋ] *adj* voljan
willingness [ˈwiliŋnis] *n* voljnost
will power [ˈwilpauə] *n* snaga volje
wilt [wilt] *v* uvenuti
wimp [wimp] *n* slabić
win [win] *v* (**won**) 1. pobediti; pobijediti 2. odneti; odnijeti
wind [wind] *n* vetar; vjetar
wind [waind] *v* (**wound**) 1. naviti 2. vijugati se
windmill [ˈwindmil] *n* vetrenjača; vjetrenjača
window [ˈwindəu] *n* prozor
windowpane [ˈwindəupein] *n* prozorsko okno
windscreen [ˈwindskri:n] *n* vetroban; vjetroban
windscreen wiper [ˈwindskri:n ˌwaipə] *n* brisač stakla
windshield [ˈwindʃi:ld] *n* (US) vetroban; vjetroban
windward [ˈwindwə:d] *adj* u pravcu vetra/vjetra
windy [ˈwindi] *adj* vetrovit; vjetrovit
wine [wain] *n* 1. vino 2. **red wine** crno vino 3. **white wine** belo vino; bijelo vino 4. **table wine** stono vino; stolno vino 5. **dry wine** oporo vino 6. **sweet wine** desertno vino 7. **sparkling wine** iskričavo vino
wing [wiŋ] *n* krilo
wink [wiŋk] *v* mignuti
winner [ˈwinə] *n* dobitnik
winnow [ˈwinəu] *v* ovejati; ovijati
winter [ˈwintə] *n* zima
winter sports *pl* zimski sportovi
winter time *n* zimsko doba
wipe [waip] *v* obrisati

wipe out *v* zbrisati
wiper [´waipə] *n* brisač
wire [´waiə] *n* 1. žica 2. **barbed wire** bodljikava žica
wiring [´wajriŋ] *n* električni vodovi
wisdom [´wizdəm] *n* mudrost
wise [waiz] *n* mudar
wisecrack [´waizkræk] *n* duhovita primedba; duhovita primjedba
wish [wiʃ] 1. *n* želja 2. *v* poželeti; pozeljeti
wit [wit] *n* 1. um 2. smisao za humor 3. *see* **wits**
witch [witʃ] *n* veštica; vještica
witchcraft [´witʃkra:ft] *n* vračanje
witch hunt *n* lov na veštice/vještice
with [wið] *prep* 1. s, sa 2. od 3. za 4. kod
withdraw [wið´drɔ:] *v* (**withdrew, withdrawn**) 1. povući (se) 2. ispisati (se) 3. **to withdraw money** podići novac iz banke 4. **to withdraw from use** povući iz cirkulacije/opticaja
withdrawal [wið´drɔ:əl] *n* 1. povlačenje 2. ispis 3. (fin.) podizanje novca iz banke
withdrawn [wið´drɔ:ən] *adj* povučen
wither [´wiðə] *v* uvenuti
withhold [wið´həuld] *v* zadržati
within [wi´ðin] 1. *prep* u kući 2. *adv* unutra
without [wi´ðaut] 1. *prep* bez 2. **without a doubt** bez sumnje 3. **without fail** zasigurno 4. *adv* van 5. a da ne
with regard to *prep* u pogledu
withstand [wið´stænd] *v* izdržati
witness [´witnis] 1. *n* svedok; svjedok 2. **to bear witness**

posvedočiti; posvjedočiti 3. *v* prisustvovati
wits [´wits] *pl* pamet
witty [´witi] *adj* duhovit
wives [waivz] *see* **wife**
wizard [´wizəd] *n* mađioničar
wobble [´wɔbl] *v* klimati se
woe [wəu] *n* jad
woke, woken [wəuk; wəukn] *see* **wake**
wolf [wulf] *n* (**wolves**) vuk
woman [´wumən] *n* (*pl* **women**) žena
womankind [wumənkaind] *n* žene
womb [wu:m] *n* materica
women [´wimin] *see* **woman**
won [wʌn] *see* **win**
wonder [´wʌndə] 1. *n* čudo 2. *v* čuditi se
wonderful [´wʌndəfl] *adj* čudesan
woo [wu:] *v* udvarati (se)
wood [wud] *n* 1. drvo 2. šuma
wooden [´wudn] *adj* drven
woods [wudz] *n* šuma
woodwork [´wudwə:k] *n* drvenarija
wool [wul] *n* vuna
woollen [´wulən] *adj* vunen
word [wə:d] *n* 1. reč; riječ 2. **in other words** drugim rečima 3. **to have a word** razgovarati (**with** s) 4. **to keep one's word** održati reč/riječ
wording [´wə:diŋ] *n* formulisanje
word processing *n* obrada teksta
word processor *n* samočitač
wore [wɔ:] *see* **wear**
work [wə:k] 1. *n* rad, posao 2. *v* raditi 3. **out of work** nezaposlen
workable [´wə:kəbl] *adj* obradljiv
workday [´wə:kdei] *n* radni dan
worker [´wə:kə] *n* radnik
work force *n* radna snaga

workman [ˈwəːkmən] *n* radnik

workmanship [ˈwəːkmənʃip] *n* veština; vještina

work off *v* skinuti

work out *v* 1. izraditi 2. završiti se 3. (spor.) trenirati

workplace [ˈwəːkpleis] *n* radno mesto; radno mjesto

workshop [ˈwəːkʃɔp] *n* 1. radionica 2. simpozijum

work to rule *v* usporavanje rada

world [wəːld] 1. *adj* svetski; svjetski 2. *n* svet; svijet

World Bank *n* Svetska banka; Svjetska banka

World Cup *n* Svetski kup; Svjetski kup

World Health Organization *n* Svetska zdravstvena organizacija; Svjetska zdravstvena organizacija

world power *n* svetska sila; svjetska sila

World War One *n* prvi svetski rat; prvi svjetski rat

World War Two *n* drugi svetski rat; drugi svjetski rat

worldwide [wəːldˈwaid] *adj/adv* širom sveta

worm [wəːm] *n* crv

worn [wɔːn] *see* **wear**

worn out *adj* 1. pocepan 2. umoran

worried [ˈwʌrid] *adj* zabrinut

worry [ˈwʌri] 1. *n* briga 2. *v* zabrinuti 3. brinuti se

worrying [ˈwʌrijiŋ] *adj* zabrinjavajući

worse [wəːs] *adj* gori

worsen [ˈwəːsn] *v* pogoršati (se)

worship [ˈwəːʃip] 1. *n* obožavanje 2. *v* obožavati

worst [wəːst] *adj* najgori

worth [wəːθ] 1. *adj* vredan; vrijedan 2. *n* vrednost; vrijednost

worthless [ˈwəːθlis] *adj* bezvredan; bezvrijedan

worthwhile [wəːθˈwail] *adj* vredan; vrijedan

worthy [ˈwəːði] *adj* dostojan

would [wuːd] *see* **will**

would-be [ˈwuːdbiː] *adj* nazovi-

wound [waund] *see* **wind**

wound [wuːnd] 1. *n* rana 2. *v* raniti

wounded [ˈwuːndid] *adj* ranjen

wove, woven [wəuv; wəuvn] *see* **weave**

wrangling [ˈræŋgliŋ] *n* prepirati se

wrap [ræp] *v* 1. zaviti 2. pakovati

wrapper [ˈræpə] *n* zane

wrapping paper *n* pakpapir

wrap up *v* uviti

wreath [riːθ] *n* venac; vijenac

wreck [rek] 1. *n* olupina 2. *v* slupati

wreckage [ˈrekidʒ] *n* olupine

wrench [rentʃ] 1. *n* ključ 2. *v* istrgnuti

wrestle [ˈresl] *v* rvati se

wrestler [ˈreslə] *n* rvač

wrestling [ˈresliŋ] *n* rvanje

wretched [ˈretʃid] *adj* jadan

wriggle [ˈrigl] *v* praćakati se

wrinkle [ˈriŋkl] *n* bora

wrinkled [ˈriŋkəld] *adj* mreškast

wrist [rist] *n* ručni zglob

wristwatch [ˈristwɔtʃ] *n* ručni sat

writ [rit] *n* (leg.) sudski nalog

write [rait] *v* (**wrote, written**) (na)pisati

write down *v* zapisati

write-off *n* 1. olupine 2. (fin.) otpis

write off *v* (fin.) otpisati

writer [ˈraitə] *n* pisac

writhe [raið] *v* previjati se

writing [ˈraitiŋ] *n* pismo

written [ˈritn] *adj* 1. pisan 2. *see* write

wrong [rɔŋ] 1. *adj* pogrešan 2. *n* nepravda 3. *adv* pogrešno 4. *v* naneti nepravdu; nanijeti nepravdu

wrongdoer [ˈrɔŋduːə] *n* vinovnik zla

wrongdoing [ˈrɔŋduːiŋ] *n* zločin

wrongful [ˈrɔŋfəl] *adj* kriv

wrote [rəut] *see* write

wry [rai] *adj* 1. kriv 2. suv; suh

X

xenophobia [ˌzenəˈfəubjə] *n*
ksenofobija
xenophobic [ˌzenəˈfəubik] *adj*
ksenofobski
xerox [ˈzerɔks] 1. *n* fotokopija 2. *v*
fotokopirati
Xmas [ˈeksməs] *n* Božić
X-rated [ˈeksreitid] *adj*
pornografski
X-ray [ˈeksrei] 1. *n* rendgenski
snimak 2. to take an x-ray
snimiti rendgen aparatom
X-ray machine [ˈeksrei,rum] *n*
rendgenski aparat
X-ray room [ˈeksrei,rum] *n* rendgen
sala

Y

yacht [jɔt] *n* jahta
yachting [jɔtiŋ] *n* jedrenje
yam [jæm] *n* jam
yank [jænk] *v* trgnuti
yard [jɑːd] *n* 1. jard 2. radilište 3. (US) bašta
yawn [jɔːn] 1. *n* zev; zijev 2. *v* zevati; zijevati
year [jiə] *n* 1. godina 2. the year before last pretporšle godine 3. last year prošle godine 4. this year ove godine 5. next year iduće godine 6. the year after next da dvije godine 7. leap year prestupna godina 8. financial year, fiscal year budžetska godina
yearly [ˈjiəli] 1. *adj* godišnji 2. *adv* svake godine
yearn [jəːn] *v* čeznuti
yearning [ˈjəːniŋ] *n* čežnja
year-round [jiəˈraund] *adj* preko godine
yeast [jiːst] *n* kvasac
yell [jel] 1. *n* vika 2. *v* viknuti
yellow [ˈjeləu] *adj* žut
yellow fever *n* žuta groznica
yes [jes] da
yes-man [ˈjesmæn] *n* dakavac
yesterday [ˈjestədei] *n/adv* 1. juče; jučer 2. the day before yesterday prekjuče; prekjučer
yesterday's [ˈjestədeiz] *adj* jučerašnji
yet [jet] 1. *adv* još 2. već 3. as yet dosada 4. *conj* a ipak
yield [jiːld] 1. *n* plod 2. *v* doneti; donijeti 3. predati (se)
yoghurt, yogurt [ˈjɔgət] *n* kiselo mleko/mlijeko
yolk [jəuk] *n* žumance
you [juː] *pro* 1. ti, tebe, tebi 2. vi, vas, vama
young [jʌŋ] *adj* 1. arami 2. sabo
your, yours [jɔː; jɔːz] 1. tvoj 2. vaš
yourself [jɔːˈself] (*pl* **yourselves**)se sebe, ti tam sam sebe
youth [juːθ] 1. *adj* omladinski 2. *n* omladina 3. mladost
youthful [ˈjuːθfl] *adj* mladalački
youth hostel *n* omladinsko prenoćište
Yugoslav [ˌjuːgəuˈslɑːv] 1. *adj* jugoslovenski; jugoslavenski 2. *n* Jugosloven; Jugoslaven
Yugoslavia [ˌjuːgəuˈslɑːvijə] *n* Jugoslavija
Yugoslavian [ˌjuːgəuˈslɑːvijən] *adj* jugoslovenski; jugoslavenski
Yuletide [ˈjuːltaid] *n* Božić

Z

zany [ˈzeini] *adj* smešan; smiješan
zap [zæp] *v* bombardovati
zeal [ziːəl] *n* revnost
zealous [ˈzeləs] *adj* revnostan
zebra [ˈzebrə] *n* zebra
zenith [ˈzeniθ] *n* zenit
zeppelin [ˈzepəlin] *n* cepelin
zero [ˈziərəu] **1.** *adj* nulti **2.** *n* nula
zigzag [ˈzigzæg] **1.** *adj* cikcak **2.** *n* cikcak **3.** *adv* krivudavo
zinc [ziŋk] *n* cink
zip [zip] *n* zip
zip code [ˈzipkəud] (US) *n* poštanski broj
zipper [ˈzipə] *see* **zip**
zip up *v* zatvoriti
zodiac [ˈzəudiæk] *n* zodijak
zonal [ˈzəunəl] *adj* zonski
zone [zəun] *n* zona
zoo [zuː] *n* zoološki vrt
zoological [ˌzuːɔˈlɔdʒikl] *adj* zoološki
zoological gardens *see* **zoo**
zoologist [zuːˈɔlədʒist] *n* zoolog
zoology [zuːˈɔlədʒi] *n* zoologija
zoom [zuːm] **1.** *n* zum-sistem **2.** *v* zujati

Appendices

Appendix 1:

ENGLISH IRREGULAR VERBS

Infinitive	Past tense	Past participle
arise *ustati*	arose	arisen
awake *probuditi*	awoke	awoken
be *biti*	was/were	been
bear *nositi*	bore	borne
beat *izbiti*	beat	beaten
become *postati*	became	become
begin *početi*	began	begun
bend *saviti*	bent	bent
bet *opkladiti se*	bet, betted	bet, betted
bid *ponuditi*	bid, bade	bid, bidden
bind *vezati*	bound	bound
bite *ujesti*	bit	bitten
bleed *krvariti*	bled	bled
blow *duvati*	blew	blown
break *slomiti*	broke	broken
breed *roditi*	bred	bred
bring *doneti; donijeti*	brought	brought
build *izgraditi*	built	built
burn *spaliti*	burnt, burned	burnt, burned
burst *raskinuti*	burst	burst
buy *kupiti*	bought	bought
cast *baciti*	cast	cast
catch *uloviti*	caught	caught
choose *izabrati*	chose	chosen
cling *držati se*	clung	clung
come *doći*	came	come
cost *koštati*	cost	cost
creep *puziti*	crept	crept
cut *seči; sječi*	cut	cut
deal *postupati*	dealt	dealt
dig *kopati*	dug	dug
dive *zaroniti*	dived; dove	dived; dove
do *uraditi*	did	done
draw *vući*	drew	drawn
dream *sanjati*	dreamt, dreamed	dreamt, dreamed
drink *ispiti*	drank	drunk

drive *voziti*	drove	driven
dwell *stanovati*	dwelt, dwelled	dwelt, dwelled
eat *pojesti*	ate	eaten
fall *pasti*	fell	fallen
feed *nahraniti*	fed	fed
feel *osetiti; osjetiti*	felt	felt
fight *boriti se*	fought	fought
find *naći*	found	found
flee *pobeći; pobjeći*	fled	fled
fling *baciti*	flung	flung
fly *leteti; letjeti*	flew	flown
forbid *zabraniti*	forbade, forbad	forbade, forbad
forecast *prognosticirati*	forecast, forecasted	forecast, forecasted
forget *zaboraviti*	forgot	forgotten
freeze *smrznuti*	froze	frozen
get *dobiti*	got	got; (US) gotten
give *dati*	gave	given
go *ići*	went	gone
grind *samleti; samljeti*	ground	ground
grow *porasti*	grew	grown
hang *obesiti; objesiti*	hung, hanged	hung, hanged
have *imati*	had	had
hear *čuti*	heard	heard
hide *skriti*	hid	hidden
hit *udariti*	hit	hit
hold *držati*	held	held
hurt *povrediti; povrijediti*	hurt	hurt
input *ubaciti (informacije)*	input, inputted	input, inputted
keep *držati*	kept	kept
kneel *kleknuti*	knelt, kneeled	knelt, kneeled
know *(po)znati*	knew	known
lay *položiti*	laid	laid
lead *voditi*	led	led
lean *nasloniti*	leant, leaned	leant, leaned
leap *skočiti*	leapt, leaped	leapt, leaped
learn *naučiti*	learnt, leaned	learnt, learned
leave *otići*	left	left
lend *pozajmiti*	lent	lent
let *pustiti*	let	let
lie *ležati*	lay	lain
light *upaliti*	lit, lighted	lit, lighted
lose *izgubiti*	lost	lost

make *napraviti*	made	made
mean *značiti*	meant	meant
meet *sresti*	met	met
misunderstand *pogrešno shvatiti*	misunderstood	misunderstood
mow *kositi*	mowed	mown, mowed
overthrow *oboriti*	overthrew	overthrown
pay *platiti*	paid	paid
prove *dokazati*	proved	proved; proven
put *metnuti*	put	put
quit *napustiti*	quit, quitted	quit, quitted
read *pročitati*	read [red]	read [red]
rend *razderati*	rent	rent
rid *otarasiti*	rid	rid
ride *jahati*	rode	ridden
ring *zvoniti*	rang	rung
rise *dići se*	rose	risen
run *trčati*	ran	run
saw *testerisati*	sawed	sawn; sawed
say *kazati*	said	said
see *videti; vidjeti*	saw	seen
seek *tražiti*	sought	sought
sell *prodati*	sold	sold
send *poslati*	sent	sent
set *staviti*	set	set
sew *sašiti*	sewed	sewn, sewed
shake *potresti*	shook	shaken
shear *ostrići*	sheared	shorn, sheared
shed *proliti*	shed	shed
shine *svetleti; svijetliti*	shone	shone
shoot *ustreliti; ustrijeliti*	shot	shot
show *pokazati*	showed	shown, showed
shrink *skupiti*	shrank, shrunk	shrunk
shut *zatvoriti*	shut	shut
sing *pevati; pjevati*	sang	sung
sink *potonuti*	sank	sunk
sit *sedeti; sjedjeti*	sat	sat
sleep *spavati*	slept	slept
slide *kliznuti*	slit	slit
sling *baciti*	slung	slung
slit *proseći; prosjeći*	slit	slit
smell *osetiti; osjetiti*	smelt, smelled	smelt, smelled

sow *posejati; posijati*	sowed	sown, sowed
speak *govoriti*	spoke	spoken
speed *ubrzati*	sped, speeded	sped, speeded
spell *spelovati*	spelt, spelled	spelt, spelled
spend *potrošiti*	spent	spent
spill *prosuti*	split, spilled	spilt, spilled
spin *vrteti se; vrtjeti se*	spun	spun
spit *pljuvati*	spat; spit	spat; spit
split *rascepiti; rascijepiti*	split	split
spoil *pokvariti*	spoilt, spoiled	spoilt, spoiled
spread *širiti*	spread	spread
spring *skočiti*	sprang	sprung
stand *staviti*	stood	stood
steal *ukrasti*	stole	stolen
stick *nabosti*	stuck	stuck
sting *ubosti*	stung	stung
stink *smrdeti; smrdjeti*	stank, stunk	stunk
strike *udariti*	struck	struck
strive *težiti*	strove	strived, striven
swear *zakleti se*	swore	sworn
sweep *pomesti*	swept	swept
swell *oteći*	swelled	swollen, swelled
swim *preplivati*	swam	swum
swing *njihati se*	swung	swung
take *uzeti*	took	taken
teach *naučiti*	taught	taught
tear *pocepati; pocijepati*	tore	torn
tell *reći*	told	told
think *misliti*	thought	thought
thrive *cvetati; cvjetati*	thrived, throve	thrived
throw *baciti*	threw	thrown
thrust *zabosti*	thrust	thrust
tread *ići, gnječiti*	trod	trodden, trod
undergo *pretrpeti; pretrpjeti*	underwent	undergone
understand *razumeti; razumjeti*	understood	understood
undertake *preduzeti; poduzeti*	undertook	undertaken
undo *ukinuti*	undid	undone
wake *probuditi (se)*	woke, waked	woken, waked
wear *nositi*	wore	worn
weave *satkati*	wove	woven
weep *plakati*	wept	wept
wet *pomokriti*	wet, wetted	wet, wetted

win *pobediti; pobijediti*	won	won
wind *naviti*	wound	wound
wring *iscediti; iscijediti*	wrung	wrung
write *[na]pisati*	wrote	written

Appendix 2:

SERBO-CROATIAN VERBS

Infinitive	1st person sing. pres.	Past participle
biti *to be*	jesam	bio
činiti *to do*	činim	činio
čitati *to read*	čitam	čitao
dati *to give*	dajem	dao
dobiti *to get*	dobim	dobio
doći *to come*	dođem	došao
doneti; donijeti *to bring*	donesem	doneo; donio
držati *to hold*	držim	držao
gledati *to look at*	gledam	gledao
govoriti *to speak*	govorim	govorio
gurati *to push*	guram	gurao
hodati *to walk*	hodam	hodao
hteti; htjeti *to want*	hoću	hteo; htio
imati *to have*	imam	imao
ići *to go*	idem	išao
izgubiti *to lose*	izgubim	izgubio
jesti *to eat*	jedem	jeo
kupiti *to buy*	kupim	kupio
misliti *to think*	mislim	mislio
moći *to be able*	mogu	mogao
ostati *to stay*	ostajem	ostao
otvoriti *to open*	otvorim	otvorio
pitati *to ask*	pitam	pitao
piti *to drink*	pijem	pijo
početi *to begin*	počnem	počeo
pomaknuti *to move*	pomaknem	pomaknuo
pomoći *to help*	pomognem	pomogao
poslati *to send*	pošaljem	poslao
praviti *to make*	pravim	pravio

raditi *to work*	radim	radio
reći *to say*	reknem	rekao
smijati se *to laugh*	smijem se	smijao sam se
spavati *to sleep*	spavam	spavao
staviti *to put*	stavim	stavio
trčati *to run*	trčim	trčao
uzeti *to take*	uzmem	uzeo
videti; vidjeti *to see*	vidim	vidio
voleti; voljeti *to like/love*	volim	volio
voziti *to drive*	vozim	vozio
vući *to pull*	vućem	vukao
zatvoriti *to close*	zatvorim	zatvorio
znati *to know*	znam	znao
želeti; željeti *to want*	želim	želio

Appendix 3:

USEFUL PHRASES AND VOCABULARY

good morning	**dobro jutro**
good afternoon	**dobar dan**
good evening	**dobro veče; dobra večer**
good night	**laku noć**
hello	**zdravo**
goodbye	**doviđenja**
how are you?	**kako ste?**
fine, thanks!	**dobro, hvala!**
excuse me!	**izvinite!**
sorry!	**pardon!**
I don't understand	**ne razumem/razumjem**
help!	**upomoć!**
yes	**da**
no	**ne**
please	**molim**
thank you	**hvala**
thank you very much	**puno hvala**
sir	**gospodin**
madam	**gospođa**
miss	**gospođica**

| What is your name? | **Kako se zovete?** |
| My name is.... | **Zovem se . . .** |

Cardinal numbers

zero	0	nula, ništica
one	1	jedan
two	2	dva
three	3	tri
four	4	četiri
five	5	pet
six	6	šest
seven	7	sedam
eight	8	osam
nine	9	devet
ten	10	deset
eleven	11	jedanaest
twelve	12	dvanaest
thirteen	13	trinaest
fourteen	14	četrnaest
fifteen	15	petnaest
sixteen	16	šesnaest
seventeen	17	sedamnaest
eighteen	18	osamnaest
nineteen	19	devetnaest
twenty	20	dvadeset
twenty one	21	dvadeset (i) jedan
twenty two	22	dvadeset (i) dva
thirty	30	trideset
forty	40	četrdeset
fifty	50	pedeset
sixty	60	šezdeset
seventy	70	sedamdeset
eighty	80	osamdeset
ninety	90	devedeset
hundred	100	sto
one hundred and one	101	sto (i) jedan
one hundred and ten	110	sto (i) deset
two hundred	200	dvesta; dvjesta
three hundred	300	trista, tri stotine; tristo
four hundred	400	četiristo

five hundred	**500**	petsto
six hundred	**600**	šesto
seven hundred	**700**	sedamsto
eight hundred	**800**	osamsto
nine hundred	**900**	devetsto
thousand	**1000**	hiljada; tisuću
two thousand	**2000**	dvije hiljade/tisuće
ten thousand	**10,000**	deset hiljada/tisuća
one hundred thousand	**100,000**	sta hiljada/tisuća
million	**1,000,000**	milion; milijun

Ordinal numbers

first	**1st**	prvi
second	**2nd**	drugi
third	**3rd**	treći
fourth	**4th**	četvrti
fifth	**5th**	peti
sixth	**6th**	šesti
seventh	**7th**	sedmi
eighth	**8th**	osmi
ninth	**9th**	deveti
tenth	**10th**	deseti

once	**jedanput, jedamput**
twice	**dvaput**
three times, thrice	**triput**

one half	**pola**
one quarter	**jedna četvrtina**
one third	**jedna trećina**

Weights and measures

kilometre; kilometer	**kilometar**
metre; meter	**metar**
mile	**milja**
foot	**stopa**
yard	**jard**
fathom	**hvat**

gallon	**galon**
litre	**litar; litra**
kilogramme; kilogram	**kilogram**
gramme; gram	**gram**
pound	**funta**
ounce	**unca**

Time

second	**sekund; sekunda**
minute	**minut; minuta**
hour	**sat**
day	**dan**
week	**nedelja; nedjelja**
fortnight	**dve nedelje; dva tjedna**
month	**mesec; mjesec**
year	**godina**
century	**vek; vijek**

morning	**jutro**
noon	**podne**
afternoon	**popodne**
evening	**veče**
night	**noć**
midnight	**ponoć**

the year before last	**pretprošle godine**
last year	**prošle godine**
this year	**ove godine**
next year	**sledeće godine; slijedeće godine**
the year after next	**za dve godine; za dvije godine**

three days before	**pre tri dana; prije tri dana**
the day before yesterday	**prekjuče; prekjučer**
yesterday	**juče; jučer**
today	**danas**
tomorrow	**sutra**
the day after tomorrow	**prekosutra**
three days hence	**za tri dana**
four days hence	**za četiri dana**

Days of the week

Monday	**ponedeljak; ponedjeljak**
Tuesday	**utorak**
Wednesday	**sreda; srijeda**
Thursday	**četvrtak**
Friday	**petak**
Saturday	**subota**
Sunday	**nedelja; nedjelja**

Months of the year

	Serbian	Croatian
January	**januar**	**siječanj**
February	**februar**	**veljača**
March	**mart**	**ožujak**
April	**april**	**travanj**
May	**maj**	**svibanj**
June	**jun(i)**	**lipanj**
July	**juli**	**srpanj**
August	**avgust**	**kolovoz**
September	**septembar**	**rujan**
October	**oktobar**	**listopad**
November	**novembar**	**studeni**
December	**decembar**	**prosinac**

Star signs

Sagittarius	**Strelac; Strijelac**
Capricorn	**Jarac**
Aquarius	**Vodolija; Vodenjak**
Aries	**Ovan**
Virgo	**Devica; Djevica**
Cancer	**Rak**
Leo	**Lav**
Libra	**Vaga**
Scorpio	**Škorpion**
Gemini	**Blizanci**
Taurus	**Bik**
Pisces	**Riba**

Other East European Language Titles from Hippocrene ...

BOSNIAN-ENGLISH/ENGLISH-BOSNIAN DICTIONARY AND PHRASEBOOK
171 pages • 1,500 entries • 3¾ x 7 • 0-7818-0596-1 • $11.95pb • (691)

BULGARIAN-ENGLISH COMPREHENSIVE DICTIONARY
1,050 pages • 47,000 entries • 6¾ x 9¼ • 0-7818-0507-4 • $90.00 2-vol set • (613)

BULGARIAN-ENGLISH/ENGLISH-BULGARIAN COMPACT DICTIONARY
322 pages • 8,000 entries • 3 x 4¾ • 0-7818-0535-X • $8.95pb • (623)

BULGARIAN-ENGLISH/ENGLISH-BULGARIAN PRACTICAL DICTIONARY
323 pages • 8,000 entries • 4⅜ x 7 • 0-87052-145-4 • $14.95pb • (331)

BEGINNER'S BULGARIAN
207 pages • 5½ x 8½ • 0-7818-0300-4 • $9.95pb • (76)

CZECH-ENGLISH/ENGLISH-CZECH CONCISE DICTIONARY
594 pages • 7,500 entries • 0-87052-981-1 • $11.95pb • (276)

CZECH-ENGLISH/ENGLISH-CZECH STANDARD DICTIONARY
10TH REVISED EDITION
1,072 pages • 40,000 entries • 5½ x 8½ • 0-7818-0653-4 • $39.50hc • (740)

CROATIAN-ENGLISH/ENGLISH-CROATIAN DICTIONARY AND PHRASEBOOK
This useful book includes a dictionary of over 1,000 words, plus chapters covering such subjects as travel and transportation, getting around, food and drink, healthcare, and much more.
160 pages • 1,800 entries • 3¾ x 7 • 0-7818-0810-3 • $11.95pb • (111) • *April 2000*

THE BEST OF CROATIAN COOKING

Croatia's distinctive culinary tradition combines central European, Mediterranean, and Near Eastern influences. These 200 easy-to-follow recipes are adapted for the North American kitchen.

200 pages • 5½ x 8¼ • 0-7818-0804-9 • $24.95hc • (435)

MACEDONIAN-ENGLISH/ENGLISH-MACEDONIAN CONCISE DICTIONARY

180 pages • 10,000 entries • 4 x 6 • 0-7818-0516-3 • $14.95pb • (619)

SERBIAN-ENGLISH/ENGLISH-SERBIAN CONCISE DICTIONARY

394 pages • 7,500 entries • 4 x 6 • 0-7818-0556-2 • $14.95pb • (326)